W9-AAJ-028

The Ancient Civilizations of Mesoamerica

The Ancient Civilizations of Mesoamerica

A Reader

Edited by

Michael E. Smith
and
Marilyn A. Masson

BLACKWELL
Publishers

Copyright © Blackwell Publishers Ltd 2000
Editorial matter and organization copyright © Michael E. Smith and Marilyn A. Masson 2000

First published 2000

2 4 6 8 10 9 7 5 3 1

Blackwell Publishers Inc.
350 Main Street
Malden, Massachusetts 02148
USA

Blackwell Publishers Ltd
108 Cowley Road
Oxford OX4 1JF
UK

Library of Congress Cataloging-in-Publication Data
The ancient civilizations of Mesoamerica: a reader / edited by Michael E. Smith and
Marilyn A. Masson.
    p. cm.
    Includes bibliographical references and index.
    ISBN 0–631–21115–2 (hb: alk. paper) — ISBN 0–631–21116–0 (pb: alk. paper)
    1. Indians of Mexico—History.   2. Indians of Mexico—Social life and customs. 3.
Indians of Mexico—Antiquities.   4. Indians of Central America—History.   5. Indians of
Central America—Social life and customs.   6. Indians of Central America—Antiquities.   I.
Smith, Michael Ernest, 1953– II. Masson, Marilyn A.

    F1219. A594 2000
    972'.01—dc21   99–048855

British Library Cataloguing in Publication Data
A CIP catalogue record for this book is available from the British Library.

Typeset in Sabon 9.5/11pt
by Kolam Information Services Pvt Ltd, Pondicherry, India

Printed in Great Britain
by TJ International, Padstow, Cornwall

This book is printed on acid-free paper.

Contents

Notes on Contributors

Frances F. Berdan (Department of Anthropology, California State University, San Bernardino) has published ten books and more than 60 articles on the ancient Aztecs, colonial Mexico, and contemporary native Mexican cultures. Her recent books include *The Codex Mendoza* (with P. R. Anawalt, 4 vols, University of California Press, 1992) and *The Emperor's Mirror: Understanding Cultures through Primary Sources* (with R. J. Barber, University of Arizona Press, 1998).

Michael Blake (Department of Anthropology, University of British Columbia) is an archaeologist whose research has concentrated on the origins of complex society in preclassic Mesoamerica, and more recently, along the Fraser River of British Columbia. He is the editor of *Pacific Latin America in Prehistory: The Evolution of Archaic and Formative Cultures* (Washington State University Press, 1999).

Elizabeth M. Brumfiel (John S. Ludington Trustees Professor at Albion College) is an archaeologist specializing in ancient Aztec culture. She was the Distinguished Lecturer in Archaeology for the American Anthropological Association in 1991, and she presented the David L. Clarke Memorial Lecture at the University of Cambridge in 1997. Brumfiel has edited four volumes, including *Production and Power at Postclassic Xaltocan* (University of Pittsburgh Monographs in Latin American Archaeology, forthcoming), *The Economic Anthropology of the State* (University Press of America, 1994), and *Specialization, Exchange and Complex Societies* (with T. K. Earle, Cambridge University Press, 1987).

John E. Clark (Department of Anthropology, Brigham Young University) is Director of the New World Archaeological Foundation. His research interests include ancient technology, replication experiments, craft specialization and trade, political economy, the organization of labor and technology, the origins of hereditary inequality, ancient art, personhood, and moral and political philosophy. Current projects concern Folsom lithic technology and lifeways, and Mesoamerican Early and Middle Formative civilizations. He has published numerous articles and books.

George L. Cowgill (Department of Anthropology, Arizona State University) is an archaeologist whose principal research interests include Mesoamerica (especially central Mexico), ideational and sociopolitical aspects of ancient societies, mathematical and computer methods in archaeology, and sociocultural factors affecting human fertility in Third World societies. Recent publications include "State and society at Teotihuacan, Mexico" (*Annual Review of Anthropology*, 1997) and *The Collapse of Ancient States and Civilizations* (with N. Yoffee, University of Arizona Press, 1988).

Heinz Dehn is retired from the Department of Geology at the University of Pittsburgh.

Arthur A. Demarest (Ingram Professor of Anthropology, Vanderbilt University) specializes in the archaeology and cultural evolution of Mesoamerica and South America. His books include *Viracocha: The Nature and Antiquity of the Andean High God* (Peabody Museum Monographs,

1981), *Ideology and Pre-Columbian Civilizations* (with G. W. Conrad, School of American Research Press, 1992), and *Religion and Empire: The Dynamics of Aztec and Inca Expansionism* (with G. W. Conrad, Cambridge University Press, 1984). He is co-editor of the Proyecto Arqueológico Regional Petexbatun (6 vols, 1989–99) and is currently authoring and editing several books including the new Vanderbilt Institute of Mesoamerican Archaeology Monograph Series.

Robert D. Drennan (Department of Anthropology, University of Pittsburgh) is an archaeologist whose research centers on the development of early complex societies, especially chiefdoms, which he has investigated in the field in Mexico, Colombia, and China. He is the author of *Statistics for Archaeologists, a Commonsense Approach* (Plenum, 1996), *Fábrica San José and Middle Formative Society in the Valley of Oaxaca* (University of Michigan, Museum of Anthropology, 1972), and *Chiefdoms in the Americas* (with C. Uribe, University Press of America, 1987), among other publications.

Gary M. Feinman (Department of Anthropology, Field Museum of Natural History) is the co-director of ongoing field research projects in Oaxaca, Mexico, and Shandong, China. He recently has authored and edited a number of books, including *Archaic States* (with J. Marcus, School of American Research Press, 1998), *Ancient Oaxaca* (with R. E. Blanton, S. A. Kowalewski, and L. M. Nicholas, Cambridge University Press, 1999), *Pottery and People* (with J. M. Skibo, University of Utah Press, 1999), and *Settlement Pattern Studies in the Americas: Fifty Years since Viru* (with B. R. Billman, Smithsonian Institution Press, 1999).

Philip T. Fitzgibbons teaches at the Franciscan University of Stuebenville, Ohio.

Kent V. Flannery (James B. Griffin Professor of Anthropological Archaeology, University of Michigan, Museum of Anthropology) is a member of the National Academy of Sciences and winner of the A. V. Kidder Medal in American Archaeology. His books include *Guila Naquitz* (Academic Press, 1985), *Zapotec Civilization* (with J. Marcus, Thames and Hudson, 1996), and *Flocks of the Wamani* (with J. Marcus and R. G. Reynolds, Academic Press, 1989).

David A. Freidel (Department of Anthropology, Southern Methodist University) is an archaeologist who since the late 1960s has conducted research at many sites in Mexico and Belize. His work has focused on the origins of civilizations, political history, and the cosmology of living and past Maya societies. He has authored many articles and books, including *A Forest of Kings* (with L. Schele, William Morrow, 1990), *The Maya Cosmos: Three Thousand Years on the Shaman's Path* (with L. Schele, J. Parker, and William Morrow, 1993), and *Archaeology at Cerros, Belize, Central America* (with R. Robertson, Southern Methodist University Press, 1986).

William A. Haviland (Emeritus Professor of Anthropology, University of Vermont) has worked in the archaeology of Mesoamerica and North America since the late 1950s. He is the author of many articles and books, including *Excavations in Small Residential Groups of Tikal: Groups 4F-1* (Tikal Report No. 19, University of Pennsylvania, 1985), *Anthropology* (Holt Rinehart, 1999), *Cultural Anthropology* (Harcourt Brace, 1998), and *The Original Vermonters: Native Inhabitants Past and Present* (with M. W. Power, University of New England Press, 1994).

Cynthia Heath-Smith (Institute for Mesoamerican Studies, University at Albany, SUNY) is an archaeologist interested in the interaction of complex societies with their natural environments, particularly in highland central Mexico. Her publications include "Excavations of Aztec urban houses at Yautepec, Mexico" (*Latin American Antiquity* 10, 1999).

Thomas R. Hester (Department of Anthropology, University of Texas) is Director of the Texas Archeological Research Laboratory. His recent publications include *Field Methods in Archeology* (with H. J. Shafer and K. L. Feder, Mayfield Press, 7th edn, 1997) and several papers on Maya and Texas archaeology. His research interests include stone tool studies, hunters and gatherers, and culture contact in Spanish colonial missions.

Kenneth G. Hirth (Department of Anthropology, Pennsylvania State University) is an archaeologist who has worked in several areas of Mexico and Honduras. A winner of the Award for Excellence in Lithic Studies from the Society for American Archaeology in 1998, his publications include *Archaeological Research at Xochicalco* (2 vols, University of Utah Press, 1999), *Trade and Exchange in Early Mesoamerica* (University of New Mexico Press, 1984), and *Eastern Morelos and Teotihuacan: A Settlement Survey* (Vanderbilt University Publications in Anthropology, 1980).

Linda Manzanilla (Director of the Instituto de Investigaciones Antropológicas, Universidad Nacional Autónoma de México) is author or editor of eleven books and 74 articles and book chapters on the emergence of early urban societies and states in Mesopotamia, Egypt, Mesoamerica, and the Andean region, and on interdisciplinary approaches for domestic archaeological research. She has received the Mexican Academy of Sciences Award (1990), the Alfonso Caso Award for the Best Archaeological Research (1993), and the Presidential Award of the Society for American Archaeology (1996).

Joyce Marcus (Elman R. Service Professor of Cultural Evolution, University of Michigan, Museum of Anthropology) is a member of the National Academy of Sciences and the American Academy of Arts and Sciences. Among her recent books are *Mesoamerican Writing Systems* (Princeton University Press, 1992), *Women's Ritual in Formative Oaxaca* (University of Michigan, Museum of Anthropology, 1998), and *Archaic States* (with G. M. Feinman, School of American

Research Press, 1998). Her research interests include comparative states, urbanism, and the origins of writing.

Marilyn A. Masson (Department of Anthropology, University at Albany, SUNY) is an archaeologist whose current research focuses on the postclassic Maya in Belize. Her major interests lie in the dynamics of secondary state formation and the analysis of economic systems at the household, community, and regional levels. She is author of the forthcoming book, *In the Realm of Nachan Kan: Postclassic Maya Archaeology at Laguna de On, Belize* (University Press of Colorado).

Peter Mathews (La Trobe University, Australia) has been a leading figure in the field of Maya epigraphy and archaeology since the late 1970s, and his research has focused on the political organization, hieroglyphic record, and dynasties of the classic-period Maya. A MacArthur Fellow, Mathews is co-author of *The Code of Kings* (with Linda Schele, Scribner, 1998) and *La escultura de Yaxchilán* (Instituto Nacional de Antropología e Historia, Mexico, 1997).

Patricia A. McAnany (Department of Archaeology, Boston University) has been involved in field research in the Maya lowlands since 1981. From 1990 to 1998 she directed archaeological investigations at the site of K'axob in Belize, focusing on the genesis of ancestor veneration and of ancient Maya strategies of wetland use. More recently, she has been investigating ancient settlement and patterns of ritual cave use in the Sibun River Valley of Belize. In addition to producing numerous book chapters and journal articles she co-edited *Prehistoric Maya Economies of Belize* (JAI Press, 1989), and is author of *Living with the Ancestors: Kinship and Kingship in Ancient Maya Society* (University of Texas Press, 1995).

Hattula Moholy-Nagy (Museum of Anthropology, University of Michigan) is a Research Associate at the University of Pennsylvania Museum interested in pre-Columbian Mesoamerican material culture.

Among her recent publications are "The misidentification of Mesoamerican lithic workshops" (*Latin American Antiquity* 1, 1990), "Middens, construction fill, and offerings: evidence for the organization of classic-period craft production at Tikal, Guatemala'" (*Journal of Field Archaeology* 24, 1997), and "Mexican obsidian at Tikal, Guatemala" (*Latin American Antiquity* 10, 1999).

Linda M. Nicholas (Department of Anthropology, Field Museum of Natural History) is an author of *Ancient Oaxaca* (with R. E. Blanton, G. M. Feinman, and S. A. Kowalewsky, Cambridge University Press, 1999). Since about 1980 she has investigated archaeological settlement patterns, prehispanic land use, and craft production in the Valley of Oaxaca, Mexico.

John M. D. Pohl (resident in Los Angeles) specializes in the study of ancient Mexican painted books called codices. He has worked extensively as an archaeologist in the United States, Canada, England, France, Mexico, and Central America. A recent book by him is *Exploring Mesoamerica* (Oxford University Press, 1999). In addition to his scholastic endeavors, Dr Pohl works as a documentary and feature film writer-producer and designs museum exhibitions for American Indian tribal organizations throughout the United States.

F. Kent Reilly III (Department of Anthropology, Southwest Texas State University) is a prehistorian whose interests converge on the religion, art, and visual validation of elite authority in New World chiefdoms and early states, particularly in Mesoamerica. He was a guest curator of the Princeton University exhibition, "The Olmec World: Art, Ritual, and Rulership" and contributor to its catalog. He has published articles on the ecological origin of Olmec symbols, the influence of Olmec symbols on the iconography of Maya rulership, and the origin and function of the Olmec symbol system.

Prudence M. Rice (Professor of Anthropology and Acting Director of the Office of Research Development and Administration, Southern Illinois University, Carbondale) is a former President of the Society for American Archaeology (1991–3), founding editor of the journal *Latin American Antiquity* (1991–4), recipient of the Society's Award for Excellence in Ceramic Studies, and current member of the US Cultural Property Advisory Committee. Her research interests include the lowland Maya, contact- and colonial-period Latin America, and ceramic analysis.

Linda Schele (1942–98, formerly John D. Murchison Regents Professor of Art at the University of Texas) conducted ground-breaking research on Maya hieroglyphs and art, which revolutionized our understanding of dynastic histories and cosmological beliefs. She received the Tania Proskouriakoff Award from the Peabody Museum (Harvard University), and co-authored a number of important books, including *The Blood of Kings* (with M. Miller, George Braziller, 1986), *A Forest of Kings* (with D. A. Freidel, William Morrow, 1990), *The Maya Cosmos* (with D. A. Freidel and J. Parker, William Morrow, 1993), and *The Code of Kings* (with P. Mathews, Scribner, 1998).

Harry J. Shafer (Department of Anthropology, Texas A&M University) is an archaeologist whose research includes lithic technology, the archaeology of the American Southwest, and the lowland Maya. He received the Award for Excellence in Lithic Studies from the Society for American Archaeology in 1995, and has published many articles, monographs, and book chapters reporting on his research in Maya lithic technology, and Mimbres and Texas archaeology.

Michael E. Smith (Department of Anthropology, University at Albany, SUNY) is an archaeologist interested in the economic and social organization of ancient states, particularly the Aztecs. He has published numerous professional articles and several books, including *The Aztecs* (Blackwell Publishers, 1996), *Economies and Polities in the Aztec Realm* (with M. G. Hodge; Institute for

Mesoamerican Studies, 1994), and *Archaeological Research at Aztec-period Rural Sites in the Mexican State of Morelos, Mexico* (University of Pittsburgh Monographs in Latin American Archaeology, 1992).

B. L. Turner II (Higgins Professor of Environment and Society in the Graduate School of Geography and George Perkins Marsh Institute, Clark University) is a geographer whose research interests are human—environment relationships, in which he focuses on three main topics: the ancient Maya, smallholder cultivation in the tropics, and global land-use and cover change. He is a member of the National Academy of Sciences and American Academy of Arts and Sciences.

Thomas M. Whitmore (Department of Geography, University of North Carolina) is a geographer primarily interested in the cultural ecology, demography and agriculture of pre-Columbian Amerindian population groups in Middle America. His research interests include the dynamics of Amerindian population collapse in the immediate post-contact era in Central Mexico and the Yucatan. His publications include *Disease and Death in Early Colonial Mexico: Simulating Amerindian Depopulation* (Westview, 1992) and "Famine vulnerability in the contact-era Basin of Mexico: a simulation" (with B. J. Williams, *Ancient Mesoamerica* 9, 1998).

Marcus C. Winter (Centro INAH Oaxaca, Instituto Nacional de Antropología e Historia) was director of the Monte Alban Proyecto Especial from 1992 to 1994, and more recently has been preparing publications on those excavations. Recent publications include "Monte Alban and Teotihuacan" (in *Rutas de intercambio en Mesoamérica*, 1998) and *Arqueología de la costa de Oaxaca: Asentamientos del período Formativo en el valle del Río Verde inferior* (with A. A. Joyce and R. G. Mueller, Centro INAH Oaxaca, 1998).

PREFACE

This reader has two intended audiences. The first readership is anyone interested in learning about the ancient civilizations of Mesoamerica. We have included important works by major scholars that cover a wide range of topics, cultures, and time periods for Mesoamerica. The organization of the book differs from that of most general texts on ancient Mesoamerica, which tend to proceed chronologically and regionally. Our feeling is that readers who want details on particular sites or cultures can find that information in a variety of books and articles, both specialized and general in approach. The bibliographies of the chapters and the section introductions contain many examples of such works. We have instead chosen to proceed thematically by comparing and contrasting fundamental principles of social and cultural organization among the ancient Mesoamerican civilizations.

The civilizations of ancient Mesoamerica shared basic patterns of social organization, economics, political organization, and ritual, and these patterns can be obscured in accounts that proceed from culture to culture. We are not claiming that all Mesoamerican cultures were identical or even highly similar. The similarities and differences among these cultures are highly informative for the anthropological study of comparative states and ancient civilizations generally. There were hundreds of separate languages and a great deal of social and cultural variation in Mesoamerica. Nevertheless, we feel that the synthetic and cross-cultural approach of this volume, structured topically by organizational principles of society, rather than by time period, can

best illuminate the nature of Mesoamerican cultures. In the introductions to each section we attempt to synthesize important aspects of both current and historically relevant research on various topics relevant to the themes of the sections. The section introductions outline issues covered in the articles that follow, pose questions for discussion, and provide references for readers who wish to pursue topics in greater detail.

Our second audience is students enrolled in courses on ancient Mesoamerica. There are several general textbooks available for such courses, and numerous more specialized books are also commonly used. The goal of this book is not to serve as a substitute for a textbook, but rather to present case studies and alternative interpretations. These articles expose students to examples of the basic professional literature on Mesoamerica so that they can learn about (and argue about) the basic data of ancient Mesoamerica and how that data is used to construct our knowledge of the past.

We have each used the articles in this book as readings for the course, "Mesoamerican Archaeology" at the University at Albany. This class, which we alternate teaching, is taken by both advanced undergraduates (with diverse majors) and beginning graduate students. The overall organization of the class is chronological and regional, following the standard format used by many such courses and by the major textbooks. We have taught the course both with a textbook and alternatively with other more specialized books, in all cases supplemented by readings. This course organization necessitates assigning the chapters out of order, which does not seem to bother the students too much.

We have used a variety of articles to supplement the textbooks and lectures. Usually one or two articles are assigned each week, and the class breaks into small groups to discuss them (sometimes with a discussion leader chosen in advance). From a large group of such articles, we have selected the chapters in this reader as the most appropriate for our two audiences. These chapters have all been "tested" in at least one class. Some of our criteria for choosing these articles include:

- Articles by major researchers on significant topics.
- Articles that present new and interesting data and conclusions.
- Articles that are well written and interesting to students.
- Articles that raise issues conducive to class discussion.

Not all of the articles in this reader have all of these traits. Some of them are favorites with the students, and a few are disliked for one reason or another. We do not agree with all of the points made in the articles. But they are all examples of good empirical research, they offer a diversity of approaches, and all have something to offer students and others interested in gaining insight into the ancient civilizations of Mesoamerica. Selecting these articles was rather difficult, since many fine works by other scholars would also have been valuable additions to this collection. Because space limitations did not allow us to be comprehensive, we have instead endeavored to assemble a representative cross-section "sample" of fine research on Mesoamerican civilizations. The references cited and discussed in the editors' introductory sections attest to the volume of exciting and significant research now occurring within this vast and diverse region. We hope that this collection will inspire students of Mesoamerican civilizations to pursue additional readings and research on their own.

We would like to thank John Davey of Blackwell for suggesting this reader in the first place, and Susan Rabinowitz for shepherding it through the compilation, writing and production processes. We owe a debt of gratitude to the students who have taken Anthropology 433/533 over the past few years and have shared their opinions, both positive and negative, on these and other articles. We thank our colleagues at other universities who responded to our request for input on course organization and content, we thank the authors of the chapters for writing them in the first place and for providing copies of their illustrations, and finally we thank our colleagues at Albany who have made this an exciting place to study ancient Mesoamerica.

ACKNOWLEDGMENTS

The editors and publishers wish to thank the original publishers of the contributions to this book, which are listed below alphabetically by authors.

Berdan, Frances F., "Principles of Regional and Long-distance Trade in the Aztec Empire," from *Smoke and Mist: Mesoamerican Studies in Memory of Thelma D. Sullivan*, ed. Josserand, J. Kathryn and Dakin, Karen (British Archaeological Reports, International Series, no. 402, Oxford, 1988)

Brumfiel, Elizabeth M., "Figurines and the Aztec State: Testing the Effectiveness of Ideological Domination," from *Gender and Archaeology*, ed. Wright, Rita P. (University of Pennsylvania Press, Philadelphia, 1996)

Clark, John, E. and Blake, Michael, "The Power of Prestige: Competitive Generosity and the Emergence of Rank Societies in Lowland Mesoamerica," from *Factional Competition and Political Development in the New World*, ed. Brumfiel, Elizabeth M. and Fox, John W. (Cambridge University Press, 1994)

Cowgill, George L., "State and Society at Teotihuacan, Mexico," from *Annual Review of Anthropology* 26 (1997)

Demarest, Arthur A., "Ideology in Ancient Maya Cultural Evolution: The Dynamics of Galactic Polities." This article was originally published in *Ideology and Pre-Columbian Civilizations*, edited by Demarest, Arthur A., and Conrad, Geoffrey W. School of American Research Advanced Seminar Series. Copyright 1992 by the School of American Research, Santa Fe, New Mexico

Drennan, Robert D., Fitzgibbons, Philip T., and Dehn, Heinz, "Imports and Exports in Classic Mesoamerican Political Economy: The Tehuacan Valley and the Teotihuacan Obsidian Industry," from *Research in Economic Anthropology* 12 (1990) (Jai Press Inc., Greenwich, 1990)

Feinman, Gary M. and Nicholas, Linda, M., "New Perspectives on Prehispanic Highland Mesoamerica: A Macroregional Approach," *Comparative Civilizations Review* 24 (1991)

Flannery, Kent V. and Winter, Marcus C., "Analyzing Household Activities," from *The Early Mesoamerican Village*, ed. Flannery, Kent V. (Academic Press Inc., New York, 1976)

Freidel, David A. and Schele, Linda, "Kingship in the Late Preclassic Maya Lowlands: The Instruments and Places of Ritual Power," from *American Anthropologist* 90 (1988) (Reproduced by permission of the American Anthropological Association from *American Anthropologist* 90: 3, September 1988. Not for further reproduction)

Haviland, William A. and Moholy-Nagy, Hattula, "Distinguishing the High and Mighty from the Hoi Polloi at Tikal, Guatemala," from *Mesoamerican Elites: An Archaeological Assessment*, ed. Chase, Diane A. and Chase, Arlen F. (University of Oklahoma Press, Norman, 1992)

Hirth, Kenneth G., "Militarism and Social Organization at Xochicalco, Morelos," from *Mesoamerica After the Decline of Teotihuacan AD 700–900*, ed. Diehl, Richard and Berlo, Janet (Dumbarton Oaks Publications, Washington DC, 1989)

Manzanilla, Linda, "Corporate Groups and Domestic Activities at Teotihuacan", from *Latin American Antiquity* 7 (1996) (© Society for American Archaeology [SAA], Washington DC)

Marcus, Joyce, "On the Nature of the Mesoamerican City," from *Prehistoric Settlement Patterns: Essays in Honor of Gordon R. Willey*, ed. Vogt, Evon Z. and Leventhal, Richard M. (University of New Mexico Press, Albuquerque, 1983)

Marcus, Joyce and Flannery, Kent V. "Ancient Zapotec Ritual and Religion: An Application of the Direct Historical Approach," from *The Ancient Mind: Elements of Cognitive Archaeology*, ed. Renfrew, Colin and Zubrow, Ezra B. W. (Cambridge University Press, 1994)

Masson, Marilyn, "Postclassic Maya Ritual at Laguna de On Island, Belize," from *Ancient Mesoamerica* 10 (1999)

Mathews, Peter, "Classic Maya Emblem Glyphs," from *Classic Maya Political History: Hieroglyphic and Archaeological Evidence*, ed. Culbert, T. Patrick (Cambridge University Press, 1991)

McAnany, Patricia A., extract from "Ancestors and the Archaeology of Place," from *Living with the Ancestors: Kinship and Kingship in Ancient Maya Society* (University of Texas Press, 1995)

Pohl, John M. D., "The Four Priests: Political Stability," from Chapter 2 of *The Politics of Symbolism in the Mixtec Codices* (Vanderbilt University Publications in Anthropology, no. 46, Department of Anthropology, Vanderbilt University, Nashville)

Reilly, F. Kent III, "Art, Ritual and Rulership in the Olmec World," from *The Olmec World: Ritual and Rulership* (The Art Museum, Princeton University, Princeton, NJ, 1995)

Rice, Prudence M., "Economic Change in the Lowland Maya Late Classical Period," from *Specialization, Exchange, and Complex Societies*, ed. Brumfiel, Elizabeth M. and Earle, Timothy K. (Cambridge University Press, 1997)

Shafer, Harry J. and Hester, Thomas R., "Lithic Craft Specialization and Product Distribution at the Maya Site of Colha, Belize," from *World Archaeology* 23 (1991) (Routledge, 1991)

Smith, Michael E. and Heath-Smith, Cynthia, "Rural Economy in Late Postclassic Morelos: An Archaeological Study," from *Economies and Polities in the Aztec Realm*, ed. Hodge, Mary G. and Smith, Michael E. (Institute for Mesoamerican Studies, Albany, 1994)

Whitmore, Thomas M. and Turner, B. L. II, "Landscapes of Cultivation in Mesoamerica on the Eve of the Conquest," from *Annals of the Association of American Geographers* 82 (1992) (Blackwell Publishers, Cambridge, MA, 1992)

Introduction:
Mesoamerican Civilizations

Marilyn A. Masson and Michael E. Smith

Mesoamerica, the area of Mexico and northern Central America, was the setting for some of the most spectacular developments of the ancient world. For example, the ancient Maya peoples developed an advanced glyphic writing system coupled with an extremely accurate calendar and the mathematical concept of zero. The Aztecs built one of the largest cities in the world – Tenochtitlan – whose many thousands of inhabitants were supported by some of the most productive agricultural methods ever devised. The ancestors of the Aztecs and Mayas invented a technique for working obsidian (volcanic glass) that produced blades with the sharpest edges known to science. Although these and other major achievements grab the attention of many readers today, archaeologists are most interested in the civilizations of Mesoamerica for another reason. The ancient peoples of Mesoamerica established numerous successful ways of life and participated in some of the most significant transitions of the human past on their own with little contact with peoples of other regions.

Two of the most important cultural transitions of the ancient world were the domestication of food crops, and the evolution of complex societies characterized by cities and centralized state government. These transitions occurred independently in several parts of the world, and the cultures of Mesoamerica provide fascinating case studies for comparison with other areas. The chapters in this book emphasize the second of these transitions, sometimes called the "urban revolution" (Childe 1950) or the

rise of civilization. In anthropology, the term "civilization" is used to refer to the culture of state-level societies. Several chapters focus on the Formative or Preclassic period, after the domestication of crops but before the rise of states and cities, exploring the dynamics of rising social complexity. Some chapters examine the nature of the earliest state-level societies in different parts of Mesoamerica (during the Classic period), and others focus on the later civilizations of the Postclassic Period. Our decision to largely ignore the processes of domestication and initial settled life does not mean that these were not important processes. Rather, we have chosen to emphasize the time periods and sites that have been the scene of the greatest amount of fieldwork and research. Readers interested in domestication and agricultural origins can consult some of the sources listed in the References below.

Archaeologists and other scholars have made tremendous strides in the study of the ancient civilizations of Mesoamerica in recent decades. Numerous sites have been excavated, an even larger number have been located through surveys, and the chronological sequences of cultural development are now known for most parts of Mesoamerica. We can now read Maya writing for the first time (Coe 1992), and numerous documents from the era of the Spanish conquest have revealed details of life at that time. As a result of these advances, researchers now have a good foundation to study important processes in the ancient social organization, economy, politics, and religion of the many diverse Mesoamerican civilizations. The chapters that follow provide the reader with a good cross-section of current and recent research.

Mesoamerica as a Culture Area

The term Mesoamerica is usually applied to a culture area covering much of Mexico and northern Central America. Although over 200 native languages were spoken in ancient Mesoamerica (Justeson and Broadwell 1996; Kaufman 1976), the cultures of this area shared a number of traits that distinguished them from peoples to the north and south. Among these traits were a reliance upon a triad of crops (maize, beans, and squash), religion involving worship at monumental centers, belief in multiple gods, a common ritual calendar of 260 days, and economies based upon market-place exchange. These and other traits were first used to define Mesoamerica as a culture area by Paul Kirchoff in 1943 (published in English in Kirchoff 1952). His approach made sense in terms of theories of cultural change common in early twentieth-century anthropology. Distinctive "cultural areas" were defined by lists of traits, and when individual traits occurred in widely separated areas, processes of migration or "diffusion" were invoked as explanations. From this perspective, the fact that diverse peoples throughout Mesoamerica shared so many traits was due to early migrations of peoples, and to vague processes of diffusion of traits from central or core areas to other areas (see Willey and Sabloff 1993).

By the 1960s archaeologists had become dissatisfied with diffusion and migration as explanations for cultural similarities and differences. The ecological and materialist orientation of the practitioners of the "new archaeology" in the 1960s and 1970s (Trigger 1989; Willey and Sabloff 1993) led to an expansion of fieldwork throughout Mesoamerica (Bernal 1979; Willey and Sabloff 1993). Archaeologists such as Richard Adams, Wendy Ashmore, Ignacio Bernal, Richard Blanton, Michael Coe, William

Coe, Kent Flannery, Richard MacNeish, Eduardo Matos, René Millon, Dennis Puleston, Don Rice, Prudence Rice, Jeremy Sabloff, William Sanders, Gordon Willey, and others focused on local and regional issues and did not give much thought to the larger question of Mesoamerica as a culture area (for an exception, see Sanders and Price 1968). In the 1980s and 1990s some archaeologists have turned again to large-scale processes and events to reexamine the concept of Mesoamerica from a new perspective based upon world systems theory. In this approach, Mesoamerica is an area whose diverse cultures were fragmented into many independent states but were linked together through processes of commerce and stylistic interaction (e.g. Blanton and Feinman 1984; Blanton et al. 1993). The paper by Feinman and Nicholas (chapter 10) is one of the clearest statements of this perspective, some version of which is shared today by most Mesoamericanists.

Mesoamerican cultures inhabited a variety of environmental zones, including lowland tropical forests, rugged mountain slopes, and flat highland river valleys. Villages and regions tended to specialize in locally available resources, leading to active commerce between settlements. This trade linked the diverse cultures and regions together and contributed to the spread of the basic Mesoamerican economic and religious ideas. Mesoamerica can be divided into two primary environmental categories: the highlands and the lowlands (figure 1). The influence of geography on cultural formation is clearly visible in Mesoamerica. Highland Mesoamerica refers primarily to the Sierra ranges of Central Mexico which provide numerous large intermontane valleys that were the home of a vast array of valley-based polities throughout the Mesoamerican past. Sanders and Price (1968) emphasized the heterogeneous nature of Mesoamerican highland environments. Considerable differences in resources may be found from one habitable valley to the next and from the valley floors to the upland mountainous zones which surrounded pockets of human habitation. This "pocketing"

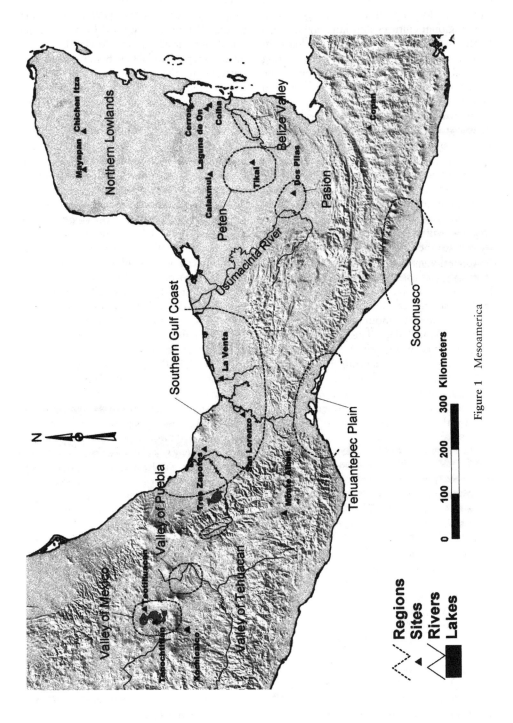

Figure 1   Mesoamerica

of terrain and human societies contributed to the development of a great range of distinct regional cultures and language groups in the highlands. For example, at least 16 dialects of Zapotec are identified among cultural groups living in and around the Valley of Oaxaca today (Justeson and Broadwell 1996; Suárez 1983).

Two of the largest and most heavily studied of the highland valleys are the Valley of Oaxaca and the Valley of Mexico. These regions are of key interest to archaeologists studying the origins of the state in Mesoamerica because the most highly centralized, urbanized, and powerful civilizations developed in these valleys. The size and resources of these valleys permitted high population levels, rich farming capacities, and considerable resources diversity needed for the sustenance of major centralized states. In between major river valley polities of highland Mesoamerica, numerous small polities also developed in mountainous zones and smaller upland valleys. These more marginal environments were not as conducive to urbanization and the centralization of political and economic functions, but these cultures, such as the Mixtec, were highly complex, economically influential, and during the Postclassic period, politically aggressive and successful.

The lowlands of Mesoamerica includes the Veracruz Gulf Coast, the Pacific coastal plains of Tehuantepec and the Socunusco, and the Maya area of the Yucatan peninsula, parts of Chiapas, Mexico, Belize, and Honduras. Maya peoples also inhabited highland zones in Chiapas and western Guatemala. The lowlands are referred to as the hot country ("tierra caliente"), and they are generally far more tropical and moist than the Central Mexican highlands. The lowlands, particularly the Maya area, have been characterized as a zone of "relative geographical uniformity" compared to the highlands which had more diverse resources located in close proximity (Sanders and Price 1968: 237; Rathje 1972: 372). The Maya lowlands are comprised of relatively open terrain with less topographic boundaries than highland Mexico regions, which are more bounded and circumscribed by surrounding mountain ranges. Sanders and Price (1968: 237–8) suggested that reliance on swidden (slash and burn) agriculture in the lowlands encouraged dispersed and less urbanized settlement patterns in the Maya area; furthermore, a lower diversity of exportable resources across this region served to curtail the development of export production in comparison with the highlands (Sanders and Price 1968: 204). In contrast, they argued, the more densely concentrated highland urban centers developed more co-dependent economic symbioses with neighboring regions, and developed centralized control of agricultural production and economic exchange (Sanders and Price 1968: 191). Building upon these ideas, Rathje (1972: 375) suggested that the development of lowland Maya centers in the tropical interior "core" zones like the Peten region occurred as part of a strategy to ensure and control the importation of valuable highland commodities from outlying "buffer" zones which were in greater contact with highland merchants.

Although Rathje (1972: 379) felt that there were shortages of basic items needed for existence in inland lowland zones, more recent works suggest that the dispersed nature of Maya settlement appears to be related to the richness of the lowland environment, which provided many habitable zones that were suitable for settlement as they supplied ample water, fertile soils, chipped stone, clays for ceramics, and other essentials (Freidel 1986; McAnany 1989). This affluent environment allowed a greater degree of community autonomy and localized control of agricultural and commodity production than was possible for highland communities more intimately tied to large political centers. Rathje may have been correct, however, in supposing that the rise of "core" Maya centers was partly related to their interest in acquiring highland commodities, although these trade items may have been more destined for prestige and the expression of power than for everyday use (Blanton et al. 1996).

Though it is now known that some Maya settlements did engage in intensive agriculture (Turner and Harrison 1983; Pohl 1990)

Table 1 Chapters classified by location and time period

Location	Time period	Authors	Chapter
Highlands	Formative	Flannery and Winter	1
	Formative	Marcus and Flannery	19
	Classic	Manzanilla	4
	Classic	Drennan et al.	8
	Classic	Cowgill	15
	Epiclassic	Hirth	16
	Postclassic	Berdan	9
	Postclassic	Smith and Heath-Smith	11
	Postclassic	Pohl	17
	Postclassic	Brumfiel	22
	Synthetic	Feinman and Nicholas	10
Lowlands	Formative	Clark and Blake	12
	Formative	Reilly	18
	Formative	Freidel and Schele	20
	Formative/Classic	Shafer and Hester	6
	Classic	Haviland and Moholy-Nagy	2
	Classic	Rice	7
	Classic	Mathews	13
	Classic	Demarest	14
	Classic	McAnany	23
	Postclassic	Masson	21
Comparative	Synthetic	Marcus	3
	Postclassic	Whitmore and Turner	5

and Maya centers were more densely settled than previously thought, Sanders and Price's fundamental characterizations and contrasts of Maya lowland environment and political structure compared to highland civilizations remain useful and provocative models which guide ongoing research in these regions. Articles in this volume provide examples of research within both the highlands and the lowlands which could serve as fuel for discussions of the differences in cultural organization among Mesoamerican states. The greater centralization of highlands polities does not imply that these cultures were superior, although they may have been more administratively complex with more stable dynasties (Blanton et al. 1996). Further discussions of similarities and differences of highlands or lowlands societies are offered in the introductions to each section of this reader and in the articles themselves (see also Miller 1983). The distribution of chapters between the highlands and the lowlands is shown in table 1.

Topics Covered in Articles in this Reader

These articles may be organized along three themes beyond the highland/lowland distinction discussed above: (1) principles of sociocultural organization, (2) methodology and data analysis, and (3) time period or degree of social complexity. The first theme represents the organization of this reader. The introductions written for each of these sections discuss aspects of cultural institutions for Mesoamerica in general and as they are reflected in the articles which follow. Selections in Part I examine various aspects of social institutions, particularly household organization and activities, social class, and other kin-based dimensions of social life. Part II groups the articles around the theme of economic organization. Issues addressed in this section include rural economies, local exchange, community-based craft specialization, wealth differences, and long-distance trade. Part III

Table 2 Chapters classified by data and methods used

Category	Authors	Chapter
Excavation	Flannery and Winter	1
	Haviland and Moholy-Nagy	2
	Manzanilla	4
	Shafer and Hester	6
	Rice	7
	Drennan et al.	8
	Smith and Heath-Smith	11
	Clark and Blake	12
	Marcus and Flannery	19
	Masson	21
	Brumfiel	22
Survey	Feinman and Nicholas	10
Ethnohistory	Berdan	9
Epigraphy	Mathews	13
	Pohl	17
Excavation/Iconography	Cowgill	15
	Hirth	16
	Freidel and Schele	20
	Reilly	18
Synthetic	Marcus	3
	Whitmore and Turner	5
	Demarest	14
	McAnany	23

presents articles on Mesoamerican political organization, including such themes as the size and stability of Maya city-states, the basis for power in the Formative period and at Teotihuacan, and the role of various institutions in political affairs such as military orders and offices of priesthood. The section on religious organization, Part IV, touches upon a number of themes in recent research. These include the origins and meaning of public religious art in Olmec society, the links between the religious beliefs at Spanish contact and sacred institutions documented hundreds of years earlier in the Mesoamerican past, the vestiges of Maya kingship, aspects of household religion and ideology, and the roots of religious belief in the metaphors central to daily agricultural life.

The articles in this reader can also be grouped by the types of data and methods that are emphasized (table 2). The majority of the chapters emphasize excavation, tradi-

tionally the major technique of archaeological fieldwork in Mesoamerica. Regional survey, which became an important method in Mesoamerica following early work by Gordon Willey (Willey et al. 1965) and William Sanders (1965), is represented in one chapter here (Feinman and Nicholas, chapter 10). Readers can consult some of the many excellent reports on regional surveys for more information on this method and its contributions to Mesoamerican studies: Blanton 1978; Blanton et al. 1982; de Montmollin 1988; Kowalewski et al. 1989; Parsons et al. 1982; Sanders et al. 1979. Ethnohistory, the use of documentary evidence on conquest-period societies, forms the foundation for one chapter; Berdan employs information from Spanish and Nahuatl administrative documents and the reports of Spanish priests and other observers to reconstruct aspects of Aztec exchange. Ethnohistory also plays a major role in other chapters, including Pohl (chapter 17), Marcus and Flannery (chapter 19), Brumfiel (chapter 22), and McAnany (chapter 23).

Epigraphy, the study of ancient inscriptions and writing systems, is the primary focus of two chapters. Mathews reviews some of the recent advances in Maya decipherment, and Pohl uses information from the Mixtec painted histories (known as codices) to reconstruct political and ritual institutions. Two chapters, by Reilly (chapter 18) and Freidel and Schele (chapter 20) make extensive use of art and epigraphic evidence in conjunction with data from exavation. Four chapters combine the results of archaeological excavations with studies of iconography (the symbolism of pictorial images and elements), and four chapters are syntheses of several kinds of data from different regions. These methodological categories are somewhat artificial, since nearly all of the chapters use more than one kind of data and more than one method. This interdisciplinary focus of much research is one of the strengths of Mesoamerican studies today.

Date	Period
AD 1500	Postclassic
AD 1000	
AD 500	Classic
0	
500 BC	Formative or Preclassic
1000 BC	
1500 BC	
2000 BC	
〇	Archaic
〇	
8000 BC	
〇	Paleoindian
〇	
〇	
20000 BC	

Figure 2

Brief Outline of Mesoamerican Cultural Development

Paleoindian and archaic periods, 15000–2000 BC

Those aspects of Mesoamerica which define it as a cultural region begin in the Formative period (see figure 2). Prior to this time, the Paleoindian and Archaic cultures of Mesoamerica, while regionally distinctive in their adaptations to the mosaic of microenvironments within this vast region, were following trends of development that parallel those observed in pre-sedentary societies throughout the New World. The timing of the initial peopling of the New World has been hotly debated in recent years, but a consensus is now appearing that the well-known Clovis culture (8000–9000 BC) was not the earliest human presence in the New World. Well-dated pre-Clovis sites such as Meadowcroft rockshelter in the eastern United States, Monte Verde in Chile, and sites in the

Amazon basin show the presence of hunters and gatherers in these areas back to 13000–14000 BC and probably earlier (Dillehay 1989, 1996; Meltzer 1995; Meltzer et al. 1997; Roosevelt et al. 1996). Although the earliest sites in Mesoamerica are not as firmly dated yet (Gruhn 1977; Lorenzo and Mirambell 1986a, 1986b), people must have been living in the region by 15000 BC at least. The campsites of small social groups of this period which subsisted on hunting of large and small game and harvesting a range of plant resources can be difficult to locate, as they may be deeply buried or completely eroded away. Research emphasis has not concentrated on this period in Mesoamerica to the same degree that it has in North and South America.

The Archaic period in Mesoamerica extends from around 8000–2000 BC. This long period of cultural adaptation represents an even greater temporal interval than that of settled agricultural cultures which are the focus of this volume. Cultures in the Mesoamerican region during the Archaic period are accordingly highly diverse across space and time. A general trend, observed throughout the Americas, is observed in gradual development of regionally-specific adaptations to local ecological resources and a gradual diversification of dietary strategies after the extinctions and warming trends that marked the end of the Pleistocene. As regional cultures settled down and increased in number, familiarity with local resources led to the deliberate horticultural cultivation of wild foods such as beans, squash, amaranth, peppers, and wild maize (*teosinte*). Over time, people's selection of optimal qualities in plant resources led to the domestication of maize and other crops (Flannery 1973, 1985; Harlan 1992; Pohl et al. 1996). Maize took several thousand years to evolve into a productive cob and kernel size that was large enough to represent a viable staple crop for the sustenance of full-time agricultural populations (Benz and Iltis 1990; Galinat 1985; McClung de Tapia 1992). Some Late Archaic Mesoamerican societies appear to have focused on the exploitation of abundant aquatic resources and wetland horticultural production of crops like manioc as well as versions of maize, beans, squash, and other cultigens (Hester et al. 1996; MacNeish 1986; Pohl et al. 1996; Stark 1981; Voorhies 1976).

The formative period
(2000 BC–AD 200)

The beginning of the Formative period in Mesoamerica, which began at different points in time throughout different regions of the highlands and lowlands, is marked by the adoption of a fully agricultural economy, the establishment of permanently occupied, sedentary villages, and the use of the first pottery containers. These traits appeared first on the Pacific coast of southern Mexico and Guatemala in the Locona and Ocos cultures (Clark and Blake, chapter 12). The ceramic vessels of these cultures are very well made and stylistically elaborate, more so than one might think for their early date.

Clark and Blake suggest that the ceramics were used in ritual feasts that were part of the political dynamics of early ranked societies in that region. The Formative way of life, comparable to that of the Neolithic period in the Old World, was successful and soon spread over most of Mesoamerica.

Midway through the Formative period, complex chiefdoms developed in several parts of Mesoamerica. The best known of these was the Olmec culture, located along the Gulf Coast of Mexico. The site of San Lorenzo (1600–800 BC) consisted of a cluster of neighborhoods whose occupants constructed the first monumental architecture in Mesoamerica. They modified the natural landscape into artificial platforms and constructions that symbolized the emergence of political power among the Olmec. Stoneworkers at San Lorenzo carved huge basalt heads and many smaller sculptures of people and animals. Jaguars, serpents, and eagles, worshipped as gods by the Olmec, would later become important supernatural symbols in many Mesoamerican cultures. Another Olmec site, La Venta (1200–400 BC), was an early monumental center that had an elaborate series of buried offerings and tombs as well as monumental sculptures similar to San Lorenzo. Elements of the Olmec art style were shared by chiefdoms in other parts of Mesoamerica, including San José Mogote in Oaxaca, Chalcatzingo in central Mexico, and Teopantecuanitlan in Guerrero.

By around 1000 BC, chiefdoms had developed in many regions of Mesoamerica. The best studied Formative chiefdoms were in the Valley of Oaxaca; chapters here by Flannery and Winter (chapter 1) and Marcus and Flannery (chapter 19) describe some of this research (see also Flannery 1976; Flannery and Marcus 1983; Marcus and Flannery 1996). Around 500 BC, fundamental changes appear in the archaeological records of many regions as the line between chiefdoms and early states was crossed. A number of powerful, centralized state capitals emerged at this time, including Teotihuacan and Monte Alban in the highlands, and Nakbe and El Mirador in the Maya lowlands, and Izapa and Kaminaljuyu in the Pacific Guatemalan region. These early states engaged in considerable interregional trade and stylistic interaction, linking the diverse regions of Mesoamerica together more closely than had been the case earlier. This was also the time when writing systems were developing in several areas, including the Gulf Coast (Justeson and Kaufman 1993), the Maya region (Coe 1992), and Oaxaca (see below).

Classic period (AD 200–900)

Advanced civilizations developed in many parts of Mesoamerica during the Classic period. Three of the most notable were Monte Alban, Teotihuacan, and the lowland Maya. Monte Alban, a hilltop city built by the Zapotec culture in the Valley of Oaxaca, had a majestic ceremonial plaza lined with palaces and temples. Most people lived in small houses built around patios on stone terraces on the slopes below the plaza. The Zapotecs devised one of the earliest writing systems in Mesoamerica, in which carved stone reliefs were used to keep track of calendrical knowledge and dynastic history. The earliest texts record conquests and sacrifices, and later texts describe possible diplomatic and commercial relations between Monte Alban and Teotihuacan (Marcus 1992).

Teotihuacan (AD 200–700), an urban center of 200,000 inhabitants in the Valley of Mexico, was the largest city in the world outside of China during the fifth through seventh centuries. Its powerful rulers built a carefully planned settlement using a grid pattern arranged around a long north-south ceremonial avenue lined with temples and other monumental civic buildings (Cowgill, chapter 15). People lived in standardized single-story apartment complexes, many of which housed workshops that produced a variety of products of obsidian (volcanic glass) and other materials (Manzanilla, chapter 4). Teotihuacan controlled a small empire in the central Mexican highlands, but its economic and religious influence reached the far corners of Mesoamerica,

including the royal cities of the lowland Maya.

Classic-period Maya civilization developed in the lowland tropical forests of southern Mexico, Guatemala, and Belize. The spectacular jungle cities of the Maya, with monumental temple-pyramids and rich offerings, have attracted considerable attention from archaeologists and the public. The Maya were organized into small states that fought and traded with one another (Mathews, chapter 13; Demarest, chapter 14). Maya writing, carved on stone monuments, was the most advanced writing system in Mesoamerica. Inscriptions record the history of dynasties and show an impressive knowledge of astronomy and mathematics, which were used to devise a variety of calendars. One such calendar, the long count, was an accurate count of days that has been correlated with the modern calendar, allowing scholars to reconstruct the dates of key events in Maya dynastic history (Mathews, chapter 13). In the ninth century AD, Classic lowland Maya civilization collapsed. Major cities were abandoned and some aspects of elite culture, such as the long count calendar, dropped out of use. The Maya collapse, which was brought about by a combination of historical events, ecological stresses, and long-term processes of change inherent in many state societies, ushered in the Postclassic period in Mesoamerica.

Postclassic period (AD 900–1520)

Some aspects of Classic lowland Maya civilization endured beyond the "collapse" in the cities of the Puuc culture of northern Yucatan. From AD 600 to AD 1100, the Puuc peoples built ornate architectural centers such as Uxmal and Chichen Itza in a distinctive, elaborate style that is found within a confined zone of northwestern Yucatan. For the majority of the eleventh and twelfth centuries, or the Early Postclassic period, the large city of Chichen Itza dominated parts of northern Yucatan through the elimination of the majority of its competitors and its control of international trade off the Yucatan peninsula. Chichen Itza was an important center in the Early Postclassic world system that linked large parts of Mesoamerica together with bonds of economic exchange (Kepecs et al. 1994). Postclassic communities in the southern Maya lowlands were linked to this extensive sphere of economic exchange through coastal trading sites. Coastal and riverine zones were heavily settled at this time, and affluent communities appear to have taken advantage of new economic opportunities created in the wake of collapse. Some centers, like Lamanai in Belize, never collapsed (Pendergast 1986). This was a time of transition and adaptation, and each subregion of the Maya lowlands appears to have reacted somewhat differently.

The Late Postclassic period in northern Yucatan began around AD 1200, when, according to historical accounts, the capital of Mayapan overthrew Chichen Itza and took over its role in long-distance trade. At least by this time, society in the Maya lowlands was organized into small states which were variously integrated and centralized. Mayapan appears to have been allied with east coast peninsular sites such as Cozumel, Tulum, and various Belize sites (Freidel and Sabloff 1984). Further to the south, the highlands of Guatemala witnessed the cultural and political florescence of the Quiché Maya and other groups.

In the Mexican highlands, many states rose and fell during the Postclassic period. The Mixtec of Oaxaca are one of the better-known cultures of this period, due to the preservation of several of their codex fold-out bark paper books. These codices provide remarkable records of Mixtec myths and history (Pohl, chapter 17; see also Byland and Pohl 1994). After the fall of Teotihuacan in central Mexico, large fortified cities such as Xochicalco, Cacaxtla, and Cholula ruled central Mexico (AD 750–950). This era, called the Epiclassic period in central Mexico, was a time of intense warfare and conflict, shown by the hilltop positions of large cities and a militaristic iconography (Hirth, chapter 16). The fall of these militaristic states was followed by the rise of the Toltec civilization (AD 950–1150), centered

at the city of Tula (Diehl 1983; Healan 1989).

In the twelfth century, the Nahuatl-speaking Aztec peoples migrated into central Mexico from a homeland somewhere in the north. The Aztecs began by founding small city-states ruled by hereditary elites. After several centuries of growth and economic expansion, the Aztec group known as the Mexica established an empire from their island capital Tenochtitlan in the Valley of Mexico. The Aztec empire expanded rapidly by conquering city-states throughout northern Mesoamerica, although the Aztecs were unsuccessful in their wars against the Tarascans, a contemporary imperial civilization located in western Mexico. Tenochtitlan grew into a large and rich metropolis of 200,000 people. The Aztecs devised a new writing system to record their conquests, imperial tribute, and rituals. The Aztec economy exhibited a high degree of complexity at all levels, from the extensive institutions of long-distance trade (Berdan, chapter 9) to the active domestic economies of provincial households (Smith and Heath-Smith, chapter 11). The Aztec state developed an imperial ideology that promoted its greatness and its invincibility (Townsend 1979), but there are indications that many or most subjects did not share that ideology (Brumfiel, chapter 22). Neither did the enemies of the Aztecs, such as the Tarascans. The Tarascans forged a powerful Postclassic empire in west Mexico based in part on their control of trade and production of luxury goods and tools made of bronze (Hosler 1994; Pollard 1993). When the expanding Aztec and Tarascan empires encountered each other in the late fifteenth century AD, they fought to a standstill. Several decades later, neither one could stand up to the invading Spaniards.

The Spanish colonial period (1520–1820)

In 1519, at the height of the glory of Aztec civilization, the Spaniard Hernando Cortés marched into Tenochtitlan and within two years the city was in ruins and the Aztecs' defeated. Within a few decades almost all of Mesoamerica's core political regions were firmly under Spanish control. The Spaniards came to Mesoamerica to get rich and to save the souls of the Indians, and the changes that took place in the wake of their wars of conquest were enormous. Aztec and Maya kings were stripped of their power, commoners were put to work in mines and plantations, native religions were suppressed, and people died by the millions of epidemic diseases brought from Europe. The Spaniards tore down native temples and cities and built their own churches and cities over the ruins. These and other changes are discussed in numerous works, including Burkhart (1989), Chance (1989), Cook (1991), Foster (1960), Gibson (1966), Lockhart (1992), and Carmack et al. (1996).

In spite of the processes of conquest and domination by the Spanish empire, the native peoples of Mesoamerica survived. Some groups quickly learned Spanish and joined the colonial society, others retreated into the jungles or mountains and resisted accommodation for centuries (Jones 1989, 1999), but most groups devised ways of coping with the new conditions somewhere between these extremes. Although most information about colonial-period Mesoamerica comes from written documents, archaeologists are playing an increasingly important role in studying native adaptations to colonial rule, particularly in rural areas (e.g. Gasco et al. 1997; Graham et al. 1989; Charlton and Fournier 1993). The ancient cultures of Mesoamerica did not die off during the colonial period; today Nahuatl, Maya, Zapotec, and other native languages are still flourishing. These cultures are not remnants of ancient groups; they are modern indigenous peoples with rich histories including pre-Spanish, Spanish colonial, and modern.

Sources of information

There are a number of textbooks that provide detailed treatments of the development of ancient Mesoamerican cultures through time. The most comprehensive is Weaver (1993), notable for its detailed coverage of sites and regional sequences; see also Adams (1991). Blanton et al. (1993) is a more analytical, problem-oriented treatment of ancient Mesoamerica. Two texts by Coe (1993, 1994) together furnish a readable and informative coverage of Mesoamerica. Other major textbooks include Henderson (1997) and Sharer (1994) on the Maya, Smith (1996) on the Aztecs, Marcus and Flannery (1996) on the Zapotecs, and Carmack et al. (1996) on Mesoamerica from ancient to modern times. The group of papers in this reader provide a supplement to broader textbooks by providing examples of original and primary research on the evolution and organization of the ancient civilizations of Mesoamerica.

REFERENCES

Adams, Richard E. W. 1991. *Prehistoric Mesoamerica*. Revised edn. University of Oklahoma Press, Norman.

Benz, Bruce F. and Hugh H. Iltis. 1990. Studies of Archaeological Maize, I: The Wild Maize from San Marcos Cave Re-examined. *American Antiquity* 55: 500–11.

Bernal, Ignacio. 1979. *A History of Mexican Archaeology: The Vanished Civilizations of Middle America*. Thames and Hudson, New York.

Blanton, Richard E. 1978. *Monte Alban: Settlement Patterns at the Ancient Zapotec Capitol*. Academic Press, New York.

Blanton, Richard E. and Gary M. Feinman. 1984. The Mesoamerican World System. *American Anthropologist* 86: 673–82.

Blanton, Richard E., Gary M. Feinman, Stephen A. Kowalewski, and Peter N. Peregrine. 1996. A Dual-Processual Theory for the Evolution of Mesoamerican Civilization. *Current Anthropology* 37: 1–14.

Blanton, Richard E., Stephen Kowalewski, Gary M. Feinman, and Jill Appel. 1982. *Monte Alban's Hinterland, Part I: The Prehispanic Settlement Patterns of the Central and Southern Parts of the Valley of Oaxaca*. University of Michigan, Museum of Anthropology, Memoirs, no. 15. University of Michigan, Museum of Anthropology, Ann Arbor.

Blanton, Richard E., Stephen A. Kowalewski, Gary M. Feinman, and Laura M. Finsten. 1993. *Ancient Mesoamerica: A Comparison of*

Change in Three Regions. 2nd edn. Cambridge University Press, New York.

Burkhart, Louise M. 1989. *The Slippery Earth: Nahua–Christian Moral Dialogue in Sixteenth-Century Mexico.* University of Arizona Press, Tucson.

Byland, Bruce E. and John M. D. Pohl. 1994. *In the Realm of 8 Deer: The Archaeology of the Mixtec Codices.* University of Oklahoma Press, Norman.

Carmack, Robert M., Janine Gasco, and Gary H. Gossen (eds). 1996. *The Legacy of Mesoamerica: History and Culture of a Native American Civilization.* Prentice-Hall, Englewood Cliffs, NJ.

Chance, John K. 1989. *Conquest of the Sierra: Spaniards and Indians in Colonial Oaxaca.* University of Oklahoma Press, Norman.

Charlton, Thomas H. and Patricia Fournier-García 1993. Urban and Rural Dimensions of the Contact Period, Central Mexico, 1521–1620. In *Ethnohistory and Archaeology: Approaches to Postcontact Change in the Americas,* edited by J. Daniel Rogers and Samuel M. Wilson, pp. 201–20. Plenum Press, New York.

Childe, V. Gordon. 1950. The Urban Revolution. *Town Planning Review* 21: 3–17.

Coe, Michael D. 1992. *Breaking the Maya Code.* Thames and Hudson, New York.

—— 1993. *The Maya.* 5th edn. Thames and Hudson, New York.

—— 1994. *Mexico: From the Olmecs to the Aztecs.* 4th edn. Thames and Hudson, New York.

Cook, Noble David and W. George Lovell (eds). 1991. "Secret Judgments of God:" Old World Disease in Colonial Spanish America. University of Oklahoma Press, Norman.

de Montmollin, Olivier. 1988. *Settlement Survey in the Rosario Valley, Chiapas, Mexico.* New World Archaeological Foundation Papers 57. New World Archaeological Foundation, Salt Lake City.

Diehl, Richard A. 1983. *Tula: The Toltec Capital of Ancient Mexico.* Thames and Hudson, New York.

Dillehay, Tom D. 1989. *Monte Verde, A Late Pleistocene Settlement in Chile. Volume 1: A Paleoenvironment and Site Context.* Smithsonian Institution Press, Washington, DC.

—— 1996. *Monte Verde, A Late Pleistocene Settlement in Chile. Volume 2: The Archaeological Context and Interpretation.* Smithsonian Institution Press, Washington, DC.

Flannery, Kent V. 1973. The Origins of Agriculture. *Annual Review of Anthropology* 2: 271–310.

—— 1985. *Guila Naquitz: Archaic Foraging and Early Agriculture in Oaxaca, Mexico.* Academic Press, New York.

Flannery, Kent V. (ed.). 1976. *The Early Mesoamerican Village.* Academic Press, New York.

Flannery, Kent V. and Joyce Marcus (eds). 1983. *The Cloud People: Divergent Evolution of the Zapotec and Mixtec Civilizations.* Academic Press, New York.

Foster, George M. 1960. *Culture and Conquest: America's Spanish Heritage.* Viking Fund Publications in Anthropology 27. Wenner-Gren Foundation for Anthropological Research, New York.

Freidel, David A. 1986. New Light on a Dark Age: Terminal Classic Lowland Maya: Successes, Failures, Aftermaths. In *Late Lowland Maya Civilization: Classic to Postclassic,* edited by Jeremy A. Sabloff and E. Wyllys Andrews, pp. 409–30. University of New Mexico Press, Albuquerque.

Freidel, David A. and Jeremy A. Sabloff. 1984. *Cozumel: Late Maya Settlement Patterns.* Academic Press, New York.

Galinat, Walton C. 1985. Domestication and Diffusion of Maize. In *Prehistoric Food Production in North America,* edited by Richard I. Ford, vol. 75, pp. 245–78. Anthropological Papers. University of Michigan, Museum of Anthropology, Ann Arbor.

Gasco, Janine, Greg Charles Smith, and Patricia Fournier-García (eds). 1997. *Approaches to the Historical Archaeology of Mexico, Central and South America.* The Institute of Archaeology, University of California, Los Angeles.

Gibson, Charles. 1966. *Spain in America.* Harper and Row, New York.

Graham, Elizabeth, David M. Pendergast, and Grant D. Jones. 1989. On the Fringes of Conquest: Maya–Spanish Contact in Colonial Belize. *Science* 246: 1254–9.

Gruhn, Ruth and Alan Lyle Bryan. 1977. *Los Tapiales: A Paleo-Indian Campsite in the Guatemalan Highlands.* Proceedings 121(3). American Philosophical Society, Philadelphia.

Harlan, Jack R. 1992. *Crops and Man.* 2nd edn. Crop Science Society of America, Madison, WI.

Healan, Dan M. 1989. *Tula of the Toltecs: Excavations and Survey.* University of Iowa Press, Iowa City.

Henderson, John S. 1997. *The World of the Ancient Maya.* 2nd edn. Cornell University Press, Ithaca.

Hester, Thomas R., Harry B. Iceland, Dale B. Hudler, and Harry J. Shafer. 1996. The Colha Preceramic Project: Preliminary Results from the 1993–1995 Field Season. *Mexicon* 18: 45–50.

Hosler, Dorothy. 1994. *The Sounds and Colors of Power: The Sacred Metallurgical Technology of Ancient West Mexico.* MIT Press, Cambridge.

Jones, Grant D. 1989. *Maya Resistance to Spanish Rule.* University of New Mexico Press, Albuquerque.

—— 1999. *The Conquest of the Last Maya Kingdom.* Stanford University Press, Stanford.

Justeson, John S. and George A. Broadwell. 1996. Language and Languages in Mesoamerica. In *The Legacy of Mesoamerica: History and Culture of a Native American Civilization*, edited by Robert M. Carmack, Janine Gasco and Gary H. Gossen, pp. 379–406. Prentice-Hall, Englewood Cliffs.

Justeson, John S. and Terrence Kaufman. 1993. Decipherment of Epi-Olmec Hieroglyphic Writing. *Science* 259: 1703–11.

Kaufman, Terrence. 1976. Mesoamerican Indian Languages. In *Encyclopedia Britannica, Macropedia*, vol. 11, pp. 956–63. Encyclopedia Britannica, New York.

Kepecs, Susan, Gary M. Feinman, and Sylviane Boucher. 1994. Chichen Itza and its Hinterland: A World-Systems Perspective. *Ancient Mesoamerica* 5: 141–58.

Kirchoff, Paul. 1952. Mesoamerica: Its Geographical Limits, Ethnic Composition, and Cultural Characteristics. In *Heritage of Conquest*, edited by Sol Tax, pp. 17–30. The Free Press, New York.

Kowalewski, Stephen A., Gary M. Feinman, Laura Finsten, Richard E. Blanton, and Linda M. Nicholas. 1989. *Monte Alban's Hinterland, Part II: Prehispanic Settlement Patterns in Tlacolula, Etla, and Ocotlan, The Valley of Oaxaca, Mexico.* Memoirs, no. 23. Museum of Anthropology, University of Michigan, Ann Arbor.

Lockhart, James. 1992. *The Nahuas After the Conquest: A Social and Cultural History of the Indians of Central Mexico, Sixteenth Through Eighteenth Centuries.* Stanford University Press, Stanford.

Lorenzo, José Luis and Lorena Mirambell. 1986a. Preliminary Report on Archaeological and Paleoenvironmental Studies in the Area of E1 Cedral, San Luis Potosí, Mexico, 1977–1980. In *New Evidence for the Pleistocene Peopling of the Americas*, edited by Alan Bryan, pp. 107–13. Center for the Study of Early Man, Orono, ME.

—— 1986b. *Tlapacoya: 35,000 Años de Historia del Lago de Chalco.* Colección Científica 155. Instituto Nacional de Antropología e Historia, Mexico City.

MacNeish, Richard S. 1986. The Preceramic of Middle America. *Advances in World Archaeology* 5: 93–129.

Marcus, Joyce. 1992. *Mesoamerican Writing Systems: Propaganda, Myth, and History in Four Ancient Civilizations.* Princeton University Press, Princeton.

Marcus, Joyce and Kent V. Flannery. 1996. *Zapotec Civilization: How Urban Society Evolved in Mexico's Oaxaca Valley.* Thames and Hudson, New York.

McAnany, Patricia. 1989. Economic Foundations of Prehistoric Maya Society: Paradigms and Concepts. In *Prehistoric Maya Economies of Belize*, edited by Patricia A. McAnany and Barry L. Isaac, pp. 347–72. Research in Economic Anthropology, Supplement, vol. 4. JAI Press, Greenwich, CT.

McClung de Tapia, Emily. 1992. The Origins of Agriculture in Mesoamerica and Central America. In *The Origins of Agriculture: An International Perspective*, edited by C. Wesley Cowan and Patty Jo Watson, pp. 143–71. Smithsonian Institution Press, Washington, DC.

Meltzer, David J. 1995. Clocking the First Americans. *Annual Review of Anthropology* 24: 21–45.

Meltzer, David J. et al. 1997. On the Pleistocene Antiquity of Monte Verde, Southern Chile. *American Antiquity* 62: 659–63.

Miller, Arthur G. (ed.). 1983. *Highland–Lowland Interaction in Mesoamerica: Interdisciplinary Approaches.* Dumbarton Oaks, Washington, DC.

Parsons, Jeffrey R., Elizabeth M. Brumfiel, Mary H. Parsons, and David J. Wilson. 1982. *Prehispanic Settlement Patterns in the Southern Valley of Mexico: The Chalco-Xochimilco Region.* Memoirs 14. Museum of Anthropology, University of Michigan, Ann Arbor.

Pendergast, David A. 1986. Stability Through Change: Lamanai, Belize from the Ninth to the Seventeenth Century. In *Late Lowland Maya Civilization: Classic to Postclassic*, edited by Jeremy A. Sabloff and E. Wyllys Andrews, pp. 223–50. University of New Mexico Press, Albuquerque.

Pohl, Mary D. (ed.). 1990. *Ancient Maya Wetland Agriculture: Excavations on Albion Island, Northern Belize.* Westview Press, Boulder.

Pohl, Mary D. et al. 1996. Early Agriculture in the Maya Lowlands. *Latin American Antiquity* 7: 355–72.

Pollard, Helen P. 1993. *Tariacuri's Legacy: The Prehispanic Tarascan State.* University of Oklahoma Press, Norman.

Rathje, William L. 1972. Praise the Gods and Pass the Metates: A Hypothesis of the Development of Lowland Rainforest Civilization in Mesoamerica. In *Contemporary Archaeology: A Guide to Theory and Contributions*, edited by Mark P. Leone, pp. 365–92. SIU Press, Carbondale.

Roosevelt, Anna C. et al. 1996. Paleoindian Cave Dwellers in the Amazon: The Peopling of the Americas. *Science* 272: 373–84.

Sanders, William T. 1965. The Cultural Ecology of the Teotihuacan Valley. Unpublished report, submitted to Department of Anthropology, Pennsylvania State University.

Sanders, William T., Jeffrey R. Parsons, and Robert S. Santley. 1979. *The Basin of Mexico: Ecological Processes in the Evolution of a Civilization*. Academic Press, New York.

Sanders, William T. and Barbara J. Price. 1968. *Mesoamerica: The Evolution of a Civilization*. Random House, New York.

Shafer, Harry J. and Thomas R. Hester. 1983. Ancient Maya Chert Workshops in Northern Belize, Central America. *American Antiquity* 48: 519–43.

Sharer, Robert J. 1994. *The Ancient Maya*. 5th edn. Stanford University Press, Stanford.

Smith, Michael E. 1996. *The Aztecs*. Blackwell, Oxford.

Stark, Barbara L. 1981. The Rise of Sedentary Life. In *Archaeology*, edited by Jeremy A. Sabloff, vol. 1, pp. 345–72. Handbook of Middle American Indians, Supplement. University of Texas Press, Austin.

Suárez, Jorge A. 1983. *The Mesoamerican Indian Languages*. Cambridge University Press, New York.

Townsend, Richard F. 1979. *State and Cosmos in the Art of Tenochtitlan*. Studies in Pre-Columbian Art and Archaeology 20. Dumbarton Oaks, Washington, DC.

Trigger, Bruce G. 1989. *A History of Archaeological Thought*. Cambridge University Press, New York.

Turner, B. L., II and Peter D. Harrison (eds). 1983. *Pulltrouser Swamp: Ancient Maya Habitat, Agriculture, and Settlement in Northern Belize*. University of Texas Press, Austin.

Voorhies, Barbara. 1976. *The Chantuto People: An Archaic Period Society of the Chipas Littoral, Mexico*. New World Archaeological Foundation Papers 41. New World Archaeological Foundation, Provo.

Weaver, Muriel Porter. 1993. *The Aztecs, Maya, and their Predecessors: Archaeology of Mesoamerica*. 3rd edn. Academic Press, San Diego.

Willey, Gordon R., William R. Bullard, John Glass, and James Gifford. 1965. *Prehistoric Maya Settlements in the Belize Valley*. Papers 54. Peabody Museum of American Archaeology and Ethnology, Cambridge.

Willey, Gordon R. and Jeremy A. Sabloff. 1993. *A History of American Archaeology*. 3rd edn. W. H. Freeman, San Francisco.

PART I

The Organization of Society

Editors' Introduction

Archaeologists approach the study of ancient Mesoamerican social organization from a variety of perspectives. The most direct method is to focus on sites – places where people once lived or carried out other activities. Settlement sites occur in many different sizes and forms, and each region had a characteristic pattern of settlement units. The most fundamental settlement unit was the house, and the excavation and analysis of domestic features and artifacts is known as "household archaeology." The methods of household-and community-based archaeology can tell us much about the differences in lifestyle between the rich and the poor, an important topic in the class-stratified societies of ancient Mesoamerica. Another way to study Mesoamerican social organization is to focus on cities and urbanism. Mesoamerican cities were among the most spectacular of the ancient world, but beyond their impressive monumental architecture these sites provide important insights into the people who built and inhabited them. An additional approach to ancient social organization is to examine the way in which gender structured social and cultural life. We use these themes – settlement hierarchy, houses and households, social classes, urbanism, and gender – to organize the following introduction to the chapters on ancient Mesoamerican social organization.

The Settlement Hierarchy

Mesoamerican settlements exhibited a great diversity of sizes and forms, from the smallest peasant hut to the largest imperial capital city. Each society had a hierarchy of settlements that reflected basic scales of social, economic, and political organization. In general, more complex societies had a greater number of tiers of settlement size. In the Formative period, before the development of states, settlement hierarchies were limited to one or two levels consisting of small centers and supporting communities. The clearest description of a Formative Mesoamerican settlement hierarchy is found in *The Early Mesoamerican Village* (Flannery 1976). In this influential study, Kent Flannery and his colleagues identified two levels of settlement for early Oaxaca: the house and the village (Flannery and Winter, chapter 1). This description of settlements remains useful after the Formative period, although in many areas additional levels are added to the settlement hierarchy, such as hamlets, secondary centers, and primary centers or cities.

The Classic lowland Maya settlement hierarchy had five levels in many areas: the house, the patio group, the cluster, the minor center, and the major center (Ashmore 1981). Maya minor and major centers had ritual and elite residential precincts that were the foci of communal activity. At the lowest levels, however, the Formative and Classic hierarchies were quite similar: both start with the house or dwelling as the basic unit, and both add a grouping of houses (village and cluster) as an important level above the household. Hierarchical organization was unevenly distributed across the landscape of Mesoamerica, and some areas such as parts of Belize, lacked the large urban centers of the central Maya lowlands (King and Potter 1994).

The notion that settlement hierarchies reflect social complexity was used by some archaeologists in the 1970s and 1980s as a method to identify state-level societies with settlement pattern data. Working in the Near East, Henry Wright and Gregory Johnson (Wright 1986; Wright and Johnson 1975) proposed that because states have multi-level administrative hierarchies, they should exhibit multiple levels of settlement size, and proposed the number four as the requisite number of levels needed to qualify as a state. This method did not fare well in Mesoamerica, however. Teotihuacan, one of the most powerful states of the Mesoamerican past, had fewer than four levels of settlement in its hinterland (Sanders et al. 1979); its complex administrative hierarchy was simply not accompanied by many different sizes of sites. Teotihuacan was a unique case, however, in that its growth was accomplished by forcibly moving much of the rural population of the Valley of Mexico into the new urban center. Archaeologists now recognize that although Wright and Johnson's method cannot claim universal application, settlement hierarchies do provide important information about ancient societies and their political complexity (see, for example, Kowalewski 1990).

The concept of settlement patterns is important because it forms a basic framework for virtually all archaeological fieldwork. Archaeologists conducting regional surveys locate sites of varying sizes and then must identify the nature of the site hierarchy (e.g. Ashmore 1981; Blanton et al. 1982; Kowalewski et al. 1989; Sanders et al. 1979). Excavations are then interpreted in light of the nature of the settlement unit being studied. In this book, the chapters by Flannery and Winter (chapter 1), Marcus (chapter 3), Feinman and Nicholas (chapter 10), Smith and Heath-Smith (chapter 11), and Mathews (chapter 13) all discuss aspects of settlement hierarchies in various regions of Mesoamerica. We suggest that students consider this concept in evaluating all of the chapters, however. Ask yourself what type of settlement unit is being described, and how the settlement level affects the contents of each chapter.

Houses and Households

Mesoamerican peoples lived in many different types of dwellings, from small shelters to huge palaces. Since the publication of *The Early Mesoamerican Village* (Flannery 1976) Mesoamericanists have devoted considerable energy to the excavation of residential structures. This work was part of a broad trend in the social and historical sciences that focused attention on the household as an important unit of social analysis (Netting et al. 1984; Yanagisako 1979). Households, defined as the people living together in a dwelling, are one of the primary units of social organization in most state-level societies. The members of a household not only share a house, but they also typically cooperate in activities of reproduction, socialization, economic production, and ritual. Although the concepts of household (residents of a dwelling) and family (a basic kinship group) are similar, scholars have found the term household to be more useful since a single dwelling may have contained a combination of kin and non-kin who nevertheless worked together cooperatively. Scholars in many disciplines found that by focusing on households, they gained considerable insight into the workings of contemporary, historic, and ancient societies.

There is a basic difficulty in applying the household concept in archaeology, however. Archaeologists excavate and study *houses*, not households. Although we sometimes find burials of household members, we never obtain direct evidence of a household as a group of people. Archaeologists must use their data to infer that a social group such as household once inhabited a given structure. This is done by reconstructing the activities conducted by household members (chapters 1 and 4), and by using archaeological remains to reveal something of the social conditions of the inhabitants of ancient houses (chapters 2, 7, 11, 12, and 21). The household approach is perhaps most useful for providing a series of comparable social units whose activities and conditions can be compared within and between sites to illuminate past social organization (Smith and Heath-Smith, chapter 11). One of the benefits of an emphasis on houses is that it turns the attention of archaeologists away from pyramids, tombs, and royalty and towards the lives of the rest of society.

Archaeological household analysis begins with a house. Details of size, location, layout, and construction materials can provide important clues about a house's ancient inhabitants. The basic domestic activities of households typically occupy indoor and outdoor spaces that are larger than the actual dwelling, so archaeologists must excavate and analyze this larger area. Flannery and Winter (chapter 1) pioneered this approach by including features, activity areas, and burials that surround a house as part of what they initially called the "household cluster." Flannery (1983) later suggested that the phrase "household cluster" be abandoned in favor of "household unit" as a clearer archaeological unit that cannot be confused with the settlement cluster concept discussed under settlement hierarchies above.

Smith and Heath-Smith (chapter 11) studied household units by excavating midden (garbage) deposits adjacent to houses at rural Aztec sites. Unlike Formative Oaxaca houses where many artifacts appear to have been deposited near the places of use on house floors (chapter 1), these rural Aztec houses had been picked clean when their last inhabitants moved to nearby villages after the Spanish conquest (chapter 11). This contrast illustrates the important role of "formation processes" in the study of ancient houses and households (Hayden and Cannon 1983; Schiffer 1987). Although people without any training in archaeology sometimes assume that all sites are like Pompeii with abundant artifacts located in the places where they were originally used, in fact most sites had quite different formation processes which make social interpretations difficult. For example, Smith and Heath-Smith found that some late-period houses had early-period potsherds resting on their floors. This puzzling finding was explained by the

nature of the walls and the way they decomposed. The late-period walls of these peasant houses had been made of sun-dried adobe (mud) bricks that had been manufactured from mud dug out from near the houses. The mud included postsherds from earlier periods, which became embedded in the bricks. When the bricks melted after abandonment of the houses, these early sherds ended up resting on the late floors of the houses. Obviously these artifacts cannot be used to analyze the activities of the late-period inhabitants of the houses (Smith 1992: 79–105).

The Early Mesoamerican Village initiated the "household archaeology" approach in Mesoamerica; later studies in this vein are included Manzanilla (1986), Santley and Hirth (1993), and Wilk and Ashmore (1988). In addition to Flannery and Winter (chapter 1), many of the chapters in this section focus on aspects of houses and the activities and conditions of ancient Mesoamerican households. Students should ask themselves just how the architectural characteristics of Mesoamerican houses, from the small Formative huts of Oaxaca to the huge apartment compounds of Teotihuacan, can inform us about the nature of the people who once lived in those structures.

Social Classes

Social inequality was a basic fact that had a direct effect on all aspects of life in ancient Mesoamerica. Mesoamerican societies differed in the extent of their inequality in wealth, power, and status, and these patterns can be studied archaeologically. Although some type of inequality is found in every human society, it is only in states that inequality became pronounced and institutionalized. Social classes refer to categories of people in state societies who differ dramatically in terms of wealth, power, and status. Thus we would say that Formative villages had a moderate level of inequality but no social classes (see Clark and Blake, chapter 12), whereas the states of the Classic and Postclassic periods had true social classes (see Haviland and Moholy-Nagy, chapter 2; Smith and Heath-Smith, chapter 11; Cowgill, chapter 15).

The basic two-class division in ancient Mesoamerica, as in most ancient civilizations, included a small upper class and everyone else. The terms elite and commoner are widely used to refer to these two fundamental social classes. Estimates of the size of the elite class in ancient Mesoamerican civilizations range from 2 per cent to 10 per cent of the total population (e.g. Smith 1994). It has been suggested that among the Classic Maya there may have been a middle class between the commoners and elites (Chase and Chase 1992). Chase (1992), for example, argues for such a middle class toward the end of the Classic period at Caracol based on the growing numbers of tombs in dispersed residential contexts and broad distributions of luxury items at that site which he claims are too abundant to simply represent an elite class expansion. Other archaeologists reject this claim as unsupported by the evidence. Instead of a middle class, Marcus (1993), for example, emphasizes variations within the commoner and elite classes. William Sanders (1992) has argued that the Aztecs were the only Mesoamerican state with an emerging middle class, and that this group was made up of merchants (see also Smith 1996). A similar argument for the development of a new Postclassic merchant class has also been made for the Maya area (Sabloff and Rathje 1975).

Recent fieldwork has made it clear that not all farmers were poor peasants, and not all craft workers lived in urban centers. In other words, the rural hinterlands of larger centers were sometimes the setting for complex social institutions and prosperous commoner households. Recent excavations at Classic Maya sites have uncovered evidence of affluent, relatively autonomous producer settlements dispersed across the landscape in zones like northern Belize (Hester and Shafer 1983) and the Peten and Usumacinta (Rands and Bishop 1980; Freidel 1981; Rice, chapter 7). These may suggest the existence of an affluent middle tier of society in parts of the Maya area (King and Potter

1994) or geographic "pockets" where class concepts were less well defined than elsewhere in the lowlands (McAnany 1995: 155). Such dispersed communities were largely self-sufficient with regard to their subsistence economy, and land-holding and resource-controlling lineages appear to have wielded considerable power independent of the domains of current political centers (McAnany 1995: 144–56; McAnany, chapter 23 below). Similarly, Smith and Heath-Smith (chapter 11) report evidence for social complexity and prosperity in a rural Aztec setting. Whether these cases best fit with a two-class or a multi-class model is not yet clear. What we can say it that archaeologists now possess the data to evaluate models of ancient social classes and social inequality, but clear and consistent criteria must be applied in site comparisons. The chapter by Haviland and Moholy-Nagy (chapter 2) is an example of the kind of approach that needs to be taken to study social class structure archaeologically.

As pointed out by Haviland and Moholy-Nagy, archaeologists have traditionally used three types of information to study social stratification in ancient societies: burials, architecture, and artifacts. In most societies, one's treatment after death depends upon one's position in life. The poor generally get simple burials, while the rich and mighty often get major monuments. Archaeologists have found this pattern in nearly all ancient civilizations (Trigger 1993), and the Classic Maya are no exception. Burials can also provide information on health and disease which may relate to past patterns of social class. Residential architecture is one of the most visible signs of social inequality. Some ancient Mesoamerican palaces that housed kings and nobles were huge elaborate compounds, whereas at the opposite end of the social spectrum commoners often lived in small, simple houses. Because elites and the lower commoners had vastly different lifestyles, the artifacts that they used often differed as well (Smith 1987). Among the Maya, for example, many luxury goods (such as polychrome pottery) were used in far greater proportions by the elite, and these can serve as markers of elite residence or activity. Among the Aztecs, however, both utilitarian and luxury goods circulated widely, and even the most valuable items are recovered in excavations of commoner houses (Smith and Heath-Smith, chapter 11).

Elites wielded considerable power in ancient Mesoamerican civilizations. An elite class that is hereditary and defined by native legal concepts is called a nobility (Bloch 1961). Ethnohistoric documents show that Aztec elites certainly fit this definition (Smith 1986), and it is probably applicable to earlier elites as well. Because of their larger and more elaborate houses and their positions at the top of the social hierarchy, ancient nobles are more easily visible archaeologically than are ancient commoners. Analysis of the activities and conditions of the nobility can shed considerable light on the organization of power within a society (Chase and Chase 1992). One characteristic of Mesoamerican elites is that individual members maintained social connections across political borders. Elites typically married spouses from other polities, and elites from independent states (including sometimes warring states) typically gathered together for important social occasions such as royal rites of accession, weddings, and funerals. This practice led to the spread of common tastes, practices, and styles among widely scattered elites and this process accounts for many of the patterns of stylistic similarity within and between regions. These elite interactions were an important part of the political process in Mesoamerican societies (see the introduction to part III).

Nobles monopolized the positions of government in most or all Mesoamerican state-level societies, and they probably owned or controlled most of the land. These characteristics gave them considerable political and economic power, but the details of the extent of their control and influence are usually uncertain, leading to considerable argumentation and debate among scholars. For example, to what extent did elites have a power base independent of the state? Did they control commerce and exchange to the same extent that they controlled land and government? These are difficult questions to answer with archaeological data, and the opinions of individual archaeologists often depend upon their theoretical orientation. Brumfiel and Earle (1987), for example, have identified three theoretical positions on the role of elites in controlling craft production and trade. In the *adaptationist* approach of the cultural ecologists, elites served as managers of the economy in roles that benefited everybody. In contrast, elites were more exploitative in the *political* approach, controlling the economy for their own gain. Finally, the *commercial* approach suggests that major aspects of the economy were not under elite control at all. Students should ask which of these approaches seem to best fit the evidence in the chapters in this book. There is no single right answer, no single interpretation that works for all Mesoamerican civilizations. There was considerable variety in the patterns of social stratification and the roles of elites, and each civilization needs to be analyzed on its own terms for these traits.

Urbanism

Although almost anyone would agree that the huge metropolis of Teotihuacan was a city, not everyone has accepted the Classic Maya settlements as true cities because of their small population sizes and low population densities (e.g. Sanders and Price 1968). But just what do we mean by city? Several alternative definitions have been proposed for ancient cities and towns, and one's choice of definition influences one's interpretations of the ancient cultures of Mesoamerica. One of the most influential approaches to ancient urbanism was the *ecological approach*, introduced to Mesoamerica by William T. Sanders as part of the "new archaeology" program of the 1960s and 1970s (Sanders and Price 1968; Sanders and Santley 1983). Cities and towns were viewed as part of a society's adaptation to the natural environment, and research focused on issues such as subsistence (where did urbanites get their food?), settlement patterns (how are urban settlements distributed across the landscape?), economic organization (what was the role of craft specialists in cities?), and population size.

In the ecological perspective, cities are defined as settlements with a large population, dense population nucleation, and high internal social diversity. The huge central Mexican cities of Teotihuacan and Tenochtitlan were seen by Sanders as the most highly developed urban centers in Mesoamerica, whereas most other Mesoamerican cultures, including the Classic Maya, had settlements that were either not truly urban in nature, or else were less urbanized than these large imperial capitals. Many archaeologists were dissatisfied with Sanders's ecological approach because they felt that the Classic Maya centers were in fact true cities, even if they did not closely resemble Teotihuacan or Tenochtitlan. This dissatisfaction led to the adoption of the *functional approach* to urbanism by most Mesoamericanists (Mathewson 1977).

The functional approach to urbanism developed in the 1970s through a combination of settlement pattern research and influences from the field of economic geography. The initial applications of this approach, from Richard E. Blanton (1976, 1978, 1981) and Stephen A. Kowalewski (1982; Kowalewski et al. 1983), emphasized regional economic functions. Economic activities tend to concentrate in specific settlements called central places, which often comprise a hierarchy of function (and size) on a regional level. In this approach, a city is a high-level central place that performs a large number and variety of economic services for a large hinterland, whereas smaller central places called towns have fewer economic functions and serve smaller areas.

In the 1980s the functional approach was broadened by the addition of non-economic functions such as administration and religion, following suggestions in Richard Fox's influential book, *Urban Anthropology* (Fox 1977). This expanded functional view was applied to Mesoamerica by Joyce Marcus (chapter 3), and was later adopted by

Sanders and David Webster as well (Sanders and Webster 1988). One advantage of the functional perspective is that is focuses attention on a variety of types of urban settlement. Not all Mesoamerican cities were identical. Some emphasized craft production (e.g. the Aztec city of Otumba – Charlton et al. 1991), others were imperial capitals focused on administration and trade (e.g. Teotihuacan – see Cowgill, chapter 15 – or Tzintzuntzan – see Pollard 1977), whereas many Mesoamerican cities combined ritual and political functions. This latter pattern, codified by Fox as the "regal-ritual city" type, was probably the most common kind of urban center in Mesoamerica. Another advantage of the functional approach is that smaller Mesoamerican cities, such as those of the Classic Maya, can be viewed as fully urban in nature and not relegated to a less-than-urban status just because they were not as large as Teotihuacan or Tenochtitlan.

The article here by Joyce Marcus (chapter 3) was a ground-breaking early statement of the expanded functional approach, and it remains the single most comprehensive comparative analysis of Mesoamerican urbanism. Its main drawback is that only a limited number of cities are included. Additional insights into Marcus's three main case studies (Teotihuacan, Monte Alban, and Tikal) can be found in chapters 2, 4, 8, 10, and 15 here; students should ask how Marcus's ideas apply to other cities included in this volume (see especially chapters 7, 11, 15, and 16).

Gender

Until recently, many studies of ancient civilizations, in Mesoamerica and elsewhere, tended to ignore the roles and position of women in society. It was simply assumed that the important actors in society were men, and women's activities were given little attention. Along with the rise in feminist scholarship generally, archaeologists began to pay more attention to issues of gender and women's roles in ancient societies (e.g. Brumfiel 1992; Claasen and Joyce 1997;

Wright 1996). Flannery and Winter's paper (chapter 1) was an early attempt to segregate the remains of domestic activities into male and female categories. Their interpretation of male and female work areas is open to question, however, since it is based on a single analogy and does not take into account the formation processes that shaped the nature of the artifact deposits.

Because of the existence of ethnohistoric documentation, the Aztecs have figured heavily in discussions of gender in ancient Mesoamerica. Unfortunately, written descriptions of Aztec women and their activities and roles are quite sketchy and even contradictory. The Spanish priests who compiled most of the available descriptions of Aztec society had little first-hand knowledge of Aztec women. The primary domain of women was in the home, and the friars rarely entered people's homes (Burkhart 1996). The result of our scanty knowledge has been heated debate over the status of women in Aztec society. Some authors (e.g. Nash 1978; Rodríguez-Shadow 1991) have seen Aztec women as "systematically exploited, demeaned, and controlled by both brutal coercion and psychological terror" (Brumfiel, chapter 22, describing the work of María Rodríguez-Shadow), whereas others have argued that Aztec gender roles were complementary or parallel in that women controlled important domains within Aztec society, particularly domestic production (e.g. McCafferty and McCafferty 1988; Brumfiel 1991; Kellogg 1995a: 88–103, 1995b, 1996). Brumfiel (chapter 22) reviews these positions and provides new archaeological data that help clarify the position of women in Aztec society.

REFERENCES

Ashmore, Wendy (ed.). 1981. *Lowland Maya Settlement Patterns*. University of New Mexico Press, Albuquerque.

Blanton, Richard E. 1976. Anthropological Studies of Cities. *Annual Review of Anthropology* 5: 249–64.

——1978. *Monte Alban: Settlement Patterns at the Ancient Zapotec Capitol*. Academic Press, New York.

——1981. The Rise of Cities. In *Archaeology*, edited by Jeremy A. Sabloff, vol. 1, pp. 392–400. Handbook of Middle American Indians, Supplement. University of Texas Press, Austin.

Blanton, Richard E., Stephen Kowalewski, Gary M. Feinman, and Jill Appel. 1982. *Monte Alban's Hinterland, Part I: The Prehispanic Settlement Patterns of the Central and Southern Parts of the Valley of Oaxaca*. University of Michigan, Museum of Anthropology, Memoirs, no. 15. University of Michigan, Museum of Anthropology, Ann Arbor.

Bloch, Marc. 1961. *Feudal Society*. 2 vols. University of Chicago Press, Chicago.

Brumfiel, Elizabeth M. 1991. Weaving and Cooking: Women's Production in Aztec Mexico. In *Engendering Archaeology: Women and Prehistory*, edited by Joan M. Gero and Margaret W. Conkey, pp. 224–51. Blackwell, Oxford.

——1992. Breaking and Entering the Ecosystem: Gender, Class, and Faction Steal the Show. *American Anthropologist* 94: 551–67.

Brumfiel, Elizabeth M. and Timothy K. Earle. 1987. Specialization, Exchange, and Complex Societies: An Introduction. In *Specialization, Exchange, and Complex Societies*, edited by Elizabeth M. Brumfiel and Timothy K. Earle, pp. 1–9. Cambridge University Press, New York.

Burkhart, Louise M. 1996. Mexica Women on the Home Front: Housework and Religion in Aztec Mexico. In *Indian Women of Early Mexico: Identity, Ethnicity, and Gender Differentiation*, edited by Susan Schroeder, Stephanie Wood, and Robert Haskett, pp. 25–54. University of Oklahoma Press, Norman.

Charlton, Thomas H., Deborah L. Nichols, and Cynthia Otis Charlton. 1991. Aztec Craft Production and Specialization: Archaeological Evidence from the City-State of Otumba, Mexico. *World Archaeology* 23: 98–114.

Chase, Arlen F. 1992. Elites and the Changing Organization of Classic Maya Society. In *Mesoamerican Elites: An Archaeological Assessment*, edited by Diane Z. Chase and Arlen F. Chase, pp. 30–49. University of Oklahoma Press, Norman.

Chase, Diane Z. and Arlen F. Chase (eds). 1992. *Mesoamerican Elites: An Archaeological Assessment*. University of Oklahoma Press, Norman.

Claasen, Cheryl and Rosemary A. Joyce (eds). 1997. *Women in Prehistory: North America and Mesoamerica*. University of Pennsylvania Press, Philadelphia.

Flannery, Kent V. (ed.). 1976. *The Early Mesoamerican Village*. Academic Press, New York.

Flannery, Kent V. 1983. The Tierras Largas Phase and the Analytical Units of the Early Oaxacan Village. In *The Cloud People: Divergent Evolution of the Zapotec and Mixtec Civilizations*, edited by Kent V. Flannery and Joyce Marcus, pp. 43–5. Academic Press, New York.

Fox, Richard G. 1977. *Urban Anthropology: Cities in their Cultural Settings*. Prentice-Hall, Englewood Cliffs.

Freidel, David A. 1981. The Political Economics of Residential Dispersion Among the Lowland Maya. In *Lowland Maya Settlement Patterns*, edited by Wendy Ashmore, pp. 371–85. University of New Mexico Press, Albuquerque.

Hayden, Brian and Aubry Cannon. 1983. Where the Garbage Goes: Refuse Disposal in the Maya Highlands. *Journal of Anthropological Archaeology* 2: 117–63.

Hester, Thomas R. and Harry J. Shafer. 1983. Ancient Maya Chert Workshops in Northern Belize, Central America. *American Antiquity* 48: 519–43.

Kellogg, Susan. 1995a. *Law and the Transformation of Aztec Culture, 1500–1700*. University of Oklahoma Press, Norman.

—— 1995b. The Woman's Room: Some Aspects of Gender Relations in Tenochtitlan in the Late Pre-Hispanic Period. *Ethnohistory* 42: 563–76.

—— 1996. From Parallel and Equivalent to Separate but Unequal: Tenochca Mexica Women, 1500–1700. In *Indian Women of Early Mexico*, edited by Susan Schroeder, Stephanie Wood, and Robert Haskett, pp. 123–44. University of Oklahoma Press, Norman.

King, Eleanor and Daniel Potter. 1994. Small Sites in Prehistoric Maya Socioeconomic Organization: A Perspective from Colha, Belize. In *Archaeological Views from the Countryside: Village Communities in Early Complex Societies*, edited by Glenn Schwartz and Steven Falconer, pp. 64–90. Smithsonian Institution Press, Washington, DC.

Kowalewski, Stephen A. 1982. The Evolution of Primate Regional Systems. *Comparative Urban Research* 9: 60–78.

—— 1990. The Evolution of Complexity in the Valley of Oaxaca. *Annual Review of Anthropology* 19: 39–58.

Kowalewski, Stephen A., Richard E. Blanton, and Gary M. Feinman. 1983. Boundaries, Scale and Internal Organization. *Journal of Anthropological Archaeology* 2: 32–56.

Kowalewski, Stephen A., Gary M. Feinman, Laura Finsten, Richard E. Blanton, and Linda M. Nicholas. 1989. *Monte Alban's Hinterland, Part II: Prehispanic Settlement Patterns in Tlacolula, Etla, and Ocotlan, The Valley of Oaxaca, Mexico*. Memoirs, no. 23. Museum of Anthropology, University of Michigan, Ann Arbor.

Manzanilla, Linda (ed.). 1986. *Unidades Habitacionales Mesoamericanas y Sus Areas de Actividad*. Universidad Nacional Autónoma de Méxio, Mexico City.

Marcus, Joyce. 1993. Ancient Maya Political Organization. In *Lowland Maya Civilization in the Eighth Century AD*, edited by Jeremy A. Sabloff and John S. Henderson, pp. 111–84. Dumbarton Oaks, Washington, DC.

Mathewson, Kent. 1977. Maya Urban Genesis Reconsidered: Trade and Intensive Agriculture as Primary Factors. *Journal of Historical Geography* 3: 203–15.

McAnany, Patricia A. 1995. *Living With the Ancestors: Kingship and Kingship in Ancient Maya Society*. University of Texas Press, Austin.

McCafferty, Sharisse D. and Geoffrey G. McCafferty. 1988. Powerful Women and the Myth of Male Dominance in Aztec Society. *Archaeological Review from Cambridge* 7: 45–59.

Nash, June. 1978. The Aztecs and the Ideology of Male Dominance. *Signs* 4: 349–62.

Netting, Robert McC., Richard R. Wilk, and R. J. Arnould (eds). 1984. *Households: Comparative and Historical Studies of the Domestic Group*. University of California Press, Berkeley.

Pollard, Helen P. 1977. An Analysis of Urban Zoning and Planning in Prehispanic Tzintzuntzan. *Proceedings of the American Philosophical Society* 121: 46–69.

Rands, Robert L. and Ronald L. Bishop. 1980. Resource Procurement Zones and Patterns of Ceramic Exchange in the Palenque Region, Mexico. In *Models and Methods in Regional Exchange*, edited by Robert E. Fry, vol. 1, pp. 19–46. Papers. Society for American Archaeology, Washington, DC.

Rodríguez-Shadow, María J. 1991. *La mujer azteca*. 2nd edn. Universidad Nacional Autónoma de México, Mexico City.

Sabloff, Jeremy A. 1997. *The Cities of Ancient Mexico: Reconstructing a Lost World*. Revised edn. Thames and Hudson, New York.

Sabloff, Jeremy A. and William L. Rathje. 1975. The Rise of a Maya Merchant Class. *Scientific American* 233: 72–82.

Sanders, William T. 1992. Ranking and Stratification in Prehispanic Mesoamerica. In *Mesoamerican Elites: An Archaeological Assessment*, edited by Diane A. Chase and Arlen F. Chase, pp. 278–91. University of Oklahoma Press, Norman.

Sanders, William T., Jeffrey R. Parsons, and Robert S. Santley. 1979. *The Basin of Mexico: Ecological Processes in the Evolution of a Civilization.* Academic Press, New York.

Sanders, William T. and Barbara J. Price. 1968. *Mesoamerica: The Evolution of a Civilization.* Random House, New York.

Sanders, William T. and Robert S. Santley. 1983. A Tale of Three Cities: Energetics and Urbanization in Pre-Hispanic Central Mexico. In *Prehistoric Settlement Patterns: Essays in Honor of Gordon R. Willey,* edited by Evon Z. Vogt and Richard Leventhal, pp. 243–91. University of New Mexico Press, Albuquerque.

Sanders, William T. and David Webster. 1988. The Mesoamerican Urban Tradition. *American Anthropologist* 90: 521–46.

Santley, Robert S. and Kenneth G. Hirth (eds). 1993. *Prehispanic Domestic Units in Western Mesoamerica: Studies of the Household, Compound, and Residence.* CRC Press, Boca Raton.

Schiffer, Michael B. 1987. *Formation Processes of the Archaeological Record.* University of New Mexico Press, Albuquerque.

Smith, Michael E. 1986. The Role of Social Stratification in the Aztec Empire: A View From the Provinces. *American Anthropologist* 88: 70–91.

—— 1987. Household Possessions and Wealth in Agrarian States: Implications for Archaeology. *Journal of Anthropological Archaeology* 6: 297–335.

—— 1992. *Archaeological Research at Aztec-Period Rural Sites in Morelos, Mexico. Volume 1, Excavations and Architecture/Investigaciones Arqueológicas en Sitios Rurales de la Epoca Azteca en Morelos, Tomo 1, Excavaciones y Arquitectura.* University of Pittsburgh Memoirs in Latin American Archaeology 4. University of Pittsburgh, Pittsburgh.

—— 1994. Economies and Polities in Aztec-period Morelos: Ethnohistoric Introduction. In *Economies and Polities in the Aztec Realm,* edited by Mary G. Hodge and Michael E. Smith, pp. 313–48. Institute for Mesoamerican Studies, Albany.

—— 1996. *The Aztecs.* Blackwell, Oxford.

Trigger, Bruce G. 1993. *Early Civilizations: Ancient Egypt in Context.* The American University in Cairo Press, Cairo.

Wilk, Richard R. and Wendy Ashmore (eds). 1988. *Household and Community in the Mesoamerican Past.* University of New Mexico Press, Albuquerque.

Wright, Henry T. 1986. The Evolution of Civilizations. In *American Archaeology, Past and Future,* edited by David J. Meltzer, Don D. Fowler, and Jeremy A. Sabloff, pp. 323–65. Smithsonian Institution Press, Washington, DC.

Wright, Henry T. and Gregory A. Johnson. 1975. Population, Exchange and Early State Formation in Southwestern Iran. *American Anthropologist* 77: 267–89.

Wright, Rita P. (ed.). 1996. *Gender and Archaeology.* University of Pennsylvania Press, Philadelphia.

Yanagisako, Sylvia. 1979. Family and Household: The Analysis of Domestic Groups. *Annual Review of Anthropology* 8: 161–206.

CHAPTER 1

Analyzing Household Activities

Kent V. Flannery and Marcus C. Winter

Perhaps the smallest spatial unit of archeological analysis is the *activity area*, and we have deferred it until now because we feel it makes more sense to discuss it in terms of the household cluster. Activity areas are spatially restricted areas where a specific task or set of related tasks has been carried on, and they are generally characterized by a scatter of tools, waste products, and/or raw materials; a feature, or set of features, may also be present. Even where activity areas are not clearly present, Mesoamerican archeologists have generally recognized *activity sets* – "tool kits" used for the performance of a specific task.

For example, in his excavations at Ticomán in the Valley of Mexico, George Vaillant (1931: 416–19) found two burials accompanied by what seem to be kits for specific craft activities, both dating to the Late Formative period (figure 1.1). Skeleton 17, an elderly male(?), had been buried with what Vaillant described as a "leatherworker's kit." Among the tools

> were found two spongy horn grainers or chisels, much worn and with both ends shaved down to edges. These might have been used to detach the flesh from the hide. Their function was supplemented by three small obsidian scrapers. For perforating holes in the leather there were three large bone awls made from deer radii, the distal portions of which were smoothed to a point. Two bodkins were used presumably to push the thread or sinew through the holes perforated by the awls. A small shovel-tipped tool of bone has no explic-

able use unless for fine work in the preparation of the hide or as an implement for weaving mats and baskets.
>
> *(Vaillant 1931: 313)*

Burial 17 also had in his lap a set of 16 pocket gopher mandibles, which may well have been part of the same tool kit; each contains one sharp, chisel-ended incisor tooth. (Vaillant considered them too "brittle" to be utilitarian, but this is an underestimate of the gopher incisor.)

Skeleton 34, also an elderly male, was buried with a kit of 15 stone and 11 bone tools for "finer work, like perhaps the tailoring of a hide." Interestingly, Skeleton 34 is shown as having been buried in a seated, upright position with the tools near his feet – a position that suggests to us that he was buried in a bell-shaped pit whose outlines Vaillant did not detect. The tool kit is described as follows:

> Thirteen obsidian blades and flakes provided for the cutting of the material. Two small bone awls served to perforate it and a needle equipped with an eye took care of the sewing. Six bird fibulae [*sic*][1] were probably blanks from which other needles could be manufactured. A hollow bone cut at one end might have been a needle case, and a battered bone, much used, served no explicable use. Needles with eyes were almost always associated in graves with blades of obsidian, so that there must have been a tailoring industry, although whether it was in hide or textiles cannot be decided on the archeological evidence.
>
> *(Vaillant 1931: 313–14)*

Reprinted from Kent V. Flannery and Marcus C. Winter. 1976. Analyzing Household Activities. In *The Early Mesoamerican Village*, edited by Kent V. Flannery (Academic Press, New York), pp. 34–45.

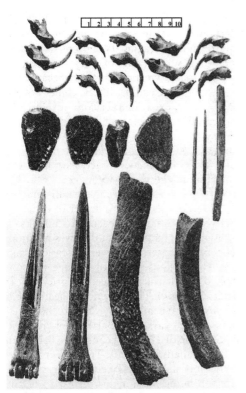

Figure 1.1 Formative "leather-worker's kit" associated with Skeleton 17 at Ticomán, Valley of Mexico. Top three rows: 15 gopher mandibles. Fourth row, left to right: 3 obsidian scrapers; 1 frag. pottery disc; 2 small bone bodkins; 1 bone chisel. Bottom row, left to right: 2 awls of deer metapodial; 2 hide grainers of deer antler. (After Vaillant 1931: Plate XCI.)

Three other Middle or Late Formative burials at Ticomán were accompanied by tool kits which, although not as elaborate as those with Skeletons 17 and 34, also seem to be "sets of tailoring implements." All three burials were male. One middle-aged female, Skeleton 48, also had a single bone bodkin and an obsidian blade. On the basis of Vaillant's data one could at least propose – as a hypothesis for future testing – that, at any one time, there were several households at Ticomán engaged in leather working or tailoring as a part-time specialty. Moreover, one could propose that this particular task was more often than not a male activity.

Such clues to the organization of household activity cannot be obtained from a study of the artifacts alone. They can be obtained only from contextual data, such as activity areas or activity sets. For more data on the household tools of the Formative Valley of Mexico, we can refer the reader to an important synthesis by Paul Tolstoy (1971).

Variation between households

Although Mesoamerican archeologists have very rarely carried out definitive functional analyses of Formative tools (as, for example, microscopic edge-wear analyses of stone artifacts), they have usually done a good job of describing and illustrating the tools they have found. Such are the continuities of rural Mesoamerican Indian life that ethnographic analogy has frequently been used, with considerable justification, in the interpretation of Formative artifacts. Customarily, variation in artifact assemblages has been presented by site and level, or by site and time period.

Once houses or household clusters have been identified, however, still another kind of variation is available for study: *the variation in activities between households*. In this section, we will briefly discuss the variation between households at 1500–500 BC in the region we know best, the Valley of Oaxaca. Wherever possible, we will point out what seem to be analogous activity areas or tool kits from other Formative sites mentioned in the archeological literature. Our discussion is intended to raise possibilities, rather than to be exhaustive.

Household activities in formative Oaxaca

We have no way of estimating the adequacy of our Oaxaca sample. We have drawn on the 3 best-preserved houses from Barrio del Rosario, Huitzo; the 10 best-preserved houses at San José Mogote; the 6 best-preserved household clusters at Tierras Largas; a single house from San Sebastian Abasolo; 2 hours from Santo Domingo Tomaltepec; and our 30 best-preserved bell-shaped pits.

The data from this sample have encouraged us to *tentatively* divide household activities in early Oaxacan villages into four categories, as follows:

1 *Universal household activities.* These are activities represented either by tools, features, or activity areas, for which there was some evidence at every reasonably complete house in our sample; we might predict, therefore, that these activities were carried out by every household in the valley.

2 *Possible household specialization.* Some types of tools seemed to be of nearly universal distribution, but the activity areas where they were manufactured were found at only one or two houses. We interpret these as activities carried out at every village, but perhaps by only one or two households in each village.

3 *Possible regional specialization.* Some activities are represented at only two of our five excavated villages; at those two villages, however, they are represented at virtually every house. Such activities may be regional specialities which were carried out by certain villages in only one part of the valley, with virtually every household in those villages participating.

4 *Possibly unique specializations.* Certain activities are known from only one village in our sample. At each of these villages, however, they are present in more than one house or household cluster. We suspect that at least one of these activities may be unique to a single residential ward or *barrio* at the largest early village in the valley. Let us now give a few examples of each of these categories.

Universal Household Activities

Food procurement, preparation, and storage apparently were carried on by every household during the period 1500–500 BC. No extensively excavated household cluster failed to yield evidence of the following: (1) fragments of grinding stones (*metates* and/or *manos*); (2) storage pits; (3) fragments of large storage jars, some with a 5- or 10-gallon capacity; (4) bones of cottontail rabbit; (5) carbonized kernels or cupule fragments of maize; and (6) fragments of pottery charcoal braziers. Where any of these ingredients were missing, we suspect it was because the house or household cluster could not be extensively excavated because of disturbance, poor preservation, or lack of time. What this suggests is that each household was probably autonomous in terms of certain basic subsistence practices during the millennium between 1500 and 500 BC, regardless of any part-time specialization.

Nevertheless, there is a degree of variation between households, even in "universal" subsistence practices, that deserves mention. For example, virtually every flotation sample from a house floor or storage pit contained corn kernels and seeds of prickly pear fruit (*Opuntia*). The presence of beans (*Phaseolus*) or avocado pits (*Persea*), however, was quite variable. Barrio del Rosario Huitzo yielded many beans, San Sebastián Abasolo many avocados; Tierras Largas had only modest amounts of either. Our samples are too numerous for this merely to be the result of sampling error. More likely, there was variation in the species chosen for cultivation by each household.

Similarly, although virtually every house contained cottontail bones, and usually bones of dog and mud turtle as well, amounts of deer bone varied considerably. Houses at San José Mogote and Tierras Largas had high numbers of deer bone, while Huitzo and Abasolo had less. Perhaps the greatest variety in hunted species occurred at Fábrica San José, a piedmont barranca site with good access to mountain hunting lands. Clearly, a village's physical location strongly influenced its access to certain kinds of game; in later periods, status considerations determined how much deer meat a household received (Spores 1965: 969).

While grinding stones and storage jars were common in households, it was decidedly uncommon to find them complete and in good shape. Occasionally, they were forgotten and left behind in good condition, as in Feature 57 at Tierras Largas. This feature consisted of two parts. Feature 57a was a small bell-shaped pit that contained a complete *mano* and *metate*, a large complete jar, a broken figurine, a piece of carbonized wood or matting, and a portion of a second jar. Feature 57b consisted of a complete *mano* and *metate* lying on a small pile of sand which probably resulted from the digging of the adjacent pit.

Certain kinds of tool preparation may also be classified as universal household activities. Particularly common in all houses were a series of chipped-stone tools and waste debris, including cores and core fragments of locally available chert or quartz. Most of the tools are small utilized flakes and flake fragments, though large (approximately 5 cm long) flakes with secondary retouch are sometimes found. Most, if not all, households seem to have had access to local stone, and each household may have produced its own cutting and scraping tools. Antler tines (also present in some household clusters) were evidently used for pressure flaking.

Not quite as common were obsidian flakes and, at least as early as 1050 BC, prismatic obsidian blades. Apparently important for cutting tasks, obsidian seems to have been available to all households, though no obsidian sources occur in the Valley of Oaxaca.

Bone needles made from split deer long bones occur with many household clusters, and may have been used for sewing, basket making, or some other tasks. Some houses had several needles, but no "kits" of needles (such as those at Ticomán) have been found.

Another common household tool was the *piscador* or "cornshucker." Made from a sharpened deer metapodial, this awl-like tool is identical to *piscadores* used today by Oaxaca farmers to slit open cornhusks, or remove kernels from cobs; the wear pattern is identical as well.

Analogous activities in other areas

A glance at Paul Tolstoy's descriptions of utilitarian artifacts from the Valley of Mexico (Tolstoy 1971) suggests that many of the same tools – *metates, manos*, antler tine pressure flakers, deer metapodial cornhuskers, and so on – must have characterized early villages in that region as well. The same is true of MacNeish, Nelken-Terner, and Johnson's (1967) descriptions of tools from early villages at Tehuacán, Puebla. Perhaps the most striking difference is that villagers in the valleys of Mexico, Puebla, and Tehuacán made hundreds of chipped stone points for lances or atl-atl darts, while Oaxacan villagers seem to have done virtually all their deer hunting without chipped-stone projectile points. Despite such regional differences, and despite our lack of information on the horizontal (house-by-house) distribution of utilitarian artifacts in areas such as the Valley of Mexico, the available data leads us to suspect the general range of "universal household activities" was similar in all these regions.

If we turn to the tropical lowlands, there are also some noticeable regional differences. Perhaps the clearest is the fact that, in some coastal areas, it was fishing, rather than land-mammal hunting, that contributed the bulk of the animal bone in the household cluster. Nevertheless, such artifacts as *metates, manos, piscadores*, and antler tine pressure flakers were still common at lowland villages like Chiapa de Corzo (Lee 1969) or San Lorenzo (Coe, personal communication). Indeed, such regional differences as occur do not alter our overall impressions that households of 1500–500 BC were (1) generally autonomous with regard to food procurement, preparation, and storage, but (2) interdependent with regard to a series of part-time crafts that only certain households conducted.

Possible Household Specialization

Certain kinds of flint tool manufacture may have been carried out by specific households within each village, not as a full-time specialty but as a form of interhousehold cooperation between relatives and affines. For example, Feature 184 at the village of Tierras Largas was a bell-shaped pit that contained an unusually high number of small chert flakes and flake fragments, undoubtedly the waste debris from stone tool manufacture by pressure retouch. Over 300 pieces were recovered, along with a bifacial tool that was probably broken during manufacture. Perhaps each small village had one or two persons sufficiently skilled at pressure flaking to provide the rest of the village with certain tools. Our evidence from other pits and houses would suggest that the average villager rarely did more than pick up a conveniently sharp flake and use it without deliberate retouch.

Certain kinds of bone tool manufacture may have been similarly organized. Feature 140 at Tierras Largas was a bell-shaped pit that contained an unusual cache of deer bone, including at least one complete, unmodified long bone, and several other long bones that had been cut to produce socket-type handles, bone rings, and other tools. Although all households used bone tools, this was the only feature that indicated that one or two households might have done a great deal of the village's bone tool manufacture.

Ground-and-polished cell manufacture also may have been a household specialty; several residential wards at San José Mogote had such households. One, dating to ca. 1150 BC, contained a finished celt, a partially completed celt, and a large quartz pebble which clearly had been used to polish the celt bits (figure 1.2). Nearby was a stone pounder which probably had been used

Figure 1.2   Artifacts from Early Formative celt-working activity areas at San José Mogote, Oaxaca; a, b, and c were all found together.
(a) Partially finished celt; (b) finished but unused celt; (c) and (d) quartz cobbles used first for pecking out celts, then polishing them (with the smooth facet shown on face of cobble).

to peck out the shape of the celt before polishing. The celts were of green metamorphic rock, while the polisher was of even harder quartz.

Analogous activities in other regions

The "leather-working kits" included with certain burials at Ticomán in the Valley of Mexico suggest that that activity may have been a household specialization. Out of Vaillant's sample of 43 adult burials, only 5 males had such kits (and 1 female had what *might* be a smaller version). Or stated differently, 5 out of the 16 middle-aged to elderly burials definitely identified as "male" had leather-working kits. Leather working, therefore, might have been carried on by fewer than a third of the households at Ticomán.

Possible Regional Specialization

Certain kinds of shell ornament production may have been restricted to households in the north-western, or Etla, region of the Valley of Oaxaca during Early Formative times. Two villages in that region – Tierras Largas and San José Mogote – have evidence of shell working in almost every house of the period 1150–850 BC that has been extensively excavated. Very few houses from other excavated villages of that time period have yielded shell-working activity areas, although finished shell ornaments appear at all other villages.

A "typical" shell-working activity area at San José Mogote would be an area of 1–2 sq m, small enough to suggest that a single individual (rather than a group) was at work. Such areas were usually in the corner of a house, and they were littered with small flint chips and fragments of cut and discarded shell. They would usually include 1 or more chert knives or burins (for cutting shell) and from 1 to 10 small chert drills or perforators (for drilling shell) (see figure 1.3). They would also usually include fragments of ornaments which broke in the process of manufacture, as well as "undesirable" parts trimmed off such shells as *Spondylus* (spiny oyster) or *Pinctada* (pearl oyster).

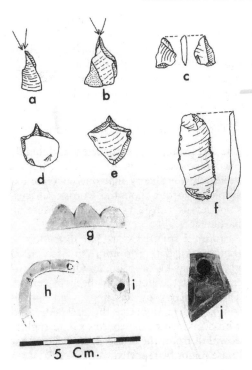

Figure 1.3 Artifacts and workshop debris from Early Formative shell-working activity areas at San José Mogote, Oaxaca. (a) and (b) Chert burins for cutting shell; (c) chert graver; (d) and (e) small chert drills; (f) utilized chert flake; (g) fragment of cut and engraved shell ornament; (h) broken fragment of mother-of-pearl holder for magnetite mirror; (i) fragment of shell bead; (j) broken fragment of drilled pearl oyster.

Certain kinds of feather working may have had a similar regionally restricted distribution. Two (or possibly three) Early Formative bell-shaped pits from different household clusters at the village of Tierras Largas yielded the bones of macaw – most likely the military macaw (*Ara militaris*), whose blue-green feathers were widely prized in Pre-Columbian times. Wing bones seem to have been cut in such a way as to preserve the feathers. Since Early Formative villages in other parts of the valley have not produced macaw remains, the accumulation and/or working of these feathers may have been restricted to the Etla region, or possibly even restricted to households at Tierras Largas alone.

Salt making was restricted to villages near saline springs, our best-studied example being Fábrica San José (Drennan 1972). As early as 1300 BC, the area was visited briefly, probably to obtain salt, but no houses were built. During the Middle Formative, the production of salt by boiling brackish spring water in pottery jars was evidently a common activity, with many jars retaining a mineral crust. Another small site called Las Salinas, founded near a saline spring not far away, may have been a salt-making village at 900–800 BC.

Analogous activities in other regions

Salt making was probably one of Formative Mesoamerica's most widespread regional specializations. Suitable localities varied from the brackish springs of the Tehuacán Valley and the shores of saline Lake Texcoco in the Valley of Mexico to the fossil lagoons and estuaries of the coastal low lands...

The manufacture of metates from suitable volcanic rock may have been a regional specialization in still other areas. At the Early Formative village of Coapexco, near Amecameca in the Valley of Mexico, Tolstoy and Fish (1973: 18) report atypically large numbers of *metates* and *manos*, including numerous unfinished specimens in and around the houses.

Formative sites near obsidian flows in other parts of Mesoamerica may have had similar regional specializations. Shook and Proskouriakoff (1956) mention *obsidian-working areas* at Middle Formative sites near Guatemala City; the Valley of Mexico is rich in such areas, but, so far, none have been reported for the early village period in which we are interested. Places near which early obsidian working might be expected include Guadalupe Victoria, Puebla; Otumba, Valley of Mexico; Zinapécuaro, Guanajuato; and El Chayal, Guatemala.

We cannot help feeling that there must be many more such regional specializations in early villages than are reported in the literature. Perhaps, at the time, the excavators who ran across them assumed that they would not be of interest to anyone else.

Possibly unique specializations

Magnetite mirror production may have been restricted to one set of households in one residential area at the village of San José Mogote during the period 1150–850 BC Rare examples of finished mirrors have been found at four other villages – Fábrica San José, Hacienda Blanca, Tomaltepec, and Tierras Largas – but no areas of mirror manufacture have been found anywhere outside a small area (Area A) on the eastern edge of San José Mogote. On one small field in this area, intensive surface collection turned up more than 500 fragments of magnetite, hematite, and related iron ores.

A "typical" magnetite working area at San José Mogote might be an area 1–2 sq m in extent, once again suggesting that production was by individuals rather than groups. In addition to scattered lumps of unused iron ore (presumably rejected because of flaws or inappropriate cleavage planes), such an activity area might include a number of small flat mirrors, about the size of a thumbnail, which had broken during manufacture. Polishers of quartz or hematite (both of which are harder than magnetite) were sometimes present. Nearby might be found "mirror holders" of pearl oyster – shell artifacts with spaces just the right size for a small magnetite mirror. Whether these "holders" were made by the same individuals who made the mirrors is not yet clear. However, some shell working was carried on in the same household clusters with the magnetite working.

Mirror-polishing activity areas were typically inside houses. What is more, in Area A at San José Mogote, as many as four stratigraphically superimposed levels contained such activity areas, suggesting that four generations of households had the same part-time specialty. In no other Early Formative residential ward have such mirror-working areas so far been discovered.

We are sure that similar situations – spatially restricted, specialized activities which span several generations in the same residential area – must occur at other early Mesoamerican villages, but they are hard to find in the literature. Indeed, we have written this chapter largely in the hope that fellow archeologists will bring new activity areas and new tool kits to our attention, or point out to us ones we have overlooked.

The Recording of Household Activities

The preceding is an abridged and highly oversimplified review of a very complex topic. On the theory that one concrete example is worth a thousand words of discussion, let us consider one actual house in particular.

House 2 in Area C at San José Mogote (figure 1.4), dating to approximately 1000 BC, is a convenient example. Only the eastern half of the house had been preserved. The long axis of the house ran north–south, with a door on the east side, and with a midden to the south of (and slightly downhill from) the house. Here is how that house might be reported:

Number: House 2.
Length: Approximately 5 m (N–S) from corner post to corner post.
Width: Unknown (west half disturbed by modern adobe makers).
Post pattern: Two corner posts (in the NE and SE corners) represented by postmolds, both framed by lines of stones. Post diameters, 20 cm.
Construction: Wattle and daub, with white, limey clay surfacing. A row of foundation stones lines the east side, except in the doorway, which is 1.1 m wide. Two particularly large stones flank the doorway. Charred *Phalaris* (reed canary grass) present, probably from roof thatch. Floor, stamped clay with a light surface of clean sand.
Major items plotted on floor: Impression, containing silica exoskeleton of twilled *petate* or sleeping mat, near NE corner. Restorable outleaned wall bowl (Vessel 3), near wall N. of door. Restorable cylindrical bowl (Vessel 1), near wall S. of door. Restorable pottery charcoal brazier (Vessel 2), lying crushed in front of doorway.

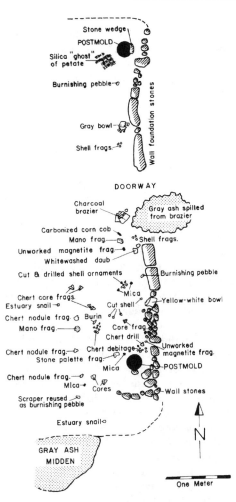

Figure 1.4 East half of House 2 in Area C at San José Mogote, Oaxaca, with artifacts and features plotted *in situ*. (West half not preserved.)

Nearby is a small charred corn-cob. The spilled ash from Vessel 2, when floated, produced six corn kernels, many cob fragments, two prickly pear fruit seeds, one burnt cane fragment, and two unidentifiable seeds.

Activity areas: Apparent shell-working area, covering about 1.5 sq m in SE corner. The artifacts include three fragments of chert nodules; two cores and five core fragments; and two separate concentrations of chert waste flakes 60 cm apart. One of the latter includes a chert burin,

while the other includes a chert drill. There are numbers of cut and drilled shell ornament fragments and shell waste, primarily freshwater mussel. Two unused shells of *Cerithidium* (an estuary snail) and one *Anomalocardia* shell are present. Apparently the worker started with chert nodules and raw shell, made his own flake cores, then made his own burins and drills from the flakes, and finally worked the shell. Included in this activity area are several possibly unrelated items, including an unworked chunk of iron ore (another occurs near the door); a stone palette fragment; a broken fragment of ground stone *mano* (another occurs near the door); and two quartz pebble burnishers, one made on a former scraper. *Associated feature*: A gray ashy midden outside the house, to the south and downslope. When floated, it produced 17 maize kernels, many cob fragments, 1 possible cucurbit seed, and 3 chile pepper seeds.

Possible "Male" and "Female" work Areas in Oaxaca Houses

Now we must raise one more possibility, which cannot yet be confirmed because our sample of houses is too small. That is the possibility that there may be an intermediate level of analysis between the activity area or feature, and the house or household cluster. That level would be the "male" or "female" work area.

A very nice ethnographic model for such work areas can be drawn from Evon Vogt's study of the highland Maya of Zinacantan, Chiapas (figure 1.5). According to Vogt (1969: 83–4):

Although Zinacanteco houses contain no interior walls or partitions, they are conceptually divided into "rooms" or living spaces. These are defined by the location of the hearth and associated objects that are owned and used by the women, and by the location of the interior house altar and associated objects owned and used by men. The house altar is nearly always constructed against the wall; others are located in corners but with one edge against the wall opposite the hearth.

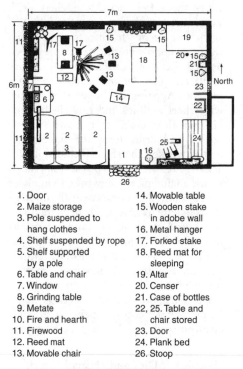

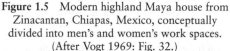

1. Door
2. Maize storage
3. Pole suspended to hang clothes
4. Shelf suspended by rope
5. Shelf supported by a pole
6. Table and chair
7. Window
8. Grinding table
9. Metate
10. Fire and hearth
11. Firewood
12. Reed mat
13. Movable chair
14. Movable table
15. Wooden stake in adobe wall
16. Metal hanger
17. Forked stake
18. Reed mat for sleeping
19. Altar
20. Censer
21. Case of bottles
22, 25. Table and chair stored
23. Door
24. Plank bed
26. Stoop

Figure 1.5   Modern highland Maya house from Zinacantan, Chiapas, Mexico, conceptually divided into men's and women's work spaces. (After Vogt 1969: Fig. 32.)

In houses without interior altars, the men's possessions still tend to be clustered in the living space opposite the hearth.

The hearth, with a fire that almost never dies (except when the members of the household are away for extended periods of time), is a focal point for women's work, as well as for family interaction, since men and children sit by the fire for warmth and also eat near the fire.

On the basis of Vogt's data, one could predict that a future archeologist, excavating a Zinacanteco house that had been hastily abandoned, would find objects owned and used by men near the altar, objects owned and used by women near the hearth. However, some men's objects could well occur intermingled with women's objects because of the family interaction near the hearth, just mentioned.

There are obvious problems in applying the Zinacanteco model to houses of the Formative period. For example, Early Formative houses in the Valley of Oaxaca usually had no hearths; instead, they had portable pottery braziers which could be moved from place to place within the house. Moreover, very few early houses show anything resembling an altar; one or two Early Formative household clusters in Oaxaca had possible ritual features.

On the other hand, we have no doubt that even these early households had "objects owned and used by men" and "objects owned and used by women," and the distribution of these within the house well might have been patterned. Thus, early houses could have been "conceptually divided" into work areas with men's tools and male-related features, work areas with women's tools and female-related features, and areas of overlap due to family interaction.

Our candidates for women's tools include *metates* and "two-hand" *manos*; pottery charcoal braziers; pots showing a crust where maize had been soaked in lime; some hammerstones for food preparation; deer bone cornhuskers; spindle whorls; sewing (as opposed to leather-working) needles; and so on. We suspect that most of the flint chipping was done in male work areas, and that antler tine pressure flakers, projectile points, and many kinds of chert bifaces and scrapers were men's tools. On the basis of the Ticomán data already mentioned, we suspect many bone hide-working tools (fleshers, beamers, etc.) also were used by men, along with tools for land clearance (celts), weapon manufacture (shaft smoothers, burins), and a variety of extractive tasks. Men also may have used some kinds of small "one-hand" *manos*, as well as hammerstones for celt manufacture.

In at least some early houses from Oaxaca, we do note a tendency for our presumed "women's tools" to occur to one side of the midline as one enters the house, while presumed "men's tools" occur to the other side. In House 1 at Tierras Largas (figure 1.6), most chert cores, scrapers, areas of retouch flakes, and at least one

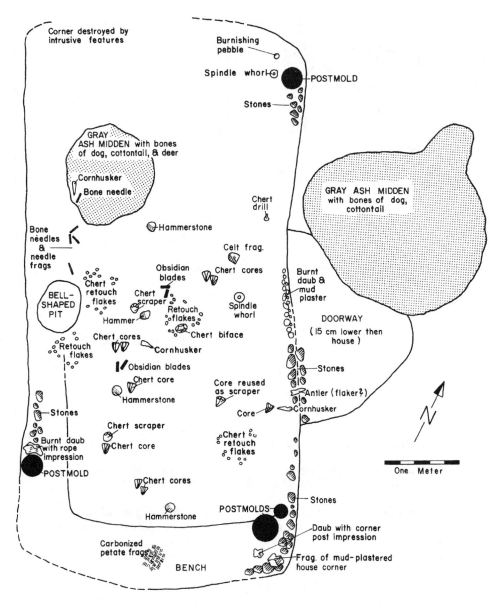

Figure 1.6   Plan of House 1 in Area A at Tierras Largas, Oaxaca, with selected artifact categories plotted on floor and intrusive features omitted. Late San José phase, ca. 900 BC.

biface lay in front of or to the left of the door as one would enter. All bone needles, deer bone cornhuskers, and pierced sherd discs (probably spindle whorls) lay in front of or to the right of the door as one would enter. In addition, a gray ash deposit from cooking activity occurred in the "right half" of the

house, and contained a needle and a deer bone cornhusker.

Most of the chert working in House 2 at San José Mogote (figure 1.4) also was concentrated to the left of the door as one entered: cores, nodules, debitage, and utilized flakes. In front of the door was a

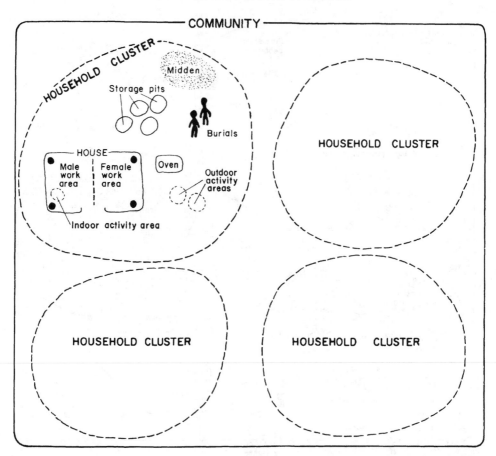

Figure 1.7 Diagram showing the relationship between the analytical levels of activity area; feature; male or female work area; house; household cluster; and community.

smashed charcoal brazier with food debris, and more food remains occurred to the right of the door. Coextensive with, and possibly related to, the chipped stone scatters was a shell-working area, only one of many craft areas associated with presumed "men's tools" in early Oaxaca villages. It was most often in these "men's work areas" that burins and drills were made, shell and mica were cut and drilled, and ritual ornaments polished or burnished. One suspects, therefore, that this was an activity carried on by males in their free time, away from the hunt or the *milpa*. Obviously, to demonstrate this convincingly we need a much larger sample of houses; our sample is not yet statistically significant.

Indeed, obtaining an adequate sample of men's and women's work areas will be difficult, for only a small percentage of houses are sufficiently undisturbed; in many, the floor debris is so kicked around that the areas are blurred. Nevertheless, we believe that the search for this intermediate analytic level is worth the effort, in terms of its potential for illuminating sexual division of labor in the Formative (figure 1.7).

NOTE

1 This is a misidentification by Vaillant. The bones are not even all bird bones, and one appears to be a dog fibula. All do, however, look like good needle blanks.

REFERENCES

Aufdermauer, J. 1970. Excavaciones en dos sitios preclásicos de Moyotzingo, Puebla, *Comunicaciones* 1: 9–24. Fundacion Alemana para la Investigación Cientifica, Puebla.

Borhegyi, S. F. 1965a. Archaeological synthesis of the Guatemalan highlands. In *Handbook of Middle American Indians*, vol. 2, edited by R. Wauchope and G. R. Willey, pp. 3–58. Austin: University of Texas Press.

—— 1965b. Settlement patterns of the Guatemalan highlands. In *Handbook of Middle American Indians*, vol. 2, edited by R. Wauchope and G. R. Willey, pp. 59–75. Austin: University of Texas Press.

Coe, M. D. 1961. La Victoria: An early site on the Pacific coast of Guatemala. *Papers of the Peabody Museum of Archaeology and Ethnology* vol. 53. Harvard University, Cambridge, Mass.

—— 1968. San Lorenzo and the Olmec civilization. In *Dumbarton Oaks Conference on the Olmec*, edited by E. P. Benson, pp. 41–71. Washington, DC: Dumbarton Oaks.

Coe, M. D., and K. V. Flannery. 1967. Early cultures and human ecology in south coastal Guatemala. *Smithsonian Contributions to Anthropology* No. 3. Smithsonian Institution, Washington, DC.

Drennan, R. D. 1972. Excavations at Fábrica San José, Oaxaca, Mexico. Mimeographed preliminary report. Ann Arbor, Mich.

Flannery, K. V. 1964. The middle formative of the Tehuacán Valley. Unpublished Ph.D. dissertation, University of Chicago.

—— 1968. Archeological systems theory and early Mesoamerica. In *Anthropological Archeology in the Americas*, edited by B. J. Meggers, pp. 67–87. Washington, DC: Anthropological Society of Washington.

Flannery, K. V., M. C. Winter, S. Lees, J. Neely, J. Schoenwetter, S. Kitchen, and J. C. Wheeler. 1970. Preliminary archeological investigations in the Valley of Oaxaca, Mexico, 1966–1969. Mimeographed preliminary report. Ann Arbor, Mich.

Hall, D. W., G. A. Haswell, and T. A. Oxley. 1956. *Underground Storage of Grain*. British Colonial Office, Pest Information Laboratory, Dept. of Scientific and Industrial Research. London: HM Stationery Office.

Lee, T. A., Jr. 1969. The artifacts of Chiapa de Corzo, Chiapas, Mexico. *Papers of the New World Archaeological Foundation* No. 26. Provo, Utah.

Lowe, G. W. 1959. Archaeological exploration of the upper Grijalva River, Chiapas, Mexico. *Papers of the New World Archaeological Foundation* No. 2 (Pub. no. 3). Provo, Utah.

MacNeish, R. S. 1954. An early archaeological site near Pánuco, Vera Cruz. *Transactions of the American Philosophical Society* 44 (n.s.): 539–641.

—— 1962. *Second Annual Report of the Tehuacán Archaeological-botanical Project*. R. S. Peabody Foundation for Archaeology, Andover, Mass.

—— (n.d.) Excavations at site Ts-381. Manuscript to appear in a future volume of *The Prehistory of the Tehuacán Valley*. Austin: University of Texas Press.

MacNeish, R. S., A. Nelken-Terner, and I. W. Johnson. 1967. *The Prehistory of the Tehuacán Valley*, edited by R. S. MacNeish, vol. 2: *Nonceramic Artifacts*.

Naroll, R. 1962. Floor area and settlement population. *American Antiquity* 27: 587–9.

Piña Chán, R. 1958. Tlatilco, vol. 1: *Serie Investigaciones*. Instituto Nacional de Antropología e Historia. Mexico City.

Sanders, W. T. 1965. The cultural ecology of the Teotihuacán Valley. Dept. of Anthropology, Pennsylvania State University, University Park. Mimeograph.

Shook, E. M. and T. Proskouriakoff. 1956. Settlement patterns in Meso-America and the sequence in the Guatemalan highlands. In *Prehistoric Settlement Patterns in the New World*, edited by G. R. Willey, pp. 93–100. *Viking Fund Publications in Anthropology* No. 23. New York: Wenner-Gren.

Spores, R. 1965. The Zapotec and Mixtec at Spanish contact. In *Handbook of Middle American Indians*, vol. 3 edited by R. Wauchope and G. R. Willey, part 2, pp. 962–87. Austin: University of Texas Press.

Tolstoy, P. 1971. Utilitarian artifacts of central Mexico. In *Handbook of Middle American Indians*, vol. 10, edited by R. Wauchope, G. F. Ekholm, and I. Bernal. Austin: University of Texas Press.

Tolstoy, P. and S. K. Fish. 1973. Excavations at Coapexco, 1973. Mimeographed preliminary report. Dept. of Anthropology, Queens College (CUNY), New York.

Vaillant, G. C. 1930. Excavations at Zacatenco. *Anthropological Papers*, vol. 32: part 1. American Museum of Natural History, New York.

—— 1931. Excavations at Ticomán. *Anthropological Papers*, vol. 32: part 2. American Museum of Natural History, New York.

—— 1935. Excavations at El Arbolillo. *Anthropological Papers*, vol. 35: part 2. American Museum of Natural History, New York.

—— 1941. *Aztecs of Mexico*. New York: Doubleday, Doran.

Vogt, E. Z. 1969. *Zinacantan: A Maya Community in the Highlands of Chiapas*. Cambridge, Mass.: Belknap Press (Harvard University).

Walter, H. 1970. Informe preliminar sobre una excavación realizada en el sitio preclásico de San Francisco Acatepec, Puebla, Mexico. *Communicaciones* No. 1: 25–36. Fundación Alemana para la Investigación Científica, Puebla.

Whalen, M. E. 1974. Excavations at Sto. Domingo Tomaltepec, Oaxaca, Mexico. Mimeographed preliminary report. Dept. of Anthropology, University of Michigan, Ann Arbor.

Willey, G. R., W. R. Bullard, J. B. Glass, and J. C. Gifford. 1965. Prehistoric Maya settlements in the Belize valley. *Papers of the Peabody Museum of Archaeology and Ethnology*, vol. 54. Harvard University, Cambridge, Mass.

Winter, M. C. 1970. Excavations at Tierras Largas (Atzompa, Oaxaca): A preliminary report. In Preliminary archeological investigations in the Valley of Oaxaca, Mexico, 1966–1969, edited by K. V. Flannery, Mimeographed preliminary report. Ann Arbor, Mich.

—— 1972. Tierras Largas: A formative community in the Valley of Oaxaca, Mexico. Unpublished Ph.D. dissertation, University of Arizona, Tucson.

CHAPTER 2

Distinguishing the High and Mighty from the Hoi Polloi at Tikal, Guatemala

William A. Haviland and Hattula Moholy-Nagy

Although the existence of a ruling elite among the Maya of the Classic period (AD 250–900) is now accepted by virtually everyone (e.g. Schele and Miller 1986), it has not always been so. Back in the late 1950s, when archaeological work was just getting underway at Tikal, the idea that ancient Maya society was essentially classless claimed considerable support (Haviland 1966: 38–40). In this view, ably championed by Evon Vogt and others at Harvard University, positions of leadership were filled on a rotating basis by people who had accumulated the resources necessary to take up residence in a major center and discharge the duties of various civic and ceremonial offices. Once in office, their funds were soon exhausted, whereupon these individuals returned to normal lives in their home communities. Being somewhat skeptical of all this, those of us engaged in the investigation of residential structures at Tikal began early on to look for the kinds of evidence that might indicate the presence of a full-time ruling class at the site. Such evidence was indeed forthcoming, allowing us to answer the question: what was the archaeological signature of Tikal's ruling class?

The presence of social elites in human societies is manifest in a number of ways: what people have to say about others in their society (verbal evaluation); who associates with whom and how; and observable differences in lifestyles and life chances. Archaeologically, data on the latter two are usually easiest to come by, but, for a variety of reasons, these are cruder indicators of class standing that the other two. Although perhaps less evident, information on patterns of association still may be retrievable. Most difficult to deal with is verbal evaluation, although decipherment of the glyphs is shedding light on how the elite were regarded (at least by themselves) in ancient Maya society. However... we shall concentrate on what archaeology has to tell us about the high and mighty of Tikal's society. Even so, some reference to other sources of information cannot (and should not) be avoided, and a definitive understanding of this center's aristocracy will require input from epigraphers and art historians, as well as archaeologists.

Class and Housing

In the category of lifestyles, the high and mighty in stratified societies usually live in more imposing houses than do the hoi polloi. At Tikal, there was considerable variation in residential architecture, as has been noted in numerous publications (e.g. Haviland 1965: 17, 1966: 31, 1970: 190, 1978: 180). Houses themselves show an unbroken range of variation all the way from simple pole-and-thatch buildings without supporting platforms, through structures of varying

Reprinted from William A. Haviland and Hattula Moholy-Nagy. 1992. Distinguishing the High and Mighty from the Hoi Polloi at Tikal, Guatemala. In *Mesoamerican Elites: An Archaeological Assessment*, edited by Diane A. Chase and Arlen F. Chase (University of Oklahoma Press, Norman), pp. 50–60.

complexity, to massive, all masonry range-type structures or "palaces." Similarly, associated buildings such as family shrines vary widely in floor area and quality of construction (e.g. Haviland 1982: 428; Becker 1986: 81, 83). Though not all palaces built entirely of masonry were houses (e.g. Jones 1969; Harrison 1986: 55), some clearly were (Haviland 1981: 93), and it is reasonable to assume that those who inhabited such imposing edifices were of considerably higher standing than those who lived in smaller houses built partially or wholly of perishable materials. Although palace groups differ considerably in the number of buildings included and the complexity of their arrangement – compare, for example, the Central Acropolis (Harrison 1986: fig. 9) with Group 7F-1 (Haviland 1985: fig. 5) – they do tend to command more space per living unit than do lower class household groups (cf. Haviland 1981, 1988). They also tend to protect the privacy of their occupants to a greater degree; for instance, various stairs, stairblocks, screens, and gateways seem to have been added to the Central Acropolis for no other purpose than to preserve the privacy of those who lived there (Harrison 1970: 186–94). Finally, palace groups also have more outbuildings, probably including storehouses, kitchens, and servants' quarters as well as private shrines (e.g. Haviland 1981; Harrison 1986: fig. 17). While separate kitchens, storehouses, or shrines may sometimes be found in non-elite settings (e.g. Haviland 1965: 21; Becker 1986: 83), servants' quarters never are.

Although major palaces are not confined to epicentral Tikal, they are far more prominent there than elsewhere (Puleston 1983: 24). At the very heart of the city is the Central Acropolis, in which the ruling family probably lived. Consistent with this, Peter Harrison (1970: 270, 1986: 55) has noted the suitability of Str. 5D-46, one of the earliest Central Acropolis palaces, for "family residence." This edifice resembles Str. 7F-32, for which a residential function is firmly established (Haviland 1981, in press). Found beneath the west stairway of 5D-46, on its axis, was Cache 198, con-

tained within a carved vessel with fitted lid bearing the name, with emblem glyph, of one of Tikal's Early Classic kings (Coggins 1975: 208; Jones and Satterthwaite 1982: 126). The rest of this inscription is now known to refer to the dedication of this man's house (Linda Schele, personal communication, 1990). The burial of Early Classic kings in and beneath nearby temples on the North Acropolis parallels the interment of men who once lived in Str. 7F-32 beneath the nearby temple Str. 7F-30 (Haviland 1985: 39, in press).

Whether or not Str. 5D-46 was the only royal residence on the Central Acropolis is so far not settled. Although a number of other probable residential palaces are present, Harrison (1970: table 15, 1986: 55) is inclined to interpret them as places where priests and boys in training lived. On the other hand, the early establishment of Str. 5D-46 and the manner in which the acropolis subsequently grew through addition and accretion is suggestive of an expanding extended family of great wealth and power. Overall, the pattern duplicates on a larger scale the same developmental cycle that has been described for smaller household units (Haviland 1988). Given the proximity of the royal living quarters to what C. Jones argues was Tikal's marketplace (Coe 1967: 73; Jones, Coe, and Haviland 1981: 307), one wonders if the residents of the Central Acropolis didn't control what went on there; certainly they were strategically located to do so.

In addition to the Central Acropolis, epicentral Tikal includes a ring of palaces – many (perhaps even most) of which were probably elite residences – that stretch in an arc from Str. 4D-14 south and east through the South Acropolis, thence north and east to Strs. 5E-1 and 4E-44 through 48 (Puleston 1983: 24–5). There is no concentration of palaces elsewhere at Tikal remotely like this, suggesting that the bulk of the nobility resided at the civic and ceremonial heart of the ancient city. Some (if not all) of the few widely separated palaces that occur at some distance from Tikal's center also housed people of high rank, one of the better known being Group 7F-1, the "Dower House" group on which two preliminary articles have appeared (Haviland 1981, 1985). This was established by the family of a deceased noble who was probably of the ruling lineage, perhaps a ruler himself (perhaps the eighteenth successor of Yax Moch Xoc, anchoring ancestor of the Tikal dynasty; Haviland in press). Apparently banished from the center of power, his survivors nonetheless retained their upper-class standing. They were even able to evict and tear down the houses of people who were obsidian workers – a relatively low-status occupation at Tikal (Haviland et al. 1985) – in order to build new living quarters for themselves (Haviland in press). Other such palace groups, unlike Group 7F-1, may have been occupied by nobles who were responsible for the administrative affairs of their localities, but who were answerable to the lords of Tikal (Haviland 1981: 117).

Class and Burial

Heads of elite households, when they died, were regularly placed in tombs or graves reminiscent of tombs, usually beneath a temple. The most spectacular examples are, of course, those of the North Acropolis and vicinity, which contained the bodies of men who in life were probably housed on the Central Acropolis. On the basis of glyphic evidence, two of these tombs have been identified as those of the rulers Animal Skull and Ah Cacao ("Ruler A"), and the others are almost certainly those of earlier and later kings (Jones and Satterthwaite 1982: 124–30). Unlike the burials of lower-class individuals (e.g. Haviland et al. 1985: 141–53), these royal graves are far larger than required to contain the body of the deceased as well as all the other objects that were placed with it. In death, as in life, the high and mighty were able to command more space than the hoi polloi. In addition, tombs were engineered in such a way as to prevent earth or other fill from entering (lower-class people, by contrast, were almost always buried with dirt in the face). Some idea of the planning, time, and

effort that went into constructing the last resting places of kings is illustrated by Burial 195 – that of the ruler Animal Skull – and Burial 23 – possibly that of Shield Skull. The former, a truly cavernous, vaulted chamber, required removal of the entire face of Str. 5D-32-2nd and its replacement by 32-1st (Coe 1990: 565). Similarly, extensive destruction of Str. 5D-33-2nd's midline preceded construction of Burial 23's commodious vaulted chamber, which had to be placed so as to avoid impinging on the earlier Burial 48 (Coe 1990: 537, 540). Following the tomb's completion, Str. 5D-33-1st was built above it, over what remained of the earlier temple.

Royal tombs were not only expensive to build, but were expensive to stock as well. Unlike lower-class burials, which rarely include more than three pottery vessels (often used or damaged ones at that), accompanied by one or two other items such as spindle whorls or other mundane household belongings, those of kings usually include large quantities of fine pottery vessels, as well as other items never found in lower-class graves. Some of the vessels appear to have been treasured heirlooms (e.g. Coggins 1975: 153), while others were specially commissioned for the burial (Coggins 1975: 515). Other objects invariably present in North Acropolis tombs are beads of jade and *Spondylus* shell, stingray spines, and red pigment dusted or painted over the body as well as associated objects. Specific to the earliest tombs, although they appear sporadically in later ones, are small anthropomorphic stone sculptures, greenstone and shell face masks, imitation pearl pendants carved from nacreous shell, and other worked marine shells. Added in Early Classic times (AD 250–550) were large earplugs of stone or shell, pyrite mosaic mirrors, sets of scraped out and perforated *Spondylus* valves, carved jade beads and pendants, vases of alabaster and calcite, true pearl pendants, unmodified marine shells and other marine invertebrates (including corals, sponges, bryozoans, and gorgonians), and painted wooden sculptures, trays, and bowls. After AD 550, other types of durable items accompanied elite corpses: jade mosaic vases, headbands made of small jade flares, bracelets and anklets of jade cylinder beads, bone, and/or shell objects interpreted as handles for fans, sets of bones inscribed with hieroglyphs, and jaguar pelts (identified from the groups of toe bones left in the skins, which either cushioned or covered the deceased). Two other hallmarks of elite burial were placement of masses of chert and obsidian debitage over the tomb and (until ca. AD 524) placement of human sacrificial victims within.

Other examples of elite-class burials are those beneath Strs. 7F-30 and 31 in Group 7F-1 (Coggins 1975: 215–32, 233–6, 312–29, 420–8; Haviland in press). The earliest of these, Burial 160, is fully comparable in its construction and contents to the North Acropolis tombs and contains the body of a man who may have been one of Tikal's rulers (Haviland in press). Subsequent burials are probably those of this man's descendants and thus collateral relatives of Tikal's later rulers (Haviland 1985: 38). Although their graves are not as large and elaborate or as richly stocked as Burial 160, they are still tomblike in their construction, contain items reminiscent of those in royal tombs, and outclass all other Tikal burials save those at the site center. As usual with high-status burials of men, those of Group 7F-1 were placed in funerary shrines (often beneath them). While the heads of lower-class households were also interred in such shrines on occasion, this was not regularly done – nor were the overlying edifices as imposing as those of the aristocracy. Thus, inhumation in or beneath a temple by itself does not connote elite-class standing; what counts is the grave's size and quality of construction, the quantity and quality of objects placed within it, and the impressiveness of the structure built above it.

Class and Belongings

As one would expect, artifacts recovered from excavations in and around residential palaces reflect the high standing of those who lived in them, although not so obviously as do the objects recovered from elite burials. For one thing, highly valued items of the sort found in tombs were rarely discarded with the detritus of day-to-day living. For another, the presence of live-in servants of lower class than those they served (e.g. Haviland 1981, in press) more or less ensures that their trash has mixed with that of their elite masters. Differences between upper-class and lower-class litter may be further obscured by the occasional presence in and around relatively humble dwellings of objects made for elite consumption by commoner craft specialists; the presence of so much shell debris in Group 4F-1 (Haviland et al. 1985), for example, is a case in point. Marine shell is usually quite scarce in refuse associated with simple houses of pole and thatch at Tikal, but because people who lived in Group 4F-1 were professional shell workers, evidently a low-status occupation, bits and objects of marine shell are well represented in their trash. A final complication is that living debris is rarely found that has not been contaminated to one degree or another by construction fill. The problem here is that trash was constantly being recycled in new construction, so that artifacts used at one location might ultimately wind up somewhere else. While it is probably safe to assume that much of the fill in residential groups was originally discarded by occupants of those same groups, our experience at Tikal is that the larger the construction, the less likely it is that there was sufficient debris available locally to use as fill. Thus, to build large palaces, the high and mighty probably found it necessary to commandeer the trash of the hoi polloi.

Allowing for these difficulties, objects from houses of whatever size and construction within the confines of Tikal may be separated into three categories: basic domestic items invariably present in living debris (including manos, metates, cores, ovate and elongate bifaces, irregular retouched, used and unused flakes, prismatic blades, and – except for Early Classic deposits – figurines); items commonly but not invariably present (censers, centrally perforated sherds, bifacial blades, pointed retouched flakes, hammer-stones, and rubbing stones); and items rarely present (all other classifiable artifacts). In palace groups, more of the common types are present, and in greater numbers, than in smaller domestic groups. Conversely, such basic items as figurines, prismatic blades, debitage, and in fact any kind of workshop debris are usually more abundant in and around small structures. Outside of workshop situations, finds of rare artifacts are few and far between in small domestic groups, but occur in greater numbers and diversity around palaces. The same is true of those basic or common types most easily made from locally available raw materials that were instead made of imported luxury materials (obsidian or imported chert, for example, rather than local chert; the only basic or common type of chipped stone artifact almost always made of obsidian was the prismatic blade).

One especially noteworthy difference in refuse from the Central Acropolis, compared to smaller domestic groups, is its relatively high content of artifacts of bone, as well as unworked bone. For example, though present in Groups 4F-1 and 4F-2 (Haviland et al. 1985: 176–7), unworked animal bones were proportionately more common in the Central Acropolis, suggesting that the elite ate more meat than did less exalted members of society. The highest proportion of unburied, unworked human remains found at Tikal was also from the Central Acropolis. Their presence here, as elsewhere in Mesoamerica (e.g. Storey 1985), poses an interesting problem for analysis.

In ceramics, our impression is that there is a higher frequency of decorated, mostly polychrome pottery from palace groups than from smaller domestic groups; unfortunately, the Tikal Project did not record the relative frequency of such pottery for each residential situation (data for a few lower-class groups may be found, however, in Haviland 1963). C. C. Coggins (1975: 203) suggests that the many Manik polychrome and fine blackware sherds found in Central Acropolis fills relate to the royal residence, Str. 5D-46. Similarly, in Group 7F-1, pieces of carved cache bowl lids in living debris clearly discarded by occupants of the palace (Str. 7F-32) are not the sorts of things normally found around lower-class houses (Haviland in press), suggesting that some pottery in elite households consisted of specially commissioned, one-of-a-kind pieces.

In sum, the kinds of objects necessary for day-to-day living found their way into the refuse generated by those who lived in imposing palaces, as well as those who lived in far humbler dwellings. Although objects most obviously indicative of wealth and power are not often found in such trash, qualitative and quantitative differences suggestive of richness can nonetheless be seen when artifact inventories from palace groups are compared with those from smaller domestic groups.

Class and Osteology

Further insights into the lifestyles of the high and mighty come from analysis of human skeletons. For this, the Tikal burials have been divided into three categories: those from major palace groups (including the tombs of the North Acropolis and vicinity); those from small domestic groups; and those from intermediate structure groups that fall between these two extremes (reflected by this arrangement is the fact that the hoi polloi did not constitute a single nonelite class, but were themselves stratified). As one might expect, there is evidence that people of noble rank had customs and performed tasks unique to themselves. The lower limb bones of the aristocrats are platymeric and mesocnemic, those of people who lived in small domestic groups are mesocnemic but only moderately platymeric, and those of the occupants of intermediate domestic groups are platycnemic and moderately platymeric, reflecting functional differences. These varied shapes represent a response on the part of the bones to differences in ways that people were using their leg muscles. In the same vein, a supratrochlear foramen is found much more often among the elite than among any other segment of the population.

The particular activities that these differences reflect are, unfortunately, unknown.

Skewed skulls, known only from the Central Acropolis, may indicate some cradling practice unique to the members of the aristocracy. Moreover, deliberate alteration of normal head shape, though not restricted to aristocrats, was adopted by high-ranking women before it was taken up by others of their sex. Similarly, among men, the custom was adopted first by those of high social position. Evidently, the hoi polloi were following a fashion trend set by the high and mighty. The same may be indicated by the social and temporal distribution of squatting, as opposed to sitting on raised seats. Squatting facets disappear first on the bones of the elite, followed by those on the bones of people who lived in intermediate domestic groups. The occupants of smaller domestic groups continued to the end to squat sufficiently to leave marks on their bones.

In the category of life chances, data on stature indicate a more favorable nutritional environment for the people of higher rank than for the rest of the population. Because of their favored circumstances (including among other things greater access to animal protein, as already noted), aristocrats were best able to realize their full growth potential. Those who were least able lived in small domestic groups, while the stature of residents of intermediate domestic groups falls in between. Contrary to first impression (Haviland 1967), in Early as well as Late Classic times, people buried in tombs were usually taller than those from intermediate domestic groups, who in turn were generally taller than those from small domestic groups (see figure 2.1). Degrees of robustness seem to have been unevenly distributed in the population in like manner. To reinforce all this, there are hints from the skeletons that life expectancy was somewhat better for the elite than for other members of society. Here is one example of how Tikal's inscriptions can help us; unless the Maya were lying (always a possibility in records written for political purposes), at least two rulers of Tikal (Ruler A and Ruler B), if not more, lived to ages in excess of sixty years (Jones 1977: 39, 53). By contrast, highest mortality for nonelite men seems to have been in the forties.

Origins of the Tikal Elite

At Tikal, the high and mighty became easily distinguishable from the hoi polloi in the last hundred years BC. Although large scale public architecture, in the form of a solar observatory (Str. 5C-54) made its appear-

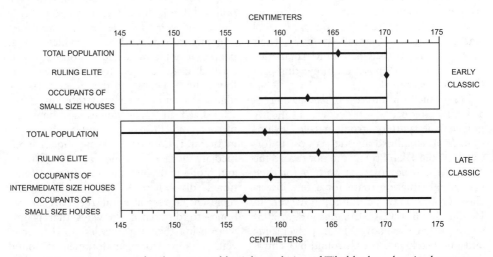

Figure 2.1 Stature ranges for the recovered burial population of Tikal by broad societal segments and periods.

ance a few centuries earlier (Laporte and Fialko 1990), this by itself does not signify the presence of a discrete elite segment of society. Nor is the facade text of Temple VI, which apparently projects dynastic rule at Tikal back several centuries before Christ (Jones and Satterthwaite 1982: 117), to be trusted; this more likely reflects an official Late Classic "party line" than reality. On the other hand, P. Mathews's (1985: 31) proposed date for the beginning of the Tikal dynasty, AD 238, is undoubtedly too late.

An emerging elite at Tikal is probably best revealed by the sequence of burials. Not until ca. 100 BC do we have what might be called a proto-tomb (Coe 1965: 8–9). Although this was preceded perhaps 100 years earlier by the burial of a young adult accompanied by jade and shell beads, as well as stingray spines (Coe 1965: 8), this individual's grave was otherwise not at all tomblike. Not until 50 BC do the first full-fledged tombs appear, in which individuals were laid to rest with their elite belongings, *without* earth covering their bodies or dirt in their faces, in chambers far larger than needed for mere containment of the corpse and associated materials (Coe 1965: figures 6, 10). Paintings on the wall of the earliest sepulcher, and on the exterior of the shrine built above the second one, depict individuals with the trappings of royalty (Coe 1965: figures 9, 12). Worth noting, too, is evidence for the existence of monumental stone carving at this same time (Jones and Satterthwaite 1982: 117), a favorite medium in the Classic period for aggrandizement of the elite. That these people held considerable authority as early as 50 BC is suggested by the placement of extra bodies with them in their earliest tombs.

In the earliest tomb, the two skeletons display artificial alterations of head shape. Twenty-five years later, it shows up in a woman from a small domestic group. By the very beginning of the first century AD, the marked differences in physical stature and robustness between social classes had developed. Although the beginnings of the Central Acropolis go back to the time of the earliest North Acropolis tombs, we don't know what kind of houses the new elite occupied, but by AD 379 at the very latest they were living in palatial residences built entirely of masonry.

As Haviland (1972: 13) suggested some years ago, Tikal's elite may have emerged as certain lineages, able to monopolize important civic and ceremonial positions, were ranked above other lineages, to form the basis of an upper class. An apparent link between the early ruling Jaguar Paw lineage and the architectural complex of which the solar observatory was a part (Laporte and Fialko 1990) suggests that control of important astronomical ritual may have played a key role in their rise to power.

If members of the important lineages tended to intermarry, then they would have constituted an endogamous caste. Hints to this effect are afforded by the presence of a dwarf in a North Acropolis tomb, the fact that certain vertebral anomalies as presently known were confined to the elite, and the fact that wormian bones – for which a genetically set potential may be involved – appear more often in these people than in others. Taken together, these might suggest congenital anomalies showing up in a family line through time. Here again, the glyphs help us out, by indicating that this kind of intermarriage between royal lineages did in fact take place. For example, C. C. Coggins (1975: 576) has argued that a daughter of Tikal's Ruler A married a lord at Piedras Negras. Ruler A himself seems to have married a woman, "Lady Yellowbird," whose sister is depicted on a stela from El Peru (Coe 1990: 855). She seems not to have been his sole wife, however, for the mother of his son, Ruler B, has a different name (Jones and Satterthwaite 1982: 129). On the lintels of Temple IV, Ruler B is noted as being in his fourth katun of life (i.e. between sixty and eighty years old) in 9.15.10.0.0 or AD 741 (Jones and Satterthwaite 1982: 103). Therefore, he was born no later than AD 681, earlier than the time of Lady Yellowbird's death (Coe 1990: 855). If the practice of polygyny was a royal prerogative, as this implies, we have found no archaeological evidence at Tikal to confirm it.

The Mexican Connection

At Tikal, the authority of the elite may have rested in part on a connection with the central Mexican site of Teotihuacan. This is reflected in the architecture of certain buildings and burials at Tikal, the presence of Mexican motifs in some of the monumental and ceramic art found in elite contexts (royal tombs and dynastic monuments, for example), and the presence of limited amounts of green obsidian from sources near Teotihuacan. C. C. Coggins (1980: 734–6) has noted that the reign of Curl Nose, who came to power at Tikal in AD 379, is associated with a number of traits, practices, and symbols of central Mexican origin. Under his successor, a fusion of these foreign and indigenous Mayan elements took place, a phenomenon repeated later under the auspices of Ruler A (Coggins 1975: 401–2, 444–5, 450, 452). More recently, some sort of connection between those who ruled at Tikal before Curl Nose and Teotihuacan has been described (Laporte and Fialko 1990). Thus, over the many centuries of Tikal's existence, there seem to have been periodic surges of influence emanating from central Mexico, which appear to have affected the local elite more than other segments of society.

Like the elite of Postclassic Yucatan, those in power at Tikal may have espoused some form of what D. Freidal (1985: 303) has called a "cult of foreignness." In Yucatan, the nobility went so far as to proclaim their ethnic distinctness from everyone else and periodically quizzed one another on their own esoteric lore to prove that no others had infiltrated their ranks. Whether or not they went to such an extreme at Tikal is not known, but Coggins (1987) suggests that signs of a special ritual language, reminiscent of that used by later Yucatecans in their periodic interrogations of one another, can be detected in the inscriptions of the Classic period. At Tikal and elsewhere, being able to claim some sort of Mexican connection may have had the same aura that the claim of Toltec descent had for the ruling class of Late Postclassic Mexico.

Conclusions

What, then, do we know about Tikal's high and mighty? That they lived and acted the way members of a favored socioeconomic class usually do: they seem to have eaten better, lived longer, and wielded more power than the hoi polloi. Their housing was more substantial, permitted them to command more in the way of personal space for themselves (as their tombs did in death), and was arranged in such a way as to minimize their contact with people of lower standing in society. Consistent with this, marriage seems to have been with others of their own kind. Their needs were catered to by live-in servants, and they were able to afford more belongings, and of better quality, than less exalted members of society. Finally, they engaged in different activities than did people of lower standing.

Symbolic of their position in society were certain of their belongings, their housing, where they lived, their physical appearance, how they were treated in death as well as in life, and undoubtedly much more. This is where analysis of the entire corpus of Tikal art – nonelite as well as elite – will help us enormously to understand the full range of symbolic indicators (class differences in clothing, to cite just one example) and the meanings behind much of the symbolism. Here iconographic analysis of tomb contents, now being pursued by C. C. Coggins, shows promise of revealing much about elite worldviews. These sorts of analysis, however, have yet to be completed and we can all look forward to them.

REFERENCES

Becker, Marshall. 1986. Household Shrines at Tikal, Guatemala: Size as a Reflection of Economic Status. *Revista Española de Antropologia Americana* 14: 81–5. Madrid.

Chase, Arlen F. and Diane Z. Chase. 1992. Mesoamerican Elites: Assumptions, Definitions, and Models. In *Mesoamerican Elites: An Archaeological Assessment*, edited by D. Z.

Chase and A. F. Chase, pp. 3–17. University of Oklahoma Press, Norman.

Coe, William R. 1965. Tikal, Guatemala and Emergent Maya Civilization. *Science* 147: 1401–19.

—— 1967. *Tikal: A Handbook of the Ancient Maya Ruins*. University Museum, University of Pennsylvania, Philadelphia.

—— 1990. *Excavations in the Great Plaza, North Terrace, and North Acropolis of Tikal*. Tikal Report No. 14, University of Pennsylvania, University Museum, Philadelphia.

Coggins, Coggins C. 1975. Painting and Drawing Styles at Tikal: An Historical and Iconographic Reconstruction. Ph.D. dissertation, Harvard University, Cambridge.

—— 1980. The Shape of Time: Some Political Implications of a Four-Part Figure. *American Antiquity* 45: 727–39.

—— 1987. Pure Language and Lapidary Prose. Paper presented at symposium, New Theories on the Ancient Maya, University of Pennsylvania, University Museum, Philadelphia.

Freidel, David A. 1985. New Light on a Dark Age: A Summary of Major Themes. In *The Lowland Maya Postclassic*, edited by Arlen F. Chase and Prudence M. Rice, pp. 285–309. University of Texas Press, Austin.

Harrison, Peter D. 1970. The Central Acropolis, Tikal, Guatemala: A Preliminary Study of the Functions of its Structural Components during the Late Classic Period. Ph.D. dissertation, University of Pennsylvania, Philadelphia.

—— 1986. Tikal: Selected Topics. In *City-States of the Maya: Art and Architecture*, edited by Elizabeth Benson, pp. 45–71. Rocky Mountain Institute for Pre-Columbian Studies, Denver.

Haviland, William A. 1963. Excavation of Small Structures in the Northeast Quadrant of Tikal, Guatemala. Ph.D. dissertation, Department of Anthropology, University of Pennsylvania, Philadelphia.

—— 1965. Prehistoric Settlement at Tikal, Guatemala. *Expedition* 7(3): 15–23.

—— 1966. *Maya Settlement Patterns: A Critical Review*. Middle American Research Institute Publication 26, pp. 21–47. Tulane University, New Orleans.

—— 1967. Stature at Tikal, Guatemala: Implications for Ancient Maya Demography and Social Organization. *American Antiquity* 32: 316–25.

—— 1970. Tikal, Guatemala and Mesoamerican Urbanism. *World Archaeology* 2: 186–98.

—— 1972. A New Look at Classic Maya Social Organization at Tikal. *Ceramica de Cultura Maya* 8: 1–16.

—— 1978. On Price's Presentation of Data on Tikal. *Current Anthropology* 19: 180–1.

—— 1981. Dower Houses and Minor Centers at Tikal, Guatemala: An Investigation into the Identification of Valid Units in Settlement Hierarchies. In *Lowland Maya Settlement Patterns*, edited by W. Ashmore, pp. 89–117. University of New Mexico Press, Albuquerque.

—— 1982. Where the Rich Folks Lived: Deranging Factors in the Statistical Analysis of Tikal Settlement. *American Antiquity* 47(2): 427–9.

—— 1985. Population and Social Dynamics: The Dynasties and Social Structure of Tikal. *Expedition* 27(3): 34–41.

—— 1988. Musical Hammocks at Tikal: Problems with Reconstructing Household Composition. In *Household and Community in the Mesoamerican Past*, edited by R. Wilk and W. Ashmore, pp. 121–34. University of New Mexico Press, Albuquerque.

—— In press. *Excavations in Group 7F–1: An Elite Residential Group of Tikal*. Tikal Report No. 22, University of Pennsylvania, University Museum, Philadelphia.

Haviland, William A. et al. 1985. *Excavations in Small Residential Groups of Tikal: Groups 4F–1 amd 4F–2*. Tikal Report No. 19, University of Pennsylvania, University Museum, Philadelphia.

Henderson, John S. 1992. Elites and Ethnicity along the Southeastern Fringe of Mesoamerica, In *Mesoamerican Elites: An Archaeological Assessment*, edited by D. Z. Chase and A. F. Chase, pp. 157–68. University of Oklahoma Press, Norman.

Jones, Christopher. 1969. The Twin Pyramid Group Pattern: A Classic Maya Architectural Assemblage at Tikal, Guatemala. Ph.D. dissertation, University of Pennsylvania, Philadelphia.

—— 1977. Inauguration Dates of Three Late Classic Rulers of Tikal, Guatemala. *American Antiquity* 42: 28–60.

Jones, Christopher, William Coe, and William Haviland. 1981. Tikal: An Outline of its Field Study (1956–1970) and a Project Bibliography. In *Supplement to the Handbook of Middle American Indians*, edited by J. A. Sabloff, pp. 296–312. University of Texas Press, Austin.

Jones, Christopher and Linton Satterthwaite. 1982. *The Monuments and Inscriptions of Tikal: The Carved Monuments*. Tikal Report No. 33, Part A, University Museum Monograph 44, University Museum, University of Pennsylvania, Philadelphia.

Kowalewski, Stephen, Gary Feinman, and Laura Finsten. 1992. The Elite and Assessment of

Social Stratification in Mesoamerican Archaeology. In *Mesoamerican Elites: An Archaeological Assessment*, edited by D. Z. Chase and A. F. Chase, pp. 259–77. University of Oklahoma Press, Norman.

Laporte, Juan P. and V. Fialko. 1990. New Perspectives on Old Problems: Dynastic References for the Early Classic at Tikal. In *Vision and Revision in Maya Studies*, edited by Flora S. Clancy and Peter D. Harrison, pp. 33–66. University of New Mexico Press, Albuquerque.

Matthews, Peter. 1985. Maya Early Classic Monuments and Inscriptions. In *A Consideration of the Early Classic Period in the Maya Lowlands*, edited by Gordon R. Willey and Peter Mathews, pp. 5–54. Institute for Mesoamerican Studies Publication 10, State University of New York at Albany.

Puleston, Dennis. 1983. *The Settlement Survey of Tikal*. Tikal Report No. 13. University Museum Monograph 48. University Museum, University of Pennsylvania.

Schele, Linda and Mary E. Miller. 1986. *The Blood of Kings: Dynasty and Ritual in Maya Art*. Kimbell Art Museum, Fort Worth.

Storey, Rebecca. 1985. An Estimate of Mortality in a Pre-Columbian Urban Population. *American Anthropologist* 87: 519–35.

CHAPTER 3

On the Nature of the Mesoamerican City

Joyce Marcus

Each city, like every other object in nature, is, in a sense, unique.

(Wirth 1925: 175)

In my opinion, it is exciting that the evolutionary histories of two of our most important nuclear regions appear to have been so different, suggesting that culture change in the direction of increased scale and complexity can occur in varied ways. I suggest that the cultural ecologists should do as others have and view this variety as a source of stimulation for theory-building, rather than deny that variety exists simply for the sake of fitting everything into a single explanatory scheme.

(Blanton 1980: 148)

One of the most spectacular settlement types of pre-Columbian Mesoamerica was the city. The Mesoamerican city – if I may attempt to accommodate two contrasting positions – was both the result of social change (Sjoberg 1960) and a source of further change (Redfield 1941). We now have detailed studies of cities such as Teotihuacan, Tula, Monte Alban, Tikal, Dzibilchaltun, and others, but as yet no overall synthesis of urbanism in ancient Mesoamerica has emerged. I began this paper with the notion of Harris and Ullman (1945) that "each city is unique in detail but resembles others in function and pattern," and I hoped to discover some patterns shared by all Mesoamerican cities – something, in other words, that would distinguish them from cities in other parts of the world. Instead, I found that what Mesoamerican cities shared, they also shared with cities elsewhere, and that in their own diversity they mirrored much of the diversity in the rest of the world.

One problem in the study of Mesoamerican cities is an unconscious bias that results from our much greater knowledge of central Mexican sites (such as Teotihuacan, Tula, and Tenochtitlan) than of other sites. In the minds of some, these great centers, with their particular regional tradition and their overwhelming commercial aspect, have become *the* model for what a Mesoamerican city should look like. This is unfortunate, for no other Mesoamerican city does look exactly like them. I can be grouped with Blanton (1980) in finding this fact exciting rather than disappointing, and in this paper I will emphasize the differences as well as the similarities among Nahua, Zapotec, Mixtec, and Maya cities.

I will first consider models for the *form* of the city proposed by sociologists and cultural geographers, giving some idea of their

Reprinted from Joyce Marcus. 1983. On the Nature of the Mesoamerican City. In *Prehistoric Settlement Patterns: Essays in Honor of Gordon R. Willey*, edited by Evon Z. Vogt and Richard M. Leventhal (University of New Mexico Press, Albuquerque), pp. 195–242.

applicability to Mesoamerica. I will then consider the ways in which various Indian groups of Mesoamerica classified their own cities and hinterlands, based on linguistic and ethnohistoric data, and discuss the relationship between their classifications and those of Western social scientists. Next I will discuss variations in the *function* of the city, especially in respect to its position in a hierarchy, following this with a detailed comparison of three of our best-known Mesoamerican cities. Finally, I will look for similarities and differences in some of the remaining cities of that region.

Formal Models

There are almost as many classificatory schemes for cities as there are cities. In general terms, however, most schemes have been based on (1) *size* (either of the population, or area covered by the city, or some combination of the two that provides a density figure); (2) *location* (as coastal or riverine, on a valley floor or mountaintop, and so forth); (3) *function* (market center, religious center, port of trade, defensive stronghold, or other); (4) *position in a hierarchy* including other settlements that are supraordinate, subordinate, or coordinate; or (5) *form*, including the morphological characteristics of the city, which may in fact reflect any or all of the other four variables mentioned above.

Because it takes other variables into account, morphology is one of the possible frameworks for approaching the archaic city. The simplest formal dichotomy is that between *planned* and *unplanned* cities (Doxiadis 1968: 347). Planned cities frequently display a formality expressed in rectangular components (such as straight roads, a gridiron street pattern, rectangular city blocks, and repetitive units of standard sizes). Unplanned cities, on the other hand, often display a lack of formality and are characterized by radial growth, as opposed to the axial growth of planned cities. In addition, unplanned or "natural" cities may be built on the "sector plan" to be described below. It should be noted, however, that many Mesoamerican cities combine both aspects, having a clearly planned "inner city," which is the locus for public secular and religious structures, and an unplanned "outer city," which shows haphazard residential growth.

Three cities that make clear the differences to be found in Mesoamerica are Teotihuacan, Dzibilchaltun, and Monte Alban. Teotihuacan covered 20 square kilometers with a population estimated at 125,000–200,000 persons by AD 600 (Millon 1976: 212). It was built, if not on an actual grid, at least on a cruciform plan whose major axes are an east–west highway and the north–south Street of the Dead, intersecting at the Ciudadela. While Millon (1976) has suggested that "successive additions to a basic cruciform plan... may give more of an impression of the realization of a master plan than was actually the case," Jeffrey Parsons (personal communication) points to survey evidence for planned growth: early in the city's history, the Street of the Dead was extended 5 kilometers north–south, and the main east–west highway was laid out 2–3 kilometers to the west and 6 kilometers to the east, well in advance of additional settlement along those avenues. Indeed, these major axes even seem to have determined the arrangement of some rural settlements nearby.

By contrast, Dzibilchaltun, covering 19 square kilometers and with a population estimated at 42,000 persons by AD 900 (Kurjack 1974), had neither a gridiron plan nor a layout based on cruciform streets carrying people into and out of the site center. One can detect an inner zone with a heavier concentration of vaulted architecture around the Cenote Xlacah, beyond which are concentric rings with ever-decreasing densities of vaulted architecture as one moves outward. While Kurjack has defined these rings as a "central group" (0.25 square kilometers), a "central aggregate" (3 square kilometers), a "peripheral sphere" (13 square kilometers), and an area "without vaulted architecture" (less than 3 square kilometers), they are clearly the result of unplanned growth on the "concentric model" to be described below.

Monte Alban, covering 6.5 square kilometers with a population conservatively estimated at 30,000 persons by AD 600 (Blanton 1978), is not laid out on a grid, nor is there any readily apparent geometric pattern to its growth. While Monte Alban has an extensive system of pre-Columbian roads, crossing *barrancas* by means of impressive masonry roadbeds, none of the major traffic arteries serve any of the major public buildings. Indeed, Blanton's ekistic studies show that the Main Plaza is in one of the areas of most limited access as far as the road system is concerned, providing a striking contrast to the Ciudadela at Teotihuacan, where cruciform avenues converge (Blanton 1981). But while Monte Alban seems to have grown haphazardly according to the "sector model" to be described below, its Main Plaza or "downtown" area is definitely planned. Archaeological evidence, however, shows that this planned complex of parallel north–south rows of public buildings and palaces was imposed, 300–500 years after the founding of the city, on an earlier linear pattern that shows much less in the way of planning (Flannery and Marcus 1983).

In addition to illustrating the degree of planning or lack of it that one may encounter in Mesoamerica, these three cities contain the four parts basic to all settlements, as defined by Doxiadis (1968: 19): (1) the homogeneous parts, (2) the central part, (3) the circulatory parts, and (4) the special parts. An example of (1) would be the multifamily apartment compounds at Teotihuacan or the apsidal residences in the outermost zones at Dzibilchaltun, while the Main Plaza at Monte Alban and the Cenote Xlacah zone at Dzibilchaltun would be examples of (2). Examples of (3) would be the cruciform streets of Teotihuacan, the winding mountain roads of Monte Alban, and the *sacbeob*, or causeways, at Dzibilchaltun. Marketplaces, sweatbaths, and ball courts are examples of the "special parts" covered by (4), and here our three cities differ considerably. Millon (1976) believes that the "Great Compound" across from the Ciudadela at Teotihuacan was a marketplace; however, no marketplace has been demonstrated conclusively for Monte Alban (nor would its mountaintop location be a sensible choice for one). Teotihuacan has no known ball court, while Monte Alban has several.

Let us now consider a further set of models for the morphology of the ancient city, developed over the past half-century by sociologists and urban geographers. Obviously, these models are not universally accepted. In preparing this paper I discovered that the longer one attempts to devise a scheme for the ancient city, the more one is forced to ignore important "exceptions." The result is that the exceptions, as well as the variance they represent, go unexplained. Complicating the situation further is the fact that cities with similar functions may have different morphologies, while cities with similar forms may have different functions. Indeed, some students of urbanism feel the similarities in function may be easier to detect than those in form:

As far as morphology is concerned ancient and modern cities share only traits of so general a character that they are virtually useless for classificatory or analytical purposes.... If structural regularities are ultimately elucidated, then it is practically certain that they will be manifested in shared functions and in trends in systemic change rather than in form.
(Wheatley 1972: 601)

The Concentric Model

The concentric model was developed by E. W. Burgess in 1923, based upon the idea that most cities have a single center from which growth moves outward, giving rise to concentric zones similar to those already described for Dzibilchaltun. Burgess's model (based on Chicago and other modern cities) included a central business district, a zone in transition, an inner zone of workers' residences, an outer zone of middle- and upper-class residences, and a commuters' zone (figure 3.1); one of the features of this model is that socially mobile individuals move outward geographically as they move upward on the socioeconomic scale (Burgess 1925: 51–3). The model has since been altered by several scholars, one of the rele-

vant modifications being that homogeneous
urban zones rarely occur in the predicted
ideal "rings" around the city center; particular types of land use may occur in localized
areas not forming a strictly continuous ring
(see below).

As so altered, the model fits the vast
majority of cities in Mesoamerica, most of
which have a central zone of monumental
public buildings surrounded by roughly concentric zones of increasingly unimpressive
architecture. Thus, Dzibilchaltun, Mitla,
Coba, Zaculeu, and Yucuñudahui all fit the
model to a greater or lesser degree. Let us
move on, however, to a further modification, namely, the sector model.

The Sector Model

The sector model is most often associated
with the work of Homer Hoyt (1939), who
maintained that once there were differences
in land use near the center of a growing city,
they would be maintained as the city
expanded outward. Thus, these sectors of

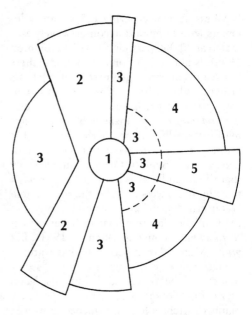

Figure 3.2   The sector model. 1. city center:
central business district; 2. manufacturing
district; 3. low-status residences; 4. medium-
status residences; 5. high-status residences.
(Redrawn from Harris and Ullman 1945: fig. 5.)

specific land-use type can grow outward as
pie-shaped wedges that crosscut Burgess's
concentric rings (figure 3.2). Geographers
have discovered that the sector model can
be applied most readily to residential districts; for example, once an area of high-
status households has been established near
the city center, new high-status residences
will be constructed contiguous to them, perhaps growing outward axially along one of
the major streets leading to and from the
center or growing outward radially on all
edges of the high-status zone. Alternatively,
one sector or quarter of the city may remain
high status rather than forming a continuous
ring. Such a situation may also occur with
sectors traditionally occupied by craftsmen,
foreigners, and the like. There may, however, be a gradation outward within each
sector, as for example in the degree of eleg-
ance of high-status residences or the size of
workshops, leading many geographers to
regard the sector model as a modification
of the concentric model rather than to see

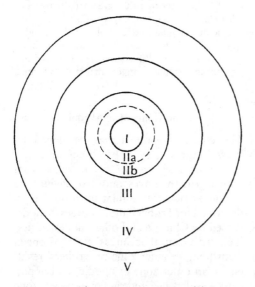

Figure 3.1   The concentric zone model. I. city
center or central business district; II. zone in
transition: a. inner belt: factory district, b. outer
belt: retrogressing neighborhoods; III. zone of
workers' residences; IV. zone of middle-class
residences; V. commuters' zone.
(Redrawn from Burgess 1925: 51, Chart 1.)

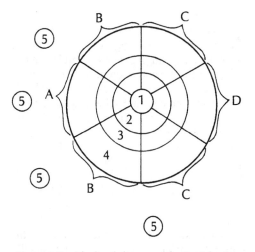

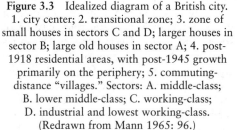

Figure 3.3 Idealized diagram of a British city.
1. city center; 2. transitional zone; 3. zone of
small houses in sectors C and D; larger houses in
sector B; large old houses in sector A; 4. post-
1918 residential areas, with post-1945 growth
primarily on the periphery; 5. commuting-
distance "villages." Sectors: A. middle-class;
B. lower middle-class; C. working-class;
D. industrial and lowest working-class.
(Redrawn from Mann 1965: 96.)

the two as mutually exclusive alternatives.
In fact, geographers are now finding that a
combination of the sector and concentric
models describes a "typical" British city
(see figure 3.3) (Mann 1965).

In the Old World, the sector model nicely
fits the Early Dynastic cities of Iraq's Diyala
River basin (R. McC. Adams 1966: 98),
where the high-status residences occur
along the broad streets running north–south
and east–west from the central area of monumental architecture. The rectangular "city
blocks" thus formed were filled with low-
status residences, whose only access to the
main streets was through narrow, twisting
alleys that occasionally emerged between
two high-status houses. In Mesoamerica,
the sector model fits Teotihuacan, whose
axial growth and grid pattern promoted the
construction of high-status residences along
main arteries such as the Street of the Dead,
and where residential wards of craftsmen
sharing the same economic specialty arose
(Millon 1976). Monte Alban, divided into

more than a dozen residential wards in Per-
iod IIIb (Blanton 1978), is another candidate.
Other cities with sector patterns include
Xochicalco, Tenochtitlan, and possibly Tula.

Finally, some geographers have concluded
that Burgess's concentric model best typified
the urbanization process, while Hoyt's sector model is more appropriate for describing
the spatial distribution of social classes
(Anderson and Egeland 1961; Olsson
1965: 9). This reinforces the notion that
cities can simultaneously display both patterns to a greater or lesser degree.

The Multiple Nuclei Model

Developed by Harris and Ullman (1945),
this model represents a further modification
of the concentric model (again, the two
models are not mutually exclusive). Harris
and Ullman suggest that some cities have a
cellular structure in which distinctive patterns of land use have evolved around
certain focal points or *nuclei* within the context of an urban area (figure 3.4). Rather

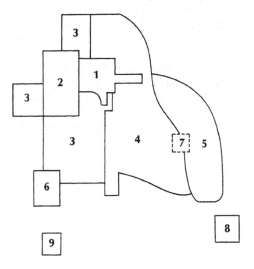

Figure 3.4 The multiple nuclei model.
1. central business district; 2. wholesale light
manufacturing; 3. lower-status residential;
4. medium-status residential; 5. higher-status
residential; 6. heavy manufacturing; 7. outlying
business district; 8. residential suburb;
9. industrial suburb.
(Redrawn from Harris and Ullman 1945: fig. 5.)

than having a single, dominant "downtown" area, these cities have a series of virtually equal nuclei that, once established, may be maintained for long periods and give the city a pattern of growth compatible with concentric or sector expansion. In some cities these nuclei have existed from the city's beginning; in others, they have developed as the growth of the city has stimulated migration and specialization (Harris and Ullman 1945: 14). One example cited by Harris and Ullman is that of London, in which the area of the medieval city now is the center for financial and commercial activities and the area near the Palace of Westminster serves as the center for political administration. The number of nuclei that result from various historical developments varies greatly from city to city, but generally speaking, once these nuclei have appeared, several factors involving distinctive land-use patterns reconfirm and maintain these distinctive foci.

In attempting to apply this to Mesoamerican sites, we can initially think of each discrete plaza group as a nucleus or focal point. There are clear differences in the number, size, form, and arrangement of plaza groups at different sites. There are sites that have a single, very large, dominant central plaza; cities with such a single center by definition do not have multiple nuclei. Another pattern, however, would constitute multiple nuclei, namely, a site with many "separate but equal" plaza groups. Of course there are limitations to these classificatory schemes. For instance, do plaza groups that are fairly equal in size (and in their types of structures) serve the same functions? If they replicate one another's functions, do they then serve a different segment of society? On the other hand, if plaza groups do have different functions, do they serve the same segment of society?

In this paper, we shall reserve the term *multiple nuclei* for sites that display many "separate but equal" plaza groups. One major, still-unresolved problem is whether these plazas were constructed sequentially or simultaneously.

If we examine the literature for sites with multiple nuclei, most of the examples that come immediately to mind are so-called secondary or tertiary centers in the lowland Maya area. Seibal (figure 3.5), Altar de Sacrificios, Tzum (figure 3.6), and Uaxactun all seem to be centers composed of various plaza groups, none of which is *completely* dominant and central in the sense that those terms apply to the Main Plaza at Monte Alban. Kaminaljuyu may be a highland Maya example (Sanders 1974: figure 1). From outside the Maya area, further cases of multiple nuclei may appear at Huamelulpan in the Mixteca Alta (Gaxiola 1976) and Lambityeco and Reyes Etla in the Valley of Oaxaca.

While the evolution and causes of this multiple nuclei pattern are not universally apparent, I would like to point to a pattern in the lowland Maya area that may be of social and political significance. The cities displaying large numbers of "separate but equal" plaza groups are frequently on the secondary (or lower) level of the site hierarchy. The major cities I have identified on the basis of emblem glyphs as being primary centers or regional capitals in AD 731 (Marcus 1973, 1976) – Tikal, Copan, Palenque, or Calakmul – do not seem to display this pattern; all appear to have a single major complex of public buildings that dominates all others. If we assume, as the hieroglyphic texts seem to suggest, that the various small plaza groups at secondary and tertiary centers were constructed by a series of rulers, this distinctive pattern may suggest something about the differences in government between capitals and their dependencies.

Indian Views of the City

We have seen how varied are the models for the city used by geographers and sociologists, and the degree to which they describe or fail to describe Mesoamerican cities. But there is another set of models we have not yet considered: those used by the Indians of Mesoamerica themselves, which differ considerably from those used by Western scholars. It has long been known that while Westerners try to define the city on the

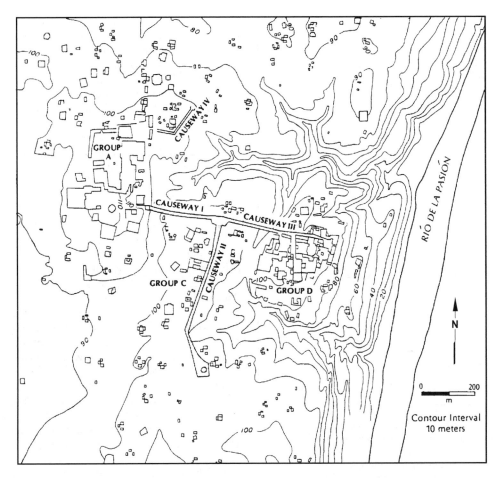

Figure 3.5 The central part of Seibal, El Peten, Guatemala. Located on high terrain, Groups A, C, D, and unlettered group are linked by causeways I–IV.
(Redrawn and adapted from Willey et al. 1975: fig. 3.)

basis of such variables as population size, percentage of population not engaged in extractive subsistence activities, or presence of public institutions such as markets, post offices, and banks, non-Western peoples may use very different criteria. Among the Yoruba of West Africa, for example, it is the presence of an *oba*, or sacred king, living in an *afin*, or royal palace, which defines the important unit, an *ilú*. And an *ilú* is an administrative unit that does not stop at the walls of a nucleated settlement or "city" in our terms, but extends out into farmland that supports and sustains it (Krapf-Askari 1969). In this section I will consider such

native categories among the sixteenth-century Nahuatl (Molina 1571), Mixtec (M. E. Smith 1973), Zapotec (Córdova 1578), and Maya (Martínez Hernández 1929).

The key Nahuatl word was *altepetl*, which meant not only *pueblo* but also *pueblos de todos juntamente, rey,* and *provincia*. In addition, *altepetl* served as the root for numerous other words such as *altepetlianca, sujeto o comarca de ciudad; altepenayotl, principal ciudad que es cabeza de reyno; altepetenametica, ciudad cercada de muro;* or *altepetequipanoliztli, obra pública o oficio público*. The term clearly referred not only to a nucleated settlement (in our

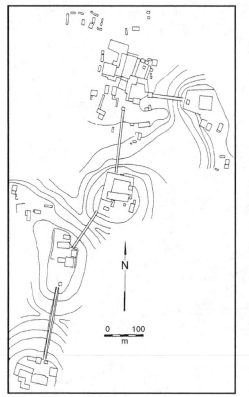

Figure 3.6   The central section of Tzum,
Campeche, Mexico, divided into five well-
defined groups connected by *sacbeob*; all but one
of the groups are on promontories. (Redrawn and
adapted from von Euw 1977: 48–9.)

terms, a town or city), but also to its ruler,
its inhabitants, and the territory ruled,
including outlying dependencies and land-
holdings. As such, it is difficult to remove
the city from its political landscape, regional
hierarchy, and spatial and cultural context.

The relevant Mixtec term was *ñuu*,
"town, place where something exists, the
city, or the town site" (Smith 1973: 39).
There was an additional term, *tayu*, which
could mean city, town, palace, or province,
and was a geographical substantive used in
the names of boundaries or for sites smaller
than towns. Once again, as in the case of the
Aztec altepetl, we see the conceptual association of the ruler and his residence, the
town or city, and the surrounding countryside governed by the ruler – much like the

Yoruba concept of *ilú*. What was important
was not so much where the city ended and
the countryside began, but where the lands
of one *cacique* ended and another's began.

For the Valley Zapotec in 1578, the term
queche meant *pueblo grande o pequeño, o
ciudad* or simply a *población de gente*, a
populated place. Like the Aztec altepetl,
the Zapotec *queche* also served as the root
for a number of other words, such as *que-
chenahuini, aldea* (literally, small populated
place); *tobilaoqueche, pueblo, estancia de
otro*; *quechenatale, pueblo, estancia grande
de mucha gente*; and *quizahaqueche, provincia* (once again showing us that a province was defined as the territory controlled
by a ruler of a city or major town). The
Isthmus Zapotec today still use essentially
the same term, *guidxi*, for a city or town
(Pickett 1959).

For the Yucatec Maya, the basic term was
cah, town, place (Martínez Hernández
1929: 164). A city or large town of importance was *noh cah*, a small town *chan cah*,
while a village was *chan chan cah*. A larger
unit was *cacab*, a town and the land belonging to it, a township, a commune, while
baalcah meant world in which they live,
and the town and its inhabitants (Brinton
1882: 262). Once again we see that the
land, people, and minor settlements controlled by one ruler who lived at a city or
major town was the meaningful unit.

Interestingly, the word for town or city in
Quiche and Pokom is *tinamit*, apparently of
Nahuatl origin, and in many contexts
thought to refer to fortified towns (J. Fox
1978). Speaking about *tinamit*, Miles (1957:
771) states, "the town name extended over
all lands 'belonging' to it; the names of hamlets and areas were subsumed."

What can we learn from this exercise in
sixteenth-century ethnohistory?   Among
other things, we can see that the archaeologist or geographer who draws a line
separating "the city" from its politically controlled territory may be performing an act
that is heuristically useful for his settlement
pattern analysis, but that does not conform
to the reality of the Mesoamerican Indian
world. The concentric, sector, and multiple

nuclei models proposed by economists, sociologists, and geographers do describe various Mesoamerican cities and may even give us clues as to why certain cities grew as they did, but these were not the patterns that were of paramount interest to the Indian. What was most important to him was the fact that he belonged to a particular region controlled by a specific native ruler, to whom he owed allegiance and tribute and from whom he received protection and civic-ceremonial leadership. And unless the ruler's city of residence had a wall around it (see below), the boundary between it and the countryside it dominated was far less striking to the Indian then than the archaeologist today.

We can also learn from these sixteenth-century sources that the Indian viewed his ruler's community as at the top of a *hierarchy* of communities; hence all the terms for *sujetos*, for *cabezas de reynos*, or for small settlements that were *estancias de otros*.

It was probably the residence of the ruler, rather than any size difference per se, that placed many cities at the tops of their respective hierarchies. In addition, however, to the obvious political hierarchies among Mesoamerican towns and cities, there were also commercial, religious, and military hierarchies. Let us now look at some of these.

The City within its Hierarchy

Those of us who grew up in the industrial West are conditioned to think of cities at the head of commercial or economic hierarchies. We would be wise, however, not to expect the same from ancient cities. R. Fox (1977) reminds us that in the pre-industrial world, cities were often ranked not on the basis of their position in a series of economic or transportation nodes, but on their position in a hierarchical network of political power or ritual status.

Despite the changes wrought by the industrial revolution, traces of this pattern can be seen today. Washington, DC, a city with no notable commercial emphasis, is part of none of our states and yet is superior to all of them in political power (R. Fox

1977: 28). An example from Mesoamerica would be Monte Alban, a city also detached (or *disembedded*, to use the term Blanton has employed) from the economic network of secondary and tertiary centers in the Valley of Oaxaca, yet politically superior to all of them (Blanton 1976a, 1978). The city of Benares ranks as one of the holiest in northern India, a position that reflects an urban hierarchy based on ritual criteria (R. Fox 1977). A Mesoamerican example would be Mitla, a city that was at the top of the Zapotec ritual hierarchy without necessarily being high in the political hierarchy (Marcus 1978). Though it was one of the largest nucleated communities in the Postclassic Valley of Oaxaca and the seat of the paramount priest of the Zapotec "church," Mitla paid tribute in goods and services to Zaachila, the political capital of the valley. And Zaachila, for its part, illustrates another principle of preindustrial society: the capital need not be the largest site in the region. The ethnohistoric documents leave no doubt that Zaachila was the seat of power of the dynasty bearing its name, yet settlement pattern surveys (Kowalewski 1983) show that the Late Postclassic occupation encompassed only a few hectares – a complex of palaces atop a huge mound that accumulated for the most part in earlier periods. It is further illustration of a point we made earlier, namely, that the capital is wherever the king lives.

Hierarchies therefore can be based on political and administrative status, economic status, or ritual and religious status. Occasionally all three of these converge, as in the case of the metropolis of Teotihuacan, but such cases are in the minority and should not (as we have already said) be used as the model for all Mesoamerican cities. For most of those cities, a part of their distinctive character derives from the extent to which these various statuses are present, and when several are present, the degree to which one may be dominant over another. Analysis of the latter may give clues to the nature of local society.

For example, R. Fox (1977: 34) expects that under conditions of weak state power and high urban economic dependency, the "ideological functions" of the city will be primary, and the cities will typically be what he calls "regal-ritual" cities. Such cities would correspond to the concept of "ceremonial center" developed by Wheatley (1971) for the urban centers of China during the Shang Period, places that provided a residence for the royal family and temples for the surrounding populace without providing major economic services. It remains to be seen whether the concept of "ceremonial center" widely used in the Maya area is analogous, or whether two different phenomena have been described by the same term (Willey 1956).

To return to R. Fox's dichotomy, he further expects that when the state is strong and the economy is autonomous, the mercantile roles are primary. This would presumably brand Teotihuacan, Tenochtitlan, Tula (and possibly Cholula) as urban centers associated with strong states, although, as we have seen, most of these centers were at the top of their respective political and religious hierarchies as well.

Apart from these huge, multifunctional urban centers, we can imagine various combinations of political, religious, and commercial roles that would account for some of the differences in *function* (as opposed to *form*) that we see in ancient Mesoamerican cities. Monte Alban, Yucuñudahui, and Xochicalco are examples of "regal-ritual" cities, where the administrative and religious roles are dominant over the commercial; significantly, this is one of the types of city most frequently defended by walls and/or moats. Guiengola in the Isthmus of Tehuantepec would be an example of a fortified administrative center that not only has no commercial focus, but has relatively few religious functions as well. Xicalango, Cozumel, Itzamkanac, and Nito would be some possible examples of ports of trade (Scholes and Roys 1948; Sabloff and Rathje 1975), where the commercial aspect overrides both ritual and political-administrative functions. Pilgrimage centers such as Izamal, Chalma, and Juquila have an overwhelmingly ritual focus; while Mitla, despite its

place at the head of the Zapotec religious hierarchy, was also a market center of several square kilometers.

Before proceeding to a detailed comparison of three Mesoamerican cities, I would briefly like to discuss the methods used for studying site hierarchies. Much of the recent work on ancient hierarchies and urban networks has employed techniques of spatial or regional analysis such as the nearest neighbor statistic (for example, Earle 1976), central place models (Johnson 1972; Blanton 1978), and the rank-size rule (Blanton 1976b). While I agree . . . that there have been overenthusiastic abuses of such techniques, we should remember that they were originally designed not to "reduce man to a statistic," but to detect patterns that are not visible to the naked eye and that can be combined with more humanistic observations that *are* visible. Moreover, these techniques are not, as some misinformed critics have suggested, applicable only to marketing hierarchies. The principles of clustering, random spacing, and equidistant spacing are basic to modern ecology; in fact, prairie dogs digging burrows and sandhill cranes feeding in marshes can be shown to exhibit spacing as regular as a hexagonal central-place lattice (Earle 1976). In a recent review of regional analysis in archaeology, Johnson has perhaps best laid these criticisms to rest, pointing out that such things as "movement minimization, activity agglomeration and centralization, functional settlement hierarchies, and regular settlement spatial distributions may occur *in the absence of market institutions*" (1977: 495; emphasis mine).

In other words, competition for tribute, efforts to minimize travel time, and similar considerations are present in administrative and religious hierarchies as much as in commercial ones. I have shown that the Maya secondary centers that mention the emblem glyphs of Calakmul and Tikal, for example, occur almost equidistantly spaced from their respective primary centers (Marcus 1976). I do not believe we can ignore this regularity of spacing just because it almost certainly reflects an administrative and religious hierarchy (as well as intersite competition for tribute and manpower), rather than results from a market system for which there is no archaeological evidence. Similarly, we need to know more about the differences in rank–size relationships within the state hierarchies below Teotihuacan, Monte Alban, Tikal, Calakmul, Palenque, and Seibal even though they cannot be presumed to have a commercial basis.

Teotihuacan, Monte Alban, and Tikal: A Functional Comparison

Teotihuacan, Monte Alban, and Tikal, all great Mesoamerican cities, illustrate the differences displayed by such places in terms of the relative importance of administrative, commercial, and religious status.

Though all three were administrative cities, they differed in the accessibility of the administrative buildings. I have already mentioned that Teotihuacan has two major streets more than 5 kilometers long, which converge at the Ciudadela (figure 3.7), which Millon (1976) feels was the administrative center of the city. Across the Street of the Dead, to the west, is an open area called the Great Compound, which Millon feels may have been the location of a major marketplace. Thus, both the main focus of administrative functions and what is *possibly* the main focus of marketing activity at Teotihuacan occur at what would be the point of highest accessibility in ekistic, or "traffic flow" terms. Large numbers of people could be, and probably were, conducted into this area from the outer city and the surrounding countryside.

The situation at Monte Alban is quite different. Here there was an extensive ancient network of roads (figure 3.8), some running for more than a kilometer, others for only a few hundred meters, occasionally supported by retaining walls or cut into the side of a slope (Blanton 1978: figure 4.4 and p. 64). These Blanton has divided into major roads (3–8 meters in width) and minor roads (2–3 meters in width). Two major roads (E and F) seemed to have handled most of the traffic, running midway through the major residential zone; another major road (G)

connects the hill of Monte Alban proper with nearby Atzompa, the northernmost part of the site. Significantly, the Main Plaza (figure 3.9) was one of the areas of least accessibility, avoided by all major and virtually all minor roads; in addition, during the Late Classic the Plaza could be reached only through three small entrances at the corners. The areas of absolutely lowest accessibility in ekistic terms were the ruler's residence and associated small temples (presumably used by the royal family) on the North Platform, apparently one of the areas of important administrative decision making. No market has yet been identified at Monte Alban, and most of the suitable open areas in zones of high road accessibility occur on the perimeter slopes of the city. Thus, we have one city whose administrative and (possible) commercial center was highly accessible, and another that fits Fox's concept of a "regal-ritual" city, for it has no clear economic focus and its administrative center is of very restricted access.

Tikal presents us with still a third pattern, although admittedly, no one has done a detailed ekistic analysis of it. Like a number of other lowland Maya sites, Tikal's public buildings and elite residences were constructed on natural promontories or artificial acropolises, and some of these were connected by elevated causeways that run through low-lying areas or *bajos*. For example, the Maudslay causeway links Building Group H with Temple IV, while the Tozzer causeway connects Temple IV to an area west of the Main Plaza; the Maler causeway connects the East Plaza to Group H; and the Méndez causeway links the Temple of the Inscriptions Group to the area east of the Central Acropolis (Carr and Hazard 1961). The Maler, Méndez, and Tozzer causeways all lead to the center of Tikal (figure 3.10). All the Tikal causeways are raised roads, and some are of great width. The Méndez causeway is 60 meters wide and a kilometer long, while the Maudslay causeway averages between 39 and 58 meters in width. This question remains, however: for whom were these causeways intended? Does their width indicate that there was a heavy

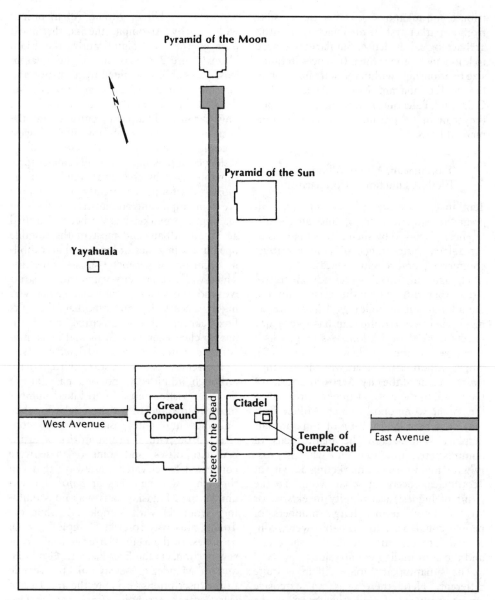

Figure 3.7 A view of central Teotihuacan. The north–south axis is the Street of the Dead (approximately 15° 25′ east of north), while the east–west axis corresponds to the East and West Avenues. (Redrawn and greatly simplified from Millon 1967: 46.)

flow of common people to public places of high accessibility, in the manner of the Street of the Dead at Teotihuacan? Or were they merely elegant streets that carried rulers and religious functionaries between temples of limited access in a "regal-ritual" setting?

As striking as the differences in traffic patterns between Teotihuacan and Monte Alban, so too were the differences in economic specialization and craft activity. Over 500 craft workshops have been located by Millon and Cowgill at Teotihuacan, and

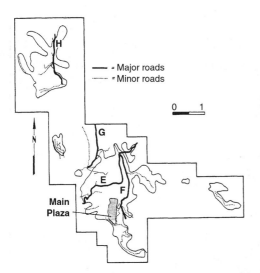

= Major roads

····· = Minor roads

0   1

Figure 3.8 Reconstruction of the pre-Columbian road system at Monte Alban, Oaxaca. (Redrawn from Blanton 1978: fig. 4.4.)

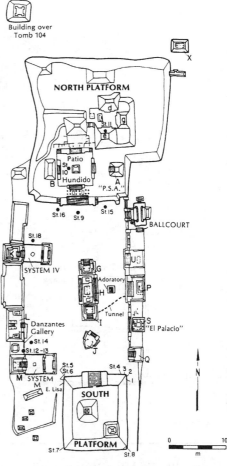

Figure 3.9 The Main Plaza at Monte Alban, Oaxaca. (A synthesis based on the work of several investigators, including Richard Blanton's most recent mapping.)

Millon (1976: 233) estimates that at least 400 of the city's apartment compounds were occupied primarily by craftsmen. In addition there were "perhaps another 200 or 300 apartment compounds, some of whose occupants were engaged in craft activities" (Millon 1976). While the primary craft seems to have been obsidian working (over 300 workshops), there were an additional 200 workshops for ceramics, figurines, slate, basalt, and shell. Both rural surveys (Sanders 1965; Parson 1971; Blanton 1972) and urban studies (Cowgill 1974) suggest that virtually all the artisans in the Valley of Mexico were drawn out of the countryside and into the metropolis, where they were organized into huge compounds of 60–100 persons.

The concentration of craftsmen into the largest urban center is one alternative mode of organization, and since Tula and Tenochtitlan appear (on the basis of available knowledge) to have had similar concentrations, we might describe this as a "central Mexican" or "Basin of Mexico" pattern. One consequence of this hyperurbanism and high commercial emphasis, however, is that the site hierarchy below Teotihuacan is notably lacking in centers of "secondary" or

"intermediate" size: there is an enormous drop-off between Teotihuacan (pop. 125,000–200,000) and the next largest settlements (pop. 1,500–3,000), suggesting that the metropolis had virtually monopolized the administrative, religious, and commercial functions for the Basin of Mexico. What this means is that a rank-size graph for the Basin's site hierarchy (drawn on the basis of population) is remarkably concave (Blanton 1976b: figure 10), lacking the "lognormal" slope of a hierarchy in which secondary centers are about half the size of primary

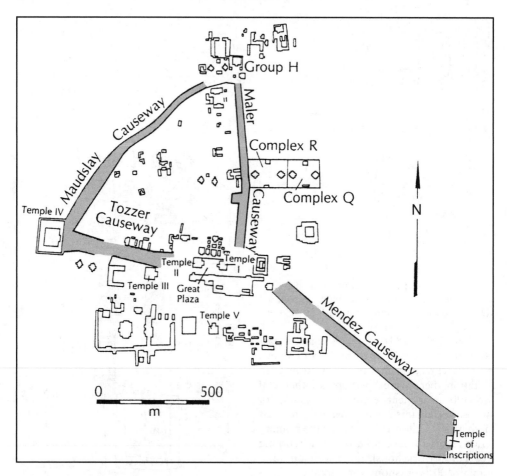

Figure 3.10   The Maler, Méndez, and Tozzer causeways leading to the central section of Tikal, El Peten, Guatemala. (Redrawn from Carr and Hazzard 1961.)

centers, tertiary centers are about one-third the size of primary centers, and so on.[1]

By contrast, Monte Alban did *not* choose to concentrate craftsmen within the city, reveals no evidence of large compounds housing such specialists, and has a site-size hierarchy that is closer to "lognormal." Monte Alban had 2,500 occupied terraces, but there are secondary centers with over 1,000, and tertiary centers with over 500; lower-level administrative centers might reach 40 hectares, and there were villages of 5 hectares and hamlets of 1 hectare. This was not because Oaxaca had no craft specialists, but because it had chosen an alternative arrangement: in the Valley of

Oaxaca, craft specialists in the Classic Period as well as today tend to specialize *by village*. For example, surveys of the valley floor and piedmont by Blanton, Kowalewski, and Feinman are showing abundant evidence of specialized pottery production by village or town, so much so that it may soon be possible to specify which ceramic types were made at which site (Feinman 1980, 1982). Even as early as Monte Alban I, when Santo Domingo Tomaltepec (Whalen 1976) was only a "third-order" administrative center in the Tlacolula arm of the valley, it was already a significant producer of fine gray pottery. Two Monte Alban I households excavated by Whalen at Tomaltepec had in their courtyards a total of four two-chambered reduced-firing kilns fueled by oak, the largest single concentration of kilns known for Period I. At the same time, Feinman says there is little evidence for ceramic production at Monte Alban during Periods I and II. Although some kilns are known from Period IIIb at Monte Alban proper (Winter and Payne 1976), and there is some evidence that Atzompa was an important producer of ceramics, the survey evidence suggests that pottery production at Monte Alban proper was no more intensive, given its size, than at any of the valley floor pottery centers studied by Feinman. In fact, the percentage of craftsmen at the nearby Early Formative site of San Jose Mogote may have been higher than that at Monte Alban. Certainly Monte Alban did not drain the countryside of craftsmen as Teotihuacan seems to have, nor did it have any compound-sized ceramic workshops such as the 100–150 concentrated at Teotihuacan (Millon 1976: 232). Fewer than a dozen kiln wasters were found in Blanton's entire survey of Monte Alban (1978). Even today the pattern in Oaxaca is for craft specialization by village, with Atzompa making green-glaze ware, Coyotepec black ware, Teotitlan del Valle blankets, Jalieza belts, Teitipac metates, and Guelavia baskets.

There are abundant precedents for this alternative craft pattern in the ancient world, one of the principal examples coming from the Shang dynasty in China (Chang 1968). The capital city, Cheng-chou, was a walled area of only 3.2 square kilometers (half the size of Monte Alban), almost the prototypical "regal-ritual" city. Outside, not inside, the walled city were the homes of the commoners and craft specialists, even those craftsmen (such as the bronze-smiths) who enjoyed a high social status. Each village in the countryside seems to have had a different occupational speciality, thereby promoting a high degree of economic interdependence among villages and between the city and the village, without producing the urban concentration of craftsmen that characterized Teotihuacan. This alternative might thus be called the "Oaxacan" or

"Shang Chinese" pattern; and significantly, the Shang city, like Monte Alban, was a place with palaces, ancestral halls, and ceremonial areas, but without a strong commercial focus.

Obviously, I do not mean to give the impression that Monte Alban was without craftsmen. In fact, numerous areas of craft activity were found in Blanton's subdivision 2 (1978) which includes the Main Plaza and contiguous high-status residential terraces and public buildings. These areas included higher concentrations of marine shell, obsidian, jade, mica, serpentine, malachite, and ocher, and Blanton suggests that during Period IIIb (the most populous) there were perhaps 900–1,800 persons involved in obsidian working and 133–266 involved in shell working, with perhaps 10 percent of the total population engaged in some kind of craft. His argument, however, is that this level of craft activity was largely designed to meet the consumption needs of the city, rather than to carry on the massive commercial export made possible by Teotihuacan's having craftsmen as 25 percent of its population. In my opinion, Blanton's argument would be even clearer had he not used the term *workshops*, which conjures up visions of the compounds of 60–100 persons seen at Teotihuacan. What Blanton is referring to are actually only surface scatters of craft debris of the type called "chipping areas" or "scatters of waste flakes" elsewhere in Mesoamerica.

Before leaving this topic, I would like to correct some errors in a recent article by O'Brien and associates (1980), which implies (1) that a site cannot be a city unless there is evidence for economic specialization, and (2) that Blanton found no such evidence because he did not record stone tools. Both assertions are false. Stone tools of numerous kinds were recorded on the 10-page survey form filled out for every terrace by Blanton (for example, every metate found during the survey can be located to a terrace by use of the computer printout accompanying the text). In addition, hundreds of areas of economic specialization have been found – but, as noted, they are located in villages around the valley, rather than concentrating in the city. And as we have seen in Shang China and Oaxaca, having an urban concentration of crafts is only one of several alternatives.

At Tikal, our information is somewhat less rich, although not as poor as that for the lowland Maya area in general, where "no unequivocally identified pottery workshops have been discovered" (Fry 1979: 495). The best evidence comes from Group 4G-1 at Tikal, where quantities of figurine molds, figurines, bowls, and decorated serving vessels have been found (Fry 1979). Other possible ceramic workshops were found in excavations carried out adjacent to one of the causeways of the northern Tikal earthworks (Puleston and Callender 1967).

That occupational specialists existed at some Maya centers is not questioned; however, we are still very uncertain about the residential quarters they occupied and do not know whether they were dispersed throughout all settlements at different levels of the hierarchy, or restricted to some barrios at some sites of the regional hierarchy. The presence of such specialists is attested to by the discovery of masons' tool kits from Muna and Dzibilchaltun (Andrews and Rovner 1973), but we still do not know where these plaster workers or other craft specialists dwelt. It has been suggested that since the two tool kits were found as caches, the structures above them may once have housed the masons. At Muna the 13 artifacts constituted the total offering below the plaster floor of a building dating to the Pure Florescent Period. The Dzibilchaltun cache was found in Structure 742, an unvaulted rectangular building. The function of these caches or the "symbolic jewelers' work kits" (Andrews 1961: figure 2) is still not clear, but craftsmen or occupational specialists may have participated in the dedication of a building on which they had worked.

Obsidian and flint workshops have also been uncovered at Tikal (Becker 1973: 398–9); 176 flint biface-ovates have been found in Group 4F-1, while another 118 came from Group 4F-2. Approximately 26 percent of the total Tikal flint biface-ovates were located within these groups. The hypothesis that these two groups of structures were occupied by flint knappers is derived from the high number of flint tools and waste flakes. Another group (Group 4H-1) may be the residence of Tikal potters. Possible evidence for residences of woodworkers, masons, and tanners/leatherworkers also exists. There is still no evidence, however, that all those living within a particular sector of the site or group of contiguous residences practiced the same occupational specialization. In fact, Becker (1973: 404) concludes that "at Tikal there does not appear to be any clustering of specialists nor any correlation between size and location within the site."

Given the presence of craft specialists at Tikal, the important question still remains: were they simply meeting the consumption needs of the city, as Blanton feels Monte Alban's craftsmen were, or were they producing on a scale suitable for commercial export, as Millon feels the Teotihuacanos were? Until evidence to the contrary is presented, I suspect the former. That does not mean that occasional fine pieces made at Tikal did not reach other sites. But it does mean that there was probably no commercial industry at Tikal on the scale of the obsidian industry at Teotihuacan.

What was the nature of the site hierarchy below Tikal? We know the names of some of its secondary and tertiary dependencies (Marcus 1976), and a rank–size graph has been produced by Adams and Jones (1981: figure 3) to show that they approach a log-normal slope. Instead of size, Adams and Jones use as the index of center size "the number of courtyards plus two times the number of acropolises (large composite structures) present in the contiguous built-up area of a given site" (p. 309).

A further basis on which Teotihuacan, Monte Alban, and Tikal can be compared is their fortifications. In my search of the literature I repeatedly found suggestions that fortified cities were more likely to have a stronger administrative focus than

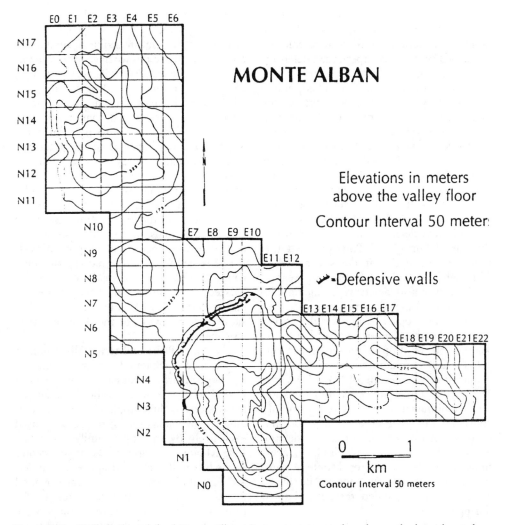

Figure 3.11   Walls built to defend Monte Alban, Oaxaca, constructed on the gentle slopes located on the western and northern sides. (Redrawn from Blanton 1978: fig. 1.3.)

commercial focus, and certainly these three cities show nothing to contradict that. Teotihuacan, surely the most clearly "commercial" of the three, is undefended. Obviously, at its peak its sheer size would have made it an unlikely object for attack, but even its early stages are undefended, and its location suggests that defense was not even a consideration.

Monte Alban sits on a clearly defensible series of hills and in addition has a series of inner and outer defensive walls (figure 3.11)

on the least precipitous slopes (Blanton 1978: 52). On its northern and western boundaries, "twin" (parallel) stone masonry walls run for approximately 3 kilometers, averaging 4–5 meters in height and reaching 20 meters in width where they cross barrancas coming down the mountainside. Excavations into one of these walls yielded stone and sherd fill, which suggests it was constructed in Period Ic (or at least in Period II with Ic fill). Two smaller walls, both later in date, run for 130–250 meters on the southern edge of the hill called Monte Alban Proper (Blanton 1978: figure 1.3). While these walls have no moats, in contrast to those at Xochicalco (discussed later in this paper), their defensive function is suggested by their position on the slopes that are most easily climbed, and is reinforced by the militaristic nature of the monumental inscriptions of Monte Alban I–IIIa (Marcus 1980).

At Tikal, a system of "earthworks" was discovered by Puleston and Callender (1967). These earthworks are located 4.5 kilometers north of the center of the city and 8.8 kilometers to the southeast of the center (Puleston 1974: 303). There is a clear drop-off in settlement density as one crosses these earthworks, and Puleston used this to define the limits of the site at Tikal. Although he initially interpreted these earthworks as primarily defensive in function, he later indicated that they might have served as the "emic" demarcation for the social, political, and religious entity that was Tikal, with the drop-off in settlement outside the earthworks representing the "etic" demarcation (Puleston 1974; Demarest 1978: 102). Other suggested functions are the delimiting of a zone of tribute or tax collection, and the control of trade and exchange, neither of which rules out defense as an additional function. Similar suggestions have been made for Monte Alban's walls, but would seem not to be likely, since the city expanded far beyond them during Period III.

Finally, we come to the religious roles of these three cities. More than a century ago, Fustel de Coulanges (1864) stunned European scholars by his revelations of the extent to which religion had permeated the ancient cities of Greece and Rome, a fact true of most archaic cities, but one that tends to be forgotten in our age of secular and commercial cities. From the *lares* and *penates* and the sacred hearth fires of the Roman household to the shared sacrifices of kin groups and the great temples of the city center, religion affected every level of the classical world. It was at least as omnipresent in Mesoamerica, where, Braidwood and Willey (1962: 350) have argued, the shrine

or early temple may be as old as sedentary life.

Two of the most striking similarities among the three cities we have been comparing are (1) the frequency of temples and (2) the general uniformity of their ground plan. All featured temples that had two rooms – an inner or more sacred chamber and an outer or less sacred room; frequently, the inner room was higher than the outer and had additional features such as altars or basins set in the floor (Marcus 1978). Ethnohistoric data suggest that these temples were designed in such a way that worshippers could enter the outer room only, while the actual rituals or sacrifices were conducted in the inner room by professionals (Marcus 1978). An alternative, the one-room temple, appeared in the cities of the Mixteca Alta (Spores 1984) and on the east and central coast of Yucatan in the Postclassic Period, but was not the dominant type elsewhere.

The Main Plaza at Monte Alban had at least a dozen such temples, and one patio on the North Platform (designated by Blanton [1978] as the least accessible spot on the entire site) has three small temples that, judging by their location, were probably used exclusively by the royal family. Even San Jose Mogote, a regional secondary center in the hierarchy below Monte Alban in Period II, had at least 10 such temples around its main plaza. Circular burned areas on the floor indicate that incense burners were periodically lit in the center of the outer room, on the step ascending to the inner room, or in the center of the inner room; occasionally, the inner room contains fragments of ripple-flaked obsidian sacrificial knives or of dozens of lancetlike obsidian blades for bloodletting rituals.

Maya temples show greater diversity than do Zapotec temples, but even at Tikal the two-room temple atop its steep-sided pyramid is common; the variant three-room temple has two inner rooms, the innermost presumably being the most sacred. The Tikal temples have very massive walls and a single doorway to the outside; the inner room may be 20–30 centimeters higher than the outer. One other feature occasionally found is an altar or bench set against the rear wall of the innermost room. In the Late Classic and Early Postclassic Periods, the outer room gradually became more open, as the Maya were able to construct either round or square columns instead of the massive temple walls, broken by a single doorway, that characterize Tikal, Copan, and Quirigua. Exactly how many temples there were at Tikal at any one time would be difficult to determine without further excavation for dating, but in addition to Temples I–V on their towering pyramids, there are countless smaller platforms and acropolises, each supporting 2–20 temples.

Despite its commercial focus, Teotihuacan takes the prize: there were more than 100 temples (or religious structures) along the Street of the Dead alone, according to Millon (1973: figure 7). In addition to these presumably "public" structures, Millon (1976: 216) has survey evidence that every multifamily apartment compound (of which there were an estimated 2,200) included one or more prominently located temple platforms. This means that every residential unit of 60–100 persons had its own local shrine or temple – a level of kin group participation in religion that rivals the ancient Mediterranean cities studied by Fustel de Coulanges. Moreover, there is a possible overlap even between the religious and commercial subsystems. At least some of the craft specialists at Teotihuacan spent part of their time making obsidian implements within a walled precinct west of and attached to the Moon Pyramid and therefore "directly within the jurisdiction of a temple community" (Millon 1976: 231); this, Millon feels, may have been part of "the larger involvement of the state in obsidian working" (Millon 1976). If we assume – as we must if the sixteenth-century *relaciones geográficas* are to be taken into account – that one of the many functions of obsidian blades was ritual bloodletting (it is, realistically, one of the few uses for which obsidian is superior to flint), then this involvement of the temple community makes sense. It means that a great proportion of the obsidian blades used in autosacrifice all over Mexico may have been produced under temple supervision in what Millon feels was surely one of Mesoamerica's most sacred cities. Lest it be thought that this is an isolated and therefore dubious case, I can add that surveys by Kowalewski (personal communication) now suggest that one major area of obsidian blade production in the Late Postclassic Oaxaca Valley is centered around the sacred city of Mitla.

To summarize: Monte Alban and Tikal differ from Teotihuacan in that their administrative and religious functions are far more overt than any commercial functions they may have had. Of the two, Monte Alban is more striking in the way its loci of administrative decision making are removed from public access. Teotihuacan not only made those loci readily accessible, but it also had commercial functions that are spectacularly apparent in spite of its hundreds of temples. The city is striking in the possible linkage of its religious and commercial functions. To ignore these differences would be to ignore clues to important variations in the Maya, Zapotec, and Teotihuacano political systems.

Some Features of Mesoamerican Cities

In this final section I will briefly review some of the other cities in Mesoamerica, noting the presence of some features similar to those seen at the three great centers just discussed.

Layout and street plan

Several other cities, primarily in the highlands, show the cruciform plan displayed by Teotihuacan. The later Nahua city of Tenochtitlan, for example, was divided into great quarters (figure 3.12) marked off by four avenues following the cardinal directions out from the ceremonial precinct (Calnek 1976). A major temple was located in each of the city quarters, and each quarter was in turn divided into barrios or *tlaxillacalli*. The barrio was the primary

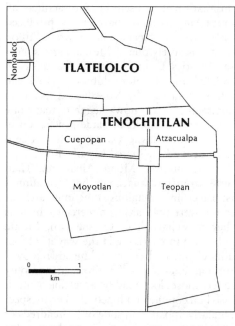

Figure 3.12   The quadrants of Tenochtitlan, the Aztec capital. (Redrawn from Calnek 1976: Map 20.)

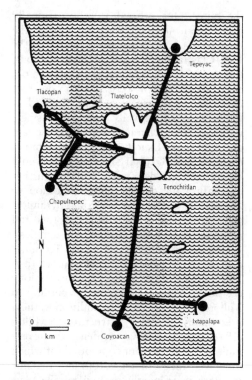

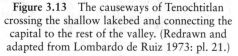

Figure 3.13   The causeways of Tenochtitlan crossing the shallow lakebed and connecting the capital to the rest of the valley. (Redrawn and adapted from Lombardo de Ruiz 1973: pl. 21.)

component or territorial unit for the internal administration within the quadrant.

That this was not the model for all Nahua cities, however, is shown by the contemporary city of Tlatelolco, which lacked the cruciform plan (Calnek 1976: 296–301). Here there were between 15 and 20 *barrios grandes*, each of which was subdivided into *barrios menores*. Similarly, the earlier Nahua city of Tula lacks the cruciform plan and seems instead to have grown through unplanned expansion and accretion (Diehl 1974: 13).

Another feature displayed by Tenochtitlan and reminiscent of Teotihuacan is the extension of its major streets into the surrounding countryside – in this case, as causeways crossing areas of shallow lakebed (figure 3.13). The major north–south axis was the long causeway running south from Tepeyac through Tlatelolco to the center of Tenochtitlan and on to Coyoacan. The major east–west axis ran from Tlacopan into Tenochtitlan, but there it ended, for a canoe trip was required to continue east to

Texcoco. A third causeway branched southeast to Ixtapalapa, and where it split off from the Tenochtitlan–Coyoacan causeway, there was a two-towered "redoubt" surrounded by a high wall with two gates. This suggests that the southern approach to Tenochtitlan was "fortified," or at the least, that traffic from that direction was regulated (Soustelle 1964: 35).

No Maya site displays the cruciform plan of a Teotihuacan or Tenochtitlan, although rectilinear plazas provide the organization for smaller units and sections within the city. Many lowland Maya districts, however, share with Tenochtitlan a causeway linking two different cities. These are the famous *sacbeob* (*sac*, white, + *be* road), the longest known of which runs 100 kilometers between the sites of Coba and Yaxuna (Villa Rojas 1934). The *sacbe* linking Ake and Izamal runs for 32 kilometers (Roys and

Shook 1966; Kurjack and Andrews 1976: 318), while that linking Uci and Cansahcab runs for 16 kilometers (Kurjack and Andrews 1976).

Palaces

Since the city was frequently the place of residence for the native lord, the palace is one of the features most commonly found there. It is, however, also one of the most variable in ground plan; therefore we can barely hint at its variability here. The observed differences seem to me to reflect differences in the size of the royal family and/or entourage and its relationship to the rest of the population; these clues should be followed up more carefully at a later date.

In Oaxaca, the Classic Period palace was rectangular and consisted of a large sunken patio surrounded by rooms of different sizes, some with sleeping benches, others with kitchenlike features. Frequently, a curtain wall shielded the interior from public scrutiny, and the most impressive palaces were entered by way of a colonnaded porch (Flannery and Marcus 1983). In the Postclassic, some palaces had a series of interconnected patios rather than one large one, as in the case of the Palace of the Six Patios at Yagul (figure 3.14) (Bernal and Gamio 1974).

At Teotihuacan, the term *palace* is too general to reflect the probable diversity of its residents and building plans. For example, Millon suggests that the Palace of the Sun served as the residence for the high priest or priests of the Sun Pyramid (1973: figure 19a). Sometimes attached to the back of a temple or a platform along the Street of the Dead, such "palaces" are really closed compounds with their own interior temple, patios, courtyards, and rooms; as such, they are similar to the apartment compounds already mentioned above.

As we move to the Ciudadela, the administrative center for the city, however, another

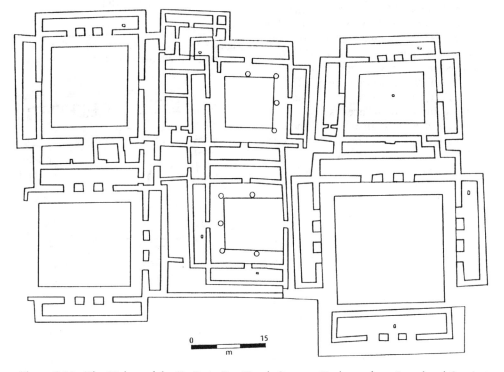

0 ━━━━━━ 15
m

Figure 3.14 The "Palace of the Six Patios" at Yagul, Oaxaca. (Redrawn from Bernal and Gamio 1974: plan 2.)

pattern emerges. It is here that Armillas (1964: 307) suggested that the rulers of Teotihuacan lived, and here Millon (1976) has identified twin palaces with identical ground plans. On this basis, Millon has suggested that Teotihuacan may have had dual rulers, a pattern known from the Aztec Period (Carrasco 1971). This interesting suggestion should certainly be followed up, because we have additional ethnohistorical data that suggest that the Toltec also had a history of dual rulership.

While the rectangular palace with the interior courtyard is one of the most widespread types, the Maya area has provided a strikingly different type: the agglutinated palace. This is a long, narrow structure consisting of modular units set in sequence, each facing outward and generally without the interconnecting doorways that characterize central Mexican palaces. While there may be three or four of these agglutinated structures sharing a large patio, their linear plan is quite different from anything seen in Oaxaca or the Basin of Mexico. One of the most striking is Structure D at the site of Nakum (Tozzer 1913), a single building over 120 meters long and consisting of 44 rooms arranged in two rows, each room opening directly on the outdoors (figure 3.15). The Nunnery Quadrangle at Uxmal has four such agglutinated palaces set around a major court more than 60 × 40 meters in extent (figure 3.16). Other examples occur at Tikal, Uaxactun, and Yaxchilan.

Palaces are both places of residence for the royal family and places for conducting some of the affairs of state. Central Mexican palaces had courtyards and what seem to be audience halls for conducting state business (as in the case of the Mitla palaces), but here the Maya palaces offer another alternative. Some "range structures" of Tikal's Central Acropolis have at least two stories and appear to be both residential and administrative in function. In the Tikal case, W. R. Coe (1967: 62–3) has suggested that the ground floor of the palace may have been devoted to conducting affairs of state, while the upper story was the residence for the royal family.

Figure 3.15 An "agglutinated palace" at Nakum, Guatemala. (Redrawn from Tozzer 1913: fig. 55.)

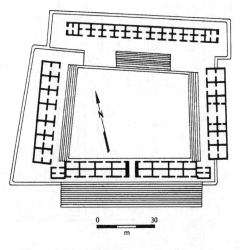

Figure 3.16 The Nunnery Quadrangle at Uxmal, Yucatan, composed of four buildings that delimit a central patio, which is approximately rectangular. (Redrawn from Marquina 1951: pl. 236.)

Temples

Temples are one of the most common features of Mesoamerican cities, and as we have seen, also one of the most standardized. The architectural evolution of temples is similar when one compares the Maya region, central Mexico, and the Oaxaca highlands (figure 3.17).

In the Maya area, for example, Spinden (1957) has suggested that a simple room with the door in the center of one of its long sides was the starting point for the temple. This grew to a lime-plastered, single-room building with thick walls of stone and perhaps some stucco modeling or mural painting. The next stage was a two-room structure with one room directly behind the other. Gradually, the inner room evolved into a kind of sanctuary, with the outer chamber becoming an open-air portico; the outer wall of the latter changed to a set of pierlike supports that eventually became columns. In some cities, such as Tikal, the addition of another interior room led to a three-room temple (figure 3.17); at Tulum and Xelha, on the other hand, the older one-room temple survived or reappeared (Lothrop 1924).

In Oaxaca, the original lime-plastered, one-room public building of the Early Formative evolved into a two-room Classic Period temple very much like those at Maya sites (Flannery and Marcus 1976; Marcus 1978). While data for the Basin of Mexico are more sketchy, a similar evolution evidently took place there, for many of the Teotihuacan temples have the same plan. At Teotihuacan, however, there developed a pattern of twin temples that was to characterize later Nahua cities. Millon (1976: 238) points out that the Pyramid of the Sun, for example, once supported twin temples; and the Aztec centers at Tenochtitlan and Tenayuca had them as well. At Tenayuca, in fact, one can see "accelerated" evolution from a single rectangular room with a small altar along the back wall to the standard two-room temple, whose outer room has a square column at either side of the doorway. The twin temples of Tenayuca are placed side by side atop a truncated pyramid (Marquina 1951). The significance of the twin temples to the Nahua-speaking world has yet to be fully worked out, and like the concept of dual rulership, it represents an interesting contrast to the rest of Mesoamerica.

It is probably significant that the plan of the temples is one of the least varied and most conservative of all Mesoamerican features from region to region, being far more predictable than the form of the palace, the plan of the city, or the degree of urban concentration of craft specialists.

Workshops and craft activity areas

Data on this topic are fragmentary and are likely to remain so until more urban studies such as those by Millon, Cowgill, and Blanton have been carried out. As previously stated, our best sequence of cities with concentrations of craftsmen is that of Teotihuacan – Tula – Tenochtitlan.

Workshops discovered at Tula include those processing obsidian, other forms of chipped stone, and pottery figurines (Diehl 1974: 13–15). In addition, some storerooms at Tula contain imported ceramics from as far away as the Nicoya Peninsula, suggesting three possibilities: (1) resident foreign merchants, (2) considerable long-distance trade, or (3) Toltec merchants who (like forerunners of the Aztec *pochteca*) traveled as far as Costa Rica (Diehl, Wynn, and Lomas 1974).

Tenochtitlan was famous for its *tolteca*, a collective term for different categories of craftsmen whose skills were sometimes attributed to the legacy of Tula and the ruler-deity Quetzalcoatl. Tenochtitlan continued the tradition of drawing craftsmen into the city from the whole Basin of Mexico and indeed from far beyond it. For example, the lapidaries were said to be from Xochimilco (Sahagún 1959: bk. 9); the feather workers were from Amantlan, a former town that later became a ward or sector of Tenochtitlan; and the goldsmiths were said to be Tlapanec-speaking Yopi, a people who

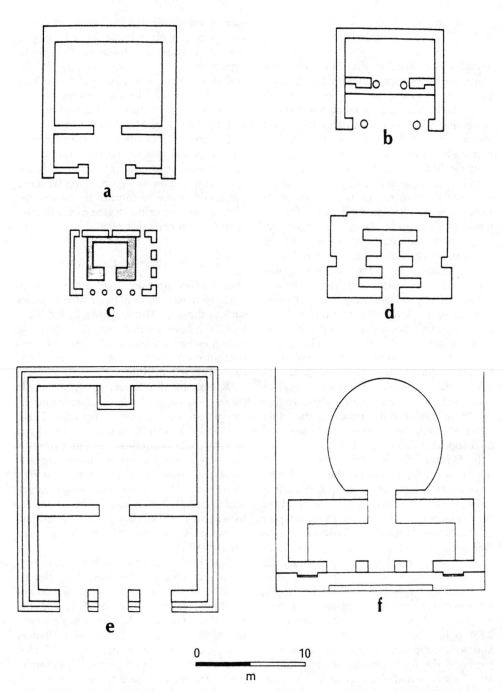

Figure 3.17 Various Mesoamerican temple plans. (a) Yayahuala, Teotihuacan, Mexico. (Redrawn from Séjourné 1966: fig. 47); (b) Mound X, Monte Alban, Oaxaca (Marcus 1978: fig. 2); (c) Temple of the Frescos, Tulum, Mexico. (Redrawn from Lothrop 1924: fig. 70); (d) Temple I, Tikal, Guatemala. (Redrawn from Séjourné 1966: fig. 48); (e) Tenayuca, Mexico. (Redrawn from Marquina 1951: pl. 51); (f) Malinalco, Mexico. (Redrawn from Séjourné 1966: fig. 47.)

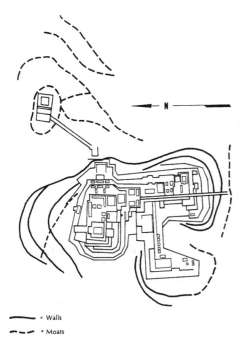

= Walls

= Moats

Figure 3.18 Central part of Xochicalco, Morelos, Mexico. (Redrawn and adapted from Armillas 1951: fig. 1; Marquina 1951: pl. 39.)

did not speak Nahuatl. Many of the Tenochtitlan craftsmen lived in distinct sections of the city and had their own festivals, rituals, and patron deities. Nevertheless, at least some of the craftsmen worked directly for the king or the state (Díaz del Castillo 1950: vol. 1, 349), in the manner hypothesized by Millon for some Teotihuacan obsidian workers. Absent from Tenochtitlan, however, were the large multifamily compound workshops seen at Teotihuacan, for Calnek (1976) describes the residences of the Aztec capital as being much smaller.

Fortifications and city walls

Hundreds of Mesoamerican sites have walls, but not all walled sites are cities, and not all city walls are necessarily fortifications. Some small walled sites, like the Fortress of Mitla and the site of Tepexi el Viejo (Gorenstein 1973) probably served principally as redoubts to which city populations retreated in time of war.

One city-sized Mexican site with significant fortifications is Xochicalco, built on the top of a series of promontories "protected by a citadel, ramparts, and dry-moats" (Armillas 1951: 78–9). It has been divided by Armillas into (1) a religious center on the steep hill with the Temple of the Feathered Serpent, surrounded by ramparts and moats; (2) a citadel atop a nearby peak, also surrounded by moats, and linked to the religious center by a paved road or causeway lined with protective walls; and (3) a habitation area situated on flat ground surrounded by deep ravines on the north and west (figure 3.18).

Xochicalco contrasts with Monte Alban in that it does not have a great outer wall enclosing an area of 3–4 square kilometers, nor does it have the pattern seen at some Maya sites (see below), where a defended "inner city" nestles within an undefended "outer city." Instead, the city displays a carefully worked-out plan for the spatial segregation of activities, each with its own defensive system. The religious center has three concentric walls with a moat inside them on the north, and two concentric walls with a moat outside them on the south; the citadel has a "ring system" of at least four moats. The residential area, on the other hand, is defended only by natural ravines.

A different pattern appears at the city of Mayapan in the northern Maya lowlands (figure 3.19). A single city wall appears to enclose not only the temples, the other ceremonial edifices, and the residences of the nobility, but also a very substantial percentage of the ordinary residences as well. The total circumference of this wall is 9.1 kilometers, enclosing an area of 4.2 square kilometers that contains more than 3,500 individual structures (Jones 1952; Shook 1952). Pollock and associates (1962: 204) estimate that perhaps 140 of these were religious or administrative buildings, while at least 2,100 were residences, the remaining number being additional structures associated with the residences. While one explanation for the wall (which has seven major and five minor entrances) is that it served to

(a)

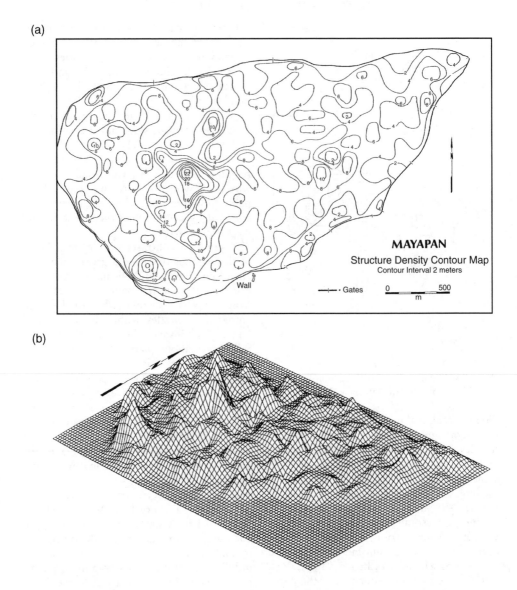

(b)

Figure 3.19   Two views of Mayapan, Yucatan.

(a) A contour map showing general structure density was devised by plotting all *numbered* structures on the Jones (1952) map. The numbers associated with the contour lines refer to the number of structures per hectare. The highest density of structures occurs to the left of center and corresponds to the "site center." Other high-density areas occur in the western and southern half of the site, while the eastern half is less densely covered by buildings.

(b) A perspective block diagram viewing the structure density topography from an angle 50° east of south from a map unit distance of 500 and from an elevation angle of 30. In this diagram, the peaks correspond to the areas of highest structure density inside the wall. The Surface II graphic system (revision 1) developed by Sampson (1978) was employed. Structure proveniences were put into digital notation using equipment of the Department of Geography, University of Michigan, Ann Arbor. Special thanks to Dr. Richard A. Taketa for help with the equipment and graphic programs and to Francis E. Smiley for generating many different maps, including both of those on these two pages.

defend the seat of government, an alternative explanation is that it delimited the boundary of the city for administrative purposes. There are structures outside the wall, but as in the case of Tikal, their density is far less. Some ethnohistoric evidence suggests that Mayapan might once have had a second, inner enclosure surrounding the Temple of Kukulcan and the residences of the Maya lords, plus those of their servants and visitors (Landa 1941). One problem with the concept of the wall as dividing administrative units is the fact that (as mentioned in an earlier section) we have little reason to believe the Maya thought of the city as greatly distinct from the rest of the territory ruled by one royal family.

Another relevant site of the Yucatan peninsula is the one whose very name, Tulum, means "wall, fortress, or entrenchment" (Pío Pérez 1866–77). The "Great Wall" of Tulum forms three sides of a rectangle enclosing the temples, palaces, and administrative structures; the fourth side of the rectangle is a cliff overlooking the sea. Inside the Great Wall is another walled area called the "Inner Enclosure," which serves a group of seven structures, most of them primarily religious in function. As in the case of Mayapan, there are residences outside the walls of Tulum, but without the density seen within the walls.

Tulum (figure 3.20) illustrates that not all walls are for defense. According to Lothrop (1924: 90), the Inner Enclosure wall merely separates a series of civic-religious structures from the secular parts of the city and played no defensive role. On the other hand, he readily assigned defensive functions to the Great Wall, which is 717 meters long, 6 meters wide, and 3–4.5 meters high, with a diagonal extension running another 378 meters from the southwest corner to the sea (1924: 90).

Obviously, there are at least two basic patterns in Mesoamerican fortified cities. In some cases, only the "center" of the city – the civic and religious structures, and the

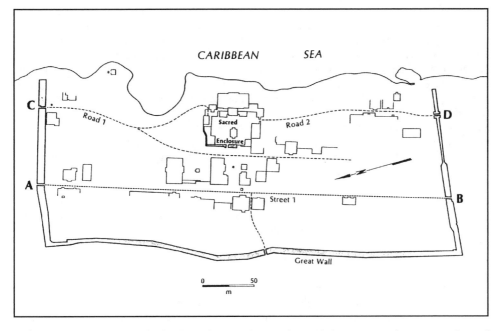

Figure 3.20 The central part of Tulum, showing clear evidence of planning. One long street is located on the west side running north–south between entrances (A, B) in the arms of the "Great Wall"; shorter roads lead to the "Sacred Enclosure" from the other northern entrance (C) and southern entrance (D). (Redrawn and adapted from Lothrop 1924: pl. 25.)

palaces and elite residences – are defended. In other cases, all (or virtually all) of the city is walled, including the residences of the common people. Mesoamericanists would do well to consider the implications of these two patterns in terms of possible sociopolitical differences.

Summary and Conclusions

What, then, can we say about the nature of the Mesoamerican city? First of all, we cannot provide a definition that will distinguish it from other culture areas, for Mesoamerican cities display, in microcosm, much of the diversity of ancient cities elsewhere. Central Mexico shows the urban concentration of craftsmen typical of many Sumerian cities, and in the case of some obsidian workers at Teotihuacan, may even have displayed the linkage of temple and craftsmen shown by the coppersmiths and seal cutters of the temple precinct of Ur. Oaxaca, on the other hand, shows the village-by-village craft specialization and "regal-ritual" cities typical of China during the Shang dynasty. Some Mixtec rulers shifted residences (and hence capitals) as often as the Achaemenid kings, who traveled seasonally from Susa to Persepolis to Hamadan. Xochicalco had moats and earthworks as cleverly designed as those of any fortified city of the ancient Levant. Some Mesoamerican cities had administrative centers as accessible as the Forum at Rome; some were as inaccessible as the Forbidden Inner City of Peking.

As for *functional* patterns, I found no Mesoamerican city to be without temples, and some had hundreds. This suggests that Mesoamerican cities were most frequently at the head of the regional religious hierarchy, a fact rarely taken into consideration. Religion penetrated to every level of urban society in Mesoamerica: the individual performed autosacrifice, his kin group had its own temple, his rural countrymen helped maintain public temples at the city, and the royal family had its own place of worship.

Although the case of Mitla and Zaachila reminds us that the capitals of the religious and political hierarchies could be separate in a spatial sense, my impression is that the city's function as administrative center was a very close second to religious center in frequency. Even here there is great diversity among planned and unplanned administrative capitals, defended and undefended capitals, cities with one major palace complex and those with dual palaces or many palaces of approximately equal size.

The city's function as commercial center is only third in frequency in my opinion, but here we are hampered because there have been few attempts to determine rigorously whether the commodities produced by a city are for its own consumption (with some surplus for trade) or for export over a wide area. Here I think we can see one pattern that links Teotihuacan, Tula, and Tenochtitlan into a regional tradition, quite distinct from the pattern seen to the south at Monte Alban, Yucuñudahui, and possibly Xochicalco. Following R. Fox, we might see the central Mexican pattern as one of very strong states with great economic autonomy, and the pattern in the southern Mexican highlands as one of weaker states with a high dependency on tribute from their hinterlands and a greater need to fortify their administrative capitals.

I have examined the wide range of functions that characterize Mesoamerican cities, and where possible I have selected representative cases. It is clear that a city may have been established to fulfill certain needs under specific conditions, and that these are not immutable. Cities may change, add to, or elaborate upon their functions over time. Cities may also lose functions; for example, ports may become obstructed with silt, and port cities may lose their commercial functions; mining towns and cities may be abandoned after the minerals are exhausted. Thus, cities have a plurality of functions, and the prominence of one over another is what we have yet to clarify for most Mesoamerican cities. One way to illustrate the diversity as well as the relative importance of (in this case) three functions – religious, commercial, and administrative – is to construct an equilateral triangle whose sides represent the functions as variables

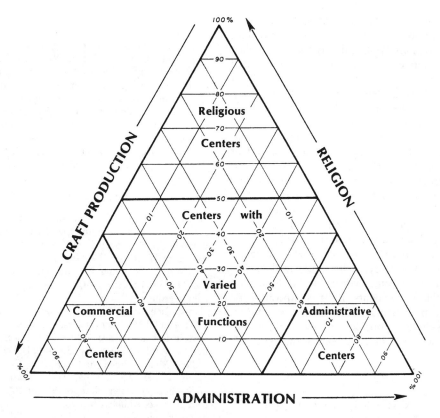

Figure 3.21 An equilateral triangle illustrating the diversity and relative importance of various urban functions. For example, a city in which the three functions – religious, commercial, and administrative – were *equally* represented would be found in the center of the triangle.
(Redrawn and adapted from Beaujeu-Garnier and Chabot 1967: fig. 6.)

(figure 3.21). A city can be defined graphically according to its essential function by the place it occupies inside such a triangle (Beaujeu-Garnier and Chabot 1967: 114).

As for the *formal* patterns proposed by geographers, I feel they tell us more about how cities grew than about their functions. All Mesoamerican cities display some degree of concentricity, and several show the sector pattern of growth, especially those with major streets or traffic arteries. Perhaps one of the most intriguing patterns is that of multiple nuclei, and I would really like to know why it appears with such frequency in lowland Maya secondary and tertiary centers.

I said at the outset that the more rigorously one tries to define the Mesoamerican city, the more one is forced to ignore import-

ant "exceptions." If we define it as a large population center with one or more palaces and one or more temples, we include most examples; but if we add a marketplace or a high level of urban craft specialization, we exclude most of the mountaintop "regal-ritual" cities. If we become more specific, we could lose sites such as Guiengola, all of the pilgrimage centers, and all the ports of trade. Many scholars would like to see 10,000 persons as the lower population limit for a city, but Monte Alban had an estimated population of only 8,000 in Period Ia, and Sjoberg (1960) reminds us that many important cities in the ancient world had populations of only 5,000.

Our problem is simple: we are trying to define the city so as to satisfy Western social scientists, not Mesoamerican Indians. For the Mesoamerican Indian, the important unit was the political territory controlled by a native ruler. It contained "populated places," simply referred to as "big" or "little," or as "small places subject to big places." The city dweller did not verbally distinguish himself from the rural dweller as did the Roman urbanite from whom our notion of "city" comes. The capital was where the ruler's palace was, the religious hierarchy began at the largest temples, and the markets could be several or none. Until we devise a way to accommodate our cumbersome typology to the Indian's view of the cultural landscape, that is, until we stop trying to treat Mesoamerica as if it were a twentieth-century, secular industrial society, we will find ourselves in the same position as the participants in a symposium on African urbanism described by Horace Miner. "Everyone knows what a city is," said Miner (1967: 3), "except the experts."

NOTE

1 The rank-size rule is given by Haggett (1972: 283) as follows:

Assume a set of cities ranked in size from the largest (l) downward. In its simplest form, the rank-size rule states that the population of a given city tends to be equal to the population of the largest city divided by the rank of the given city.

$$P_r = \frac{P_l}{R}$$

P_r = the population of the r th city
P_l = the population of the largest city
R = the size rank of the r th city in the set

Contributors to the volume Prehistoric Settlement Patterns provided me with thoughtful comments during our fruitful week in Austria. Very special thanks to Evon Z. Vogt and Lita Osmundsen for making the evenings particularly memorable. The sessions during the day brought back memories of the Maya seminar discussions led by Gordon R. Willey at Harvard in the late sixties; as one might expect, many of the same settlement pattern problems persist.

In the field my Oaxaca colleagues – Richard Blanton, Gary Feinman, Stephen Kowalewski, and others – made valuable suggestions that substantially aided me while I was trying to put my thoughts together during those evenings of rum and coke along with chile-covered peanuts.

Here in Ann Arbor, F. E. Smiley took great care in completing all of the illustrations for this article, and I appreciate his desire for perfection. Susan Gregg aided us with the graphics equipment.

REFERENCES

Adams, Richard E. W. 1983. Ancient Land Use and Culture History in the Pasion River Region. In Prehistoric Settlement Patterns: Essays in Honor of Gordon R. Willey, edited by Evon Z. Vogt and Richard M. Leventhal, pp. 319–36. University of New Mexico Press, Albuquerque.

Adams, Richard E. W. and Richard C. Jones. 1981. Feudal Models for Classic Maya Civilization. In Lowland Maya Settlement Patterns, edited by Wendy Ashmore, pp. 335–50. University of New Mexico Press, Albuquerque.

Adams, Robert McC. 1966. The Evolution of Urban Society: Early Mesopotamia and Prehistoric Mexico. Aldine, Chicago.

Anderson, Theodore R. and Janice A. Egeland. 1961. Spatial Aspects of Social Area Analysis. American Sociological Review 26: 392–8.

Andrews, E. Wyllys IV. 1961. Preliminary Report on the 1959–1960 Field Season, Middle American Research Institute, Miscellaneous Series No. 11. Tulane University, New Orleans.

Andrews, E. Wyllys IV and Irwin Rovner. 1973. Archaeological Evidence on Social Stratifications and Commerce in the Northern Maya Lowlands: Two Mason's Tool Kits from Muna and Dzibilchatun. Publications vol. 31. Middle American Research Institute, New Orleans.

Armillas, Pedro. 1951. Mesoamerican Fortifications. Antiquity 25: 77–86.

—— 1964. Northern Mesoamerica. In Prehistoric Man in the New World, edited by J. D. Jennings and E. Norbeck, pp. 291–329. University of Chicago Press, Chicago.

Beaujeu-Garnier, J. and G. Chabot. 1967. Urban Geography. Longmans, Green, London.

Becker, Marshall Joseph. 1973. Archaeological Evidence for Occupational Specialization Among the Classic Period Maya at Tikal, Guatemala. American Antiquity 38(4): 396–406.

Bernal, Ignacio and Lorenzo Gamio. 1974. *Yagul: El Palacio de los Seis Patios*. Universidad Nacional Autónoma de Mexico, Mexico City.

Blanton, Richard E. 1972. *Prehispanic Settlement Patterns of the Ixtapalapa Peninsula Region, Mexico*. Occasional Papers in Anthropology No. 6. Pennsylvania State University, University Park.

—— 1976a. Anthropological Studies of Cities. *Annual Review of Anthropology* 5: 249–64.

—— 1976b. The Role of Symbiosis in Adaptation and Socio-Cultural Change in the Valley of Mexico, In *The Valley of Mexico: Studies in Pre-Hispanic Ecology and Society*, edited by E. R. Wolf, pp. 181–201. University of New Mexico Press, Albuquerque.

—— 1978. *Monte Alban: Settlement Patterns at the Ancient Zapotec Capital*. Academic Press, New York.

—— 1980. Cultural Ecology Reconsidered. *American Antiquity* 45(1): 145–51.

—— 1981. The Rise of Cities. In *Supplement to the Handbook of Middle American Indians*, vol. 1, edited by J. A. Sabloff, pp. 392–402. University of Texas Press, Austin.

Braidwood, Robert J. and Gordon R. Willey. 1962. Conclusions and Afterthoughts. In *Courses Toward Urban Life: Archaeological Considerations of Some Cultural Alternates*, edited by R. J. Braidwood and G. R. Willey, pp. 33–59. Viking Fund Publications in Anthropology 32. Wenner-Gren Foundation, New York.

Brinton, Daniel G. 1882. *The Maya Chronicles*. Library of Aboriginal American Literature No. 1. Philadelphia.

Burgess, Ernest W. 1925. The Growth of the City: An Introduction to a Research Project. In *The City*, by R. E. Park, E. W. Burgess, and R. D. McKenzie, pp. 47–62. University of Chicago Press, Chicago.

Calnek, Edward E. 1976. The Internal Structure of Tenochtitlan. In *The Valley of Mexico: Studies in Pre-Hispanic Ecology and Society*, edited by E. R. Wolf, pp. 287–302. University of New Mexico Press, Albuquerque.

Carr, Robert F. and James E. Hazard. 1961. *Map of the Ruins of Tikal, El Peten, Guatemala*. Tikal Reports No. 11, Museum Monographs of the University Museum, University of Pennsylvania, Philadelphia.

Carrasco, Pedro. 1971. Social Organization of Ancient Mexico, In *Archaeology of Northern Mesoamerica, Part I. Handbook of Middle American Indians*, edited by G. F. Ekholm and I. Bernal, pp. 349–75. University of Texas Press, Austin.

Caso, Alfon so. 1935. *Las Exploranciones en Monte Alban, 1934–1935*, Instituto Panamericano de Geografía e Historia. Publicacion 18, Mexico, DF.

Chang, Kwang-Chih. 1968. *The Archaeology of Ancient China*. Yale University Press, New Haven.

Coe, William R. 1967. *Tikal: A Handbook of the Ancient Maya Ruins*. University Museum, University of Pennsylvania, Philadelphia.

Cordova, Fray Juan de. 1578. *Vocabulario en Lengua Zapoteca*, edited by P. Charte and A. Ricardo. Reprinted 1942. Mexico City.

Cowgill, George L. 1974. Quantitative Studies of Urbanization at Teotihuacan, In *Mesoamerican Archaeology: New Approaches*, edited by N. Hammond, pp. 363–96. University of Texas Press, Austin.

Demarest, Arthur A. 1978. Interregional Conflict and "Situational Ethics" in Classic Maya Warfare. In *Codex Wauchope: Festschrift in Honor of Robert Wauchope*, edited by M. Edmonson and W. Creamer, pp. 101–11. Tulane University, New Orleans.

Díaz del Castillo, Bernal. 1950. *Historia Verdadera de la Conquista de la Nueva España*. Mexico City.

Diehl, Richard A. (ed.). 1974. *Studies of Ancient Tollan: A Report of the University of Missouri Tula Archaeological Project*. University of Missouri Monographs in Anthropology 1. Department of Anthropology, University of Missouri, Columbia.

Diehl, Richard A., Jack T. Wynn, and Roger Lomas. 1974. Evidence for Toltec Trade with Central America. *Archaeology* 27: 182–7.

Doxiadis, Constantinos A. 1968. *Ekistics: An Introduction to the Science of Human Settlements*. Oxford University Press, London.

Earle, Timothy K. 1976. A Nearest Neighbor Analysis of Two Formative Settlement Systems, In *The Early Mesoamerican Village*, edited by K. V. Flannery, pp. 196–223. Academic Press, New York.

Feinman, Gary M. 1980. The Effects of Changing Administrative Organization on Ceramic Production in the Prehispanic Valley of Oaxaca, Mexico. Ph.D. dissertation, City University of New York.

—— 1982. Patterns in Ceramic Production and Distribution, Periods I through V, In *Monte Alban's Hinterland, Part I. Prehistory and Human Ecology of the Valley of Oaxaca*, edited by K. V. Flannery and R. E. Blanton. Memoirs of the Museum of Anthropology No. 15, University of Michigan, Ann Arbor.

Flannery, Kent V. and Joyce Marcus. 1976. Evolution of the Public Building in Formative Oaxaca, In *Cultural Change and Continuity: Essays in Honor of James Bennett Griffin*, edited by C. Cleland, pp. 205–21. Academic Press, New York.

Flannery, Kent V. and Joyce Marcus (eds). 1983. *The Cloud People: Divergent Evolution of the Zapotec and Mixtec Civilizations of Oaxaca, Mexico*. Academic Press, New York.

Fox, John W. 1978. *Quiche Conquest: Centralism and Regionalism in Highland Guatemalan State Development*. University of New Mexico Press, Albuquerque.

Fox, Richard G. 1977. *Urban Anthropology*. Prentice Hall, Englewood Cliffs, New Jersey.

Fry, Robert E. 1979. The Economics of Pottery at Tikal, Guatemala: Models of Exchange for Serving Vessels. *American Antiquity* 44(3): 494–512.

Fustel de Coulanges, Numa Denis. 1864. *The Ancient City*. Doubleday, New York (1963).

Gaxiola, Margarita. 1976. Excavaciones en San Martín Huamelulpan, Un Sitio de la Mixteca Alta, Oaxaca. Master's thesis, Escuela Nacional de Antropología e Historia.

Gorenstein, Shirley. 1973. Tepexi el Viejo. *Transactions of the American Philosophical Society* 63(1). Philadelphia.

Haggett, Peter. 1972. *Geography: A Modern Synthesis*. Harper and Row, New York.

Harris, Chauncy D. and Edward L. Ullman. 1945. The Nature of Cities. *Annals of the American Academy of Political and Social Sciences* 242: 7–17.

Hoyt, Homer. 1939. *The Structure and Growth of Residential Neighborhoods in American Cities*. US Government Printing Office, Washington, DC.

Johnson, Gregory A. 1972. A Test of the Utility of Central Place Theory in Archaeology. In *Man, Settlement, and Urbanism*, edited by P. J. Ucko, R. Tringham, and G. W. Dimbleby, pp. 769–85. Duckworth, London.

—— 1977. Aspects of Regional Analysis in Archaeology. *Annual Review of Anthropology* 6: 479–508.

Jones, Morris R. 1962. *Map of the Ruins of Mayapan, Yucatan, Mexico*. Carnegie Institution of Washington, Department of Archaeology Current Reports No. 1. Washington, DC.

Kowalewski, Stephen A. 1983. Monte Alban V. Settlement Patterns in the Valley of Oaxaca. In *The Cloud People: Divergent Evolution of the Zapotec and Mixtec Civilizations of Oaxaca,*

Mexico, edited by K. V. Flannery and J. Marcus, pp. 285–8. Academic Press, New York.

Krapf-Askari, Eva. 1969. *Yoruba Towns and Cities: An Inquiry into the Nature of Urban Phenomena*. Clarendon Press, Oxford.

Kurjack, Edward B. 1974. *Prehistoric Lowland Maya Community and Social Organization – A Case Study at Dzibilchaltun, Yucatan, Mexico*. Middle American Research Institute Publication 38. Tulane University, New Orleans.

Kurjack, Edward B. and E. Wyllys Andrews V. 1976. Early Boundary Maintenance in Northwest Yucatan, Mexico. *American Antiquity* 41(3): 318–25.

Landa, Fray Diego de. 1941. *Relacíon de las Cosas de Yucatán: A Translation*, edited by Alfred M. Tozzer. Papers of the Peabody Museum of Archaeology and Ethnology 18. Harvard University, Cambridge.

Lombardo de Ruiz, Sonio. 1973. *Desarollo Urbano de Mexico–Tenochtitlan Según las Fuentes Históricas*. Instituto Nacional de Antropología e Historia, Departmento de Investigaciones Historicas, Mexico City.

Lothrop, Samuel K. 1924. *Tulum: An Archaeological Study of the East Coast of Yucatan*. Carnegie Institute of Washington Publication 335. Washington, DC.

Mann, Peter H. 1965. *An Approach to Urban Sociology*. Routledge Kegan Paul, London.

Marcus, Joyce. 1973. Territorial Organization of the Lowland Classic Maya. *Science* 180(4089): 911–16.

—— 1976. *Emblem and State in the Classic Maya Lowlands: An Epigraphic Approach to Territorial Organization*. Dumbarton Oaks, Washington, DC.

—— 1978. Archaeology and Religion: A Comparison of the Zapotec and the Maya. *World Archaeology* 10(2): 171–91.

—— 1980. Zapotec Writing. *Scientific American* 242(2): 50–64.

Marquina, Ignacio. 1951. *Arquitectura Prehispánica*. Memorias 1 del Instituto Nacional de Antropología e Historia. Mexico City.

Martínez Hernández, Juan (ed.). 1929. *Diccionario de Motul: Maya Español*. Attributed to Fray Antonio Ciudad Real and Arte de Lengua Maya by Fray Juan Coronel. Talleres de la Compañía Tipográfica Yucateca, Merida.

Miles, Susanna W. 1957. The Sixteenth-Century Pokom-Maya: A Documentary Analysis of Social Structure and Archaeological Setting. *Transactions of the American Philosophical Society* 47(4): 731–81.

Millon, Rene. 1967. Teotihuacan. *Scientific American* 216(6): 38–48.

—— 1973. *Urbanization at Teotihuacan, Mexico. Volume 1, Part I. The Teotihuacan Map.* University of Texas Press, Austin.

—— 1976. Social Relations in Ancient Teotihuacan. In *The Valley of Mexico: Studies in Prehispanic Ecology and Society,* edited by Eric R. Wolf, pp. 205–48, University of New Mexico Press, Albuquerque.

Miner, Horace. 1967. The City and Modernization: An Introduction. In *The City of Modern Africa,* edited by H. Miner, pp. 1–20. Pall Mall Press, London.

Molina, Alonso de. 1571. *Vocabulario en Lengua Castellana y Mexicana.* 2nd edn (facsimile), reprinted 1977. Editorial Porrúa, Mexico City.

O'Brien, Michael J., Dennis E. Lewarch, Roger D. Mason, and James A. Neely. 1980. Functional Analysis of Water Control Features at Monte Alban, Oaxaca, Mexico. *World Archaeology* 11: 342–55.

Olsson, Gunnar. 1965. *Distance and Human Interaction: A Review and Bibliography.* Regional Science Bibliography Series No. 2. Research Institute, Philadelphia.

Parsons, Jeffrey R. 1971. *Prehispanic Settlement Patterns in the Texcoco Region, Mexico.* Memoirs of the Museum of Anthropology No. 3. University of Michigan, Ann Arbor.

Pickett, Velma. 1959. *Castellano–Zapotec, Zapotec–Castellano: Dialecto del Zapotec del Istmo.* Serie de Vocabularios Indígenas 3. Secretaría de Educación Pública, Mexico City.

Pío-Pérez, Juan. 1866–77. *Diccionario de la Lengua Maya.* Merida.

Pollock, H. E. D. 1962. Introduction. In *Mayapan, Yucatan, Mexico,* by H. E. D. Pollock, Ralph Roys, Tatiana Proskouriakoff, and A. L. Smith, pp. 1–24. Carnegie Institute of Washington Publication 619. Washington, DC.

Puleston, Dennis E. 1974. Intersite Areas in the Vicinity of Tikal and Uaxactun. In *Mesoamerican Archaeology: New Approaches,* edited by Norman Hammond, pp. 303–11. Duckworth, London.

Puleston, Dennis E. and Donald W. Callender, Jr. 1967. Defensive Earthworks at Tikal. *Expedition* 9(3): 40–8.

Redfield, Robert. 1941. *The Folk Culture of Yucatan.* University of Chicago Press, Chicago.

Roys, Lawrence and Edwin M. Shook. 1966. *Preliminary Report on the Ruins of Ake, Yucatan.* Memoirs of the Society for American Archaeology No. 20.

Sabloff, Jeremy A. and William L. Rathje (eds). 1975. *A Study of Changing Pre-Columbian Commercial Systems: The 1972–1973 Season at Cozumel, Mexico.* Monographs of the Peabody Museum No. 3. Harvard University, Cambridge.

Sahagun, Fray Bernardino de. 1959. *Florentine Codex: General History of the Things of New Spain: Book 9–The Merchants.* Translated by A. J. O. Anderson and C. E. Dibble. Monographs of the School of American Research, University of Utah Press, Salt Lake City.

Sampson, Robert J. 1978. *Surface II Graphics System.* Series on Spatial Analysis No. 1. Kansas Geological Survey. Original edition 1975. Lawrence, Kansas.

Sanders, William T. 1965. *The Cultural Ecology of the Teotihuacan Valley: A Preliminary Report of the Results of the Teotihuacan Valley Project.* Pennsylvania University, University Park.

—— 1974. Chiefdom of State: Political Evolution at Kaminaljuyu, Guatemala. In *Reconstructing Complex Societies: An Archaeological Colloquium,* edited by C. B. Moore, pp. 97–121. Supplement to the Bulletin of the Schools of Oriental Research No. 20. Cambridge, Massachusetts.

Scholes, Frances V. and Ralph L. Roys. 1948. *The Maya Chontal Indians of Acalan-Tixchel: A Contribution to the History and Ethnography of the Yucatan Peninsula.* Carnegie Institute of Washington Publication 560. Washington, DC.

Séjourné, Laurette. 1966. *Arquitectura y Pintura en Teotihuacán.* Siglo Veintiuno Editores, Mexico City.

Shook, Edwin M. 1952. *The Great Wall of Mayapan.* Carnegie Institute of Washington Department of Archaeology Current Reports No. 2. Washington, DC.

Sjoberg, Gideon. 1960. *The Preindustrial City, Past and Present.* Free Press, Glencoe, Illinois.

Smith, Mary Elizabeth. 1973. *Picture Writing from Ancient Southern Mexico: Mixtec Place Signs and Names.* University of Oklahoma Press, Norman.

Soustelle, Jacques. 1964. *The Daily Life of Aztecs on the Eve of the Spanish Conquest.* Penguin Books, New York.

Spinden, Herbert J. 1957. *Maya Art and Civilization.* Indian Hills, Colorado.

Spores, Ronald. 1984. *The Mixtecs in Ancient and Colonial Times.* University of Oklahoma Press, Norman.

Stuart, George E., J. C. Scheffler, Edward B. Kurjack, and J. W. Cottier. 1979. *Map of the Ruins of Dzibilchaltun, Yucatan, Mexico*. Middle American Research Institute Publication 47. Tulane University, New Orleans.

Tozzer, Alfred M. 1913. *A Preliminary Study of the Ruins of Nakum, Guatemala*. Memoirs of the Peabody Museum of Archaeology and Ethnology, vol. 5, no. 2. Harvard University, Cambridge.

Villa Rojas, Alfonso. 1934. The Yaxuna–Coba Causeway. Carnegie Institute of Washington Publication 436. *Contributions to American Archaeology* 2(9): 187–308.

von Euw, Eric. 1977. *Corpus of Maya Hieroglyphic Inscriptions*, vol. 4, part 1. Peabody Museum of Archaeology and Ethnology. Harvard University, Cambridge, Massachusetts.

Whalen, Michael E. 1976. Excavations at Santo Domingo Tomaltepec: Evolution of a Formative Community in the Valley of Oaxaca. Ph.D. dissertation, University of Michigan.

Wheatley, Paul. 1971. *The Pivot of the Four Quarters: A Preliminary Enquiry into the Origins and Character of the Ancient Chinese City*. Harvard University, Cambridge.

——1972. The Concept of Urbanism. In *Man, Settlement, and Urbanism*, edited by P. J. Ucko, R. Tringham, and G. W. Dimbleby, pp. 601–37. Duckworth, London.

Willey, Gordon R. 1956. Problems Concerning Prehistoric Settlement Patterns in the Maya Lowlands. In *Prehistoric Settlement Patterns in the New World*, edited by Gordon R. Willey, pp. 1–2. Viking Fund Publications in Anthropology No. 23. Wenner-Gren Foundation, New York.

Willey, Gordon R., William R. Bullard, Jr., John B. Glass, and John C. Gifford. 1965. *Prehistoric Maya Settlements in the Belize Valley*. Papers of the Peabody Museum of Archaeology and Ethnology, vol. 54. Harvard University, Cambridge.

Winter, Marcus C. and William O. Payne. 1976. Hornos Para Ceramic Halados en Monte Alban. *Boletín del Instituto Nacional de Antropología e Historia* 16: 37–40.

Wirth, Louis. 1925. A Bibliography of the Urban Community. In *The City*, edited by R. E. Park, E. W. Burgess, and R. D. McKenzie, pp. 161–228. University of Chicago Press, Chicago.

CHAPTER 4

Corporate Groups and Domestic Activities at Teotihuacan

Linda Manzanilla

The Prehispanic cities of the central highlands of Mexico were planned settlements that served as capitals of large states. As the locus of huge demographic concentrations, they were manufacturing and exchange centers as well. Many were multiethnic centers that took advantage of the occupational skills of foreign groups; many were strategically situated with respect to resources. As one of the first urban developments in Mesoamerica, Teotihuacan was conceived as the archetype of the Mesoamerican civilized city. It was the most sacred realm, the mythic Tollan where crafts flourished.

One of the hallmarks of Teotihuacan civilization, from the third century AD onward, is the presence of multifamily compounds. These multiroom residential structures present an ideal opportunity to examine the nature and diversity of urban social segments. We know practically nothing about urban life in the Basin of Mexico before AD 200, with the exception of some partial data on earth floors and from a one-room house in TC-49 (Charlton 1969) that resembles the local Formative houses of the village of Cuanalan (Charlton 1969; Manzanilla 1985). For the Tlamimilolpa phase (AD 200–350/ 400), elements of urban planning at Teotihuacan are clearly defined, as are indicators of domestic life in apartment compounds (Millon 1973) (figure 4.1). Several examples of these have been studied since Linné's (1934) extensive excavations at Xolalpan

(figure 4.2); these include Tlamimilolpa (figure 4.3), Atetelco, Tepantitla, La Ventilla, Tetitla (figure 4.4), Yayahuala (Séjourné 1966b), Zacuala (Séjourné 1966b), Bidasoa, San Antonio Las Palmas, El Cuartel, and Structure 15B:N6W3 at Oztoyahualco (figure 4.5). We also have information from Tlajinga 33 (Storey 1983, 1987, 1991, 1992; Storey and Widmer 1989; Widmer 1991) and Maquixco Bajo (TC8) in the southern outskirts of the city (Sanders 1966, 1994, 1995), as well as from domestic structures in the foreign wards of the city (Rattray 1987, 1988, 1993; Spence 1989, 1992, 1994).

In the following section I describe the methodology that was used for the activity area analyses at Oztoyahualco. The subsequent discussions consider the nature of the Teotihuacan apartment compounds and the evidence for different activities, as indicated through the articulation of chemical, botanical, faunal, and artifactual analyses (Manzanilla 1987, 1993b; Manzanilla et al. 1990).

Oztoyahualco 15B:N6W3: Methodological Approaches

From 1985 to 1988 we carefully dissected an apartment compound at Oztoyahualco 15B:N6W3 (figure 4.5), at the northwestern boundary of the city, in Millon's N6W3 square (Manzanilla 1993b), as part of an intensive interdisciplinary project. We knew that stucco floors were scrupulously

Reprinted from Linda Manzanilla. 1996. Corporate Groups and Domestic Activities at Teotihuacan. *Latin American Antiquity* 7: 228–46. Copyright © Society for American Archaeology [SAA], Washington DC.

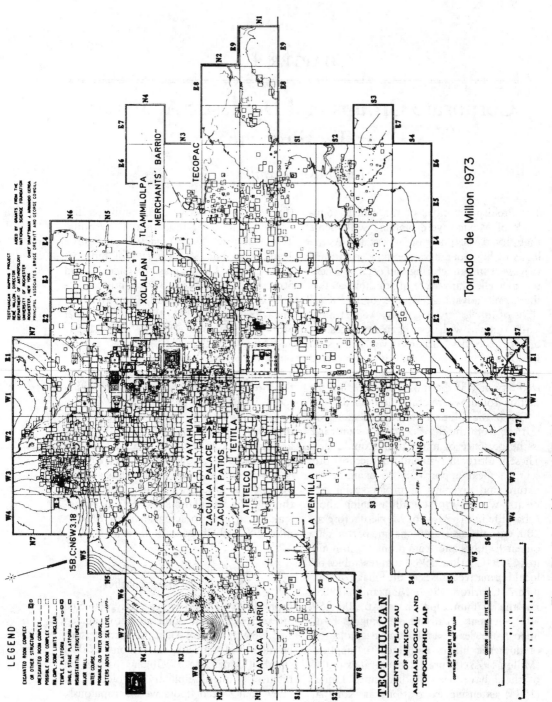

Figure 4.1 Map of the city of Teotihuacán showing location of some of the compounds.

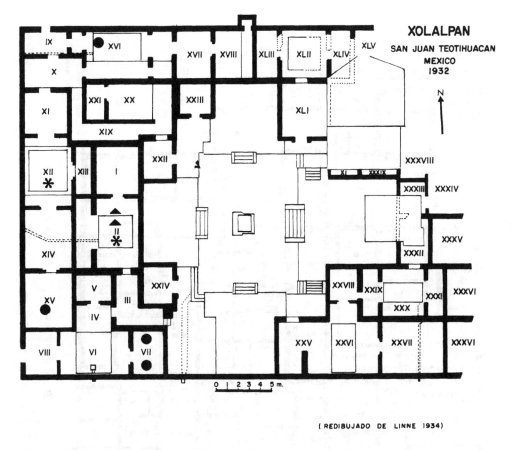

Figure 4.2 Map of Xolalpan (Linné 1934), with placement of burials.

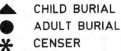

swept in the ancient domestic setting, so we would not have abundant macroscopic remains for our analysis. We thus planned a strategy that took into consideration chemical traces of activities on the plastered floors, as well as microscopic evidence related to these activities.

After the geophysical, geochemical, and archaeological plotting of surface materials, we chose mound 15B:N6W3 to begin a detective-like analysis of each room. We gathered architectural and funerary data as Linné (1934, 1942) did for Tlamimilolpa and Xolalpan, Séjourné (1966b) for Tetitla,

Yayahuala, and Zacuala, and as Piña Chán (1963) and Vidarte did for La Ventilla. We plotted the distribution of artifacts on floors as Monzón (1989) did for San Antonio Las Palmas, as Sánchez Alaniz (1989) did for Bidasoa, and as Sanders (1966, 1994, 1995) did for Maquixco Bajo. We also screened and analyzed flotation samples as Widmer did for Tlajinga 33 (Storey and Widmer 1989; Widmer 1987). These studies were supplemented with fine-grained analyses of phytoliths and pollen, botanical and faunal macrofossils, and chemical compounds on floors, as well as micro-artifactual distributions (Barba

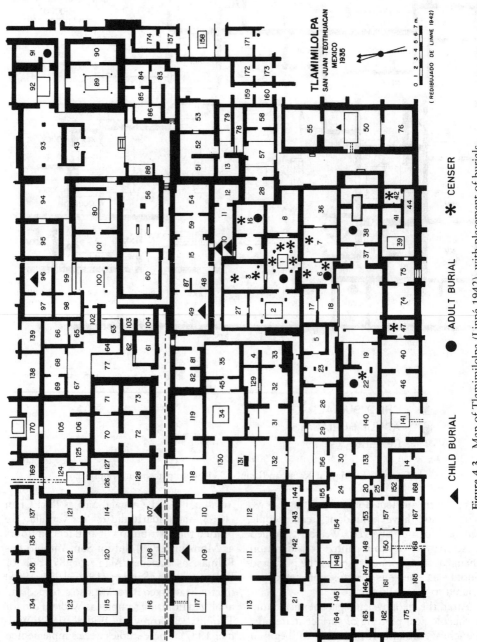

Figure 4.3 Map of Tlamimilolpa (Linné 1942), with placement of burials.

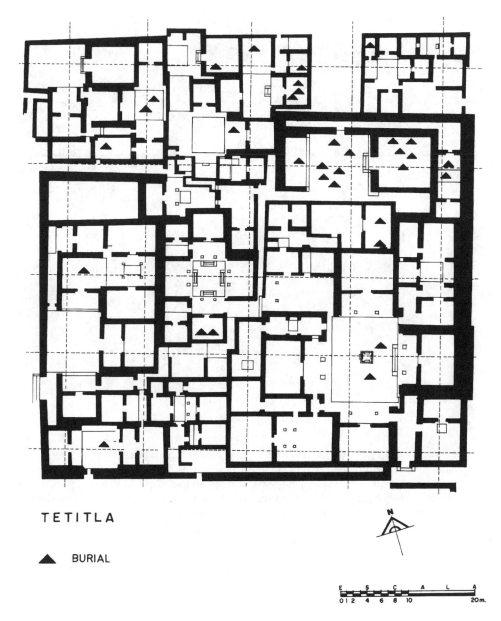

TETITLA

▲ BURIAL

(Redibujado de Séjourné 1966)

Figure 4.4 Map of Tetitla (Séjourné 1966b), with placement of burials.

et al. 1987; Manzanilla 1988–9, 1993b; Manzanilla and Barba 1990). In this manner, we obtained the anatomy of an apartment compound during Xolalpan times (ca. AD 550). This case serves as reference for the reconsideration of socioeconomic variations in domestic compounds at Teotihuacan.

Because the Oztoyahualco 15B:N6W3 compound was abandoned and the residents took most of their goods with them, we

Figure 4.5   Aerial photograph of Oztoyahualco 15B:N6W3 taken by the author.

found only traces of some "de facto refuse" in certain rooms, and some exceptional cases of *locus agendi* areas (Manzanilla 1986a, 1986b, 1988–9) (figure 4.6). During the excavation process, we isolated discrete distributions that appear to represent activity areas. These normally were delimited structurally, representing offerings or burial cavities excavated in the floors, associations of storage vessels, or concentrations of artifacts or faunal remains in the corners of the rooms. These potential activity areas exhibited specific sets of artifactual characteristics that were then compared with the distribution of the biological elements and chemical compounds to gain an idea of the set of activities associated with each room.

One of the methodological approaches that was most useful in assessing past activities was the chemical analysis of the stucco floors of the compound. Barba (1986: Barba

and Manzanilla 1987; Ortiz and Barba 1993) has demonstrated in ethnographic as well as archaeological examples that stucco floors trap chemical compounds derived from specific activities that are repeatedly enacted in a structure. At Oztoyahualco 15B:N6W3 we collected samples to a depth of 5 cm in each square meter of the stucco floor. The following tests were completed on each sample:

Phosphates. This semiquantitative test is based on the intensity of blues that appear on the surface of filter paper, which reflects the quantity of phosphate in each sample. Areas where organic refuse was abundant tend to have high phosphate values.

Carbonates. The quantity of carbonates present in the sample was estimated based on its reaction to hydrochloric

Figure 4.6 Ceramic plate and mortar on top of floor of room C40.

acid. A scale from one to five was employed to measure the level of intensity of these reactions. Leaving natural calcium carbonate deposition aside, carbonate concentrations could be derived either from tortilla preparation, or from stucco and limestone processing.

Levels of pH. These were determined by routine procedures that are used for soils in a water solution; they were measured with a combined electrode. The presence of fire in the vicinity of a stucco floor increases pH values.

Color. Soil samples were compared using a Munsell Soil Color Chart. Color can be an indicator of organic material; a change in color also can signify where a fire has been lighted.

Specific chemical tests for sodium and iron were used in locations where it was expected that particular activities had been enacted. For example, iron concentrations are derived from agave processing or from the butcher-

ing of animals. Organic and inorganic chemical analyses also were undertaken on specific types of ceramic vessel bottoms. These provided further information on food preparation and consumption.

Apartment Compounds

Apartment compounds generally consist of several rooms at slightly different levels, arranged around open spaces (courtyards, refuse areas, and light wells) that serve as places for ritual, rainwater collection, partial refuse disposal, and light provision. The compounds contain different apartments joined by passages for circulation. They have domestic sanctuaries, and the entire compound is enclosed within an exterior wall (see figures 4.2–4.4).

It is believed that these compounds were occupied by corporate groups sharing kinship, residence, and occupation. It has been archaeologically ascertained that craftspeople dedicated to the manufacture of different products lived in separate compounds (Millon 1968; Spence 1966). In mapping activities shared by all households in our compound, we found additional data supporting this idea. Unfortunately our fossil DNA tests on the burials at Oztoyahualco 15B:N6W3 (Millones 1994) did not provide sufficient collagen to evaluate kinship ties between individuals of each household.

The apartment compounds at Teotihuacan vary considerably in surface area. Some are very large, such as Tlamimilolpa (Linné 1942), Yayahuala, Zacuala Palace, and Tetitla (ca. 3,600 m^2; Séjourné 1966b); others are medium size, such as Tlajinga 33 (2,280 m^2; Storey 1992), Bidasoa (1,750 m^2 at S2E4; Sánchez Alaniz 1989), Xolalpan (more than 1,344 m^2; Linné 1934), and Mound 1–2 in TC8 at Cerro Calaveras (1,500 m^2; Sanders 1966, 1994). Other compounds are much smaller, such as the one we excavated at Oztoyahualco 15B:N6W3 (slightly more than 550 m^2), Mounds 3 and 4 at TC8 (340 and 529 m^2, respectively; Sanders 1966), and the one excavated by Monzón at San Antonio Las Palmas (280 m^2, at N7W3; Monzón 1989).

Individual household sectors within the compound could be distinguished either by taking into consideration the circulation

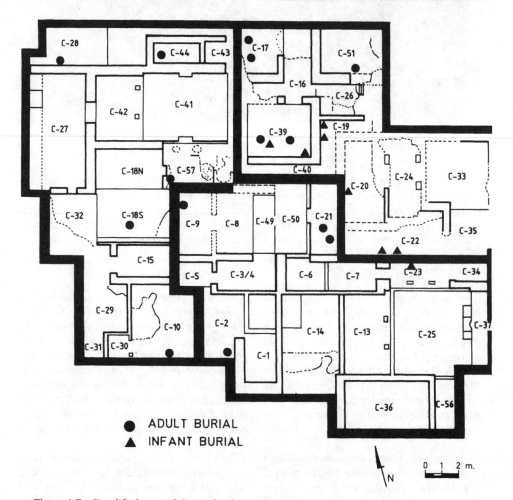

ADULT BURIAL

INFANT BURIAL

Figure 4.7 Simplified map of Oztoyahualco 15B:N6W3 with the three proposed sections and placement of burials.

alleys or access points (Sanders 1994: 19–37), or by mapping the different food consumption loci for each nuclear household. The Oztoyahualco 15B:N6W3 compound had three sections (figure 4.7) that we propose were related to three households (Ortiz and Barba 1993; Ortiz 1990). Each apartment included a zone for food preparation and consumption, sleeping quarters, storage areas, sectors for refuse, patios for cult activities, and funerary areas. Additionally, there were zones in which the entire family group or compound group (all the households in an apartment compound; see Sempowski 1994: 9–10) gathered to share activities, particularly those related to ritual and perhaps the curation of domestic animals.

We suspect that members of different household units participated in specialized activities related to the larger urban setting. In the compound that we studied, the whole compound group likely specialized in the stucco plastering of neighboring three-temple plazas and perhaps of other structures at Oztoyahualco. Other compound groups in the city seem to have been devoted to the production of certain ceramic wares, textile manufacture, obsidian or lapidary working, or even painting activities. I review some of these data below.

Evidence for Different Activities

Three building levels were detected: two of Teotihuacan date (Late Tlamimilolpa and Late Xolalpan) overlayed by two Aztec houses (one on the southeastern corner, on top of C36, and the other in the western portion on top of C18). This article only deals with the Late Xolalpan occupation.

Food processing and consumption

At Oztoyahualco 15B:N6W3 we located three kitchen sectors (C3-4, C15, and C19), recognized by dark red stains on the floor, a reduction of carbonate values, and a considerable increment of pH in the place where the portable stove stood. Ash augmented the pH in the stain zone. This area was surrounded by a semicircular band of

phosphates (Manzanilla and Barba 1990; Ortiz 1990; Ortiz and Barba 1993) (figure 4.8). The phosphate band suggests that this also was a major consumption area. In some cases, grinding instruments were found near the characteristic dark red stains. Access to storage rooms also was nearby. Plant and animal remains provide further support for food processing and consumption. Subsistence remains included rabbit, hare, young and adult deer bones, charred agave spines, *Panicum*, charred maize remains, squash phytoliths, and charred prickly pear seeds.

In one of these kitchens, C3–4, the door provided access to a small service patio (a medium-size open space where refuse was swept and where rainwater probably was collected). The patio drained to the north, where we found a band of refuse from the consumption area (e.g. turkey remains). The phosphate value was high near the drain, where all the small-grained refuse was concentrated.

Other Teotihuacan apartment compounds had similar access to plant resources, including maize, amaranth, beans, squash, chili peppers, *Chenopodium, Portulaca, Physalis*, cactus, Mexican hawthorn (*Crataegus mexicana*), and Mexican cherries (*Prunus capuli*) (González 1993; Manzanilla 1985, 1993b; McClung 1979, 1980: 162–3; Storey 1992: 64) (figure 4.9). Other plants used for medicinal purposes, fuel, and construction include purslane, wild potatoes, wild reeds, umbelliferous plants, white sapodilla, pine, oak, juniper, ditch reeds, and bulrushes. Yet the greater abundance of *Nicotiana* at San Antonio Las Palmas (Monzón 1989), avocado at Teopancazco (McClung 1979), and cotton at Tlamimilolpa (Linné 1942) and Teopancazco (McClung 1979) suggest differential access to certain foreign botanical resources associated with manufacturing and ritual consumption.

Tetitla (Séjourné 1966b) and Maquixco Bajo-Mound 3 (Sanders 1994: 63) were rich in agave end-scrapers, probably for *pulque* production. Sizable differences were noted in the number of scrapers per compound. For example, the three small compounds in Maquixco Bajo had 243 scrapers,

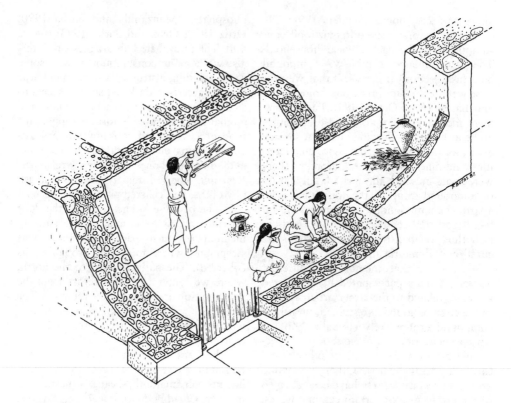

Figure 4.8   Artistic reconstruction of activities in C3-4 and C5 as drawn by Fernando Botas.

while Oztoyahualco 15B:N6W3 had only 6. Likewise, 93 projectile points were recovered at Maquixco Bajo compared to only 10 at Oztoyahualco 15B:N6W3. These differences may reflect specialized procurement activities at the former. In contrast, mano and metate distribution was more even. We recovered 8 metates and 13 manos in the Oztoyahualco 15B:N6W3 compound (Hernández 1993); Sanders (1994: 66) found 29 metates and 35 manos in all three compounds at Maquixco Bajo, with a rough estimate of 8 to 10 metates and 12 manos per compound.

In general, important faunal resources included rabbits, hares, deer, dogs, and turkey, supplemented with duck and fish (Sanders 1994: 31; Starbuck 1975; Valadez Azúa 1993; Valadez and Manzanilla 1988). At Oztoyahualco, we recorded a wide variety of rabbit and hare species (*Sylvilagus floridanus*, *Sylvilagus cunicularius*, *Sylvilagus*

audobonii, *Romerolagus diazi*, and *Lepus callotis*). We even detected young individuals, so we have proposed a breeding locus for rabbits in C10 (see figure 4.7). We also recovered four young dogs, often in child burials (Valadez Azúa 1993; Valadez and Manzanilla 1988); thus we also have proposed that the residents raised dogs.

The abundance of rabbit and hare bones also has an ideological counterpart in a small rabbit sculpture that stood on a temple model in one of the ritual courtyards (C33), probably as a patron deity (figure 4.10). Rabbit feet appear to have been ritually cut in C9 as part of a group ritual held in a small destroyed temple (at C57) (Hernández 1993; Manzanilla 1988–9, 1993b; Manzanilla and Ortiz 1991).

Storey (1992) and Widmer (1987) found large amounts of rabbits, turkey eggs, small birds (such as quail and pigeon), as well as small freshwater fish at Tlajinga 33, and low

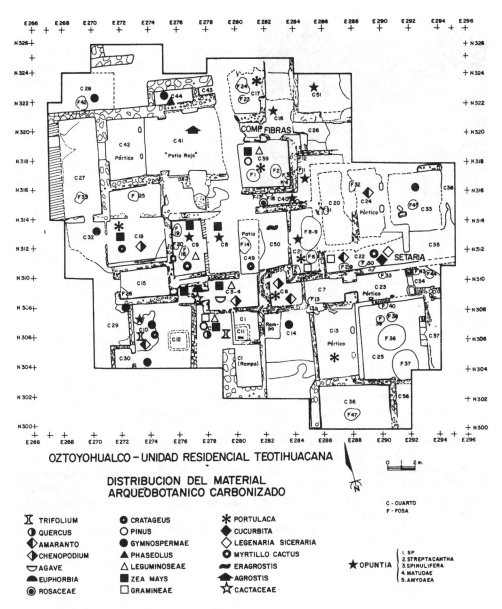

Figure 4.9 Location of carbonized archaeobotanical material on Oztoyahualco 15B:N6W3. (González 1993: fig. 429.)

counts of deer, dog, and turkey. It is particularly interesting that Storey (1992) suggests turkey eggs could have been obtained externally, without necessarily breeding turkey at Tlajinga 33.

In Xolalpan times, there could have been shortages in meat distribution in response to population pressure. One of the relevant responses may have been the breeding of rabbits together with turkeys and dogs at Oztoyahualco. Another possible response was the consumption of freshwater fish at Tlajinga 33. However, we have no way as yet to compare the number of individuals of

Figure 4.10   Model of a temple (10×7.6 cm) and small rabbit sculpture (probably a patron deity) found in courtyard C33.

each faunal species per unit area in the apartment compounds, because the only thorough data yet published is that of Oztoyahualco 15B:N6W3 (Valadez Azúa 1993; Valadez and Manzanilla 1988).

Starbuck (1975: 181–2) suggested that between the Terminal Preclassic (last centuries BC) and the end of the Classic period (first seven centuries AD), a change from locally available animal resources to a reliance upon a much-expanded support area, probably encompassing most of the Valley of Mexico took place. He also proposed a decrease in the importance of deer during the Classic horizon. There are, however, some points of disagreement, because our experience at the Late and Terminal Formative village of Cuanalan, in the southern Teotihuacan Valley, shows that a wide variety of lake, land, and mountain resources were consumed (Manzanilla 1985). This range of resource exploitation continued in Classic-period Teotihuacan.

Even though approximately the same faunal and floral species are represented in all the apartment compounds, the quantities varied. Tetitla showed an unprecedented diversity of birds (as well as a particular richness in botanical species); Yayahuala had a wide variety of marine mollusks (as well as a high proportion of *Chenopodium* and amaranth); the consumption of small birds and freshwater fish was high in

Tlajinga 33; and Oztoyahualco 15B:N6W3 relied heavily on several species of rabbits and hares. At present, the degree to which these data reflect differential access to faunal and floral resources cannot be determined, because many other alternatives related to group choice and ideology have not yet been considered. One difference between compounds can be pointed out: the presence of different hunting techniques represented in the technological repertory. For example, Tetitla had projectile points of various sizes that would have permitted the residents to cope with small, medium, and large animals (Séjourné 1966b: fig. 117). Even though Linné only published offerings from burials, the projectile points at Xolalpan (Linné 1934: figs 258, 259, 263, 264, 293–7, 298–311) and Tlamimilolpa (Linné 1942: figs 247, 252, 263–71) show similar size ranges. On the contrary, Oztoyahualco 15B:N6W3 only had projectile points of medium and large size, which were found in conjunction with many examples of blow-gun projectiles, perhaps for hunting small animals (Hernández 1993). Linné (1942: 187) also found blow-gun projectiles at Tlamimilolpa.

Storage

At Oztoyahualco 15B:N6W3, two storage sectors were adjacent to two of the food consumption areas already mentioned. In C5, San Martín storage amphorae were present, together with several plant macrofossils dominated by charred maize, non-carbonized Leguminosae, charred *Chenopodium*, cactus, *Euphorbia*, and noncarbonized *Ipomoea*. The quantity of *Casimiroa* pollen (95 percent) indicates that there was surely a mass of stored *Casimiroa*. This plant had medical uses in Prehispanic times, and early chroniclers reported that it had hypnotic and somnific effects (Barba et al. 1987). In line with its use for storage, the floor surface in C5 did not indicate intense utilization or activity. Chemical values revealed no more than a slight rise in phosphates. The other storage sector (C18) was a large room situated in the western portion of the compound; it housed 11.47 percent of the sherds recovered from the compound, particularly San Martín orange storage vessels, together with red, orange, and brown jars, nine *candeleros*, two figurines, and some fragments of mother-of-pearl (*Pinctata mazatlanica*).

Partly a consequence of the small number of recent extensive excavations, few storage rooms have been identified in apartment compounds. Room 89 at Tlajinga 33 was probably a storeroom; *Argemone* sp., Malvaceae, Leguminosae, and plant fibers were found there (Storey and Widmer 1989: 414). Séjourné (1966a: 29, *láminas* 6 and 7) describes a room with storage vessels at Tetitla. Sanders (1994: 31–3) identifies Rooms 2 and 3 of Mound 3 at Maquixco Bajo as possible storage areas for *Spondylus calcifer.*

Butchering and refuse sectors

At Oztoyahualco 15B:N6W3 all the southern rooms had evidence of butchering; several rabbit and hare remains were found, together with high phosphate values. Only one other context had similar findings. In a corner of a room (C9) to the east of the service courtyard, we found 12 obsidian blades near rabbit, rodent, and mollusk remains, and high phosphate and pH values (Manzanilla 1988–9).

In other compounds, nonplastered open areas at the fringes of the compound may have served as refuse disposal and butchering areas. In Tlajinga 33, Storey and Widmer (1989: 410) mention three depositional areas: patios, courtyards, and open unroofed areas with packed earth floors located at the peripheries of the compounds.

Manufacture and construction

Edge rejuvenation and prismatic blade extraction was carried out in many compounds. Prismatic blade cores have been found at Maquixco Bajo (Sanders 1994, 1995), Oztoyahualco 15B:N6W3 (Hernández 1993), and Xolalpan (Linné 1934: figs

325, 327). But core-to-blade ratios were variable. For example, at Maquixco Bajo 37 prismatic cores (Sanders 1994: 66) and 304 prismatic blades were recovered (Santley et al. 1995: 483). In contrast, at Oztoyahualco 15B:N6W3, only 9 prismatic cores were found, compared to 349 prismatic macroblades and 342 prismatic blades (Hernández 1993: 461).

Plaster polishing also was important at Oztoyahualco 15B:N6W3. This activity was detected in the northern sector of the compound, where some graves that cut into the plaster floor were intended to be recovered again with stucco. Yet the compound was abandoned before this task was concluded. The calcium carbonate mixture was already prepared, with a basalt polisher on top of it. There were 42 polishers and 16 polisher fragments in our compound (a total of 58), an abundance that indicates a probable group occupation (figure 4.11). Fewer of these artifacts (40) were obtained from the three compounds in Maquixco Bajo (Sanders 1994: 66).

Crespo Oviedo and Mastache de E. (1981) proposed that there were two sites in the Tula region that could be considered Zapotec settlements where lime was obtained for plastering Teotihuacan: El Tesoro and Acoculco. Spence (1992) supported this idea by proposing that the Zapotec controlled the mining, processing, and importation of lime to the city. Our research at Oztoyahualco 15B:N6W3 does not support this interpretation. We have concluded that parts of the northwestern district of the ancient city had direct links with settlements in the Tula region, and that our compound was perhaps more related to Chingú (Díaz O. 1980), a Teotihuacan settlement also located in the limestone area near Tula. The number of plaster "polishers" made of volcanic scoria (*tezontle*) per square meter could be used to differentiate the relevance of this activity in apartment compounds, assuming that Linné and Séjourné saved all the specimens found. Tetitla had .19 polishers per square meter; the Oztoyahualco compound, .10; Xolalpan, .04; and Tlamimilolpa, .01.

Figure 4.11   A sample of stucco polishers found at Oztoyahualco 15B:N6W3.

Other craft activities also varied by compound. Lapidary work involving green-stone, slate, and onyx, marine-shell working, and ceramic manufacture, particularly of San Martín Orange ware, were clearly represented at Tlajinga 33 (Krotser and Rattray 1980; Storey 1991; Widmer 1991).

Several figurine molds were found at Xolalpan (Linné 1934: figs 199–208); and stone celts for cutting wood were particularly abundant in Grave 1 at that compound (Linné 1934: figs 246–56). Different kinds of pigments for painting walls, pottery, and probably codices, as well as spindle whorls and needles, were recorded at Xolalpan. Tlamimilolpa (Linné 1942) also had evidence of textile manufacture, as well as basket making and fiberwork. Tetitla (Séjourné 1966b) is represented by bone instruments for working hides and polishing pottery.

With respect to figurine production, the Oztoyahualco compound only had 132 figurines and figurine fragments from Teoti-huacan times (Manzanilla 1993b: 358–69), very few in comparison, for example, to Maquixco Bajo, where Kolb (1995) mentions 2,150 figurines for the same time period. Within the Oztoyahualco com-pound, each household or family unit appears to have used different ceramic wares. Matte and Red Hematite wares are associated with Household 1. Household 2 used black, brown, Copa, Granular, and San Martín wares. Household 3 had a concentration of range and Thin Orange wares. These patterns may reflect differential access to pottery production in the urban setting for each nuclear household.

Cult areas

It has been proposed that a superimposition of deities on two levels occurred for the first time at Teotihuacan. Lineage gods were patrons of lines of descent, and above them was the deity Tlaloc as god of place, protector of territory, and patron of the city and the caves (López Austin 1989).

Among the deities present at Teotihuacan, the Fire God (Huehuetéotl), who was known from the Formative horizon, always appears associated with the eastern portions of apartment compounds. Another deity present in domestic contexts is the Fat God, generally represented in figurines or appliquéd on tripod vessels. The Butterfly Deity is depicted on incense burners and is

Figure 4.12   Burial 8 in a pit (90 cm in diameter) in C21, with dismantled theater-type censer around the body.

probably linked to death and fertility. In particular, the impressive theater-type censer we found accompanying the burial of an adult male (figure 4.12) had butterfly wings in the chest of the main figure (figure 4.13) and displayed a wide array of food and economically important plants (Manzanilla and Carreón 1991) (figure 4.14).

In domestic contexts, the state god Tlaloc was represented in figurines with goggles and elaborate headdresses, as well as on Tlaloc vases (figure 4.15) and on a "handled cover" (figure 4.16). However, at Oztoyahualco 15B:N6W3, we also had evidence of patron gods related to particular families. A stucco rabbit sculpture was found on a miniature Teotihuacan temple-shaped shrine (made of basalt) in one of the ritual patios (see figure 4.10).

There were three ritual courtyards in the Oztoyahualco compound, each corresponding to a household; the largest one (C41) probably also served the compound group as a whole and was called the "Red Court-

yard," due to its mural paintings (figure 4.17). It was the only one with a central altar in its lower construction level. The second one (Courtyard 25) had evidence of theater-type censers; many Aztec pits in this courtyard disturbed offerings or burials. The third one (Courtyard 33) contained the miniature temple with the rabbit sculpture mentioned above (see figure 4.10).

Some activity areas related to ritual preparation were detected around these courtyards. At Oztoyahualco 15B:N6W3, in the corner of C9 (near the main shrine), a concentration of 58 obsidian prismatic blade fragments, a basalt hammerstone, and a limestone half sphere (with radial cutting marks probably caused by the continuous cutting of rabbit and hare limbs) (figure 4.18) were found (Hernández 1993; Manzanilla 1993b). There also were numerous funerary and offering pits, particularly in the eastern half of the compound. The northeastern household (Household 3) had the most burials, and also the greatest

Figure 4.13 Theater-type censer found around Burial 8. (height of the lid: 34.5 cm, height of the main figure: 18.5 cm.)

Figure 4.14 Representations of squash flowers and fruits, tamales, cotton, maize corn cobs, and other economically important plants and processed food that surrounded the censer's lid. (pieces 3–5.1 cm.)

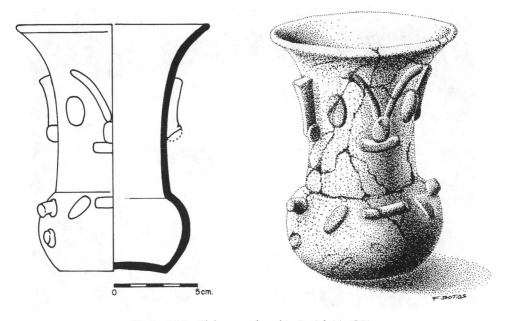

Figure 4.15 Tlaloc vase found in Burial 4 in C51.

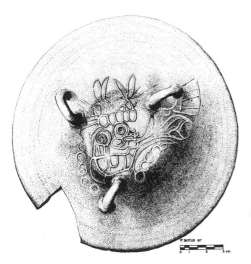

Figure 4.16 Tlaloc representations on a
"handled cover."

quantities of foreign fauna: bear, jaguar, mother-of-pearl, and other marine shells (including *Spondylus calcifer*).

Religion should be seen as a sphere of sociopolitical integration organized into a hierarchy in which the patron gods of house-

hold groups and barrios, occupational deities, the gods of specific priestly groups, and state deities (such as Tlaloc) are superimposed (Manzanilla 1993a). Teotihuacan society was integrated mainly through religion. The conception of the four courses of sacred space permeated the domestic domain of Teotihuacan (Manzanilla 1993b). Spatial patterning seems to have been established for the disposition of functional sectors, which extended beyond the framework of the nuclear household. Thus, in general, storage zones were found to the west; those for refuse to the south; funerary areas were concentrated in the middle of the eastern sector (although exceptions exist); and neonate burials were located primarily on a north–south band, in the eastern third of the compound. The affinity for order so patently manifest in the grid system of the city finds its correspondence on the domestic level as well.

Burials and foreign raw materials

Burials are common in domestic contexts. However, with the exception of Tlajinga 33

Figure 4.17   The main courtyard (C41) of Oztoyahualco 15B:N6W3 (5.5 × 4.5 m).

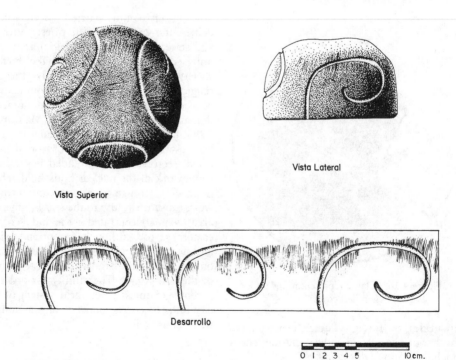

Vista Superior

Vista Lateral

Desarrollo

Figure 4.18   A limestone half-sphere found in C9 in association with prismatic blade fragments and rabbit and hare limb bones.

and probably La Ventilla, the number of adults interred in each compound is too low, relative to the area of the compound, to account for most of its inhabitants. For example, 7 burials are recorded for Xolalpan, 13 for Tlamimilolpa, and 18 for the compound at Oztoyahualco 15B:N6W3 (see figure 4.7). Perhaps other adults, particularly women, were buried elsewhere.

Certain burials in each compound had rich offerings. Burial 8 at Oztoyahualco (see figure 4.12) was exceptional, for it contained a 22-year-old male adult with an intentionally deformed skull that was associated with an impressive theater-type incense burner (see figures 4.13 and 4.14) (Manzanilla and Carreón 1991). In what seems to represent a funerary ritual, the incense burner appliqués were removed from the lid, and all were placed around the deceased. The chimney was deposited toward the west, with the lid and the figure to the east of the skull. Representations of plants and sustenance (ears of corn, squash, squash flowers, cotton, tamales, tortillas, and perhaps amaranth bread) were placed to the south; the four-petaled flowers, roundels representing feathers, and mica disks were situated to the east and west.

Although Oztoyahualco 15B:N6W3 had only 18 burials, fewer than were found at Tlajinga 33 (Storey 1983, 1987, 1992) or La Ventilla "B" (Serrano and Lagunas 1974), there are important conclusions regarding these data. We hypothesized that there were three nuclear households at Oztoyahualco. The first household, in the southeastern section, is represented by only three burials. The second, in the western portion of the compound, also has three burials, all adults. The third, in the northeastern section, has 11 burials, of which 6 represent new-born babies (figure 4.19) and children (see Storey 1986).

This overrepresentation of burials belonging to particular sectors of the apartment compounds is also noted for Xolalpan (see figure 4.2), where nearly all the burials are concentrated in the southwestern section. At Tlamimilolpa (see figure 4.3), nearly all are grouped in the central-southern section; at Tetitla (see figure 4.4), they are concentrated in the northeastern section. It seems there is one family that is well represented with respect to funerary practices; the rest are underrepresented.

Each household at Oztoyahualco 15B:N6W3 had one or two burials that stood out because of their grave goods (Burial 8 for unit 1, Burial 13 for unit 2, and probably Burials 10 and 1 for unit 3). Burial 8 was the most outstanding of the compound group as a whole.

Theater-type censers were used frequently at Xolalpan (where they are found in the altar and in a western courtyard) and Tlamimilolpa (where they are grouped around Burial 4 and kept in caches, ready for ritual use). Decorated tripods also are common at Xolalpan and Tlamimilolpa, but very rare – although present – at Oztoyahualco. Probably one difference lies in the presence of Maya fine wares in the western portion of Xolalpan and in the central part of Tlamimilolpa, possibly due to their proximity to the Merchants' Barrio. Other imported wares, such as Thin Orange and Granular wares, are present in all compounds. Exotic raw materials such as mica, slate, and marine shells, were present in burials at Xolalpan, Tlamimilolpa, and Oztoyahualco, although there are differences in quantity and in the proportion of Pacific vs. Atlantic shell species.

Conclusion

At Oztoyahualco 15B:N6W3 there was, in general, a clear differentiation among the various sectors of the structure. The southern sector was associated with refuse. Areas for food preparation and consumption, as well as the sleeping quarters, were set around the central portion of the compound. The eastern sector was rich in funerary and ritual components. The western sector was devoted to storage. Finally, the northwestern sector had the largest courtyard, probably the compound's meeting place.

The compound was transformed by closing circulation alleys and accesses when the

Figure 4.19   Burial 11, a new-born baby inside a bowl (23 cm in diameter) found in C22.

family structure changed. Distributional maps of all types of archaeological materials – ceramic types, obsidian, polished stone, bone, antler, and shell, as well as chemical compounds, pollen, phytoliths, seeds, and faunal macrofossils – help identify activities and choices particular to each nuclear household.

1 Matte and Red Hematite wares and symbols of the Butterfly God are associated with Household 1, situated to the south. This household has the largest concentration of prismatic blades and is the locus for the ritual butchering of rabbits.

2 Household 2, to the west, used black, brown, Copa, Granular, and San Martín wares. It was characterized by rabbits and hares held in captivity, the butchering of animals for consumption, and activities where side- and end-scrapers were used. Foreign wares and minerals were more prevalent in the household, as were symbols of fire.

3 Household 3, to the northeast, was the poorest in pottery diversity, having a concentration of orange and Thin

Orange wares, together with Tlaloc symbols. Differences between the ceramic assemblages associated with each household may indicate either differences in access among households and/or domestic distinctions in ritual and other activities.

One of the great problems in comparing the Oztoyahualco compound with others excavated at Teotihuacan is that, in the latter cases, a high percentage of the data comes from small-scale excavations, with no context control. Comparing these data with those collected during the controlled, large-scale excavations at Oztoyahualco can only be handled through presence/absence.

When we take into consideration the presence/absence of botanical and faunal resources, as well as exogenous raw materials, we conclude that differences in access were relatively slight between compounds. There may be a whole range of socioeconomic possibilities, with no clear-cut distinctions between groups in the urban setting. One may think that there are differences in quantities, but the problem is the comparability of the samples.

However, differences exist among the specialized activities enacted by household groups of different compounds. Dominant activities also vary by households, suggesting group and family specializations. Differences in the number of high-status products, particularly decorated ceramic tripods or mural paintings, and variability in the quality of construction itself have been noted.

One household in each compound seems to have been the most active in linking the household group to the urban hierarchy. The preponderance of Tlaloc cult items (Tlaloc vases, figurines, and representations in "handled covers") in Household 3 suggests its members served this role for Oztoyahualco 15B:N6W3.

If Millon (1981: 209) is right in proposing that the apartment compounds are a byproduct of state decisions to control the population of the city, then further research might focus on the articulation between these social units and urban organization as a whole at Teotihuacan. It also may be worth considering whether the inefficiency of the state bureaucracy, and its inflexibility to change, which may ultimately have caused its collapse (Millon 1988), was in part provoked by the difficulty of harmonizing the interests of such a vast array of ethnic, occupational, and social groups.

ACKNOWLEDGMENTS

I thank the reviewers and editors for their enriching comments on the article. I also thank the following people for their participation in particular studies in my project: Luis Barba and Agustín Ortiz for the geophysical and geochemical prospection, as well as for the chemical studies of stucco floors: Raúl Valadez for the paleofaunal analysis; Neusa Hidalgo, Javier González, and Emily McClung de Tapia for the paleobotanical data: Beatriz Ludlow and Emilio Ibarra for the pollen information: Judith Zurita for the phytolith analysis; Magalí Civera and Mario Millones for the osteological, as well as the DNA, analysis; Cynthia Hernández for the lithic analysis; Miguel Angel Jiménez for the ceramic distributional maps; Edith Ortiz for the domestic ideology research, and the Graphic Department of the Institute of Anthropological Research of the National Autonomous University of Mexico (particularly Fernando Botas, César Fernández, and José Saldaña) for their invaluable help. This interdisciplinary research was funded by the Institute of Anthropological Research of the National Autonomous University of Mexico (UNAM), and carried on thanks to a permit from the Consejo de Arqueología of the Instituto Nacional de Antropología e Historia.

REFERENCES

Barba, L. A. 1986. I. La química en el estudio de áreas de actividad. *Unidades habitacionales mesoamericanas y sus áreas de actividad*, edited by L. Manzanilla, pp. 21–39. Arqueología, Serie Antropológica 76. Instituto de Investigaciones Antropológicas, Universidad Nacional Autónoma de México, Mexico City.

Barba, L., B. Ludlow, L. Manzanilla, and R. Valadez. 1987. La vida doméstica en Teotihuacan. Un estudio interdisciplinario. *Ciencia y desarrollo* 77, año 13, pp. 21–32. Consejo Nacional de Ciencia y Tecnología. Mexico City.

Barba, L. and L. Manzanilla. 1987. Superficie/excavación: Un ensayo de predicción de rasgos arqueológicos desde la superficie. en Oztoya-hualco. *Antropológicas* 1: 19–46.

Charlton, T. H. 1969. Sociocultural Implications of House Types in the Teotihuacan Valley, Mexico. *Journal of the Society of Architectural Historians* 28(4): 284–90.

Crespo Oviedo, A. M. and A. G. Mastache de E. 1981. VII. La presencia en el área de Tula, Hidalgo, de grupos relacionados con el Barrio de Oaxaca en Teotihuacan. In *Interacción cultural en México central*, edited by E. C. Rattray, J. Litvak, and C. Díaz O., pp. 99–104. Universidad Nacional Autónoma de México, Mexico City.

Díaz O., C. L. 1980. *Chingú: Un sitio clásico del área de Tula, Hgo*. Colección Científica 90. Instituto Nacional de Antropología e Historia, Mexico City.

González, J. 1993. A. Estudio del material arqueobotánico de Oztoyahualco. Capítulo 14. Macrofósiles botánicos, fitolitos y polen. In *Anatomía de un conjunto residencial teotihuacano en Oztoyahualco*, vol. 2, edited by L. Manzanilla, pp. 661–73. Instituto de Investigaciones Antropológicas, Universidad Nacional Autónoma de México, Mexico City.

Hernández, C. 1993. Capítulo VII. La lítica. In *Anatomía de un conjunto residencial teotihuacano en Oztoyahualco*, vol. 1, edited by L. Manzanilla, pp. 388–467. Instituto de Investigaciones Antropológicas, Universidad Nacional Autónoma de México, Mexico City.

Kolb, C. C. 1995. Teotihuacan Period Figurines: A Typological Classification, Their Spatial and Temporal Distribution in the Teotihuacan Valley. In *The Teotihuacan Valley Project: The Teotihuacan Occupation of the Valley*, part 2: *Artifact Analyses*, edited by W. T. Sanders, pp. 275–465. Occasional Papers in Anthropology No. 20. Matson Museum of Anthropology, Pennsylvania State University, University Park.

Krotser, P. and E. Rattray. 1980. Manufactura y distribución de tres grupos cerámicos de Teotihuacan. *Anales de Antropología* 17: 91–104. Universidad Nacional Autónoma de México.

Linné, S. 1934. *Archaeological Researches at Teotihuacan. Mexico*. Publication I. Ethnographical Museum of Sweden, Stockholm.

—— 1942. *Mexican Highland Cultures: Archaeological Researches at Teotihuacan, Calpulalpan and Chalchicomula in 1934–35*. New Series, Publication 7. Ethnographical Museum of Sweden, Stockholm.

López Austin, A. 1989. 1. La historia de Teotihuacan. In *Teotihuacan*, pp. 13–35. El Equilibrista, Citicorp/Citibank, Mexico City.

McClung de Tapia, E. 1979. Plants and Subsistence in the Teotihuacan Valley AD 100–750. Ph.D. dissertation, Brandeis University. University Microfilms, Ann Arbor.

—— 1980. Interpretación de restos botánicos procedentes de sitios arqueológicos. *Anales de Antropología* 17: 149–65. Universidad Nacional Autónoma de México.

Manzanilla, L. 1985. El sitio de Cuanalan en el marco de las comunidades pre-urbanas del Valle de Teotihuacan. In *Mesoamérica y el Centro de México*, edited by J. Monjarás-Ruiz, E. Pérez Rocha, and R. Brambila, pp. 133–78. Colección Biblioteca del Instituto Nacional de Antropología e Historia. Instituto Nacional de Antropología e Historia, Mexico City.

—— 1986a. Introducción. In *Unidades habitacionales mesoamericanas y sus áreas de actividad*, edited by Manzanilla, pp. 9–18. Arqueología. Serie Antropológica 76. Universidad Nacional Autónoma de México, Mexico City.

—— 1986b. *La constitución de la sociedad urbana Mesopotamia.: Un proceso en la historia*. Serie Antropológica 80. Universidad Nacional Autónoma de México, Mexico City.

—— 1988–9. The Study of Room Function in a Residential Compound at Teotihuacan, Mexico. *Origini, Giornate in onore di Salvatore Maria Puglisi* 14: 75–86. Universitá La Sapienza, Rome.

—— 1993a. The Economic Organization of the Teotihuacan Priesthood: Hypotheses and Considerations. In *Art, Ideology, and the City of Teotihuacan*, edited by J. C. Berlo, pp. 321–38. Dumbarton Oaks, Washington, DC.

Manzanilla, L. (ed.). 1987. *Cobá, Quintana Roo. Análisis de dos unidades habitacionales mayas del horizonte clásico*. Arqueología. Serie Antropológica 82. Universidad Nacional Autónoma de México, Mexico City.

—— 1993b. *Anatomía de un conjunto residencial teotihuacano en Oztoyahualco*, 2 vols. Universidad Nacional Autónoma de México, Mexico City.

Manzanilla, L. and L. Barba. 1990. The Study of Activities in Classic Households: Two Case Studies from Coba and Teotihuacan. *Ancient Mesoamerica* 1(1): 41–9.

Manzanilla, L. and E. Carreón. 1991. A Teotihuacan Censer in a Residential Context: An Interpretation. *Ancient Mesoamerica* 2(2): 299–307.

Manzanilla, L. and A. Ortiz. 1991. Los altares domésticos en Teotihuacan: Hallazgo de dos fragmentos de maqueta. *Cuadernos de Arquitectura Mesoamericana* 13: 11–13. Universidad Nacional Autónoma de México, Mexico City.

Manzanilla, L., A. Ortiz, C. Hernández, M. A. Jiménez, E. Ortiz, and M. Cortina. 1990. Nuevos procedimientos para el análisis de áreas de actividad en arqueología. *Antropológicas* 5: 13–27. Universidad Nacional Autónoma de México, Mexico City.

Millon, R. 1968. Urbanization at Teotihuacan: The Teotihuacan Mapping Project. *Actas y Memorias del 37 Congreso Internacional de Americanistas* 1: 105–20. Argentina 1966. Departamento de Publicaciones Científicas Argentinas, Buenos Aires.

—— 1973. *Urbanization at Teotihuacan, Mexico 1, Part 1: The Teotihuacan Map*. University of Texas Press, Austin.

—— 1981. Teotihuacan: City, State and Civilization. In *Handbook of Middle American Indians, Supplement 1: Archaeology*, edited by V. Bricker and J. A. Sabrott, pp. 198–243. University of Texas Press, Austin.

—— 1988. The Last Years of Teotihuacan Dominance. In *The Collapse of Ancient States and Civilizations*, edited by N. Yoffee and G. Cowgill, pp. 102–64. University of Arizona Press, Tucson.

Millones, M. 1994. Paleoparentesco en la Ciudad de los Dioses. Los entierros de Oztoyahualco. Unpublished thesis in physical anthropology. Escuela Nacional de Antropología e Historia, Mexico City.

Monzón, M. 1989. *Casas prehispánicas en Teotihuacan*. Instituto Mexiquense de Cultura. Toluca, Mexico.

Ortiz Butrón, A. 1990. Oztoyahualco: Estudio químico de los pisos estucados de un conjunto residencial teotihuacano para determinar áreas de actividad. Unpublished thesis in archaeology, Escuela Nacional de Antropología e Historia, Mexico City.

Ortiz Butrón, A. and L. Barba. 1993. Capítulo 13. La química en los estudios de áreas de actividad. In *Anatomia de un conjunto residencial teotihuacano en Oztoyahualco*, vol. 2, edited by L. Manzanilla, pp. 617–60. Universidad Nacional Autónoma de México, Mexico City.

Piña Chán, R. 1963. Excavaciones en el Rancho "La Ventilla." In *Teotihuacan*, edited by I. Bernal, pp. 50–2. Instituto Nacional de Antropología e Historia, Mexico City.

Rattray, E. C. 1987. Los barrios foráneos de Teotihuacan. In *Teotihuacan: Nuevos datos, nuevas síntesis y nuevos problemas*, edited by E. McClung de Tapia and E. C. Rattray, pp. 243–73. Universidad Nacional Autónoma de México, Mexico City.

—— 1988. Nuevas interpretaciones en torno al Barrio de los Comerciantes. *Anales de Antropología* 25: 165–82. Universidad Nacional Autónoma de México, Mexico City.

—— 1993. *The Oaxaca Barrio at Teotihuacan*. Monografías Mesoamericanas 1. Instituto de Estudios Avanzados, Universidad de las Américas, Puebla, Mexico.

Sánchez Alaniz, J. I. 1989. Las unidades habitacionales en Teotihuacan: El caso de Bidasoa. Unpublished thesis in archaeology, Escuela Nacional de Antropología e Historia, Mexico City.

Sanders, W. T. 1966. Life in a Classic Village. In *Teotihuacan Onceava Mesa Redonda*, pp. 123–47. Sociedad Mexicana de Antropología, Mexico City.

Sanders, W. T. (ed.). 1994. *The Teotihuacan Valley Project: The Teotihuacan Occupation of the Valley, Part I. The Excavations*. Occasional Papers in Anthropology No. 19. Matson Museum of Anthropology, Pennsylvania State University, University Park.

—— 1995. *The Teotihuacan Valley Project: The Teotihuacan Occupation of the Valley. Part 2: Artifact Analyses*. Occasional Papers in Anthropology No. 20. Matson Museum of Anthropology, Pennsylvania State University, University Park.

Santley, R. S., J. M. Kerley, and T. P. Barrett. 1995. Teotihuacan Period Obsidian Assemblages from the Teotihuacan Valley. In *The Teotihuacan Valley Project: The Teotihuacan Occupation of the Valley. Part 2. Artifact Analyses*, edited by W. T. Sanders, pp. 466–83. Occasional Papers in Anthropology No. 20. Matson Museum of Anthropology, Pennsylvania State University, University Park.

Séjourné, L. 1966a. *Arqueología de Teotihuacan: La cerámica*. Fondo de Cultura Económica, Mexico City.

—— 1966b. *Arquitectura y pintura en Teotihuacan*. Siglo XXI, Mexico City.

Sempowski, M. L. 1994. Part I. Mortuary Practices at Teotihuacan. In *Mortuary Practices and Skeletal Remains at Teotihuacan*, edited by M. L. Sempowski, and M. W. Spence. pp. 1–314. Urbanization at Teotihuacan, Mexico 3. University of Utah Press, Salt Lake City.

Serrano, C. and Z. Lagunas. 1974. Sistema de enterramiento y notas sobre el material osteológico de La Ventilla, Teotihuacan, México. *Anales del Instituto Nacional de Antropología e Historia* 7a: 105–44. Instituto Nacional de Antropología e Historia, Mexico City.

Spence, M. W. 1966. Los talleres de obsidiana de Teotihuacan. In *XI Mesa Redonda: El Valle de*

Teotihuacan y su entorno, pp. 213–18. Sociedad Mexicana de Antropología, Mexico City.

—— 1989. Excavaciones recientes en Tlailotlacan, el Barrio Oaxaqueño de Teotihuacan. *Arqueología* 5: 81–104. Instituto Nacional de Antropología e Historia, Mexico City.

—— 1992. A Comparative Analysis of Ethnic Enclaves. Paper presented at the 57th Annual Meeting of the Society for American Archaeology, Pittsburgh.

—— 1994. Part II. Human Skeletal Material from Teotihuacan. In *Mortuary Practices and Skeletal Remains at Teotihuacan*, edited by M. L. Sempowski and M. W. Spence, pp. 315–453. Urbanization at Teotihuacan, Mexico 3. University of Utah Press, Salt Lake City.

Starbuck, D. 1975. Man–Animal Relationships in Pre-Columbian Central Mexico. Unpublished Ph.D. dissertation, Department of Anthropology, Yale University, New Haven, Connecticut.

Storey, R. 1983. The Paleodemography of Tlajinga 33: An Apartment Compound of the Pre-Columbian City of Teotihuacan. Ph.D. dissertation, Pennsylvania State University, University Park. University Microfilms International, Ann Arbor.

—— 1986. Perinatal Mortality at Pre-Columbia Teotihuacan. *American Journal of Physical Anthropology* 69: 541–8.

—— 1987. A First Look at the Paleodemography of the Ancient City of Teotihuacan. In *Teotihuacan: Nuevos datos, nuevas síntesis, nuevos problemas*, edited by E. McClung de Tapia and E. C. Rattray, pp. 91–114. Arqueología, Serie Antropológica 72. Universidad Nacional Autónoma de México, Mexico City.

—— 1991. Residential Compound Organization and the Evolution of the Teotihuacan State. *Ancient Mesoamerica* 2(1): 107–18.

—— 1992. *Life and Death in the Ancient City of Teotihuacan. A Modern Paleodemographic Synthesis*. University of Alabama Press, Tuscaloosa.

Storey, R. and R. J. Widmer. 1989. Household and Community Structure of a Teotihuacan Apartment Compound: S3W1:33 of the Tlajinga Barrio. In *Households and Communities*, edited by S. MacEachern, D. J. W. Archer, and R. D. Garvin, pp. 407–15. Archaeological Association of the University of Calgary, Calgary, Alberta.

Valadez Azúa, R. 1993. Capítulo 15. Macrofósiles faunísticos. In *Anatomía de un conjunto residencial teotihuacano en Oztoyahualco*, vol. 2, edited by L. Manzanilla, pp. 729–825. Universidad Nacional Autónoma de México, Mexico City.

Valadez, R. and L. Manzanilla. 1988. Restos faunísticos y áreas de actividad en una unidad habitacional de la antigua ciudad de Teotihuacan. *Revista Mexicana de Estudios Antropológicos* 34(1): 147–68.

Widmer, R. J. 1987. The Evolution of Form and Function in a Teotihuacan Apartment Compound: The Case of Tlajinga 33. In *Teotihuacan: Nuevos datos, nuevas síntesis, nuevos problemas*, edited by E. McClung de Tapia and E. C. Rattray, pp. 317–68. Universidad Nacional Autónoma de México, Mexico City.

—— 1991. Lapidary Craft Specialization at Teotihuacan: Implications for Community Structure at 33:S3W1 and Economic Organization in the City. *Ancient Mesoamerica* 2(1): 131–47.

PART II

Economic Organization

Editors' Introduction

Some of the most notable achievements of the ancient Mesoamerican peoples were in the realm of economics. Farmers worked out numerous different ways to grow maize and other crops, including a form of cultivating swampy lands – raised fields – that had some of the highest yields of any ancient agriculture anywhere. The technology of many crafts was quite advanced, particularly obsidian (volcanic glass) and bronze metallurgy. Trade and exchange were highly developed, with professional merchants making journeys of hundreds of miles to obtain goods that were sold in busy marketplaces using several types of currency.

The ancient civilizations of Mesoamerica had complex and dynamic economies. The economy is traditionally divided into three realms: production, distribution, and consumption. *Production* includes subsistence (agriculture, gathering, etc.), extraction of raw materials, and the manufacture of goods. *Distribution or exchange* describes the ways in which raw materials and commodities are exchanged between and within social groups, and *consumption* concerns the way that goods are used or consumed by people. The chapters in this section cover these aspects of the economy for a variety of Mesoamerican cultures. Some of the key commodities or goods in ancient Mesoamerica – such as ceramics, obsidian, and chert – preserve well, and archaeologists have made great advances in reconstructing aspects of their production, exchange, and consumption. Other goods that are highly perishable – such as feathers, cacao, and textiles – are known to have been important from documentary sources. The study of ancient economics goes beyond these three topics, however, to include larger issues of how whole economies work as systems, how economic processes are related to political and social patterns, and how they change through time.

Agriculture

Mesoamerican agriculture was based on a group of food crops domesticated in the region during the Archaic period (see the general introduction to this volume). Maize or corn was the staple crop that supplied most of the calories and a good part of the protein of the traditional Mesoamerican diet. The importance of maize in Mesoamerica is hard to overstate because of its role in protein supply. In most traditional diets around the world, people get the bulk of their calories from a staple grain and their protein from meat, fish, or dairy products. The ancient cultures of the Old World had a variety of domesticated animals to provide protein, including cows, pigs, sheep, goats, and chickens; their calories typically came from wheat, barley, or rice. In Mesoamerica, however, the only fully domesticated animals were dogs, turkeys, and bees, although the Maya kept "tame" deer and peccaries in their yards. Dogs and turkeys were both eaten, but their small size limited their usefulness as sources of protein for growing populations. To make up for the lack of domesticated animals, the Mesoamerican peoples used a variety of wild food resources, and they relied extensively upon maize, a crop with some very special characteristics.

Maize has high concentrations of most of the essential amino acids that the human body needs to synthesize proteins, but two are lacking and another is chemically bound and not readily available. It turns out that beans have high quantities of the missing nutrients, and by eating maize and beans together at the same meal, people could obtain a "complete" and health supply of protein. To free the chemically-bound amino acid, Mesoamericans soaked their maize in an alkali solution (made by adding powdered limestone to water) before grinding the kernels. These two practices – serving maize and beans together and soaking the maize – are deeply ingrained traits that not only produce delicious meals but also ensure that maize provides adequate protein for human needs. The Mesoamerican diet, followed from Early Formative times through the present, is one of the few traditional world cuisines that can provide adequate protein without heavy supplements of meat or dairy products (Coe 1994; Katz et al. 1974).

Just as maize was eaten in a variety of forms in ancient (and modern) Mesoamerica – including tortillas, tamales, and other forms – the crop was grown under a variety of agricultural systems. The clearest influence on variation in farming systems was environmental. The diverse environments of Mesoamerica presented differing challenges to farmers, and people were creative in devising systems of cultivation to take advantage of each area's characteristic patterns of rainfall, soils, temperature, topography, and other features. Whitmore and Turner (chapter 5) illustrate the great variation in Mesoamerican agricultural systems for the Late Postclassic period by following three imaginary transects that cut across the area's major environmental zones. The study of ancient agricultural systems is a major focus of current research in Mesoamerica, and it is becoming clear that most or all of the conquest-era farming methods described by Whitmore and Turner were also used back to the Classic and Formative periods as well (Fedick 1996; Killion 1992; Rojas Rabiela and Sanders 1985; Scarborough and Isaac 1993; Wilken 1987).

Another important kind of variation in Mesoamerican agricultural systems is based upon the concept of intensification. "Intensive agriculture" refers to techniques that rely upon heavy inputs of labor in order to achieve high productivity per unit of land. Non-intensive (or extensive) agricultural methods, such as slash-and-burn, have lower yields, but it takes less labor to produce a given amount of food (Boserup 1965). People generally prefer to use non-intensive methods, since they require less labor. However, people can be forced to intensify their farming where populations are high and traditional non-intensive methods cannot produce enough food. All ancient state-level societies relied upon one or more methods of intensive agriculture because of their large populations (relative to non-state societies such as tribes). Also, the presence of social stratification in a society typically requires intensive agriculture, since the elite and various occupational specialists do not actually farm for themselves. In fact, ancient elites used institutions such as rent and tribute to force commoner farmers to intensify their farming in order to produce more goods for the elite's support and benefit.

In Mesoamerica, the major forms of intensive agriculture were canal irrigation (Doolittle 1990; Scarborough and Isaac 1993), terracing (Donkin 1979; Turner 1983), and raised fields (Sluyter 1994). Whitmore and Turner (chapter 5) describe these methods for the Late Postclassic period, and Smith and Heath-Smith (chapter 11) present archaeological information on Aztec-period terraces in Morelos (see also Smith and Price 1994). The social implications of agricultural intensification have been the subject of much debate in the social sciences generally, and in Mesoamerica specifically. One Mesoamerican example is the extent and role of raised field cultivation among the Classic Maya (see e.g. Adams et al. 1990; Chapin 1988; Pohl 1990; Pohl et al. 1996; Pope and Dahlin 1989; Siemens 1990; Sluyter 1994; Turner and Harrison 1983).

Craft Production

The technology and organization of craft production are major topics of research for all ancient civilizations. There are two reasons for this. First, many craft industries leave clear material remains that are easily recovered in excavations, and archaeologists have been very successful at reconstructing the details of ancient production of ceramics, lithics, and other materials. Second, craft production is an important component of ancient economies. For many decades, one of the hallmarks of archaeologists' definitions of state-level society has been the presence of specialized occupations (e.g. Childe 1950; Clark and Parry 1990), and craft specialization is one such occupation that can be studied archaeologically.

Of the various ancient crafts of Mesoamerica and elsewhere, chipped-stone tool production is one of the easiest to study because it is a "subtractive" process. The craftsperson begins with a large piece of stone and gradually removes, or subtracts, flakes to produce the desired tools. In the process, many waste flakes are produced, and their analysis provides abundant information about the locations and nature of the technological process. This kind of subtractive industry can be compared to "additive" industries such as ceramic production, where a variety of raw materials are brought together and combined to make the final product. When a potter is done making a series of pots, only a few materials remain for the archaeologists to find – supplies of raw clay, a few scrapers, smoothers and other tools, and perhaps molds or kilns. These latter items are reused numerous times and thus do not occur in large quantities. When a knapper is done making a series of stone tools, on the other hand, he or she has typically produced thousands of waste flakes that are considered garbage and will be discarded accordingly.

One of the most dramatic craft industries of ancient Mesoamerica was the chert tool industry at the Maya site of Colha. As described by Shafer and Hester (chapter 6), Colha is located on top of the most extensive deposit of high-grade chert in Mesoamerica, called the chert-bearing zone of Belize. Knappers at Colha mined this chert and produced literally millions of tools that were traded widely in the central Maya lowlands during all time periods. The archaeological deposits at Colha are unmatched in scale by workshop deposits elsewhere in the New World – with heaps of refuse comprised of as much as 150 cubic meters of chert flakes with little soil or other debris.

Although the Colha chert industry is one of the clearest cases of high-volume, specialized craft production in Mesoamerica, several archaeologists have criticized the findings of Shafer and Hester and claimed that this was not really specialized production, or that the production locations were not really workshops. Mallory (1986), for example, attacked an early article (Shafer and Hester 1983), arguing that it was unlikely that a small site without monumental architecture could have extensive specialized production, an inference that is clearly incorrect (see Shafer and Hester 1986). Later, Moholy-Nagy (1990) questioned the identification of lithic workshops at a number of Mesoamerican sites, including Colha, suggesting that the dense lithic debris deposits were not located in the original place where tools had been manufactured. Hester and Shafer (1992) responded that "identifying precise manufacturing loci is less important than assessing the overall scale of production at a site and that site's role in regional settlement systems" (p. 243); in any case, the Colha chert debris piles were almost certainly at or very close to the location where the debris was produced by knappers.

Colha is not alone as a case of well-documented specialized craft production that has been hotly debated; the Teotihuacan obsidian industry is another example. Obsidian tools and flakes are abundant and widely distributed at Teotihuacan, which is located very close to several of the major central Mexican obsidian source areas. Furthermore, obsidian from these sources has been found in Classic-period contexts at sites throughout Mesoamerica (see e.g. Drennan et al., chapter 8). Most archaeologists have concluded that obsidian production for both local use and for export was a major industry at Teotihuacan (Santley 1984, 1989; Spence 1981, 1987; see also Cowgill, chapter 15). Nevertheless, this view was challenged by Clark (1986), who suggested that the many "workshops" that Spence had reported at Teotihuacan may in fact represent dumps of debris of utilized blades that had been used by the city's occupants for other activities. Formal "workshop" areas should exhibit piles of unmodified production debris, as at Colha. It is possible, however, that production debris at Teotihuacan was later used for other purposes, making it difficult to identify the original workshop areas.

In our view, the original models of large-scale, specialized production at Colha and Teotihuacan were correct, although the various critiques make valuable points about the evidence and methods used to study lithic production. Part of the problem may be the very concept of "specialization" itself. In an important paper, Costin (1991) showed that the term specialization is commonly used to refer to at least four different aspects of the process of craft production, and different authors may emphasize different aspects. Costin's four components of specialization are: *intensity* (the nature of labor input, whether full-time or part-time); *scale* (the size and organization of facilities, from home-based work to industrial factories); *concentration* (the location and density of production locations); and *context* (whether specialists work independently for the market, or work under the direction and sponsorship of an elite patron, a pattern called "attached" production). To these we might add the notion of *production process*, referring to the organization of the various tasks that go into craft production (e.g. does one person complete the entire process, or are different tasks done by different people or in different locations?). Since the term "specialization" means so many different things, we suggest that archaeologists are better served by concen-trating on the individual components rather than arguing about whether craft production at particular sites was "specialized" or not.

Chert and obsidian chipped stone tools were some of the most important utilitarian goods in the economies of ancient Meso-america. Another important utilitarian item was ceramic vessels. Rice (chapter 7) reviews evidence for the production and exchange of ceramics in the lowland Maya economy. She shows that much ceramic production occurred in small settlements outside of the large Classic Maya cities (see also Rands and Bishop 1980). This finding, along with the Colha chert industry, supports the models of rural social and economic complexity discussed in the introduction to part I above. Brumfiel (1987) has shown that among the Aztecs, utilitarian goods were produced by part-time specialists, often living in rural areas (Smith and Heath-Smith, chapter 11), whereas luxury goods (defined as expensive items not used for utilitarian tasks in daily life) tended to be produced by full-time urban specialists attached to elite patrons (see Costin 1991 on "attached specialization"). Ethnohistoric sources on the Aztecs describe several types of full-time specialists who made luxury goods, largely for elite consumption. These included feather-workers, stone sculptors, and goldsmiths (Smith 1996: ch. 4). Several authors have suggested similar arrangements for the production of fancy Classic Maya polychrome vessels, with the difference that the artists may have been low-ranking nobles rather than commoners attached to noble patrons (Ball 1993; McAnany 1993; Reents-Budet 1994, 1998).

Exchange

Exchange or trade has been a major topic of research for ancient Mesoamerica, because like craft production, exchange was an important process that often left clear archaeological evidence. As pointed out in the general introduction to this volume, the varied environments of Mesoamerica led people in individual settlements and regions to specialize in particular products, which they exchanged with peoples in other areas. The volume and nature of trade in Mesoamerica were limited by the available technology of transport. Although the concept of the wheel was known in Mesoamerica (as shown by wheeled toys found at many sites), it was not applied to working vehicles because of the absence of draft animals and the mountainous terrain in many areas. Transport by water was limited to coastal regions and a few major rivers. This left human carriers as the major means of transporting goods between regions. Compared to travel by water and wheeled vehicles, human carriers are a very "expensive" means of transport since they must be fed, sometimes from the loads they are carrying. This led to an emphasis on high-value, low-bulk goods for long-distance exchange in Mesoamerica (Drennan 1984; Rice, chapter 7).

Although the kings of powerful states could command that bulky grains and other foodstuffs be brought from great distances, this was probably rare in ancient Mesoamerica. The Aztec empire, the most powerful state in ancient Mesoamerica, did receive grains as tribute from distant provinces (Berdan and Anawalt 1997), but the quantities were small and their significance may have been more symbolic than real. In fact, most of the food to feed the inhabitants of Tenochtitlan came from its immediate hinterland in the Valley of Mexico (Parsons 1976). This was typical of Mesoamerican cities, most of which obtained food from their nearby regions. The general pattern was for food and bulky utilitarian goods to be obtained locally and exchanged within individual regions, whereas luxury goods and other high-value, low-bulk items were exchanged over large distances (Rice, chapter 7). Of all of the basic utilitarian goods used in Mesoamerican households, one stood out from this pattern as an important long-distance trade good – obsidian.

Obsidian is unusual compared to other domestic goods like pottery vessels or grinding stones in that a large number of finished tools can be made from a relatively modest amount of raw material. As a result, obsidian can be easily transported and made an excellent trade good. As a naturally occurring volcanic glass, obsidian only occurs in a few regions of Mesoamerica. The obsidian from each geological source area has a distinctive chemical fingerprint consisting of characteristic quantities of minor inclusions called "trace elements." When analyzed chemically for these trace elements, obsidian artifacts can be assigned to their geological place of origin, thereby allowing the reconstruction of trade connections. The most accurate technique for doing this is known as neutron activation analysis, which has been applied to a number of sets of artifacts in Mesoamerica (e.g. Cobean et al. 1991). The difficulty with this method is that it requires expensive sophisticated instruments that are not widely available, and the cost to archaeologists can be quite high. There are several simpler and less expensive techniques that are not as precise as neutron activation analysis but can still accurately source most obsidian artifacts. Of these, X-ray fluorescence is the most commonly used for sourcing Mesoamerican obsidian (e.g. Jackson and Love 1991; Pollard and Vogel 1994). This is the method used by Drennan et al. (chapter 8) in their study of Classic-period highland obsidian trade.

One of the implications of the obsidian research described in chapter 8 is that ancient Mesoamerican exchange systems could be complex and multifaceted. This point is made even more explicitly in Berdan's article (chapter 9) on the organization of long-distance trade among the Aztecs. Full-time Aztec guild-based merchants known as *pochteca* are described in Fray Bernardino de Sahagún's *Florentine Codex* (Sahagún 1950–82), and these are well known to students of the Aztecs. Other types of Aztec merchants are very poorly known, and Berdan describes the scattered references to these. Again, the implication is that the Aztec economy was quite complex and multi-layered.

Berdan's chapter points out the need to look at exchange on a variety of levels. The smallest level is the local environment of a settlement, where much of the food and other resources typically originate. The next level is the region, which corresponds to an area integrated by extensive exchange relationships. In Mesoamerica at the time of the Spanish conquest, regions were held together economically through systems of periodic markets (Freidel 1981; Smith 1996: ch. 5). Merchants traveled among local markets buying and selling, and people attended their local market on the weekly market day (every five days in the ancient Mesoamerican calendar). Several types of currency were used, including cacao beans for small purchases and cotton textiles for more costly items. Regional market systems remained important in Mesoamerica in the Colonial and modern periods, and they are still prominent features in most parts of Mesoamerica today (Cook and Diskin 1976). How far back can market systems be traced prior to the Late Postclassic period? This is a difficult question to answer, although many archaeologists believe that markets were common at least back to the Classic period (e.g. Blanton et al. 1993; Freidel 1981; Hirth 1998).

Although most exchange took place between settlements and households within regions, long-distance exchange between regions was also important for luxury goods, obsidian, textiles, and sometimes other goods. This larger scale of exchange was almost always conducted between independent states. Although long-distance trade did take place within large polities such as the Aztec empire (Berdan, chapter 9), these polities also engaged in exchange with peoples and states outside of their territory. For example, bronze bells and tools manufactured in the Tarascan territory of Michoacan have been found in Aztec sites in central Mexico (Hosler 1994; Hosler and Macfarlane 1996), even though these two empires were hostile and in a state of constant warfare. When exchange between independent states is extensive and important to the individual societies, scholars often employ a world-systems approach to help understand the dynamics of such systems. Feinman and Nicholas (chapter 10) illus-

trate this approach for ancient Mesoamerica, contrasting the world systems approach with the cultural ecology approach and applying it to central Mexico in Aztec times and to Oaxaca at various periods.

The notion that exchange should be studied at a variety of levels, from the local to the macroregional, is implicit in many of the chapters in this section. Good case studies of this approach in Mesoamerica include Flannery (1976) and McAnany (1991). Can ethnohistoric details of Aztec exchange systems be projected back into the past, to Teotihuacan, Monte Alban, or the Maya? There is as yet no scholarly consensus on this point, and students should consider this question when reading the chapters in this section.

Consumption

Consumption refers to the ways in which people consume or use goods. After tools, pots, and other goods are manufactured they are exchanged, and after they are exchanged most of these goods are brought home and used in domestic contexts. Once household goods were broken or worn out, many ancient peoples (in Mesoamerica and elsewhere) simply tossed them out into their yard, where they formed garbage heaps called middens for archaeologists to find (Hayden and Cannon 1983; Schiffer 1987). The artifacts in these middens provide direct evidence for household consumption patterns, often revealing information about the activities and conditions of the people whose garbage is studied. The reconstruction of activities is one of the basic approaches in the study of ancient consumption patterns. Sometimes artifacts and features are arranged spatially so that particular "activity areas" can be identified, as in chapters 1 and 4 above (see also Kent 1987). In other cases, the remains of individual activities have been heavily disturbed so that particular locations or activity areas cannot be identified. Then the archaeologist must analyze middens and reconstruct general patterns of activities and conditions, as in Smith and Heath-Smith's study of rural Aztec domestic contexts (chapter 11).

In the reconstruction of consumption patterns, one of the first tasks is to determine the uses or functions of artifacts. Archaeologists rely heavily on ethnographic analogy for this, particularly in areas like Mesoamerica where many traditional practices have survived in remote and rural areas (Deal 1998; Lesure 1998). In addition to basic domestic items such as ceramic cooking and serving vessels, obsidian and chert tools, and grinding stones, Smith and Heath-Smith identify a number of special-purpose artifacts such as whorls and bowls for spinning cotton thread, "bark beaters" for manufacturing paper, and censers for burning incense. These artifacts document a wide variety of household activities beyond the basic necessities of food and shelter.

The functions and significance of particular goods sometimes changed over time, and archaeologists must be alert to identify this process. Obsidian in the Maya area is a good example. Rice (chapter 7) suggests that during the Classic period, obsidian was a luxury good in the Maya lowlands. Household cutting tasks were performed most often with chert from Colha and other production areas, and the small number of obsidian blades and their contexts suggests that they were used in elite rituals of bloodletting (Freidel 1986a; Spence 1996). Later, in Postclassic times, obsidian became more widely available and it was transformed from a luxury good to a utilitarian good. This contrasts with the situation in central Mexico, where obsidian blades were utilitarian goods throughout the Prehispanic period.

Another important component of consumption is the study of variation in wealth and status. As discussed in part I, class differences are often expressed in domestic artifact inventories (Haviland and Moholy-Nagy, chapter 2). Smith and Heath-Smith (chapter 11) provide an Aztec case study of this phenomenon. At these rural sites, elite and commoner residences are clearly differentiated by architecture, and these class distinctions can be seen in the household artifacts. Surprisingly, no single category of material was found only in elite contexts,

and even the most valuable long-distance trade items (jade beads and bronze tools) were often recovered at commoner houses. Nevertheless, elites and commoners differed in the quantities of particular types of imported and decorated ceramic vessels (see also Freidel 1986b).

Economic Processes and Issues

Once the individual components of ancient economies – production, exchange, and consumption of particular goods – have been reconstructed, attention turns to larger issues, such as how whole economies worked as systems, how economic processes related to other social processes, and how economies changed through time. At this higher level of analysis, there is ample opportunity for argument. For example, the role of elites and the state in controlling the economy has been debated for decades. Brumfiel and Earle's (1987) three models of elites and the economy (see above) are relevant here. Did elites manage the economy for everyone's benefit, did they control the economy for their own gain, or were large parts of the economy outside of elite control? We urge students to consider these three models in reading the chapters in this section; this should provide ample opportunity for discussion and debate.

REFERENCES

Adams, R. E. W., J. P. Culbert, W. E. Brown, P. D. Harrison, and L. J. Levi. 1990. Rebuttal to Pope and Dahlin. *Journal of Field Archaeology* 17: 241–4.

Ball, Joseph W. 1993. Pottery, Potters, Palaces, and Polities: Some Socioeconomic and Political Implications of Late Classic Maya Ceramic Industries. In *Lowland Maya Civilization in the Eighth Century* AD, edited by Jeremy A. Sabloff and John S. Henderson, pp. 243–72. Dumbarton Oaks, Washington, DC.

Berdan, Frances R. and Patricia Reiff Anawalt (eds). 1997. *The Essential Codex Mendoza*. University of California Press, Berkeley.

Blanton, Richard E., Stephen A. Kowalewski, Gary M. Feinman, and Laura M. Finsten. 1993. *Ancient Mesoamerica: A Comparison of*

Change in Three Regions. 2nd edn. Cambridge University Press, New York.

Boserup, Esther. 1965. *The Conditions of Agricultural Growth: The Economics of Agrarian Change Under Population Pressure*. Aldine, Chicago.

Brumfiel, Elizabeth M. 1987. Elite and Utilitarian Crafts in the Aztec State. In *Specialization, Exchange, and Complex Societies*, edited by Elizabeth M. Brumfiel and Timothy K. Earle, pp. 102–18. Cambridge University Press, New York.

Brumfiel, Elizabeth M. and Timothy K. Earle. 1987. Specialization, Exchange, and Complex Societies: An Introduction. In *Specialization, Exchange, and Complex Societies*, edited by Elizabeth M. Brumfiel and Timothy K. Earle, pp. 1–9. Cambridge University Press, New York.

Chapin, Mac. 1988. The Seduction of Models: Chinampa Agriculture in Mexico. *Grassroots Development* 12: 8–17.

Childe, V. Gordon. 1950. The Urban Revolution. *Town Planning Review* 21: 3–17.

Clark, John E. 1986. From Mountains to Molehills: A Critical Review of Teotihuacan's Obsidian Industry. In *Economic Aspects of Prehispanic Highland Mexico*, edited by Barry L. Isaac, vol. 2, pp. 23–74. Research in Economic Anthropology, Supplement. JAI Press, Greenwich, CT.

Clark, John E. and William J. Parry. 1990. Craft Specialization and Cultural Complexity. In *Research in Economic Anthropology*, edited by Barry L. Isaac, vol. 12, pp. 289–346. JAI Press, Greenwich, CT.

Cobean, Robert H., James R. Vogt, Michael D. Glascock, and Terrence L. Stocker. 1991. High-Precision Trace Element Characterization of Major Mesoamerican Obsidian Sources and Further Analysis of Artifacts from San Lorenzo Tenochititlan, Mexico. *Latin American Antiquity* 2: 69–91.

Coe, Sophie D. 1994. *America's First Cuisines*. University of Texas Press, Austin.

Cook, Scott and Martin Diskin (eds). 1976. *Markets in Oaxaca*. University of Texas Press, Austin.

Costin, Cathy L. 1991. Craft Specialization: Issues in Defining, Documenting, and Explaining the Organization of Production. *Archaeological Method and Theory* 3: 1–56.

Deal, Michael. 1998. *Pottery Ethnoarchaeology in the Central Maya Highlands*. University of Utah Press, Salt Lake City.

Donkin, R. A. 1979. *Agricultural Terracing in the Aboriginal New World*. Viking Fund Publications in Anthropology 56. University of Arizona Press, Tucson.

Doolittle, William E. 1990. *Canal Irrigation in Prehistoric Mexico: The Sequence of Technological Change*. University of Texas Press, Austin.

Drennan, Robert D. 1984. Long-Distance Transport Costs in Pre-Hispanic Mesoamerica. *American Anthropologist* 86: 105–12.

Fedick, Scott L. (ed.). 1996. *The Managed Mosaic: Ancient Maya Agriculture and Resource Use*. University of Utah Press, Salt Lake City.

Flannery, Kent V. 1976. Empirical Determination of Site Catchments in Oaxaca. In *The Early Mesoamerican Village*, edited by Kent V. Flannery, pp. 103–16. Academic Press, New York.

Freidel, David A. 1981. The Political Economics of Residential Dispersion Among the Lowland Maya. In *Lowland Maya Settlement Patterns*, edited by Wendy Ashmore, pp. 371–85. University of New Mexico Press, Albuquerque.

—— 1986a. The Mesoamerican World. *Latin American Research Review* 21: 231–41.

—— 1986b. New Light on a Dark Age: Terminal Classic Lowland Maya: Successes, Failures, Aftermaths. In *Late Lowland Maya Civilization: Classic to Postclassic*, edited by Jeremy A. Sabloff and E. Wyllys Andrews, pp. 409–30. University of New Mexico Press, Albuquerque.

Hayden, Brian and Aubry Cannon. 1983. Where the Garbage Goes: Refuse Disposal in the Maya Highlands. *Journal of Anthropological Archaeology* 2: 117–63.

Hester, Thomas R. and Harry J. Shafer. 1992. Lithic Workshops Revisited: Comments on Moholy-Nagy. *Latin American Antiquity* 3: 243–9.

Hirth, Kenneth G. 1998. The Distributional Approach: A New Way to Identify Marketplace Exchange in the Archaeological Record. *Current Anthropology* 39: 451–76.

Hosler, Dorothy. 1994. *The Sounds and Colors of Power: The Sacred Metallurgical Technology of Ancient West Mexico*. MIT Press, Cambridge.

Hosler, Dorothy and Andrew Macfarlane. 1996. Copper Sources, Metal Production and Metals Trade in Late Postclassic Mesoamerica. *Science* 273: 1819–24.

Jackson, Thomas L. and Michael W. Love. 1991. Blade Running: Middle Preclassic Obsidian Exchange and the Introduction of Prismatic Blades at La Blanca, Guatemala. *Ancient Mesoamerica* 2: 47–60.

Katz, S. H., M. L. Hediger and L. A. Valleroy. 1974. Traditional Maize Processing Techniques in the New World. *Science* 184: 765–73.

Kent, Susan (ed.). 1987. *Method and Theory for Activity Area Research: An Ethnoarchaeological*

Approach. Columbia University Press, New York.

Killion, Thomas (ed.). 1992. *Gardens of Prehistory: The Archaeology of Settlement Agriculture in Greater Mesoamerica*. University of Alabama Press, Tuscaloosa.

Lesure, Richard G. 1998. Vessel Form and Function in an Early Formative Ceramic Assemblage From Coastal Mexico. *Journal of Field Archaeology* 25: 19–36.

Mallory, John K. 1986. "Workshops" and "Specialized Production" in the Production of Maya Chert Tools: A Response to Shafer and Hester. *American Antiquity* 51: 152–8.

McAnany, Patricia A. 1991. Structure and Dynamics of Intercommunity Exchange. In *Maya Stone Tools: Selected Papers From the Second Maya Lithic Conference*, edited by Thomas R. Hester and Harry J. Shafer, pp. 271–93. Prehistory Press, Madison, WI.

—— 1993. The Economics of Social Power and Wealth Among 8th Century Maya Households. In *Lowland Maya Civilization in the Eighth Century* AD, edited by Jeremy A. Sabloff and John S. Henderson, pp. 65–89. Dumbarton Oaks, Washington, DC.

Moholy-Nagy, Hattula. 1990. The Misidentification of Mesoamerican Lithic Workshops. *Latin American Antiquity* 1: 191–215.

Parsons, Jeffrey R. 1976. The Role of Chinampa Agriculture in the Food Supply of Aztec Tenochtitlan. In *Cultural Change and Continuity: Essays in Honor of James B. Griffin*, edited by Charles Cleland, pp. 233–57. Academic Press, New York.

Pohl, Mary D. (ed,). 1990. *Ancient Maya Wetland Agriculture: Excavations on Albion Island, Northern Belize*. Westview Press, Boulder.

Pohl, Mary D. et al. 1996. Early Agriculture in the Maya Lowlands. *Latin American Antiquity* 7: 355–72.

Pollard, Helen P. and Thomas A. Vogel. 1994. Late Postclassic Imperial Expansion and Economic Exchange within the Tarascan Domain. In *Economies and Polities in the Aztec Realm*, edited by Mary G. Hodge and Michael E. Smith, pp. 447–70. Institute for Mesoamerican Studies, Albany.

Pope, Kevin O. and Bruce H. Dahlin. 1989. Ancient Maya Wetland Agriculture: New Insights from Ecological and Remote Sensing Research. *Journal of Field Archaeology* 16: 87–106.

Rands, Robert L. and Ronald L. Bishop. 1980. Resource Procurement Zones and Patterns of Ceramic Exchange in the Palenque Region,

Mexico. In *Models and Methods in Regional Exchange*, edited by Robert E. Fry, vol. 1, pp. 19–46. Papers. Society for American Archaeology, Washington, DC.

Reents-Budet, Dorie. 1994. *Painting the Maya Universe: Royal Ceramics of the Classic Period*. Duke University Press, Durham, NC.

—— 1998. Elite Maya Pottery and Artisans as Social Indicators. In *Craft and Social Identity*, edited by Cathy Lynne Costin and Rita P. Wright, pp. 71–89. Archaeological Papers of the American Anthropological Association, vol. 8. American Anthropological Association, Washington, DC.

Rojas Rabiela, Teresa and William T. Sanders (eds). 1985. *Historia de la Agricultura: Epoca Prehispánica – Siglo XVI*. 2 vols. Instituto Nacional de Antropología e Historia, Mexico City.

Sahagún, Fray Bernardino de. 1950–82. *Florentine Codex, General History of the Things of New Spain. 12 books. Translated and edited by Arthur J. O. Anderson and Charles E. Dibble*. School of American Research and the University of Utah Press, Santa Fe and Salt Lake City.

Santley, Robert S. 1984. Obsidian Exchange, Economic Stratification, and the Evolution of Complex Society in the Basin of Mexico. In *Trade and Exchange in Early Mesoamerica*, edited by Kenneth G. Hirth, pp. 43–86. University of New Mexico Press, Albuquerque.

—— 1989. Obsidian Working, Long-Distance Exchange, and the Teotihuacan Presence on the South Gulf Coast. In *Mesoamerica After the Decline of Teotihuacan, AD 700–900*, edited by Richard A. Diehl and Janet C. Berlo, pp. 131–51. Dumbarton Oaks, Washington, DC.

Scarborough, Vernon L. and Barry L. Isaac (eds). 1993. *Economic Aspects of Water Management in the Prehispanic New World*. Research in Economic Anthropology, Supplement 7. JAI Press, Greenwich, CT.

Schiffer, Michael B. 1987. *Formation Processes of the Archaeological Record*. University of New Mexico Press, Albuquerque.

Shafer, Harry J. and Thomas R. Hester. 1983. Ancient Maya Chert Workshops in Northern Belize, Central America. *American Antiquity* 48: 519–43.

—— 1986. Maya Stone-Tool Craft Specialization and Production at Colha, Belize: Reply to Mallory. *American Antiquity* 51: 158–67.

Siemens, Alfred H. 1990. Reducing the Risk: Some Indications Regarding Pre-Hispanic Wetland Agriculture Intensification from

Contemporary use of a Wetland/Terra Firm Boundary Zone. In *Central Veracruz Archaeology: Researching the Ecological Basis for Sustainable Agriculture*, edited by Steven R. Gliessman, pp. 233–50. Springer-Verlag, New York.

Sluyter, Andrew. 1994. Intensive Wetland Agriculture in Mesoamerica: Space, Time and Form. *Annals of the Association of American Geographers* 84: 557–84.

Smith, Michael E. 1996. *The Aztecs*. Blackwell, Oxford.

Smith, Michael E. and T. Jeffrey Price. 1994. Aztec-Period Agricultural Terraces in Morelos, Mexico: Evidence for Household-Level Agricultural Intensification. *Journal of Field Archaeology* 21: 169–79.

Spence, Michael W. 1981. Obsidian Production and the State in Teotihuacan. *American Antiquity* 32: 769–88.

——— 1987. The Scale and Structure of Obsidian Production in Teotihuacan. In *Teotihuacán: Nuevos Datos, Nuevas Síntesis, Nuevos Problemas*, edited by Emily McClung de Tapia and Evelyn C. Rattray, pp. 439–50. Universidad Nacional Autónoma de México, Mexico City.

——— 1996. Commodity or Gift: Teotihuacan Obsidian in the Maya Region. *Latin American Antiquity* 7: 21–39.

Turner, B. L., II. 1983. *Once Beneath the Forest: Prehistoric Terracing in the Río Bec Region of the Maya Lowlands*. Westview Press, Boulder.

Turner, B. L., II and Peter D. Harrison (eds). 1983. *Pulltrouser Swamp: Ancient Maya Habitat, Agriculture, and Settlement in Northern Belize*. University of Texas Press, Austin.

Wilken, Gene C. 1987. *Good Farmers: Traditional Agricultural Resource Management in Mexico and Central America*. University of California Press, Berkeley.

CHAPTER 5

Landscapes of Cultivation in Mesoamerica on the Eve of the Conquest

Thomas M. Whitmore and B. L. Turner II

The Columbian Encounter opened the world to the treasures of Amerindian plant domestication, the impacts of which would be global in reach and range far beyond agriculture per se. The potato, for example, increased the caloric base of northern Europe, facilitating its exponential population growth after 1750, while maize, manioc, sweet potato, and peanut became dietary mainstays for much of the rest of the world (Hamilton 1976: 856–7, 860). Amerindian cotton was literally the fabric of the industrialization of textiles (Sauer 1976: 818), and tobacco claims the dubious distinction of "vice of choice" for much of the world.

Less well known is that these and other Amerindian domesticates of global significance (e.g. avocado, bean, cacao, chile, papaya, squash, and tomato) coevolved with equally impressive systems of cultivation. Long before the Columbian Encounter, Amerindian agriculturalists had developed technologies and management practices with which to crop a wide range of environments and ecological conditions, giving rise to a variety of landscapes of cultivation. This variety was particularly evident in Mesoamerica, where advanced material culture and state organization extended from the southern border of the Bajío in Central Mexico southeastward to Guatemala, including parts of Belize, Honduras, Nicaragua, and Costa Rica (figure 5.1). Some of these cultivated landscapes consisted of intermingled or patchwork-like microsystems, fine-tuned to small-scale environmental variations, while others were dominated by zonal patterns keyed to the broad environmental zones created by elevation, aspect, and slope.

The *conquistadores* marveled at these landscapes, even as they sowed the seeds of change. A new rendering of the land emerged at a pace only slightly slower than that of the conquest itself. Within fifty years of Columbus's initial landfall, Spanish hegemony over Middle America (the Caribbean, Mexico, and Central America) was complete and, in the course of the sixteenth century, most of the cultivated landscapes of Mesoamerica had been forever altered from their former condition. This alteration followed not only from changes in control of the land, but from the introduction of exotic biota, technologies, and management practices as well.

The cultivated landscapes of the preconquest Amerindians and the implications of their transformation, especially in Mesoamerica, have been the subject of rather polarized views, many of which have been empirically uninformed. Amerindian agriculture has not always been fully appreciated, the scale of environmental degradation associated with Spanish transformation of this agriculture has been overstated at times, and the contrasting ideologies of

Reprinted from Thomas M. Whitmore and B. L. Turner II. 1992. Landscapes of Cultivation in Mesoamerica on the Eve of the Conquest. *Annals of the Association of American Geographers* 82: 402–25.

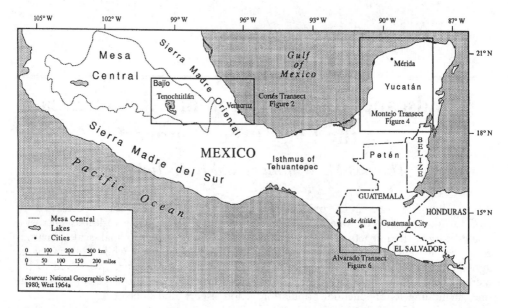

Figure 5.1   Mesoamerica, locating Cortés, Montejo, and Alvarado transects. (Adapted from National Geographic Society 1980 as base map only, and West 1964a for other locational information.)

nature between the two cultures has been oversimplified.

Here we explore the indigenous cultivated landscapes that were witnessed by the Spanish adventurers as they existed about the time of the Columbian Encounter. Our primary objective is to illustrate the variety of these landscapes through the examination of three transects traversing different environmental and sociopolitical terrain. Each transect approximates the course of one of the initial Spanish entradas through this diverse region: the "Cortés transect" extends to central Mexico from the Gulf coast, the "Montejo transect" traverses the Yucatán peninsula from north to south, and the "Alvarado transect" climbs into highland Guatemala from the Pacific coastal plain (figure 5.1). Second, we broadly sketch the major changes that took place in these landscapes during the first phase of Spanish domination and some of the forces that shaped these changes. Our intent is neither to mythologize the accomplishments of the Amerindians nor to vilify the conquerors, but to illustrate the magnitude and breadth of the changes that took place in the cultiv-

ated landscapes of Mesoamerica as a result of the Columbian Encounter.

The Cortés Transect

Cortés and his small band probably first saw the snowcapped summit of Orizaba (5,639 m) from ship's deck in the vicinity of modern Veracruz, Mexico. From that vantage point, they were observing the eastern flanks of the Aztec empire, a domain that stretched east–west from the Gulf of Mexico to the Pacific Ocean and north–south from the Bajío to the Isthmus of Tehuantepec (figures 5.1 and 5.2). More properly identified with the "Triple Alliance" of the city states of Tenochtitlán, Texcoco, and Tacuba in the Basin of Mexico (Gibson 1964: 17), the empire has taken its popular name from the dominant Mexica (Tenochtitlán) and their mythical homeland, Aztlan. The Alliance commanded a political and economic realm unparalleled in Mesoamerican history, complete with a supreme ruler, professional armies and merchants, and a system of taxation and marketing that siphoned the wealth of the empire into its lacustrine

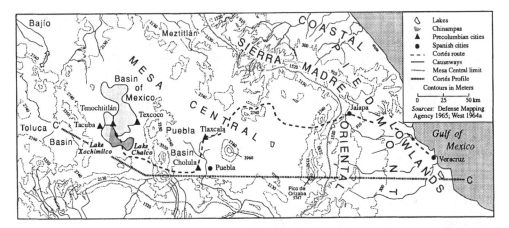

Figure 5.2 Cortés Transect, showing Central Mexico, Cortés's route, and the path of the Cortés Profile C–C′ (see Figure 5.3). (Adapted from US Defense Mapping Agency 1965 as a base map and West 1964a for other locational information.)

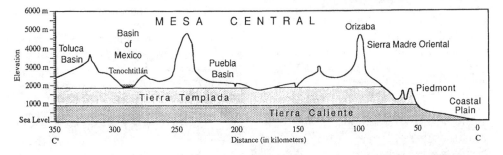

Figure 5.3 Cortés Profile, showing vertical relief along C–C′ transect, as noted in Figure 5.2. (Based on figure 5.2.)

heart. Population estimates for Central Mexico, roughly corresponding with the empire, range from < 10 million–>50 million (Denevan 1992: 77–84).

This transect parallels the Cortés route and crosses virtually every major climatic and agroecological zone in Mesoamerica: the hot and humid *tierra caliente* of the Gulf Coast Plains, the *tierra templada* (temperate land) of the coastal piedmont and the basins on the *altiplano* or Mesa Central, and the upper reaches of the sierras that separate the basins from one another (figures 5.2 and 5.3). Each of these broad realms, with the exception of the cold lands and steep slopes of the sierras, was orchestrated and transformed into landscapes of cultivation.

Gulf coastal plain and piedmont

The area of the Spaniards' landfall was inhabited by the Totonac who mastered the seasonal rhythm and environmental variation of the coastal plain and piedmont to produce crops for local subsistence as well as tribute, and possible commerce, with the Aztec empire (Barlow 1949; Hassig 1985: 114, 115; Stark 1990: 269). The coastal plains and hills offered a complex mosaic of microenvironmental opportunities and constraints for agriculture. The cultivated landscapes encountered in this complex natural terrain consisted of a patchwork of different cultivation types interspersed with forests and scrub land. It is even likely that the forests were managed and may have sheltered orchards. The Totonac orchestrated their year-round cultivation with the spatial and temporal variations in soil-water conditions, working the well-drained lands during the rainy season, and the inundated lands in the dry season (Siemens et al. 1988; Siemens 1992; Wilkerson 1983: 58). The landscape configured by these practices led Spaniards to describe the low-lands around Zempoala as "a garden with luxuriant vegetation" (Diaz del Castillo 1956: 87).

The mainstay of Totonac agriculture (and Mesoamerican agriculture generally) was rainfed cultivation or *temporal*. In the Gulf Coast area, such cultivation dominated the well-drained, usually sloping, terrain and incorporated terraces with rock-walled, earthen, and probably also earth and *maguey* (*metepantli*) embankments (Rojas Rabiela 1988: 118; Sluyter 1990: 20–37, 51–3; Wilkerson 1983: 64, 76).

Perhaps as important, however, were a variety of wetland adaptations that allowed cultivation during the marked dry season (Siemens 1983: 87, 1990: 117; Vivió Escoto 1964: 212; West 1964b: 58). In some instances, the margins of wetlands and levees were cultivated as water receded in the dry season, facilitated by the use of small drainage ditches. In others, more elaborate networks of canals were used to create field systems in wetlands proper. Siemens (1982, 1983) believes that these more elaborate networks may also have functioned in a flood-recessional manner. Contemporary flood-recessional cultivation in the Gulf Coast (and elsewhere) does not employ the elaborate and major canal networks found in the relics of the ancient systems. Thus we suspect that the cultivation associated with wetlands proper may have functioned through most of the year rather than only during recession of the floods.

Relics of walls and embankments on dry-lands and fields and canals in wetlands are abundant in the Gulf Coast area, although dating their continued use up to the eve of conquest is difficult to establish (Sluyter

1990; Siemens 1982, 1983). Indeed, Siemens et al. (1988: 107) found evidence that at least one wetland system in Veracruz was probably abandoned 500–700 years before the Columbian Encounter. Further southeast, however, Spanish accounts describe conditions that imply wetland cultivation in the sixteenth century (Pohl 1985). This evidence, the relatively large populations along portions of the Gulf Coast (López de Gómara 1964: 91; Stark 1978: 214–19; Wilkerson 1983: 55), and the amount of tribute extracted by the Aztec from the area (Barlow 1949), lead us to suspect that many of the relic agricultural features found throughout the Gulf Coast zone may have been operating at the time of Spanish contact. These issues require further investigation. In addition, Wilkerson (1983: 81) speculates that runoff and other types of irrigation were used in the area.

It can also be presumed that two types of orchard-gardens were found in the area: the ubiquitous *solar* or *calmil*, carefully tended household gardens providing vegetables, fruits, condiments, medicinals, and fiber products (Siemens 1983: 97); and orchards, especially of cacao and various fruits grown for commercial purposes and tribute (Bergmann 1969: 86, 88; Millon 1955: 705; Schmidt 1977: 57; Stark 1974: 204, 210, 1978: 215). Orchard species may have been cultivated as special plots (see Montejo Transect), and/or they may have been integrated within managed forests as described by Alcorn (1984) for the modern Huastec.

Field management practices were probably similar to those used in the *altiplano*, including *montones* (mounded soil) or *camellones* (ridged or furrowed soil) and possibly transplanting from seedbeds (*almácigos* or *tlalacalli*) (Rojas Rabiela 1988: 33, 74–5, 82; Schmidt 1977: 57). While maize dominated, ethnohistorical and ethnographic analogs suggest that fields were intercropped with beans, squash, cotton, maguey (*Agave spp.*), *tuna* (*Opuntia spp.*) or root crops (Rojas Rabiela 1988: 93; Sluyter 1990: 56, 62; Stark 1974: 205, 1978: 216).

Sierra Madre Oriental

The eastern versant of the Sierra Madre Oriental presented a formidable escarpment separating the Gulf coastal plains and piedmont from the mineral wealth and cooler climates on the *altiplano*. Its ascent took the Spaniards from the *tierra caliente* to the *tierra templada* and, ultimately the *tierra fría* beyond the 2,000–3,000 m saddle of the range (figure 5.2). The slope is steep and rugged throughout, dissected by the deep, narrow canyons of the Gulf-bound streams (West 1964b: 52–3). Much of the mountain slope receives large amounts of orographically-induced rainfall (2000 mm–3000 mm annually), giving rise to cloud forests near the crest (Vivió Escoto 1964: 201).

This escarpment was an agricultural transition zone perhaps shaped less by agroecological conditions than by declining population pressures between the piedmont and the upper slopes. The piedmont apparently was a landscape of terraces, and Siemens (1990: 145) quotes a nineteenth-century German resident who described "terraces...on every slope." As slopes grew steeper, however, the intensity of cultivation diminished to a shifting type, although fog moisture in the dry season supported two maize crops annually in a single field in some locations (Rojas Rabiela 1988: 78). Gutiérrez Ruvalcaba (1994: 135) notes sixteenth-century cultivation frequencies in the Sierra Madre Oriental of 1:8–1:10 (i.e. 1 year of cultivation and 8–10 years of fallow for each *milpa* plot). Another source notes shorter cycle periods (1:4–1:5) for the same region (the Colonial-era province of Meztitlán on the present-day Hildago-Veracruz border [Rojas Rabiela 1988: 62]).[1] Local inhabitants also may have employed a vertical zonation strategy, cultivating plots at different elevations to reduce risk and augment production (Gutiérrez Ruvalcaba 1994; Siemens 1990: 144).

Mesa Central

Crossing the Sierra, the Spaniards entered the great semiarid volcanic basins and ranges of the Mesa Central, encountering landscapes that they found more familiar and appealing than those of the *tierra caliente* (figures 5.2 and 5.3). Here, a large Amerindian population was arranged in settlement hierarchies dominated by city-states whose hinterlands spread across basin floors and up the surrounding slopes. Agriculture formed the basis of subsistence and commerce among city-states and was central to the tribute extracted by the Aztec.

The Mesa Central is composed of broad, flat-floored basins ringed by imposing volcanoes and broad slopes (West 1964b: 42, 47), many of which offered fertile soils for agriculture (Stevens 1964: 195–296; West 1964b: 47). Most of this area is above 1800 m (figures 5.2 and 5.3). Here, Mesoamerican crop production was limited by recurrent frosts and low levels of precipitation (Sanders et al. 1979: 230) (mean annual precipitation ranges from 250 mm to 1,000 mm) combined with high annual variability (Vivió Escoto 1964: 199). Paradoxically, poor interior drainage gave rise to various wetlands on the basin floors.

While each basin differed according to its features and occupation, commonality of use gave rise to a characteristic pattern of cultivated landscapes.[2] The upper *sierras* remained in forest, a source of wood and regulator of water. Below the forest line, rainfed terraced and semiterraced cultivation dominated. Various forms of floodwater irrigation were pursued within ephemeral water courses and along lands adjacent to them, including the edges of the basins' floors into which the drainages emptied. On the basin floor proper, where poor drainage was common, various kinds of wetland cultivation were adapted to the perihumid conditions.

Small clusters of villages and hamlets were scattered across the landscape. Their intensively cultivated gardens produced food crops, condiments, ornaments, and medicinal plants (Evans 1990: 117, 126; Palerm 1955; Rojas Rabiela 1988: 92–3, 1991: 109–10). Specialized orchards of avocado, *nopal de grana* (the cacti hosting the cochineal insect used for red dye, *Opuntia* spp.), *maguey* (agave or century plant, *Agave spp.*), *tejocote* (Mexican hawthorn, *Crataegus mexicana*), *capulín* (capulin cherry, *Prunus capuli*) and other fruits occupied favored niches (Rojas Rabiela 1988: 93, 1991: 112–18).

Rainfed cultivation dominated spatially, although its forms were adapted to the varying terrain.³ Upper and lower slopes were embraced by flights of sloping *metepantli* (semi-terraces) which preserved soil and soil moisture (Donkin 1979: 131; Patrick 1985; Rojas Rabiela 1988: 118–19; Sanders 1981: 192). More than a simple slope adjustment, *metepantli* incorporated food and fiber production into the terrace by using *maguey* or *nopal* cacti as berm anchors (Evans 1990: 125; Patrick 1985: 542; Wilken 1979). Maize, beans, and squash were the mainstays of slope cultivation, but Mesoamerican cultivators grew a large variety of other cultigens, including amaranth (*Amaranthus annuus*), *chía* (*Salvia hispanica*), tomato, beans, squash, and chiles.

Perhaps the most common irrigation works were weirs or check dams that captured silt and water within intermittent drainages, or that spread water onto adjacent lands for floodwater irrigation (Donkin 1979: 42, 44; García Cook 1985; Parsons 1971: 220; Rojas Rabiela 1988: 120, 1985: 202, 1991: 102; Sanders et al. 1979: 222–81; Wolf and Palerm 1955: 266). Perhaps it was these features in Cholula that Cortés described in 1520: "the farmlands are very fertile and they have much land and the greater part is irrigated" (1945: 146). In some cases, this technique was extended to valley floors, which were straddled by broad terraces that could be fed by channel runoff water (Donkin 1979: 44; Rojas Rabiela 1988: 120; Sanders et al. 1979: 253; Wolf and Palerm 1955).

Small dams and diversion weirs coupled with canals provided permanent irrigation water from springs or permanent streams in selected locations (Armillas et al. 1956; Doolittle 1990: 115; Millon 1957; Rojas Rabiela 1985: 198, 1988: 121; Sanders et al. 1979: 260–2). Thousands of small con-

tour bench terraces in the Basin of Mexico are thought to have been irrigated in this way (Donkin 1979: 44; Sanders et al. 1979: 251–2). In some cases, lengthy canals, complete with aqueducts that spanned intervening *barrancas* (gullies), attest to the use of permanent irrigation (Doolittle 1990: 127; Donkin 1979: 42, 44; Parsons 1971: 220; Wolf and Palerm 1955: 266). At least one instance of the canalization and relocation of the flow of a large stream for irrigation is known in the Basin of Mexico (Doolittle 1990: 115–20). While terracing was located throughout the Mesa Central, its association with elaborate irrigation infrastructures has only been well documented for the Basin of Mexico.

Many of the seasonal and permanent wetlands and shallow lakes in the interior of the valleys of Tlaxcala, Mexico, and perhaps Puebla were transformed into a network of canals and planting surfaces (wetland fields) on which year-round cultivation could be practiced (Parsons 1971: 220; Rojas Rabiela 1985: 208; Sanders 1972: 131–2; Sanders et al. 1979: 275; Wilken 1969, 1987). In some cases, hierarchial systems of canals channeled excessive water to the interior, creating drained fields along the periphery of lakes or wetlands.

The latter form of wetland cultivation reached its zenith among the *chinampas*, or "floating gardens," of the Basin of Mexico, occupying thousands of hectares of the southern freshwater lakes of Chalco and Xochimilco (Armillas 1971: 653; Sanders et al. 1979: 275; West and Armillas 1952: 171) (figure 5.2). The actual *chinampa* was a narrow artificial island (a raised field), anchored by trees along its edges, and constructed from lake muck and biotic materials dredged from the shallow lakes themselves (Wilken 1985: 42). The effect was to raise the planting surface relative to the water in the bordering canals, providing subsurface irrigation at all times, but also facilitating surface irrigation if needed. Canals were regularly cleaned, and the aquatic muck was used to fertilize the fields (Armillas 1971: 653; Palerm 1973; West and Armillas 1952: 171; Wilken 1985: 42).[4]

By the sixteenth century, *chinampas* were part of a state-designed and controlled hydraulic system that included dikes and sluice gates controlling water level and quality in the southern parts of the lacustrine network (Palerm 1973). Not only did dikes protect the two southern lakes from brackish Lake Texcoco, but an adjacent section of that lake was diked as well, making *chinampa* agriculture possible on the islands of the Aztec capital (figure 5.2) (Calneck 1972; Parsons 1976: 253; Sanders et al. 1979: 154).

Individually and as a system, *chinampas* required significant labor input to construct and maintain, but they combined very high productivity with risk-reduction (Armillas 1971: 660; Coe 1964: 98; Moriarty 1968: 473; Parsons 1976: 244–6; Sanders 1972: 133; Sanders et al. 1979: 390). Irrigation reduced problems of drought, and the presence of water mitigated frost hazard. *Chinampas* were probably double-cropped, using different cultigens and transplantation from seedbeds (Rojas Rabiela 1985: 165, 1988: 79–80). Few cultivation systems in the world could match their sustained level of productivity.

The Montejo Transect

The Yucatán Peninsula, home to the lowland Maya, provided a radically different experience for the Spaniards (figures 5.1 and 5.4) As in the Mexican case, the northern Yucatán was well peopled, and the Maya were both skilled cultivators and active in long-distance trade (Andrews 1983; Chamberlain 1948; Farriss 1984). Nevertheless, by such measures as the number and spatial domain of city-states, and level of sociopolitical organization and affluence (as measured by the scale and quality of monumental architecture), the condition of the lowland Maya in Yucatán at the time of contact was not on par with that of their Classic Period ancestors of some 500–700 years earlier (Chase and Rice 1985; Jones 1989; Turner 1983a, 1983b).

The Yucatán is composed of two environmental domains (figures 5.4 and 5.5) over which a common set of cropping practices were differentially employed in association with differing intensities of occupation. The peninsula is a large limestone shelf with extreme karst conditions, dominated by a tropical wet-dry climate (*tierra caliente*) in which rainfall increases considerably from the northwest to the southeast (Finch 1965; Wilhelmy 1981; Wilson 1980). The northern periphery of the peninsula is a relatively flat, lowly elevated plain, but starting with the Puuc Hills (figures 5.3 and 5.4), a rolling hill or upland area extends southward into the Péten (Guatemala). Everywhere in the north, extremely shallow and rocky soils, an absence of surface water, and a pronounced dry season impeded agriculture.

At the time of the Columbian Encounter, the northern low plains were moderately to heavily occupied. In contrast, the central and southern uplands, an area that was once the heart of the Classic Maya civilization (Culbert 1973; Turner 1990a), were very sparsely settled in 1492 (Jones 1989; Means 1917; Scholes and Roys 1968; Turner 1990a, 1990b).

Northern and coastal plains

Spaniards officially discovered the Yucatán in 1517 (Chamberlain 1948: 61–4; Clendinnen 1987: 17–18; Means 1917) only to find that at least two Spaniards, survivors of a shipwreck, were present among the Maya. One of these men refused to return to his former comrades, but led the Maya in subsequent military encounters against them (Chamberlain 1948: 61–4; Means 1917). The Spaniards bypassed the Yucatán for Mexico, so that the initial conquest awaited 1527, while subjugation of the peninsula followed some twenty years later (Farriss 1984: 12). Led by Francisco de Montejo (the Elder), the first *entrada* began on the northeastern coast of the peninsula and marched inland. The transect that we follow here roughly corresponds to the north–south course of Montejo's route, with some liberties taken to include the interior uplands which Montejo's party apparently avoided because of its sparse occupation.

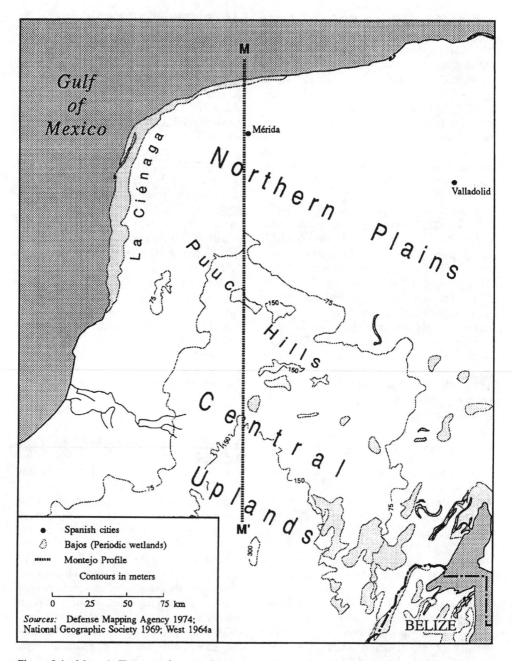

Figure 5.4 Montejo Transect, showing the Northern Yucatán, and the path of the Montejo Profile, M-M' (see figure 5.5). (Adapted from US Defense Mapping Agency 1974 and National Geographic Society 1969 as base maps, and West 1964a for other locational information.)

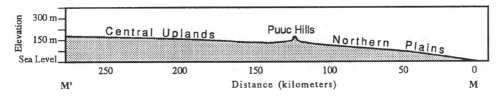

Figure 5.5 Montejo Profile, showing vertical relief along M–M' transect, as noted in figure 5.4. (Based on figure 5.4.)

The littoral of northern Yucatán was extremely important economically to the Maya, who had converted coastal wetlands (the ciénaga) into the center of Mesoamerican salt production and trade. Salt was apparently transported by canoe along the coasts to Mexico and Central America (Andrews 1983). The settlements controlling salt production lay inland, spread throughout the northern plains, as was most of the Maya population. Here the Spaniards encountered large numbers of Maya, arranged in small-sized polities consisting of sizable villages and well-tended landscapes.

These villages and their lands had a common morphology. A small plaza and public monument, usually a small pyramid or some other shrine, marked the center of a village, from which homesteads, each demarcated by stone walls enclosing orchard-gardens, radiated outward (the elite lived closest to the center) (Clendinnen 1987; Gómez-Pompa et al. 1987). Homesteads gave way to open- or outfields in various stages of fallow, which in turn gave way to forest, much of which may have been managed. Here, culling and related activities may have supported forms of agroforestry (*pet kot*) (Gómez-Pompa et al. 1987). This spatial arrangement was repeated across the northern plains, with the apparent exception of savanna areas.

Spanish documents refer to both "plantations" and "orchard-gardens" in the area, using the former designation frequently for elite-owned "cacao" stands situated on the edges of Maya towns (Tozzer 1941: 194–5; Scholes and Roys 1968: 171–2).[5] The spatial arrangement and concentration of these plots may have given the impression of

extensive orchards. Maya horticultural practices were not well documented by the Spaniards, other than reports that the elite used slaves and servants to care for their orchards, and evidence of monocropping or plantation-like labor organization is lacking (Scholes and Roys 1968: 171–2).

Orchard-gardens played an important role among the Maya and the Amerindians of *tierra caliente* in general (Killion 1992). Much of the Maya food supply was grown in orchard-gardens, as testified by their spatial extent and the quantity of remains of orchard-gardens species taken from excavations of Maya middens (Turner and Miksicek 1984). Indeed, Gómez-Pompa and colleagues (1987) argue that the unusual distribution of useful species currently found within ancient walled plots throughout Yucatán are remnants of ancient orchard-gardens (see also Folan et al. 1979). Individual trees and groves were apparently privately owned and inherited (Millon 1955: 700; Scholes and Roys 1968: 171–2).

Landa referred to the use of agaves, chiles, beans, and cotton in house gardens (Tozzer 1941: 194–5). Maya orchard-gardens included a large variety of native trees, shrubs, and other species adapted to the wet-dry tropical climate of the plains (Clendinnen 1987: 141; Chamberlain 1968: 52; Scholes and Roys 1968: 171–2, 328; Tozzer 1941: 179, 230). These included agave and cotton, avocado, nance (*Brysonima crassifolia*), allspice (*Pimenta dioica*), guava (*Psidium guajava*), sapodilla (*Manilkara zapote*), and mamey zapote (*Calocarpum mammosum*).

The prevalence of orchard-gardens notwithstanding, the staple crop of the northern Maya at the time of the Columbian

Encounter was maize. Considerable documentation by earlier chroniclers indicates that the bulk of it was produced in fields distant from the walled homesteads and orchard-gardens, although walls may have been present in these "outfields" (walls without occupation structures are common; see Freidel and Leventhal 1975). The cultivation practices in these "outfields" are uncertain, as is the intensity of cultivation. In the mid-1500s, Landa noted that the Maya prepared the land from January to April (in the dry season), planted with a digging stick, and cultivated by "collect[ing] together refuse and burn[ing] it in order to sow" (indicating shifting cultivation?); but they also had "improved" lands and "kept the land well cleared and free from weeds" (indicating nonshifting cultivation?) (Tozzer 1941: 62, 64, 97; Landa 1937: 38).

Because of the level of population and the well-defined boundaries of villages and provinces in the north, we suspect that a short-fallow rotational system was used in which plot preparation focused on burning collected and dried vegetation in order to provide essential phosphorus for the soil before the rains began in April. Plots were first sowed to maize and subsequently intercropped with squash and nitrogen fixing beans.[6] Interestingly, the region was known for its cotton and hemp production at the time of conquest, although virtually no descriptions of its cultivation exist. Weeding dominated the growing-season labor until the fall harvest.

The outfields of each village were apparently separated from those of the next by forest which, in addition to possible agroforestry activities, formed a reserve for wood fuel, hunting, and tame animals. Deer were, perhaps, the most important of the semi-tame animals, apparently controlled from birth through biological imprinting, and later herded from the village to feed in the forest (Means 1917: 30; Tozzer 1941: 127).

The uplands

Compared to the northern plains, the rolling karst hills of the central peninsular area must have been a disappointment and aggravation to the Spaniards, for here the population thinned dramatically (Means 1917; Scholes and Roys 1968: 333), and the tropical forest provided a frontier refuge for Maya fleeing Spanish control. The distinctive cultivated landscape of the northern plain was replaced in the uplands by extensive swidden systems, possibly similar to those described by ethnographers in the nineteenth and twentieth centuries.[7] This slash-and-burn or milpa (literally cornfield) method involved basically the same tools and crops as in the north, but utilized longer fallow cycles and lower labor inputs, especially for weeding. New plots were cut in January to allow the woody species to dry sufficiently for burning before the rains of April. After several seasons of cultivation, a plot was abandoned for a protracted period to escape the concentration of pests and weeds there and to allow regrowth of a secondary forest.

The role of orchard-gardens in the uplands during this period is not clear. They may have existed around larger settlements, but references to activity of this kind are sparse. House gardens were undoubtedly common. The forests were very much the product of past Maya activities and were well stocked with economic species from which extensive collecting took place.

Alvarado Transect

Pedro de Alvarado led the Spanish entrada into the highland Maya realm of Guatemala in 1524, charting a route southeastward from the Mesa Central, following the Pacific coastal plain, before turning northward into the well-defended highlands of present day Guatemala (figures 5.1 and 5.6). Following the experience of Cortés, Alvarado brought thousands of Aztec and Tlaxcalan warriors to subdue the Maya, who fought the invasion in a series of bloody battles. The Spaniards found a populous highlands divided into provinces of different ethnolinguistic Maya stock. Each province had hereditary rulers, but no overarching state was present,

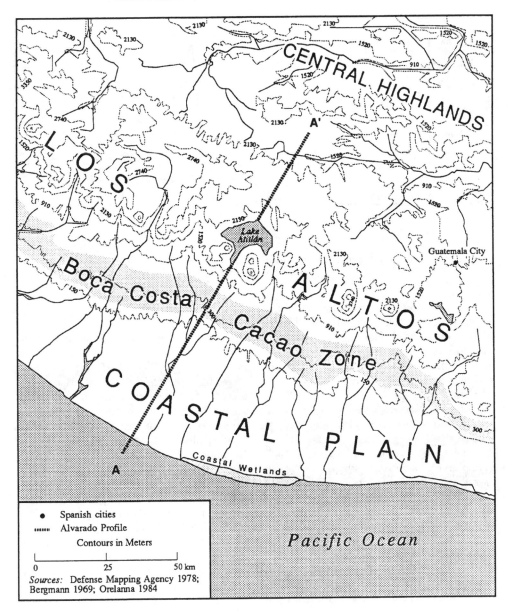

Figure 5.6 Alvarado Transect, showing southwestern Guatemala, and the path of the Alvarado Profile, A–A′ (see figure 5.7). (Adapted from US Defense Mapping Agency 1978 as a base map and Bergmann 1969 and Orelanna (1984) for other locational information.)

nor were there many large cities of the material majesty found in the Aztec realm. The region, however, contained some of the finest agricultural soils in Mesoamerica and the low lands of its Pacific versant gave the Spaniards a preview of yet another source of wealth – estate production of cacao.

The climb from the Pacific Coast to the homelands of the highland Maya transverses

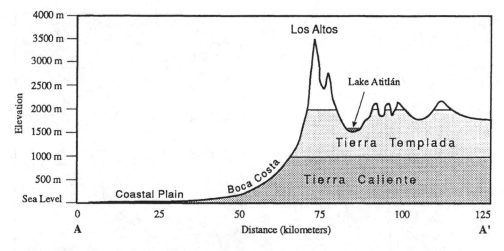

Figure 5.7   Alvarado Profile, showing vertical relief along A–A′ transect, as noted in figure 5.6.
(Based on figure 5.6.)

an array of broad agroecological zones associated with elevation (West 1964a: 373). The Coastal Plain (La Costa) and the Boca Costa or piedmont comprise a 40–50 km-wide strip between the ocean and highlands proper (figures 5.6 and 5.7). The coastal plain (up to about 100 m elevation) and the lower Boca Costa (about 100 m–460 m elevation) are *tierra caliente* while the upper Boca Costa (about 460–1,500 m elevation) is *tierra templada*. Precipitation increases inland and with elevation, such that portions of the Boca Costa receive in excess of 2,000 mm annually (Vivió Escoto 1964: figure 10). Around 1000 m elevation, the mountain front rises steeply to cinder cones and composite volcanos, some of which exceed 3,000 m. Above the 1,500 m contour and to the interior of the versant is Los Altos, the highland volcanic axis, composed of small depressions and calderas surrounded by volcanoes (more than twenty in Guatemala alone). Lake Atitlán occupies such a caldera at 1566 m. The peaks are in clouds and mist much of the time and average annual precipitation there reaches 3,000 mm–4,000 mm. To the northern end of the Alvarado transect the volcanic axis gives way to the lower-elevated and drier central highlands.

Boca costa

Very little is known about Amerindian agriculture on the narrow coastal plain proper. In contrast, the Boca Costa was a zone so prized for its agricultural fertility that Amerindian groups vied with one another for its control. The southwest portion of the Boca Costa was part of the greater Soconusco (also spelled Soconosco, Xoconusco, and Xoconocho) region, extending into southeastern Chiapas state in Mexico. This region was renowned for producing and widely exporting the finest cacao in Mesoamerica (Bergmann 1969: 86; Gasco and Voorhies 1989: 289; MacLeod 1973: 68–79; Millon 1955: 702). Cacao is a delicate species that requires moist but well-drained soils, shade, protection from high winds, and warm temperatures (mean temperatures between 18° C and 32° C, without frost) (Gasco 1987: 157). Owing to these needs, major orchard zones were below 650 m (Orellana 1984: 70) where annual precipitation totals ranged between 1,150 mm–2,500 mm. Pronounced dry seasons necessitated irrigation. Cacao was commonly germinated using seedbeds (*almácigos*) and replanted to orchards (Rojas Rabiela 1988: 82). Another species, *Theobroma tricolor*, is hardier, but it is not clear that it was grown extensively in the

Boca Costa. Major cacao began about 30 km inland on the alluvial fans. Bergmann (1969: 89) suggests that this interior location was a response to the drier conditions approaching the ocean, but it also corresponds with the well-drained agricultural soils of the alluvial fans characteristic of this piedmont.

Cacao was produced over a wide area, perhaps in an orchard or plantation-like pattern. The Spaniards referred to estates and gardens or orchards of cacao, terms that imply not only monocropping conditions but possibly irrigation as well (Armillas 1949: 88; Bergmann 1969: 90; Millon 1955; Rojas Rabiela 1988: 92; Zamora Acosta 1985: 182). Cacao was intensively tended, its care including the use of shade trees (e.g. *madera negra* [*Gliricidia maculata* H. B. and K.] or *coxote* [*G. sapium*]) and protection from predators and theft (Lange 1971: 240–4; Millon 1955: 704; Orellana 1984: 70; Stone 1977: 85–6; Rojas Rabiela 1988: 92).

The immense value of the cacao to Mesoamericans was in its use as a thick beverage or gruel. Such was the importance of this food that the cacao bean served as a medium of exchange in Mesoamerica, used in virtually any commodity or service transaction (Millon 1955; Bergmann 1969: 85–6). Elites controlled the production of and trade in cacao in the Boca Costa, although this control did not require actual occupation of the piedmont. Highland Maya communities governed some of the production in the Boca Costa, while Náhuatl-speaking groups within the piedmont may have served to ensure the flow of cacao to Aztec Mexico (Bergmann 1969: 89; Orellana 1984). At the time of the Spanish conquest, the Aztec extracted tribute from Soconusco and Boca Costa by taxing the towns controlling production, regardless of their location. The Boca Costa also offered a full array of agriculture, producing other foods and fibers. Maize was double- and even tripled-cropped in some locales (Fuentes and Guzmán 1882: 64; Zamora Acosta 1985: 182), undoubtedly through the use of irrigation. It is also possible that orchards producing

other crops than cacao were present. The spatial extent of this production onto the southern versant proper (between the cacao zone and Los Altos) is not well understood. The slope is very steep and rugged, and it appears to have been sparsely occupied at contact relative to the lands above and below. The southern versant may have been used for extensive cultivation as a "spill over" zone for farmers ascending from the Boca Costa or descending from Los Altos.

Los altos

In addition to the ubiquitous house gardens, rainfed cultivation was practiced on both terraced and nonterraced fields in the slopes and depressions of Los Altos. Many slopes were intensively cultivated without terracing, particularly where mounding (*montones*) or ridging (*camellones* contouring the slope) were apparently sufficient to impede erosion (see Wilken 1987: 129–44). Although Alvarado spoke of a highly developed agriculture, Spanish descriptions of practices associated with *temporal* are vague, making it difficult to distinguish shifting from permanent cultivation (Zamora Acosta 1985: 178; Palerm and Wolf 1962: 336). The *Annals of the Cakchiquels* (ca. 1559–81) mentions cut-and-burn techniques, but not rotation of fields, leading to various interpretations about the implied frequency of cultivation (Feldman 1985: 29; Orellana 1984: 69). The apparently extensive use of mounding, along with the use of a hoe-like instrument and a scraper-like rake for weeding, led Feldman (1985: 29–30) to conclude that a rainfed system, more intensive than slash and burn, was prevalent in Los Altos.

Terracing was practiced throughout the highlands (Orellana 1984: 27–9), although specific references to Los Altos are few. Remnants of pre-Hispanic terracing exist in the central highlands, and the practice may have been followed at the time of conquest (Guzmán 1962: 398). The distribution of the relic features may reflect soil distinctions between the volcanic axis of Los Altos and the more northerly central highlands or it may reflect differential Spanish impacts. Documentation of terrace remains in the volcanic axis zone is slim, however. Lothrop (1933) found relic terraces around Lake Atitlán but did not designate their function for agriculture as opposed to house sites.

Highland Maya terracing, in general, served the same functions as described in the Cortés transect. Where associated with the *tablón*, however, irrigation was common. The *tablón* (literally, plank) is a raised-garden plot (20–65 cm in height), usually rectangular in shape with inwardly sloping sides, accompanied by irrigation channels (Mathewson 1984; Wilken 1971: 435). If on a sufficient slope, the *tablón* is constructed on terraces with the irrigation channel located at the base of each terrace wall. *Tablones* in use today are especially frequent around the edges of Lake Atitlán and on the northern slopes above the lake, although they can be found elsewhere in the highlands (Altee 1968; Wilken 1987). While no direct evidence yet confirms the use of *tablones* in the pre-Hispanic highlands, two facts strongly suggest that they were a major component of highland Maya agriculture. The first is that each of the structural elements of *tablones* was known and used by the Maya; the second is that the current distribution coincides with contact-era social and environmental conditions that would have promoted their use (Mathewson 1984: 17–20; Orellana 1984: 69; Wilken 1971: 435–6). It is likely that *tablón* systems constituted many of the gardens described in Spanish accounts.

The principal crops grown were those prevalent throughout the highlands of Mesoamerica. According to Feldman (1985: 26), at least seven varieties of maize, three of squash, nine of beans, tobacco, and, perhaps, sweet potato have been identified in Los Altos in prehistoric context. Studies of highland Maya communities by Stadelman (1940) and others indicate the presence of a much greater variety of maize, much of which is assumed to have been present in antiquity.

The Lake Atitlán Basin was a microcosm of the highland landscapes in general at contact times, including its occupation by at least three Maya groups: the Cakchiquel in the north and east sides, the Tzutujuil on the south side and Pacific slopes, and the Quiché on the north and west sides (Lothrop 1933: 3). The cultivated landscape here appeared as a mosaic of practices associated more with slope than with climatic variation or with elevation. The upper, broad slopes of the basin were apparently under intensive rainfed cultivation, complete with cascading *monotones* and *camellones*. Further down the basin, where drainage systems facilitated irrigation but the steepness of slope increased significantly (particularly on the northern side of the lake), ranks of terraced *tablones* continued down towards the lake. Near lake level, almost all the small deltas of the drainages were also converted into *tablones* (see Mathewson 1984).

The Fate of the Cultivated Landscapes

The repercussions of the Conquest spread swiftly throughout Mesoamerica during the first century of the Hispanic era, leaving few, if any, cultivated landscapes untouched (Butzer 1991). The conquerors reapportioned land and labor under conditions of rapid Amerindian depopulation and reconstituted agriculture through the introduction of European technologies and biota. The conquered retained, where possible and appropriate, their crops and cropping techniques. Ultimately, however, both conquerors and conquered borrowed extensively, if differentially, from one another, and the reconfigured landscapes that resulted were not so much one culture's cultivated landscape replacing another's but their union or "hybrid" landscapes.[8]

Causes of the transformations

The Conquest of Mesoamerica set in motion a series of processes, intentional and otherwise, that penetrated every facet of the physical and spiritual world of the Amerindian, with many of the results having significant ramifications on cultivated landscapes. We cannot treat all of these processes here, but focus on three clusters of them that were especially significant in a direct way: the Amerindian depopulation, the introduction of exotic biota and technologies, and the reordering of land and the rural economy.

The scale of Amerindian depopulation that accompanied the introduction of Old World pathogens by the Spaniards is nothing short of phenomenal, remaining unparalleled in demographic history.[9] This demographic tragedy affected agriculture in at least two ways. The landesque capital (terracing, irrigation, wetland systems) of the intensive cropping systems of the Amerindian could not be sustained with such losses in labor, leading to the decay of many cultivated landscapes (Cook and Borah 1979: 169), with the concomitant environmental degradation that typically follows from the lack of upkeep. This decay contributed to the larger process of land abandonment which, in turn, weakened Amerindian claims to land and led to Spanish land appropriation (e.g. Licate 1981).

The introduction of Old World biota and technologies, part of what Crosby (1972) calls the Columbian Exchange, had wide-ranging impacts on the landscape because of the new land-uses associated with them and the expansion of these uses into areas extensively utilized by Amerindians. Among the most dramatic were those of range livestock, previously unknown in Mesoamerica. The population explosion of grazing animals early in the sixteenth century is claimed by many to have contributed to accelerated erosion on agricultural lands, increased siltation, more frequent and profound flooding, and losses of harvests due to predatory herds and the physical trampling of the fields (Brand 1961: 133; Chevalier 1963: 93; Cook and Borah 1979: 169; Crosby 1972: 76–77; Gibson 1964: 305; Morrisey 1951: 116; Simpson 1952; Super 1988: 26). Chevalier (1963: 93) claims that entire communities in the Mesa Central were forced to move, in part because of live-stock damage to croplands, and the land so abandoned may well have contributed to the growth in cattle and sheep *estancias* (ranches) during the early sixteenth century (Chevalier 1963: 83; Licate 1981: 114–15).

Such impacts may have been more short-lived than conventional wisdom asserts. Gibson (1964: 281), among others (e.g. Butzer and Butzer, personal communication), notes that the Spanish Crown invoked law and policy directed at preserving Amerindian lands and cultivation, although these efforts were apparently at odds with the forces of depopulation, resettlement, land abandonment, and local appropriation (Licate 1981: 113). Discovery of silver in the north and the cattle producers' adaptions of their production strategies to the new lands, led to a livestock industry that spread northward into lands that were less intensively used in pre-Columbian times, producing an economy that was relatively in tune with the environments in question (Butzer and Butzer).

The critical point for our discussion is that much land that was once under Amerindian cultivation (in the highland domain) or was sparsely utilized (north of Mesoamerica proper or in lands abandoned because of depopulation) was rapidly put to a new, exotic use. The land-cover impacts associated with this land-use change are vividly illustrated in the Gulf Coast area, where cattle and sheep production was pursued on pastures created by burning forest and on former wetland fields; in either case, these were formerly Amerindian cultivated landscapes, altered to new use (Siemens 1992).

Hispanic crop introductions also redefined the lands to be cultivated and the form of cultivation on them (Hassig 1985: 221). The use of plow and draft animals, for example, placed a premium on level or gently sloped lands with good soil depth and drainage and large field size (Cook and Borah 1979: 171). In contrast, pre-Columbian coa-based cultivation was particularly suitable for use in shallow soils and small fields, and on steep slopes.[10] The shift to plow cultivation and the abandonment of cultivated lands owing to depopulation and resettlement may have altered the overall proportion of valley bottom to upper slope cultivation relative to pre-Hispanic times.

Spanish preferences for European foods also played a part. Wheat cultivation was carried across the *altiplano* from the Puebla basin to the northern silver mines (Gibson 1964: 322; Chevalier 1963: 51–4; Super 1988: 32) because of the demand for wheat bread. This pursuit led the Spaniards to introduce irrigation in the Bajío and other arid lands on the margins of Mesoamerica, and to rework Amerindian irrigation in the Basin of Mexico to allow winter (dry season) cultivation (Chevalier 1963: 70: Butzer and Butzer; Davis 1990). The environmental impacts of these shifts in agriculture are insufficiently documented so that more pointed assessments constitute speculation.

Plantation crops for trans-Atlantic commerce emerged in the lowlands, although large-scale plantations were not the norm (Butzer 1991: 210). The most important of the crops in terms of landscape change was sugarcane, which the Spaniards introduced wherever ecologically suitable (Chevalier 1963: 74). Cortés himself established a sugarcane plantation in the lowlands west of Tuxtla as early as 1528 (Barrett 1970: 11). For the most part, sugarcane production in the *tierra caliente* was undertaken on small estates, as was Spanish-controlled production of cacao, cotton, tobacco, and dyes (MacLeod 1973: 220–4). By the close of the sixteenth century, sugarcane production also spread into warmer upland locales, such as in Morelos where large-scale plantations were established (Barrett 1970: 4; Super 1988: 37), and where it may have helped to displace Amerindian cultivation (Chevalier 1963: 82).

These changes were intertwined with those stemming from the reordering of land and labor. By the mid-sixteenth century, significant land holdings had accrued to the Spaniards and, interestingly, to Amerindian elites in some areas (Gibson 1964; Licate 1981; Simpson 1952). Amerindian labor was siphoned off for work on large Spanish

estates, and the *encomienda* (grants for the control of Amerindian labor) refocused production goals, and in some cases, the location of Amerindian settlements. After mid-century, full-blown resettlement schemes (the *congregación*) relocated much of the remaining rural population (Cline 1949). The impacts of these activities were to reduce Amerindian cultivation in some locales and increase land pressures on others.

Landscapes transformed and traditions retained

Three very broad patterns of transformation of cultivated landscapes followed throughout Mesoamerica and beyond. The humid *tierra caliente* (save the northern Yucatán) was virtually abandoned, allowing major forest regeneration. The few remaining Amerindians in these lowlands, armed with the introduction of steel cutting tools, increasingly moved towards labor-saving swidden cultivation. The Spaniards, on the other hand, introduced small scale estates devoted to plantation crops, both introduced and native, followed by livestock production. The *tierra templada* witnessed widespread abandonment and destruction of Amerindian agricultural landscapes and the emergence of new ones. The general pattern of this transformation involved the disuse of some land, the disproportional redistribution of other lands to the Spaniards, and an investment in large-scale plow and wheat cultivation and livestock production drawing on Amerindian labor. Finally, cultivation and livestock rearing expanded into the more arid segments of Mesoamerica and the lands beyond, especially to the north, and later into Central America.

Indigenous landscapes dominated by labor-intensive cultivation, especially terraces and wetland systems, were particularly affected. Terrace systems were abandoned throughout the upper piedmonts of the Mesa Central of Mexico (Cortés transect), Los Altos of Guatemala (Alvarado transect), and somewhat later in the piedmont of the

Gulf Coast (Cortés transect) (Donkin 1979: 35–6). These extensively distributed systems of slope modification simply could not be maintained in the face of Amerindian depopulation and relocation (Cook and Borah 1979: 168; Donkin 1979: 36) and with the increasing focus of cultivation in valleys and lower basins.

Similarly, wetland agriculture, the productive heart of some pre-Columbian landscapes, also faded in significance. It did so for several reasons beyond those of population collapse and labor shortage. Indigenous wetland agriculture was not well understood by the Spaniards, was not central to their vision of appropriate land use, and was not suited for plow or wheat production. Moreover, it occupied lands potentially suitable for plow and livestock production, if properly drained (Cook and Borah 1979: 171; Hassig 1985: 221). Interestingly, deterioration of the Amerindian systems upslope lead to increased sedimentation and other problems that apparently degraded some wetland systems below (Gibson 1964: 305; López Ríos 1988). Owing to these and other factors, wetland agriculture almost disappeared from the Mesa Central (Cortés transect), except for the *chinampas* of Lakes Chalco and Xochimilco in the Basin of Mexico (which would decay slowly) and the drained fields in the Tlaxcalan valley. Wetland systems, other than ephemeral flood-recessional practices, also disappeared in the Gulf Coast Plain (Cortés transect), although their demise may have been underway previous to the Conquest.

In the Yucatán (Montejo transect), the Spaniards developed extensive cattle estates, utilizing both Maya agricultural lands and forest (Farriss 1984: 32).[11] This not only disrupted the well-developed cultivated landscape of the Maya, but, along with depopulation, the introduction of steel cutting tools, and Maya "escape" to the forests outside of Spanish control, probably led to the disintensification of Maya cultivation from rotational to shifting cultivation.[12] The rearranged landscape was composed of large estates interspersed with small villages,

following a form of *milpa* cultivation that has continued to the present.

Most of the cultivated landscapes that escaped major change lay on the margins of Spanish interests or control. For example, agriculture in the expanse of the lowland tropical forest between the Maya highlands (Alvarado transect) and northern Yucatán (Montejo transect) remained more or less as it had been at contact, that is extensive swidden cultivation. One landscape prized by the Spaniards that survived more or less in its pre-Hispanic form, at least under the first phase of Spanish domination, was that of the cacao-producing Boca Costa and Soconusco (Alvarado transect). The Spaniards were quick to realize the importance of cacao among Mesoamericans and, later, its value for international trade (Hamilton 1976: 860–1). They took control of cacao-producing zones largely through the *encomienda*, the effect of which was to leave the form of production largely intact.

The reconfiguring of the cultivated landscapes did not mean that Amerindian agricultural practices and technologies were lost; many survived as integral components of the new landscapes. Perhaps the most important of these was the omnipresent *calmil*. Small household gardens remained central to Amerindian and peasant agriculture throughout the contact and colonial periods (and are still maintained), albeit with European additions. Field-scale surface modifications, especially camellones and *montones*, also endured well, especially where maize cultivation persisted without the plow. These features were so common in the Mesa Central in the sixteenth century that any parcel of cultivated land was referred to as a *camellón* and even abandoned lands were known as "acamellonada" (i.e. filled with planting mounds) (Rojas Rabiela 1988: 42–3). The *metapantli* (maguey-anchored terraces) also survived (Patrick 1977), perhaps because of the ease of upkeep of the retaining wall, although it was much more spatially restricted than in precontact times (Donkin 1979). Vestiges of drained fields, raised fields, and *tablones* also weathered the conquest, but in highly localized areas. The survival of the *tablón* in Guatemala (Alvarado transect) was due in part to its use on steep and narrow lands not suited for other forms of cultivation, and, as Mathewson (1984: 24–5) implies, because it may have been appropriated by the Spaniards for their own horticultural needs. Finally, various extensive rotational systems contined to be employed, especially in the *tierra caliente* and in areas that were and remained sparsely utilized. In some cases, extensive agriculture may have been introduced anew in so-called refuge areas – regions where the indigenous population fled to avoid Spanish laws, taxes, or culture, such as the sparsely inhabited interior of the Maya lowlands.

These Amerindian systems were combined with Hispanic ones to create the new cultivated landscapes of New Spain. In some cases, systems of either origin were distributed across a landscape according to the differing socioeconomic and environmental circumstances present (e.g. Spanish-dominated bottom lands and Amerindian-dominated slope lands). More common, however, the various systems themselves were modified by exchanges in biota and technology. The new cultivated landscapes, therefore, were a product of agricultural systems lost, added, modified through exchange, and redistributed across the terrain.

Transformations in Perspective

What became known as *La leyenda negra* (the Black Legend) encapsulated long-standing beliefs about Spanish civilization and its conquests in the New World, perhaps overstating its barbarism and brutality relative to other societies. In recent years, another legend related to the Columbian Encounter has emerged: what might be called *La leyenda verde*. This Green Legend mythologizes the achievements and qualities of Amerindian cultures, especially their agriculture. Such interpretations, especially in the popular literature (e.g. Sale 1990; Weatherford 1988), attribute Amerindian decision making in agriculture and land-

scape alterations to cultural values placed on the conservation of nature or on the need for harmony with nature as much as or more than to the need for food, fiber, and tribute, the desire for wealth, or the response to sociopolitical conflict and change. An idealized Amerindian experience of using nature in a benign way is contrasted with a European penchant for controlling or raping nature for profit. This polarization errs in several fundamental ways as applied to the cultivated landscapes of Mesoamerica and New Spain. It fails to appreciate sufficiently the nature and scale of agricultural production in preconquest Mesoamerica and, hence, the scale and magnitude of its associated environmental changes, and it tends to inflate the environmental damage associated with the cultivated landscapes of New Spain.

The peoples of Mesoamerica engineered nature into regional mosaics comprised of diverse systems of cultivation which contributed to extensive land modification and conversion. The particular systems and the landscapes in which they were embedded were the result of real and perceived needs in the context of the cultural and environmental constraints and opportunities. These systems served first to feed the large populations, but also to sustain elites and oppressive political structures, engage in commerce, and pay tribute. Polities fought one another for the control of the land and the wealth that came from its cultivation. Production shortfalls, even prolonged famines, were common throughout Mesoamerica (e.g. Hassig 1981), and changes in socioeconomic conditions led to localized decay, abandonment, and replacement of particular agricultural landscapes, ofttimes leading to environmental degradation (e.g. see Williams 1972).

The Columbian Encounter constituted an abrupt, even brutal, change in population, biota, technological capacity (especially in transportation), and, to a much lesser extent, political economy that recast Amerindian cultivated landscapes. The swiftness of change as well as the changes themselves exacerbated environmental damage as some systems were abandoned and others reconstituted, but ultimately a series of "*mestizo*" cultivated landscapes emerged that were more or less ecologically sustainable. It is difficult to compare these pre- and post-Columbian landscapes in terms of such attributes as land and labor productivity or environmental damage. In general however, Amerindian systems may have been more land productive (output per unit area and time), while Spanish systems were higher in labor productivity. The exception to this characterization, of course, was Amerindian shifting cultivation.

This reality does not demean the accomplishments of the Amerindian cultivator, nor does it diminish the impact of the Columbian Encounter. Rather, it directs us to understand the Encounter from a position of balance. Both the pre- and postcontact landscapes of cultivation were constructed for the purpose of extracting from nature, and as the pressures for this extraction varied, so did the kind and scale of local landscape transformation. Where and when these pressures were high in Mesoamerica, extensive alterations of environments took place. The denudation of the tropical forests of the Maya lowlands before 1000 AD and the complete transformation of the Basin of Mexico, especially during Aztec times, are clear examples. We can assign the negative environmental impacts of the emergent landscapes of New Spain to an inherent view of nature embedded within Hispanic and European culture, only in a polemic that fails to understand the material circumstances that drive agricultural change. A more balanced view of this collision of worlds forces us to recognize that environmental degradation invariably follows the abandonment of well-adjusted intensive systems and the experimentation with rapidly evolving new systems. This was so before the Columbian Encounter and remains so today.

ACKNOWLEDGMENTS

Much of the research behind this work was supported by a grant from the National Endowment for the Humanities. We are indebted to Karl W. Butzer, William M. Denevan, William E. Doolittle, Kent Mathewson, William B. Meyer, Ylena Ogneva, Alfred Siemens, Andrew Sluyter, and the anonymous reviewers for their comments and critiques of this manuscript during various stages of preparation. We thank Heather Henderson for assistance in preparing the final manuscript, and Patti Neumann for preparing the maps and figures.

NOTES

1 See the Montejo Transect for descriptions of swidden or slash-and-burn cultivation (also called *tumba y roza*, signifying long fallow, and *barbecho*, signifying short fallow).

2 This section is based largely on information from two large city-state provinces encountered along the Cortés route, Tlaxcala and Cholua (in the present Mexican states of Tlaxcala and Puebla), and from the Basin of Mexico (including parts of the present day Mexican states of México and the Distrito Federal) (figure 5.2).

3 For the details of the construction, morphology, and functioning of most the systems described for the Mesa Central, see Wilken's (1987) thorough assessment of modern-day systems, many, if not most, of which have their origins in pre-Columbian times, and Rojas Rabiela's (1988) excellent treatment of early postcontact indigenous systems.

4 The construction of *chinampas* has been the subject of considerable discussion, because few, if any, have been built in modern times. No less an authority than Humboldt refers to "the chinampas, that Europeans call floating gardens. There are two types: some are moveable ... others are closely fixed to the margins" (1966: 134). Some have interpreted references to "floating gardens" as references to *chinampas* proper, while others believe that they refer to the canoes filled with transplantings (on route to *chinampas*) or to gathered vegetation floated across the lakes for various purposes. See the following for details and more on the *chinampas* dispute: Apenas 1943: Bancroft 1914 [1887]; Bernal 1973; Acosta 1880; Gibson 1964; Leicht 1937; López Ríos 1988; Wilken 1985.

5 Spanish documents notwithstanding, the northern Yucatán is not generally considered to have been a major source of cacao (*Theobroma cacao* or *T. bicolor*) at contact times

(Bergmann 1969). Indeed, the Yucatán's hydrological conditions seem unsuitable for extensive production. The sole direct evidence of cacao from the Yucatán is a rare variety only known in the Lacandon region of Mexico (Gómez-Pompa, et al. 1990).

6 Landa (Tozzer 1941: 196) mentioned the presence of root crops, probably *jicama* (*Pachyrihizus erosus* L.), but the significance of root crops in the north at contact times is suspect. The soils of the plains are extremely thin, incapable of supporting adequate root and tuber growth. No reports of the use of mounding (*montones*), which might indicate major root crop cultivation, exist for the lowland Maya realm at this time.

7 For descriptions of contemporary swidden agriculture throughout the Maya lowlands, see Carter 1969; O. Cook 1921; Emerson and Kempton 1935; Hester 1954; Higbee 1948; Redfield and Avilla 1934; Roys 1943.

8 Licate (1981: 1, 133) refers to this hybridization as giving rise to "Mexican" landscapes in the Mesa Central. We have refrained from using this term because two of our transects deal with cultural or political units that are not Mexican.

9 Perhaps fueled by the controversy that still surrounds the scale of the Amerindian depopulation, the literature related to the Amerindian population decline is too large to fully cite here. See Denevan (1992) for a useful bibliography and a thorough overview of the issue. Simulation exercises indicate that depopulation probably approached 90 percent by 1600 (Whitmore 1991, 1992).

10 A prevalent theme asserts that Amerindians typically favored wetlands and slopes because non-inundated, level terrain (between slope and shore) was not suited to their nonplow cultivation technologies. This assessment is too simple. Nonplow cultivators are known to have cultivated almost every conceivable terrain (Turner and Brush 1987), given the need to do so.

11 The development of agricultural estates for the monocropping of *henequen* (sisal) did not emerge in the Yucatán until the nineteenth century (Farriss 1984: 34).

12 We are not certain of the impact of metal tools on the frequency of swidden or *milpa* cultivation in the region. One argument holds that the ease of cutting trees with steel tools promoted more extensive systems of cultivation, and that the more strenuous labor involved in felling trees with stone tools would have favored more frequent cultivation of the same plot. Incidentally, Landa (Tozzer 1941: 121) reported that the Maya had metal hatchets, but it is not certain that they were used in agriculture.

REFERENCES

Acosta, Joseph de. 1880 [1590]. *The Natural and Moral History of the Indies*. London: Hakluyt Society. 1880.

Alcorn, Janice B. 1984. *Haustec Mayan Ethnobotany*. Austin: University of Texas Press.

Altee, Charles B., Jr. 1968. *Vegetable Production in Guatemala*. Washington: US Agency for International Development.

Andrews, Anthony P. 1983. *Maya Salt Production and Trade*. Tucson: University of Arizona Press.

Apenas, Ola. 1943. The pond in our backyard. *Mexican Life* 19(60): 15–18.

Armillas, Pedro. 1949. Notas sobre sistemas de cultivo en Mesoamérica. *Anales del Instituto Nacional de Anthropología e Historia* 3: 85–113.

——1971. Gardens on swamps. *Science* 174(4010): 653–61.

Armillas, Pedro, Palerm, Angel, and Wolf, Eric R. 1956. A small irrigation system in the valley of Teotihuacan. *American Antiquity* 21(4): 396–9.

Bancroft, Hubert H. 1914 (1887). *The History of Mexico, being a Popular History of the Mexican People from Earliest Primitive Civilization to the Present Time*. San Francisco: Bancroft Co.

Barlow, R. H. 1949. *The Extent of the Empire of the Culhua Mexica*. Ibero-Americana 28. Berkeley: University of California Press.

Barrett, Ward. 1970. *The Sugar Hacienda of the Marqueses del Valle*. Minneapolis: University of Minnesota Press.

Bergmann, John F. 1969. The distribution of cacao cultivation in pre-Columbian America. *Annals of the Association of American Geographers* 59: 85–96.

Bernal, Ignacio. 1973. *Mexico before Cortez: Art History and Legend*. New York: Doubleday Anchor Press.

Brand, Donald D. 1961. The early history of the range cattle industry in northern mexico. *Agricultural History* 35(3): 132–9.

Butzer, Karl W. 1991. Spanish colonization of the new world: Cultural continuity and change in Mexico. *Erdkunde* 45(3): 204–19.

——1992. Transfer of the Mediterranean livestock economy to New Spain: Adaptations and consequences. Paper presented at the SCOPE

Scientific Symposium on Principles, Patterns, and Processes: Some Legacies of the Columbian Encounter, Sevilla, Spain.

Butzer, Karl W. and Butzer, Elisabeth. 1992. Personal communication, January.

Calneck, Edward E. 1972. Settlement patterns and chinampa agriculture at Tenochtitlán. *American Antiquity* 37(1): 104–15.

Carter, William E. 1969. *New Lands and Old Traditions: Kekchi Cultivators in the Guatemalan Lowlands.* Latin American Monograph 6. Gainesville: University of Florida Press.

Chamberlain, Robert S. 1948. *The Conquest and Colonization of Yucatan, 1517–1550.* Publication 582. Washington: Carnegie Institution of Washington.

Chase, Arlen F. and Rice, Prudence M. 1985. *The Lowland Maya Postclassic.* Austin: University of Texas Press.

Chevalier, F. 1963. *Land and Society in Colonial America,* ed. L. B. Simpson; trans. A. Eustis. Berkeley: University of California Press.

Clendinnen, Inga. 1987. *Ambivalent Conquests: Maya and Spaniard in Yucatan, 1517–1570.* Cambridge: Cambridge University Press.

Cline, H. F. 1949. Civil congregations of the Indians in New Spain, 1598–1606. *The Hispanic American Historical Review* 29(3): 349–69.

Coe, M. D. 1964. The chinampas of Mexico. *Scientific American* 211(1): 90–8.

Cook, O. F. 1921. Milpa agriculture: A primitive tropical system. *Annual Report of the Smithsonian Institution,* 1919: 302–26.

Cook, Sherburne F. and Borah, W. 1979. Indian food production and consumption in Central Mexico before and after the conquest (1500–1650). In *Essays in Population History, Mexico and California,* vol. 3. Berkeley: University of California Press.

Cortés, Hernán. 1945. *Cartas y relaciones.* Buenos Aires: Emecé Editores, SA.

Crosby, Alfred W., Jr. 1972. *The Columbian Exchange: Biological and Cultural Consequences of 1492.* Contributions in American Studies 2. Westport, CT: Greenwood.

Culbert, T. Patrick. 1973. *The Classic Maya Collapse.* Albuquerque: University of New Mexico Press.

Davis, Clint. 1990. Water control and settlement in colonial Mexico's first frontier: The bordo system of the eastern Bajío. *Yearbook, Conference of Latin Americanist Geographers* 16: 73–81.

Denevan, W. M. 1992 [1976]. *The Native Population of the Americas in 1492.* Madison: University of Wisconsin Press.

Diaz del Castillo, Bernal. 1956. *The Discovery and Conquest of Mexico,* trans. A. P. Maudslay. New York: Farrar, Straus and Giroux.

Donkin, R. A. 1979. *Agricultural Terracing in the Aboriginal New World.* Tucson, AZ: University of Arizona Press for the Wenner-Gren Foundation for Anthropological Research, Inc.

Doolittle, William E. 1990. *Canal Irrigation in Prehistoric Mexico: The Sequence of Technological Change.* Austin: University of Texas Press.

Emerson, R. A. and Kempton, J. H. 1935. Agronomic investigations in Yucatan. *Yearbook of the Carnegie Institution of Washington* 34: 138–42.

Evans, Susan T. 1990. The productivity of maguey terrace agriculture in central Mexico during the Aztec period. *Latin American Antiquity* 1(2): 117–32.

Farriss, Nancy M. 1984. *Maya Society under Colonial Rule: The Collective Enterprise of Survival.* Princeton, NJ: Princeton University Press.

Feldman, Lawrence H. 1985. *A Tumpline Economy: Production and Distribution Systems in Sixteenth-century Eastern Guatemala.* Culver City, CA: Labyrinthos.

Finch, William A. Jr. 1965. The karst landscape of Yucatan. Ph.D. dissertation, University of Illinois.

Folan, W. J., Fletcher, L. A., and Kintz, E. R. 1979. Fruit, fiber, bark, and resin: social organization of a Maya urban center. *Science* 204: 697–701.

Freidel, David A. and Leventhal, Richard M. 1975. The settlement survey. In *A Study of Changing pre-Columbian Commercial Systems: The 1972–1973 Season at Cozumel, Mexico,* ed. J. A. Sabloff and W. L. Rathje, pp. 60–76. Monograph 3. Peabody Museum of Archaeology and Ethnology. Cambridge: Harvard University.

Fuentes y Guzmán, D. and de Francisco, Antonio. 1882. *Historia de Guatemala, o recordation florida: Natural vecino y regidor perpetuo de la cindad de Guatemala.* Madrid: Biblioteca de los Americanistas.

García Cook, Angel. 1985. Historia de la tecnología agrícola en el altiplano central desde el principio de la agricultura hasta el siglo XIII. In *Historia de la agricultura: Epoca prehispánica-siglo XVI,* ed. Teresa Rojas Rabiela and William T. Sanders, pp. 7–75. Mexico City: Instituto Nacional de Antropología e Historia.

Gasco, Janine. 1987. Cacao and the economic integration of native society in colonial Soconusco, New Spain. Ph.D. dissertation, University of California, Santa Barbara.

Gasco, Janine and Voorhies, Barbara. 1989. The ultimate tribute: The role of the Soconusco as an Aztec tributary. In *Ancient Trade and Tribute*, ed. Barbara Voorhies, pp. 48–94. Provo: University of Utah Press.

Gibson, Charles. 1964. *The Aztec under Spanish Rule: A History of the Indians of the Valley of Mexico 1519–1810*. Stanford, CA: Stanford University Press.

Gómez-Pompa, Arturo, Flores, Jose Salvador, and Aliphat Fernández, Mario. 1990. The sacred cacao groves of the Maya. *Latin American Antiquity* 1(3): 247–57.

Gómez-Pompa, Arturo, Flores, Jose Salvador, and Sosa, Victoria. 1987. The "pet kot": A man-made tropical forest of the Maya. *Interciencia* 12(1): 10–15.

Gutiérrez Ruvalcaba, Ignacio. 1994. Ecología y agricultura en Metztitlán, siglos XVI y XVII. In *Agricultura indígena: Pasado y presente*, ed. Teresa Rojas Rabiela, pp. 129–41. Mexico City: CIESAS, Ediciones de las Casa Chata.

Guzmán, Louis E. 1962. Las terrazas de los antiguos mayas montañeses. *Revista Interamerican de Ciencias Sociales*, 2nd epoch, vol. 1(3): 398–406.

Hamilton, Earl J. 1976. What the new world gave the economy of the old. In *First Images of America*, vol. 2, ed. Fredi Chiappelli, Michael J. B. Allen, and Robert L. Benson, pp. 853–84. Berkeley: University of California Press.

Hassig, Ross. 1981. The famine of one rabbit: Ecological causes and social consequences of a pre-Columbian calamity. *Journal of Anthropological Research* 37: 171–82.

—— 1985. *Trade, Tribute, and Transportation: The Sixteenth-century Political Economy of the Valley of Mexico*. Norman: University of Oklahoma Press.

Hester, Joseph A. 1954. Natural and cultural bases of ancient Maya subsistence. Ph.D. dissertation, University of California, Los Angeles.

Higbee, Edward. 1948. Agriculture in the Mayan homeland. *Geographical Review* 48: 457–64.

Humboldt, Alexander von. 1966. *Ensayo politico sobre el reino de la nueva España*, ed. Juan A. Ortega y Medina. Mexico City: Editorial Porrua, SA.

Jones, Grant D. 1989. *Maya Resistance to Spanish Rule: Time and History on a Colonial Frontier*. Albuquerque: University of New Mexico Press.

Killion, T. 1992. *Gardens of Prehistory*. University, AL: University of Alabama Press.

Landa, Diego de. 1937 [1566]. *Yucatán Before and After the Conquest*, trans. W. Gates. New York: Dover Publications.

Lange, Frederick W. 1971. *Culture History of the Sapoa River Valley of Costa Rica*. Occasional Papers in Anthropology 4. Beloit, WI: Logan Museum of Anthropology, Beloit College.

Leicht, Hugo. 1937. Chinampas y almácigos flotantes. *Anales del Instituto de Biología (UNAM)* 5(3): 375–86.

Licate, Jack A. 1981. *Creation of a Mexican Landscape: Territorial Organization and Settlement in the Eastern Puebla Basin 1520–1605*. Department of Geography Research Papers 201. Chicago: University of Chicago.

López de Gómara, Francisco. 1964. *Cortés: The Life of the Conqueror by his Secretary*, trans. and ed. Lesley Byrd Simpson. Berkeley: University of California Press.

López Ríos, Georgina Florencia. 1988. *Sistema agrícola de chinampa: Perspectiva agroecológica*. Mexico City: Universidad Autónoma Chapingo.

Lothrop, Samuel K. 1933. *Atitlán: An Archaeological Study of Ancient Remains on the Borders of Lake Atitlán, Guatemala*. Publication 444. Washington: Carnegie Institute of Washington.

MacLeod, Murdo J. 1973. *Spanish Central America: Socioeconomic History, 1520–1720*. Berkeley: University of California Press.

Mathewson, Kent. 1984. *Irrigation Horticulture in Highland Guatemala: The Tablón System of Panajachel*. Boulder, CO: Westview.

Means, Philip A. 1917. *History of the Spanish Conquest of Yucatán and of the Itzás*. Papers of the Peabody Museum of American Archaeology and Ethnology, Harvard University, vol. 8. Cambridge, MA.

Millon, René F. 1955. Trade, tree cultivation, and the development of private property in land. *American Anthropologist* 57(4): 698–712.

—— 1957. Irrigation systems in the valley of Teotihuacán. *American Antiquity* 23(2): 160–6.

Moriarty, J. R. 1968. Floating gardens (chinampas) agriculture in the old lakes of Mexico. *America Indígena* 28(2): 461–84.

Morrisey, Richard J. 1951. The northward expansion of cattle ranching in New Spain, 1550–1600. *Agricultural History* 25(3): 115–21.

National Geographic Society. 1980. *Mexico and Central America* (map). Washington.

—— 1989. *Land of the Maya* (map). Washington.

Orellana, Sandra L. 1984. *The Tzutujil Mayas: Continuity and Change, 1250–1630*. Norman: University of Oklahoma Press.

Palerm, Angel. 1955. The agricultural bases of urban civilization in Mesoamerica. In *Irrigation Civilizations: A Comparative Study*, ed. J. H. Steward, pp. 28–42. Pan American Union Social Science Monographs 1. Washington.

—— 1973. *Obras hidráulicas prehispánicas en el sistema lacustre del valle de Mexico*. Cordoba, Mexico City: Instituto Nacional de Anthropología e Historia.

Palerm, Angel and Wolf, Eric. 1962. Potencial ecológico y desarrollo cultural de mesoamerica. *Revista Interamerican de Ciencias Sociales*, 2nd epoch, 1(2): 322–45.

Parsons, Jeffery R. 1971. *Prehistoric Settlement Patterns in the Texcoco Region, Mexico*. Memoirs, no. 3, of the Museum of Anthropology, Ann Arbor: University of Michigan.

—— 1976. The role of chinampa agriculture in the food supply of Aztec Tenochtitlán. In *Cultural Change and Continuity: Essays in Honor of James Bennett Griffin*, ed. Charles E. Cleland, pp. 233–57. New York: Academic Press.

Patrick, L. 1977. A cultural geography of the use of seasonally dry, sloping terrain: The metepantli crop terraces of central Mexico. Ph.D. dissertation, University of Pittsburgh.

—— 1985. Agave and zea in highland central Mexico: The ecology and history of the Metepantli. In *Prehistoric Intensive Agriculture in the Tropics*, vol. 2, ed. T. S. Farrington, pp. 539–46. Oxford: BAR. International Series, 232.

Pohl, Mary. 1985. An ethnohistorical perspective on ancient Maya wetland fields and other cultivation systems in the lowlands. In *Prehistoric Lowland Maya Environment and Subsistence Economy*, ed. M. D. Pohl. Papers of the Peabody Museum of Archaeology and Ethnology, Harvard University, vol. 77, pp. 34–45. Cambridge, MA.

Redfield, Robert and Avila, R. 1934. *Chan Kom: A Maya Village*. Publication 488. Washington: Carnegie Institution of Washington.

Rojas Rabiela, Teresa. 1985. La technología agrícola mesoamericana en el siglo XVI. In *Historia de la agricultural epoca prehispánica-siglo XVI*, ed. Teresa Rojas Rabiela and William T. Sanders, pp. 129–232. Mexico City: Instituto Nacional de Antropología e Historia.

—— 1988. *Las siembras de ayer: La agricultura indígena del siglo XVI*. Mexico City: Secretaría de Educación Pública y Centro de Investigaciones y Estudios Superiores en Antropología Social.

—— 1991. La agricultura en la Epoca prehispánica. In *La agricultura en tierras mexicanas, desde sus orígenes hasta nuestros días*, ed. Teresa Rojas Rabiela, pp. 15–138. Mexico, D.F.: Editorial Erijalbo S.A. de C.V.

Roys, Ralph L. 1943. *The Indian Background of Colonial Yucatan*. Publication 548. Washington: Carnegie Institution of Washington.

Sale, Kirkpatrick. 1990. *The Conquest of Paradise: Christopher Columbus and the Columbian Legacy*. New York: A. Knopf.

Sanders, William T. 1972. The agricultural history of the basin of Mexico. In *The Valley of Mexico*, ed. Eric R. Wolf, pp. 101–59. Albuquerque: University of New Mexico Press.

—— 1981. Ecological adaptation in the basin of Mexico: 23,000 BC to present. In *Archaeology: Handbook of Middle American Indians*, ed. J. A. Sabloff, pp. 147–97. Austin: University of Texas Press.

Sanders, Williams, T., Parsons, J. R., and Santley, R. S. 1979. *The Basin of Mexico: Ecological Processes in the Evolution of a Civilization*. New York: Academic Press.

Sauer, Jonathan D. 1976. Changing perception and exploitation of New World plants in Europe, 1492–1800. In *First Images of America*, vol. 2, ed. Fredi Chiappelli, pp. 813–32. Berkeley: University of California Press.

Schmidt, Peter J. 1977. Un sistema de cultivo intensivo en la cuenca del río Nautla, Veracruz. *Boletín del Instituto Nacional de Anthropología e Historia* 3(20): 50–60.

Scholes, France V. and Roys, Ralph L. 1968 [1948]. *The Maya Chontal Indians of Acalan-Tixchel: A Contribution to the History and Ethnography of the Yucatan Peninsula*. Norman: University of Oklahoma Press.

Siemens, Alfred H. 1982. Modelling pre-hispanic hydroagriculture on levee backslopes in northern Veracruz, Mexico. In *Drained Field Agriculture in Central and South America*, ed. J. P. Darch, pp. 27–54. Oxford: British Archaeological Reports International Series 189.

—— 1983. Oriented raised fields in central Veracruz. *American Antiquity* 48(1): 85–102.

—— 1990. *Between Summit and Sea. Central Veracruz in the Nineteenth Century*. Vancouver: University of British Columbia Press.

—— 1992. Land use succession in the Gulf lowlands on Mexico: A long view. Paper presented at the SCOPE Scientific Symposium on Principles, Patterns, and Processes: Some Legacies of the Columbian Encounter. Seville, Spain.

Siemens, Alfred H. et al. 1988. Evidence for a cultivar and a chronology from patterned wetlands in central Veracruz, Mexico. *Science* 242: 105–7.

Simpson, L. B. 1952. *Exploitation of Land in Central Mexico in the Sixteenth Century*. Ibero-Americana 36. Berkeley: University of California Press.

Sluyter, Andrew. 1990. Vestiges of upland fields in central Veracruz: A new perspective on its Pre-columbian human ecology. MA thesis, University of British Columbia.

Stadleman, Raymond. 1940. *Maize Cultivation in Northwestern Guatemala*. Contributions to American Anthropology and History. Publication 523, pp. 83–263. Washington: Carnegie Institution of Washington.

Stark, Barbara L. 1974. Geography and economic specialization in the lower Papaloapan, Veracruz, Mexico. *Ethnohistory* 21(3): 199–221.

—— 1978. An ethnohistoric model for native economy and settlement patterns in southern Veracruz, Mexico. In *Prehistoric Coastal Adaptation: The Economy and Ecology of Maritime Central America*, ed. Barbara L. Stark and Barbara Voorhies, pp. 211–38. New York: Academic Press.

—— 1990. The Gulf coast and central highlands of Mexico: Alternative methods for interaction. *Research in Economic Anthropology* 12: 243–85.

Stevens, Rayfred L. 1964. The soils of Middle America and their relation to Indian people and cultures. In *Natural Environments and Early Cultures*, vol. 1. Handbook of Middle American Indians, ed. Robert C. West, pp. 265–315. Austin: University of Texas Press.

Stone, Doris. 1977. *Pre-Columbian Man in Costa Rica*. Cambridge: Harvard University Peabody Museum Press.

Super, John C. 1988. *Food, Conquest, and Colonization in Sixteenth-century Spanish America*. Albuquerque: University of New Mexico Press.

Tozzer, Alfred M. 1941. *Landa's Relación de las cosas de Yucatán*. Peabody Museum, Paper 18 (translation). Cambridge: Harvard University.

Turner, B. L. II. 1983a. Comparisons of agrotechnologies in the Basin of Mexico and central Maya lowlands: Formative to the classic Maya collapse. In *Highland–lowland Interaction in Mesoamerica: Interdisciplinary Approaches*, ed. A. G. Miller, pp. 13–47. Washington: Dumbarton Oaks Research Library and Collection.

—— 1983b. *Once Beneath the Forest: Prehistoric Terracing in the Río Bec Region of the Maya Lowlands*. Dellplain Latin American Series 13, Boulder, CO: Westview Press.

—— 1990a. Population reconstruction for the central Maya lowlands: 1000 BC to AD 1500. In *Precolumbian Population History in the Maya Lowlands*, ed. T. P. Culbert and D. S. Rice, pp. 301–24. Albuquerque: University of New Mexico Press.

—— 1990b. The rise and fall of population and agriculture in the central Maya lowlands: 300 BC to present. In *Hunger in History: Food Shortage, Poverty, and Deprivation*, ed. L. F. Newman, pp. 178–211. Cambridge, MA: Basil Blackwell.

Turner, B. L. H. and Brush, S. B. 1987. *Comparative Farming Systems*. New York: Guilford Press.

Turner, B. L. H. and Miksicek, Charles H. 1984. Economic plant species associated with prehistoric agriculture in the Maya lowlands. *Economic Botany* 38: 179–93.

US Defense Mapping Agency. 1965. *Operational Navigational Chart, J-25*. Washington.

—— 1974. *Operational Navigational Chart, J-24*. Washington.

—— 1978. *Operational Navigational Chart, K-25*. Washington.

Vivió Escoto, Jorge A. 1964. Weather and climate of Central Mexico. In *Natural Environment and Early Cultures*, vol. 1. Handbook of Middle American Indians, ed. Robert C. West, pp. 187–215. Austin: University of Texas Press.

Weatherford, Jack. 1988. *Indian Givers: How the Indians of the Americas Transformed the World*. New York: Fawcett Columbine.

West, Robert C. 1964a. The natural regions of middle America. In *Natural Environments and Early Cultures*, vol. 1. Handbook of Middle American Indians, pp. 363–83. Austin: University of Texas Press.

—— 1964b. Surface configuration and associated geology of Middle America. In *Natural Environments and Early Cultures*, vol. 1, Handbook of Middle American Indians, pp. 33–83. Austin: University of Texas Press.

West, Robert C. and Armillas, Pedro. 1952. Las chinampas de México. Poesía realidad de los "jardines flotantes." *Cuadernos Americanos* 50: 165–82.

Whitmore, Thomas M. 1991. A simulation of the sixteenth-century population collapse in the Basin of Mexico. *Annals of the Association of American Geographers* 81(3): 464–87.

—— 1992. *Disease and Death in Early Colonial Mexico: Simulating Amerindian Depopulation*. Dellplain Latin American Geography Series. Boulder, CO: Westview Press.

Wilhelmy, Herbert. 1981. *Welt und Umwelt der Maya*. Munich: R. Piper and Co.

Wilken, Gene C. 1969. Drained field agriculture: An intensive farming system in Tlaxcala, Mexico. *The Geographical Review* 59: 215–41.

—— 1971. Food-producing systems available to the ancient Maya. *American Antiquity* 36: xx.

—— 1979. Traditional slope management: An analytical approach. In *Hill Lands: Proceedings of an International Symposium*, pp. 416–21. Morgantown: West Virginia University Books.

—— 1985. A note on buoyancy and other dubious characteristics of the "floating" chinampas of Mexico. In *Prehistoric Intensive Agriculture in the Tropics*, ed. I. S. Farrington, pp. 31–48. International Series 232. Oxford: British Archaeological Reports.

—— 1987. *Good Farmers: Traditional Agricultural Resource Management in Mexico and Central America*. Berkeley: University of California Press.

Wilkerson, S. Jeffrey K. 1983. So green like a garden: Intensive agriculture in ancient Veracruz. In *Drained Field Agriculture in Central and South America*, ed. J. P. Darch, pp. 55–90. International Series 189. Oxford: British Archaeological Reports.

Williams, Barbara J. 1972. Tepetate in the Valley of Mexico. *Annals of the Association of American Geographers* 62(4): 618–26.

Wilson, Eugene M. 1980. Physical geography of the Yucatán peninsula. In *Yucatán, a World Apart*, ed. E. H. Moseley and E. D. Terry, pp. 5–40. University, AL: University of Alabama Press.

Wolf, Eric C., and Palerm, Angel. 1955. Irrigation in the old Acolhua domain, Mexico. *Southwestern Journal of Anthropology* 11: 265–81.

Zamora Acosta, Elias. 1985. *Los Mayas de las tierras altas en el siglo XVI; Tradición y cambio en Guatemala*. Seville: Diputación Provincial de Sevilla.

CHAPTER 6

Lithic Craft Specialization and Product Distribution at the Maya Site of Colha, Belize

Harry J. Shafer and Thomas R. Hester

Introduction

This paper presents a case-study of prehistoric lithic craft specialization among the ancient Maya of northern Belize, central America. The focus is on mass production of stone tools at the site of Colha and the distribution of these products to Maya consumers outside the site area.

Colha is situated in the northern part of a restricted outcrop zone of chert. As we shall detail, these chert resources were used for more than 2,000 years by the Maya occupants of the site in craft-specialized stone tool production. The evidence for lithic craft specialization takes the form of extensive debitage deposits that are the byproduct of chipped stone tool manufacture. The details on the various aspects of craft specialization at Colha can be found in Shafer and Hester (1983, 1986a) Hester and Shafer (1989), Shafer (1983a, 1985), Hester (1985), Roemer (1984), Drollinger (1989), and Michaels (1986, 1989).

Craft specialization defined

We have used the term 'craft specialist' to define an individual who repeatedly manufactures a craft product for exchange. Production in craft-specialized communities exceeds that needed for household use. The degree of specialization depends upon the amount of time devoted to the craft and to the quantity of production. Production efficiency and standardization are other criteria that have been used to define craft specialization (Roemer 1984: 67, 68).

Why did stone tool craft specialization occur at the site of Colha? The extensive chert-bearing zone (hereafter CBZ) in which it is located (figure 6.1) encompasses a large area of good quality chert, readily accessible. Indeed a few other workshop sites are known within the CBZ, both north and south of Colha, though none appears to have achieved the level of production attributed to Colha. We believe that the concentrated nature of the workshop deposits at Colha, and the other workshop sites, the standardization of production of only a few formal tool classes, and a substantial body of evidence of tool consumption in sites lying outside the CBZ production zone, all support a model of restricted access and control of the chert resources.

Whether the production was governed by supply and demand, under the control of the elite or simply by the craftsmen themselves, is presently unknown. Ethnographic parallels from New Guinea (cf. Burton 1984, 1989) will be offered below as a basis for a model suggesting that production of CBZ formal tools may indeed have been determined by the craftsmen themselves.

Chert-bearing zone

The chert-bearing deposits (CBZ) of northern Belize lie in a region of about 181 km^2

Reprinted from Harry J. Shafer and Thomas R. Hester. 1991. Lithic Craft Specialization and Product Distribution at the Maya Site of Colha, Belize. *World Archaeology* 23: 79–97.

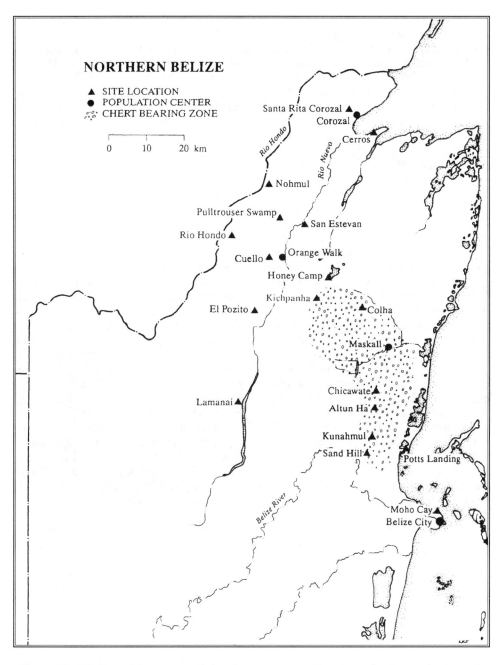

Figure 6.1 Northern Belize: extent of chert-bearing zone and locations of major production and consumer sites.

(Hester and Shafer 1984: 159). The cherts are derived from Ecocene and Miocene limestones; the best available map of chert distribution appears in Wright et al. (1959). However, we define the CBZ here as being restricted to surface outcrops of nodular chert; this definition has been derived largely from Colha Project regional surveys (Hester and Shafer 1984). Concentrations of both nodular and tabular chert are exposed either directly on the surface or in erosional features in the limestone. Chert is also known to occur in at least three separate strata, as revealed in modern quarry pits in the CBZ (Tobey 1986). Color and texture vary in different levels; the finer cherts occur deeper, while coarser varieties are found usually in upper deposits. Colors range from a golden hue to a mottled or banded brown and gray material. Trace element characterization studies have shown the chemical composition of the cherts to be sufficiently variable so as to distinguish specific outcrops or locales (Tobey 1986). Exploitation of the CBZ cherts can be traced back to Paleoindian (9000–6000 BC) and Archaic (preceramic: 6000–2000 BC) times, but is most intensive during the Maya Preclassic and Classic periods (Hester and Shafer 1984).

While the most extensive utilization of chert occurs at the northern and southern ends of the CBZ, our regional surveys have shown that most settlements in the zone did not exploit the local resources at the level of craft specialists. On the northern end of the CBZ is Colha, unmatched by any other Maya site in the region in terms of the number, size, density, and volume of production evidenced by its workshop deposits. Also at the northern end of the zone is Kichpanha, where one minor and one major lithic workshop have been found. In the southern part of the CBZ lie the sites of Kunahmul (Kelly 1980; Taylor 1980), and Chicawate (Kelly 1980). Finally, in the central portion of the CBZ, minor workshop activity has been documented at sites near Maskall (Gibson 1982) (figure 6.1).

Colha

The most visible example of prehistoric lithic craft specialization in the New World is found at Colha. Colha was first briefly studied by the Corozal Project (Hammond 1973) and has been the focus of investiga-

tions by members of the Colha Project since 1979 (a joint effort of the University of Texas at San Antonio, Texas A & M University, Centro Studi Ricerche Ligabue, Venice, and the University of Texas at Austin). It covers about 6 km^2 and contains several hundred mounds. Most are small 'house' mounds and *plazuela* mound groups (an arrangement of small 'house mounds' on a low platform); there are several 'plaza' groups consisting of large mounds (presumably elite residences), a small monumental center, and more than 100 chert debitage mounds and deposits.

Chronological data on Maya exploitation of the CBZ resources at Colha is the most complete for any site in the region (Hester 1985; Hester and Shafer 1989). Significant chert utilization, and manufacture of formal tools for distribution beyond Colha, began in the Middle Preclassic (1000–300 BC). However, evidence for lithic craft specialization and large-scale production is most evident in the Late Preclassic (300 BC–AD 250), the Late Classic (AD 600–850), and the Early and Middle Postclassic (AD 900–1250) periods (Hester 1985; Shafer and Hester 1986a). Michaels (1986, 1989) has described the Early Postclassic specialization. However, since the latter represents a different level of utilization and is separate from the long-lived local Maya craft specialization at the site, we will deal here only with the Preclassic and Classic materials.

Extensive surface exploitation, and likely shallow pit mining, accompanied the production of formal tools in the Middle Preclassic. Colha was a village of Maya farmers at this time, but excavations have produced data on shell bead making (using burin-spall drills) and clear indication of the manufacture of formal tools (such as the 'T-shaped adze'; figure 6.2) that exceeded the needs of the community. As noted later, there is evidence of distribution of Middle Preclassic products to other Maya sites in Belize and we suspect that during the span of ca. 800–300 BC, chert exploitation and craft specialization had reached the level of a 'cottage industry' (Shafer and Hester 1986a).

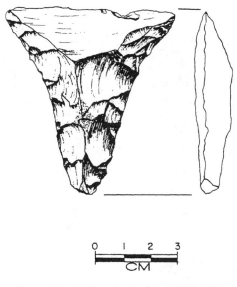

0   1   2   3
CM

Figure 6.2 T-shaped adze from the Middle Preclassic at Colha.

At some time during the Late Preclassic (and Terminal Preclassic) era, intensive production of formal tools began at Colha. These activities created extensive debitage deposits, both workshop mounds and massive linear deposits, that are concentrated on the terraces of the water catchment basins (aguadas) occurring throughout the site. These debitage deposits (at least thirty-six have been mapped) vary in thickness from 0.7 to 2 m. Structurally, they usually overlie low platforms faced with a single course of cobbles, or are superimposed over middens and activity areas of Middle Preclassic or early Late Preclassic age.

The Late Preclassic debitage deposits (as well as those of the Late Classic) are composed of 95–9 percent pure debitage resulting from biface thinning and striking platform preparation (Drollinger 1989; Shafer and Hester 1986a), as well as of numerous aborted failures of formal tool manufacture (Shafer 1985; Drollinger 1989). The deposits also include a light scattering of Chicanel sphere ceramics and occasional pieces of limestone rubble. Matrix analysis of the debitage deposits has docu-

mented both the standardization of tool manufacture and the volume of production (Roemer 1984; Drollinger 1989; Shafer and Hester 1986a). Further, it has been demonstrated that initial quarry reduction of bifaces was conducted elsewhere (Hester and Shafer 1984) and that rough bifaces or 'quarry blanks' were transported to the workshops for thinning and shaping as formal artifacts.

Quantitative debitage samples were drawn from each excavation to calculate the debitage density and to formulate production estimates. Standard samples of 8,000 cm^3 were taken from each 20 cm level of an excavation unit. Drollinger (1989) and Roemer (1984) provide quantitative figures on the flake density of the Late Preclassic and Late Classic workshop deposits respectively.

Drollinger (1989) examined three 8,000 cm^3 samples of debitage from Operation 2024, a Late Preclassic workshop. The average weight of each sample was 5,137 gm; the average number of flakes (larger than 6 mm) per cubic meter was 603,000. Drollinger (1989) thus estimated that the workshop contained 432,954,000 pieces of lithic debitage.

By comparison, Roemer (1984) studied seven 8,000 cm^3 samples from a Terminal Classic workshop known as Operation 2007. The average weight for each was 7,680 gm or 960,000 gm of debitage per cubic meter. He also counted all flakes larger than 3 mm in one of the samples, a total of 36,649, and calculated that this debitage deposit contained 4,956,125 pieces per cubic meter.

In Late Preclassic workshop production at Colha, the craft specialists focused on four formal tools. The most common was the large oval biface (celt or axe blade; figure 6.3). Second in frequency was the tranchet bit tool (figure 6.4; Shafer 1983b; Hester 1985), which probably served several functions, especially as axes or adzes (Nash 1986). A third formal tool is a long, parallel-sided biface (biconvex in cross section) that may have been used as an adze in woodworking (ibid.).

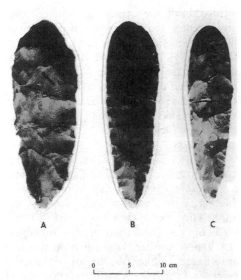

Figure 6.3 Large oval bifaces refitted from manufacturing failures found in the Late Preclassic workshops at Colha.

While these three formal tools served in secular or domestic contexts, a fourth formal tool – the stemmed macroblade (figure 6.5) – was used in both secular and non-secular functions.

Another non-secular product of the Late Preclassic workshops was the 'eccentric', which makes its first appearance in ancient Maya material culture in the Late Preclassic (Gibson 1986). Fragments of eccentrics broken in manufacture are found scattered in the workshop deposits. These strangely-shaped, often large, lithic artifacts (figure 6.6) are found at Colha and at consumer sites in ritual caches and in burials. While their precise function remains a mystery, they most likely had symbolic importance and are sometimes depicted in Maya art (McKinney 1984; Schele and Miller 1986).

In terms of lithic technology, the tranchet bit tool is a unique artifact in the assemblage. These tools were made by obtaining a large macroflake (ca. 20–30 cm long and 15–20 cm wide), and shaping and preparing the proximal (bulbar) end for the removal of a long, curved flake (tranchet flake). If the tranchet flake was removed successfully,

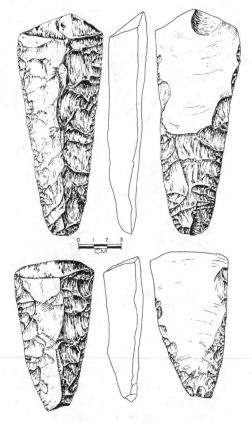

Figure 6.4 Tranchet bit tools from the Late Preclassic at Colha.

then the remainder of the preform was shaped to the desired length, width, and thickness (Shafer 1983b). Thus to manufacture one tranchet bit tool, the removal of at least one tranchet flake – the 'primary tranchet flake' – is required, but often a second – the 'secondary tranchet flake' – was needed because the first was not removed with the desired effects. Primary tranchet flakes are easily recognized since they carry the flake scars, and distinctive platform preparation flakes, of the proximal end of the parent macroflake. Secondary tranchet flakes bear the facets of the previous (primary) tranchet flake removal. Since a minimum of one primary flake was required, one method of estimating the production of tranchet bit tools is to count the primary tranchet flakes found in the workshop deposit.

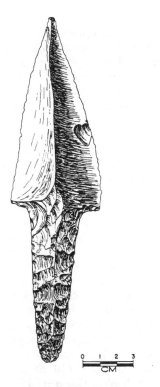

Figure 6.6 Late Preclassic eccentric from Colha.

Figure 6.5 Stemmed macroblade from the Late Preclassic at Colha.

We conducted such a calculation for one Late Preclassic debitage mound, Operation 4001, with a total volume of about 150 m³. All tranchet flakes were kept and counted for each of the levels in two 2 × 2 m units, each with an average depth of 1.4 m. A total of 4,847 tranchet flakes was recovered and primary tranchet flakes numbered 563 (58.2 per cent) of the study sample (n = 1034). Assuming (1) that 58.2 per cent of all of the tranchet flakes are primary; (2) there is a random distribution of primary to secondary tranchet flakes in the deposit; and (3) there was no loss of primary to secondary flakes, it is possible to estimate the *minimum* number of tranchet bit tools produced in the workshop. A total of 5.6 m³ of fill is represented in the two excavation units that yield 4,847 tranchet flakes. Fifty-eight per cent of 4,847 divided by 5.6 m³ yields a total of 503.7 tranchet flakes per cubic meter – or the minimum number of tranchet bit tools

produced, and represented by that volume of debitage. Given the estimated workshop volume of 150 m³, we estimate that 75,562 tranchet bit tools were produced at this one workshop alone.

Oval biface production at Operation 4001 must have been at least equal to that of the tranchet bit tool production, judging from the frequency of both biface thinning flakes and biface failures. If this assumption is correct, then a minimum of 150,000 tools of these two forms was produced at the 4001 workshop.

We have used these production estimates from Operation 4001, combined with additional data from Operations 2006 and 2024, to calculate an approximate volume of tool production for the Late Preclassic period (Shafer and Hester 1986a). We estimate that at least 4.5 million oval bifaces and tranchet bit tools were produced during this period at Colha (note: this estimate does not include the narrow bifaces or stemmed macroblades, the other two important formal tool classes). Chronological studies suggest a time span for the workshops of about 250 years, with an average production volume of 18,000 tools per year.

The population at Late Preclassic Colha, in the 1 km² core area, has been estimated about 600 persons (Eaton 1982). If we assume that one in five was a mature male, suggesting 120 males at any one time, each male would have had to average 150 tools per year to achieve a production rate of 18,000 tools a year. This production estimate is far in excess of what was needed for local consumption. Indeed, it is most likely that a much smaller number of the males were craft specialists and were capable of producing many more tools per person than indicated above. In comparison, Burton's (1984) study of quarrying and axe making in Papua New Guinea led him to estimate that, among the Tungei people of the Wahgi Valley, 200 men produced ten axes every five years, or 40,000 axes per century (he felt a more realistic estimate was 300,000 per century). He observed that such a volume of axes was 'easily swallowed up' by the existing trade with the agricultural population in the hinterlands (Burton 1984: 244). The New Guinea axes were, when finished, ground stone tools that were likely more durable and longer lived than the thinner, chipped stone bifaces made at Colha. This fact would suggest a shorter use-life and higher replacement rate for the Maya tools.

Colha stood alone in the Late Preclassic as the major supplier of chert tools in northern Belize (indeed, only one other Late Preclassic workshop is known outside Colha, that recently excavated at Kichpanha; John Cross, personal communication). Production at Colha undoubtedly continued through the Terminal Preclassic/Early Classic, but this is difficult to gauge, given the temporal overlap of diagnostic sherds within the workshops (it should be obvious that workshops are notoriously hard to date, as they contain no organic materials and only rarely pieces of obsidian that can be used for hydration analysis).

We can be more specific about intensive production of stone tools, however, during the Late Classic (and its final, or Terminal, phase). More than thirty Late Classic workshops and debitage deposits have been recorded and some of these are equal in size to those of the Late Preclassic (figure 6.7). The Colha lithic tradition continued, notably in the technology and production of oval bifaces and tranchet bit tools. However, the Late Classic oval bifaces tend to be smaller and narrower than the Late Preclassic examples (Hester 1985; Shafer and Hester 1986a). The tranchet bit tools continued to be made, as were eccentrics, though the latter were usually either notched blades or small bifacial forms. One distinctive Late Classic artifact is the 'general utility biface'. This is a celt or axe form that has a thick, diamond-shaped cross section and a carefully shaped bit. The variety of wear patterns seen on it at Colha suggest that it was a hafted axe used for a wide range of functions, from cutting wood to shaping stone blocks. A core-blade technology is in place by Terminal Classic times. The products are blades and stemmed projectile points made on blades (Roemer 1984). These points were presumably used on spears launched by spear-throwers (*atlatls*) and their intensive production could mark a period of warfare within the region.

The Southern Chert-Bearing Zone

Chert workshops occur at several sites in the southern part of the CBZ (figure 6.1). In the central part of the zone they are scattered in the vicinity of the town of Maskall. In the south the Colha regional survey recorded ninety-five mounds at the site of Kunahmul, seven of which were chert workshops or debitage deposits. This Late Classic site is situated around a large lagoon, with a substantial monumental center to its north, and thirty-four mounds and platforms on its south side (Kelly 1980). The debitage mounds were also on the south, doubtless due to the outcrops in the area of brown ledge chert (15–20 cm thick), as well as large nodules of gray mottled chert that ranged up to 60 cm or more in diameter.

Figure 6.7   A Late Classic workshop at Colha; *above*, view of workshop, Operation 1001; *below*, profile of excavation unit in the workshop.

The seven chert workshops at Kunahmul were tested and found to be somewhat different structurally than those at Colha. One major difference was that all stages of lithic production were present, versus the thinning and shaping stages found in Colha workshops. The tool assemblage included oval bifaces, tranchet bit tools, and stemmed blades.

Quantitative studies of one test pit indicated that the production rate for tranchet bit tools was considerably lower than at Colha. At Operation 4, the density of tranchet flakes per cubic meter was only 950. If we use the same calculations as for Colha, a total of 553 tranchet bit tools was produced for each cubic meter of debitage at Kunahmul.

At Chicawate (Rockstone Pond) is an area ca. 2 km north of the well-known Maya center of Altun Ha (Pendergast 1981) in which eight chert debitage deposits were recorded (Kelly 1980). The chert outcrops are in a series of linear ridges, the debitage deposits occurring either along the outcrops or as veneers over small mounds. The actual extent of these workshops is unknown. None was thoroughly tested, though shovel tests in each revealed deposits averaging 40–50 cm thick (Kelly 1980). Two of the deposits were outstanding in terms of their length, each measuring ca. 100 m. Identifiable ceramics suggest they are of Late Classic date, which is consistent with their associated tool assemblage (e.g. the same formal tools found at Colha Late Classic workshops occur at Chicawate). It is also possible, though it cannot be documented at this time, that Chicawate was comparable to Colha in terms of *Late Classic* lithic craft production.

Distribution of Colha Products

Temporal and spatial distribution

During their study of the lithic industry of Colha, the authors examined lithic assemblages from other parts of Belize. Using the variables of chert color, banding, and texture, and the technology of manufacture at the site of Colha, we have defined the distribution through time and space of Colha products in northern Belize and adjacent areas. We have been careful to identify these materials as 'Colha-like', or as derived from the 'CBZ', though we are confident that most of such artifacts are from Colha. Obviously, such links cannot be positively established without trace element studies (Tobey 1986). What seems clear, however, is that Colha is *the* major production center in Middle and Late Preclassic times, with technology and production levels so distinctive that identification of 'Colha' products at consumer sites is likely to be highly accurate. In the Late Classic, other workshop sites such as Kunahmul and Chicawate are known in the region, albeit with much lower production levels than Colha, and our attributions of materials from consumer sites are better couched in terms like 'derived from the CBZ'.

The external distribution of Colha lithic artifacts has been extensively reviewed by Hester and Shafer (1989) and space does not permit full discussion here. We have recognized two levels of tool consumption: 'utilitarian' and 'ritual'. The mass-produced artifacts from Colha, such as the oval bifaces and tranchet bit tools, fall into the utilitarian realm. The eccentrics and finely-made stemmed macroblades are found in ritual or non-secular contexts, particularly caches or tombs. Further, we have identified two areas of Maya consumers. The first is the 'primary consumer area' located largely in northern Belize, as well as parts of central and coastal Belize, and apparently into southern Quintana Roo (Mexico); high frequencies of distinctive Colha artifacts, both utilitarian and ritual occur in the farming areas (McAnany 1986), communities, and centers within this region. The other occurrences of Colha artifacts are in the 'peripheral consumer area' in western and southern Belize, as well as some sites in the Peten (Guatemala); at these sites, including Pacbitun (Belize), Tikal, and El Mirador (Peten), the most common artifact form derived from Colha or the CBZ is the large-stemmed macroblade, of both Preclassic and Classic date.

We have offered several perspectives on the nature of demand and exchange related to these two consumer areas (Hester and Shafer 1989). The primary consumer area lies largely outside the chert-bearing zone where local lithic sources were of chalcedony of generally poor quality. Colha tools were procured and utilized in a variety of ways, as the analyses of Shafer (1983a) and McAnany (1986) have demonstrated. The artifacts left Colha in their standardized mass-produced form and the consumer adapted them to the needs at hand. For example, a hafted large oval biface found in the Rio Hondo area, the so-called 'Puleston Axe' (figure 6.8; Shafer and Hester 1986b), bears wear suggestive of use in cutting woody materials or plants. Use of identical tools in agriculture or ground-working activities is documented at Pulltrouser Swamp (Shafer 1983a), but there is also good evidence for the use of these tools as axes, for chopping and clearing activities. The tranchet bit tools, once in the hands of the Maya consumers, also saw different

uses, sometimes as adzes, but also as axes (Shafer 1983b). The overriding pattern, however, is that of *recycling* of these tools. As they broke or wore out, the Maya consumer fashioned them into other tools (e.g. hammerstones). At practically every site in the primary consumer area, recycling is present; knowledge of the Colha production system allows us to incorporate the recycled fragments into their original categories.

Stemmed macroblades and eccentric lithics also occur in the primary consumer area, usually as grave goods (e.g. at Santa Rita Corozal; Chase and Chase 1986) and as cache items (e.g. at Nohmul; Hammond et al. 1987; personal communication). We should point out that not all stemmed macroblades went into the ritual/elite realm; some occur in utilitarian contexts, used as knives or for other tasks (Shafer 1983a; Nash 1986).

The time range involved in the distribution of Colha products within the primary consumer area is of considerable interest. It is now clear that the lithic specialists at Colha were producing tools for broad distribution during the Middle Preclassic (perhaps as early as 800–1000 BC). The artifacts are highly distinctive and reflect specific technological attributes (as well as skills). They include: the 'T-shaped adze' (figure 6.2); truncated macroblades used as bores for burin spalls for shell bead drills; a biface with a wedge-shaped bit; and small oval bifaces (celts). These occur in the Middle Preclassic deposits at Cuello. The absence of debitage attributable to their manufacture, and the clear Colha origin of both the chert and the technology, attest to their derivation from craft specialists at Colha. One of the 'T-shaped adzes' has been found as far south as the Sibun River in southern Belize (Hester and Shafer 1989).

The Late Preclassic (through Terminal Preclassic) utilization of Colha-produced tools has been documented in a number of publications, summarized by Hester and Shafer (1989). Indeed, this is the period for which we have the strongest evidence of mass production and widespread distribution, issues returned to below. There is the

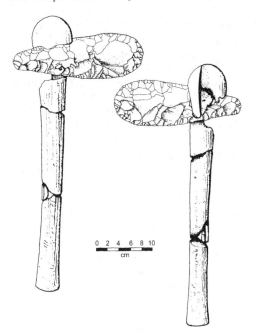

0 2 4 6 8 10
cm

Figure 6.8 A hafted stone tool from northern Belize ('Puleston axe'). (From Shafer and Hester 1986b.)

recently excavated Late Preclassic work-shop at Kichpanha (John Cross, personal communication), associated with a ceremonial complex and suggested to have been under elite control. It apparently produced oval bifaces and tranchet bit tools for local use.

To the long list of Late Preclassic consumer sites already known (Cuello, Nohmul, San Estevan, Cerros, El Pozito, Santa Rita Corozal, Pulltrouser Swamp), we can now add a Late Preclassic settlement on the shores of Honey Camp Lagoon (figure 6.1). A surface collection in the Lowie Museum, University of California, Berkeley (Meighan and Bennyhoff, MS; Hester, notes) includes tranchet bit tools (resharpened), macroblades, oval bifaces, stemmed macroblades (some much used), a single tranchet flake, and numerous recycled bifaces – an assemblage mirroring the sites listed above.

The presence or absence of stone tool production at Colha in the Early Classic is presently unresolved. However, by Late and Terminal Classic times, workshops were clearly in production and standardized artifact forms were again being widely distributed in the primary consumer area. Most distinctive of the Late Classic are small oval bifaces, general utility bifaces, and eccentrics. In the Terminal Classic, the blade workshops noted earlier in this paper produced stemmed blade dart points and these are found at various sites outside Colha. For example, at Potts Landing in central coastal Belize, these stemmed blades and small oval bifaces, make up almost all of the formal lithics (Meighan and Bennyhoff, MS; Hester, notes on materials at the Lowie Museum, University of California, Berkeley). Some of these may be derived from Late Classic workshops at nearby Kunahmul or even Chicawate.

Discussion

With the beginning of standardized stone tool production at Colha in the Middle Preclassic, and its termination (at least from standpoint of mass production) in the Terminal Classic, there is an almost 2,000-year record of production and distribution.

In viewing the distribution of Colha lithics in the peripheral consumer area, it appears that the site of Colha was the source of almost all formal tools during the Late Preclassic, and perhaps into the Early Classic. These are accompanied by locally made non-formal tools, usually of chalcedony. However, by the Late Classic, Colha may have been but one, albeit probably the largest, of the production sites. As we have speculated in earlier papers (cf. Shafer and Hester 1983), Colha may have lost its control over lithic production, perhaps due to the rise of Altun Ha. Notably, the southern CBZ workshops are in the vicinity of that major site.

Given these broad patterns and the clear evidence of craft specialization and mass production at Colha, what can we say about the reasons for the rise (and persistence) of lithic production, its control, and the modes of exchange? Production appears to correlate chronologically with the rise of Maya civilization and with the increase of population and the attendant intensification of agriculture. Colha was suitably located, with permanent water (Rancho Creek), nearby agricultural lands and abundant chert. But what initially sparked lithic craft specialization here and what enhanced it to the scale of mass production by Late Preclassic times? Why were generations of craft specialists tied to Colha for so long? Was production controlled by the elite or by the craft specialists themselves? At Kichpanha, there seems to be an example of an elite-controlled workshop, but at Colha, with its more numerous workshops, that level of control is far from clear. We have noted in earlier papers the analogies that can be drawn from craft-specialized communities elsewhere (Reina and Hill 1978), but these are often modern communities in different cultural and economic situations (e.g. the pottery-producing communities of highland Guatemala). However, a recent paper by Burton (1989) and one by Salvatori (1986) provide data on axe production in New Guinea. Burton (1984) notes the nature of quarry control, although this is not particularly relevant to the Colha situation, given the vast expanse of chert resources in the CBZ. Burton (1989: 258), on the other hand, has obtained data from native participants in axe-exchange networks in Papua New Guinea that raise some interesting issues with regard to Colha lithic production. For example, he notes that 'axe production was not . . . driven by the subsistence needs of an ever-growing hinterland of neolithic agriculturalists, but by buoyant exchange values in the immediate vicinity of their territory, a zone of some 20 km at most' (1989: 258). Indeed, axe-making was 'a personal endeavor that helped in assembling brideprices and gaining prestige through carefully tended exchange relationships' (1989: 258). Whatever the local view of the benefits of axe-making, the axes usually made their way into a trade system that extended over a 250 km radius (Burton 1984). He notes (1984: 234): 'Nowhere were these operations [mining, axe production, trade] directed by a central authority; they were co-operative ventures in so-called egalitarian, tribal societies'. Of course, the Colha situation must have been considerably different, although perhaps not drastically so in terms of Middle Preclassic social organization. By the Late Preclassic, all of the social, political and economic structures of Maya civilization were in place, and lithic production is unlikely to have existed, especially at the level of Colha mass-production, for the benefit of local craft specialists. Colha's 'primary consumer area' – for artifacts of all sorts – extended over a radius of at least 75 km. Its 'peripheral consumer area', notable for the distribution of stemmed macroblades, was at least 150 km in radius, to the south and west. However, the knowledge and control of quarries in New Guinea and the organization of axe-making at the community level fit rather well with what McAnany (1986: 266) describes as 'very localized pools of knowledge regarding resource location and production skills', as well as 'entrenchment of resources extraction and commodity production skills' (1986: 267), characteristics of her defined

'interpolity exchange network' hypothesized for northern Belize. She believes that the larger communities could have served as central marketplaces, with 'barter as the circulation mechanism' (McAnany 1986: 109). Such trade may have been carried out by 'petty traders' (cf. Feldman 1978), who moved limited types of goods over short distances (McAnany 1986: 269).

Conclusions

An archaeological case-study of ancient Maya lithic craft specialization has been presented. Communities with such craft specialists have been documented in the chert bearing zone of northern Belize. These communities, Colha and Kichpanha in the northern end of the zone, and Kunahmul and Chicawate in the southern part, produced tools in excess of that which was needed for local consumption. Colha was the major production center and far outdistances any other known site in production during the Late Preclassic and Late Classic periods.

Examination of collections from contemporaneous sites in the surrounding region indicates that large numbers of formal tools, identical to those produced in the chert-bearing zone, were being used by Maya consumers. Formal tool production has not been documented in the consumer sites, at least not to the extent or degree that would account for the rates of formal tool consumption at these sites.

The formal tools, produced and consumed, fall into two functional categories – utilitarian and non-utilitarian. The geographic distribution of the utilitarian tools was mainly in the immediate region ('primary consumer area') while the range for the non-utilitarian tools (stemmed macroblades and eccentrics) extended farther ('peripheral consumer area').

The archaeological documentation of craft specialization in ancient Maya culture has provided considerable fuel for generating economic models of production and exchange. Control of production may have been governed in one of several ways, by the elite, by merchants, or perhaps the crafts-men themselves. We have suggested that at the site level Colha was in control of pro-duction in the Late Preclassic (and likely earlier), while the community and center at Altun Ha assumed control by the Late Clas-sic. While control of production may have been under the supervision of a 'ruling elite', it is more likely that the political sphere (dominated by a major center such as Altun Ha) controlled a given territory, and by inference the *resource* (the chert-bearing areas) itself. It is suggested, based on ethno-graphic data from New Guinea, that the actual volume of production was in the hands of the craft specialists. Certainly considering that the technology and skill was handed down from generation to gen-eration, the production was probably line-age-based.

ACKNOWLEDGMENTS

For preparation of illustrations, we wish to thank Kathy Roemer, Pam Headrick, Kathryn Reese-Taylor and Daniel Julien. Plate 4 is courtesy of Giancarlo Ligabue and Erizzo Editrice, Venice. We are grateful to the collaborating institutions involved in the Colha Project (University of Texas at San Antonio, Texas A&M University, Univer-sity of Texas at Austin, Centro Studi Ricerche Ligabue, Venice) and we are particularly appre-ciative of support provided over the years by the National Endowment for the Humanities, the National Geographic Society, Earthwatch, and the American Philosophical Society, along with numerous private donors. Finally, we want to express our thanks to our archaeological colleagues working in Belize and adjacent areas; they have been very kind to share their lithic data with us.

REFERENCES

Burton, J. E. 1984. Quarrying in a tribal society. *World Archaeology* 16: 234–47.
——1989. Repeng and the salt-makers: 'Ecological trade' and stone axe production in the Papua New Guinea Highlands. *Man* (n.s.) 24: 255–72.
Chase, D. Z. and Chase, A. F. 1986. *Offerings to the Gods: Maya Archaeology at Santa Rita Corozal*. Orlando: University of Central Florida.

Drollinger, H. D., Jr. 1989. An investigation of a Late Preclassic chert workshop for Colha, Belize. Master's thesis, Department of Anthro-pology, Texas A&M University.
Eaton, J. D. 1982. Colha: An overview of archi-tecture and settlement. In *Archaeology at Colha, Belize: The 1981 Interim Report*, ed. T. R. Hester, H. J. Shafer, and J. D. Eaton, pp. 11–20. San Antonio: Center for Archaeological Research, The University of Texas at San Antonio, and Centro Studi Ricerche Ligabue, Venezia.
Feldman, L. H. 1978. Moving merchandise in protohistoric central Quahtemallan. In *Meso-american Communication Routes and Cultural Contacts*, ed. T. A. Lee, Jr. and C. Navarrete, pp. 7–17. Provo: Papers of the New World Archae-ological Foundation.
Gibson, E. C. 1982. Excavation of a Late Classic Maya workshop near Maskall, Belize. In *Archaeology at Colha, Belize: The 1981 Interim Report*, ed. T. R. Hester, H. J. Shafer, and J. D. Eaton, pp. 181–6. San Antonio: Center for Archaeological Research, the University of Texas at San Antonio, and Centro Studi Ricerche Ligabue, Venezia.
——1986. Diachronic patterns of lithic produc-tion, use and exchange in the Southern Maya lowlands. Doctoral dissertation, Harvard Uni-versity.
Hammond, N. (ed.). 1973. *British Museum–Cambridge University Corozal Project 1973 Interim Report*. Cambridge: Centre of Latin American Studies, Cambridge University.
Hammond, N., Donaghey, S., Gleason, C., Sta-neko, J., Van Tuerenhout, D., and Kosakowsky, L. 1987. Excavations at Nohmul, Belize 1985. *Journal of Field Archaeology* 14: 257–82.
Hester, T. R. 1985. The Maya lithic sequence in northern Belize. In *Stone Tool Analysis: Essays in Honor of Don E. Crabtree*, ed. M. Plew, J. Woods, and M. Pavesic, pp. 187–211. Albuquer-que: University of New Mexico Press.
Hester, T. R. and Shafer, H. J. 1984. Exploitation of chert resources by the ancient Maya of north-ern Belize. *World Archaeology* 16: 157–73.
—— and ——1989. The ancient Maya craft community at Colha, Belize and its external relationships. *Texas Papers on Latin America* 89–11. Austin: Institute of Latin American Stu-dies, the University of Texas at Austin.
Kelly, T. C. 1980. The Colha regional survey. In *The Colha Project Second Season, 1980 Interim Report*, ed. T. R. Hester, J. D. Eaton, and H. J. Shafer, pp. 51–70. San Antonio: Center for Archaeological Research, the University of

Texas at San Antonio and Centro Studi Ricerche Ligabue, Venezia.

McAnany, P. 1986. Lithic technology and exchange among wetland farmers of the eastern Maya lowlands. Doctoral dissertation, Department of Anthropology, University of New Mexico, Albuquerque.

McKinney, W. W. 1984. Representations of lithic artifacts in Maya art. Manuscript on file with the authors.

Meighan, C. W. and Bennyhoff, J. A. MS: Excavations in British Honduras. Manuscript dated 1952 on file with the authors.

Michaels, G. H. 1986. A description and analysis of Early Postclassic lithic technology at Colha, Belize. Master's thesis, Department of Anthropology, Texas A&M University.

—— 1989. Craft specialization in the Early Postclassic of Colha. *Research in Economic Anthropology, Supplement* 4: 139–83.

Nash, M. A. 1986. A functional analysis of two lithic tool collections from Colha, Belize. Master's thesis, Department of Anthropology, Texas A&M University.

Pendergast, D. M. 1981. *Excavations at Altun Ha, Belize (1964–1970)*, vol. 2. Toronto: Royal Ontario Museum.

Reina, R. E. and Hill, R. M. 1978. *Traditional Pottery of Guatemala*. Austin: University of Texas Press.

Roemer, E. R. 1984. A Late Classic Maya workshop at Colha, Belize. Master's thesis, Department of Anthropology, Texas A&M University.

Salvatori, S. 1986. Le asce di pietra dei Papua Pigmei. In *Indonesia: La Grande Deriva Etnica*, ed. G. M. Rozoni, pp. 145–52. Venice: Erizzo Editrice.

Schele, L. and Miller, M. E. 1986. *The Blood of Kings*. Fort Worth: Kimball Art Museum.

Shafer, H. J. 1983a. The lithic artifacts of the Pulltrouser area: Settlements and fields. In *Pulltrouser Swamp, Ancient Maya Habitat, Agricul-*ture *and Settlement in Northern Belize*, ed. B. L. Turner II and P. D. Harrison, pp. 212–45. Albuquerque: University of New Mexico Press.

—— 1983b. The tranchet technique in lowland Maya lithic production. *Lithic Technology* 12: 57–68.

—— 1985. A technological study of two Maya workshops at Colha, Belize. In *Stone Tool Analysis: Essays in Honor of Don E. Crabtree*, ed. M. G. Plew, J. C. Woods, and M. G. Pavesic, pp. 277–315. Albuquerque: University of New Mexico Press.

Shafer, H. J. and Hester, T. R. 1983. Ancient Maya chert workshops in northern Belize, Central America. *American Antiquity* 48: 519–43.

—— and ——1986a. Maya stone-tool craft specialization and production at Colha, Belize: Reply to Mallory. *American Antiquity* 51: 148–66.

—— and —— 1986b. Ancient Maya hafted stone tool from northern Belize. *Working Papers in Archaeology* 3. San Antonio: Center for Archaeological Research, the University of Texas at San Antonio.

Taylor, A. J. 1980. Excavations at Kunahmul. In *The Colha Project Second Season, 1980 Interim Report*, ed. T. R. Hester, J. D. Eaton, and H. J. Shafer, pp. 241–50. San Antonio: Center for Archaeological Research, University of Texas at San Antonio and Centro Studi Ricerche Ligabue, Venezia.

Tobey, M. H. 1986. Trace element investigations of Maya chert from Belize. *Papers of the Colha Project*, 1. San Antonio: Center for Archaeological Research, the University of Texas at San Antonio.

Wright, A. C., Romney, D. H., Arbuckle, R. H., and Vial, V. E. 1959. *Land Use in British Honduras*. Colonial Research Publication 24. London: HMSO.

CHAPTER 7

Economic Change in the Lowland Maya Late Classic Period

Prudence M. Rice

In this paper I synthesize available data on the production and exchange of two important goods in ancient Maya society, pottery and obsidian. In treating these goods, I address not the parts they played in the development of complex society, but rather their structural roles in a society that had already achieved complex levels of organization: southern lowland Maya civilization in the Late Classic period.

This focus has several advantages for understanding the particular relationships between commodity production and exchange in Maya society, as well as more general interactions of economic, political, social, and technological changes. Pottery and obsidian are useful because – aside from their ubiquity – these materials represent, respectively, non-elite versus elite, or 'subsistence' and 'wealth' goods among the Classic Maya. Comparisons and contrasts between these two categories of commodities thus permit relatively broad-based insights into economic behavior. In addition, the Late Classic period of the southern Maya lowlands is the pinnacle of that civilization, followed by what is traditionally viewed as an abrupt 'collapse'. It is increasingly clear, however, that the 'collapse' was largely a failure of the economic role or power base of elites; it was felt to varying degrees in different parts of the area; and rather than being a sudden disaster at the end of the Late Classic, it was instead a socioeconomic transition observable through changes in commodity production and distribution evident *during* the Late Classic. This transition provides the backdrop for the investigation of the relationship between declining elite political power and economic organization. A look at pottery and obsidian among the Late Classic lowland Maya is thus instructive for understanding the changing roles in a complex society of different kinds of goods, produced and distributed by different means, in periods of political, economic, and social transformation.

The period of interest here, the Late Classic, is customarily divided into three parts: the early Late Classic, or Tepeu 1 (AD 600–700); the late Late Classic, or Tepeu 2 (AD 700–830); and the Terminal Classic, or Tepeu 3 (AD 830–950). The spatial context for the Late Classic lowland Maya political and settlement organization appears to be the *region*, a territorial expanse surrounding a civic–ceremonial center. Epigraphic (Marcus 1976) and settlement (Adams and Jones 1981; Bove 1981) data suggest that after AD 534 the southern lowlands can be divided into four major divisions, each dominated by a 'capital' or 'primary' civic–ceremonial center. Beneath these capitals exists a hierarchy of several subsidiary administrative levels of secondary and tertiary (or 'major' and 'minor') centers, and relatively dispersed populations of individual or extended households.

Reprinted from Prudence M. Rice. 1987. Economic Change in the Lowland Maya Late Classic Period. In *Specialization, Exchange, and Complex Societies*, edited by Elizabeth M. Brumfiel and Timothy K. Earle (Cambridge University Press, New York, reprinted 1997), pp. 76–85.

Despite decades of research into Late Classic Maya history at these large civic–ceremonial centers, however, there is distressingly little that is securely known about the relationship of Maya sociopolitical organization to economic production, either agricultural or commodity (see Marcus 1983a). The lack of real understanding of the economic system is all the more ironic given the prominence of trade theories in explaining both the rise and the fall of southern lowland Maya society (Rathje 1972; Webb 1973). Well known among these is the argument linking the rise of elites in 'core' versus 'buffer' zones of the lowlands to the long-distance procurement of so-called 'basic resources,' such as obsidian, salt (Andrews 1983), and basalt, supposedly necessary for tropical lowland agrarian societies (Rathje 1972, 1973).

Lowland Maya economies in the Classic period were integrated on the local and regional (rather than interregional) levels (Adams 1977a: 147). The foci of these regional economies are generally thought to be the large civic–ceremonial centers: it has been hypothesized that the centers 'functioned largely... [in] economic networks that dealt heavily in both subsistence goods and utilitarian craft products' (Culbert 1977: 512; also Folan, Kintz, and Fletcher 1983: 149). Little evidence exists, however, to support a strong directive role for Classic centers in regional economies, at least in terms of traditional archaeological indicators of centralized systems of production and exchange. That is, the Classic lowland civic–ceremonial centers have no structures clearly identifiable as storehouses or markets, although the open plazas have been suggested to be areas for fairs or markets (Coe 1967: 73; Folan et al. 1983: 49–64; Freidel 1981: 378, and 1986). Nothing suggests that the writing system was used to record transactions, yields, tribute, or other economic affairs. Nor have workshops been found in concentrations in the centers that would indicate barrio-like organization (cf. Folan et al. 1983: 149–60), administrative control of production (i.e. taxation), and/or a desire on the part of artisans to establish themselves in proximity to a market. Instead, the pattern is one of non-urban, geographically dispersed lowland craft-production locales, a pattern which has parallels with the village specialization found in highland Maya groups today (Smith 1976: 341–2) as well as in ancient highland Mexico (see Marcus 1983b: 216–18; Freidel 1981: 376–8).

The evidence (albeit mostly negative) suggests that the Classic Maya had neither a hierarchically organized market economy nor an economy based on centrally administered production and exchange on a large scale. Instead, they relied primarily on low-level specialization and redistributive mechanism(s), probably based on kin relations. 'Certain goods and services are given the head of kin groups, who in turn redistribute these items in return for still other goods and services' (Adams 1977a: 147), 'with goods controlled by the upper classes exchanged for services by lower classes' (Adams 1977a: 155). The situation is thus similar to the 'staple finance' system proposed for the Hawaiian chiefdoms (Earle 1978), in which direct exchange rather than strict marketing principles was a primary feature of maintenance of relationships of producers to non-producers.

Pottery Production and Distribution

Occupational specialization in the Maya lowlands is a matter of no little interest to archaeologists (Adams 1970; Becker 1973, 1983; Haviland 1974; Shafer and Hester 1983). A variety of different specialties has been proposed, and in some cases even specific residence compounds and lineage type social organization have been suggested for certain occupations (Haviland 1974). Most attention has been directed toward pottery production (see Fry 1981 for a review). Elaborate human-figure polychrome vases associated with sumptuous tombs are the most widely appreciated examples of the Classic Maya potters' skilled artistry. These would have functioned as 'wealth' goods, being circulated – sometimes between regions (Adams 1977b) – by gift-giving at the time of elite funerals or other ceremonial occasions. Yet

simpler polychrome and monochrome
slipped serving vessels, together with vast
quantities of unslipped utilitarian jars, were
manufactured and used in large quantities
throughout the Maya realm.

It is the production and exchange of these
goods, rather than the burial vases, that
have been most intensively investigated by
Mayanists. These studies are limited to
inferring economic processes primarily on
the basis of differential spatial occurrence
of the artifacts, but it should be noted that
locations of recovery reflect the patterns of
use or 'consumption' of the pottery, rather
than the actual economic processes by
which it circulates. More precise studies of
production, which are a necessary prelude
to study of commodity distribution, are not
yet possible because actual manufacturing
loci (kilns) have not been located in the lowlands (see P. Rice 1986a).

The data base for most of what is known
about pottery production in the Classic
period in the southern Maya lowlands
proceeds from technological and physico-
chemical studies of pottery, principally
from two sites (figure 7.1). These sites are
Palenque, in Chiapas, Mexico, and Tikal in
Peten, Guatemala; to these might also be
added data from a third site, Lubaantun, in
southern Belize. It should be noted here that
Tikal and Palenque are two of the four Late
Classic Maya political capitals or 'super-
centers' (Marcus 1976, 1983a: 465), while
Lubaantun is a small center lacking carved
monuments (Hammond 1975) and is thus
below the fourth order in the lowland site
hierarchy. All three sites have smaller minor
or 'satellite' centers within their domains.

At Palenque, the analyses focused on the
distribution (in an area with a radius of
approximately 50 km from the center) of
utilitarian vessels, serving wares, and special
purpose pottery, characterized by inclusions
and trace elemental composition (Rands and
Bishop 1980; Bishop 1980; Bishop and
Rands 1982; Bishop, Rands, and Harbottle
1979). At Tikal, frequency/distance graphs
of technological and stylistic characteristics
of formal/functional pottery classes were
used to study pottery distribution within a

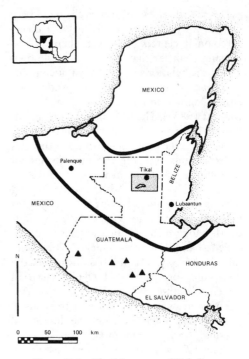

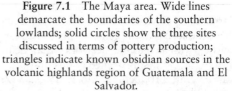

Figure 7.1 The Maya area. Wide lines
demarcate the boundaries of the southern
lowlands; solid circles show the three sites
discussed in terms of pottery production;
triangles indicate known obsidian sources in the
volcanic highlands region of Guatemala and El
Salvador.

transect extending 12 km north and south
from the site center (Fry 1979, 1980; Fry
and Cox 1974; see also Becker 1983: 40).
The transect sampled a 'sustaining area' of
123 sq km (Haviland 1970: 190). A possible
locus of serving-ware pottery production
north of the site was hypothesized on the
basis of the distribution of muscovite pastes
along the transect. At Lubaantun, trace elemental analyses were performed on pottery
from the center and on local clays in order
to identify resources and examine production (Hammond 1982: 228; Hammond,
Harbottle, and Gazard 1976).

On the basis of these studies, it can be
suggested that production of pottery vessels
seems to have been in the hands of multiple
sub-regional and local specialists residing in
the peripheries of the centers or at some

distance from them. At Palenque, for example, most of the Late Classic utilitarian pottery (jars and basins) was made within the Sierras and Plains zones, up to 20 km to the north of the center. At Tikal, the hypothesized location for production of serving wares of micaceous pastes was approximately 8 km north of the site center. At Lubaantun most vessels were produced within 6 km of the site. No definite workshops have been located at these sites, and there is no indication of participation at the level of full-time, barrio-like craft organization. The non-center locations and the lack of capital investment suggest that potters combined their part-time craft activities with involvement in agricultural production.

The products of the potters (at least within non-elite wares) were diverse form classes. For example, the producers using micaceous pastes at Tikal manufactured serving vessels but not wide mouthed jars (Fry 1979); at Palenque, the phytolith-bearing clays of the Plains were used for figurines and utilitarian jars, while the micaceous clays of the Sierras were used for serving vessels (Rands and Bishop 1980: 34, 42). Thus these data support ethnographic models drawn from the Maya highlands (McBryde 1947; Reina and Hill 1978) of community specialization by vessel forms.

The Classic civic–ceremonial centers were largely consumers rather than producers of pottery, particularly of utilitarian or serving wares. The centers themselves produced and distributed only small quantities of pottery, and that was principally 'non-utilitarian' or 'elite'. For example, the potters who are suggested to have resided at Group 4H-1 in the Tikal center produced 'censers, simple polychrome vessels, whistles and figurines, and probably...ceramic masks' (Becker 1983: 40). At Palenque, the paste group associated with the center itself was used primarily for incensario supports, cache vessels, figurines, and some serving wares (Rands and Bishop 1980: 43). At Lubaantun figurines seem to have been the principal products of manufacture within the center (Hammond 1975: 371–4). Hammond suggests the possibility of a workshop for mak-

ing or painting polychrome pottery within the Lubaantun ceremonial precinct, mentioning the likelihood that here as at other small provincial centers the painting might have been done by traveling artists who decorated locally made vessels (Hammond 1982: 227). Distinctive 'Codex Style' polychrome vases probably were produced only at the largest Peten centers (see Robicsek and Hales 1981). Prestigious ceramic items produced within the centers may have been manufactured under direct elite administration, commission, or patronage.

The areas of distribution of the vessel shape categories produced in the different manufacturing loci are highly variable, reflecting both demand (including rates of breakage and replacement) and the existence of competing producers. In general, however, the areas are rather small. For example, at Tikal slipped bowls of the micaceous paste were apparently circulated primarily within 15 km of their hypothesized source (Fry 1981: 161); unslipped widemouthed jars were made of a large variety of pastes and were rarely distributed in areas more than 4–5 km from their presumed source. These jars may have been produced by individual households (Fry 1979: 495).

These data can be used to evaluate two alternative models of pottery exchange proposed on the basis of general reconstructions of Maya settlement and sociopolitical relations (Rands 1967). One model is 'inward-looking,' and postulates similar ceramic assemblages occurring at sites throughout the sustaining area of a major center (such as Palenque or Tikal) by virtue of that site acting as an economic central place for local exchange (analogous with 'solar' marketing systems, for example). Outside the sustaining area the sites would have individually differentiated assemblages. The alternative 'outward-looking' model hypothesizes great variability among the ceramic assemblages of local communities resulting from independent exchange relationships and individual patterns of non-center oriented economic ties. Evaluations of these models, as well as other observations on the nature of lowland Maya pottery manufacture drawn from the studies at the three sites, are revealing as to the nature of production and distribution of utilitarian goods in general in the Late Classic period.

Available data concerning the exchange and distribution of ceramic goods conform more closely to the 'outward-looking' model than to the 'inward-looking' model (cf. Marcus 1983a: 477), and it cannot be clearly demonstrated that political centers exerted any region-wide influence in the production or distribution of most classes of pottery. Graphs of frequency of utilitarian vessel classes against distance from the civic–ceremonial centers do not indicate true 'supply-zone' behavior. Elite (or 'wealth') items seem to be the single exception, showing distribution curves interpreted as typical of centralized exchange (Rands and Bishop 1980: 33; Fry 1980: 12). Recent studies (Hodder 1974; Hodder and Orton 1976; Renfrew 1977) caution, however, that reciprocity versus redistribution, and redistribution versus market exchange, may not be distinguishable on the basis of fall-off curves alone. The multimodality of the Maya pottery distribution graphs – and particularly the differences in occurrence of micaceous wares in comparing North Tikal with Central Tikal (Fry 1979: 509) – tends to suggest that 'non-economic' or non-centralized and unmeasured factors were operating to control the circulation of these wares. One such factor is kinship; another – status differences – was controlled in Fry's studies.

The spatial patterns of occurrence of pottery from different locations of manufacture within a region could be explained in theory by market models or by redistribution. Rands and Bishop, however, declined to accept either the 'inward' or the 'outward' models of ceramic exchange on the basis of their Palenque data. They concluded that the pottery produced at the center itself does not 'enter a regional exchange system; sharp decrement occurs at a short distance from the site, a pattern which fails to conform well to either of the models unless the 'sustaining area' is defined in severely circumscribed terms' (Rands and Bishop 1980: 43). The same is true at Tikal, where not only the

presence of markets but the operation of a money economy has been claimed (Becker 1983: 42). Despite advocating a complex market system at Maya centers, Fry (1980: 16) concluded from his examination of ceramic data at Tikal that 'even the largest Classic Maya sites, such as Tikal, were apparently not the major nodes of redistribution of craft items as many had anticipated.'

In addition to these difficulties in assessing the role of the large centers in Late Classic ceramic production and distribution, other factors complicate the picture. Although the non-center spatial location of production of utilitarian and serving ware pottery seems to have been stable during the course of the Late Classic period, changes are evident in production organization. Evidence from Tikal suggests that the number of producers increased and the pottery assemblage became more varied (in both technological and stylistic attributes) between the early and late Late Classic periods (Fry 1979: 509, especially figs 3 and 4). At Palenque, this same tendency is also apparent in the increased ceramic diversity in four paste/form combinations in the late Late Classic Murcielagos complex (Rands and Bishop 1980: figs 12–16). There is also a tendency toward production of increasingly regionalized lowland polychrome styles from the early to the late part of the Late Classic period. Variability and regionalization are particularly evident in the succeeding Terminal Classic Period, when highly localized ceramic assemblages characterize the largely 'rural' lakes area of central Peten (P. Rice 1986b). Stylistic sharing is conspicuous only between the largest central Peten sites, such as Tikal, Yaxha (center), and Uaxactun; for example, the distinctive feather or 'dress shirt' motif is common on Terminal Classic polychromes at these large centers, but this motif was not found in rural assemblages in the lakes area.

Obsidian Procurement and Distribution

Although pottery provides little evidence of an integrated market system existing on regional or extra-regional levels in the lowlands, the fact remains that a tremendous variety of non-local or exotic goods is spread throughout the area, at sites which appear to have been composed of all socioeconomic statuses. Obsidian is one category of exotica that is not only ubiquitous in the lowlands, but is particularly useful as a vehicle for studying long-distance exchange processes (see Nelson 1983). The stone occurs naturally only in the volcanic highlands of Guatemala and Mexico some 350 or more miles (500 km) to the south and west (fig. 7.1), and probably traveled much of the distance to the southern lowlands by overland human transport. Its widespread occurrence in the lowlands bespeaks some organized procurement system for non-local goods.

Despite the analytical advantages of obsidian's ubiquity and the ability to identify its specific highland sources through provenience analyses (Stross, Hester, Heizer, and Jack 1976; Stross, Sheets, Asaro, and Michel 1983; Nelson 1983; Nelson, Sidrys, and Holmes 1978; P. Rice, Michel, Asaro, and Stross 1985), there are some unanswered questions in Maya obsidian exchange studies. An important one concerns the locus of control of the exchange: did it reside with lowland polities or in the highlands? Most lowland archaeologists ignore the latter, and accept a major role for the large lowland centers in both the organization of its procurement (i.e. its 'production') and the control of its local distribution.

It is generally posited that obsidian, like other exotic goods, was acquired by lowland 'central places,' i.e. the large civic–ceremonial centers such as Tikal, Uaxactun, Palenque, and Yaxha, from which it circulated to smaller and/or less influential areas (Sidrys 1976, 1977; Nelson 1983). The stone was probably brought in from the highlands in the form of large polyhedral cores rather than fragile finished blades, because of the ease and efficiency of bulk transport. It is not known, however, if cores then were moved from the large centers out into the hinterland, with blades being produced at individual smaller centers, or if

blades were manufactured only at the importing centers themselves and exchanged, the cores never leaving the immediate area of the procuring site. (As with pottery, few if any obsidian workshops are known in the lowlands, and processes of exchange have to be inferred from spatial disposition, which more directly reflects patterns of 'consumption' and use.) Whatever the mechanism or form of movement, it is generally thought that the spatial occurrence of obsidian in the lowlands reflects central place redistribution. Provenience analyses of obsidians from several lowland sites have revealed that the centers seem to have exploited multiple highland sources simultaneously; the reason for this may be to ensure a steady supply of the stone in case of trade disruptions (Stross et al. 1983), or to acquire different stone for different kinds of tools and uses (Moholy-Nagy, Asaro, and Stross 1984: 116).

Obsidian is a paradoxical commodity in the Maya lowlands if one compares theories concerning its procurement against the realities of its spatial occurrence. On the one hand, it has been regarded as a 'basic' resource essential for the efficient practice of the maize subsistence economy in the lowland rainforest environment (Rathje 1972). This hypothesis is founded on the ubiquity of obsidian, its sharp cutting edges (presumably necessary for cutting trees and/or harvesting the grain), and the inferred unavailability of local chippable stone that could serve as a substitute. If the hypothesis were indeed true, it would be expected that greater quantities of obsidian would be found in rural residential and non-elite contexts outside the limits of the ceremonial centers, in the areas of primary agricultural production (see Stoltman 1978: 20, 27).

This expectation is not at all fulfilled, however. Considerably greater quantities of obsidian are found in and around large centers than at more peripheral locations, as much as five times more per capita (Sidrys 1976: 458–60; see also Moholy-Nagy et al. 1984). As a consequence, obsidian is usually identified as an elite 'wealth' commodity by its manufacture into special unusual flaked forms, such as animals or human profiles, called 'eccentrics'; also, incised obsidians appear to be a peculiar elite item manufactured only at Tikal and are found virtually nowhere else in the lowlands (Moholy-Nagy et al. 1984: 109). Not only are most obsidians recovered from large centers, but most of them come from special deposits as opposed to general midden or fill. Their use in special ritual, such as bloodletting, or extravagant caching on special ceremonial occasions (for example burials or dedications of stelae or temples; see Moholy-Nagy et al. 1984: table 1), or 'potlatching' (Sidrys 1976: 461), further supports obsidian's primarily elite, ceremonial, and 'wealth' status.

All of these features argue for centralized procurement and control of the material by elites. As wealth, obsidian procurement and distribution may have been a narrowly guarded perquisite of high status, the stone being obtained for purposes of making offerings on ceremonial occasions. Local movement of obsidian into rural areas surrounding the centers would have been through redistribution by means of a patronage system and/or kin relations. It is significant that long-distance trade activities are thought to have been controlled and/or led by elites in the Late Classic period (Thompson 1964), as they were at the time of contact. It has been hypothesized additionally that in the Classic period the material served as a 'currency,' or exchange equivalent, in international 'cartel-like' highland–lowland trade systems in Mesoamerica (Freidel 1986).

A wider perspective on the role of this wealth commodity in Maya society can be gleaned from an obsidian data base that represents a broader geographical, temporal, and socioeconomic range of Maya society than those previously available. Such a context is provided by the obsidians from the Central Peten Historical Ecology Project (CPHEP), an archaeological survey project in the lakes area of Peten, Guatemala (Deevey, Rice, Rice, Vaughan, Brenner, and Flannery 1979; D. Rice and P. Rice 1980, 1982, 1984). Although in comparison with work at the large civic–ceremonial centers, the CPHEP excavations yielded minuscule

quantitites of obsidian, the sampling of 'rural' residential structures through a long period of time in these six lake basins (figure 7.2) results in a broad context for investigating and interpreting changes in obsidian distribution (P. Rice 1984; P. Rice et al. 1985).

The occurrence of obsidian around two lakes, Yaxha and Sacnab, conforms to patterns found in other areas of the Maya lowlands: it is heavily concentrated near centers. Nearly three-quarters of the total obsidian recovered from all periods in this pair of lakes comes from excavations in a single survey transect, the one immediately west of the center of Yaxha (D. Rice 1976: 323). Yaxha, a large, thriving site on the north shore of the lake, was a secondary-level ceremonial locus in the Late Classic lowland hierarchy (Marcus 1983: 465, table 1) with architectural ties to Tikal. The same transect adjacent to the center also accounts for all obsidian cores recovered from pre-Late Classic contexts, suggesting heavy elite involvement in the importation, use, and distribution of obsidian in the area prior to the Late Classic period.

The CPHEP excavations suggest, however, that the role of obsidian in the Maya economy was changing in Late Classic times. First, it was becoming more available to rural residents. In the Late Classic, obsidian was less concentrated in the single transect west of the Yaxha center, and was correspondingly more equitably distributed around the basin (table 7.1). Second, its absolute availability in the lake basins actually diminished, a situation which was paralleled at Central Tikal, where the ratio of obsidian to flint declined from 52:1 in Tepeu 1 to 13:1 in Tepeu 2 (Moholy-Nagy 1975: 517). Third, only in the Late Classic are fragments of exhausted prismatic cores or core fragments of obsidian recovered from transects other than the one adjacent to the Yaxha center. This suggests that during this time the cores themselves may have circulated, in addition to the finished blades (P. Rice 1984).

Further evidence for a changed role of (or access to) obsidian in the Late Classic comes from elsewhere in the southern lowlands.

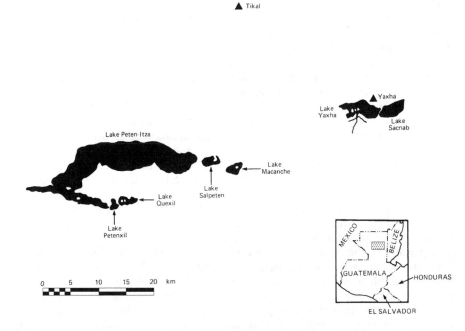

Figure 7.2 The lakes region of central Peten, showing the six lake basins included in the Central Peten Historical Ecology Project (CPHEP) archaeological and ecological studies, and some of the centers in or near the basins. Lake Peten-Itza, the largest of the lakes in the area, was not included in the survey project.

Table 7.1 Ratio of obsidian to occupation in the Yaxha–Sacnab lake basins

	Preclassic		*Early Classic*		*Late Classic†*	
	Obs	*Occ**	*Obs*	*Occ**	*Obs*	*Occ**
Lake Yaxha	9	16	19	27	36	71
Yaxha Op. 2	87	18	54	11	69	24
Lake Sacnab	6	15	19	18	9	27
TOTAL	102	49	92	56	114	122
% Yaxha obs. in Op. 2	90.6%		73.9%		65.7%	
Ratio of obs. per occ.	2.08		1.64		0.93	

† Late Classic figures do not include the Terminal Classic period, AD 830–950.
* 'Occ' refers to the number of excavated occupational or constructional episodes dated to that period. Data from D. Rice and P. Rice 1980: table 1.

For example, at Becan, a fortified center in Campeche, Mexico, 130 of 147 obsidian blades come from within the site center; of the other thirteen phased obsidians recovered outside the site walls, twelve are from Late Classic or Terminal Classic contexts and only a single blade was found outside the center prior to that time (Stoltman 1978: table 5). Additional insights come from Rathje's (1973: table 30 and fig. 57) analysis of 1,009 burials from thirteen southern low-land sites. These burials evidenced a signi-ficant drop in the use of obsidian as a grave offering between the early (Tepeu 1) and late (Tepeu 2) portions of the Late Classic period (table 7.2). At Central Tikal, although obsi-dian appears *more* frequently in Tepeu 2 tombs, it declines in use in special deposits, such as structure or stelae caches (Moholy-Nagy 1975: 515).

These data draw attention to the fact that the social and economic status of this com-modity alters during the Late Classic. The possibility exists that models of centralized obsidian importation and exchange, focus-ing on the large political centers as ad-ministrators of this activity, may not be appropriate for the Late Classic period. Either direct access to (or distribution of) cores rather than solely to blades was newly manifest in these areas, or non-center or rural locations were able to import this material. In other words, the traditional sta-tus of obsidian as an elite-controlled 'wealth' commodity seems to be changing during the Late Classic.

Discussion

This summary of data on the economics of obsidian and pottery in the southern Maya lowlands in the Late Classic period provides a useful basis for comparing production and distribution of utilitarian and prestige (or 'subsistence' and 'wealth') goods, and for looking at changes in economic organiza-tion in the context of a sociopolitical system

Table 7.2   Percentage of grave goods in 1,009 southern lowland burials (after Rathje 1973: table 30)

	Pre-classic	Early Classic	Tepeu 1	Tepeu 2
Exotics				
Obsidian	5.8	14.7	20.5	3.8
Shell	24.0	23.3	22.2	14.1
Jade	23.1	22.1	18.1	15.4
Local				
Pottery	51.9	51.6	56.7	65.4

in transition. The Classic Maya economy seems to show parallels with that suggested for Hawaii (Earle 1978: ch. 6) in being a decentralized system based on 'staple finance' and redistribution of locally pro-duced and stored commodities. 'Wealth' in the Maya system – like Hawaiian feather cloaks – existed in several forms, only one of which, obsidian, is investigated here. The organization of production and distribution of pottery and obsidian underwent some transformations between the early and late parts of the Late Classic period. This shift signifies broader changes in lowland Maya political economies, and these changes demand some explanation. The questions are all the more compelling because the Late Classic period preceded the 'collapse' of Classic civilization in the southern lowlands.

In the southern Maya lowlands in the Late Classic, observed changes in the pro-duction and distribution of pottery and obsidian include: an increased number of producers of pottery from the early (Tepeu 1) to the late (Tepeu 2) period; increasing regional and local variability in techno-logical and stylistic (including formal) attri-butes of pottery from the early to the late period; broader spectrum availability of obsidian, a prestige good; and a decline in the absolute availability of obsidian during the Late Classic as opposed to earlier peri-ods. The first three changes suggest wider participation in a more commercialized economy. Increased variability in technolo-gical and stylistic attributes of pottery has been linked with heightened competition between producers, and decreased adminis-trative control of ceramic production (Fein-man 1985). The more even distribution of obsidian cores and artifacts also suggests diminished administrative control over its procurement and distribution.

It is useful to probe further into why these changes in production occurred in the Maya Late Classic period, in terms of the general dynamics between social and political change, and economic organization. Smith (1976: 334), for example, notes that relaxed administration and free competition between producers are associated with stable and secure political systems that are not threatened by local economic independence. The other side of the coin is described by Feinman (1985), who observes in Oaxaca a correlation of political interference and increased administration of large-scale ceramic production industries with population nucleation and periods of probable localized food shortages that may have caused social stresses.

The Late Classic in the southern Maya lowlands was a period of instability and transition, with evidence of demographic shifts (D. Rice and P. Rice 1982), political conflict, and warfare (indicated on inscriptions; Marcus 1976). The elite class expanded in size (Willey and Shimkin 1973: 483–4), moving to establish new centers and erecting more and more carved monuments at these sites. Household residential plans were increasingly variable, suggesting broad differences in labor investment in their establishment and in the activities carried out therein (see Wilk and Rathje 1982: 632). Polychrome pottery styles became increasingly localized, perhaps as a result of favored artisans having been moved as part of the retinue of elite households. The growth of elites doubtless placed tremendous burdens of production on the non-elites in order to support the attendant ceremonial activities.

Climaxing the social, political, and demographic instability was the so-called 'Maya collapse,' the ninth- and tenth-century cessation of patterns of conspicuous consumption among the elite. The traditional catastrophist view of sudden 'collapse' and depopulation is strictly applicable only to the elites and the largest centers, however. The CPHEP data from the rural lakes area show that in this peripheral region the events were much less dramatic, and there is greater evidence for population and craft continuity (D. Rice 1986; P. Rice 1986b). Thus, if the Late Classic period is viewed not as the *peak* of the civilization prior to its collapse, but simply as a phase of a complex society preceding a transformation of the system, some of the data on commodity production and distribution can be seen in a broader framework.

It is plausible to suggest that the increased numbers of people moving into ceramic manufacture in the Late Classic were exercising one option for coping with social and economic (especially agricultural) insecurity: diversification. There is no evidence to suggest that pottery production had ever been a tightly controlled full-time specialization; thus there was probably a certain fluidity of membership in producing groups over time. It is particularly likely that in times of economic stress, manufacture of low-value/ high-consumption goods (such as utilitarian pottery vessels) would become an attractive way of augmenting one's livelihood. The need for these goods would be relatively continuous, in contrast to the probably fluctuating demand for splendid polychromes on the part of the stressed elites, thus making it a comparatively secure occupation to adopt. Furthermore, pottery-making might have been especially opportune in highly populated areas suffering some degradation in agricultural productivity as a result of heavy farming in earlier periods.

The greater numbers of producers in Tepeu 2 times would contribute to increased variability of the products (see P. Rice 1981: 226), and the marked regionalization of pottery styles and compositions in the late Late Classic and Terminal Classic periods bears this out. Diversification in pottery production was not limited solely to utilitarian pottery, however. During the Terminal Classic in the lakes area, a widespread 'tradeware,' Pabellon Modeled-Carved type of Fine Orange Ware (see Bishop and Rands 1982), was imitated in at least four distinct pastes at Yaxha (P. Rice 1986b), suggesting that innovations in production extended to localized copying of exotic prestige materials.

With respect to obsidian, changes in spatial distribution are significant in light of the long-recognized phenomenon that after the Late Classic period, obsidian became more widely available to the inhabitants of the lowlands in the Postclassic period. Sidrys (1976, 1977) sees this as 'devaluation' resulting from the ease of Postclassic waterborne trade; Freidel (1986) feels that obsidian ceased to serve as a currency in the Postclassic (being replaced by lowland products such as cacao and cotton cloth; see also Piña Chán 1978: 43–4).

Although obsidian is found in far greater quantities in large centers such as Tikal in the Late Classic than in rural or non-elite regions, there is an overall decline in absolute availability from Tepeu 1 to Tepeu 2 times. This decline suggests the early stages of failure of the organization of procurement (see also Rathje, Gregory, and Wiseman 1978: 168). Such failure may be a consequence of the elites having to cope with increasingly frequent political or economic crises (warfare, crop failures, etc.) within their territories by the end of the Late Classic, and a forced retrenchment policy with respect to far-flung long-distance exchange. In addition, it may reflect changes in the economies of polities in the highlands near the obsidian sources (see, for example, Zeitlin 1982).

A look at the distribution of several categories of exotics in lowland burials (table 7.2) suggests that both factors were involved. Shell, jade, and obsidian, for example, all decreased in Tepeu 2 burials as compared to Tepeu 1, being supplanted by locally made polychrome pottery (Rathje 1973: 448–9). These three commodities are all highland materials (much shell is from the Pacific coast; Tourtellot 1978: 80–1), and their decline in the Late Classic may be a function of problems internal to the highlands rather than a deterioration of the economic power or international standing of lowland elites. At the same time, the reduction in obsidian is more dramatic than that in shell or jade. This reduction must also be considered in light of the fact that in the Tepeu 2 or Terminal Classic period a new obsidian source, Ixtepeque, in eastern Guatemala, began to be used again after a long hiatus, and continued as the major source through the Postclassic (P. Rice et al. 1985).

Another non-local item of interest in Late Classic Peten is a distinctive fine-grained brown chert from northern Belize, over 150 km distant. Only very small quantities

(fifty-nine pieces) of this distinctive brown chert were recovered in CPHEP excavations in the lakes area (Aldenderfer 1991, and personal communication), so it was never a very abundant commodity in the region. Nonetheless, three observations are significant with respect to the occurrence of this commodity in the early and late Late Classic periods. First, of the seventeen pieces of brown chert that can be phased within the Late Classic, only two were from Tepeu 1 deposits, while fifteen were from the late Late Classic or Tepeu 2 period (an additional seventeen were from 'general' Late Classic deposits that could not be further subphased). Brown cherts continued to occur in Postclassic deposits in the lakes, with twenty-one pieces being recovered. Second, brown cherts showed no tendency to be concentrated around the Yaxha center, as did obsidian, suggesting that it was not a prestige good. The greater quantity of this non-local chert in the late Late Classic period is evidence that exotic goods continued to circulate in the lowlands, even in the rural lakes area, and the major change in commodities concerns the role of obsidian as a 'wealth' item. Third, the investigators of Colha, Belize, the area of specialized production of artifacts from this chert, note that during the Late Classic period the number of workshop sites increased, although there may have been diminished per capita participation in lithic production (Shafer and Hester 1983: 540). This observation parallels the patterns of economic diversification hypothesized here for Peten during the Late Classic.

These changes in the distribution of ceramic and exotic lithic (obsidian and chert) materials in the lowlands are significant in light of the strong likelihood that in the Postclassic period both the organization of long-distance coastal trade and production of important cacao and cotton cloth commodities were controlled by lowland elites. Together, they suggest the first steps of a general restructuring of the procurement system for non-local goods in the southern lowlands during the late Late Classic. The wider distribution of obsidian in late Late

Classic[1] and Postclassic times, I would argue, reflects one element of this reorganization: the conversion of obsidian from a 'wealth' good to a utilitarian good. Its new status is evident in the changed patterns of procurement and distribution in the 'rural' lakes area, and in the decline of its use in burials and caches in a geographically broader sample of centers. Such a conversion may have been necessitated by the increasing size of the Maya elite class and the consequent difficulties in establishing rights of inheritance to land and titles. Under less stressful conditions, the procurement, distribution, and use of obsidian in elite rituals such as bloodletting, in offerings to the gods, and on ceremonial occasions such as stela dedications, played an important role in demonstrating access to these privileges. With the strain on elites during the Late Classic period, however, the right to engage in such ritual, the nature of the ritual itself, and/or the rights and abilities to acquire the material, may have been transformed.

It is doubtful that the changed status of obsidian was a complete 'devaluation'. It was used in increasing quantities in Tepeu 2 tombs at Central Tikal (Moholy-Nagy 1975: 515), which suggests that elites at this large center may have maintained its status as a prestige good. Not totally devalued or democratized, obsidian in the late Late Classic may have undergone a process of gradual decontrol that culminated in the Postclassic period, at which time the stone had lost its status as 'wealth,' ritual offering, and 'currency.' At the same time, its commerce drew broader participation (though still within the elite sector), perhaps among 'petty elites' who were not inheriting land or rule. These individuals, lacking other alternatives, could have constituted an additional (and potentially disruptive) burden at the upper echelons of an already stressed economic system. Broader access to obsidian and its commerce may have been an outgrowth of patronage or gift-giving relationships, and institutionalized as means of accommodating a burgeoning secondary elite social segment.

Conclusions

Economic pressures within southern lowland societies in the late Late Classic (or Tepeu 2) period are reflected most dramatically in the decontrol of obsidian, a former item of 'wealth,' and its possible redefinition as a utilitarian commodity in the Postclassic period. But what are more interesting are the parallels between the changes in production of both pottery and obsidian at this time in response to the changes in the social system. Production and distribution of both goods appears to have become more widespread and decentralized, involving more individuals who were presumably seeking to increase their economic well-being by taking on new or additional productive pursuits. This transition may be viewed as a harbinger of the later commercialization of Mesoamerican economies, highland and lowland, evident in the succeeding Postclassic period. It is probably safe to say, however, that the two activities, obsidian trade and pottery production, were not alternatives effectively open to everyone. That is, rural non-elites would not have been able to enter into long-distance obsidian commerce, while elites at the large centers were unlikely to adopt utilitarian pot-making in order to fill the family coffers.

Finally, it remains to explain why the Mayas' economic response to political instability was decreased rather than increased control of production and distribution, contrary to expectations discussed above. Maya rulers at the large centers seem to have had no tradition of tight control of utilitarian commodity production underlying their power base in the Late Classic. Power rested in the genealogies of the rulers, not in their administration of production and distribution of utilitarian goods within their realms. For this reason, arguments linking the rise of southern lowland elites to trafficking in exotic but supposedly 'basic' commodities such as salt, obsidian, and volcanic stone metates (Rathje 1972, 1973) call attention to an empirical correlation, but do not constitute a satisfactory explanation of the phenomenon.

This leads to broader questions of lowland Maya economic organization. It was observed recently that 'The economic implications of regional centers have been particularly neglected, and one can only conclude that most Mayanists consider such centers to have functioned almost entirely in the political realm' (Culbert 1977: 512). On the basis of the political and settlement hierarchies, Mayanists have tried valiantly to force their artifactual data into an idealized central place economic model, for example a hierarchical solar or dendritic model typical of the Chiapas and Guatemalan highlands today (Smith 1976: 339–48). Although the characteristics of the organization of production seem to fit such systems in the lowland Maya Classic period, the degree of commercialization of the distribution system does not.

Yet Mayanists have been slow to acknowledge the implications of their findings. The distribution of pottery, taken together with the absence of clear archaeological evidence for marketplaces or 'supply zone' behavior at these centers, provides little support for commercialized exchange in the Classic period. Noncentralized marketing, reciprocal exchange, 'outward-looking' models, or 'basically autonomous localized marketing' (Fry 1981: 149) may be more appropriate explanatory constructs for Classic lowland Maya economic systems. Because hierarchization is only one of three structural attributes of distribution systems, Mayanists may find it more profitable to focus on the others – networks and inclusiveness (Smith 1976: 314). As has been remarked recently (Marcus 1983a: 466; see also 1983b: 209–10), 'political, religious, and economic hierarchies may not be co-extensive' among the Maya.

NOTE

1 This wider spatial distribution may be more apparent than real, however. It could result in part from the growth and dispersion of elites into more of the area between the large centers,

as is registered in the distribution of elite 'dower house' residences (Haviland 1981), the growing prominence of new satellite centers (Marcus 1976), and the large numbers of stelae erected between AD 751 and 771 (Willey and Shimkin 1973: 461). Nevertheless, these late Late Classic elites apparently did not have access to the same quantities of obsidian and did not dispose of it in the same conspicuous manner as did their predecessors.

Furthermore, whether or not the decline of obsidian in burials indicates a decline in real *availability* of the good is another question; it may simply signal changing mortuary customs. The entire issue of the procurement and distribution of exotics in the Late Classic is extremely complex (see Tourtellot and Sabloff 1972; Rathje, Gregory, and Wiseman 1978: 168), particularly as they relate to highland–lowland interactions.

REFERENCES

Adams, Richard E. W. 1970. Suggested Classic Period Occupational Specialization in the Southern Maya Lowlands. In *Monographs and Papers in Maya Archaeology*, edited by W. R. Bullard, Jr. Papers of the Peabody Museum, Harvard University, Cambridge.

——1977a. *Prehistoric Mesoamerica*. Little, Brown and Co., Boston.

——1977b. Comments on the Glyphic Texts of the 'Altar Vase.' In *Social Process in Maya Prehistory*, edited by Norman Hammond. Academic Press, New York.

Adams, Richard E. W. and Jones, R. C. 1981. Spatial Patterns and Regional Growth among Classic Maya Cities. *American Antiquity* 46: 301–22.

Aldenderfer, Mark S. 1991. The Structure of Rural Lithic Assemblages of the Late Classic in the Central Peten Lakes Region, Guatemala. In *Maya Stone Tools*, edited by Thomas R. Hester and Harry J. Shafer. Prehistory Press, Madison.

Andrews, Anthony P. 1983. *Maya Salt Production and Trade*. University of Arizona Press, Tucson.

Becker, Marshall J. 1973. Archaeological Evidence for Occupational Specialization Among the Classic Period Maya at Tikal, Guatemala. *American Antiquity* 38(4): 396–406.

——1983. Indications of Socialization Class Differences Based on the Archaeological Evidence for Occupational Specialization Among the Classic Maya at Tikal, Guatemala. *Revista*

Española de Antropología Americana 13: 29–46.

Bishop, Ronald L. 1980. Aspects of Ceramic Compositional Modeling. In *Models and Methods in Regional Exchange*, edited by Robert Fry, pp. 47–65. SAA Papers No. 1, Society for American Archaeology, Washington, DC.

Bishop, Ronald L. and Rands, Robert L. 1982. Maya Fine Paste Ceramics: A Compositional Perspective. In *Analyses of Fine Paste Ceramics, Excavations at Seibal, Department of Peten, Guatemala*, edited by Jeremy A. Sabloff. Peabody Museum Memoirs, vol. 15, Harvard University, Cambridge.

Bishop, Ronald L., Rands, Robert L., and Harbottle, Garman. 1979. *A Ceramic Compositional Interpretation of Incense-Burner Trade in the Palenque Area, Mexico*. Brookhaven National Laboratory Report BNL-26787. Upton, New York.

Bove, Frederick J. 1981. Trend Surface Analysis and the Lowland Classic Maya Collapse. *American Antiquity* 46: 93–112.

Coe, William R. 1967. *Tikal: A Handbook of the Ancient Maya Ruins*. Philadelphia, University Museum, Philadelphia.

Culbert, T. Patrick. 1977. Maya Development and Collapse: An Economic Perspective. In *Social Process in Maya Prehistory*, edited by Norman Hammond. Academic Press, New York.

Deevey, Edmund S., Jr., Rice, Don S., Rice, Patricia M., Vaughan, H. H., Brenner, Mark, and Flannery, M. S. 1979. Mayan Urbanism: Impact on a Tropical Karst Environment. *Science* 206: 298–306.

Earle, Timothy K. 1978. *Economic and Social Organization of a Complex Chiefdom: The Halelea District, Kaua'i Hawaii*. Anthropological Paper No. 63. The University of Michigan Museum of Anthropology, Ann Arbor.

Feinman, Gary M. 1985. Changes in the Organization of Ceramic Production in Prehispanic Oaxaca, Mexico. In *Decoding Prehistoric Ceramics*, edited by Ben A. Nelson, pp. 195–223. Southern Illinois University Press, Carbondale.

Folan, William J., Kintz, Ellen R., and Fletcher, Laraine A. 1983. *Coba: A Classic Maya Metropolis*. Academic Press, New York.

Freidel, David A. 1981. The Political Economics of Residential Dispersion Among the Lowland Maya. In *Lowland Maya Settlement Patterns*, edited by Wendy Ashmore, pp. 371–82. University of New Mexico Press, Albuquerque.

—— 1986. Terminal Classic Lowland Maya: Successes, Failures, and Aftermaths. In *Late Lowland Maya Civilization: Classic to Postclassic*, edited by Jeremy A. Sabloff and E. Wyllys Andrews V. University of New Mexico Press, Albuquerque.

Fry, Robert E. 1979. The Economics of Pottery at Tikal, Guatemala: Models of Exchange for Serving Vessels. *American Antiquity* 44: 494–512.

—— 1980. Models of Exchange for Major Shape Classes of Lowland Maya Pottery. In *Models and Methods in Regional Exchange*, edited by Robert E. Fry, pp. 3–18. SAA Papers No. 1, Society for American Archaeology, Washington, DC.

—— 1981. Pottery Production-Distribution Systems in the Southern Maya Lowlands. In *Production and Distribution: A Ceramic Viewpoint*, edited by H. Howard and E. L. Morris. BAR International Series 120, Oxford.

Fry, Robert E. and Cox, S. 1974. The Structure of Ceramic Exchange at Tikal, Guatemala. *World Archaeology* 6: 209–25.

Hammond, Norman. 1975. *Lubaantun, A Classic Maya Realm*. Peabody Museum Monographs No. 2, Harvard University, Cambridge.

—— 1982. *Ancient Maya Civilization*. Rutgers University Press, New Brunswick.

Hammond, Norman, Harbottle, Garman, and Gazard, T. 1976. Neutron Activation and Statistical Analysis of Maya Ceramics and Clays from Lubaantun, Belize. *Archaeometry* 18: 147–68.

Haviland, William A. 1970. Guatemala and Mesoamerican Urbanism. *World Archaeology* 2: 186–97.

—— 1974. Occupational Specialization at Tikal, Guatemala: Stoneworking-Monument Carving. *American Antiquity* 39: 494–6.

—— 1981. Dower Houses and Minor Centers at Tikal, Guatemala: An Investigation into the Identification of Valid Units in Settlement Hierarchies. In *Lowland Maya Settlement Patterns*, edited by Wendy Ashmore, pp. 89–117. University of New Mexico Press, Albuquerque.

Hodder, Ian R. 1974. Regression Analysis of Some Trade and Marketing Patterns. *World Archaeology* 6: 172–89.

Hodder, Ian R. and Orton, Clive R. 1976. *Spatial Analysis in Archaeology*. Cambridge University Press, Cambridge.

Marcus, Joyce. 1976. *Emblem and State in the Classic Maya Lowlands: An Epigraphic Approach to Territorial Organization*. Dumbarton Oaks, Washington, DC.

—— 1983a. Lowland Maya Archaeology at the Crossroads. *American Antiquity* 48: 454–88.

—— 1983b. On the Nature of the Mesoamerican City. In *Prehistoric Settlement Patterns: Essays in Honor of Gordon R. Willey*, edited by Evon Z. Vogt and Richard M. Leventhal. University of New Mexico Press and Peabody Museum, Albuquerque and Cambridge.

McBryde, Felix W. 1947. *Cultural and Historical Geography of Southwest Guatemala*. Institute of Social Anthropology 4, Smithsonian Institution, Washington, DC.

Moholy-Nagy, Hattula. 1975. Obsidian at Tikal, Guatemala. *Actas del XLI Congreso Internacional Americanistas*, Mexico, 1: 511–18.

Moholy-Nagy, Hattula, Asaro, Frank, and Stross, Fred. 1984. Tikal Obsidian: Sources and Typology. *American Antiquity* 49: 104–17.

Nelson, Fred W. Jr., Phillips, David A. Jr., and Barrera Rubio, Alfred. 1983. Appendix A: Trade Element Analysis of Obsidian Artifacts from the Northern Maya Lowlands. *In Investigations at Edzná, Campeche, Mexico, Vol. 1, part 1: The Hydraulic System*, edited by Ray T. Matheny, Deanne L. Gurr, Donald W. Forsyth, and F. Richard Hauck, pp. 205–39. Papers, Vol. 46. New World Archaeological Foundation, Provo, UT.

Nelson, Fred W., Sidrys, Raymond, and Holmes, R. D. 1978. Trace Element Analysis by X-ray Fluorescence of Obsidian Artifacts from Guatemala and Belize. In *Excavations at Seibal, Department of Peten, Guatemala: Artifacts*, edited by Gordon R. Willey. Peabody Museum Memoirs No. 14, Harvard University, Cambridge.

Piña Chán, Roman. 1978. Commerce in the Yucatan Peninsula: The Conquest and Colonial Period. In *Mesoamerican Communication Routes and Cultural Contacts*, edited by Thomas A. Lee, Jr. and Carlos Navarrete. Papers of the New World Archaeological Foundation No. 40. Brigham Young University, Provo.

Rands, Robert L. 1967. Ceramic Technology and Trade in the Palenque Region, Mexico. In *American Historical Anthropology*, edited by Carroll L. Riley and Walter W. Taylor, pp. 137–51. Southern Illinois University Press, Carbondale.

Rands, Robert L. and Bishop, Ronald L. 1980. Resource Procurement Zones and Patterns of Ceramic Exchange in the Palenque Region, Mexico. In *Models and Methods in Regional Exchange*, edited by Robert E. Fry, pp. 19–46. SAA Papers No. 1, Society for American Archaeology, Washington, DC.

Rathje, William L. 1972. Praise the Gods and Pass the Metates: A Hypothesis of the Development of Lowland Rainforest Civilization in Middle America. In *Contemporary Archaeology*, edited by Mark P. Leone, pp. 365–92. Illinois University Press, Carbondale.

—— 1973. Classic Maya Development and Denouement: A Research Design. In *The Classic Maya Collapse*, edited by T. Patrick Culbert, pp. 405–54. University of New Mexico Press, Albuquerque.

Rathje, William L., Gregory, David A., and Wiseman, Fred M. 1978. Trade Models and Archaeological Problems: Classic Maya Examples. In *Mesoamerican Communication Routes and Cultural Contacts*, edited by Thomas A. Lee, Jr. and Carlos Navarrete. Papers of the New World Archaeological Foundation No. 40. Brigham Young University, Provo.

Reina, Ruben E. and Hill, Robert M., II. 1978. *The Traditional Pottery of Guatemala*. University of Texas Press, Austin.

Renfrew, Colin. 1977. Alternative Models for Exchange and Spatial Distribution. In *Exchange Systems in Prehistory*, edited by Timothy Earle and Jonathan Ericson, pp. 71–90. Academic Press, New York.

Rice, Don S. 1976. The Historical Ecology of Lakes Yaxha and Sacnab, El Peten, Guatemala. Ph.D. dissertation, Pennsylvania State University, State College.

—— 1986. The Peten Postclassic: A Settlement Perspective. In *Late Lowland Maya Civilization: Classic to Postclassic*, edited by Jeremy A. Sabloff and E. Wyllys Andrews V. University of New Mexico Press, Albuquerque.

Rice, Don S. and Rice, Prudence M. 1980. The Northeast Peten Revisited. *American Antiquity* 45: 432–54.

——, —— 1982. The Central Peten Historical Ecology Project. Final Summary report, 1979, 1980, and 1981 season. MS, files of the authors.

——, —— 1984. Lessons from the Maya. *Latin American Research Review* 19: 7–34.

Rice, Prudence M. 1981. Evolution of Specialized Pottery Production: A Trial Model. *Current Anthropology* 22: 219–40.

—— 1986a. *Maya Pottery Techniques and Technology*. Ceramics and Civilization 1, American Ceramic Society.

—— 1986b. The Peten Postclassic: Perspectives from the Central Peten Lakes. In *Late Lowland Maya Civilization: Classic to Postclassic*, edited by Jeremy A. Sabloff and E. W. Andrews V. University of New Mexico Press, Albuquerque.

Rice, Prudence M., Michel, H. V., Asaro, Frank, and Stross, Fred. 1985. Provenience Analysis of Obsidian from the Central Peten Lake region, Guatemala. *American Antiquity* 50: 591–604.

Robicsek, Frances and Hales, Donald M. 1981. *The Maya Book of the Dead: The Ceramic Codex*. University of Virginia Museum, Charlottesville.

Shafer, Harry J. and Hester, Thomas R. 1983. Ancient Maya Chert Workshops in Northern Belize, Central America. *American Antiquity* 48: 519–43.

Sidrys, Raymond. 1976. Classic Maya Obsidian Trade. *American Antiquity* 41: 449–64.

—— 1977. Mass-Distance Measures for the Maya Obsidian Trade. In *Exchange Systems in Prehistory*, edited by Timothy Earle and Jonathan Ericson, pp. 91–107. Academic Press, New York.

Smith, Carol A. 1976. Exchange Systems and the Spatial Distribution of Elites: The Organization of Stratification of Agrarian Societies. In *Regional Analysis: Volume II, Social Systems*, edited by Carol A. Smith, pp. 309–74. Academic Press, New York.

Stoltman, James B. 1978. *Lithic Artifacts from a Complex Society: The Chipped Stone Tools from Becan, Campeche, Mexico*. Occasional Paper 2: 1–30, Middle American Research Institute, New Orleans.

Stross, Fred H., Hester, Thomas R., Heizer, Robert F., and Jack, R. N. 1976. Chemical and Archaeological Studies of Mesoamerican Obsidians. In *Advances in Obsidian Glass Studies: Archaeological and Geochemical Perspectives*, edited by R. E. Taylor, pp. 240–58. Noyes Press, Park Ridge.

Stross, Fred H., Sheets, Payson, Asaro, Frank, and Michel, Helen. 1983. Precise Characterization of Guatemalan Obsidian Sources, and Source Determination of Artifacts from Quirigua. *American Antiquity* 48: 323–46.

Thompson, J. Eric S. 1964. Trade Relations between the Maya Highlands and Lowlands. *Estudios de Cultura Maya* 4: 13–49.

Tourtellot, Gair. 1978. Getting What Comes Unnaturally: On the Energetics of Maya Trade. In *Papers on the Economy and Architecture of the Ancient Maya*, edited by Raymond Sidrys. Monograph no. 8, Institute of Archaeology, University of California, Los Angeles.

Tourtellot, Gair and Sabloff, Jeremy A. 1972. Exchange Systems among the Ancient Maya. *American Antiquity* 37: 126–35.

Webb, Malcolm C. 1973. The Peten Maya Decline Viewed in the Perspective of State Formation. In *The Classic Maya Collapse*, edited by T. Patrick Culbert, pp. 367–404. University of New Mexico Press, Albuquerque.

Wilk, Richard R. and Rathje, William L. 1982. Household Archaeology. *American Behavioral Scientist* 25: 617–39.

Willey, Gordon R. and Shimkin, Demitri B. 1973. The Maya Collapse: A Summary View. In *The Classic Maya Collapse*, edited by T. Patrick Culbert, pp. 457–501. University of New Mexico Press, Albuquerque.

Zeitlin, Robert N. 1982. Toward a More Comprehensive Model of Interregional Commodity Production. *American Antiquity* 42: 260–75.

CHAPTER 8

Imports and Exports in Classic Mesoamerican Political Economy

The Tehuacan Valley and the Teotihuacán Obsidian Industry

Robert D. Drennan, Philip T. Fitzgibbons, and Heinz Dehn

Introduction

Teotihuacán has long been recognized as the pinnacle of Classic Mesoamerican urbanism – a city of such size as to have no conceivable rival among its Mesoamerican contemporaries. Stylistic links between Teotihuacán and virtually every part of Mesoamerica are often noted. At one time, scholars took the simple presence of these stylistic links as clear evidence of a vaguely defined domination of all Mesoamerica by Teotihuacán. Fortunately, that time is now past, and discussion of such domination without careful attention to the political, economic, social, military, or ideological reality behind it is not taken seriously.

We focus here on the economics of relationships between Teotihuacán and places outside the Basin of Mexico. Our point of departure is the contrast between two views of these relationships, recently elaborated in a series of papers which illustrate the enormous advances made in the study of such issues within the last few years – advances we measure not so much in resolution of contentious issues as in sophistication of questions asked and rigor applied in efforts to provide answers. The two contrasting views concern the importance and economic role of imported and exported goods to Teotihuacán. More than simply accurate reconstruction of economic activities at one site is at issue. The debate really concerns the nature of Classic-period economies in Mesoamerica and the significance of "interstate commerce," of economic interrelationships between developing states and distant regions occupied either by similar states or much smaller-scale, simpler societies. Such external economic relationships are often taken to be critical factors in the development of complex societies, not only in Mesoamerica but in other parts of the world, as well.

Models of Teotihuacán Obsidian Export

As far as Teotihuacán is concerned, attention is very heavily focused on obsidian, and not just because obsidian is particularly easy for archaeologists to work with. On the one hand, Robert Santley and various co-authors (Sanders and Santley 1983; Santley 1983, 1984; Santley et al. 1986) see Teotihuacán's economy as "the hub of a vast

Reprinted from Robert D. Drennan, Philip T. Fitzgibbons, and Heinz Dehn. 1990. Imports and Exports in Classic Mesoamerican Political Economy: The Tehuacan Valley and the Teotihuacán Obsidian Industry. *Research in Economic Anthropology* 12: 177–99.

commercial 'empire'" (Santley 1983: 69); they build a detailed and carefully justified model on the traditional view of a Teotihuacán of such overwhelming proportions that it dominated much or all of Mesoamerica. According to this model, the bulk of Teotihuacán's economy was focused on producing and distributing basic necessities within close range of the city, as required by the limited possibilities of transportation in Prehispanic Mesoamerica (Sanders and Santley 1983: 246–9; cf. Drennan 1984b).

One commodity had special properties, however, that made it an exception to this local economic focus: obsidian. Because of its restricted source distribution, the proximity of one of the best sources to Teotihuacán, its superiority to available substitutes, its low bulk, its ease of production in large quantities, and its relatively low rate of use, obsidian was an ideal focus for an industry of pan-Mesoamerican proportions (Sanders and Santley 1983: 249–56). This industry maintained monopolistic control of all or most of Mesoamerica's obsidian production and distribution (Santley 1983: 107–8), in part by "discriminatory pricing" practices (Sanders and Santley 1983: 285–6; Santley 1984: 67–73), and returned a huge profit to the city. This profit is seen as the major element in the Teotihuacán elite's extraordinary ability to accumulate capital (Sanders and Santley 1983: 284; Santley 1983: 107); it directly underwrote the building of the Pyramid of the Sun and other monumental construction projects (Santley 1984: 72). This contribution to Teotihuacán's economic capital made the difference that allowed Teotihuacán to develop into a city whose scale far exceeded that of any of its contemporaries. (Later, Tula and then Tenochtitlán are seen as playing out the same economic dynamic [Sanders and Santley 1983: 282].) The capital generated by obsidian export was of such fundamental importance to Teotihuacán's economy that, when the monopoly was threatened by developing rival centers in the Late Classic, Teotihuacán collapsed (Santley 1983: 111–12).

Evidence offered in support of this model includes the usual lists of places in Meso-america where green Pachuca obsidian and stylistic evidence of Teotihuacán contact occur (Santley 1983: 86–7); estimates of production rates and costs, relying on Spence's (1967, 1981, 1984) identification of obsidian workshops at Teotihuacán; and estimates of consumption rates from excavations at Loma Torremote and Maquixco (Santley 1983: 60–1). The fundamental notions of this model, at least, are consistent with Charlton's (1978, 1984) and Millon's (1970: 1081–2; 1973: 45) reconstructions of the importance of obsidian in the economy of the central Mexican highlands. Kurtz (1987) has presented a model that deals in greater detail with just how a sizable import/export sector, focused largely on export of obsidian, might have affected the development of Teotihuacán's economy. At least to the extent that Kurtz's model emphasizes the unique opportunity that obsidian export afforded Teotihuacán, Santley (1987) finds this model consistent with his own. We should add that both Santley (personal communication 1987; Santley and Pool, n.d.) and Sanders (personal communication 1987) now disavow some aspects of the obsidian-export-for-profit model, particularly as far as the most distant regions are concerned.

On the other hand, John Clark (1986: 65–8) sets forth at least a sketch of a model denying such an economic dynamic. In his approach, production of obsidian artifacts at Teotihuacán was for a local market. Items exchanged at long distance were almost exclusively prestige goods, and quantities were quite small. Teotihuacán's relations with the rest of Mesoamerica were largely between elites of the various regions. They did not involve domination of distant regions by Teotihuacán in an economic or any other sense. Rather, Teotihuacán stylistic elements that appear in widely scattered regions represent the willing emulation of Teotihuacán and proud display of its symbols by local elites who thereby bolstered their own political positions. By similar token, the goods that Teotihuacán acquired from distant regions were of political rather than economic importance. They did not represent capital accumulation but were part of the conspicuous consumption of elites. Teotihuacán elites could have distributed such prestige goods to subordinates, thereby helping to maintain their political control of the important means of accumulating capital – which were at home, not abroad (cf. Blanton and Feinman 1984: 676–8).

In marshaling evidence, Clark focuses heavily on questioning the identification of obsidian workshops at Teotihuacán, and he arrives at vastly lower estimates of Teotihuacán's obsidian output than those that have been current in the literature for the last ten years or more. He also argues (Clark 1986: 64) that the quantity of green obsidian or other identifiable Teotihuacán goods in distant regions is quite small and restricted to elite contexts.

Implications for Obsidian Consumption in the Tehuacán Valley

In discussion of Teotihuacán's obsidian industry, the focus has often been on evidence of production, simply because that is the evidence available in largest quantity. While the presence of obsidian from various identified sources among the artifacts of different sites is often recognized, small sample sizes and inappropriate methods of sample selection often impede efforts to discuss patterns of distribution or consumption except in vague terms. In this section, we make an initial report on results of obsidian sourcing studies of Tehuacán Valley materials that provide relevant evidence of consumption.

The two approaches just outlined provoke rather different expectations concerning patterns of obsidian consumption in the Tehuacán Valley. If the Teotihuacán obsidian industry served a major capital-raising function, then its profits had to be translatable into human energy – the only basis on which it makes sense to think of "profit" in the context of pre-Columbian Mesoamerica. Some of the most obvious capital investments of Teotihuacán, and indeed the principal ones mentioned by Santley (1984: 72), are its massive architectural monuments,

which required, more than anything else, an immense amount of human labor. The rulers of Teotihuacán could have used profits from the obsidian trade directly to feed those laborers if the profits arrived in the form of food staples. Elsewhere, Drennan (1984b: 106–7) has argued that overland transport of food staples on human backs can represent this kind of energy profit only for distances less than 275 km. Sanders and Santley (1983: 246–9), mainly by insisting on a higher profit margin, are more restrictive, arriving at a figure of 150 km. Taking either distance and drawing a circle around Teotihuacán delimits only a very small part of the area of the Teotihuacán obsidian monopoly postulated by Santley.

Energy profits could have been derived from greater distances only by importing goods that in some sense contain human energy in much smaller bulk than food staples do. By far the most likely candidate here is textiles, which contain enormous amounts of "frozen" human energy in relatively little bulk (see Drennan 1984a: 39, 1984b: 109). Cotton textiles are often mentioned as a luxury item in historic sources on the Late Postclassic, but translating luxury items of any kind into human labor is difficult, since their wide distribution to the kind of people who carry basket-loads of dirt to build pyramids would render them non-luxury goods. Almost as valuable in human energy terms, however, and much easier to "cash in," would be maguey fiber textiles. These, in addition, could come from arid highland regions much closer to Teotihuacán, thereby reducing wasted effort in transporting them over excessively long distances. In the excitement over elaborately decorated cotton mantles, the large number of textiles made of maguey in Aztec tribute is often overlooked (Drennan 1984b: 109).

The Tehuacán Valley is distant enough from Teotihuacán to make it an unlikely point of origin for food staples imported to Teotihuacán. It is beyond the 150 km distance, although it does lie within 275 km (figure 8.1). Thinking of the Tehuacán Valley as a producer of maguey fiber seems much more promising. Its dry climate makes

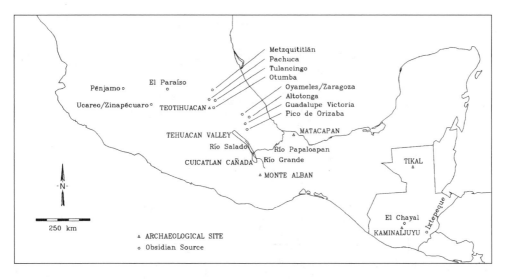

Figure 8.1 Locations of obsidian sources and archaeological sites and regions discussed.

sustaining sizable populations by maize agriculture precarious and labor-intensive, but maguey grows well. The opportunity to trade maguey textiles for high-quality obsidian should have been very attractive to inhabitants of the Tehuacán Valley. Moreover, the Tehuacán Valley falls exactly within the 200–300 km range that Santley (1984: 70) identifies as the distance at which Teotihuacán's discriminatory pricing policies ought to yield it the greatest return. It is, then, a prime region in which to see the effects on consumption of the developing Teotihuacán obsidian industry. Presumably, those effects should manifest themselves as changes in the sources from which the inhabitants of Tehuacán obtained their obsidian. During the Late and Terminal Formative – Patlachique phase or earlier at Teotihuacán, Late Santa María and the beginning of Early Palo Blanco phases in Tehuacán (see figure 8.2) – Tehuacán might be expected to rely on a variety of obsidian sources, perhaps emphasizing those located closest (Oyameles/Zaragoza, Altotonga, Guadalupe Victoria, and Pico de Orizaba). As Teotihuacán's large-scale export-oriented obsidian industry developed in the Classic–Tlamimilolpa and Xolalpan phases at Teotihuacán, and the latter Early Palo Blanco and Late

Palo Blanco phases in Tehuacán (see figure 8.2) – then Tehuacán should come to rely more heavily on obsidian procured from Teotihuacán. If, on the other hand, the export of obsidian from Teotihuacán to regions outside the Basin of Mexico was on a very small scale, there would be no reason to expect much impact on the obsidian procurement patterns of residents of the Tehuacán Valley. Elite exchanges between Teotihuacán and Tehuacán would probably be less important than those between more powerful polities on both sides, but such Teotihuacán obsidian and other goods as occurred in the Tehuacán Valley should be concentrated in elite contexts.

Three excavated sites in Tehuacán produced collections of obsidian artifacts that were sampled for source identification. The earliest of these sites, Quachilco, was a "central place" for a segment of the valley during the Late Santa María phase and the first part of the Early Palo Blanco phase. It was the only such central place that existed in the Tehuacán Valley at this time, but it probably did not dominate the entire valley (Drennan 1978: 1–9; Drennan and Nowack 1984: 148–9). Obsidian artifacts from five different excavated areas were sampled for source analysis. These excavations were all

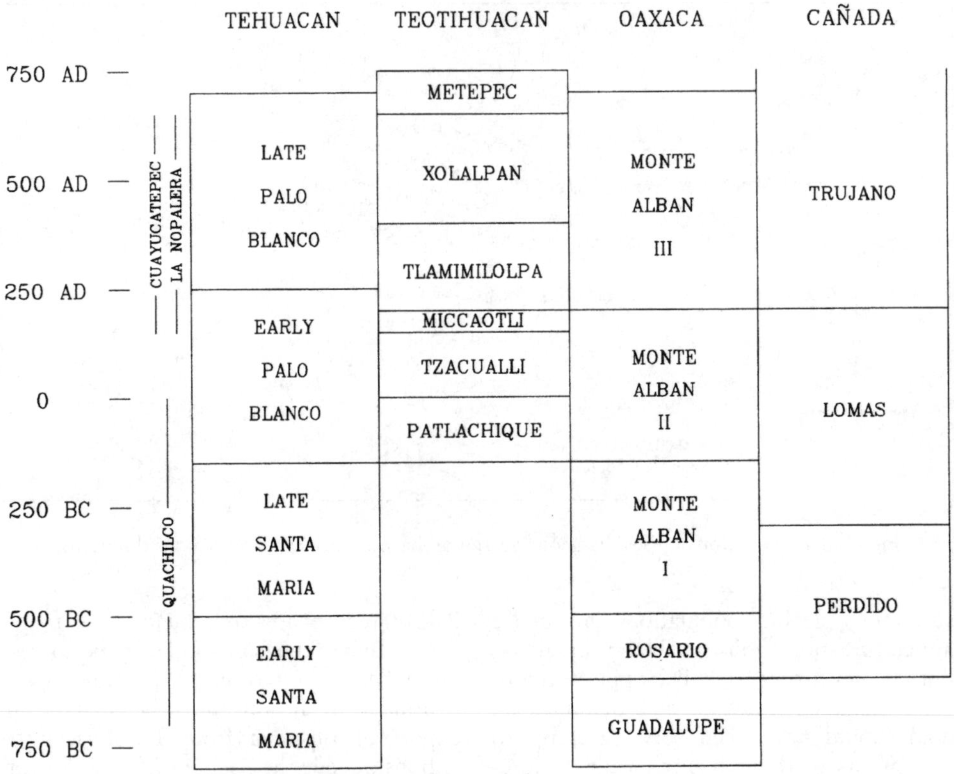

	TEHUACAN	TEOTIHUACAN	OAXACA	CAÑADA
750 AD		METEPEC		
500 AD	LATE PALO BLANCO	XOLALPAN	MONTE ALBAN III	TRUJANO
250 AD		TLAMIMILOLPA		
	EARLY PALO BLANCO	MICCAOTLI	MONTE ALBAN II	
0		TZACUALLI		LOMAS
		PATLACHIQUE		
250 BC	LATE SANTA MARIA		MONTE ALBAN I	
500 BC				PERDIDO
	EARLY SANTA MARIA		ROSARIO	
750 BC			GUADALUPE	

(Tehuacan side labels: CUAYUCATEPEC / LA NOPALERA; QUACHILCO)

Figure 8.2 Chronologies for regions discussed.

in residential areas and spanned a range of statuses and locations in the site. These collections are taken to represent Late to Terminal Formative obsidian procurement in Tehuacán.

During the ensuing Palo Blanco phase, Quachilco was abandoned, and several other centers were founded. These were hilltop fortified towns of similar size (1,000–2,500 inhabitants) that seem to have divided the valley into competing spheres of influence (Drennan and Nowack 1984: 149–50). One of them, Cuayucatepec, provided collections of obsidian artifacts from four different excavated areas, which were sampled for source analysis. As in the case of Quachilco, all excavations were in residential debris and span a range of statuses and locations in the site (Drennan 1979). These collections are taken to represent Early and Middle Classic obsidian procurement in Tehuacán.

Also during the Palo Blanco phase, several rather unusual sites appeared. The most distinctive feature of these sites is an extremely high proportion of "real" Thin Orange pottery, i.e. equivalent to "Group A" or "Core Group" or "Alpha" Thin Orange (Sotomayor and Castillo Tejero 1963; Harbottle et al., n.d.; Kolb 1986). These sites were ordinarily rather small, unimpressive in terms of public architecture, and they lacked the defensible locations and fortifications of the major Palo Blanco phase towns with which they were contemporaneous (Drennan and Nowack 1984: 154). "Real" Thin Orange pottery, while quite rare on other Palo Blanco phase sites, comprises up to 50 percent of the ceramics in residential contexts at these sites. Regardless of dispute over the location of manufacture of Thin Orange pottery, some kind of special connection, direct or indirect, between these sites and Teotihuacán is suggested. One of them, La Nopalera, provided collections of obsidian artifacts from two excavated areas, which were sampled for source analysis. These collections are taken to represent Early and Middle Classic obsidian procurement by the inhabitants of these peculiar sites.

Obsidian Sourcing Methodology

The obsidian sourcing studies we carried out were designed to provide the most accurate and precise estimates possible of proportions of consumption in the Tehuacán Valley of obsidian from various sources. Such an objective had two principal implications for the procedures used to select specimens for analysis. First, the number of artifacts whose sources were identified had to be fairly large, or else estimates of proportions of consumption could be expected to be neither accurate nor precise. Second, the artifacts to be analyzed had to be selected by a random procedure to avoid systematic bias and make possible the calculation of confidence intervals for estimates of proportions of consumption so that risks of error were known. In short, the day is past when one could select a small handful of obsidian artifacts from a collection, trying to include as many different colors as possible, and then use that sample to make conclusions about proportions of consumption of obsidian from different sources. Such a procedure has the same level of statistical validity as picking the two brightest marbles of different colors from a jar of assorted marbles and concluding, on the basis of that sample, that the jar contains 50 percent red marbles and 50 percent blue marbles.

The confidence intervals we report below, of course, refer to confidence in the accuracy with which the results of the source analysis characterize the groups of artifacts from which the samples were drawn. Our sample of artifacts was selected randomly from the three collections of obsidian artifacts enumerated above – several different excavated areas at three sites. We take these three sites to represent others in the same category: Quachilco for the Late and Terminal Formative, Cuayucatepec for the Early and Middle Classic, and La Nopalera for the unusual sites with high proportions of Thin Orange pottery. This latter is a matter of judgment, not statistics. Insofar as obsidian from different sources can be distinguished visually, the accuracy of this judgment is confirmed by study of the artifacts from other sites.

The sample comprised a total of 436 artifacts, stratified according to site, excavation area, and stratum. Another 65 obsidian artifacts were selected in similar fashion from several sites in the Cuicatlán Cañada to the south of the Tehuacán Valley. Yet another handful of artifacts were analyzed for special reasons, including a few from the Valley of Oaxaca and the Mixteca Alta. Our sample finally contained a total of 519 obsidian artifacts, which we analyzed for trace element composition to determine sources. The vast majority of the obsidian artifacts recovered were prismatic blades, although some very small utilized flakes, some debitage, and a few core fragments appeared.

A total of 59 specimens from 13 known obsidian source locations were also analyzed to provide the basis to which artifact results could be compared. These sources included major ones in Mexico, spanning the states of Puebla, Veracruz, Mexico, Hidalgo, Querétaro, Michoacán, and Guanajuato (table 8.1, figure 8.2). Sources in the highlands of Guatemala were not included because we did not expect them to be heavily represented in our artifact sample. This did turn out to be the case, although a single artifact specimen (one of a handful of Formative specimens from the Valley of Oaxaca) did not match any of the source specimens we analyzed. Its composition so strongly resembled published figures for sources in the Guatemalan highlands that there can be little doubt that it came from that source region. Most important, this artifact provided a demonstration that our methodology did not confuse artifacts from Guatemalan sources with any of the Mexican sources from which we analyzed specimens.

The specimens selected for trace element analysis were ground to powders. The

Table 8.1   Trace element analysis for source specimens[a]

Source	Mn	Fe	Zn	Rb	Sr	Y	Zr	Nb
Pénjamo, Guanajuato	433	1.50	80	180	<20	40	500	20
Zinapécuaro, Michoacán	200	0.82	40	180	<20	<20	100	<20
Ucareo, Michoacán	210	0.83	36	204	<20	20	100	<20
El Paraíso, Querétaro	250	1.90	220	220	<20	80	740	40
Metzquititlán, Hidalgo	200	1.10	30	340	50	20	200	<20
Pachuca, Hidalgo[b]	1200	1.60	200	220	<20	60	640	60
Tulancingo, Hidalgo[c]	450	1.75	180	150	<20	60	550	40
Otumba, México[d]	380	0.95	40	150	20	20	130	<20
Altotonga, Veracruz	260	0.96	40	180	<20	30	180	<20
Guadalupe Victoria, Puebla	540	0.48	30	120	90	<20	80	<20
Oyameles, Puebla	250	1.03	30	150	40	20	190	<20
Zaragoza, Puebla	250	1.01	30	150	40	20	190	<20
Pico de Orizaba, Veracruz	550	0.41	30	120	40	<20	60	<20

[a] Mean values, in parts per million, except Fe, in percent.
[b] a.k.a. Cerro de las Navajas, Rancho Guajolote, Cruz del Milagro, El Ocote.
[c] a.k.a. Pizzarín, Rancho Tenango.
[d] a.k.a. Teotihuacán, Barranca de los Estetes.

powder mounts were then subjected to X-ray fluorescence analysis on a General Electric Model 5 instrument with a single W-tube at 60 KV/50 MA, a flat reflecting crystal (LiF), and a sealed proportional counter. Readings for the elements Mn, Fe, Zn, Rb, Sr, Y, Zr, and Nb were converted by consistent procedures to approximate ppm form for comparison of artifacts and source specimens.

Results of Obsidian Sourcing

The results of the Tehuacán obsidian source analysis are summarized in table 8.2. Rather than attempt to test the significance of some of the many comparisons that table 8.2 makes possible, we have chosen to report error ranges (always of one standard error). These error ranges provide information on the significance of any difference observed in the table, since a difference of one standard error represents a significance level of about 33 percent, of two standard errors about 5 percent, and of 2.5 standard errors about 1 percent.

Throughout the sequence, the vast majority of the obsidian comes from the two closest groups of sources. The first and closest

group lies along the eastern flanks of the mountains of the Central Highlands in the states of Puebla and Veracruz. Individual sources represented are Oyameles/Zaragoza, Altotonga, Guadalupe Victoria, and Pico de Orizaba. Although Oyameles and Zaragoza are actually two different localities, they are quite close to each other, and we could not distinguish them reliably on the basis of trace element analysis. Thus, they are treated here as a single source. Only slightly more distant are the sources near Teotihuacán: Metzquititlán, Pachuca, Tulancingo, and Otumba. Only one other source is represented, Ucareo/Zinapécuaro in Michoacán. (These two localities, like Oyameles and Zaragoza, are treated as a single source here for the same reason.)

Quachilco: late to terminal formative

At Quachilco, the proportions of obsidian from the different sources are highly variable from one area of the site to another (table 8.2). Sources near Teotihuacán are well represented in all areas but one – Area H near the outer periphery of the occupied zone, where excavations produced only very sparse material of any kind and the total

Table 8.2 Percentages of obsidian from different sources at Quachilco, Cuayucatepec, and La Nopalera in the Tehuacán Valley[a]

Sources	Quachilco					Cuayucatepec				La Nopalera	
	A (25)	B (25)	F (76)	H (6)	K (103)	A (90)	D (20)	E (16)	H (28)	A (29)	B (18)
Puebla/Veracruz											
Oyameles/Zaragoza	15 ± 7	47 ± 8	1	0	8 ± 3	62 ± 4	72 ± 10	57 ± 5	85 ± 6	11 ± 6	17 ± 4
Altotonga	13 ± 6	17 ± 5	52 ± 6	100	23 ± 4	3 ± 2	3	10	0	0	0
Guadalupe Victoria	30 ± 8	9 ± 5	6 ± 2	0	23 ± 4	1	0	5	0	0	4 ± 3
Pico de Orizaba	15 ± 7	10 ± 6	0	0	7 ± 3	1 ± 1	0	0	0	4 ± 4	6 ± 3
Subtotal	72 ± 7	82 ± 7	58 ± 6	100	60 ± 5	67 ± 4	75 ± 10	72 ± 5	85 ± 6	15 ± 7	26 ± 3
Near Teotihuacán											
Metzquititlán	0	0	0	0	0	2 ± 2	9 ± 8	8 ± 5	0	4 ± 4	0
Pachuca	24 ± 7	6 ± 5	26 ± 5	0	17 ± 4	16 ± 3	3	15	10 ± 6	77 ± 8	74 ± 3
Tulancingo	0	3 ± 2	0	0	0	0	5 ± 3	5	0	0	0
Otumba	4	10 ± 6	16 ± 4	0	23 ± 4	3 ± 1	5 ± 3	0	5 ± 1	1	0
Subtotal	28 ± 7	18 ± 7	42 ± 6	0	40 ± 5	21 ± 4	16 ± 8	28 ± 5	15 ± 6	81 ± 7	74 ± 3
Other											
Ucareo/Zinapécuaro	0	0	0	0	0	12 ± 3	9 ± 8	0	0	4 ± 4	0

[a] Under each of the three sites, the capital letters stand for excavation areas and the numbers in parentheses are the numbers of obsidian artifacts sourced from each. In the body of the table, the plus or minus terms represent one standard error.

amount of obsidian recovered was only six pieces. Almost all the material from Teotihuacán sources comes from the Pachuca and Otumba localities. Except for the very small sample from Area H, the Teotihuacán sources are least important in Area B, providing 18 percent (± 7 percent) of the obsidian, and most important in Area F, providing 42 percent (± 6 percent) of the obsidian. Of the Puebla/Veracruz sources, all but Pico de Orizaba were extremely important in at least one of the site areas: Guadalupe Victoria, with 30 percent (± 8 percent) in Area A and 23 percent (± 4 percent) in Area K; Oyameles/Zaragoza, with 47 percent (± 8 percent) in Area B; and Altotonga, with 52 percent (± 6 percent) in Area F, 100 percent in Area H, and 23 percent (± 4 percent) in Area K. Even Pico de Orizaba, though not as important a provider as the others, reached more than trivial proportions in some areas of the site. In a word, the pattern to be observed in Late and Terminal Formative obsidian procurement is diversity. The importance of each source varies substantially from one area of the Quachilco site to another.

Seven core fragments were recovered from Quachilco, all from the Puebla/Veracruz sources. (Four came from Guadalupe Victoria, two from Oyameles/Zaragoza, and one from Altotonga.) Much of the material from the Puebla/Veracruz sources, then, was evidently imported in raw form for working in Tehuacán, while the material from the sources near Teotihuacán was much more likely to arrive in the form of finished prismatic blades.

Cuayucatepec: the Early to Middle Classic

The picture changes sharply as we shift our focus to the site of Cuayucatepec. First and foremost, the patterns shown by the four areas in the Cuayucatepec site are much more uniform. Sources near Teotihuacán regularly provide 10–30 percent of the obsidian used in each area. Thus, they are more important than in the one tiny sample from Area H at Quachilco, at roughly the same

level of importance as at Areas A and B at Quachilco, and they never reach the levels of importance represented in Areas F and K at Quachilco. Of the sources near Teotihuacán, Pachuca is clearly providing the most, but Metzquititlán, Tulancingo, and Otumba all contribute. Ucareo/Zinapécuaro appears for the first time, providing modest but more than trivial amounts in Areas A and D at Cuayucatepec. The most striking figures for Cuayucatepec in table 8.2, of course, are those for the Oyameles/Zaragoza source, which provides a clear and sometimes overwhelming majority of the obsidian in all four areas. The other three Puebla/Veracruz sources are very sparsely represented. Four core fragments were among the obsidian recovered at Cuayucatepec, one each from four different sources: Oyameles/Zaragoza, Altotonga, Guadalupe Victoria, and Otumba.

La Nopalera: Early to Middle Classic

Patterns in the two excavated areas of La Nopalera are, like those at Cuayucatepec, quite uniform, but they certainly do not resemble those at Cuayucatepec. At La Nopalera, the sources near Teotihuacán, and especially the Pachuca source, are overwhelmingly dominant. Oyameles/Zaragoza comes in second in both areas and, together, these two sources account for some 90 percent of the obsidian in each. Other sources are represented, but in very small amounts. No cores at all were recovered from La Nopalera, but the total amount of material of all kinds was substantially less than that from either Quachilco or Cuayucatepec as a consequence of the smaller scale of the excavations.

Evaluating Models

Quachilco, then, establishes a Late and Terminal Formative baseline for obsidian procurement in the Tehuacán Valley. All obsidian came from the relatively nearby sources in the Puebla/Veracruz or Teotihuacán groups, but source representation was highly variable, suggesting a good deal of flexibility in acquisition of this resource. The pattern shown at La Nopalera is just what we would expect for the Early to Middle Classic on the basis of a model of a large-scale Teotihuacán obsidian export industry focused on returning substantial profit to Teotihuacán, perhaps through monopolistic practices. The pattern shown at La Nopalera, however, is clearly anomalous for the Tehuacán Valley at this time. Instead, the pattern revealed at Cuayucatepec is the typical one. We can be quite confident of this because the critical difference in pattern hinges on the frequency of Pachuca obsidian, the distinctive green color of which makes it readily identifiable without recourse to trace element analysis. (The trace element analysis we did confirms the high degree of correspondence; nearly 100 percent of the obsidian we classed as green did turn out, on trace element analysis, to have come from the Pachuca source, and nearly 100 percent of the obsidian that trace element analysis linked with the Pachuca source had already been classified as green.) There are a few other sites that, like La Nopalera, have high frequencies of both green obsidian and "real" Thin Orange pottery, but they provide the exceptions to the rule that, as Teotihuacán's obsidian craft grew into an industry, the people of Tehuacán turned very heavily not to Teotihuacán but rather to the Oyameles/Zaragoza source for their obsidian.

The foregoing is most definitely not what we would expect of a Classic period obsidian production and distribution sphere controlled monopolistically by Teotihuacán – unless, of course, the Oyameles/Zaragoza source were exploited and controlled by that same monopolistic system. Precisely such control has been suggested by Santley (1983: 109–12), who sees El Tajín as a Teotihuacán "ally or colony" through which this control was effected. While postulating such circumstances fits nicely with a monopolistic, capital-generating obsidian industry model, not one shred of evidence has been produced to support the postulate. In contrast, the pattern of obsidian source reliance in the Tehuacán Valley shows two very clearly different obsidian production and distribution systems operating contemporaneously during the Classic, one focused on the Pachuca source, the other on the Oyameles/Zaragoza source. The Tehuacán sites in which the Pachuca obsidian appears also have very high proportions of "real" Thin Orange ceramics, providing an independent line of evidence linking this distribution system to Teotihuacán in one way or another. The sites where the Oyameles/Zaragoza obsidian dominates, and which represent the vast majority of the Tehuacán population, lack this Teotihuacán link. If both systems were controlled by Teotihuacán, directly or indirectly, we should not see such clear-cut separation between them on the ground in the Tehuacán Valley. Whether they can be considered rival systems or not, they certainly cannot be taken simply as proxies for one another. The evidence of obsidian consumption in the Tehuacán Valley, then, does not fit the export-for-capital-gain-through-monopolistic-control model of Teotihuacán's obsidian industry.

Neither does the evidence fit a model in which obsidian was exported from Teotihuacán largely in the context of elite exchange – at least not exchange with the elites of the Tehuacán Valley. The pattern that characterizes La Nopalera, namely, overwhelming reliance on the Pachuca obsidian source and large quantities of "real" Thin Orange pottery, is not much connected with Tehuacán's elites. The residents of La Nopalera and the few other similar sites were not of high status or much political importance in the usual sense. The foci of both these aspects of Tehuacán society were clearly in the half-dozen fortified hilltop towns, of which Cuayucatepec is one. What attracts attention is the very failure of these Teotihuacán-connected sites to mesh clearly with what seems an otherwise unremarkable local system for a relatively underdeveloped region in the Classic period. The small sizes, undefensible locations, and minimal public architecture of La Nopalera and similar sites rule them out as Teotihuacán garrisons or provincial capitals. They were certainly not sites from which either Thin Orange pottery or Pachuca obsidian was distributed to the Tehuacán Valley, because the absence of these goods at other sites is precisely what sets sites like La Nopalera apart.

An Alternative Approach

This apparent lack of connection between sites like La Nopalera and Tehuacán's local social, political, or economic system suggests yet another possibility: that these sites represent not some connection between the Tehuacán Valley and Teotihuacán but a connection between Teotihuacán and some other more distant region – a connection that simply went through Tehuacán. The Tehuacán Valley is, after all, the most direct route from Teotihuacán toward the Valley of Oaxaca, the southern Gulf Coast, and the Maya area in general. There is no real topographical obstacle between Tehuacán and Teotihuacán. The Río Salado runs down from Tehuacán to join the Río Grande flowing from the direction of Oaxaca. From this point, one can follow the Río Grande upstream and cross one major mountain ridge into the Valley of Oaxaca. Alternatively, the joined ríos Salado and Grande flow down through a narrow gorge to emerge into the Gulf Coast plain as the Río Papaloapan aimed directly at Matacapan, where strong Teotihuacán "influence" has often been noted (e.g. Santley 1983: 75–9). There is no more gradual route for climbing from the Gulf Coast to the Basin of Mexico, nor does any other provide greater possibility for the use of canoes or rafts. One can easily conjure up a vision of sites whose special connection to Teotihuacán is their involvement in moving goods to and from the city along one of its major long-distance trade routes. Whether residents were displaced Teotihuacanos, Teotihuacán agents supervising trade, local inhabitants specializing in serving Teotihuacán's merchant caravans, or independent middlemen, they would have had a special link to Teotihuacán and might well have procured not only Thin Orange pottery but also Pachuca obsidian through that link for their own use. (We can only understand the large propor-

tions of such goods at sites like La Nopalera if they were *used* there, since simply transshipping such goods to other regions would not result in disposition of them at La Nopalera.) If the movement of goods was *through* Tehuacán rather than *to* it, then the failure of sites like La Nopalera to mesh into the local system makes sense.

These thoughts lead us to a somewhat different model of the economics of Teotihuacán's long-distance foreign relations. This model also postulates export of substantial amounts of goods from Teotihuacán. The purpose is not, however, to return a profit in human energy terms (the only currency in which it makes sense to think of such a "profit" in the context of pre-Columbian Mesoamerica). Rather, the purpose is to acquire a variety of goods, almost exclusively prestige goods, which could not be obtained near the city. These goods would include such items as cacao, cotton, colorful feathers, and many others that can be produced easily in the humid lowlands but are mostly unavailable in the Central Highlands. We have direct or indirect evidence of the luxury use of such materials in various periods. If Thin Orange pottery was produced far from Teotihuacán, it might also have been acquired through such a network, but many questions remain about the source of this famous ware (Kolb 1986).

Thus far our model parallels that sketched by Clark (1986). It departs from his model, however, in recognizing that the size of Teotihuacán and the wealth and power of its elites would create a demand for prestige goods that could not easily be satisfied through low-volume elite exchange with the lowlands. Rather, Teotihuacán would need to export a substantial quantity of goods, *both elite and utilitarian*, in order to acquire sufficient supplies for its own elites without recourse to military force – which, we agree with both Santley (1983: 77) and Clark (1986: 66), is neither indicated nor likely. Although the import side of the ledger for Teotihuacán would have included almost exclusively elite goods, there is no reason to believe that this would have been true of the export side, since many of the likely imports were not, in their raw form, necessarily elite goods in the regions from which they came. Berdan (1986: 286) notes that, in such a fashion, the Aztec *pochteca* (professional traders) carried from Tenochtitlán both luxury goods from foreign elites and such items as rabbit furs and obsidian blades for commoners.

In short, this model sees Teotihuacán traders carrying obsidian and likely other goods away from Teotihuacán in some quantity, not to the regions where energy profits could best be made but to regions where goods sought by Teotihuacán's elite could be obtained. Sanders and Santley (1983: 266), among others, have noted this very aspect of the distribution of Teotihuacán "influence" through Mesoamerica and the likelihood that elite goods figured importantly in Teotihuacán imports. Some of these elite goods could have been acquired through exchanges with local elites, as Clark (1986) has emphasized, and still more acquired in barter, perhaps in markets, for utilitarian goods brought from Teotihuacán. The "sales" of utilitarian goods such as obsidian would not be at a "profit," however, but often at a staggering loss; these goods would have covered much more distance than the rival goods provided by the competitors from closer sources.

From this viewpoint, the export of obsidian was not a way for Teotihuacán's elites to accumulate capital; rather, it was one of the ways that capital, accumulated locally, was expended. The prestige goods acquired came at tremendous expense in human energy. The importance of acquiring them, however, was not easily translated into energy; it was social, religious, and political – just as in our own case with such prestige goods as imported English tableware, French wine, German cars, or looted pre-Columbian art. Blanton and Feinman (1984) also see a pre-Columbian long-distance exchange system of major economic proportions focused on luxury goods whose true importance must be measured in the social and political realm.

If such a reconstruction of the economics of Teotihuacán's foreign relations is correct, then the failure of the Teotihuacán "presence" in the Tehuacán Valley to integrate with the local political or economic system makes sense. The Tehuacán Valley was a route to other areas rather than a destination; energy profits (for which Tehuacán would have been a likely source) were not the objective, and the array of available resources for prestige goods in Tehuacán differed little from that of the Basin of Mexico.

Such a reconstruction also fits with evidence concerning the volume of trade. If there were sites with a special Teotihuacán "presence," such as La Nopalera and others in the Tehuacán Valley or the notorious Teotihuacán "enclaves" at Matacapan or Kaminaljuyú, then there were residents of a number of communities who spent much of their time in activities connected with Teotihuacán trade. Even by the most extravagant estimates of the Teotihuacán obsidian export trade, however, the transport and distribution of the obsidian does not require an enormous amount of human effort. (This very feature of obsidian is said to exempt it from the rule that economic activities of major importance focused on rather small regions.) By Santley's (1984: 68) estimate, a single itinerant obsidian merchant could supply a population of 10,125 at an average distance of 640 km (which seems quite a generous estimate of an overall average distance for Teotihuacán obsidian distribution). Santley's (1984: 72) middle estimate of the number of consumers supplied with obsidian by Teotihuacán is 3,000,000; this would require fewer than 300 such merchants. If even a third of these traders followed the Tehuacán Valley route toward the Gulf Coast, to Matacapan, and eventually to the Maya area, making an average of 4.7 trips per year (Santley 1984: 68), then a caravan of 50 merchants would come along every six weeks or so. This hardly seems a level of activity sufficient to justify specialized Teotihuacán-connected settlements (such as La Nopalera) of people earning their living through such trade. Santley's lower estimates of the number of consumers supplied with Teotihuacán obsidian would require only one or two such caravans annually, and even these lower figures have been challenged as much too high (Clark 1986).

If, as we have suggested, the special Teotihuacán-connected sites in the Tehuacán Valley owed their existence to the movement of goods, then substantially more goods must have been moved than postulated in the obsidian export-for-profit models. (Recall that the possibility for profit in those models depended on the small amount of effort required to transport obsidian.) Likewise, our suggestion implies substantially larger-scale movement of goods than is called for in models focused on small-scale exchange between elites. As noted above, trade for acquisition of prestige goods and raw materials for prestige goods could involve such a volume because of the size of Teotihuacán and the power of its elite. That volume could include not only obsidian exported from Teotihuacán, in whatever quantity, but also assorted raw and finished items of both utilitarian and elite nature. Few of these goods could possibly have had the favorable characteristics of obsidian for profitable export, but trade for acquisition of prestige goods need not be profitable – indeed, it surely was not.

Reconstructing Teotihuacán's foreign trade as aimed at acquiring certain prestige goods, even at very high costs, by exporting both elite and utilitarian goods in some quantity is also consistent with evidence from farther afield than the Tehuacán Valley. The Gulf Coast and the Maya Lowlands are especially likely sources of exotic prestige goods. If obsidian was at least among the materials traded there, then it certainly ought to be in evidence. Small-scale exchanges between elites would result in small quantities of Teotihuacán obsidian occurring especially in elite forms and contexts. A monopolistic obsidian export-for-profit system would result in very large proportions of Teotihuacán obsidian in both elite and utilitarian forms and contexts, since the artificially high prices necessary to turn a profit would depend on monopolistic control of the market, preventing utilization of obsidian from other sources. If such a monopolistic system operated

through control of the obsidian source at El Chayal by way of a Teotihuacán enclave at Kaminaljuyú, as Santley (1983: 100–1) has argued, then there should be very little Teotihuacán obsidian at all in the Maya area because it would be less profitable to transport it so far than to distribute El Chayal obsidian. If Teotihuacán exported obsidian (among other things) to trade for prestige goods, even at a very unfavorable rate, then Teotihuacán obsidian ought to appear in significant but not dominant quantities in both utilitarian and elite forms and contexts. In such a situation the quantities would be significant because a substantial amount would be needed to exchange for the substantial amounts of other goods acquired, but not dominant because of the absence of the monopoly control which would exclude obsidian from other sources.

Assessing the pattern of obsidian procurement for the Maya Lowlands is difficult: (1) because the sample of artifacts identified to source is small – a total of only 289 Early Classic artifacts (Nelson 1985; Nelson and Howard 1986), (2) because even this small sample is composed of tiny samples from many different sites, and (3) because none of the samples have been selected in such a way as to avoid bias. Indeed, most of the samples have been selected in ways that guarantee strong bias. At the moment, nothing can be done about this situation except to take the patterns observed with a grain of salt. Two sources outside Guatemala are represented in the total Early Classic sample of artifacts from the Maya lowlands in significant but certainly not dominant proportions: Pachuca (12.5 percent) and Otumba (2.4 percent). Six other Mexican sources are represented in trivial proportions (Nelson and Howard 1986). These figures, for what they are worth, clearly correspond to the expectations of the model proposed here.

At Tikal, some 4 percent of a sample of 10,950 prismatic blades were green, and, presumably, from the Pachuca source (Moholy-Nagy et al. 1984). Only 1 percent of 840 eccentrics were green but 29 percent of projectile points or knives were green. In a sample of 14 points/knives that were sourced chemically, 7 came from Otumba and one each from Pachuca, Zaragoza, and Ucareo, suggesting that the proportion of these bifacially worked artifacts imported from Teotihuacán might be quite high (Moholy-Nagy et al. 1984). The picture at Tikal, then, also confirms our expectation that obsidian from Teotihuacán should occur in significant but not dominant proportions. It occurs in both elite and utilitarian forms and contexts, but its presence is especially notable in utilitarian forms and contexts. The fact that Teotihuacán obsidian is especially common in the form of points or knives is significant. These artifacts would have been more valuable than plain prismatic blades because of the extra labor involved in making them. For Teotihuacán to emphasize points or knives in its exports to the Maya area makes sense only if the obsidian industry was functioning not to import energy profits to Teotihuacán but to export energy. Otherwise, labor input in the manufacturing process would have been minimized by concentrating on the material itself in its most economical form for transport and trade, the prismatic blade.

Oaxaca provides a final few pieces of information against which the model proposed here can be evaluated. There is little possibility in the Valley of Oaxaca for production of elite goods unavailable in the Basin of Mexico, but small-scale elite exchange with Monte Albán would not be surprising. Whatever we make of the Oaxaca ward at Teotihuacán, the carved stones of Monte Albán speak quite clearly of just such elite contacts (Marcus 1980, 1983). If the sites in the Tehuacán Valley with large quantities of Thin Orange pottery and Teotihuacán obsidian represent some kind of trade route, it likely goes down toward the Gulf Coast rather than up the Río Grande on the natural route toward the Valley of Oaxaca. At least, survey in the Cuicatlán Cañada, through which the Oaxaca route would pass (Redmond 1983), failed to reveal any more such Teotihuacán-related sites in that direction. (The other possible branch of the route, down toward the Río Papaloapan and Matacapan, passes through archaeological *terra incognita*, so we do not know whether such sites occur there.) Our source analysis of a modest sample of obsidian from the Cañada shows reliance on a large number of sources during the Late Formative, a surge in obsidian from Teotihuacán during the Terminal Formative, and

Table 8.3   Percentages of obsidian from different sources during three phases in the Cuicatlán Cañada[a]

	Perdido Phase (Late Formative) (19)	Lomas Phase (Terminal Formative) (37)	Trujano Phase (Classic) (9)
Puebla/Veracruz			
Oyameles/Zaragoza	0	11 ± 5	22 ± 9
Altotonga	84 ± 4	5 ± 2	0
Guadalupe Victoria	5 ± 2	20 ± 2	22 ± 9
Pico de Orizaba	0	10 ± 4	11 ± 7
Subtotal	90 ± 3	45 ± 6	56 ± 11
Near Teotihuacán			
Pachuca	11 ± 3	24 ± 6	22 ± 9
Tulancingo	0	4 ± 3	0
Otumba	0	16 ± 6	11 ± 7
Subtotal	11 ± 3	44 ± 7	33 ± 10
Other			
Ucareo/Zinapécuaro	0	11 ± 5	11 ± 7

[a] Numbers in parentheses for each phase are numbers of obsidian artifacts sourced from each. In the body of the table, the plus or minus terms represent one standard error.

a decline in the importance of Teotihuacán sources during the Classic (table 8.3). This parallels the situation described above for the Tehuacán Valley, except that the Oyameles/Zaragoza source fails to dominate the Cañada as it does the Tehuacán Valley during the Classic.

We also analyzed a very few artifacts from Monte Albán, where one Late to Terminal Formative artifact came from Oyameles/Zaragoza and one from Pachuca. For the Early and Late Classic, two artifacts came from Oyameles/Zaragoza and one from Pachuca. Winter (n.d.: 4) reports source analysis of four Late to Terminal Formative obsidian artifacts from Monte Albán; one came from Otumba, one from Guadalupe Victoria, and two from unidentified sources. For the Classic, one came from Pachuca and five from unidentified sources. The values reported for several trace elements suggest that some if not all these unidentified sources are in the Puebla/Veracruz group, with the Oyameles/Zaragoza locality being a prime candidate. No source specimens from this locality were analyzed by Zeitlin and Heimbuch (1978), who provided the source identifications Winter reports, but subsequent analysis confirms Oyameles/Zaragoza as the source of at least two of these five artifacts (Robert Zeitlin, personal communication 1987). Finsten (1982: 204–10) finds green obsidian comprising about 30 percent of that from surface collections in the Valley of Oaxaca for the Early Classic. This is a significant amount but, curiously, it does not decrease after the Late Classic when the economic system centered on Teotihuacán had ceased to exist. This glimpse of obsidian sources supplying Monte Albán and the Valley of Oaxaca does not suggest a Teotihuacán monopoly, but it is far from definitive. Other possible imports from Teotihuacán, such as Thin Orange pottery, are present but conspicuous principally because they are so rare.

Conclusion

Reconstruction of changing patterns of obsidian procurement and attention to the contexts in which obsidian from different sources appears, then, argue against the idea that the export of obsidian or other goods to regions outside the Basin of Mexico in any way underwrote or sustained the economy of Teotihuacán. Nevertheless, there are indications that goods were imported and exported in quantities that required significant expenditure of human effort. These activities were more important to Teotihuacán in social and political terms as an element in elite consumption than as a "profit-making" activity. We do not see our account as necessarily contradictory to Kurtz's (1987) model of the effect of imports and exports on Teotihuacán's economy. Neither does the evidence we have presented provide support for the specific dynamic envisioned by Kurtz over other alternatives. Teotihuacán's foreign trade apparently was not overwhelmingly focused on obsidian and, therefore, Teotihuacán's proximity to a high-quality source of this commodity was not of particular importance to its development.

ACKNOWLEDGMENTS

The trace element analysis of obsidian discussed here was funded by a grant from the National Science Foundation (BNS81–12161) to the University of Pittsburgh. The excavations from which the bulk of the obsidian came in the Tehuacán Valley were funded by a grant from the National Science Foundation (BNS76–82651) to the University of Michigan, by the R. S. Peabody Foundation for Archaeology, and by a grant from the Central Research Development Fund of the University of Pittsburgh. Obsidian artifacts from the Cuicatlán Cañada were provided by Charles S. Spencer and Elsa M. Redmond. Those mentioned from Monte Albán were provided by Marcus C. Winter. Source specimens were kindly provided by Robert H. Cobean from collections at the University of Missouri and by Jane Wheeler and William Farrand from collections at the University of Michigan. Jeanne Ferrary Drennan helped us in our efforts to make our message clear. We thank participants in the symposium at the 1987 annual meeting of the Society for American Archaeology, to which this paper was first presented, and especially George L. Cowgill and Barry L. Isaac, for useful and thoughtful comments. None of these people, of course, can be blamed for the uses to which we have put their cooperation.

REFERENCES

Berdan, Frances F. 1986. Enterprise and Empire in Aztec and Early Colonial Mexico. pp. 281–302 in Barry L. Isaac (ed.), *Economic Aspects of Prehispanic Highland Mexico* (Research in Economic Anthropology, Supplement 2). Greenwich, CT: JAI Press.

Blanton, Richard and Gary Feinman. 1984. The Mesoamerican World System. *American Anthropologist* 86: 673–82.

Charlton, Thomas H. 1978. Teotihuacán, Tepeapulco, and Obsidian Exploitation. *Science* 200: 1227–36.

—— 1984. Production and Exchange: Variables in the Evolution of a Civilization. pp. 17–42 in Kenneth G. Hirth (ed.), *Trade and Exchange in Early Mesoamerica*. Albuquerque: University of New Mexico Press.

Clark, John E. 1986. From Mountains to Molehills: A Critical Review of Teotihuacán's Obsidian Industry. pp. 23–74 in Barry L. Isaac (ed.), *Economic Aspects of Prehispanic Highland Mexico* (Research in Economic Anthropology, Supplement 2). Greenwich, CT: JAI Press.

Drennan, Robert D. 1978. *Excavations at Quachilco: A Report on the 1977 Season of the Palo Blanco Project in the Tehuacán Valley*. Ann Arbor: University of Michigan Museum of Anthropology, Technical Reports, No. 7.

—— 1979. Excavations at Cuayucatepec (Ts281): A Preliminary Report. pp. 169–99 in Robert D. Drennan (ed.), *Prehistoric Social, Political, and Economic Development in the Area of the Tehuacán Valley: Some Results of the Palo Blanco Project*. Ann Arbor: University of Michigan Museum of Anthropology, Technical Reports, No. 11.

—— 1984a. Long-Distance Movement of Goods in the Mesoamerican Formative and Classic. *American Antiquity* 49: 27–43.

—— 1984b. Long-Distance Transport Costs in Pre-Hispanic Mesoamerica. *American Anthropologist* 86: 105–12.

Drennan, Robert D. and J. A. Nowack. 1984. Exchange and Sociopolitical Development in the Tehuacán Valley. pp. 147–56 in Kenneth G. Hirth (ed.), *Trade and Exchange in Early Mesoamerica*. Albuquerque: University of New Mexico Press.

Finsten, Laura. 1982. The Classic–Postclassic Transition in the Valley of Oaxaca, Mexico: A Regional Analysis of the Process of Political Decentralization in a Prehistoric Complex Society. Ph.D. diss., Purdue University.

Harbottle, G., E. V. Sayre, and R. Abascal-M. n.d. Neutron Activation Analysis of Thin Orange Pottery. Mimeographed, Department of Chemistry, Brookhaven National Laboratory, Upton, NY.

Kolb, Charles C. 1986. Commercial Aspects of Classic Teotihuacán Period "Thin Orange" Wares. pp. 155–205 in Barry L. Isaac (ed.), *Economic Aspects of Prehispanic Highland Mexico* (Research in Economic Anthropology, Supplement 2). Greenwich, CT: JAI Press.

Kurtz, Donald V. 1987. The Economics of Urbanization and State Formation at Teotihuacán. *Current Anthropology* 28: 329–53.

Marcus, Joyce. 1980. Zapotec Writing. *Scientific American* 242(2): 50–64.

—— 1983. Teotihuacán Visitors on Monte Albán Monuments and Murals. pp. 175–81 in Kent V. Flannery and Joyce Marcus (eds), *The Cloud People: Divergent Evolution of the Zapotec and Mixtec Civilizations*. New York: Academic Press.

Millon, René. 1970. Teotihuacán: Completion of Map of Giant Ancient City in the Valley of Mexico. *Science* 170: 1077–82.

—— 1973. *Urbanization at Teotihuacán, Mexico, Vol. 1: The Teotihuacán Map, Part 1: Text*. Austin: University of Texas Press.

Moholy-Nagy, Hattula, Frank Asaro, and Fred H. Stross. 1984. Tikal Obsidian: Sources and Typology. *American Antiquity* 49: 104–17.

Nelson, Fred W., Jr. 1985. Summary of the Results of Analysis of Obsidian Artifacts from the Maya Lowlands. *Scanning Electron Microscopy* 1985: 631–49.

Nelson, Fred W., Jr. and David S. Howard. 1986. *Trace Element Analysis of Obsidian Artifacts from El Mirador, Guatemala*. Provo, UT: New World Archaeological Foundation Notes, no. 3.

Redmond, Elsa M. 1983. *A Fuego y Sangre: Early Zapotec Imperialism in the Cuicatlán Cañada*. Ann Arbor: University of Michigan Museum of Anthropology, Memoirs, No. 16.

Sanders, William T. and Robert S. Santley. 1983. A Tale of Three Cities: Energetics and Urbanization in Pre-Hispanic Central Mexico. pp. 243–91 in Evon Z. Vogt and Richard M. Leventhal (eds), *Prehistoric Settlement Patterns: Essays in Honor of Gordon R. Willey*. Albuquerque: University of New Mexico Press.

Santley, Robert S. 1983. Obsidian Trade and Teotihuacán Influence in Mesoamerica. pp. 69–124 in Arthur G. Miller (ed.), *Highland–Lowland*

Interaction in Mesoamerica: Interdisciplinary Approaches: A Conference at Dumbarton Oaks. Washington, DC: Dumbarton Oaks Research Library and Collection.

——1984. Obsidian Exchange, Economic Stratification, and the Evolution of Complex Society in the Basin of Mexico. pp. 43–86 in Kenneth G. Hirth (ed.), *Trade and Exchange in Early Mesoamerica*. Albuquerque: University of New Mexico Press.

——1987. Comment on The Economics of Urbanization and State Formation at Teotihuacán by Donald V. Kurtz. *Current Anthropology* 28: 344–5.

Santley, Robert S., Janet M. Kerley, and Ronald R. Kneebone. 1986. Obsidian Working, Long-Distance Exchange, and the Politico-Economic Organization of Early States in Central Mexico. pp. 101–32 in Barry L. Isaac (ed.), *Economic Aspects of Prehispanic Highland Mexico* (Research in Economic Anthropology, Supplement 2). Greenwich, CT: JAI Press.

Santley, Robert S. and Christopher A. Pool. n.d. Prehispanic Exchange Relationships between Central Mexico, the Valley of Oaxaca, and the Gulf Coast of Mexico. MS.

Sotomayor, Alfredo and Noemí Castillo Tejero (1963) *Estudio petrográfico de la cerámica Anaranjado Delgado*. Mexico, DF: Instituto Nacional de Antropología e Historia (Mexico), Departmento de Prehistoria, Publication No. 12.

Spence, Michael W. 1967. The Obsidian Industry of Teotihuacán. *American Antiquity* 32: 507–14.

——1981. Obsidian Production and the State in Teotihuacán. *American Antiquity* 46: 769–88.

——1984. Craft Production and Polity in Early Teotihuacán. pp. 87–114 in Kenneth G. Hirth (ed.), *Trade and Exchange in Early Mesoamerica*. Albuquerque: University of New Mexico Press.

Winter, Marcus C. n.d. La obsidiana en Oaxaca prehispánica. Paper presented at the Symposium "La Obsidiana en Mesoamérica," Centro Regional de Hidalgo, Instituto Nacional de Antropología e Historia, Pachuca, Hgo., Mexico City.

Zeitlin, Robert N. and Ray C. Heimbuch 1978. Trace Element Analysis and the Archaeological Study of Obsidian Procurement in Precolumbian Mesoamerica. pp. 117–59 in Dave D. Davis (ed.), *Lithics and Subsistence: The Analysis of Stone Tool Use in Prehistoric Economies*. Nashville: Vanderbilt University Publications in Anthropology No. 20.

CHAPTER 9

Principles of Regional and Long-distance Trade in the Aztec Empire

Frances F. Berdan

Trade in Aztec Mexico: it consisted of long caravans of professional merchants – merchants laden with precious goods, merchants trekking through dangerous and hostile country, merchants concluding glamorous transactions with rulers of distant states. These are the well-documented and paradoxical *pochteca*, and this is the usual twentieth-century image of Aztec trade. But it is a skewed and incomplete image.

If trade is a peaceful "method of acquiring goods that are not available on the spot" (Polanyi 1975: 133), then, in the Aztec empire, there were several levels or "layers" (Polyani 1975: 136–42) which served this end. These included state-supported foreign trade, conducted beyond the bounds of the empire; guild-regulated intra-empire trade; regional trade; and local-level trade. The complexity of the Aztec domain required these many levels of "material provisioning." Not only must the ruler and his state machinery be provisioned, but also a *macehualli*'s small household. While the basic fact is the same – both must be supplied with goods which they cannot or do not fully produce themselves – the scale and types of requirements are quite different. Indeed, they are sufficiently different to call forth distinct styles of trade.

My ultimate goal in this paper is to account for these diverse styles of trade. This requires an examination of each type in terms of its essential contextual dimensions. These distinguishing dimensions include degree of specialization, types of participants, scale of operations, trading goals, usual exchange "vehicles," types of goods traded, extent of state (or other) control, and adaptability under changing imperial conditions.

Types of Trading Ventures

Foreign Trade

While any trading activity carried on beyond the bounds of one's own familiar territory may be considered "foreign trade," I am using this term quite specifically here to refer to Aztec state-sponsored trading enterprises conducted beyond the borders of the imperial domain.

The principal actors in this business were the professional long-distance merchants, the colorful pochteca. These merchant specialists, organized into guilds,[1] were ensconced in separate *calpulli* in the major Valley of Mexico cities (see Berdan 1978). Some of these merchant groups, at least by the sixteenth century, appear to have exercised a monopoly over state-supported foreign trading ventures. We are told by the Tlatelolcan informants of the Franciscan friar Bernardino de Sahagún that the pochteca from only five Valley of Mexico cities

Reprinted from Frances F. Berdan. 1988. Principles of Regional and Long-distance Trade in the Aztec Empire. In *Smoke and Mist: Mesoamerican Studies in Memory of Thelma D. Sullivan*, edited by J. Kathryn Josserand and Karen Dakin (British Archaeological Reports, International Series, no. 402, Oxford), pp. 639–56.

commissioned by the Tenochtitlan ... er to carry state goods to foreign districts; these were the privileged pochteca from the merchant calpulli of Tenochtitlan, Tlatelolco, Uitzilopochco, Azcapotzalco and Quauhtitlan (Sahagún 1950–82: book 9, 17).[2] To be more precise, only the merchants from Tenochtitlan and Tlatelolco were actually entrusted with the Tenochca ruler's goods. The others traveled as their companions. While it goes unreported, these merchants (all from cities in Tepanec territory) may have carried the goods of the ruler of Tlacopan in these ventures. Similarly, while merchants from seven other Valley of Mexico cities were supposedly restricted from trading in the Gulf Coast lands beyond the imperial boundaries (Sahagún 1950–82: book 9, 48–9), they may have served elsewhere as extra-empire emissaries for the ruler of Texcoco – these cities were located in Acolhua country and in the southern lakeshore districts.[3] Admittedly, this is speculation. But Sahagún's grouping of the cities corresponds fairly nicely to the geographical domains of the Triple Alliance capitals: Tenochtitlan, Texcoco and Tlacopan.

Whether under Mexica, Acolhua, or Tepanec sponsorship, the pochteca operated as both state agents and private entrepreneurs in undertaking their long and arduous journey to foreign lands. They were sent with the blessing, and some actual material wealth, of the Aztec government (Sahagún 1950–82: book 9, 7–8, 17). In the most fully documented case (see pp. 7–8), merchants from Tenochtitlan were given 1,600 *quachtli* (large white cotton cloaks) by the Mexica ruler, Ahuitzotl (ruled 1486–1502). They carried these cloaks to Tlatelolco where the pochteca of the two cities exchanged gifts and then divided the cloaks equally between them. With these, they purchased the elaborately decorated articles of clothing (undoubtedly in the bustling Tlatelolco marketplace) which they were to trade with the rulers of outlying districts. The fact that the pochteca carried as "state goods" the highly embellished elite clothing rather than the more "negotiable" quachtli punctuates the political overtones of this foreign exchange. The pochteca exchanged the Mexica ruler's goods directly with the rulers of foreign districts for precious items of supposedly equal value: jade, turquoise mosaic shields, shells, tortoise shell cups, wild animal skins and a variety of feathers including the prized quetzal (Sahagún 1950–82: book 9, 17, 18–19). Throughout, these goods remained the property of the ruler, and the merchants served as his agents; an armed escort was even provided the merchants by their hosts as they traversed hostile foreign territory. It has all the trappings of a political arrangement enacted for mutual benefit.

This "mutual benefit" was not without its economic rewards. The very exchange of exclusively elite goods between Mexica emissaries and foreign rulers served to "move" these luxury items across political boundaries. While low-value subsistence goods may move fairly readily across such borders, the elite-consumables would not easily penetrate those same borders in large quantities (see below). Also, like the famed Kula Ring, might there be additional economic accompaniments to this formalized exchange? On these expeditions, the pochteca also carried personal goods for purposes of sale – they were private entrepreneurs as well as state agents. They offered costly goods (such as golden necklaces and ear plugs) for the distant elite, and less expensive items (such as rabbit fur and pointed obsidian blades) for the commoners of those districts.

While the formalized aspect of pochteca foreign exchange suggests a "port of trade" context, the inclusion of additional private merchant goods for exchange implies marketplaces (Berdan 1978: 194–5). Sahagún, elaborate in his description of the state-level transactions, regrettably fails to mention the nature of transactions involving the personal goods of the merchants. However, an unpublished document in the Archivo General de las Indias (AGI 1541: Justicia 195) mentions that Mexican Indian merchants in 1541 were trading in marketplaces (*tianguiz*) in these areas "as was their custom." In addition, contentions are made that these merchants regularly took advantage of the local inhabitants in their economic dealings, a characteristic also noted by Durán (1967: vol. 2, 357–8). This suggests that such trade was a pre-conquest pattern, and that the location for exchanges involving the personal goods of the pochteca were the marketplaces in these foreign areas. Local persons involved in such trade apparently were of both nobility and commoner status, given the types of goods carried by the Mexica merchants. According to the 1541 document, these merchants obtained cacao in these marketplaces. This is consistent with the somewhat problematic statement by Sahagún that the pochteca possessed cacao in their personal inventories after returning from their trading ventures (1950–82: book 9, 27, 30).[4]

In general, the state and private pochteca wares had a conspicuous characteristic: they were high-value, low-bulk items. It seems that the pochteca placed a premium on realizing a high return from their lengthy and dangerous ventures, ventures in which transport by foot and canoe posed "expensive" problems. Under these circumstances it can be anticipated that the 1,600 Mexica ruler's cloaks (quachtli) would be immediately exchanged by the pochteca for the more highly valued decorated cloaks, thus reducing the bulk while at the same time offering prestigious rather than strictly utilitarian textiles. Similarly, all of the elite goods, and most of the "ordinary" wares carried as private merchandise of the pochteca were manufactured, some of precious or highly localized materials such as gold, obsidian, and copper. The manufacturing "step" serves to add value to any unembellished item, again (as with the decorated cloaks) without adding to its bulk. Other goods carried by the Mexica merchants for the Gulf Coast commoners consisted of items such as cochineal, rabbit fur,[5] sewing needles, alum[6] and various herbs (Sahagún 1950–82: book 9, 8, 18), all of which may have been in great local demand with few other avenues open for supplying the region. Slaves were also brought to these districts by special high-ranking Mexica merchants – while they seem to have been in general

abundance in the Gulf coastal and Yucatan area, they were also in high demand year-round as agricultural laborers and for transport services (Scholes and Roys 1968: 29). Endemic warfare throughout the Yucatan peninsula produced a steady supply of captives for slavery, but it appears that slaves from distant regions were preferred over those from nearby areas: "since they [the Yucatecan towns] ordinarily fought with the neighboring provinces, they sold their captives and for their own service purchased slaves from more distant regions, who could less easily escape to their homes" (Roys 1972: 68).

While the pochteca tended not to carry and deal in bulky items, they did traffic in bulk. They traveled, armed, in long caravans. This provided them with some measure of protection, and also made their substantial capital investment worthwhile. For not only were the goods of the ruler and those of the individual merchant packed, but also those of other pochteca unable to undertake that particular venture (Sahagún 1950–82: book 9, 14).

Expeditions were very well organized, both at home and on the road. The guilds contained specific merchant ranks, well documented by Sahagún. This ranking system conditioned much of the individual pochteca's day-to-day life and long-term goals. Certain rights and responsibilities were restricted to merchants of particular standing: to name a few, the principal merchants received and traded the ruler's goods, "expedition leaders"[8] organized the details of trading ventures and assumed responsibility for the neophyte youths traveling with the caravan, "burden-carrying merchants"[9] were of relatively low standing and were required to carry some wares on their own backs. If the accounts related to Sahagún by the Tlatelolcan merchants are to be taken at face value, the guilds strictly controlled trading activities, accumulation of wealth, feasting and its attendant rise in social station, training, and the expectations and value orientations of their members. The elders were forever admonishing their underlings to behave in a proper pochteca manner. This is, of course, the "official script," and the actual behavior applied to these ideals may have been somewhat more casual and flexible. Nonetheless, if only out of self-interest, long-distance foreign trading ventures were planned carefully and carried the blessing of the state.

As military conquests repeatedly extended the boundaries of the empire, foreign trading, by definition, moved farther from the Triple Alliance capitals, into more distant regions. In this sense, Chapman's (1957) hypothesis that tribute replaced trade is indisputable. It is documented that Aztec merchants and state emissaries had traded goods in subsequently conquered outlying districts through market transactions and through strictly political connections with local rulers at least since the time of Motecuhzoma Ilhuicamina (ruled 1440–68).

For example, Cohuaxtlahuaca, before its conquest by the Triple Alliance, possessed a rich and attractive market. Merchants from Tenochtitlan, Texcoco, Chalco, Xochimilco, Coyoacan, Tlacopan, and Azcapotzalco obtained gold, feathers, cacao, fine gourd bowls, clothing, and thread made from rabbit fur in this market (Durán 1967: vol. 2, 185). At one time, during the reign of Motecuhzoma Ilhuicamina, 160 merchants from these cities are recorded as being present in that market (Durán 1967: vol. 2, 185). The killing of these same merchants motivated the Triple Alliance forces to conquer Cohuaxtlahuaca.

Professional merchant activity is also recorded in the district of Tututepec prior to its conquest by the Triple Alliance during the reign of Motecuhzoma Xocoyotzin (ruled 1502–20):

the lapidaries of the city of Mexico, of Tlatelolco, and of other cities heard that in the provinces of Tototepec and Quetzaltepec there existed a type of sand good for working stones, together with emery to polish them until they became bright and shining. The stone workers told King Moctezuma about this and explained the difficulties in obtaining the sand and emery from those provinces, and the high prices that were asked. Moctezuma sent messengers then to Tototepec and Quet-

zaltepec, asking as a favor that the sand be sent to the master artisans. He stated that he would send them things in return, since he wishes this to be an exchange.

(Durán 1964: 229–30)

Difficulties in conducting transactions to the satisfaction (or advantage) of the Tenochtitlan ruler (as representative of the lapidary interests) and subsequent mistreatment of the emissaries were offered by the Triple Alliance as reasons for the conquest of this province.

A further example of tribute replacing trade involves Aztec dealings with Cempoala in the province of Cuetlaxtlan.

they [the Aztecs] decided to send messengers to Cempoala in the province of Cuetlaxtla, asking the rulers there to send them some conch shells, live turtles and scallops and other curious sea products, since these people lived right next to the ocean. The Aztecs had heard about these objects and wished them for the cult of their god.

(Durán 1964: 113–14)

The Aztec officials carried with them goods for exchange. Yet they were killed, at the encouragement of the Tlaxcallan rulers, who accused the ruler of Cuetlaxtlan of being a subject of the Aztecs; this underlines the political overtones of these exchanges.

Guild-regulated intra-empire trade

These same pochteca, as members of merchant guilds, also traded extensively within the Aztec imperial territory. Indeed, it may be that most of their energies were directed to intra-empire trading ventures – they were generally safer (although not without its hazards, as the elders warned the neophytes), distances were less, and, as the empire expanded, many precious high-value goods became available to traders who never crossed the imperial borders (Matrícula de Tributos 1980: folios 10^r, 10^v, 12^r, 12^v, 13^r, 14^r, 15^v).

The hypothesis by Acosta-Saignes (1945) and Chapman (1957: 122) that trade preceded tribute also states that once an area was conquered by the Aztecs, trade by professional merchants usually ceased there. However, there is evidence that pochteca traded in marketplaces within the empire. The suggestion that merchants from Mixcoac, Texcoco, Uexotla, Coatlichan, Otompan, Xochimilco, and Chalco were prohibited from trading outside the empire necessarily implies that, of the professional merchants, these at least traded *within* the empire. We know that they traveled at least as far as Tochtepec on the southeastern edge of Aztec control – they would not have trekked so far without some anticipated gain en route. That professional merchants traded within the empire is confirmed by a statement which records the rebellion of the district of Tizauhcoac in which merchants from the cities of Texcoco and Tenochtitlan were killed (Alva Ixtlilxochitl 1965: vol. 2, 272). A similar instance of a rebellion involved the Huasteca (Durán 1967: vol. 2, 327). Indeed, Alva Ixtlilxochitl (1965: vol. 2, 190–1) states that provinces conquered by Texcoco were obligated to permit merchants to traffic within the confines of those provinces, quite as a matter of policy. Durán mentions that merchants traveled "to all the markets of the land, bartering cloth for jewels, jewels for feathers, feathers for stones, and stones for slaves, always dealing in things of importance, of renown, and of high value" (1971: 138). One such market was that of Tepeaca. This city, upon its conquest by the Aztecs, was required to hold a market on a designated day. A wide variety of goods, including rich cloaks, stones, jewels, feathers of different colors, gold, silver (and other metals), skins of jaguars and ocelots, cacao, rich loincloths, and sandals were to be sold in that market (Durán 1967: vol. 2, 162). Given the types of commodities to be available (luxury prestige goods), it is highly likely that Valley of Mexico professional merchants frequented this market. It may well have been established for purposes of making many "tropical" luxuries more accessible to those very merchants.

Pochteca (in their many "guises") are mentioned as purveyors of some goods in the great Tlatelolco market (Sahagún 1950–82: book 10 *passim*). They seemed to specialize, again, in items of high value and prestige: gold, decorated cloaks, feathers, cotton, cacao, and slaves (see ibid. pp. 59, 61, 63–4, 75). They ranged from the principal merchants (*ueicapan tlacatl*) who dealt in fine, decorated cloaks, to the wealthy slave dealers (*tecoani*) to undistinguished pochteca (dealing in gold and feathers) and *oztomeca* (providing bulky goods from the *tierra caliente*, such as cotton and cacao). These merchants, having traveled to distant parts to obtain such luxuries (or having commissioned other merchants to do so for them), would certainly frequent the most urban of all marketplaces, with its great concentration of potential noble buyers.

Some of these merchants were the same as those who traveled outside the empire on state missions. However, in their dealings in marketplaces within the empire, state "policies" affected them only indirectly: the state could mandate specific marketplace supplies, as at Tepeaca; it demanded market taxes of them as sellers of merchandise (see Berdan 1975: 208–9); and it required that the demand for their goods be limited to those of appropriate status. The guilds would have had a more direct impact on their daily life: assuring that their goals be material gain, but insisting that they not publicly display such gain when successful; controlling access to wealth through prescribed ranks, yet insisting that such wealth be dissipated through "rank-qualifying" feasts. These modes held whether trade was conducted within the imperial bounds or beyond them – under these constraints, it would have been difficult for a guild merchant to operate in an independent manner, even though his primary trading vehicle was the marketplace.

Regional and local-level trade

There can be little doubt that professional merchants operated within the confines of the empire, although determination of the actual categories of merchants involved and the extent of their enterprises is necessarily imprecise. Professional merchant middlemen did indeed operate within local, regional, and provincial contexts, quite apart from the Valley of Mexico merchant guilds.

Documentation on these merchants is, admittedly, sparse. As with most details of Aztec life, the data derives from post-Conquest sources, often reflecting post-Conquest changes in lifestyles. Regional and petty trading activities were entwined with the indigenous marketplace (*tianquiztli*) – a part of the everyday landscape which the great Colonial chroniclers and historians saw but rarely felt worthy of special detailed mention. However, for this reason and others (Berdan 1980: 37), many of the mid-sixteenth-century records that do exist may be taken as reasonably reflective of pre-Spanish conditions.[10] Especially in the outlying areas, little seems to have changed in the indigenous marketplaces during the first century of Spanish rule (Gibson 1964: 352–3; Lockhart 1976: 115). While regional entrepreneurs and petty part-time traders are recorded by Sahagún (1950–82: book 10) as active in the grand Tlatelolco marketplace, more realistic interpolations may be found by scrutinizing data from areas distant from the centers of Spanish Colonial power. Contrasting these areas to a rapidly transformed Tenochtitlan–Tlatelolco, Gibson concludes that "In the towns, Indian control lasted for longer periods" (1964: 355), "some smaller or more remote communities retained aboriginal market schedules for longer periods" (1964: 357), and in general that "Tlatelolco deteriorated more than any other of the Valley's marketplaces" (1964: 358).

That non-guild merchant middlemen were common under Aztec rule is evidenced by the description of such persons in the famed Tlatelolco marketplace (still, in the mid-sixteenth century, under Spanish rule). They had a Nahuatl designation, *tlanecuilo* in the Sahagún corpus,[11] translated as "retailer" or "dealer" by Anderson and Dibble. These traders did not deal in the full range of goods listed for the marketplace vendors. The objects of their trade were, for the most part, a far cry from the luxury wares purveyed by the guild merchants:

cacao, maize, amaranth seeds, chili, tortillas, wheat,[12] sandals, cotton, palm-fiber cloaks, painted gourd bowls, cane-carrying baskets, turkey, and salt (Sahagún 1950–82: book 10, 65–94). Five of these items included distinguishable regional varieties, some coming from the distant reaches of the empire and beyond.[13] It is significant that in all but one case (wrinkled chia), whenever regional varieties are mentioned, so also are the tlanecuilo. It may have been their special efforts which supplied the urban dwellers with such a remarkable assortment of consumer goods. Many varieties of cacao, maize, chile, cotton, and gourd bowls would have been either imported from long distances by individual merchants, or would have worked their way through successive regional marketplaces to finally reach Tlatelolco. In most cases, there would have been a combination of possibilities. For example, cacao and cotton were imported by oztomeca (guild merchants), retailed by tlanecuilo, *and* marketed by the field owners themselves. Invariably, the owners, workers, or manufacturers of a given product are listed as also selling that item in the Tlatelolco marketplace; only in these few cases are full-time merchants also mentioned. Why they are involved with these particular goods is somewhat mystifying. The five items from broadly diverse regions are understandable – the tlanecuilo gained economically by transporting and selling them, especially in the urban marketplaces. By expending this effort, the value of the item increased: this served as their means of livelihood. Of the remaining items, only the palm-fiber cloaks may have required the services of a tlanecuilo for reasons of distance. The others may have been in sufficiently great demand in the urban environment to support specialized retailers.[14]

The tlanecuilo, in a somewhat different Nahuatl guise, also appear in the market tax records for mid-sixteenth-century Coyoacan (Anderson, Berdan, and Lockhart 1976: 138–49). They appear as dealers in wood, chia, salt, and fish. Wood and wood products were a specialty of the Coyoacan marketplace, and certainly would have warranted the attention of full-time middlemen, who may also have supplied other nearby marketplaces with this necessary but heavy item. In all of these references they appear as dealers from specific places.[15] And, since the taxes seem to cover a full year's attendance at the marketplace, it may be assumed that these retailers followed a relatively consistent and well-entrenched market schedule.[16]

This is perhaps better seen in the provinces, at some distance from the great urban centers. Importantly, the localized availability of key subsistence goods seems to have had a profound effect on provincial marketplaces, or stimulated the development of professional traveling merchants at a regional level.

The localized occurrence of salt, cotton, and cacao particularly stimulated this type of activity. Both individual householders and merchants might travel over 200 kilometers for salt or cotton (PNE 1905–6: vol. 4, 204), and an undetermined distance for cacao. Merchants were particularly active in carrying salt and cotton, products which were bulky[17] and not widely produced (PNE 1905–6: vol. 4, 122, 181, 204; vol. 6, 78, 85, 112, 164, 241; Sahagún 1950–82: book 10, 84). When individual householders were involved, *they* were the ones who typically journeyed to the source of the salt, cacao or cotton; the producers of these commodities seem not to have transported their products[18] (e.g. PNE 1905–6: vol. 4, 67, 98, 103, 107, 113, 181, 223; vol. 5, 30, 130, 157, 162; vol. 6, 4, 31, 85, 143, 164, 225, 230). This is to be expected, given the great demand, limited supply, and hence high value placed on these special commodities. Given this, it may also be expected that trade in those goods would be of particular interest to professional merchants. Indeed, for Tlatelolco, Sahagún (1950–82: book 10, 84) says that the salt retailer (*iztanecuilo*) "sets out on the road, travels with it, goes from market to market." The somewhat surprising anomaly is cacao: while regional merchants were active in this trade, more commonly individual householders in the provinces may have trekked

to the *tierra caliente* to secure this prized item (PNE 1905–6: vol. 5, 181–2, 175; vol. 6, 131, 136, 164, 321).

Trade in these high-demand commodities was frequently intertwined. For example, the people of Teotitlan del Camino, external to the Aztec domain, manufactured *huipiles* and sold them to merchants who carried them to Guatemala, Chiapa, Suchitepeques, and Xoconochco. There they exchanged the huipiles for cacao, which the people of Teotitlan lacked. Nor did the people of Teotitlan grow their own cotton for their extensive *huipilli* manufacture; this they obtained from the distant Tehuantepec area (PNE 1905–6: vol. 4, 107). While the "type" of merchant involved in this intricate web is not specified, they were probably non-guild regional merchants, given the relative ease with which they would have necessarily crossed and recrossed Aztec imperial boundaries.[19]

For all these goods, salt, cotton, and cacao, the householders exchanged small surpluses of their subsistence production. This included both raw materials and manufactured items: maize, beans, chile, chia, fish, vegetables, fruits, honey, pinole, gourd bowls, mats, and cloaks (PNE 1905–6: vol. 5, 157, 181–2; vol. 6, 126, 131, 136, 164, 165, 261, 321). Likewise, full-time merchants trafficked in these more generally produced goods. However, whenever salt, cotton, or cacao were exchanged for one another, merchants were most likely to be involved in the transaction (PNE 1905–6: vol. 4, 241, 246; vol. 6, 112).

Regional merchant activity in outlying areas was extensive and lively. An excellent example comes from beyond the bounds of Aztec military control.[20] Miahuatlan in the Mixtec area became an entrepôt for the distribution of salt, brought there from Tehuantepec nearly 200 kilometers away. The full-time merchants who engaged in this distribution also dealt in fish, maize, chile, and cotton, carrying these goods from marketplace to marketplace in the Miahuatlan area (PNE 1905–6, vol. 4, 122). But the grandest marketplace of the region was at Miahuatlan, where a great *tianguiz* was held weekly (in conformity with the Spanish calendar), and reputedly *everything* was bought and sold there (PNE 1905–6: vol. 4, 126). The full-time merchants hailed from surrounding communities as well as from Miahuatlan itself: Coatlan merchants specialized in the salt trade; merchants from other unspecified communities dealt in cochineal[21] (PNE 1905–6: vol. 4, 126, 136), and the commercial entrepreneurs from Miahuatlan itself specialized in *amole*, used for cleaning clothes (PNE 1905–6: vol. 4, 126). These merchants were regionally based, and not the guild-organized pochteca from the Valley of Mexico who primarily specialized in the trading of exotic luxury goods. Such regional professional merchants probably provided the backbone of the marketplace exchange system in the provinces; still, as in Tlatelolco and Coyoacan, the majority of the vendors were those who sold small lots of their own surplus production.

Principles of Regional and Long-Distance Trade

Trading enterprises may be hierarchically ranked with respect to degree of specialization, value and types of goods traded, scale of operations, usual exchange context, extent of state or other control, and sensitivity to imperial expansion. These dimensions, applied to foreign trade, guild-regulated intra-empire trade, regional trade, and local-level trade, are summarized in table 9.1. They are ranked in that order from "large scale" to "small scale."

These several layers of trade all contributed to provisioning the people of Aztec Mexico at prescribed, desired, or feasible standards of living. Yet each made its contribution in a unique way. There are several possible factors which prompted the use of one form of trade in contrast to another. I will call these "principles of regional and long-distance trade," and will limit my discussion to three.

1 *The larger the scale of trading operations, the more intense the political boundaries.* It should be clear that it was more difficult, dangerous, and politically charged for the professional pochteca to step beyond the empire, than it was for either the regional merchant or small-scale producer–seller.[22] Certainly the main determinant here is the fact that the pochteca were themselves politically charged. Indeed, they warranted an armed escort by their hosts from the southeastern imperial borders to the port of trade Xicalanco (Sahagún 1950–82: book 9, 18). Yet even the imperially imposed tribute demands took advantage of the relatively free flow of a wide variety of goods across similar borders – the realm of the regional and local-level trader (see Berdan 1975, 1980).

2 *Persons engaging in full-time commerce, on whatever scale, gravitate toward dealing in goods which have a high exchange rate.* After all, profit is a primary motivation.[23] What kinds of commodities fall into this category, and why? The pochteca dealt heavily in items deemed luxuries in Aztec culture: precious feathers, metals, stones, and hides which were rare, alluring in appearance, and capable of manufacture into spectacular works of art (allowing further potential for an increase in value). These commodities were directed toward the highest strata of Aztec society; they constituted a profitable investment for merchants who could afford the capital outlay and deliver them from distant regions. Traffic in these high-value low-bulk luxuries also would have brought the guild-organized merchants higher returns than the regional merchants who probably could not afford the initial investment – the opportunities for wealth were greater. But regional merchants themselves, while they carried and exchanged a wide array of goods, also inclined their efforts toward locally produced, generally high-demand items to be carried across ecological boundaries: cotton, cacao, and salt.[24] These tendencies

Table 9.1

	Degree of specialization	Value/type of goods	Scale of operations	Usual exchange context	State of other control	Sensitivity to imperial expansion
Foreign trade	full-time guild members; may specialize in particular commodities (e.g. slaves, cloaks)	highest-value prestige goods and other high-demand commodities	largest-scale operators; great quantities moved in large caravans	"ports-of-trade"; associated marketplaces outside and within empire	direct state and guild controls; may serve as state agents	highly sensitive to expanding political boundaries and diplomatic relations
Guild-regulated intra-empire trade	full-time guild members; may specialize in particular commodities (e.g. slaves, cloaks)	highest-value prestige goods and other high-demand commodities	large-scale operators, but probably not as well endowed as those in foreign trade	marketplaces within empire	guild control; indirect state controls (e.g. market taxes)	sensitive to expanding borders; ability to expand operations into conquered areas
Regional trade	full-time; no merchant organization discernible; may specialize or deal in a variety of goods	"middle range," desirable utility goods	operate individually or perhaps in small groups; moderate quantities moved	marketplaces within and outside empire	indirect state controls (e.g. market taxes)	relatively insensitive – have ability to cross political borders, carrying goods in and out of empire
Local-level trade	part-time vendors; deal in surpluses of own productive efforts	low-value subsistence and craft products	small individual lots	marketplaces within and outside empire	indirect state controls (e.g. market taxes)	relatively insensitive – have ability to cross political borders, carrying goods in and out of empire

sound much like the favorable conditions for entrepreneurial trade as proposed by Rowlands (1973: 592):

The inbuilt discrepancies in the evaluation of
goods and services, either spatially and/or
between discrete spheres of exchange would
appear to present the best opportunity for
exploitation. Disparity in evaluation most frequently occurs between closed exchange
networks separated by physical barriers, ecological boundaries, distance and the operation
of different exchange mechanisms. Such a
situation can promote the activities of the specialist trader operating in strategically well-
placed communities who does not belong to
any particular network but, by supplying bar-
gaining skill and transport facilities, articu-
lates communities in different exchange
systems that would otherwise be widely separated from each other.[25]

The retailing of widely produced, low-
value products therefore did not particularly interest the merchant – except for
regionally special varieties, the marketing of items such as maize, chile, and
pottery was left to the producers themselves.

3 Merchants take advantage of not only
"naturally-occurring" exchange discrepancies (such as physical barriers and
distance), but also may create their
own. For example, elsewhere (Berdan
1980: 39, 1983) I have discussed a pattern of "sequential movement and modification of goods" in the Aztec
economy.[26] Some goods underwent a
complex process from raw material to
finished good, frequently changing
hands. This was a kind of investment
procedure, since value is added each
time an item changes hands and is pro-
ductively modified. In these procedures,
the merchant is not merely a relatively
passive conveyer, but an active agent
and frequently essential to the process.

Although ethnohistoric sources often present a monolithic picture of ancient Aztec
trade, there were indeed trading options.
Not all members of the same community

were unitary in their acquisition of necessary or desired commodities (see e.g. PNE
1905–6: vol. 6, 172, 321; Berdan 1980).
Similarly, products themselves could travel
to appropriate and needy consumers
through several channels, sometimes making "modification stops" along the way.
Indeed, for Aztec Mexico it would be hard
to imagine how both a king's palace and a
macehualli's small household could be properly supplied in the absence of these options.

NOTES

Expanded version of a paper presented in the
symposium, Production and Distribution in
Mesoamerica: Economic Models and Cases,
44th International Congress of Americanists,
September 5–11, 1982, Manchester, England. I
have further developed some of the ideas presented here, with different emphases, in Markets
in the Economy of Aztec Mexico, in S. Plattner
(ed.), Markets and Marketing (1985) and Enterprise and Empire in Aztec and Early Colonial
Mexico, in Barry Isaac (ed.), Economic Aspects
of Prehispanic Highland Mexico (1986).

1 They were allowed to create and enforce their
   own laws (within definite limits, to be sure),
   and exercise control over group membership
   and training (see Berdan 1978: 193). They
   resided in separate calpulli in at least twelve
   Valley of Mexico cities.
2 However, elsewhere Sahagún (1950–82: book
   9, 49) omits Azcapotzalco. There appears to
   have been some special cohesion among the
   merchants of these five cities, as they seem to
   have feasted among themselves more frequently than with the merchants of the other
   seven cities listed (p. 13).
3 Texcoco, Uexotla, Coatlichan, Otompan,
   Chalco, Mixcoac, and Xochimilco.
4 Cacao is the only commodity mentioned in this
   source. It is not certain that they brought the
   cacao mentioned by Sahagún from foreign districts; they might well have obtained it after
   their return to Tenochtitlan–Tlatelolco, or in
   other dealings as disguised merchants. Alvarado Tezozomoc (1975: 537) states that organized merchants (identified as oztomeca, from
   throughout the Valley of Mexico) trekked to
   "the coast" to obtain cacao, feathers, gold,
   precious stones, jaguar skins, and small birds
   with fine feathers.

5 This is *tochomitl*. According to the Relación de Mérida (Tozzer, in Landa 1966: 97 n. 433), "it is woolen yarn dyed all colors and all the Indians are very fond of it because they weave it with their cotton and white feathers in rows and they make their clothes and use it in great quantities."

6 Alum was important in dying feathers and in cleaning gold objects (Sahagún 1950–82: book 9, 95, 75, 78). For the general characteristics of alum, see ibid., book 11, 243).

7 They were greatly concerned about encountering hostilities in their journeys; they would even adorn any accompanying women slaves with military devices (*tlahuiztli*) when traveling through dangerous country (Sahagún 1950–82: book 9, 17–18).

8 *Tachcauhchiuhtiaz*: he who would lead, or become leader (Sahagún 1950–82: book 9, 14).

9 Sahagún 1950–82: book 9, 14–15. This may not be a specific designated rank, but rather the plight of those merchants relatively low in social standing and poor in material goods.

10 Nonetheless, the rapid breakdown of the pochteca was compensated by the rise of other, non-guild persons venturing into the trading business (Gibson 1964: 358–9); this ongoing process may be reflected in some of the sixteenth-century Colonial sources (e.g. in Tepoztlan, see PNE 1905–6: vol. 6, 249–50).

11 Molina (1970: 127v) defines tlanecuilo as "mohatrero, tratante, regaton, o trafagante." It is interesting (although perhaps not unanticipated) that a term suggesting swindling or fraudulent dealings is included in this definition as the first option.

12 Wheat is the only non-indigenous item listed by Sahagún for the tlanecuilo.

13 It may have been the demise of the Aztec structure and the imposition of a new political order which allowed goods to work their way into this marketplace from the regions of Michoacan, Tlaxcalla, Guatemala and the Chichimeca. Indeed, the Aztec powers maintained hostile relations with Michoacan and Tlaxcalla – nonetheless, the possibility that these items crossed even hostile borders in economic dealings should not be discounted.

14 Sahagún (1950–82: book 10, 91) also describes peddlers (*tlacocoalnamacac*) in the Tlatelolco market: these were retailers of an assortment of apparently unrelated wares.

15 The wood dealers were from Atliztaca, Atonco, Coyoacan, San Agustín, Nexpilco, and Aticpac; the chia dealers from Coyoacan,

Iztapalapa, Tetzcolca, and "Tepaneca;" the salt dealers from Izquiteca; and the fish dealers from Apcolco.

16 In pre-Conquest times, markets alternated on a variety of reported schedules, the most common being 5–day and 20–day (20 days constituting one Aztec month). See Kurtz 1974 and Hassig 1982.

17 Adams (1978: 35) states that "Only where access was had to the inland waterways of the coast could large bulk cargoes such as salt be shipped easily. Cost of commodities such as salt must have been high when transport was by means of porters."

18 This is despite Sahagún's statement that the owners of cacao groves and cotton fields sold their products in the Tlatelolco marketplace (1950–82: book 10, 65, 75). Salt was sold in that marketplace by both producers and retailers – transportation would have posed few problems, since salt was produced in several locations within the Valley of Mexico, and the extensive lake system allowed transport by canoe.

19 If this indeed reflects a pre-Colonial pattern, the merchants would have had to cross through the Aztec-controlled provinces of Cohuaxtlahuacan and Coyolapan, and into the Aztec province of Xoconochco (and out again, of course).

20 See also Berdan 1975 and Carrasco 1971: 63–4.

21 This specialization may, to some extent, reflect the strong Spanish interest in cochineal. Still, high demands for salt and amole reflect pre-Spanish patterns; this market was probably transformed slowly under Colonial rule. The Miahuatlan Relación Geográfica was dated 1580.

22 Called *tlanamacac* (lit. "seller of something") by Sahagún's informants (1950–82: book 10, *passim*).

23 Merchants may also arise where no other economic opportunities present themselves, or under political encouragement.

24 McVicker (1978: 178), investigating pre-Columbian Chiapas, describes the regional system as "characterized by the movement of utility items, which are desirable, but neither absolutely necessary nor unusually exotic."

25 See also Barth (1967: 171): "entrepreneurs will direct their activity pre-eminently towards those points in an economic system where the discrepancies of evaluation are greatest, and will attempt to construct bridging transactions which can exploit these discrepancies."

26 See Mason and Lewarch (1981) and Byland
    (1981), who propose interesting sequences for
    obsidian, and Berdan (1980: 39) for textiles.

REFERENCES

Acosta-Saignes, Miguel. 1945. *Los Pochteca.*
Acta Antropológica, vol. 1, no. 1.

Adams, Richard E. W. 1978. Routes of Com-
munication in Mesoamerica: The Northern
Guatemalan Highlands and the Peten. In
Thomas A. Lee Jr. and Carlos Navarrete (eds),
*Mesoamerican Communication Routes and
Cultural Contacts*, pp. 27–35. Papers of the
New World Archaeological Foundation No.
40. Provo, Utah.

AGI (Archivo General de las Indias, Sevilla). Justicia 195: 1541. Son los de el Fiscal contra
Alonso Lopez, vecino de la villa de Santa
Maria de la Victoria, sobre haverse titulado
visitador, y exigido a los yndios de la Provincia
de Tabasco differentes contribuciones.

Alva Ixtlilxochitl, Fernando de. 1965. *Historia
Chichimeca*. Editora Nacional, Mexico City.

Alvarado Tezozomoc. 1975. *Crónica Mexicana*.
Porrúa, Mexico City.

Anderson, Arthur J. O., Frances Berdan, and
James Lockhart. 1976. *Beyond the Codices:
The Nahua View of Colonial Mexico*. University
of California Press, Berkeley.

Barth, Fredrik. 1967. Economic Spheres in Dar-
fut. In Raymond Firth (ed.), *Themes in Economic Anthropology*, pp. 149–74. Tavistock,
London.

Berdan, Frances F. 1975. Trade, Tribute and
Market in the Aztec Empire. Unpublished
Ph.D. dissertation, the University of Texas at
Austin.

——1978. Ports of Trade in Mesoamerica: A
Reappraisal. In Thomas A. Lee Jr. and Carlos
Navarrete (eds), *Mesoamerican Communication
Routes and Cultural Contacts*, pp. 187–98.
Papers of the New World Archaeological Foun-
dation No. 40. Provo, Utah.

——1980. Aztec Merchants and Markets: Local-
level Economic Activity in a Non-industrial
Empire, *Mexicon* 2(3): 37–41.

——1983. The Reconstruction of Ancient
Economies: Perspectives from Archaeology and
Ethnohistory. In Sutti Ortiz (ed.), *Topics and
Theories in Economic Anthropology*, pp.
83–95. University Press of America, New York.

Byland, Bruce. 1981. Economy, Politics, and the
Expansion of the Aztec Empire in the Mixteca
Alta. Paper presented at the 1981 meeting of the
Society for American Archaeology, San Diego.

Carrasco, Pedro. 1971. Los Barrios Antiguos de
Cholula. In Efraín Castro Morales (ed.), *Estu-
dios y Documentos de la Región de Puebla-
Tlaxcala*, vol. 3, pp. 9–88. Instituto Poblano de
Antropología e Historia, Puebla.

Chapman, Anne. 1957. Port of Trade Enclaves in
Aztec and Maya Civilization. In Karl Polanyi, C.
Arensberg, and H. W. Pearson (eds), *Trade and
Market in the Early Empires*, pp. 114–53. The
Free Press, New York.

Durán, Diego. 1964. *The Aztecs: The History of
the Indies of New Spain*, translated by D. Heyden and F. Horcasitas. Orion, New York.

——1967. *Historia de las Indias de Nueva
España e Islas de la Tierra Firme*, 2 vols. Porrúa,
Mexico City.

——1971. *Book of the Gods and Rites and the
Ancient Calendar*, translated by F. Horcasitas
and D. Heyden. University of Oklahoma Press,
Norman.

Gibson, Charles. 1964. *The Aztecs under Spanish
Rule*. Stanford University Press, Stanford.

Hassig, Ross. 1982. Periodic Markets in Pre-
columbian Mexico. *American Antiquity* 47(2):
346–55.

Kurtz, Donald V. 1974. Peripheral and Transitional Markets: The Aztec Case. *American Ethnologist* 1(4): 685–705.

Landa, Diego de. 1941. *Relación de las Cosas de
Yucatan*, edited by A. M. Tozzer. Papers of the
Peabody Museum of American Archaeology and
Ethnology, vol. 18. Cambridge, Massachusetts.

Lockhart, James. 1976. Capital and Province,
Spaniard and Indian: The Example of Late Sixteenth-century Toluca. In Ida Altman and James
Lockhart (eds), *Provinces of Early Mexico: Variants of Spanish American Regional Evolution*,
pp. 99–123. UCLA Latin American Center Publications, Los Angeles.

Mason, Roger D. and Dennis E. Lewarch. 1981.
Structural Analysis of the Late Horizon Settlement System in the Coatlan del Rio Valley,
Morelos, Mexico. Paper presented at the 1981
meeting of the Society for American Archaeology, San Diego.

Matricula de Tributos. 1980. Facsimile edition of
the Matrícula de Tributos, with commentaries
by Frances F. Berdan and Jacqueline de Durand-
Forest. Akademische Druck u. Verlagsanstalt,
Graz.

McVicker, Donald E. 1978. Prehispanic Trade in
Central Chiapas, Mexico. In Thomas A. Lee Jr.
and Carlos Navarrete (eds), *Mesoamerican
Communication Routes and Cultural Contacts*,
pp. 177–86. Papers of the New World Archaeological Foundation No. 40. Provo, Utah.

Molina, Alonso de. 1970. *Vocabulario en Lengua Castellana y Mexicana y Mexicana y Castellana*. Porrúa, Mexico City.

PNE (Papeles de Nueva España). 1905–6. Francisco del Paso y Troncoso (ed.), *Sucesores de Rivandeneyra, Madrid*, vols 4–6.

Polanyi, Karl. 1975. Traders and Trade. In Jeremy A. Sabloff and C. C. Lamberg-Karlovsky (eds), *Ancient Civilization and Trade*, pp. 133–54. University of New Mexico Press, Albuquerque.

Rowlands, M. J. 1973. Modes of Exchange and the Incentives for Trade, with Reference to Later European Prehistory. In Colin Renfrew (ed.), *The Explanation of Culture Change: Models in Prehistory*, pp. 589–600. University of Pittsburgh Press, Pittsburgh.

Roys, Ralph L. 1972. *The Indian Background of Colonial Yucatan*. University of Oklahoma Press, Norman.

Sahagún, Bernardino de. 1950–82. *Florentine Codex: General History of the Things of New Spain*, translated by Arthur J. O. Anderson and Charles E. Dibble. University of Utah and School of American Research, Santa Fe.

Scholes, F. V. and Ralph Roys. 1968. *The Maya Chontal Indians of Acalan-Tixchel*. University of Oklahoma Press, Norman.

CHAPTER 10

New Perspectives on Prehispanic Highland Mesoamerica

A Macroregional Approach

Gary M. Feinman and Linda M. Nicholas

Many social scientists might question the potential role for archaeology in the study of world systems and macroregional political economies. After all, the principal contributions to this contemporary research domain have come from history and other social sciences (e.g. Braudel 1972; Wallerstein 1974; Wolf 1982). In addition, most of the world systems literature to date has focused on Europe and other regions of the Old World. This paper takes a somewhat novel tack, one that integrates contemporary findings in archaeology and history to expand and contribute to current debates concerning the nature of ancient world systems and interregional relations. Yet, the geographic focus is not Rome or Greece or even the area between the Tigris and Euphrates Rivers, but rather prehispanic Mesoamerica, an area that encompasses the southern two-thirds of what is now Mexico, as well as Guatemala, Belize, and parts of Honduras, Costa Rica, and El Salvador.

In approaching these issues, the authors recognize that the study of pre-Columbian peoples is not blessed with the extent of historical documentation that is available for some of the Old World regions mentioned above. However, the last several decades have witnessed rather dramatic empirical and theoretical transitions in prehispanic Mesoamerican studies, and a growing minority of archaeologists and ethnohistorians are currently addressing questions phrased in terms of world systems, long-distance exchange, and the spatial division of labor.

At the outset, the two paradigms (diffusionism and developmentalism) that dominated ancient Mesoamerican research into the 1980s are reviewed briefly. Some of the fundamental premises of both approaches are suggested to be inadequate for understanding the prehispanic Mesoamerican world. Following this theoretical grounding, a multi-scale approach that considers (and gives interpretive weight to) macroregional relations is argued to be necessary to understand the workings of this ancient world. The macroregional perspective advocated here draws interpretive insight from both prior approaches (diffusionism and developmentalism), although aspects of each framework are rejected or altered. At the same time, based on empirical analysis, significant modifications to several facets of world systems theory are advanced.

Two empirical directions are taken to examine the importance of macroregional relations in prehispanic Mesoamerica. First, the Late Postclassic period is discussed (table 10.1), focusing on the Aztec of the Central Highlands of Mexico (figure 10.1). Examination of this era allows for the integration

Reprinted from Gary M. Feinman and Linda M. Nicholas. 1991. New Perspectives on Prehispanic Highland Mesoamerica: A Macroregional Approach. *Comparative Civilizations Review* 24: 13–33.

Table 10.1 Chronological sequences for the Valley of Oaxaca and Highland Mesoamerica

		Valley of Oaxaca	Mesoamerica
	1500		
	1300	Monte Albán V	Late Postclassic
	1100		
	900	Monte Albán IV	Early Postclassic
	700	Monte Albán IIIb	Late Classic
	500	Monte Albán IIIa	Early Classic
	300		
AD	100	Monte Albán II	Terminal Formative
BC	100	Monte Albán Late I	
	300	Monte Albán Early I	Late Formative
	500	Rosario	
	700		Middle Formative
		Guadalupe	
	900	San José	
	1100		Early Formative
	1300	Tierras Largas	
	1500		

of early colonial documentary as well as archaeological information in a manner not possible for most of the rest of prehispanic Mesoamerica. Subsequently, findings from the authors' fieldwork in Mexico's Southern Highlands are used to extend interpretive arguments to earlier times and to illustrate from a diachronic perspective the greater utility of the proposed analytical framework. Through this two-pronged investigation, some of the basic parameters and attributes of the ancient Mesoamerican political economy are illustrated. This consideration of a non-Western, preindustrial macroregional system contributes to the wider debate on world systems and political economies by extending the geographical and temporal setting on which such discussions generally are held.

Theoretical Background

Prior to the 1960s, Mesoamerican archaeologists and art historians endeavored to construct a space–time continuum for the pre-Columbian past. Excavations at major urban centers helped establish sequences of ceramic and other artifactual change that were used to date sites and define episodes of cultural transition. For the most part, variation and change were judged to be stimulated by either migration or diffusion – the transmission of new ideas and innovations from other regions. In a seminal paper, Paul Kirchhoff (1943) defined Mesoamerica as a multipolity domain that shared certain ideological, social, political, and technological features. This multicultural entity was bound loosely by interregional exchanges of diffused ideas and the adoption of specific cultural traits. Significantly, many of the shared traits enumerated by Kirchhoff were either concepts (like the calendar, writing conventions, pyramid construction, and sacred beliefs) or sumptuary goods (such as cotton textiles, cacao, ear spools, nose plugs, and iron-ore mirrors) that were associated principally with elites and their lifeways, and the ritual knowledge that they controlled.

Although this early era of research was extremely important for the empirical contributions made, many critical questions were left unanswered or even unaddressed. What were the populations of these ancient centers and their hinterlands? What were the social and economic ties that bound commoners to elites and one polity to another? How did these relations change over time and vary across space? Even the construct diffusion has been found to be unsatisfactory, since it is difficult to document archaeologically and conflates such diverse activities as intermarriage, trade, warfare, and conquest. Mesoamerica was classified as a culture area, yet the behavioral referents behind these shared concepts and traits largely were unknown (Blanton and Feinman 1984). Diffusionists also tended to look almost exclusively at loosely defined outside influences to account for variation and change.

In response to these concerns, as well as larger trends in anthropological archaeology, the 1950s and 1960s witnessed a marked shift in prehispanic Mesoamerican research with the growing acceptance of the

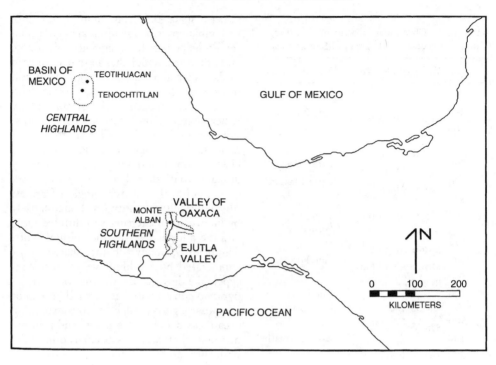

Figure 10.1   Map of Mesoamerica.

developmentalist, cultural-ecological paradigm. The reconstruction of past patterns of behavior, especially those with material referents, received greater attention. In addition to the traditional focus (temples and tombs), small villages and agricultural features increasingly were studied. Regional and urban settlement patterns provided an empirical basis for estimating past populations and demographic change, as well as for evaluating shifting human–resource relations. In Mesoamerican studies over the last four decades, these new research agendas have led to a much better understanding of what people ate, where they lived, and how their lifeways varied in space and time.

Despite notable advances, several shortcomings are evident in the developmentalist approach. Perhaps, partly in response to the outward focus of diffusionism, the developmentalists modeled change in bounded local regions or systems in which long-distance relations often were ignored. The interaction of population and environment was deemed the core from which all other aspects of cultural variability and change were to be explained. Yet in ancient Mesoamerica, as elsewhere, the findings from regional settlement studies illustrate that demographic shifts were not constant or ever increasing, nor did population change precede or coincide with episodes of disequilibrium or transition in any simple, predictable fashion (Feinman et al. 1985; Feinman 1991: 229–62). Thus, population determinism proved to be an inadequate explanation for long-term cultural transitions (Blanton 1983). Likewise, environmental factors are not sufficient to account for the significant complexity of historical variation and change in prehispanic Mesoamerica.

More specifically, the developmentalist paradigm does not explain adequately key differences in the evolutionary histories of two highland cores, the Basin of Mexico and the Valley of Oaxaca (figure 10.1) (Blanton 1978; Marcus 1983a). Nor can it account for the massive and complex episodes of transition that crossed regional boundaries and affected almost the entire culture area (such as between AD 700–900, when most extant urban centers declined greatly in size and importance while others were founded; see Diehl and Berlo 1989). Also neglected were questions concerning Mesoamerica as an area of intertwined cultural traditions. Why, for example, were luxury goods and symbolically significant items, as opposed to other kinds of materials, generally shared so widely?

Over the last decade, mesoamericanists have given increasing attention to larger-scale phenomena and processes. Yet, for the most part, these studies have not returned to trait-based diffusionism, but have concentrated on the elucidation of long-distance political and economic relations (e.g. Berdan 1980; Blanton and Feinman 1984; Drennan 1984a, 1984b; Hirth 1980; Pailes and Whitecotton 1979; Schortman and Urban 1987; Smith 1986; Spencer 1982). This interpretive shift is both a reaction to the narrow determinism of some cultural ecology positions (e.g. Sanders et al. 1979) and a reflection of larger currents in archaeology (e.g. Trigger 1984) and other fields, including history, political science, sociology, and cultural anthropology (e.g. Braudel 1972; Frank 1966; Wallerstein 1974; Wolf 1982). Yet these new intellectual currents were made possible both by several decades of materially focused archaeological fieldwork, as well as by new economic perspectives that were brought to the interpretation of the historical sources of the sixteenth century. While the former provided new quantitative findings on production, distribution, and exchange, the latter suggested the complexity of long-distance relations in the Aztec world and the significance that these interregional relations could have on the organization of local economies.

The Late Prehispanic Period in Highland Mesoamerica

In descriptions of late prehispanic Mesoamerica (ca. AD 1519), one often sees reference (e.g. Coe et al. 1986) to the "Aztec or Triple Alliance empire." Yet, as Davies (1978: 229) has argued, this best documented Mesoamerican "empire" was "hardly an empire in the true sense of the word, but an area loosely dominated for the purpose of gathering tribute...there is ample evidence of a continual process of conquest, rebellion, and reconquest." Unlike the Roman and Incan cases, the Aztec sphere had virtually no provincial infrastructure (Smith 1986). Even if one considers this relatively short-lived tribute domain to be consolidated politically, a view that glosses over considerable organizational variation in time and space, the maximal extent of the political domination never encompassed even half of Mesoamerica (Hassig 1988). Adjacent parts of the Central Mexican Highlands remained outside Aztec authority (Barlow 1949). Other tributary states, such as that of the Tarascans, coexisted elsewhere in Mesoamerica (Pollard 1987). Thus, during the late prehispanic period, Kirchhoff's multistate, multicultural domain that shared key ideological, technological, and social features was not politically dominated by a single administrative entity. Earlier core states appear to have controlled no larger portion of the macroregion than the Aztecs, and as Whitecotton and Pailes (1986: 186) have noted, "all mesoamericanists seem to agree that at no point of time was Mesoamerica a single world empire dominated by a single center."

What then linked Late Postclassic Mesoamerica, this multistate, multiethnic domain? As argued elsewhere (Blanton and Feinman 1984), luxury goods and aspects of elite knowledge were shared very widely. The specific mechanisms by which sacred information was transmitted were undoubtedly very important in linking this ancient world; however, these connections are not well understood and so will not be considered in depth here. Rather, the present focus is on the movement of goods, a topic for which one can draw on both tribute records and archaeological data. Nevertheless, as one mesoamericanist (Lee 1978: 2) reminded the field a decade ago: "religion and commerce were recognized as inter-dependent factors of Mesoamerican society as early as the beginnings of the Spanish Conquest."

Aztec long-distance tribute demands emphasized relatively light weight, precious products, such as cotton suits, feathers, jaguar pelts, cacao, tropical fruits, jewels, and metal ornaments. As with tribute, the *pochteca* and other long-distance profes-sional merchants and traders generally moved rare resources and highly crafted items rather than staple foods or other bulk goods. Likewise, similar products, as well as highly decorated pottery and obsidian ("vol-canic glass"), tend to be found archaeolog-ically at the greatest distances from their sources of origin. In contrast, grain tribute was collected by the Aztecs, but almost exclusively from areas in and adjacent to their Basin of Mexico homeland (Drennan 1984b). Even some of the obligated maize, especially from more distant domains, was not transported back to Aztec Tenochtitlan, but was used at the point of collection to feed armies on the march (Hassig 1988). Interestingly, while cotton was the most frequently demanded tributary good, it was not requested from distant Xoconocho on the Pacific coast of Guatemala. Perhaps even *mantas* were too heavy to lug to Central Mexico from this distance, and so tribute was paid in lighter and rarer goods, like animal skins, feathers, and gems (Berdan 1987).

The greater importance of precious items, rather than staples, in long-distance exchange is not surprising given the prehis-panic absence of beasts of burden and wheeled vehicles. Although significant in the Mesoamerican lowlands, water trans-portation would not have been a viable option in the highlands, except on the lake system of the Basin of Mexico. As Drennan (1984a) cogently calculated, maize trans-port by human bearers would have made little sense energetically or economically at distances greater than 275 km. Yet the com-parative significance of lightweight, high-value items in long-distance transactions leaves two important questions unanswered.

What was the effect of such goods and their movement on the regional and interregional division of labor? And did these items have a central role in the workings and reproduc-tion of the social systems of which they were part? In other words, were these goods simply elite trappings that lacked broader societal implications, or did the items have critical systemic importance (see Schneider 1977)?

In Aztec times, complex exchange webs interconnected tributary demands for pre-cious goods with expanded market trans-actions and intensified local production (Berdan 1975, 1980, 1987). For example, Aztec tributary provinces paying in cotton were not necessarily capable of producing the desired quantities of the cloth, and there-fore they were forced to obtain some, if not most, of what they had to pay from adja-cent, nontributary cotton-producing areas (Saindon 1977). In Icpatepeque, tributaries traveled more than 140 km to obtain the green feathers, gold dust, and green stone that they owed Moctezuma in tribute (Ber-dan 1975, 1980). The inhabitants of Pochu-tla on the Oaxaca coast acquired the copper for their tribute payment by trading local cotton to long-distance merchants. Some of this cotton was then traded at ports of trade and smaller marketplaces outside the tribu-tary realm (Berdan 1978, 1987). Berdan (1987: 258) has noted that some highland towns above the limits of cotton production were supplied with sufficient raw materials to become well known as textile producers. The production of another preciosity, cacao, the beans of which were used as an elite drink as well as for currency, was expanded in the Pacific lowlands late in the pre-conquest period in response to increased highland demand (Bergman 1969).

Given the large volume of raw materials imported into Tenochtitlan through tribute and trade, it is not surprising that the late prehispanic Aztec capital emerged as a cen-ter of elite craft production (Berdan 1980; Brumfiel 1987: 111). Increases in both raw resource supply and elite demand for pre-cious items undoubtedly made the full-time craft manufacture of high-status goods a less risky venture (Brumfiel 1987). Yet at the same time, the ready availability of imported, finished goods has been argued to have had a "chilling effect" on the local production of certain other craft goods (Blanton 1985; Blanton and Feinman 1984; Brumfiel 1976, 1980, 1981, 1987). For example, in the Basin of Mexico hinterlands, outside of Tenochtitlan, the ready availability through the market of non-local goods, like obsidian implements and cloth, may have undermined small-scale specialists who had produced those items earlier (Brumfiel 1987: 109). Archaeological surveys (Brumfiel 1976, 1986, 1987) in both Xico and Huexotla in the Basin of Mexico found that agricultural implements and exotic goods tended to increase in relative frequency between the Early and Late Aztec periods, while artifacts associated with local craft production declined proportionately. Thus, while small-scale craftwork diminished in the rural portion of this core, maize production intensified in areas that were well positioned to feed the growing capital (Blanton 1985; Brumfiel 1987). Blanton (1985) has argued that the spatial arrangement of powerful highland Mesoamerican states frequently may have conformed to this geographic division of labor; agrarian production was emphasized and intensified near the cores, while certain crafts were pushed toward the peripheries.

In addition, although environmental potentialities influenced the aforementioned labor and production divisions and exchange patterns, tribute demands, trade interdependencies, and marketing specialties often were not simple consequences of ecological parameters or resource availability. Rather these late prehispanic interconnections were reflective of a complex web of political and economic decisions. The remainder of this section briefly examines the second question – the role of luxury goods in Aztec society. Such sumptuary goods circulated through the Basin of Mexico via many mechanisms (long-distance trade, tribute, gift exchange, and the market), and, as already discussed, these channels often were intertwined.

Most of the elite craft goods were articles of apparel (pelts or cotton cloth) or personal adornment (nose plugs, lip plugs, necklaces, earrings, armbands, pectorals, or hair combs) (Brumfiel 1987: 111). They served as key markers of social identity that distinguished nobles from commoners, rulers from vassals, military champions from basic soldiers, and one deity from another (Anawalt 1980). Such goods were used as a principal form of patronage by the Aztec state, whose aims included the co-option of local lords and the encouragement of fealty from nobles and soldiers (Brumfiel 1987; Smith 1986). Sumptuary items were awarded to the military for battlefield successes (Blanton and Feinman 1984). Wearing such regalia in the field was a symbol of prowess in battle.

Yet, such precious goods also circulated and were exchanged during other activities that were partially or entirely autonomous of the central state. These included religious ceremonies, life-cycle rituals, alliance compacts, hospitality rites, competitive feasts, and certain patron–client relations (Brumfiel 1987; Carrasco 1971). Many changes in status (life crises) and succession required specific costumes, props, or ritual items. Often these rites were validated by the exchange of precious goods. At contact, the Spanish observed that precious goods were plentiful at Tlatelolco, central Mexico's largest market, and that some craftsmen produced high status goods almost entirely for private consumers (Sahagún 1950–69: book 9, ch. 20). Thus, the cycling of these goods was neither simply redistributive nor was it entirely controlled by the Tenochtitlan state. Furthermore, for the Aztec and their neighbors, sumptuary items were not epiphenomenal. Rather the circulation of these nonutilitarian goods affected energy flows (through altered patterns of exchange and the intensification of production), while they concurrently served key social and symbolic roles in some of the basic rites and processes of societal reproduction (Brumfiel 1987).

A Diachronic Perspective from the Southern Highlands of Oaxaca

In the following discussion, late prehispanic Mesoamerica is conceptualized as a kind of world economy albeit one linked largely by the flow of goods other than food and fuel (see Blanton and Feinman 1984; cf. Wallerstein 1974). The world economy construct is particularly appropriate if one does not assume that such systems must be dominated by a single core state (see Abu-Lughod 1989). In the subsequent section, a narrower and more diachronic perspective that relies heavily on settlement pattern research in the Valleys of Oaxaca and Ejutla in Mexico's Southern Highlands is presented (figure 10.1) (Blanton et al. 1982; Feinman and Nicholas 1988; Kowalewski et al. 1989). In reviewing this long temporal sequence, it is important to remember that the ancient polity centered at Monte Albán in the Valley of Oaxaca was just one of a large number of interacting and competing contemporaneous centers that coexisted in the prehispanic Mesoamerican world.

Through this brief synthesis of prehispanic change in the adjoining Oaxaca and Ejutla Valleys (see Feinman and Nicholas 1988, 1990, 1991, 1992), three basic points are made. First, the long-term interrelationship and the observed differences and similarities between the two valleys are not easily accountable by the diffusionist or developmentalist frameworks. Second, a multi-scale approach that incorporates macroregional considerations provides a more explanatory perspective on the noted transitions, which were by no means simple nor linear. And third, when the Ejutla region was incorporated politically into the Monte Albán state, the most important considerations appear not to have been the production of maize, but access to rarer, exotic goods, like shell and cloth, as well as defensive concerns. It is the interregional importance of high-status goods and the complexity of links that interwined trade in these goods with the production and movement of essentials like food that thematically binds this section with the prior more general discussion.

The Ejutla Valley and the Valley of Oaxaca: Introduction

Before proceeding to a discussion of prehispanic change, a short introduction to the Valleys of Oaxaca and Ejutla is in order. The larger Oaxaca Valley is the broadest expanse of flat land in Mexico's Southern Highlands. It has long been recognized as a key region of prehispanic political and demographic development (Palerm and Wolf 1957). Adjacent Ejutla, roughly one-quarter the size, is generally drier and more rolling.

Systematic regional-scale fieldwork in the Valley of Oaxaca began roughly two decades ago with Richard Blanton (1978), who mapped the ancient city of Monte Albán. Subsequent projects extended full field-by-field pedestrian coverage to a more than 2,600 km^2 contiguous area that encompasses the Oaxaca and Ejutla Valleys (Blanton et al. 1982; Feinman and Nicholas 1988; Kowalewski et al. 1989). These regional surveys have collected basic information on changing settlement patterns, land use, demographic profiles, and sociopolitical organization for the last 3,000 years of the prehispanic era. As noted previously, such projects are essential if archaeologists are to expand their vantage to material concerns that extend beyond a single excavation trench or site. Although the difficulties of translating sherd scatters to population estimates and mound complexes to civic-ceremonial behavior are obvious and severe, the data collected by these regional projects are the closest an archaeologist can get to a diachronic census, illustrating prehispanic settlement patterns at broad spatial and temporal scales. Elsewhere in discussions of these two adjacent valleys (Feinman and Nicholas 1990, 1992), excavation findings and the interpretation of ethnohistoric accounts are incorporated with the interpretation of survey results.

Long-term Change in Ejutla and Oaxaca: Expectations and Results

What might the diffusionists and the developmentalists predict for the long-term interaction between central Oaxaca and smaller Ejutla? The former might expect the pace of change in Ejutla to lag behind, yet closely reflect, that in the Valley of Oaxaca. Status items and cultural features would be received from (and hence simply mimic) those in Oaxaca, but appear later in the sequence or be present to a lesser degree. In other words, Ejutla would be a microcosm of Oaxaca. Some developmentalists might envision a similar scenario, in which the prehispanic populations of Ejutla would exhibit lesser degrees of public construction and craft specialization than found in Oaxaca, but otherwise be similar. Alternatively, other developmentalists might retrodict the increasing – albeit "inevitable" – incorporation of the Ejutla region into an ever-expanding polity centered in Oaxaca.

Although aspects of these scenarios cannot be dismissed entirely, a brief review of the prehispanic sequence reveals a more complex trajectory of transition than might be foreseen by either traditional framework (see Feinman et al. 1985; Kowalewski et al. 1989 for more complete accounts). By necessity, this abbreviated discussion focuses on empirical findings that relate to the above expectations. In conjunction with these retrodictions, survey findings indicate that the Ejutla region was occupied prehispanically at lower densities than the Valley of Oaxaca (Feinman and Nicholas 1988). The colonization of the former region also occurred at a slower pace than the larger region to the north. In the Valley of Oaxaca, a major episode of demographic growth coincided with the foundation of the large site of Monte Albán (ca. 500 BC) at the region's hub. The most rapid rate of population expansion in Ejutla occurred in the subsequent phase (300–200 BC). Sometime between 200 BC and AD 200, the Ejutla region appears to have been absorbed into the Monte Albán state. The incorporation

lasted until roughly AD 450, when the Monte Albán state weakened, precipitating major shifts in regional settlement patterns and political organization. Yet, in contrast to certain developmentalist interpretations, a single polity never again dominated the entire study region. That is, at the scale of the entire study region, there is no indication that the prehispanic polity expanded continuously through time. At conquest, political units in the Valleys of Oaxaca and Ejutla were smaller in area than the Monte Albán polity had been a millennium earlier.

To consider the Ejutla region as a simple microcosm of the Valley of Oaxaca also would be a mistake. At certain times, the population density of the Valley of Oaxaca was roughly twice that of Ejutla, while in other phases, it was many times greater. The relationship between the two regions also was far from constant through time. For centuries following the advent of sedentary villages in the Southern Highlands, Ejutla was a sparsely settled frontier of neighboring Oaxaca, but as noted above, it became an incorporated periphery between 200 BC and AD 200. Late in the prehispanic sequence, Ejutla was linked economically to Oaxaca, but it was not part of a unified political entity. In fact, the Valley of Oaxaca was not consolidated administratively at contact, and political decentralization was the rule for most of, if not the entire, period following the collapse of Monte Albán (ca. AD 650).

Monumental construction was indeed less evident overall (and even per capita) in the Ejutla region compared to Oaxaca. The specialized manufacture of utilitarian products, like pottery and chipped stone, also was less common in the smaller valley. However, this expected pattern was not found for the specialized production of rarer goods, such as exotic marine shell ornaments or cloth. Although these labor-intensive crafts were rare in both Ejutla and Oaxaca, they were considerably more abundant per capita in the smaller region. And in a pattern similar to the Basin of Mexico in Aztec times, shell working (a high-status craft) was entirely absent in

Monte Albán's immediate hinterland in the Valley of Oaxaca. Shell artifacts and debris also were proportionally more common at Ejutla sites than at Oaxaca settlements. While Ejutla does lie slightly closer to the Pacific Coast than does much of Oaxaca, both regions are at least several days' walk over high mountains to the ocean. The relative frequencies of exotic ceramics and different obsidian varieties also signal that the Ejutla and Oaxaca regions had distinctive linkages with areas outside the Southern Highlands (see Feinman and Nicholas 1990, 1992). Furthermore, these connections do not appear to have been immutable through time.

Thus, these findings suggest that Ejutla was not a microcosm of Oaxaca, that the relationship between these neighboring regions shifted over time, as did their connections to other parts of Mesoamerica. In other words, to understand the long-term trajectory of prehispanic change, one cannot look exclusively at the Valley of Oaxaca core, smaller Ejutla, or their larger context in the ancient Mesoamerican world, but at the interplay between all three (see Hall 1986).

What can be said about Monte Albán's interest in Ejutla and the nature of the first millennium AD linkage between the two regions? The results of a series of analyses, in which the relationship between demography and agricultural resources was examined (Feinman and Nicholas 1991), indicate that the Ejutla region, due to its relatively low population, could not have furnished large maize surpluses to Monte Albán at the time of its incorporation. In fact, even during the subsequent Early Classic (AD 200–450), when Ejutla's population was larger, the potential agrarian exports were fairly low (compared to other parts of the region), and the necessary transport costs would have been high. These analyses also indicate that most of the agrarian surplus required by Monte Albán was produced in the core of the valley, within a one day's round trip of the site. The greater than expected presence of cloth working and shell ornament production in Ejutla suggests that access to these lighter-weight, higher-value goods may have been of more interest (than potential maize production in Ejutla) to Monte Albán's elite. During the Early Classic period, the Ejutla region, along with the southern and eastern arms of the Valley of Oaxaca, was surrounded by a network of hilltop terrace sites. The distribution of these defendable, ridgetop sites indicates that Ejutla's incorporation may have had a defensive/military rationale as well.

Finally as discussed in more detail elsewhere (Feinman and Nicholas 1992), the settlement arrangements in the highland Valleys of Oaxaca and Ejutla seem to conform preliminarily to several of Blanton's (1985) expectations concerning the spatial division of labor. For example, for more than 1,000 years following the establishment (ca. 500 BC) of the early city of Monte Albán at the hub of the Valley of Oaxaca, agrarian production was apparently emphasized immediately around the site. This surrounding area was not particularly fertile nor well watered, rather it was proximate to the regional center, where transport costs could be minimized. Meanwhile, labor-intensive high-status craft activities, like cloth production and shell working, were much more prevalent than expected (per capita) at the margins of the study region. At present, these patterns suggest that spatial divisions in the deployment of labor in ancient Mesoamerica were neither restricted to central Mexico nor solely constrained to the Late Aztec period. Furthermore, as in the world of the Aztecs, the articulations between polities and regions also were complex and nested during the earlier Classic period (AD 200–700). For example, while Monte Albán was involved in a diplomatic, and perhaps economic, long-distance relationship with central Mexican Teotihuacan (Marcus 1983b), both centers were more closely interlinked economically and politically with smaller, less distant polities.

Conclusion

In summation, neither the developmentalist nor diffusionist positions can account adequately for the economic and political relations evident in the late prehispanic period in Mesoamerica nor for the trajectory of long-term change in the Valleys of Oaxaca and Ejutla. Rather, an approach that is more sensitive to questions of scale is required. Such a framework must consider macroregional processes; however, it also should examine smaller-scale relations, such as the interplay between humans and their lands. Whereas the developmentalists tend to focus on valleys and regions as autonomous, closed entities, the diffusionists often look to poorly defined outside influences to explain episodes of cultural transition. Clearly, an approach that embodies a more flexible view of spatial relations is necessary. Ancient Mesoamerica was the complex product of both short-range movements of maize that were necessary to support centers, like Tenochtitlan and Monte Albán, and long-distance exchanges of symbolically imbued goods, like ornaments and cloth, that linked local regions to the rest of Mesoamerica.

As seen for the Late Postclassic period, the exchange of so-called non-essential, sumptuary items was not systematically insignificant in ancient Mesoamerica. Such items played a key role in societal production and reproduction. Likewise, access to such items may have provided a critical rationale for political expansion (in the case of Monte Albán) and long-distance exchange. In fact, in this ancient world where military and transport technologies were relatively minimal, the web of interregional and interpersonal connections may have been so intertwined that access to and manipulation of highly created, exotic goods provided an important mechanism for attracting labor, thereby stimulating production and securing the control of seemingly more basic items, like food. At certain times, the crafting of such high-status goods also was part of complex and spatial segregated divisions of labor.

If a world systems or macroregional approach is to have utility beyond discussions of the capitalist world, modifications to Wallerstein's (1974) conception are necessary. As illustrated above, relatively light-weight, high-value items appear to have played a much more fundamental role in the central workings of prehispanic Mesoamerica. Hence, it would be arbitrary and hasty to ignore such items in conceptualizing the structure of ancient world systems and how these macroregions changed through time. Yet, the relative importance of low-volume, high-value exchange goods in ancient Mesoamerica may have given that world system less stability in its specific structural (e.g. core–periphery) relations than noted in other macroregional systems in which the long-distance movement of food and fuel have had a more central role. For those interested in the comparative study of civilizations, cross-cultural analyses of variation and change in world systems should form the grist for much future research.

ACKNOWLEDGMENTS

Many individuals and institutions contributed to the completion of this article and we are truly grateful to them all. The National Science Foundation generously supported the regional settlement pattern surveys of the Valleys of Oaxaca and Ejutla, while over the years necessary permissions and essential assistance were provided by both the Instituto Nacional de Antropología e Historia and the Centro Regional de Oaxaca. Many individuals helped with the settlement survey; however, Richard E. Blanton and Stephen A. Kowalewski, Principal Investigators for different stages of the project were particularly instrumental. We also wish to thank Christopher Chase-Dunn, who asked us to prepare a version of this paper for the 19th (1990) annual meeting of the International Society for the Comparative Study of Civilizations. The paper was written while the senior author had the good fortune to be a resident scholar at the School of American Research, an opportunity for which he thankfully acknowledges Douglas W. Schwartz, Jonathan Haas, and the entire SAR staff. Thomas D. Hall and Wayne Bledsoe offered valuable comments on an earlier draft of this work. Richard E. Blanton has provided continual support and intellectual stimulation over the years, for which we are both indebted.

REFERENCES

Abu-Lughod, Janet L. 1989. *Before European Hegemony: The World System* AD *1250–1350*. Oxford University Press, New York.

Anawalt, Patricia, 1980. Costume and Control: Aztec Sumptuary Laws. *Archaeology* 33: 33–43.

Barlow, Robert. 1949. The Extent of the Empire of the Culhua Mexica. *Ibero-Americana* 28. University of California Press, Berkeley.

Berdan, Francis. 1975. Trade, Tribute and Market in the Aztec Empire. Ph.D. dissertation, University of Texas, Austin.

—— 1978. Ports of Trade in Mesoamerica: A Reappraisal. In *Mesoamerican Communication Routes and Cultural Contacts*, ed. Thomas Lee, Jr. and Carlos Navarrete, pp. 187–98. Papers of the New World Archaeological Foundation 40. Brigham Young University, Provo, UT.

—— 1980. Aztec Merchants and Markets: Local-Level Economic Activity in a Non-Industrial Empire. *Mexicon* 2: 37–41.

—— 1987. Cotton in Aztec Mexico: Production, Distribution and Uses. *Mexican Studies/ Estudios Mexicanos* 3: 235–62.

Bergman, John. 1969. The Distribution of Cacao Cultivation in Pre-Columbian America. *Annals of the Association of American Geographers* 59: 85–96.

Blanton, Richard E. 1978. *Monte Albán: Settlement Patterns at the Ancient Zapotec Capital*. Academic Press, New York.

—— 1983. The Ecological Perspective in Highland Mesoamerican Archaeology. In *Archaeological Hammers and Theories*, ed. James A. Moore and Arthur S. Keene, pp. 221–31. Academic Press, New York.

—— 1985. A Comparison of Early Market Systems. In *Markets and Marketing*, ed. Stuart Plattner, pp. 399–416. Monographs in Economic Anthropology 4. University Press of America, Lanham, MD.

Blanton, Richard E. and Gary Feinman, 1984. The Mesoamerican World System: A Comparative Perspective. *American Anthropologist* 86: 673–82.

Blanton, Richard E., Stephen A. Kowalewski, Gary Feinman, and Jill Appel. 1982. *Monte Albán's Hinterland, Part I: The Prehispanic Settlement Patterns of the Central and Southern Parts of the Valley of Oaxaca, Mexico*. Memoir No. 15, Museum of Anthropology, University of Michigan, Ann Arbor.

Braudel, Fernand, 1972. *The Mediterranean and the Mediterranean World in the Age of Philip II*, 2 vols. Harper and Row, New York.

Brumfiel, Elizabeth M. 1976. Specialization and Exchange at the Late Postclassic (Aztec) Community of Huexotla, Mexico. Ph.D. dissertation, University of Michigan, Ann Arbor.

—— 1980. Specialization, Market Exchange, and the Aztec State: A View from Huexotla. *Current Anthropology* 21: 459–78.

—— 1981. Tribute Allocation and the Organization of Rural Labor in the Aztec State. Paper presented at the 80th Annual Meeting of the American Anthropological Association, Los Angeles.

—— 1986. The Division of Labor at Xico: The Chipped Stone Industry. In *Economic Aspects of Prehispanic Highland Mexico*, ed. Barry L. Isaac, pp. 245–79. Research in Economic Anthropology, Supplement 2.

—— 1987. Elite and Utilitarian Crafts in the Aztec State. In *Specialization, Exchange, and Complex Societies*, ed. Elizabeth M. Brumfiel and Timothy K. Earle, pp. 102–18. Cambridge University Press, Cambridge.

Carrasco, Pedro. 1971. Social Organization of Ancient Mexico. In *The Handbook of Middle American Indians*, vol. 10: *Archaeology of Northern Mesoamerica*, part 1, ed. Gordon F. Ekholm and Ignacio Bernal, pp. 349–75. University of Texas Press, Austin.

Coe, Michael, Dean Snow, and Elizabeth Benson. 1986. *Atlas of Ancient America*. Facts on File, New York.

Davies, Nigel. 1978. The Military Organization of the Aztec Empire. In *Mesoamerican Communication Routes and Cultural Contacts*, ed. Thomas Lee, Jr. and Carlos Navarrete, pp. 223–30. Papers of the New World Archaeological Foundation 40. Brigham Young University, Provo, UT.

Diehl, Richard A. and Janet C. Berlo (eds). 1989. *Mesoamerica after the Decline of Teotihuacan* AD *700–900*. Dumbarton Oaks, Washington, DC.

Drennan, Robert D. 1984a. Long-Distance Movement of Goods in the Mesoamerican Formative and Classic. *American Antiquity* 49: 27–43.

—— 1984b. Long-Distance Transport Costs in Pre-Hispanic Mesoamerica. *American Anthropologist* 86: 105–12.

Feinman, Gary M. 1991. Demography, Surplus, and Inequality: Early Political Formations in Highland Mesoamerica. In *Chiefdoms and their Evolutionary Significance*, ed. Timothy Earle. Cambridge University Press, Cambridge.

Feinman, Gary M., Stephen A. Kowalewski, Laura Finsten, Richard E. Blanton, and Linda Nicholas. 1985. Long-Term Demographic Change: A Perspective from the Valley of Oaxaca, Mexico. *Journal of Field Archaeology* 12: 333–62.

Feinman, Gary M. and Linda M. Nicholas. 1988. The Prehispanic Settlement History of the Ejutla Valley, Mexico: A Preliminary Perspective. *Mexicon* 10: 5–13.

—— 1990. At the Margins of the Monte Albán State: Settlement Patterns in the Ejutla Valley, Oaxaca, Mexico. *Latin American Antiquity* 1(3).

—— 1991. The Monte Albán State: A Diachronic Perspective on an Ancient Core and its Periphery. In *Precapitalist Core/Periphery Relations*, ed. Christopher Chase-Dunn and Thomas D. Hall, pp. 240–76. Westview Press, Boulder, CO.

—— 1992. Prehispanic Interregional Interaction in Southern Mexico: The Valley of Oaxaca and the Ejutla Valley. In *Resource, Power, and Interregional Interaction*, ed. Edward M. Schortman and Patricia A. Urban, pp. 75–116. Plenum, New York.

Frank, Andre Gunder. 1966. The Development of Underdevelopment. *Monthly Review* 18: 17–31.

Hall, Thomas D. 1986. Incorporation in the World-System: Toward a Critique. *American Sociological Review* 51: 390–402.

Hassig, Ross. 1988. *Aztec Warfare: Imperial Expansion and Political Control*. University of Oklahoma Press, Norman.

Hirth, Kenneth G. 1980. *Eastern Morelos and Teotihuacan: A Settlement Survey*. Publications in Anthropology 25. Vanderbilt University, Nashville.

Kirchhoff, Paul. 1943. Mesoamérica: Sus Límites Geográficas, Composición Etnica y Carácteres Culturales. *Acta Americana* 1: 92–107.

Kowalewski, Stephen A., Gary M. Feinman, Richard E. Blanton, Laura Finsten, and Linda M. Nicholas. 1989. *Monte Albán's Hinterland, Part II: The Prehispanic Settlement Patterns in Tlacolula, Etla, and Ocotlán, the Valley of Oaxaca, Mexico*. Memoir No. 23, Museum of Anthropology, University of Michigan, Ann Arbor.

Lee, Thomas A., Jr. 1978. Introduction. In *Mesoamerican Communication Routes and Cultural Contacts*, ed. Thomas Lee, Jr. and Carlos Navarrete, pp. 1–4. Papers of the New World Archaeological Foundation 40. Brigham Young University, Provo, UT.

Marcus, Joyce. 1983a. On the Nature of the Mesoamerican City. In *Prehistoric Settlement Patterns: Essays in Honor of Gordon R. Willey*, ed. Evon Vogt and Richard Leventhal, pp. 195–242. University of New Mexico Press, Albuquerque.

—— 1983b. Teotihuacán Visitors on Monte Albán Monuments and Murals. In *The Cloud People: Divergent Evolution of the Zapotec and Mixtec Civilizations*, ed. Kent V. Flannery and Joyce Marcus, pp. 175–81. Academic Press, New York.

Pailes, Richard and Joseph Whitecotton. 1979. The Greater Southwest and Mesoamerican "World" System: An Exploratory Model of Frontier Relationships. In *The Frontier: Comparative Studies*, vol. 2, ed. William Savage and Stephen Thompson, pp. 102–21. University of Oklahoma Press, Norman.

Palerm, Angel and Eric R. Wolf. 1957. Ecological Potential and Cultural Development in Mesoamerica. *Pan American Union Social Science Monograph* 3: 1–37.

Pollard, Helen Perlstein. 1987. The Political Economy of Prehispanic Tarascan Metallurgy. *American Antiquity* 52: 741–52.

Sahagún, B. de. 1950–69. *Florentine Codex: General History of Things of New Spain*, translated by A. Anderson and C. Dibble, 12 vols. School of American Research, Sante Fe (orig. 1577).

Saindon, Jacqueline. 1977. Cotton Production and Exchange in Mexico, 1427–1580. Master's thesis, Hunter College, City University of New York.

Sanders, William T., Jeffrey R. Parsons, and Robert S. Santley. 1979. *The Basin of Mexico: Ecological Processes in the Evolution of a Civilization*. Academic Press, New York.

Schneider, Jane. 1977. Was There a Pre-Capitalist World System? *Peasant Studies* 6: 20–9.

Schortman, Edward M. and Patricia A. Urban. 1987. Modeling Interregional Interaction in Prehistory. In *Advances in Archaeological Method and Theory*, vol. 11, ed. Michael B. Schiffer, pp. 37–95. Academic Press, San Diego.

Smith, Michael E. 1986. The Role of Social Stratification in the Aztec Empire: A View from the Provinces. *American Anthropologist* 88: 70–91.

Spencer, Charles S. 1982. *The Cuicatlán Cañada and Monte Albán*. Academic Press, New York.

Trigger, Bruce G. 1984. Archaeology at the Crossroads: What's New? *Annual Review of Anthropology* 13: 275–300.

Wallerstein, Immanuel. 1974. *The Modern World-System*. Academic Press, New York.

Whitecotton, Joseph and Richard Pailes. 1986. New World Precolumbian World Systems. In *Ripples in the Chichimec Sea: New Considerations of Southwestern-Mesoamerican Interactions*, ed. Frances J. Mathien and Randall H. McGuire, pp. 183–204. Southern Illinois University Press, Carbondale.

Wolf, Eric R. 1982. *Europe and the People without History*. University of California Press, Berkeley.

CHAPTER 11

Rural Economy in Late Postclassic Morelos

An Archaeological Study

Michael E. Smith and Cynthia Heath-Smith

What was life like in the rural communities of Central Mexico in the Late Postclassic period? How were these communities affected by their conquest and incorporation into the Aztec empire? Our recent archaeological fieldwork in the modern Mexican state of Morelos, Mexico, provides new information on the nature of peasant households and communities in a provincial area of the Aztec empire. We recovered evidence for a densely settled, socially complex rural landscape. Elites lived at both rural and urban sites; craft production and intensive agriculture were prominent activities, and marketplace exchange with near and distant areas was commonplace. In this paper we explore these and other economic issues as documented by the Postclassic Morelos Archaeological Project, an excavation-based study of socioeconomic conditions among rural[1] households at the sites of Cuexcomate and Capilco in western Morelos. After presenting information on household economy, we explore the implications of these data for some of the important issues in the analysis of Aztec economics, including the role of population growth, the effects of imperial conquest, and the degree of centralized political control over economic activities.

Excavations at Capilco and Cuexcomate

The Postclassic Morelos Archaeological Project excavations at Capilco and Cuexcomate were conducted in part to investigate the possibility of rural social complexity in this region. Ethnohistoric documents and prior archaeological research suggested that western Morelos had dense rural populations that were well integrated into Aztec-period exchange networks (see Smith 1994). Capilco and Cuexcomate, located about 20 km southwest of the large urban center of Quauhnahuac, were first investigated by Kenneth G. Hirth's (1994) Xochicalco Mapping Project. This preliminary research revealed a high surface visibility of Late Postclassic residential architecture and significant variability in structure-based artifact collections.

Capilco and Cuexcomate were excavated in 1986 with a research design intended to gather data on household social and economic conditions, residential architecture, and community organization (figure 11.1). Among the specific topics of investigation were the presence and role of rural elites, the nature of socioeconomic variation among households, the nature of economic

Reprinted from Michael E. Smith and Cynthia Heath-Smith. 1994. Rural Economy in Late Postclassic Morelos: An Archaeological Study. In *Economies and Polities in the Aztec Realm*, edited by Mary G. Hodge and Michael E. Smith (Institute for Mesoamerican Studies, Albany), pp. 349-76.

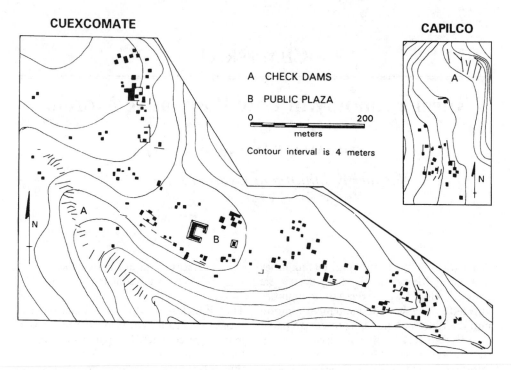

Figure 11.1   Maps of Capilco and Cuexcomate.

activities and conditions, and the impact of Aztec conquest on provincial society (Smith 1992). House foundations at these sites were visible on the surface, and random samples of houses were tested at each site to investigate site-wide patterns of variability. Selected houses were cleared completely, including large exterior areas, in order to address the issues of domestic conditions and activities in greater detail. Also, a number of nonresidential structures and features were excavated, among them a temple-platform, possible granaries, ritual deposits, and agricultural terraces. The excavations and architectural remains are described in detail in Smith (1992); preliminary discussions may also be found in Smith et al. (1989).

Three chronological periods are represented at Capilco and Cuexcomate. The Temazcalli phase (AD 1200–1350) is present in only two refuse deposits at Capilco. The Early Cuauhnahuac phase (abbreviated here as "EC") dates to AD 1350–1430, and the Late Cuauhnahuac phase ("LC") follows

from AD 1430–1550. Both sites were abandoned early in the Spanish Colonial period, probably in response to Spanish administrative decree. The chronology is based upon radiocarbon dates, stratigraphy, and quantitative ceramic seriation (see Smith and Doershuk 1991).

Environmental and Social Context

The environmental setting

Cuexcomate and Capilco are located 3 km apart near the ruins of the large Epiclassic city of Xochicalco. Today precipitation is adequate for *temporal* (nonirrigated) agriculture (900 mm per year), but the thin rocky soils around the sites limit agricultural productivity in the area. Hirth (1994) estimates the average yield of traditional nonmechanized farming in the immediate area (prior to the use of industrial fertilizers) to have been approximately 550 kg of maize per hectare. The sites are situated at the southern extreme of a large Plio-Pleistocene alluvial fan known as the Buenavista Lomas (part of the Cuernavaca Formation; see Fries 1960). Because the lomas are cut by numerous, deeply entrenched, seasonal streams, the amount of level land for cultivation is limited. Only a few very small tracts of land along the Tembembe and Cuentepec Rivers can be irrigated, in contrast to other parts of Morelos where Late Postclassic irrigation along the major rivers was extensive (Maldonado 1990; Smith 1994).

During the Epiclassic period (AD 750–950), the agricultural heartland of Xochicalco was oriented to the south rather than north into the Buenavista Lomas (Hirth 1994). The lomas supported only a few scattered settlements throughout most of the Prehispanic epoch until the Cuauhnahuac phase, when a major colonization of this area took place. Settlement of this marginal zone became possible with the construction of extensive systems of agricultural terraces of both the contour and cross-channel varieties. Thus, Cuexcomate and Capilco are located in a marginal environment without great agricultural potential.

Apart from agricultural production, other significant local economic resources include a low-grade chert used for tools, which occurs in nodules in the limestone of the adjacent Xochicalco Formation (Fries 1960), and abundant wild fig trees (*amate*) from which bark could be removed for the manufacture of paper (*amate* pollen was recovered, as were tools for papermaking). The vertisol soils provide suitable clays for a ceramics industry (jars and *comals* are made in the nearby village of Cuentepec today), but there is no direct evidence for ceramic manufacture at any of the Cuauhnahuac phase sites in the area (see Goodfellow 1990). Vesicular basalt for the manufacture of metates and other groundstone tools could have been obtained from Real del Puente, about 5 km east of Cuexcomate.

Demography

A massive population growth between the Temazcalli and EC phases in western Morelos had important effects on economic organization. There are several types of evidence for this population explosion. On a regional scale, the number of occupied sites located by Hirth's Río Chalma survey southwest of the study area jumps markedly between Temazcalli and EC times (Hirth, unpublished notes). Surface survey and mapping in the Buenavista Lomas by Osvaldo Sterpone (1988), Scott O'Mack (1991), and Michael E. Smith confirm extensive Cuauhnahuac phase occupation with few earlier sites apparent.

At the level of individual sites, demographic reconstructions for Cuexcomate and Capilco show significant population growth at this time (table 11.1). The population estimates in table 11.1 are based upon occupation patterns extrapolated from the random sample of houses at the two sites; the estimates use household size constants of 5.5 persons per house for commoners (Kolb 1985) and 11 persons per house for elite residences (see Smith [1992: 335–45] for a full discussion of the demographic data and methods). Capilco was first settled in the Temazcalli phase and continued to grow throughout the final three prehispanic phases. Cuexcomate, on the other hand, was occupied initially in EC times and rapidly grew into a minor town center of 800 persons. When the phased occupation patterns at the excavated sites are applied to unphased Middle/Late Postclassic sites located by Hirth in a 6 km² area around Xochicalco, the reconstructed population levels for the Temazcalli, EC, and LC phases are 460, 1,690, and 4,000 persons respectively. These data suggest very rapid rates of population growth in the immediate vicinity of Cuexcomate and Capilco: 1.6% annually between the Temazcalli and EC phases, and 1.0% annually between the EC and LC phases (Smith 1992).

Rural society

At the time of Spanish conquest, western Morelos was divided into a number of small city-states, all subject to the larger conquest-state of Quauhnahuac (Maldonado

Table 11.1 Demographic data for Capilco and Cuexcomate

Context	Phase		
	Temazcalli	*Early Cuauhnahuac*	*Late Cuauhnahuac*
Number of Houses			
Capilco (nonelite)	5	13	21
Cuexcomate: elite	—	4	7
Cuexcomate: nonelite	—	35	132
Number of Persons			
Capilco (nonelite)	28	72	116
Cuexcomate: elite	—	44	77
Cuexcomate: nonelite	—	193	726
Cuexcomate: total	—	237	803
Settlement Area (hectares)			
Capilco	0.14	0.60	1.15
Cuexcomate	—	9.94	14.58
Population Density (persons per hectare)			
Capilco	197	121	101
Cuexcomate	—	24	55

1990; Smith 1994). The city-state capitals nearest to Cuexcomate and Capilco were Cohuintepec (near modern Cuentepec) to the northwest, Miacatlan to the southwest, and Acatlipac to the east. We do not know, however, to which polities the excavated sites pertained. In spite of high population densities (over 600 persons per km² for the region in the LC phase) the immediate area around Cuexcomate and Capilco can be considered rural in the Cuauhnahuac phase because of a lack of cities (see note 1). In fact much of western Morelos outside of the city of Quauhnahuac (estimated population of 67,000) was rural in character since the major "urban" settlements, the city-state capitals, were quite small in size (Mason 1980; Smith 1994).

Capilco was a small settlement (figure 11.1) which grew from a tiny hamlet in the Temazcalli phase to a village of around 100 persons in LC times (table 11.1). Cuexcomate was first occupied in the EC phase and from the start was a much larger and more complex settlement containing an elite residential compound, a modest temple platform, and a central public plaza (figure 11.1). Smith (1992) suggests that its rapid growth was due to the presence of an elite

group in EC times, which probably attracted further commoner settlement (although by what means is not clear). The elite resided in a large, distinctive compound (patio group 6) with a plan similar to the standard Aztec palace layout identified by Susan Evans (1991). The inhabitants of patio group 6 are classified as elite on several bases: the large size of their residence; the high energy cost of its construction; the architectural distinctiveness of the compound relative to other houses and house groups (e.g. raised rooms, ample use of lime plaster); its resemblance to the Aztec palace plan; its location on the public plaza; and the distinctiveness of its artifactual inventories, which generally have higher frequencies of imported and decorated ceramics than other houses (see discussion in Smith 1992). Patio group 6 and several other groups are illustrated in figure 11.2.

In the LC phase, population growth continued at a somewhat slower rate, and a general decline in the standard of living occurred. Patio group 6 was abandoned, and the more modest patio group 7 was built on an adjacent side of the public plaza, probably as an elite compound. Although far less imposing or distinctive

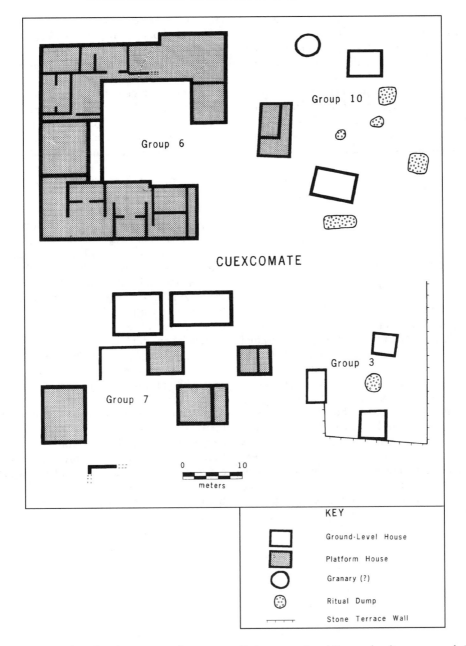

Figure 11.2 Selected patio groups at Cuexcomate. Patio groups 6 and 7 were the elite compounds in the Early Cuauhnahuac and Late Cuauhnahuac phases respectively.

than its predecessor, patio group 7 still stands out relative to contemporaneous houses in terms of its architecture and artifacts (figure 11.2).

If we make the reasonable assumption that the Cuexcomate elite resembled the ethnohistorically documented rural nobility of Morelos (e.g. Carrasco 1976; Smith

1993a), then this class probably controlled most if not all of the land in the immediate vicinity of the sites. Commoners would have been under the control of these elite, paying them tribute in goods and services. Rural commoners were probably members of the residential units known as *calpulli*. In contrast to Zorita's (1963) well-known view of the *calpulli* as an egalitarian, land-holding kin group that was outside of noble control, the Morelos *calpulli* were controlled by nobles who owned the land and extracted tribute from the commoners (Carrasco 1976; Smith 1993a).

Production

Agriculture

The bulk of the diet at Cuexcomate and Capilco was from agricultural crops. Faunal remains are scanty, suggesting that animal protein contributed little to the diet. The majority of the nonhuman bones are turkey, dog, and rabbit, with a minor contribution from deer and various small mammals and reptiles. Pollen studies show the presence of a number of wild economic species, but there are also traces of many domesticates in the household middens. Prominent domesticates include maize, tomato, squash, avocado, and several arboreal fruits (Amie Limón, personal communication). Although no cotton pollen was recovered, the cultivation of cotton can be inferred from the abundance of cotton-spinning artifacts at the sites (see below). Extensive flotation of midden sediments yielded only a few beans and maize kernels due to poor conditions of preservation (Virginia Popper, personal communication).

Both excavated sites are associated with areas of stone agricultural terrace walls (Price 1988). There is a small area of alluvial fields created by cross-channel terraces (also known as check-dams) just north of Capilco, and a small drainage on the southwest side of Cuexcomate is crossed by over 30 of these terraces (figure 11.1). Excavations and sediment analyses show that the stone walls were built up gradually over a long period of time. In one case, a short wall was built and the terrace filled in fairly rapidly by natural transport with turbulent stream flow. The wall was breached, causing a major erosion gully that was subsequently filled in again. After this, the terrace went through a long period of gradual enlargement, leading to the expansion of the cultivated field through continuous deposition by gentle stream flow. Soil analyses reveal the presence of at least two buried topsoils with elevated concentrations of organic matter and available phosphorus, coupled with a condition of general nutrient depletion in the terrace soils relative to surrounding soils; these findings provide strong evidence that these terraces were indeed farmed in the past. Artifactual remains date the terraces to the Cuauhnahuac phase in general, and one carbon date with a calibration curve intercept of AD 1476 (ETH-6309) dates the period of gradual expansion to the Late Cuauhnahuac phase (see Price and Smith [1992] for further discussion and Sandor et al. 1990 for discussion of terrace archaeology).

In addition to the cross-channel terraces, there are extensive zones of contour terracing in this area. The hillslopes that surround Cuexcomate on three sides are covered with abandoned terraces, which come up to the edge of the settled area. Both types of terraces were needed by the expanding Late Postclassic populations. A preliminary reconstruction of carrying capacity in the area around Xochicalco (Price and Smith 1992) suggests that dry farming on flat areas (without terraces) could support only about 1,200 persons in a 6 km^2 area, a population level passed by EC times (see above). The productivity of terrace agriculture has yet to be modelled for this area, but it seems likely that the extensive Cuauhnahuac phase terraces (coupled with dry farming) would have been capable of producing enough maize to support the local population as well as to fulfill regional- and perhaps imperial-level tribute requirements.

Craft production

A number of different craft products were manufactured in domestic contexts at Cuexcomate and Capilco as evidenced by production tools (ceramic spindle whorls and spinning bowls, worked sherds, basalt polishing stones and bark beaters, and copper tools), production byproducts (chert debitage), and other materials (paint stones). Quantitative data on these artifacts are listed in table 11.2, which presents mean values for various social categories by phase.[2] These social categories are Capilco houses (column A), Cuexcomate nonelite houses (column B), and Cuexcomate elite houses (column C; these are patio groups 6 and 7 in the EC and LC phases respectively).

By far the most widespread and intensive craft activity was *cotton spinning*. Ceramic spindle whorls and spinning bowls were found in every excavated domestic context. Frequencies of spinning artifacts among individual houses are illustrated graphically in figure 11.3. These graphs (and table 11.2) show little difference between elite and nonelite contexts in cotton spinning, although the elite means are lower than the

nonelite means at Cuexcomate. The major change through time was an increase in spinning artifacts at Capilco (table 11.2). Cotton textiles were important items of trade and tribute (Berdan 1987; Smith and Hirth 1988), and much of the textile production was probably destined for export. Similar patterns of abundant whorls and spinning bowls are reported for almost all known Late Postclassic sites in western Morelos (e.g. Smith and Hirth 1988).

Evidence for other types of craft production is far less visible when compared with that for cotton spinning. *Chert tools* were manufactured at both sites from locally available stone, but overall, frequencies of chert artifacts are low (table 11.2). The major material for lithic tools was imported obsidian (see below). Chert tool production debris is found in many deposits, which suggests scattered domestic manufacture. *Basalt polishing stones* are rare but widely distributed artifacts (table 11.2), recovered from 90% of the houses with large samples of excavated midden (over 4 m³).[3] We do not know what function they served, but these smoothed stones were probably a tool in some sort of craft activity. *Worked sherds* (round disks and other shapes) are rare, enigmatic artifacts that may have

Table 11.2 Mean values of craft production measures

Category	Temazcalli	Early Cuauhnahuac			Late Cuauhnahuac		
	(A)	(A)	(B)	(C)	(A)	(B)	(C)
No. of houses[a]	2	5	3	4	9	22	4
Ceramics (percentage of all vessels and artifacts)							
Spinning bowls	2.6	4.2	5.6	3.7	6.2	5.5	4.7
Spindle whorls	0.1	1.3	2.9	1.1	2.7	2.2	1.3
Worked sherds	0.2	0.2	0.4	0.1	0.1	0.4	0.5
Other (frequency per 1,000 sherds)							
Chert	7	3	14	9	5	13	7
Polishing stones	0.22	0.16	0.31	.10	0.22	0.39	—
Bark beaters	0.22	0.10	—	—	0.09	0.08	—
Paint stones	—	.03	.10	0.38	0.13	0.26	0.53
Copper tools	0.12	.10	.21	—	.03	.06	—

Note: Column headings represent types of social contexts as follows: (A) nonelite houses at Capilco, (B) nonelite houses at Cuexcomate, and (C) elite houses at Cuexcomate.
[a] Number of excavated residential middens for each social context.

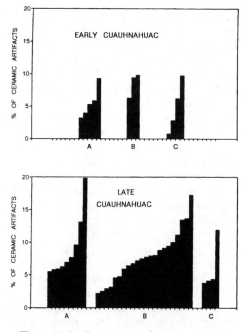

Figure 11.3 Frequencies of cotton spinning artifacts. Data are from domestic middens for the EC and LC phases. Each bar represents a single house, and the bars are grouped in three categories: (A) non-elite houses at Capilco; (B) nonelite houses at Cuexcomate; (C) elite houses at Cuexcomate.

been used in some phase of craft production – smoothing ceramic vessels is a possibility although we have no other evidence for ceramic production (see below).

The manufacture of *paper* from the bark of the *amate* tree is indicated by the presence of grooved, rectangular, basalt tools commonly known as "bark beaters." Although these tools are quite rare (table 11.2), they do occur in 70% of the houses with large samples of excavated midden, suggesting that paper production was widespread among households. *Copper and bronze artifacts*, while not common, are broadly distributed among domestic middens (table 11.2). Most of these artifacts are tools, such as needles, chisels, and awls. Jewelry and other nonutilitarian objects are not included in calculations for table 11.2. The needles were probably used with textiles, and the chisels and awls may have been

used in woodworking (Dorothy Hosler, personal communication).

Mineral paint pigments are another uncommon artifact found in midden deposits. Three colors are represented: red (hematite), yellow (limonite), and black (graphite). Of all types of evidence for craft manufacture, these items show the highest degree of spatial concentration and the strongest association with elite contexts (table 11.2). Paint stones have a minor positive association with elite contexts in both Cuauhnahuac phases. In the EC phase, four of the 12 examples of paint stones (33%) are from the elite patio group; in the LC phase, two of the 43 examples (5%) are from the elite compound and another 28 paint stones (67%) from one single house group, patio group 10. Patio group 10 is not an elite compound (based on a number of architectural and artifactual indicators), but its intensive use of paints could have been in the service of the LC elite who resided nearby. These pigments could have been used to paint manuscripts on bark paper (group 10 also has a large number of bark beaters), an activity associated with the nobility in Late Postclassic Central Mexico (Boone 1994).

Ceramic vessels and obsidian tools are the most abundant artifacts at both sites, but we have no evidence that these goods were produced at either one. Goodfellow's (1990) reconstruction of regional ceramic production and exchange suggests that multiple production centers served Cuexcomate and Capilco, but the locations of production centers have yet to be identified on the ground. Obsidian is quite abundant (we recovered over 12,000 pieces in total), but there is almost no evidence for the production of blades or other tools (Sorensen 1988). There is a production locale or workshop for prismatic blades at the nearby site of El Ciruelo from which the inhabitants of Capilco and Cuexcomate may have obtained their obsidian blades (Sorensen et al. 1989).

Exchange

All three of the major Aztec-period Central Mexican exchange mechanisms – tribute, long-distance trade, and market trade – operated in Morelos. The multilevel tribute system involved payments to local lords, to *tlatoque* at one or more levels, and to the Aztec empire. Merchants from Quauhnahuac traded as far away as Xoconochco, and *pochteca* from the Basin of Mexico traded in the small towns of western Morelos. Markets were common at all levels of the political hierarchy: Quauhnahuac had a large market, many or all city-state capitals had markets, and even some smaller towns held periodic markets (see Smith 1994 for the ethnohistoric evidence for this description). Given the existence of multiple exchange systems and the high rural population density, it is not surprising to find a high frequency of imported goods at the excavated houses.

Frequencies of the three major imports – ceramics, obsidian, and copper – are listed in table 11.3. Two patterns in these data stand out: the large number of imports and their extensive distribution among households. Averaged over all houses, imported ceramics constitute 11.7% of all domestic vessels in Temazcalli phase houses, 11.2% in EC phase houses and 8.3% in LC phase houses. Most of these imports come from the Basin of Mexico. Imports from other parts of Morelos, primarily from the Cuer-navaca area, are also common, with some sherds from the Yauhtepec area and eastern Morelos. There are a few sherds from Cholula, the Mixteca, Guerrero, and the Toluca Valley, mainly in EC phase contexts. The decline in frequency of imported ceramics from EC to LC times primarily occurs in types from the Cuernavaca area (table 11.3). During the LC phase, however, it is not possible to distinguish the polychromes of the Cuernavaca area from those of western Morelos (unlike the situation during earlier phases), and this "decline" in imports from other areas of Morelos (e.g. Cuernavaca) may be more apparent than real.

Nearly all of the obsidian recovered is of the green variety from the Pachuca source area. Domestic inventories average between 30 and 40 pieces per 1,000 sherds; the figures for ceramic vessels (not sherds) are closer to 20 pieces of obsidian per 100 vessels. Obsidian density in domestic middens averages between 25 and 50 pieces per m^3.

Not only were imports abundant, they were also widely distributed. Every excavated house had some Aztec (Basin of Mexico) ceramics, and all but one had obsidian. Copper artifacts (tools and ornaments), although rare, were also widely distributed – present in 80% of the houses with extensively excavated midden deposits (see note 3).

Table 11.3 Mean values of imported artifacts

Category	Temazcalli (A)	Early Cuauhnahuac (A)	Early Cuauhnahuac (B)	Early Cuauhnahuac (C)	Late Cuauhnahuac (A)	Late Cuauhnahuac (B)	Late Cuauhnahuac (C)
Ceramics (percentage of all vessels and artifacts)							
Aztec salt vessels	2.4	2.6	3.5	3.8	2.7	4.4	4.4
Aztec III bowls	—	0.8	2.6	5.3	0.7	1.5	2.9
Aztec spinning bowls	0.5	1.7	1.9	1.3	1.6	1.6	2.7
Other Aztec types	0.1	0.3	1.1	0.3	1.2	0.2	—
Total Aztec imports	3.0	5.4	9.1	10.7	6.2	7.7	10.0
Morelos imports	8.6	3.1	0.3	3.0	1.7	0.4	0.9
Other imports	0.1	0.4	0.3	0.9	0.2	—	—
Other (frequency per 1,000 sherds)							
Obsidian	15	20	32	38	21	45	24
Total copper	.22	.32	.21	.10	.20	.10	—

Note: Column headings represent types of social contexts as follows: (A) nonelite houses at Capilco, (B) nonelite houses at Cuexcomate, and (C) elite houses at Cuexcomate.

Although the elite houses had higher frequencies of some imports (e.g. Morelos ceramic imports in the EC phase, and Aztec III bowls in both EC and LC phases), they did not by any means monopolize these goods.

In sum, rural households at Cuexcomate and Capilco were well integrated into regional and long-distance exchange networks. Exotic goods were normal components of domestic utilitarian inventories, and a number of goods produced by these households (textiles and bark paper at least and probably agricultural goods as well) were destined for export at either the local, regional, or long-distance levels. The lack of any apparent elite monopolies suggests that exchange was most likely independent of elite control, but this is difficult to establish securely with our data.

Consumption

Evidence for elite/commoner differences in consumption practices is surprisingly scarce. No artifact categories, apart from architecture, show an exclusively elite association. Perhaps the strongest a priori candidates for sumptuary goods are luxury items of personal adornment, but none of the 19 examples of jewelry (jade beads, obsidian lip plugs, and shell pendants) were recovered in elite contexts. A number of ceramic categories do show statistical associations with the elite residences in each phase, but these are far from exclusive associations.

Based upon the cross-cultural validity of household possessions as wealth indicators (Smith 1987a), two artifactual indices were constructed to study variability among houses in wealth levels. For the first index, the architectural distinctiveness of patio groups 6 and 7 was inferred to signal the presence of elite groups in the EC and LC phases respectively. Five ceramic variables or types were chosen that best differentiated the elite from the nonelite houses at Cuexcomate in each phase; these are listed in table 11.4 (three types served in both phases). These five variables were used to construct wealth index 1,[4] a phase-specific index of wealth variation among households. Wealth index 2 was calculated to examine change over time since values of the first index are not directly comparable between phases. Index 2 is the simple sum of the frequency of local decorated ceramics and two times the frequency of imported ceramics, calculated for each house. This

Table 11.4 Mean values of wealth indices and ceramic markets of wealth

Category	Temazcalli	Early Cuauhnahuac			Late Cuauhnahuac		
	(A)	(A)	(B)	(C)	(A)	(B)	(C)
Wealth indices							
Index 1	—	−1.26	−5.03	3.83	−.50	−.77	3.11
Index 2	51.4	43.3	43.0	62.5	37.2	34.5	48.3
Ceramic types (percentage of all vessels and artifacts)							
Morelos imports	8.6	**3.1**	**0.3**	**3.0**	**1.7**	**0.4**	**0.9**
Other decorated bowls	4.0	**2.9**	**0.3**	**3.5**	**1.7**	**0.7**	**0.2**
Total bowls	48.4	**46.7**	**38.4**	**50.1**	**41.1**	**39.3**	**42.5**
Aztec III bowls	—	0.8	2.6	5.3	**0.7**	**1.5**	**2.9**
Polished red bowls	10.8	4.5	5.5	12.9	4.5	7.2	9.9
Tlahuica polychrome	11.6	**15.6**	**10.2**	**8.9**	**12.5**	**6.2**	**8.7**
Incense burners	2.6	3.3	6.1	3.7	3.1	3.2	4.7

Notes: Column headings represent types of social contexts as follows: (A) nonelite houses at Capilco, (B) nonelite houses at Cuexcomate, and (C) elite houses at Cuexcomate.

Bold figures denote the five phase-specific wealth indicators for each phase that were used in the calculation of wealth index 1.

index ranges from 19.7 to 68.2; table 11.4 shows the mean values.

The wealth indices suggest a number of conclusions on consumption patterns at Cuexcomate and Capilco. First, all three social categories (Capilco, Cuexcomate nonelite, and Cuexcomate elite) manifest an overall decline in standard of living through time. Second, the elite households show distinctive patterns of ceramic usage in both phases. Third, elite/commoner differences were much reduced in the LC phase as measured by both wealth indices. The decline in the fortunes of the elite as measured by portable artifacts is matched by the architecture: the LC elite compound is far less imposing and distinctive than the EC compound, although it is still the largest residential group at the sites in LC times. Furthermore, the lack of conformity of this compound to the Aztec palace plan suggests a lower level of involvement in long-distance elite interactions at this time.

Summary of Social and Economic Changes

The excavations at Cuexcomate and Capilco have allowed us to document a number of social and economic changes in the three phases of occupation – population growth, agricultural intensification, increasing textile production, changing configurations of long-distance trade partners, decline of the standard of living, and modifications of elite/commoner distinctions. We summarize these changes here for each of the phase transitions.

Temazcalli to Early Cuauhnahuac transition

Reconstruction of the socioeconomic system during the Temazcalli phase (1200–1350) is limited by the small number of excavated deposits from this phase (two refuse deposits at Capilco). Nevertheless, the artifacts from these deposits can be compared with the more abundant Early Cuauhnahuac (1350–1430) materials to suggest patterns of change. There was clearly a major growth

in population as Capilco expanded and Cuexcomate was founded; this pattern is repeated in Smith's (1992) demographic reconstruction for the area around the two sites, where the annual population growth rate was an estimated 1.6%. This population surge was accompanied by the construction of agricultural terraces in the study area. No pre-Cuauhnahuac agricultural terraces have been documented (Hirth 1994; Price and Smith 1992), and although only one of the check-dams at Cuexcomate can be unequivocally assigned to a phase on the basis of a chronometric date (LC), strong indirect evidence points to an EC origin for the terracing (Price and Smith 1992).

The frequencies of cotton-spinning artifacts increase dramatically from Temazcalli to EC times (table 11.2), conforming to a pattern previously documented at nearby Xochicalco and Coatetelco (Smith and Hirth 1988). This apparent growth in the textile industry was not equalled by other craft activity, most of which continued at low levels. Trade with the Basin of Mexico (as measured by imported ceramics and obsidian) increased greatly, while exchange within Morelos declined (table 11.3). Wealth index 2 declines (except for the EC elite compound), but we do not see this as indicating a drop in standards of living since the numerical decline is due almost entirely to the decline in Morelos ceramic imports (table 11.3; see note 4). Other evidence, reviewed below, points to the EC phase as a time of prosperity and expansion.

Early Cuauhnahuac to Late Cuauhnahuac transition

The rate of population growth decreased from the Early Cuauhnahuac phase (1350–1430) to the Late Cuauhnahuac phase (1430–1550), from 1.6% to 1.0%, but it was still quite high, and the magnitude of the population increase was impressive (table 11.1; see Smith 1992: 335–45). Agricultural intensification in the form of terracing continued until nearly all available land in the Buenavista Lomas was under cultivation (O'Mack 1991; Price and Smith 1992). Although productivity studies have not been carried out, it appears that the population had exceeded the carrying capacity of the land; Smith (1992: 335–45) estimates the LC population density in this area at over 600 persons per km^2.

The frequency of cotton-spinning artifacts in individual household deposits increases by 50% at Capilco, with little change at Cuexcomate. When increased population at these settlements is considered, however, the overall level of textile production increased dramatically. Several lines of evidence point to lowered standards of living in LC times. Wealth index 2 shows a decline in all social categories (table 11.4). There is less variability in artifactual wealth indicators, including a lower level of elite/commoner differences. This pattern is exhibited even more strongly in residential architecture, with elite abandonment of the imposing patio group 6 and construction of the more modest group 7 (figure 11.2). The abandonment of patio group 6 between EC and LC probably signals a major social change, but we do not know its cause or significance (see discussion below).

These changes from the Temazcalli through Late Cuauhnahuac phases are all clearly documented in the archaeological record at Capilco and Cuexcomate. Their causes and consequences are discussed below under three headings: the role of the elite, Aztec conquest, and economic growth cycles.

Processes of Change

The role of the elite

The degree of centralized political control over the economy is an important issue in Aztec economics, although with archaeological data it is difficult to distinguish state control from control by elites acting independently of the state. Brumfiel and Earle (1987) describe three models of economic organization and social complexity that help frame the issue of elite control. In

their *commercial development model*, production and exchange are relatively independent of elite interference. On the other hand, elites may take an active role in the organization of economic activity. In the *adaptationist model*, elites serve a managerial function, producing social benefits for everyone. In the *political model*, however, elites act in a controlling and monopolizing capacity, benefitting themselves primarily. In our view, the data from Cuexcomate and Capilco are most consistent with the *commercial development model*, with "bottom-up" forces primary in the generation of Postclassic economic change in this area (see Blanton 1983a; Maclachlan 1987).

The expansion of terraced farming is the most visible aspect of Postclassic agricultural change in the Cuexcomate/Capilco area. Although terracing is a more intensive practice than level-field rainwater cultivation, it is not nearly as intensive as the irrigation or raised field techniques used elsewhere in Late Postclassic Central Mexico. Following Turner and Doolittle (1978), we define intensification as agricultural change that involves increased labor investment to produce higher yields per unit of land. Terracing is generally carried out on the household level (Netting 1968, 1990; Wilken 1987), and unlike the methods of irrigation or raised field cultivation, terracing does not require or stimulate collective or centralized organization (Sanders et al. 1979; Wilken 1987). Our stratigraphic evidence for an extended period of check-dam enlargement conforms with this pattern. Netting's (1990) model of intensification (as a household-level adaptation to population pressure that does not necessarily lead to political centralization or control) seems applicable to this case. It is not necessary to invoke a model of elite control of production to account for the expansion of terracing. On the other hand, attempts by elites to increase production within their territory are a common incentive to intensification cross-culturally (e.g. Brumfiel and Earle 1987; Polgar 1975), and this possibility cannot be ruled out.

With the possible exception of the use of paint stones, there was little elite control over craft production. Textiles, paper, and other goods were manufactured at the elite compounds, but not at higher levels than at nonelite houses (table 11.2; figure 11.3). This finding surprised us, since regional ethnohistorical sources indicate that commoners went to noble compounds to spin and weave, (e.g. Cortés 1865: 542; Smith 1994); we had expected therefore to find evidence of more intensive textile manufacture in such contexts.

No imported artifacts have an exclusively elite association, although some imported ceramic types show statistical associations with elite contexts (e.g. Morelos imports in the EC phase; Aztec III in both EC and LC phases; see table 11.4). All excavated houses had access to imported ceramics and obsidian tools, and many had copper artifacts. Moreover, exotic items of rare, valuable jewelry (jade beads, obsidian earspools, shell pendants) were found almost exclusively in nonelite contexts. Apart from architecture, our analyses found no examples of sumptuary goods to distinguish elite from commoner contexts. On this basis, we see no evidence for elite control over exchange. Imports were probably obtained through the market system where noble and commoner had equal access.

In sum, there is little evidence for elite control over production or exchange activities, and a "bottom-up" economic model appears to be most appropriate for agricultural production, craft industries, and exchange. The diminished elite/commoner distinctions in the LC phase indicate that the decline in standards of living was not due to greater exploitation at the hands of the local Cuexcomate elite. Nevertheless, this and other changes from EC to LC could have resulted from exploitation by external elites centered in either Quauhnahuac and/or the Basin of Mexico. In other words, the actions of elites may have had important repercussions on rural conditions, but if so, the relevant

elite groups were not those resident at Cuexcomate.

Aztec conquest

The EC and LC phases correspond to the periods before and after western Morelos was conquered and incorporated into the Aztec empire (Smith 1987b; Smith and Doershuk 1991). We distinguish three types of effects that Aztec imperialism may have had on rural sites: the direct effects of conquest, the impact of Aztec tribute, and the indirect effects that derived from regional changes brought about by Aztec imperialism. Although all three may have played a role, we believe the indirect effects had the most significant influence on rural socioeconomic patterns.

The evaluation of the effects of Aztec conquest at Cuexcomate and Capilco is complicated by the earlier conquest of western Morelos by the Quauhnahuac polity in the 1420s (Smith 1986). The only likely direct effect of foreign conquest that we can identify is the abandonment of the patio group 6 elite compound at Cuexcomate. This could have been caused by the killing or destruction of the EC phase elite household by either the Quauhnahuac polity in the 1420s or by the Aztec empire in the late 1430s.

The direct tributary demands of the Aztec empire probably had little impact on settlements like Capilco and Cuexcomate. This area was within the territory of the Quauhnahuac conquest-state, which corresponded to the Aztec tributary province of the same name. The major tribute items paid to the Aztecs by Quauhnahuac were cotton textiles, grains, bark paper, and warrior costumes (see Smith 1994). At least three of the observed archaeological changes – increased agricultural production, increased textile manufacture, and lowered standards of living – could be direct results of Aztec tributary exploitation. Smith's (1994) quantitative reconstruction of Morelos demography and tribute, however, suggests that on the household level, imperial tribute was quite modest (the rate for cotton textiles was under one manta or piece per household per year).

Imperial tribute alone would not cause the EC to LC archaeological changes; nevertheless, the indirect effects of Aztec imperialism could have had a greater impact. In an earlier article, Smith (1986) presents a model that shows the importance of interaction between the ruling dynasties of Quauhnahuac and Tenochtitlan as a mechanism of integration within the empire. This interaction, begun before the formation of the Aztec empire, increased in intensity after the conquest of Quauhnahuac in 1438. Smith hypothesizes that the Quauhnahuac nobility used their enhanced position within the Aztec empire to increase their own tributary exploitation of provincial commoners, augmenting tribute exactions beyond the relatively modest imperial quota for their own gain.

This model does not fit Cuexcomate elite, however, whose interaction with the Basin of Mexico declined in the LC phase (as judged by architectural styles and imports) while their economic position worsened. In fact, the EC phase elite may have been wiped out during the Aztec conquest (see above). Unlike the nobility in the capital city of Quauhnahuac, the LC Cuexcomate elite did not receive the benefits of Aztec imperial elite interaction networks. Rural populations like the inhabitants of Capilco and Cuexcomate were at the bottom of the Quauhnahuac tributary hierarchy (see Smith 1994), and commoners and elite alike at these sites were probably exploited by regional elites at both city-state capitals and Quauhnahuac. The combined effects of increased tribute at the imperial and regional state levels probably contributed to the observed changes in agricultural production, textile manufacture, standard of living, and elite conditions. These indirect effects of Aztec conquest were not autonomous causes of the archaeological changes, however. Rather, they were but one component of a complex system of forces that generated economic change in Postclassic western Morelos.

An economic growth cycle

The various processes of change outlined above began in Temazcalli and EC times well before the formation of the Aztec empire in 1430, a strong argument against Aztec conquest as their primary direct or indirect cause. We interpret these changes as components of a dynamic system of economic growth characterized by complex feedback relationships. This system fueled a regional agrarian cycle of boom and bust, where initial growth, expansion, and prosperity lead to contraction, decline, and crisis.

The population increase between the Middle and Late Postclassic periods was one of the more dramatic developments of the Postclassic epoch throughout Central Mexico. This demographic process has been discussed in terms of both causal population pressure models (Sanders et al. 1979) and systemic feedback models (Blanton 1983b). The rough chronological framework in the Basin of Mexico has prevented detailed analysis, however, and much of the population pressure debate proceeds more from theoretical first principles than from empirical evidence (Smith 1993b). The greater chronological control in western Morelos permits the process of population growth to be examined more closely. Based upon our admittedly limited data, it appears that the greatest regional surge occurred in the fourteenth century (Temazcalli–EC transition), with slower but still significant growth continuing through the fifteenth century (EC–LC transition); annual regional growth rates at these two transition periods averaged 1.6% and 1.0% respectively (Smith 1992: 335–45).

The fourteenth-century surge led to large-scale colonization of the Buenavista Lomas, probably by peoples from the more productive, irrigated, alluvial areas of Central Morelos. Capilco already existed at this time, but Cuexcomate was initially settled as a relatively large center of 10 hectares with over 200 inhabitants. Agricultural terracing was required by the large number of new settlers, and population pressure was a major force leading to agricultural intensification. On the other hand, the economic success of the EC phase (see below) probably served as a feedback loop that further stimulated population growth. Once a successful terracing program was established, the economy initially would have faced labor shortages rather than land shortages, a condition favourable to demographic growth (Polgar 1975). Later, local and regional tribute demands may have contributed to the forces stimulating population growth. Eventually, by LC times, economic growth slowed down as the lomas area filled up. Continued population growth became a major contributor to lowered standards of living.

The network of interactions among demography, economic forces, and household-level craft production is an important component of this model. Many of the documented craft activities – chert tool manufacture and production activities that involved polishing stones, worked sherds and/or copper tools – were apparently performed at all or most houses for domestic purposes. These activities fit Peacock's (1982) category of "household production," or low-level domestic production for immediate household use. Two products – cotton textiles and bark paper – were also manufactured in domestic contexts but with some production for exchange beyond the immediate family. In the case of textiles, production was quite intensive (inferred from the high frequencies of spindle whorls and spinning bowls), and fits Peacock's "household industry" category in which production is carried out in domestic contexts for both use and exchange, usually by part-time producers.

Part-time, rural textile manufacture conforms to Brumfiel's (1987) model of Aztec craft production in which utilitarian items were made by part-time, independent rural artisans and luxury items by full-time urban specialists attached to noble courts. We believe, however, that the economic context of rural production differs somewhat from Brumfiel's account. She proposes (Brumfiel

1987; Brumfiel and Earle 1987: 5) that rural craft producers do not have sufficient, steady, aggregate demand to specialize full time, so they adopt farming as a buffer against fluctuations in supply and demand. On the other hand, ethnographic and historical accounts suggest that the opposite process may in fact be more common: rural farmers take up part-time craft production to supplement their income. This pattern commonly occurs under conditions of growing rural population, land shortages, and poverty that lead peasant households to try to augment their declining agricultural income with cottage industries (Arnold 1985: 171–96; Miller and Hatcher 1978; Thirsk 1961).

Data from Cuexcomate and Capilco suggest this latter process occurred in the Late Cuauhnahuac phase. The progressive decline in wealth index 2 (table 11.4) over the three phases is accompanied by increases in the frequency of cotton-spinning artifacts (table 11.2), particularly at the site of Capilco. More telling is the situation in the LC phase. In EC times, no single house stands out with excessive amounts of textile artifacts, but in LC times one nonelite house at each site exceeds the phase mean by more than two standard deviations. These houses with greatly intensified cotton spinning (houses 102 and 261) are also among the lowest in values for wealth index 1, as shown in figure 11.4. Admittedly, there is

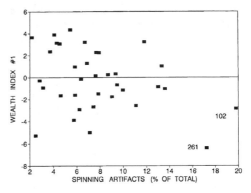

Figure 11.4   Textile artifact frequency and wealth level. Data are from Late Cuauhnahuac households at Cuexcomate and Capilco.

little overall statistical association between cotton spinning and wealth, but it may be important that the two houses with the most intensive spinning are among the poorest houses at these sites. At Capilco in the EC phase, house 102 was involved in craft production using copper tools and had the highest wealth index at that site. In the LC phase, however, both of its wealth indices plummeted and the inhabitants of house 102 intensified both textile production and the use of copper tools.

The above observations may be summarized as follows. The EC phase was a time of economic growth and general prosperity at Cuexcomate and Capilco. Population was growing and new lands were put into production with terracing. Population levels were well within the carrying capacity of terraced agriculture. Compared to Temazcalli times, trade increased with all areas except perhaps Quauhnahuac, and textile production was carried out at higher levels. A prosperous and powerful elite group was linked architecturally and stylistically with the Central Mexican elite class, and the commoners appear to have had relatively high standards of living (to judge by the wealth indices and access to imported goods). By contrast, the LC phase showed a decline in living conditions. The extremely high population density probably taxed the limits of terrace agriculture (a study of terrace chronology and productivity is badly needed). All social sectors experienced decreases in standards of living and the relative and absolute position of the LC elite was greatly reduced. The two major forces leading to this socioeconomic downturn were the demographic/agricultural crisis and the increased tribute demands of Quauhnahuac and the Aztec empire. Aztec conquest did not create the problems, but the indirect effects of Aztec imperialism must have exacerbated local troubles, adding further to the economic difficulties of rural households.

This overall pattern of development from Temazcalli through Late Cuauhnahuac times is an example of an economic cycle common in pre-industrial states with dense peasant populations. In the first half of the cycle, population grows, new lands are colonized, trade and manufacturing expand, and towns prosper. As growth continues beyond some threshold, however, the economy is transformed from a condition of excess land and a shortage of labor to one with surplus labor and a shortage of land. In this second half of the cycle, cultivable land is filled in, productivity declines, prices rise, the countryside becomes impoverished, and many peasant households take up cottage industries to supplement falling agricultural income. Two well-documented historical examples of this agrarian cycle are England in the twelfth and thirteenth centuries (Miller and Hatcher 1978) and southern France in the fifteenth and sixteenth centuries (Le Roy Ladurie 1972). In another case, Blanton et al. (1993: 50–105) present archaeological evidence for similar prehispanic growth cycles in the Valley of Oaxaca. We believe that these examples are comparable to the changes observed from the excavations at Capilco and Cuexcomate.

Conclusions

The rural economy of Late Postclassic western Morelos was more complex and dynamic than ethnohistoric accounts of Aztec society would suggest. The inhabitants of Capilco and Cuexcomate were not simple peasants toiling away to support nobles and states. Instead, these people, elites and commoners, were well connected to Central Mexican exchange networks. They carried out a variety of productive activities in addition to agriculture, and their towns and villages exhibited a high level of social heterogeneity. These patterns cannot be recovered from generalized ethnohistoric accounts of sixteenth-century Central Mexico, nor are they clear from local administrative documents from Morelos. Local social and economic conditions and the ways in which they changed through time can only be understood when detailed archaeological data are gathered and analyzed within a comparative social framework that integrates local, regional, and macroregional data into a comprehensive model.

The model of change that we propose above provides a good fit to the observed archaeological changes at Capilco and Cuexcomate. This model should be viewed as an exploratory account, however, until comparable data from other areas become available. The processes we single out as important – population growth, agricultural intensification, craft production, social stratification, and external conquest – operated at regional and macroregional scales, and this description of change at two small sites can only provide a partial view of Late Postclassic rural conditions in Central Mexico. Nevertheless, this study demonstrates the value of the household archaeology approach as a method for generating useful social and economic data. As more such studies are carried out, our models will continue to improve, and earlier normative and static accounts of Aztec rural society will be replaced by a more accurate appreciation of the dynamic and diverse nature of Aztec economies and societies.

ACKNOWLEDGMENTS

The Postclassic Morelos Archaeological Project was supported by funds from the National Science Foundation, the National Endowment for the Humanities, and Loyola University of Chicago. Permission for the fieldwork and analyses was granted by the Instituto Nacional de Antropología e Historia. We would like to thank Arqueólogos Norberto González Crespo, Joaquín García-Bárcena, Angel García Cook, and Lorena Mirambel of the Instituto for helping the project in many ways. Elizabeth Brumfiel, Frederic Hicks, and Mary Hodge provided helpful comments on an earlier draft of this paper.

NOTES

1 In this paper we use the concept "rural" as an attribute of regions (rather than as an attribute of individual settlements). A rural region is an area with a low level of urbanization in the sense that it contains few cities or else has a low proportion of the population living in cities.

2 All quantitative data on artifact distributions in this article describe materials from well-phased, domestic midden deposits associated with individual houses. Ceramic artifacts are quantified in terms of minimum numbers of vessels per type per context (based upon rim sherds), which are expressed as percentages for each context. Other artifacts are quantified in terms of abundance relative to ceramics; the measure used is frequency per 1,000 sherds. These measures are discussed in Smith (1992).

3 Out of a total of 56 well-phased, residential midden deposits at Capilco and Cuexcomate, 10 have excavated volumes greater than 4 m^3 (for a single phase). These 10 deposits cover all three phases and both sites. Because of the statistical problem of underrepresentation of rare categories in small collections, these 10 deposits are used to monitor the ubiquity of rare artifact types on a general level.

4 Two methods were used to select the five ceramic types for calculation of wealth index 1. Analysis of variance established the variables that most consistently differed between elite and nonelite houses, and comparisons of means revealed the magnitudes of the group differences. Combining the results of the two methods, the five most sensitive variables were selected for each phase. Percents were transformed to standardized Z-scores (within each phase separately), and the five scores summed, giving each house a value that ranged from −7.9 to +7.0; a score of 0 would be the "average" wealth level. The figures in table 11.4 are means by social category.

REFERENCES

Arnold, Dean. 1985. *Ceramic Theory and Cultural Processes*. Cambridge University Press, New York.

Berdan, Frances F. 1987. Cotton in Aztec Mexico: Production, Distribution, and Uses. *Mexican Studies/Estudios Mexicanos* 3: 235–62.

Blanton, Richard E. 1983a. Factors Underlying the Origin and Evolution of Market Systems. In *Economic Anthropology: Topics and Theories*, edited by Sutti Ortiz, pp. 51–66. University Press of America, Lanham, Maryland.

——— 1983b. Advances in the Study of Cultural Evolution in Prehispanic Highland Mesoamerica. *Advances in World Archaeology* 2: 245–88. Academic Press, New York.

Blanton, Richard E., Stephen A. Kowalewski, Gary M. Feinman, and Laura M. Finsten. 1993. *Ancient Mesoamerica: A Comparison of*

Change in Three Regions. 2nd edn. Cambridge University Press, New York.

Boone, Elizabeth H. 1994. Manuscript Painting in Service of Imperial Ideology. In *Aztec Imperial Strategies*, by Frances F. Berdan, Richard E. Blanton, Elizabeth H. Boone, Mary G. Hodge, Michael E. Smith, and Emily Umberger. Dumbarton Oaks, Washington, DC.

Brumfiel, Elizabeth M. 1980. Specialization, Market Exchange, and the Aztec State: A View from Huexotla. *Current Anthropology* 21: 459–78.

—— 1987. Elite and Utilitarian Crafts in the Aztec State. In *Specialization, Exchange, and Complex Societies*, edited by Elizabeth M. Brumfiel and Timothy K. Earle, pp. 102–18. Cambridge University Press, New York.

Brumfiel, Elizabeth M. and Timothy K. Earle. 1987. Specialization, Exchange, and Complex Societies: An Introduction. In *Specialization, Exchange, and Complex Societies*, edited by Elizabeth M. Brumfiel and Timothy K. Earle, pp. 1–9. Cambridge University Press, New York.

Carrasco, Pedro. 1976. Estratificación social indígena en Morelos durante el siglo XVI. In *Estratificación social en la Mesoamérica prehispánica*, edited by Pedro Carrasco and Johanna Broda, pp. 102–17. Instituto Nacional de Antropología e Historia, Mexico City.

Cortés, Hernán. 1865. Carta de Hernán Cortés, al Consejo de Indias . . . sobre la constitución de la propriedad de las tierras entre los indios (1538). In *Colección de documentos inéditos . . . de indias*, vol. 3, pp. 535–43. Real Academía de la Historia, Madrid.

Evans, Susan T. 1988. *Excavations at Cihuatecpan, an Aztec Village in the Teotihuacan Valley*. Vanderbilt University Publications in Anthropology No. 36. Vanderbilt University, Nashville.

—— 1991. Architecture and Authority in an Aztec Village: Form and Function of the Tecpan. In *Land and Politics in the Valley of Mexico*, edited by Herbert R. Harvey, pp. 63–92. University of New Mexico Press, Albuquerque.

Fries, Carl, Jr. 1960. *Geología del estado de Morelos y de partes adyacentes de México y Guerrero*. Boletín No. 60. Instituto de Geología, Universidad Nacional Autónoma de México, Mexico City.

Goodfellow, Susan T. 1990. Late Postclassic Period Economic Systems in Western Morelos, Mexico: A Study of Ceramic Production, Distribution and Exchange. Ph.D. dissertation, Department of Anthropology. University of Pittsburgh. University Microfilms, Ann Arbor.

Hirth, Kenneth G. 1994. *Ancient Urbanism at Xochicalco*. Manuscript on file at the Department of Anthropology, Pennsylvania State University.

Kolb, Charles C. 1985. Demographic Estimates in Archaeology: Contributions from Ethnoarchaeology on Mesoamerican Peasants. *Current Anthropology* 26: 581–600.

Le Roy Ladurie, Emmanuel. 1972. *The Peasants of Languedoc*. University of Illinois Press, Urbana.

Maclachlan, Morgan D. 1987. From Intensification to Proletarianization. In *Household Economies and their Transformations*, edited by Morgan D. Maclachlan, pp. 1–27. University Press of America, Lanham, Maryland.

Maldonado Jiménez, Druzo. 1990. *Cuauhnahuac y Huaxtepec: Tlalhuicas y Xochimilcas en el Morelos prehispánico*. Centro Regional de Investigaciones Multidisciplinarias, Universidad Nacional Autónoma de México, Cuernavaca.

Mason, Roger D. 1980. Economic and Social Organization of an Aztec Provincial Center: Archaeological Research at Coatlan Viejo, Morelos, Mexico. Ph.D. dissertation, Department of Anthropology, University of Texas. University Microfilms, Ann Arbor.

Miller, Edward and John Hatcher. 1978. *Medieval England: Rural Society and Economic Change, 1086–1348*. Longman, New York.

Netting, Robert McC. 1968. *Hill Farmers of Nigeria: Cultural Ecology of the Jos Plateau*. University of Washington Press, Seattle.

—— 1990. Population, Permanent Agriculture, and Polities: Unpacking the Evolutionary Portmanteau. In *The Evolution of Political Systems: Sociopolitics in Small-Scale Societies*, edited by Steadman Upham, pp. 21–61. Cambridge University Press, New York.

O'Mack, Scott H. 1991. *Final Report of the Tetlama Lienzo Project*. Report submitted to the National Geographic Society.

Peacock, D. P. S. 1982. *Pottery in the Roman World: An Ethnoarchaeological Approach*. Longman, New York.

Polgar, Steven. 1975. Population, Evolution, and Theoretical Paradigms. In *Population, Ecology, and Social Evolution*, edited by Steven Polgar, pp. 1–26. Mouton, The Hague.

Price, T. Jeffrey. 1988. Investigation of Agricultural Features at Two Rural Late Postclassic Sites in Western Morelos, Mexico. Unpublished Master's thesis, Department of Anthropology, University of Georgia.

Price, T. Jeffrey and Michael E. Smith. 1992. Agricultural Terraces. In *Archaeological Research at Aztec-Period Rural Sites in Morelos, Mexico, Volume 1: Excavations and Architecture*, by Michael E. Smith, pp. 267–92. Memoirs in Latin American Archaeology No. 4. University of Pittsburgh, Pittsburgh.

Sanders, William T., Jeffrey R. Parsons, and Robert S. Santley. 1979. *The Basin of Mexico: Ecological Processes in the Evolution of a Civilization.* Academic Press, New York.

Sandor, Jon A., P. L. Gersper, and J. W. Hawley. 1990. Prehistoric Agricultural Terraces and Soils in the Mimbres Area, New Mexico. *World Archaeology* 22: 70–86.

Smith, Michael E. 1986. The Role of Social Stratification in the Aztec Empire: A View from the Provinces. *American Anthropologist* 88: 70–91.

—— 1987a. Household Possessions and Wealth in Agrarian States: Implications for Archaeology. *Journal of Anthropological Archaeology* 6: 297–335.

—— 1987b. The Expansion of the Aztec Empire: A Case Study in the Correlation of Diachronic Archaeological and Ethnohistorical Data. *American Antiquity* 52: 37–54.

—— 1992. *Archaeological Research at Aztec-Period Rural Sites in Morelos, Mexico, Volume 1: Excavations and Architecture.* Memoirs in Latin American Archaeology No. 4. University of Pittsburgh, Pittsburgh.

—— 1993a. Houses and the Settlement Hierarchy in Late Postclassic Morelos: A Comparison of Archaeology and Ethnohistory. In *Prehispanic Domestic Units in Western Mesoamerica: Studies of the Household, Compound, and Residence,* edited by Robert S. Santley and Kenneth G. Hirth, pp. 191–206. CRC Press, Boca Raton.

—— 1993b. New World Complex Societies: Recent Economic, Social, and Political Studies. *Journal of Archaeological Research* 1: 5–41.

—— 1994. Economies and Polities in Aztec-period Morelos: Ethnohistoric Introduction. In *Economies and Polities in the Aztec Realm,* edited by Mary E. Hodge and Michael E. Smith, pp. 313–48. Institute for Mesoamerican Studies, Albany.

Smith, Michael E., Patricia Aguirre, Cynthia Heath-Smith, Kathryn Hirst, Scott O'Mack,

and T. Jeffrey Price. 1989. Architectural Patterns at Three Aztec-period Sites in Morelos, Mexico. *Journal of Field Archaeology* 16: 185–203.

Smith, Michael E. and John F. Doershuk. 1991. Late Postclassic Chronology in Western Morelos, Mexico. *Latin American Antiquity* 2: 291–310.

Smith, Michael E. and Kenneth G. Hirth. 1988. The Development of Prehispanic Cotton-Spinning Technology in Western Morelos, Mexico. *Journal of Field Archaeology* 15: 349–58.

Sorensen, Jerrell H. 1988. Rural Chipped Stone Technology in Late Postclassic Morelos, Mexico. Paper presented at the 1988 Annual Meeting, American Anthropological Association, Phoenix.

Sorensen, Jerrell H., Kenneth G. Hirth, and Stephen M. Ferguson. 1989. The Contents of Seven Obsidian Workshops Around Xochicalco, Morelos. In *La obsidiana en Mesoamérica,* edited by Margarita Gaxiola and John E. Clark, pp. 269–76. Instituto Nacional de Antropología e Historia, Mexico City.

Sterpone, Osvaldo. 1988. Late Postclassic Settlement Patterns in Northwestern Morelos. Paper presented at the 1988 Annual Meeting of the American Anthropological Association, Phoenix.

Thirsk, Joan. 1961. Industries in the Countryside. In *Essays in the Economic and Social History of Tudor and Stuart England, in Honor of R. H. Tawney,* edited by F. J. Fisher, pp. 70–88. Cambridge University Press, Cambridge.

Turner, B. L., II and William E. Doolittle. 1978. The Concept and Measure of Agricultural Intensity. *Professional Geographer* 30: 297–301.

Wilken, Gene C. 1987. *Good Farmers: Traditional Agricultural Resource Management in Mexico and Central America.* University of California Press, Berkeley.

Zorita, Alonso de. 1963. *Breve y sumaria relación de los señores de la Nueva España.* Universidad Nacional Autónoma de México, Mexico City.

PART III

Political Organization

Editors' Introduction

The study of Mesoamerican political organization has contributed significantly to evolutionary models of complex societies in anthropology. Mesoamerica is one of the few places in the world where the processes by which primary civilizations evolved out of relatively egalitarian villages can be studied. A diaspora of secondary complex societies, which are found in micro-environments extending from northern Mexico through Honduras, also provide numerous opportunities for studying systems of interaction among complex cultures of multiple linguistic and ethnic backgrounds.

Many evolutionary models of Mesoamerican cultural development follow conventional directional schemes of classification such as Service's (1962) political categories of band, tribe, chiefdom, and state (for example, Coe and Diehl 1980: 147; Blanton 1983: 83–6). Some archaeologists find the social categories of Freid (1967) – egalitarian, rank, stratified, and class society – more productive (Clark and Blake, chapter 12). Others have argued for approaches that avoid labels and focus on variability and adaptation among complex societies (Feinman and Neitzel 1984: 78; Feinman 1991: 229–30; Drennan 1991: 264). Studies of the evolution of Mesoamerican polities have been most closely linked to the interpretation of regional settlement data and the application of processual approaches in American archaeology since the 1970s (Flannery 1976; Blanton 1978; Blanton et al. 1982; Kowalewski et al. 1989; Sanders et al. 1979; Willey and Sabloff 1993). While many regions of Mesoamerica exhibit a continuum of complexity from the earliest sedentary agricultural villages to later regional states, considerable variation existed over space and time in the size, integration, economic stability, and power of regional political entities.

Anthropological research suggests that dynamic cycles of fluctuating political hierarchy may have been more common than the continuous, linear development of civilizations (McGuire 1983; Yoffee 1993; Paynter 1989; de Montmollin 1989). A landmark ethnographic study of the Kachin of Highland Burma (Leach 1964) indicates that oscillations of political centralization and decentralization can occur in long-term cycles of human adaptation, and these forms of organization are affected by population levels, environmental capacities, and internal and external forces of political competition. Leach's model of dynamic fluctuation in hierarchical development has been used as an analogy for lowland Maya political cycles (Freidel 1983).

Because of the great variation across time and space, the application of ethnographically derived typologies to archaeological cultures is not always an easy task (Feinman and Neitzel 1984; Drennan 1991). Freidel (1985: 305–8) has described the southern lowland Maya area as a cultural mosaic of economic diversity and political units representing subregions of Maya society. Spatial diversity in Mesoamerica is also found in the relationships between cultural cores and their peripheries or hinterlands (Rathje 1972; Blanton and Feinman 1984; Carmack 1996). Core areas were characterized by greater hierarchical development, whereas peripheral zones exhibited fewer hierarchical patterns (Rathje 1972; Feinman and Nicholas, chapter 10). Over time, core–periphery positions fluctuated and even reversed roles as peripheral regions developed organizational complexity. Rathje (1972: 375) has suggested that this phenomenon sometimes resulted in the collapse of core zones which were cut off from key trading resources by their peripheries.

Regional and Interregional Patterns in Mesoamerican Polities

Core zones changed over time in Mesoamerica. Often-discussed examples of political and economic cores (Carmack et al. 1996) include the Olmec heartland on the Veracruz Gulf Coast, the Classic and Postclassic-period Valley of Mexico, the Classic period Valley of Oaxaca, the Classic-period Peten region of the southern Maya lowlands, the Postclassic-period northern Yucatan, and the Tarascan core in the Pátzcuaro Basin of Michoacan in Late Postclassic times. Studies of hinterland regions and societies located in zones peripheral to these core centers are well known from Isthmian and coastal Oaxaca (Joyce 1993), mountainous zones near the Valley of Oaxaca (Redmond 1983; Feinman 1990), the southeast frontier of Mesoamerica (Joyce 1991), many parts of west Mexico (Pollard 1997; Townsend 1998), and other regions throughout Mesoamerica.

The reasons for the development of political capitals in core regions have been hotly debated in Mesoamerican archaeology. Were these zones the most suitable for sustenance of large populations, the production of surplus, state-controlled intensive agriculture, intergroup trade, urbanization, and the maintenance of a ruling class as some have suggested for the highlands (Sanders and Price 1968; Sanders et al. 1979)? Or did they represent zones of resource deficiency that evolved a complex organization in order to control trade and importation of items that were more accessible on their frontiers as others have proposed for the lowlands (Rathje 1972)? The study of Mesoamerican regional development is closely linked to the analysis of core–periphery dynamics and ways in which natural and

cultural landscapes affected the rise of powerful hierarchical societies. Complex states can develop by very different processes, and it is a challenge to archaeologists to identify the variables most significant for patterns of cultural development in the archaeological regions of Mesoamerica.

Several theoretical approaches have been applied to issues of political evolution in Mesoamerica. Sanders and Price (1968) presented an influential ecological explanation (see ch. 1). They point out that in highland Mesoamerica, the most hierarchical cultures developed in inter-montane, semi-arid valleys. These valleys were characterized by considerable resource diversity, but the limited agricultural potential of these arid zones may have encouraged the development of intensive agricultural techniques such as canal building. Sanders and Price claimed that more centralized, hierarchical polities evolved in the highlands (compared to the lowlands) because of these factors. Resource diversity encouraged symbiotic relationships between valley cultures and the intensification of interregional economic exchange (Sanders and Price 1968: 190–205). The need for hydraulic agriculture justified the existence of a political elite to oversee the construction and management of these public works (Sanders and Price 1968: 190–205).

Researchers in Oaxaca have presented an alternative approach to sociocultural evolution in this highland valley that emphasizes political forces over ecological factors. Marcus (1976a), for example, pointed to the large number of conquest monuments erected at Monte Alban at the time of its founding as evidence for the importance of power and dominance in the development of this city. Blanton (1978: 106–8) used surface artifact distributions at Monte Alban to argue that a number of polities were united in a type of confederacy at this capital. These researchers have argued consistently that environmental factors, although clearly important to any society, were not the main causal forces generating political evolution in the Valley of Oaxaca (Blanton et al. 1982, 1993; Kowalewski et al. 1989; see Feinman and Nicholas, chapter 10). Sanders and Nichols (1988) have criticized these interpretations by arguing for the importance of the environment and demography, and their article was in turn criticized by the Oaxaca researchers (Marcus 1990).

Political interaction is an important component in the analysis of Mesoamerican cultures. Two scales of interaction have received much attention: interactions within regions and interactions between regions. Interaction is often examined through the distribution of rare and valuable long-distance exchange items within and between regions. Elite members of society often showed off their status by obtaining exotic commodities and publicly exhibiting them as Clark and Blake discuss (chapter 12). High-ranking individuals distributed these items to other prestigious members of society within their community or in neighboring communities in their region. This behavior is exhibited in the limited distribution of rare items such as obsidian blades in elite and ritual contexts in the archaeological record, as Clark (1987) notes for sites in the Formative Mesoamerican lowlands.

Regional interaction can occur among autonomous polities of roughly equivalent size and power in a process identified as "peer polity interaction" by Renfrew (1986). In this model, groups of polities are linked through a common culture and various forms of interaction (both friendly and competitive), yet they maintain their political identity and independence. Behaviors identified with peer polity systems include the following (from Renfrew 1986: 8–10): competitive display in games and costuming at group gatherings; conspicuous consumption of resources by sponsoring public feasts or constructing ostentatious architectural works; ritualized forms of warfare; rapid information exchange and the spread of innovations; and elite gift exchange involving luxury goods and marriage partners. The polities of both the Maya and the Aztecs have been described as engaging in peer polity interaction with each other (Freidel 1986; Smith and Hodge 1994; Demarest, chapter 14).

From the Early Formative period on (Flannery 1968; Clark and Blake, chapter 12), interregional communication fostered a degree of long-distance emulation. In some cases, interregional influence appears to have been limited to the upper tiers of society. Long-distance interaction may have stimulated the development of elites because the possession of exotic objects and ritual knowledge helped to distinguish elites from other members of societies (Flannery 1968; Clark and Blake, chapter 12). A recent alternative view suggests that "sister" cultures may have evolved simultaneously in Formative Mesoamerica, and were in close contact with each other through elite gift exchange (Grove 1989: 9–10; Marcus 1989). The presence of symbols and objects from distant regions at a developing site is not always easily interpreted. What type of "influence" did powerful societies like the Olmec have on societies located hundreds of miles away?

A debate exists regarding the meaning of the appearance of Olmec style motifs on carved monuments or ceramics in regions distant from the Gulf Coast Veracruz Olmec heartland. Some scholars do not interpret the presence of Olmec iconograpy as evidence of direct contact with the Olmec (Grove 1989; Marcus 1989; Flannery and Marcus 1994), while others suggest an Olmec presence in foreign lands (Clark 1997: 228). The degree to which a long-distance influence permeates the utilitarian realm in the styles of domestic utensils may be one useful gauge for measuring the foreign impact on local societies, as Clark suggests (Clark 1991, 1997: 228–9; Clark and Blake 1989). Reilly's article (chapter 18) takes a moderate position with regard to the polarized debate about interregional Olmec influence. Reactions against attributing too much credit to Olmec influence on political evolution in other regions are based on evidence for the maintenance of strong local traditions alongside the appearance of Olmec-style artifacts or motifs (Grove 1989; Marcus 1989). Similar debates have occurred for other Mesoamerican cultures such as the nature of Teotihuacan's influence at Monte

Alban and Tikal (Sanders and Price 1968: 145, 204; Coggins 1979, 1983; Marcus 1976a, 1983; Schele and Freidel 1990).

The Origins of Political Complexity

This section of readings on Mesoamerican political organization begins with an article by Clark and Blake (chapter 12), who have documented one of the earliest complex cultures in Mesoamerica along the Socunusco Pacific coastal plain region. Their research identifies the origins of some political strategies observed on a larger scale by later complex polities. In the Soconusco, the development of village agriculturalists by 1800 BC was followed shortly by the development of rank societies by 1650 BC.

The archaeological record at Clark and Blake's site of Paso de la Amada shows a local developmental sequence of accelerating complexity stimulated by the acquisition of long-distance luxury objects and the adoption of an exquisite ceramic technology that was restricted to elite and ritual use. This Early Formative quest for prestige was fostered by a rich agricultural environment with the capacity for surplus production and the carrying capacity to support increasing population levels (Clark and Blake, chapter 12). These authors acknowledge the role of ecological factors in a social system that allowed for conspicuous display, competitive generosity, and other aggrandizing behavior leading to social inequalities. The early leaders appear to have depicted themselves in shamanistic postures, as observed by certain figurines which exhibit distorted facial characteristics and head mirrors (Clark 1991). Mesoamerican leaders, particularly those in lowlands societies, from this point forward often depicted themselves as intermediaries with the supernatural realm, imbued with special ritual skills enabling them to intercede on behalf of the living (Reilly 1989; Graham 1998; Freidel and Schele, chapter 20).

Lowland States

The fact that lowland complex societies such as the Olmec, Pacific coastal piedmont polities (such as Izapa), and the Maya share fundamental aspects of organization that are more similar to each other than to highland societies points to the influence of geography on the evolution of political structure. The terrain of the lowlands has been described as open or "unbounded" in comparison to the highlands (Blanton et al. 1993: 163). The Maya lowlands, for example, is an area 40 to 100 times the size of the largest highland valley polities (Blanton et al. 1993: 163). It exhibits many ecological niches in which adequate water and cultivable land can support agricultural villages. Scholars have correlated this pattern with the dispersed, non-centralized pattern of Maya settlement (Sanders and Price 1968: 134, 145; Freidel 1981). It has been further suggested that Classic-period Maya society lacked strongly differentiated social divisions (Sanders and Price 1968: 142) due to the existence of "flat" or open networks with little hierarchical development across the landscape (Blanton et al. 1993: 167). A mosaic of diverse resources across this region encouraged the development of prosperous localized industries and intercommunity and regional exchange networks (Hester and Shafer 1994; Graham 1994; Piña Chán 1978; Shafer and Hester, chapter 6; Rice, chapter 7; McAnany, chapter 23).

The political organization of Olmec society and Classic-period Maya society was centered on the institution of divine rulership. Charismatic rulers portrayed themselves in elaborate costumes and claimed to be divine intermediaries with the supernatural realm (see part IV of this reader: Reilly, chapter 18; Freidel and Schele, chapter 20). The themes of lowland public monuments and the political strategies of representation which they represent varied with the charisma and agenda of individual leaders. This individualizing form of legitimization of political power may have been responsible for the creation of a large number of monuments and a well-developed writing and calendric system (Schele and Miller 1986; Schele and Freidel 1990). A great number of inscribed monuments and murals are concerned with ensuring inheritance of the throne, a position which appears to have been vulnerable to challenge by powerful factions of society (Schele and Freidel 1990).

Demarest (chapter 14) discusses the fundamental instability of Maya kingdoms and suggests that this attribute is responsible for much of the conspicuous display of power, wealth, and divinity by Maya kings. Faced with continual threats to their rights to rule, Maya kings may have had more need for historical records and artistic programs advocating powerful and protective holy lords. The dynamics of competition were pronounced not only among factions within individual polities, but between polities as well. Escalation of competition appears to have culminated in increasing conflict and warfare among polities throughout the Classic period (Schele and Miller 1986; Schele and Freidel 1990; Demarest et al. 1997). As Mathews points out in chapter 13, the number of powerful polities increased over time during the Classic period, and this pattern reflects the escalating competitive environment of the southern Maya lowlands at this time.

The manner in which Classic-period Maya polities went through episodes of fission and fusion has been described as a property of segmentary lineage political organization (Dunham et al. 1989). Segmentary lineage dynamics have been identified in the ethnohistorical and archaeological records of the highland Postclassic Quiche Maya (Carmack 1981; Fox 1987). These systems were characterized by the joint rule or rotating rule of powerful allied lineage groups linked to territorial units. These lineage groups were autonomous yet had the capacity to centralize for military defense or expansive conquest. This political formation was based upon coalitions of kin groups, and thus it differs from traditionally defined state societies which are said to transcend kin-based affiliations. For this reason, some scholars do not feel the segmentary lineage model is appropriate for the analysis of Maya or other regional states (Marcus and Feinman 1998: 17–18). Certainly, within the

Classic period some polities were too large and too centralized to have depended solely on kin networks for their development, organization, and administration (Chase and Chase 1997). Nevertheless, from at least the Early Classic period onward, the Maya archaeological record reflects ongoing dynamic processes of both centralization and segmentation which were dependent on variables such as environmental capacity, population growth, economic security, and political stability (Freidel 1983; de Montmollin 1989). Part of these dynamics may reflect the continual conflict and negotiation of kin-based power versus kingship institutions in various sub-regions of the lowlands, as McAnany (chapter 23) suggests.

Unlike the Classic-period highland polities described below, the Maya lowlands were not centralized under a single political capital (Mathews, chapter 13). As Mathews shows, numerous relatively independent city states existed across the landscape. Each controlled supporting populations which occupied surrounding territories. The extent of these territories has been estimated by drawing thiessen polygon boundary lines midway between primary centers (Hammond 1974; Marcus 1993; Mathews, chapter 13). Supporting populations inhabited settlements of varying sizes, including smaller centers, villages, and hamlets (Adams and Smith 1981; Willey and Mathews 1991). Some of these polities were identified in Classic-period inscriptions by a particular "emblem glyph" attached to the end of ruler's titles (Marcus 1976b; Mathews, chapter 13). Mathews's article in this section provides a review of interpretations based on emblem glyph analysis, and he integrates this hieroglyphic information with settlement data from other large centers which lack emblem glyphs. He argues for the presence of a number of relatively autonomous small polities across the Classic-period landscape.

Others have claimed that these "emblem glyph polities" represent an upper tier of more powerful city-states. This model has been used to argue for the existence of larger regional states in four primary divisions of lowland Maya society (Marcus 1976b) or seven regional states as proposed by Adams (1986). Recent decipherment of glyphic texts suggests that larger alliance networks of city-states were formed at times during the Classic period (Martin and Grube 1995). Two of the largest Maya capitals which controlled territories and subsidiary centers – Tikal and Calakmul – appear to have been fierce rivals (Martin and Grube 1995). Evidence for their regional influence is found in acts of war carried out by smaller sites under their auspices, as well as other alliance-building activities such as royal visits, ritual participation, and intermarriage (Schele and Freidel 1990; Martin and Grube 1995).

Because this argument is relatively new, others reserve judgment in interpreting the organization of Maya polities into larger entities (Mathews, chapter 13). It is not currently known to what extent alliances of macropolities may have endured inbetween conquest and alliance events occasionally recorded in hieroglyphic texts. Were the economies of allied polities also linked? Geographic comparisons of ceramic types exhibit diverse ceramic inventories that suggest a fragmented political landscape comprised of relatively autonomous polities existed during the Classic period (Willey, Culbert, and Adams 1967: 310; Smith and Gifford 1965: 533). Further work is needed to see if allied polities such as those proposed by Martin and Grube (1995) were linked economically beyond the level of elite gift-giving.

The competing polities of Classic-period Maya society stand in contrast to contemporary highland polities of Monte Alban and Teotihuacan which were centralized under single powerful capitals. According to recent models of Mesoamerican political economy proposed by Blanton et al. (1996), Classic Maya society represents a "network" type of political strategy which was based on the tenuous success of persuasive leadership and the ability to maintain control over networks of exchange that facilitated the flow of prestige items essential to the maintenance of the upper tier of elites (Blanton et al. 1996). This kind of political system emphasizes differences in status among individual members of society, but does not maintain centralized control of the basic daily economy (Blanton et al. 1996). It is characterized by "individualizing" political themes that glorified the feats of historical personages.

In the Postclassic period, relatively autonomous regional polities formed long-distance alliances between the northern and southern Maya lowlands (Roys 1957; Schele et al. 1998). A more mercantile focus characterizes this period and provided a new priority for the investment of social energies (Rathje 1975; Sabloff and Rathje 1975). The northern lowlands were sequentially dominated by the centers of Chichen Itza and Mayapan (Andrews 1993), although ceramic evidence suggests that pan-lowlands north–south integration was greater after the rise of Mayapan (Masson in press). The institution of divine kingship appears to have ended by the end of the ninth century, when it was replaced by institutions emphasizing group rule, such as *multepal* (Roys 1957; Schele and Freidel 1990). Confederations of allied lineage groups and other factions appear to have divided aspects of governance through the definition of many specialized roles (Roys 1957). Although regional lords (*halach uinics*) were known in some polities, they were not the subject of monumental glorification in the Classic-period sense. Segmentary lineage organization has been suggested for the Maya highlands during the Postclassic period (Carmack 1981; Fox 1987), and these principles may have been in effect for Late Postclassic lowland polities as well (Roys 1957: 4).

Blanton et al. (1996) suggest that Postclassic Maya society in northern Yucatan was fundamentally different from that of the Classic period. These authors characterize it as a "corporate" type of political formation that emphasizes group-oriented public space, rulership that does not glorify individuals, decreased social differences in terms of material possessions of "prestige" items, and a more centralized utilitarian economy (Blanton et al. 1996). This form of organization was also more typical of many Classic- and Postclassic-period highland polities.

Highland States

The huge Classic-period city of Teotihuacan was the capital of a small empire in the central Mexican highlands, and within this domain it maintained tight military and political control over its subject peoples (Millon 1988). It may seem surprising, therefore, that the institution of rulership is almost invisible at this powerful urban center. Unlike the Classic Maya, there is little evidence for the glorification of historical individuals in the art of Teotihuacan (Cowgill, chapter 15). This polity has been described as "acephalous," with a corporate or bureaucratic-type political structure that communicated power through other group-maintaining artistic themes (Pasztory 1997). Elite lineages may have provided an important balance of power in this society, suggested in recent interpretations of Teotihuacan art and architecture (Headrick 1999). Imagery of warfare is explicit at Teotihuacan (Cabrera et al. 1991; Cowgill chapter 15) as is creation mythology (Pasztory 1997). Such themes and others attest to the power of the Teotihuacan state and the existence of a series of savvy political programs of art which reinforced such power, despite the low profile of the political agents themselves.

The political art of the Classic-period Zapotec city of Monte Alban in Oaxaca preserves some evidence of the recorded deeds of historical individuals. For example, stelae recovered from the South Platform (Caso 1928) appear to depict a captive-taking event presided over by a ruler, 12F (Marcus 1976a). Earlier in this site's history, a program of wall slabs depicting sacrificed victims and warfare appear to commemorate early important events in the site's establishment as a political capital (Marcus 1976a; Scott 1978). Other historical individuals were portrayed in the murals and monuments of Monte Alban (Caso 1965).

Although these few records do attest to the historical glorification of powerful leaders at several points in Monte Alban's history, the number of monuments is relatively small compared to many Maya centers. Rulers are most often portrayed with feline features that emphasize their political power rather than their individual identity (Marcus 1976a; Masson and Orr 1998). The degree of historical portrayal at Monte Alban falls between the scarcely visible rulership of Teotihuacan and the highly conspicuous and abundant portrayal of individual rulership of the Maya area (Masson and Orr 1998). Ethnohistoric analogy suggests that other political units, such as councils of priests, may have held important roles in the governance of Monte Alban (Whitecotton 1977: 147), perhaps in a manner not unlike the role of the four priests described by Pohl (chapter 17). The facelessness of this sort of corporate polity is emphasized in Blanton et al. (1996). Societies with corporate forms of organization appear to have been relatively more politically stable and are thought to have exhibited a centralized control of the daily economy (Blanton et al. 1996).

The highly centralized early states of highland Mesoamerica declined after AD 700 in a period referred to in some regions as the Epiclassic period. In chapter 16, Hirth provides a perspective on Epiclassic society at the emergent center of Xochicalco. Competition for the control of trade during this period resulted in considerable interpolity conflict and the establishment of formal military guilds which may have been actively involved in governance. This pattern is observed in many regions of the highlands, and military societies with far-flung trading ties are indicated in the art and archaeology of polities such as Cacaxtla, Tula, Chichen Itza, and others (Diehl and Berlo 1989).

The Epiclassic societal transformations paved the way for new forms of political organization observed in Postclassic Mesoamerica. The Mixtec codices portray a fascinating record of dynamic interactions among powerful factions of one Postclassic society. These factions included important lineage heads, war leaders, and priests (Byland and Pohl 1994; Pohl 1994). Pohl (chapter 17) examines the articulation of religious institutions such as the "Four Priests" with political and military rulers. This institution served as a mechanism for the direct involvement of powerful lineage heads in the politics of Mixtec society and reveals how political power was balanced by other important social groups. It is probable that this balance of power between lineage heads, priests, and political leaders is of great antiquity among Mesoamerican societies (Headrick 1999; Schele and Freidel 1990; McAnany 1995: 144–56; Cowgill, chapter 15), and similar patterns are observed elsewhere in Mesoamerica (Landa 1941; Roys 1957; Fox 1987).

The Aztecs of Late Postclassic central Mexico exhibited considerable complexity in their political organization. Although many accounts of this civilization stress Aztec imperialism with its conquering armies and the public sacrifice of enemy prisoners, the most important Aztec political unit was the city-state (Hodge 1997, 1998; Smith 1996; Smith and Hodge 1994). Aztec city-states were small polities consisting of a central town with a palace, pyramid, ballcourt, and market, surrounded by farmland and small villages. Each city-state was ruled by a hereditary king called a *tlatoani* who was selected by a council of high lords from among blood relatives of the former king. Renfrew's model of peer polity interaction fits the Aztec city-states well: they were linked by a common language and culture but fragmented politically, and city-states engaged in interactions both friendly (trade, elite gift-giving, and visiting) and antagonistic (warfare and conquest). Each Aztec city-state kept pictorial histories that recounted the past glories of the dynasty and the peoples of the polity. Although not as detailed as the Mixtec codices described by Pohl (chapter 17), these Aztec historical codices provide crucial insights into political history and processes (Boone 1992). Most Aztec city-states were established in the twelfth century AD. By the

fourteenth century, some polities were expanding their control by conquering neighbors and forcing them to pay tribute. The basic principle was one of indirect control; so long as the conquered city-state paid the tribute, their king and government were left intact by the dominant king. This produced a complex political landscape of numerous dynasties of varying power and renown. By the mid-fifteenth century, one Aztec city-state – Tenochtitlan, home of the Mexica ethnic group – managed to achieve a level of power and control above all others. The kings of Tenochtitlan conquered the city-states of the Basin of Mexico and then embarked on a program of conquest that would lead them as far south as the Maya area of southern Mexico (Berdan et al. 1996; Hassig 1985; Smith 1996).

The Aztec empire, as this expansionistic polity based at Tenochtitlan is known, followed the basic patterns of indirect control mentioned above. As long as they continued to pay their tribute, local kings in conquered areas were left in power. Thus city-states continued to function even though they were incorporated into the Aztec empire (Smith and Berdan 1992), and in fact these city-states kept their integrity (but not all of their activities) long after the Spanish conquest as important units of regional social organization for native peoples (Lockhart 1992). Tribute from the far-flung imperial provinces was recorded in pictorial lists, of which the early colonial Codex Mendoza (Berdan and Anawalt 1997) is a detailed copy. Vast amounts of tribute flowed into Tenochtitlan, and the city rapidly grew into the largest urban center in the ancient New World. Its rulers rebuilt the city in the image of the great ancient imperial capitals Teotihuacan and Tula and commissioned numerous monumental sculptures that proclaimed the legitimacy of their rule over Mesoamerica; the well-known stone known (incorrectly) as the "Aztec calendar stone" is an example of these propagandistic public stone monuments.

Aztec rulers drew on ancient Mesoamerican principles of kingship and political ideology, but they also devised new practices and institutions to accommodate their dynamic political setting. Unfortunately, almost all of our information on rulership and other political institutions comes from Tenochtitlan, making it difficult to know how similar or different the imperial capital was from the smaller and more typical city-states under the indirect control of Tenochtitlan. The kings of Tenochtitlan expended considerable effort in glorifying their empire through urban planning and public monuments. Rulers of individual city-states glorified their own rule and accomplishments in the painted historical codices, but they did not portray their images on stone sculptures. Thus the Aztec political system combined elements of both the lowland and highland Mesoamerican patterns.

Although the Aztec empire was highly successful in conquering regions to the south, it came up against a formidable rival in the Tarascan empire based in the city of Tzintzuntzan to the west of Tenochtitlan (Pollard 1993). Neither of these powerful empires was able to conquer the other, and they set up a fortified border with an empty area between lines of fortresses. The decisive blow to the Aztecs came when Hernando Cortés landed in Mexico in 1519. Unable to comprehend the nature of the invading Spaniards, king Motecuhzoma of Tenochtitlan wavered in his response to them, leading ultimately to the defeat of Tenochtitlan in 1521 after long battles with Spanish armies and epidemic diseases. Students should think about the similarities and differences among the polities described in these articles: was there a basic underlying Mesoamerican form of political organization, or was there too much variation to suggest such a common pattern?

REFERENCES

Adams, Richard E. W. 1986. Rio Azul. *National Geographic* 169: 420–51.

Adams, Richard E. W. and Woodruff P. Smith. 1981. Feudal Models for Classic Maya Settlements. In *Lowland Maya Settlement Patterns*, edited by Wendy Ashmore, pp. 335–49. University of New Mexico Press, Albuquerque.

Andrews, Anthony. 1993. Late Postclassic Lowland Maya Archaeology. *Journal of World Prehistory* 7: 35–69.

Berdan, Frances R. and Patricia Reiff Anawalt. 1997. *The Essential Codex Mendoza*. University of California Press, Berkeley.

Berdan, Frances F., Richard E. Blanton, Elizabeth H. Boone, Mary G. Hodge, Michael E. Smith, and Emily Umberger. 1996. *Aztec Imperial Strategies*. Dumbarton Oaks, Washington, DC.

Blanton, Richard E. 1978. *Monte Alban: Settlement Patterns at the Ancient Zapotec Capital*. Academic Press, New York.

——1983. The Foundation of Monte Alban. In *The Cloud People: Divergent Evolution of the Zapotec and Mixtec Civilizations*, edited by Kent V. Flannery and Joyce Marcus, pp. 83–6. Academic Press, New York.

Blanton, Richard E. and Gary M. Feinman. 1984. The Mesoamerican World System. *American Anthropologist* 86: 673–82.

Blanton, Richard E., Gary M. Feinman, Stephen A. Kowalewski, and Peter N. Peregrine. 1996. A Dual-Processual Theory for the Evolution of Mesoamerican Civilization. *Current Anthropology* 37: 1–14.

Blanton, Richard E., Stephen A. Kowalewski, Gary M. Feinman, and Jill Appel. 1982. *Monte Alban's Hinterland, Part I: Prehispanic Settlement Patterns of the Central and Southern Parts of the Valley of Oaxaca, Mexico*. Memoirs 15. Museum of Anthropology, University of Michigan, Ann Arbor.

Blanton, Richard E., Stephen A. Kowalewski, Gary M. Feinman, and Laura M. Finsten. 1993. *Ancient Mesoamerica: A Comparison of Change in Three Regions*. Cambridge University Press, Cambridge.

Boone, Elizabeth H. 1992. Pictorial Codices of Ancient Mexico. In *The Ancient Americas: Art from Sacred Landscapes*, edited by Richard F. Townsend, pp. 196–209. The Art Institute of Chicago, Chicago.

Byland, Bruce and John M. D. Pohl. 1994. *In the Realm of 8 Deer: The Archaeology of the Mixtec Codices*. University of Oklahoma Press, Norman.

Cabrera Castro, Ruben, Saburo Sugiyama, and George L. Cowgill. 1991. The Templo de Quetzalcoatl Project at Teotihuacan. *Ancient Mesoamerica* 2: 77–92.

Carmack, Robert M. 1981. *The Quiche Mayas of Utatlan*. University of Oklahoma Press, Norman.

——1996. Mesoamerica at Spanish Contact. In *The Legacy of Mesoamerica: History and Culture of a Native American Civilization*, edited by

Robert M. Carmack, Janine Gasco, and Gary H. Gossen, pp. 80–121. Prentice Hall, Englewood Cliffs.

Carmack, Robert M., Janine Gasco, and Gary H. Gossen. 1996. *The Legacy of Mesoamerica: History and Culture of a Native American Civilization*. Prentice Hall, Englewood Cliffs.

Caso, Alfonso. 1928. *Las Estelas Zapotecas*. Secretaria de Educación Pública. Talleres Gráficos de la Nación, Mexico City.

—— 1965. Zapotec Writing and Calendar. In *Archaeology of Southern Mesoamerica*, part 2, edited by Gordon R. Willey, pp. 931–47. Handbook of Middle American Indians, vol. 3. University of Texas Press, Austin.

Chase, Arlen F. and Diane Z. Chase. 1997. More Kin than King: Centralized Political Organization Among the Late Classic Maya. *Current Anthropology* 37: 803–10.

Clark, John E. 1987. Politics, Prismatic Blades, and Mesoamerican Civilization. In *The Organization of Core Technology*, edited by J. K. Johnson and C. A. Morrow, pp. 259–84. Westview Press, Boulder.

—— 1991. The Beginnings of Mesoamerica: Apologia for the Soconusco Early Formative. In *The Formation of Complex Society in Southeastern Mesoamerica*, edited by William R. Fowler, pp. 13–26. CRC Press, Boca Raton.

—— 1997. The Arts of Government in Early Mesoamerica. *Annual Review of Anthropology* 26: 211–34.

Clark, John E. and Michael Blake. 1989. El Origen de la Civilización en Mesoamérica: Los Olmecas y Mokaya del Soconusco de Chiapas, México. In *El Preclásico o Formativo: Avances y Perspectivas*, edited by M. Carmona Macias, pp. 385–403. Museo Nacional de Antropología e Historia, Mexico City.

Coe, Michael D. and Richard A. Diehl. 1980. *In the Land of the Olmec, Volume II: The People of the River*. University of Texas Press, Austin.

Coggins, Clemency. 1979. A New Order and the Role of the Calendar: Some Characteristics of the Middle Classic Period at Tikal. In *Maya Archaeology and Ethnohistory*, edited by Norman Hammond and Gordon R. Willey, pp. 38–50. University of Texas Press, Austin.

—— 1983. An Instrument of Expansion: Monte Alban, Teotihuacan, and Tikal. In *Highland–Lowland Interaction in Mesoamerica: Interdisciplinary Approaches*, edited by Arthur G. Miller, pp. 49–68. Dumbarton Oaks, Washington, DC.

Dahlin, Bruce Harrison. 1976. An Anthropologist Looks at the Pyramids: A Late Classic Revitalization Movement at Tikal, Guatemala. Ph.D. dissertation, Temple University.

Davies, Nigel. 1973. *The Aztecs: A History*. University of Oklahoma Press, Norman.

de Montmollin, Olivier. 1989. *The Archaeology of Political Structure: Settlement Analysis in a Classic Maya Polity*. Cambridge University Press, Cambridge.

Demarest, Arthur A., Matt O'Mansky, Claudia Wolley, Dirk Van Tuerenhout, Takeshi Inomata, Joel Palka, and Hector Escobedo. 1997. Classic Maya Defensive Systems and Warfare in the Petexbatun Region. *Ancient Mesoamerica* 8: 229–53.

Diehl, Richard A. and Janet Catherine Berlo (eds). 1989. *Mesoamerica After the Decline of Teotihuacan AD 700–900*. Dumbarton Oaks, Washington, DC.

Drennan, Robert. 1991. Pre-Hispanic Chiefdom Trajectories in Mesoamerica, Central America, and Northern South America. In *Chiefdoms: Power, Economy, and Ideology*, edited by Timothy K. Earle, pp. 263–87. Cambridge University Press, New York.

Dunham, Peter S., Thomas R. Jameson, and Richard M. Leventhal. 1989. Secondary Development and Settlement Economics: The Classic Maya of Southern Belize. *Research in Economic Anthropology*, Supplement 4: 255–92.

Feinman, Gary M. 1990. At the Margins of the Monte Alban State: Settlement Patterns in the Ejutla Valley, Oaxaca, Mexico. *Latin American Antiquity* 1: 216–46.

—— 1991. Demography, Surplus, and Equality: Early Political Formations in Highland Mesoamerica. In *Chiefdoms: Power, Economy, and Ideology*, edited by Timothy K. Earle, pp. 229–62. Cambridge University Press, New York.

Feinman, Gary M. and Jill Neitzel. 1984. Too Many Types: An Overview of Sedentary Prestate Societies in the Americas. *Advances in Archaeological Method and Theory* 7: 39–102.

Flannery, Kent V. 1968. The Olmec and the Valley of Oaxaca: A Model for Inter-Regional Interaction in Formative Times. In *Dumbarton Oaks Conference on the Olmec*, edited by Elizabeth P. Benson, pp. 129–35. Dumbarton Oaks, Washington, DC.

Flannery, Kent V. (ed.). 1976. *The Early Mesoamerican Village*. Academic Press, New York.

Flannery, Kent V. and Joyce Marcus. 1994. *Early Formative Pottery of the Valley of Oaxaca, Mexico*. Memoirs of the Museum of Anthropology, University of Michigan No. 27, Ann Arbor.

Fox, John W. 1987. *Late Postclassic State Formation*. Cambridge University Press, Cambridge.

Freid, Morton H. 1967. *The Evolution of a Political Society: An Essay in Political Anthropology*. Random House, New York.

Freidel, David A. 1981. The Political Economics of Residential Dispersion Among the Lowland Maya. In *Lowland Maya Settlement Patterns*, edited by Wendy Ashmore, pp. 371–85. University of New Mexico Press, Albuquerque.

—— 1983. Political Systems in Lowland Yucatan: Dynamics and Structure in Maya Settlement. In *Prehistoric Settlement Patterns: Essays in Honor of Gordon R. Willey*, edited by Evon Z. Vogt and Richard M. Leventhal, pp. 375–86. University of New Mexico Press, Albuquerque.

—— 1985. New Light on a Dark Age: A Summary of Major Themes. In *The Lowland Maya Postclassic*, edited by Arlen F. Chase and Prudence M. Rice, pp. 285–310. University of Texas Press, Austin.

—— 1986. Maya Warfare: An Example of Peer Polity Interaction. In *Peer Polity Interaction and Socio-Political Change*, edited by Colin Renfrew and John F. Cherry, pp. 93–108. Cambridge University Press, New York.

Graham, Elizabeth. 1994. *The Highlands of the Lowlands: Environment and Archaeology in the Stann Creek District, Belize, Central America*. Monographs in World Prehistory No. 19, Prehistory Press, Madison.

Graham, Mark Miller. 1998. The Iconography of Rulership in Ancient West Mexico. In *Ancient West Mexico: Art and Archaeology of the Unknown Past*, edited by Richard F. Townsend, pp. 191–203. Thames and Hudson, New York.

Grove, David C. 1989. Olmec: What's in a Name? In *Regional Perspectives on the Olmec*, edited by Robert J. Sharer and David C. Grove, pp. 8–14. Cambridge University Press, New York.

Hammond, Norman. 1974. The Distribution of Late Classic Maya Major Ceremonial Centres in the Central Area. In *Mesoamerican Archaeology: New Approaches*, edited by Norman Hammond, pp. 313–34. University of Texas Press, Austin.

Hassig, Ross. 1985. *Trade, Tribute, and Transportation: The Sixteenth Century Political Economy of the Valley of Mexico*. University of Oklahoma Press, Norman.

Headrick, Annabeth. 1999. The Avenue of the Dead at Teotihuacan: It Really Was. *Ancient Mesoamerica* 10: 69–86.

Hester, Thomas R. and Harry J. Shafer. 1994. The Ancient Maya Craft Community at Colha, Belize, and its External Relationships. In *Archaeological Views from the Countryside: Village Communities in Early Complex Societies*, edited by Glenn M. Schwartz and Stephen E. Falconer, pp. 48–63. Smithsonian Institution Press, Washington, DC.

Hodge, Mary G. 1997. When is a City-State? Archaeological Measures of Aztec City-States and Aztec City-State Systems. In *The Archaeology of City-States: Cross Cultural Approaches*, edited by Deborah L. Nichols and Thomas H. Charlton, pp. 209–28. Smithsonian Institution Press, Washington, DC.

—— 1998. Archaeological Views of Aztec Culture. *Journal of Archaeological Research* 6: 197–238.

Joyce, Arthur A. 1993. Interregional Interaction and Social Development on the Oaxaca Coast. *Ancient Mesoamerica* 4: 67–84.

Joyce, Rosemary A. 1991. *Cerro Palenque: Power and Identity on the Maya Periphery*. University of Texas Press, Austin.

Kowalewski, Stephen A., Gary M. Feinman, Laura Finsten, Richard E. Blanton, and Linda M. Nicholas. 1989. *Monte Alban's Hinterland, Part II: The Prehispanic Settlement Patterns in Tlacolula, Etla, and Ocotlan, the Valley of Oaxaca, Mexico*. Memoirs 23. Museum of Anthropology, University of Michigan, Ann Arbor.

Landa, Friar Diego de. 1941. *Landa's Relaciones de las Cosas de Yucatan*. Translated by Alfred Tozzer. Papers of the Peabody Museum of Archaeology and Ethnology 18. Harvard University Press, Cambridge.

Leach, Edmund R. 1964. *Political Systems of Highland Burma*. London School of Economics Monographs on Social Anthropology No. 44. The Athlone Press, London.

Lockhart, James. 1992. *The Nahuas After the Conquest: A Social and Cultural History of the Indians of Central Mexico, Sixteenth Through Eighteenth Centuries*. Stanford University Press, Stanford.

Marcus, Joyce. 1976a. The Iconography of Militarism at Monte Alban and Neighboring Sites in the Valley of Oaxaca. In *The Origins of Religious Art and Iconography in Preclassic Mesoamerica*, edited by H. B. Nicholson, pp. 123–39. University of California at Los Angeles, Latin American Center, Los Angeles.

—— 1976. *Emblem and State in the Classic Maya Lowlands: An Epigraphic Approach to*

Territorial Organization. Dumbarton Oaks, Washington, DC.

—— 1983. Teotihuacan Visitors on Monte Alban Monuments and Murals. In *The Cloud People: Divergent Evolution of the Zapotec and Mixtec Civilizations*, edited by Kent V. Flannery and Joyce Marcus, pp. 175–80. Academic Press, New York.

—— 1989. Zapotec Chiefdoms and the Nature of Formative Religions. In *Regional Perspectives on the Olmec*, edited by Robert J. Sharer and David C. Grove, pp. 148–97. Cambridge University Press, New York.

—— 1990. *Debating Oaxaca Archaeology*. Anthropological Papers, vol. 84. Museum of Anthropology, University of Michigan, Ann Arbor.

—— 1993. Ancient Maya Political Organization. In *Lowland Maya Civilization in the Eighth Century AD*, edited by Jeremy A. Sabloff and John S. Henderson, pp. 111–84. Dumbarton Oaks, Washington, DC.

Marcus, Joyce and Gary M. Feinman. 1998. Introduction. In *Archaic States*, edited by Gary M. Feinman and Joyce Marcus, pp. 3–14. School of American Research Press, Santa Fe.

Martin, Simon and Nikolai Grube. 1995. Maya Superstates. *Archaeology* 48(3): 41–6.

Masson, Marilyn A. In press. In the Realm of Nachan Kan: Postclassic Maya Archaeology at Laguna de On, Belize. Book manuscript in review, Mesoamerican Worlds Series, University of Colorado Press, Boulder.

Masson, Marilyn A. and Heather Orr. 1998. The Writing on the Wall: Political Representation and Sacred Geography at Monte Alban. In *The Sowing and the Dawning: Termination, Dedication, and Transformation in the Archaeological and Ethnographic Record of Mesoamerica*, edited by Shirley Boteler Mock, pp. 165–76. University of New Mexico Press, Albuquerque.

McAnany, Patricia A. 1989. Economic Foundations of Prehistoric Maya Society: Paradigms and Concepts. In *Prehistoric Maya Economies of Belize*, edited by Patricia A. McAnany and Barry L. Isaac, pp. 347–72. Research in Economic Anthropology, Supplement 4, JAI Press, Greenwich.

—— 1995. *Living with the Ancestors: Kinship and Kingship in Ancient Maya Society*. University of Texas Press, Austin.

McGuire, Randall H. 1983. Breaking Down Cultural Complexity: Inequality and Heterogeneity. *Advances in Archaeological Method and Theory* 6: 91–142.

Millon, René. 1988. The Last Years of Teotihuacan Dominance. In *The Collapse of Ancient States and Civilizations*, edited by Norman Yoffee and George L. Cowgill, pp. 102–64. University of Arizona Press, Tucson.

Pasztory, Esther. 1993. An Image is Worth a Thousand Words: Teotihuacan and the Meanings of Style in Classic Mesoamerica. In *Latin American Horizons*, edited by Don S. Rice, pp. 113–45. Dumbarton Oaks, Washington, DC.

—— 1997. *Teotihuacan: An Experiment in Living*. University of Oklahoma Press, Norman.

Paynter, Robert. 1989. The Archaeology of Equality and Inequality. *Annual Review of Anthropology* 18: 369–99.

Piña Chán, Román. 1978. Commerce in the Yucatec Peninsula: The Conquest and Colonial Period. In *Mesoamerican Communication Routes and Culture Contacts*, edited by T. A. Lee and C. Navarrete, pp. 37–48. Papers of the New World Archaeological Foundation 40. Brigham Young University, Provo.

Pohl, John M. D. 1994. *The Politics of Symbolism in the Mixtec Codices*. Vanderbilt University Publications in Anthropology No. 46, Nashville.

Pollard, Helen P. 1993. *Tariacuri's Legacy: The Prehispanic Tarascan State*. University of Oklahoma Press, Norman.

—— 1997. Recent Research in West Mexican Archaeology. *Journal of Archaeological Research* 5: 345–84.

Rathje, William R. 1972. Praise the Gods and Pass the Metates: A Hypothesis of the Development of Lowland Rainforest Civilizations in Mesoamerica. In *Contemporary Archaeology: A Guide to Theory and Contributions*, edited by Mark P. Leone, pp. 365–92. Southern Illinois University Press, Carbondale.

—— 1975. The Last Tango in Mayapan: A Tentative Trajectory of Production-Distribution Systems. In *Ancient Civilization and Trade*, edited by J. A. Sabloff and C. C. Lamberg-Karlovsky, pp. 409–48. University of New Mexico Press, Albuquerque.

Redmond, Elsa M. 1983. *A Fuego y Sangre: Early Zapotec Imperialism in the Cuicatlan Canada*. Museum of Anthropology, University of Michigan, Memoirs No. 16, Ann Arbor.

Reilly, F. Kent III. 1989. The Shaman in Transformation Pose: A Study of the Theme of Rulership in Olmec Art. *The Record* 48: 4–21.

Renfrew, Colin. 1986. Introduction: Peer Polity Interaction and Socio-Political Change. In *Peer Polity Interaction and Socio-Political Change*, edited by Colin Renfrew and John F. Cherry, pp. 1–18. Cambridge University Press, New York.

Roys, Ralph L. 1957. *The Political Geography of the Yucatan Maya*. Carnegie Institute of Washington Publication 613. Washington, DC.

Sabloff, Jeremy A. and William L. Rathje. 1975. The Rise of a Maya Merchant Class. *Scientific American* 233: 72–82.

Sanders, William T. and Deborah L. Nichols. 1988. Ecological Theory and Cultural Evolution in the Valley of Oaxaca. *Current Anthropology* 29: 33–80.

Sanders, William T., Jeffrey R. Parsons, and Robert S. Santley. 1979. *The Basin of Mexico: Ecological Processes in the Evolution of a Civilization*. Academic Press, New York.

Sanders, William T. and Barbara J. Price. 1968. *Mesoamerica: The Evolution of a Civilization*. Random House, New York.

Scott, John F. 1978. *The Danzantes of Monte Alban*, vols 1 and 2. Studies in Precolumbian Art and Archaeology No. 19. Dumbarton Oaks, Washington, DC.

Schele, Linda and David Freidel. 1990. *A Forest of Kings: The Untold Story of the Ancient Maya*. William Morrow, New York.

Schele, Linda, Nikolai Grube, and Erik Boot. 1998. Some Suggestions on the K'atun Prophecies in the Books of the Chilam Balam in Light of Classic-Period History. In *Memorias del Tercer Congreso Internacional de Mayistas. Instituto de Investigaciones Filológicas*, Centro de Estudios Mayas, Universidad Nacional Autónoma de México, Mexico City.

Schele, Linda and Mary Ellen Miller. 1986. *The Blood of Kings: Dynasty and Ritual in Maya Art*. George Braziller, New York, in association with the Kimbell Art Museum, Fort Worth.

Service, Elman R. 1962. *Primitive Social Organization: An Evolutionary Perspective*. Random House, New York.

Smith, Michael E. 1996. *The Aztecs*. Blackwell, Oxford.

Smith, Michael E. and Frances F. Berdan. 1992. Archaeology and the Aztec Empire. *World Archaeology* 23: 353–67.

Smith, Michael E. and Mary G. Hodge. 1994. An Introduction to Late Postclassic Economies and Polities. In *Economies and Polities in the Aztec Realm*, edited by Mary G. Hodge and Michael E. Smith, pp. 1–42. Institute for Mesoamerican Studies, Albany.

Smith, Robert E. and James C. Gifford. 1965. Pottery of the Maya Lowlands. In *Archaeology of Southern Mesoamerica*, part 1, edited by Gordon R. Willey, pp. 498–543. Handbook of Middle American Indians, vol. 2. University of Texas Press, Austin.

Townsend, Richard F. (ed.). 1998. *Ancient West Mexico: Art and Archaeology of the Unknown Past*. Thames and Hudson, New York.

Whitecotton, Joseph W. 1977. *The Zapotecs: Princes, Priests, and Peasants*. University of Oklahoma Press, Norman.

Willey, Gordon R., T. Patrick Culbert, and Richard E. W. Adams. 1967. Maya Lowlands Ceramics: A Report from the 1965 Guatemala City Conference. *American Antiquity* 32: 289–315.

Willey, Gordon R. and Peter Mathews. 1991. Prehistoric Polities of the Pasion Region: Hieroglyphic Texts and their Archaeological Settings. In *Classic Maya Political History: Hieroglyphs and Archaeological Evidence*, edited by T. Patrick Culbert, pp. 30–72. Cambridge University Press, New York.

Willey, Gordon R. and Jeremy A. Sabloff. 1993. *A History of Mesoamerican Archaeology*, 3rd edn. Freeman, San Francisco.

Yoffee, Norman. 1993. Too Many Chiefs? (or, Safe Texts for the '90's). In *Archaeological Theory: Who Sets the Agenda?*, edited by Norman Yoffee and A. Sherratt, pp. 60–78. University of Cambridge Press, Cambridge.

CHAPTER 12

The Power of Prestige

Competitive Generosity and the Emergence of Rank Societies in Lowland Mesoamerica

John E. Clark and Michael Blake

Introduction

Explanations of the origins of institutionalized social inequality and political privilege must resolve the central paradox of political life – why people cooperate with their own subordination and exploitation in non-coercive circumstances (Godelier 1986: 13). In the following pages we address this paradox for an archaeological case from Mesoamerica.

The first chiefdoms in lowland Mesoamerica, the focus of this discussion, appear to have developed some 3,300 years ago among the Mokaya in the Mazatan region of Chiapas, Mexico, during the first part of the Early Formative, 1550–1150 BC (all dates are in radio-carbon years). This period also witnessed the adoption of maize agriculture in the coastal lowlands, the founding of sedentary villages, the adoption of ceramic technology, a rapid population increase, and the beginnings of patronized craft specialization.

To explain these developments, we first offer a general model for the development of hereditary rank distinctions as the outcome of competition among political actors vying for prestige and social esteem. We then apply this model to the issues of technological and demographic change in the development of social inequality in the Mazatan region.

Resources, Prestige, and Privilege

It is difficult to imagine why people would voluntarily submit to non-egalitarian political systems. Despite this perception, the institutionalization of political privilege may have been quite simple; it may at first have been in people's best interest. Nowadays, in addressing this issue, we are hindered by hindsight and evolutionist and functionalist thinking that regards change as reaction to existing social problems. Binford (1983: 221), for example, states: "When I am faced with a question such as why complex systems come into being, my first reaction is to ask what problem people were attempting to solve by a new means." As will become clear, we disagree with this perspective. The development of social inequality was neither a problem nor a solution. Rather, it was a long-term, unexpected consequence of many individuals promoting their own aggrandizement.

Briefly, we argue that the transition from egalitarian to rank societies was a process that occurred on a regional scale under special historical and techno-environmental

Reprinted from John E. Clark and Michael Blake. 1994. The Power of Prestige: Competitive Generosity and Emergence of Rank Societies in Lowland Mesoamerica. In *Factional Competition and Political Development in the New World*, edited by Elizabeth M. Brumfiel and John W. Fox (Cambridge University Press, New York), pp. 17–30.

circumstances. The engine for change was self-interested competition among political actors vying for prestige or social esteem. We refer to such political entrepreneurs as "aggrandizers," paralleling Hayden and Gargett's (1990) term "accumulators." Over time, some aggrandizers became chiefs with institutionalized authority. Parlaying temporary prestige into legitimate authority was the key process.

Primary Assumptions

Our view of the origins of social inequality rests on several propositions concerning human action, the formation of factions, and the creation and deployment of physical and social resources. Our most critical assumptions concern culture, society, and individual behavior.

Social systems are regularized practices. They lack reason, purpose, or needs and are incapable of adaptation (Giddens 1979: 7). Only the actors within a system share these attributes and are capable of adaptive response. Purposive, motivated action becomes the point of articulation between structure and the human agent (Vincent 1978; Giddens 1979; Callinicos 1988). Importantly, such action often sparks unintended consequences for the system.

It is clear that actors are constrained by past practice (history of system and structure) and opportunities for future practice (e.g. available technology, physical and social environment, personal social networks, etc.). Each actor knows a great deal about his/her social system and its constraints and limits under varying circumstances – even to the extent that (s)he can manipulate aspects of the system for personal advantage. We presume a primary motivation of self-interested action based upon culturally bound rational choice (i.e. "minimal rationality," see Cherniak 1986). Obviously, individual motivations, desires, and reasons for action cannot be the same for everyone (Callinicos 1988). Where numerous people pursue self-interests, their interaction is characterized by frequent conflicts of interests, internal social tensions, and social constraints on behavior.

Specifically, in emergent chiefdoms or transegalitarian societies, we postulate the necessary presence of ambitious males (aggrandizers) competing for prestige within a regional setting.[1] Aggrandizers do not strive to become chiefs; the end result of political competition cannot be foreseen by participants in the system. Aggrandizers simply strive to become more influential. It is the successful deployment of resources and labor that ultimately ensures the social and political longevity of an aggrandizer, and only certain environments can sustain such behavior on a regional scale and a chronic basis (Hayden and Gargett 1990).

Competition for "prestige" consists of rivalry for continual public recognition by supporters (with access to their resources). Prestige is maintained by establishing a coalition of loyal supporters, or a faction (Salisbury and Silverman 1977; Bailey 1977). In this view, vying for prestige is the equivalent of competing for people or their labor power and support (Binford 1983: 219; see also Sahlins 1968: 89–90; Gulliver 1977: 44; Silverman 1977: 72; Price 1984). It also involves competition over the "management of meaning" and "interpretation of behavior and relationships" (Cohen and Comaroff 1976: 102); this probably relates to the emphasis on oratory among tribal leaders (Clastres 1977).

Although our argument requires the presence of a particular personality type, we consider psychology a constant. Ambitious individuals are probably present in most societies. The presence of such individuals is a necessary but insufficient condition for the transition to non-egalitarian systems.

Structure and Social System

We assume that "all social systems, whatever their structure, contain the seeds of inequality" (Josephides 1985: 1; see also Béteille 1977). We do not view social evolution as unfolding from inner forces, but we do maintain that all egalitarian systems mask fundamental structural contradictions which necessitate leveling mechanisms to assert egalitarianism (Woodburn 1982; Matson 1985; Lee 1990).

Cohen (1974: 78) argues that all social systems involve hierarchy, which suggests the presence of leadership with attendant prestige, no matter how ephemeral. In egalitarian groups, hierarchy is likely to be based on age, gender, and aptitude. Rivalries for temporary hierarchical positions develop among many of those with requisite ability to fill them. In addition to social differentiation, all societies require a system of social evaluation (Béteille 1977: 9). These two necessary conditions for any society lay the basis of social inequalities.

In our model we assume egalitarian groups or communities where great latitude exists in the degree to which individuals may maneuver for prestige, that is, societies in which prestige is possible, personal ambition is allowed, and agents have control over the fruits of some of their labor. The deployment of resources (or property) as actors see fit involves usufruct rights within a defined territory (Sack 1986; Hayden 1990).

Two more specific aspects of structure and social system inform our model. The first concerns biological reproduction. We concur with Friedman and Rowlands (1978: 204) that "reproduction is an areal phenomenon in which a number of separate social units are linked in a large system" (see Wobst 1974). Furthermore, we assume patrilocality, with patrilineal descent favored but not strictly necessary (cf. Allen 1984; Coontz and Henderson 1986).

Environment and Technology

Considerations of the environment should acknowledge actors with conventional perceptions and constructions of their "world" in symbolic interaction with other people and objects (Blumer 1969: 11). In short, "nature" (including resources, physical features, and concepts of space and distance) is subject to interpretive shifts and even manipulation by interested individuals within a given social system (Sack 1986; Helms 1988).

Using these resources, aggrandizers compete for "prestige"; *competition over physical resources is not an end in itself*. Nature is handed a passive role in this process. Resources and technology circumscribe individual choice but otherwise neither impede nor promote social competition or development.

Only certain kinds of environments and resources will sustain escalating exploitation by aggrandizers. Resources must be accessible, productive, and relatively immune to normal environmental perturbations (Coupland 1985: 219; Matson 1985) – characteristics of r-selected species, such as fish, rodents, and cereals (Hayden 1986, 1990). Resource availability and productivity determine potential levels of accumulation for social display and competition. In addition, the periodicity and extent of resource shortfalls is critical to the development of political inequality on a permanent basis.

The environment must be productive enough to support a rapidly growing labor force, the followers attached to an aggrandizer. In other words, aggrandizers fare best in "intensifiable habitats" (Price 1984: 225). Of course, the elasticity of a habitat to labor influx varies according to basic technology, social relations of production, and subsistence techniques.

Any transition to a non-egalitarian system requires the emergence of new practices as a necessary prelude to structural change. And these must be maintained and financed long enough to make the practices habitual (Berger and Luckmann 1966; Bourdieu 1977). Therefore, factional leaders must have access to important resources continuously over a period of years or even decades (Binford 1983: 219; Earle 1987: 294). One or two bad seasons can undo years of public posturing, faction-building, and prestations, with loss of face and depletion of stored resources and social credits.

While resource productivity and reliability act as relaxed restraints on individual action, they alone cannot explain the specific location, timing, or extent of social development. An equally important consideration is the geographic configuration of resources and physical features which channel communication and social interaction.

Demography, Social Interaction, and Rank

Demographic increase does not and cannot force people to invent and adopt non-egalitarian social formations (Netting 1990). Although there is a strong correlation between population size and level of sociopolitical complexity (Cohen 1985; Keeley 1988), we view population as a necessary precondition or threshold phenomenon. Population must reach a certain size and density before the complex social interactions that lead to the emergence of rank can occur.

Both intra- and inter-community interactions are essential in faction building. Interaction within (1) the community, (2) the region, and (3) various regions (the area) includes both positive and negative social discourse, from trade and marriage to warfare (Price 1977, 1984). Cooperation and competition are complementary principles. To compete effectively, aggrandizers require the cooperation and support of indebted clients, probably including many kin, and other patrons or trade partners. Competition is undertaken to maintain or enlarge this cooperative unit or interest group.

Effective competition at the community level requires aggrandizers to traffic outside their home communities and establish significant ties to individuals elsewhere, preferably other aggrandizers who also seek outside contacts. The physical and social resources and knowledge thus gained allow an aggrandizer to compete more effectively within his own community. The aggrandizer capitalizes upon innovation and risk-taking (Schmookler 1984: 28). Enhancing prestige through innovation depends on an aggrandizer's ability to convince potential beneficiaries/clients of the value of his innovations.

The conversion of external resources into social leverage locally requires (near) exclusive access to outside goods, material, or information (Gosden 1989). This also allows the aggrandizer to operate partially outside the sanctioning norms of his local group, where local norms are more ambiguous and easier to manipulate. Our model presumes a plurality of structurally similar, autonomous social groups or communities within a region and a complex web of rivalry and cooperation among aggrandizers and their supporters, in what has been called "peer polity interaction" (Renfrew and Cherry 1986).

Even the first steps of an aggrandizer's career involve interaction both within and beyond his home community. Building renown commences in the nuclear unit of production. An aggrandizer first accumulates deployable resources by the sweat of his brow, and through the efforts of his wife (wives) and children. The more wives and children the better (Coontz and Henderson 1986). Since intensified resource procurement is a consequence of increased labor input, it follows that larger families may produce larger surpluses to invest in prestige competition. Multiple wives also provide the aggrandizer with a larger group of affines for exchange partnerships (Strathern 1966: 360). In addition, multiple wives engender more offspring who later become a source of additional alliances.

The potential for social development of a community is a function of its access to *social resources*, notably people in neighboring communities and kinship structures. Such access depends upon relative topographic position within the region (Johnson 1977: 492). Some basic features of the landscape (e.g. mountains, canyons, and rough ocean) will inhibit travel and communication to some areas; other features (e.g. mountain passes, fords, and navigable rivers) funnel social contact into specific areas. Inherent potential for travel, coupled with distribution of critical resources, delimits settlement locations, sizes, population densities, permanence, and future growth. Some communities will be central and others peripheral to critical natural and social resources. So too, some people are more centrally placed than others vis-à-vis various social and physical resources and can avail themselves of this advantage. Thus, some aggrandizers will be better placed than others to mobilize resources. Those with the most numerous or strongest ties to different outside resources should be best off.

The settlement pattern may be linear or non-linear (or open). In linear settlement systems, each aggrandizer has unimpeded access to only one or two significant neigh-

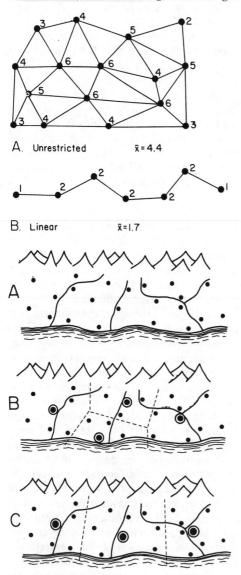

A. Unrestricted   x̄ = 4.4

B. Linear   x̄ = 1.7

A

B

C

Figure 12.1 Measures of interaction in unrestricted (A) and linear (B) networks.

boring groups, as shown in figure 12.1. In open settlement systems, however, potential for interaction varies significantly from center to periphery; a community's territory can border the territories of two to six neighboring groups. Note the difference in mean interaction between linear and open systems shown in figure 12.1. Centrally placed aggrandizers within open settlement systems enjoy an advantage with more possibilities for inter-group alliances and for manipulating the ambiguities of several different systems for their own benefit.

We expect social change at focal points of regional social interaction, or in the central sectors of open settlement systems. Rank societies emerge within a network of interacting groups. One society does not hoist itself from one social level to another; the process involves the simultaneous emergence of a network of *chiefdoms* from a network of interacting *chiefs*. In this sense, all pristine developments are secondary developments dependent on outside resources, alliances, and events. However, the process is irreversible in most instances. Because social competition is elevated to a new level among a plurality of like units, there is no practical way to reverse the process – and little incentive for doing so. Structural and systemic changes shift the conditions for future development and possibilities for action.

Perks, Persuasion, and Clientage

Returning to the question of the emergence of institutionalized inequality, why would individuals in a subordinate position surrender their liberty, equality, and fraternity to a non-egalitarian system? Traditionally, two answers have been proposed, one emphasizing voluntary "social contracts" and the other stressing "coercion" (Service 1975). Both proposals have serious flaws.

Theories of coercion often stress the importance of warfare and conquest in the construction of social inequality. Raiding does play an important role in emerging systems of inequality as one way that leaders can gain reputation and undercut the prestige of rivals (Kirch 1984: 197), seize booty that can be shared with one's followers, or even obtain captives. Of equal importance is the hostile "meaning" attributed to the exterior social environment and the increased prestige accrued by successful negotiation in that domain. But theories based upon conquest and subjugation are inappropriate for egalitarian societies (see Fried 1967: 213–23; also Otterbein 1985: ch. 2 for a cross-cultural study of war). On the other hand, social contract theories are all teleological and/or functional and thus logically flawed (see Dahrendorf 1968: 165; Fischer 1970: 155). In contrast to either of these theories, we suggest that social inequality was an unanticipated consequence of aggrandizers vying for followers.

Aggrandizers cannot force anyone to join their group or faction. Followers must be persuaded, coaxed, cajoled, begged, bribed, and otherwise won over. Consequently, aggrandizer strategies and tactics for persuasion must appear to conform to the self-interests of their followers (Doob 1983: 41; Bailey 1988). Simply put, followers tag along because they benefit from doing so, retaining the option of shifting their loyalty to other aggrandizers should enough benefits not be forthcoming (Wolf 1966: 17). The most successful aggrandizers are those who provide the most physical, social, and/or spiritual benefits to the most people on the most reliable basis. Thus, aggrandizers are strongly motivated to increase rewards through increased production and innovation.

Aggrandizers and followers, as social creditors and debtors, construct complex webs of relationships as they interact on different levels (see Lederman 1986). These relationships are in constant flux and vary according to the particular dyadic relationships considered. An aggrandizer can be creditor to his group and at the same time be indebted to other powerful partners (Strathern 1966). All successful aggrandizers begin as followers of powerful patrons and acquire prestige from their prestigious mentors.

The self-aggrandizing process is fundamentally a political one based upon the simple principle of reciprocity. We view personal generosity as the key competitive process for forging a coalition of clients (Price 1984: 224–5). Aggrandizer gifts are eventually returned by their followers in reciprocal exchanges. When this is not possible, unreciprocated benefits create obligations of social indebtedness which become deployable social resources themselves (Blau 1964; Sahlins 1968: 88; Orenstein 1980; Gosden 1989). Periodically aggrandizers must "draw on the fund of good will" (Paynter and Cole 1980: 66) created by previous acts of generosity to mobilize labor and resources. The most successful aggrandizers are those who can maintain a positive balance of generosity and "gift-credits" (Lederman 1986); they give more than they receive. This puts them in a socially superior position which, if sustained long enough, can lead to the institutionalization of social inequalities (Friedman 1975; Hayden and Gargett 1990). Apical rank societies or chiefdoms are clearly prefigured in the organization of personal followings or factions.

Rank or chiefdom societies, however, can only be said to be truly in place when special privileges get passed on to the leader's heirs. "Attention to processes of consolidation of power shifts the focus from individual actors to families" (Vincent 1978: 187). The general process of establishing succession is clear. Men of wealth, renown, and influence can create opportunities for favored dependants, "to effect differential patterns of marriage choice" (Wolf 1966: 6). Strategies for passing benefits to heirs may also involve creation of heritable wealth through patronized craft production (Clark and Parry 1990) or monopolization of important outside resources (Gosden 1989). Orenstein (1980: 76) demonstrates that "rules of inheritance" are the key; we would also add marriage rules and arrangements (Friedman and Rowlands 1978; Collier 1988). To become habitual, at least two generations are probably needed to allow for the socialization of the majority of a society's members to the changed social reality.

Summary

Our model of structural transformation considers historical antecedents (system and structure *sensu* Giddens), environment and technology, scales of social interaction, and human agency, action, and personality. It focuses upon "action" rather than "reaction" (i.e. in response to ecological variables). In particular, the main motivation is the self-interested pursuit of prestige, or competition for followers, using a strategy of competitive generosity.

Forming a coalition is inherently competitive. Successful competition involves elements of luck, chance, personality, and mobilization of social and physical resources over a continuous period. As the process depends on an unpredictable concatenation of factors and contexts negotiated in social interaction, we cannot predict *specific* timing nor precise location of initial occurrence within a generally favorable environmental and demographic milieu.

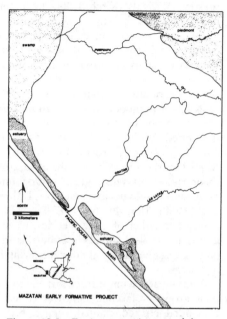

Figure 12.2   Environmental zones of the Mazatan region.

The Mokaya and the Origins of Rank

Background

The Mazatan region lies in the highly productive section of the southern Chiapas coast known as the Soconusco – an area long famed for its productivity (Voorhies 1990). Mazatan consists of closely packed environmental zones, with a narrow, low-lying coastal plain sandwiched between a linear beach/estuary complex and the formidable piedmont/Sierra Madre mountain range 20–30 km inland (figure 12.2). Specialized hamlets were located within the estuary system, but the largest Early Formative communities occupied the central strip of the coastal plain, 10–15 m above sea level. The plain is crossed by numerous abandoned river channels radiating in a semicircular fan; until twenty years ago these served as runoff channels during the rainy season and supported garden plots at the end of the dry season. These seasonal rivers and streams divided the tropical forest into a patchy mosaic of

trees, shrubs, small lagoons, and swamps, ideal for a great variety and density of small fauna. The abundance of game is implicit in the Aztec name – Mazatan, "place of the deer."

Late Archaic (Chantuto phase) shell middens in the estuary zone probably represent seasonal accumulations from occupations by residentially mobile hunter-fisher-gatherers (Voorhies 1976, 1990). Towards the end of the Late Archaic the Chantuto people engaged in long-distance exchange for highland Guatemalan obsidian (Nelson and Voorhies 1980).

The Early Formative transition began about 1550 BC, or 200 years after the last reliable data on the Archaic. The Barra phase (1550–1400 BC) witnessed the founding of sedentary villages, presumably with agriculture, and the introduction of ceramics. We refer to these Early Formative villagers as the "Mokaya," an indigenous term meaning "corn people." The estuary shell middens saw only minimal use after the Chantuto phase (Voorhies 1976), perhaps as a consequence of a shift in the settlement-subsistence system from residential mobility to sedentism.

Hints of rank distinctions first appear towards the end of the Barra phase, with more convincing evidence for the following Locona phase, beginning about 1400 BC. Briefly, the indicators of Locona rank systems are (1) a two-tiered settlement pattern comprising small villages and hamlets centered around large villages, (2) elite and non-elite domestic architecture (Blake, Clark, Feddema et al. 1993), (3) differential mortuary practices, (4) unequal access to sumptuary goods and long-distance imports, (5) attached craft specialization centered around elite housemounds, and (6) redistribution within each large community (Clark 1991). Artisans made ceramic vessels and figurines, elaborate carved stone bowls that imitated fancy ceramic forms, greenstone beads, and, perhaps, textiles and cordage.

The following events or processes are implicated in the emergence of rank in the Mazatan region: (1) a shift from residential mobility to sedentism; (2) increased emphasis on agriculture, including the adoption of highland cultigens such as corn and beans; (3) the beginnings of ceramic technology; (4) rapid population growth; and (5) the beginning of craft specialization. Rather than causal, these processes are probably all related as secondary indicators of a more fundamental process of prestige-building and competitive generosity. In the remainder of this paper we assess the roles of (1) population pressure, (2) the adoption of ceramic technology, and (3) the beginnings of agriculture in this process as it evolved in the Mazatan area.

Population pressure

As presented by Carneiro (1970), population pressure on limited resources provokes agricultural intensification and, later, when this temporary measure proves inadequate, wars of conquest and subjugation. In this view, the transition to institutionalized inegalitarianism occurs within a circumscribed zone once the limits of its carrying capacity are exceeded.

Our hypothesis of competing aggrandizers turns Malthus on his head. The objective of competitive generosity is to *attract* more followers to one's locale and to foment rapid population growth, including local increases in family sizes and fertility rates. The emergence of rank is coupled with strategies that bring more people into a zone that is well below carrying capacity (see Kirch 1984). Rank emerges in regions able to absorb this increased population without deleterious effect. Increase in local population is achieved through mechanisms such as promoting immigration, younger marriage, a higher birth rate, or even the capture of slaves. In the Mazatan area, competition among aggrandizers for secondary wives could have effectively lowered the age of marriage for women, and consequently increased the fertility rate (see Hayden 1992). We expect the emergence of rank societies to occur well below carrying capacity. The process as we see it results from a long-term distribution of benefits rather than the exercise of naked force.

The uniformity in subsistence tools and remains during the Early Formative suggests that the carrying capacity of Mazatan was virtually constant throughout this period; it may even have increased slightly as the number of fallow fields increased (creating a greater "edge" effect), and with genetic improvements in cultigens such as corn (Kirkby 1973). Survey data for the zone provide the basis for the demographic estimates shown in figure 12.3. This population curve is based upon the estimated hectares of occupation per phase for a 50 km^2 survey block of 100 percent coverage. As figure 12.3 demonstrates, the first major shift in population corresponds to the emergence of rank societies, countering the predictions of population pressure advocates. Interestingly, the next major change anticipated another important political shift in the zone – from a network of simple chiefdoms to a single paramount chiefdom.

Had the transition to rank society been prompted by population pressure, one would expect it to have taken place at or shortly after the peak of demographic

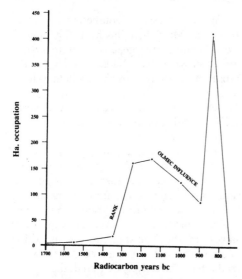

Figure 12.3 Population estimates for the Mazatan region during the Early Formative period. Estimates are based upon a 50 km² survey block.

growth (i.e. near carrying capacity). Wars of conquest, as argued by Carneiro (1970), merely reshuffle usufruct rights of critical resources rather than provide a basis for additional growth. In contrast, population growth as part of the transformation process should evince rapid change to the degree that nascent leaders compete for followers. The Mazatan data support the notion of population growth as outcome of social complexity rather than cause.

Although settlement survey coverage of adjacent areas is not complete, available data suggest that during the Early Formative period the Mazatan area was ringed by uninhabited or sparsely occupied land, signaling the absence of any environmental or social circumscription and, of equal importance, some population movement from these areas into the Mazatan region.

Ceramic technology

Technological and ecological explanations of the origins of Mesoamerican ceramics cannot account for the technical and aesthetic sophistication of the early ceramics

from coastal Chiapas and Guatemala. Barra-phase ceramics (figure 12.4) from the Mazatan area are currently the earliest securely dated examples (1550–1400 BC) in Mesoamerica, but these thin-walled, hard ceramics are finely finished and elaborately decorated (bichromes, trichromes, incised, grooved, carved, fluted, and gadrooned). This assemblage is clearly well developed, suggesting an origin and development elsewhere. Alternatively, some investigators conjecture that earlier, less complex ceramics will yet be found in the Soconusco region.

Were these early ceramics a local development, or were they brought in from elsewhere? Both Coe (1960) and Lowe (1975) speculate about Central or South American origins. But with the benefit of more complete assemblages from Mazatan and the areas to the south, we now recognize only vague similarities between the Mazatan pottery and pottery from Central and South America. Notable, however, are (1) the apparent temporal progression of the earliest ceramic assemblages as one moves northward from Ecuador to Mesoamerica (Hoopes 1987) and (2) the stylistic dissimilarities among adjacent early assemblages.

The Central and South American data suggest that the earliest Mokaya did adopt the basic ceramic technology from people to the south. Central questions, then, are (1) why they chose to adopt pottery when they did, (2) what functions the pottery served, and (3) how the process of adoption occurred. We argue that the adoption of ceramics was a result of competition among aggrandizers who brought in foreign technology and products as part of their pursuit of prestige.

To place this hypothesis in perspective, we need to consider probable historical antecedents to the adoption of ceramics. First, we postulate the presence of numerous aggrandizers within the Mazatan region and a dynamic egalitarian network – a society of complex hunter-fisher-gatherers (see Price and Brown 1985). Second, these hunter-fisher-gatherers inhabited the zone for at least 2,000 years prior to the adoption of

Figure 12.4   Reconstruction of Barra vessels from the Mazatan region.

ceramics (Blake, Clark, Voorhies, et al. 1993). Undoubtedly, the adaptation of these archaic Chantuto foragers to their tropical coastal environment already included viable container technology and food preparation techniques. The adoption of ceramic technology, therefore, involved the *replacement* of some perishable containers with ceramic vessels. Attributes of the first ceramic vessels suggest they served a specialized function.

All Barra ceramics are finely made, flat-bottomed tecomates or deep incurved bowls (figures 12.4 and 12.5). To date, no plain, unslipped, undecorated vessels have been recovered. Ceramic vessels mimic gourd forms (Lowe 1975; Marcus 1983). We suggest these first ceramic vessels copied then extant fancy gourd vessels. All the techniques used to embellish the surface of Barra pots are still used today to decorate gourds (see Lathrap 1977). Such techniques may have been used initially to decorate gourds and only later transferred to the new ceramic medium.

We postulate that aggrandizers borrowed foreign ceramic technology for personal advantage in displays of competitive feasting. The aggrandizers might have sent someone to the pottery-producing areas to learn the techniques (or gone themselves) or, alternatively, sponsored a potter to come to the Mazatan region.

But if ceramic technology was brought in fully developed, how do we explain the differences in pottery styles in the borrowing area (Mazatan) and the donor area (Central America)? If gourd vessels (which may have been elaborately decorated and expensive) were already functioning in a competitive sphere of public/ritual display, the containers most likely imitated by ceramic forms would have been stylistically elaborate and socially bounded already. That is, vessel style would already have been socially meaningful or semantically complex within special social contexts (cf. Steinberg 1977). Producing these vessels in a new and more expensive medium (fired clay) would have enhanced their value but not tampered with

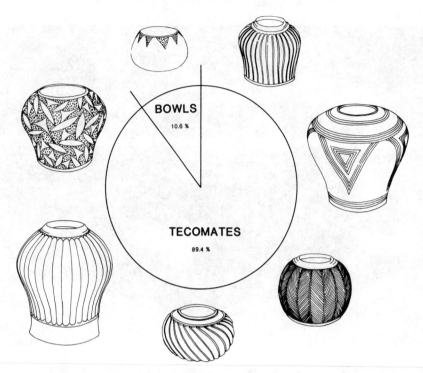

Figure 12.5   Percentages of vessel types in the Barra ceramic assemblage.

meaningful social conventions. In contrast, the direct transfer of foreign vessel forms and styles would not have been immediately meaningful, in traditional conventions, and may have been of less value to those seeking prestige through conspicuous consumption. McCracken (1987) demonstrates that material codes, unlike language codes, lack generative capacity or combinatorial freedom. To recombine the stylistic elements into a new form is to render them meaningless. The material code (or combination of elements) must be known in advance to be culturally meaningful in social interaction. Consequently, different social messages are conveyed by local and foreign styles.

Technological transfer in a milieu of competing aggrandizers can account for those aspects of ceramic technology that previous investigators found puzzling. It would explain (1) the timing of the adoption, (2) vessel style or exterior decoration, (3) vessel forms, (4) workmanship, (5) the general

function of these first ceramic vessels, and (6) the development of ceramics during the following phases. Timing was dictated by the heightened level of social competition in Mazatan. Vessel style and forms were predicated upon the style and forms of the non-ceramic ritual/feasting vessels already functioning in competitive social displays; all that changed was the base material and *some* processes of surface manipulation and finish. The sociopolitical functions of pottery also account for the superior quality of the first vessels (they were preciosities) and the unexpected absence of plain, utilitarian vessels. Functions later relegated to plain pottery continued to be performed, in the Barra phase, by gourds or *jicaras*, net bags, and baskets. Unslipped pottery became more common during the following Locona phase, a time when techniques of ceramic manufacture were more widely known and consequently less "expensive," and probably when the use of ceramic vessels in competitive displays had lost its novelty.

Figure 12.6 Reconstruction of Locona vessels from Mazatan region.

Barra vessels do not appear to have been designed or used for cooking; instead, they are appropriate for preparing and serving liquids (figures 12.4 and 12.5).[2] Large quantities of fire-cracked rock, dating to the Barra and early Locona phases, may indicate non-ceramic-vessel cooking techniques such as roasting and/or stone boiling. But during the Locona phase (figure 12.6), cooking wares were introduced, and the frequency of fire-cracked rocks declined. In sum, we suspect that ceramics were initially adopted more for their power to impress others in competitive social displays than for their culinary potential in food preparation.

We argue that the first Barra ceramics mimicked functionally specialized gourd vessels and that the range of forms increased with time as ceramic technology was applied to other functions. We would expect to see an increasing diversity of functional types over time and a greater range of execution (fancy vs. plain pottery). In addition, the per capita consumption of functionally analogous vessels should remain constant between phases. All these trends are evident in Barra phase (figures 12.4 and 12.5) and Locona phase (figures 12.6 and 12.7) ceramics.

Ceramic diversity increased through time with a Locona-phase proliferation of fancy dishes and plates as well as relatively plain tripod tecomates, perhaps used for storage and/or boiling. Consumption rates between phases, as gauged by ceramic counts per volume of excavated fill, remained remarkably constant for highly polished, slipped, decorated tecomates (table 2.1). The smaller proportion of fancy tecomates in the Locona ceramic assemblage (figure 12.7) results from the addition of new forms, including utilitarian tecomates, rather than a decreased use of fancy tecomates during the Locona phase.

Beginning of agriculture

The first clear evidence of agriculture in the Mazatan region consists of domesticates brought in from the highlands. This may be another example of aggrandizers

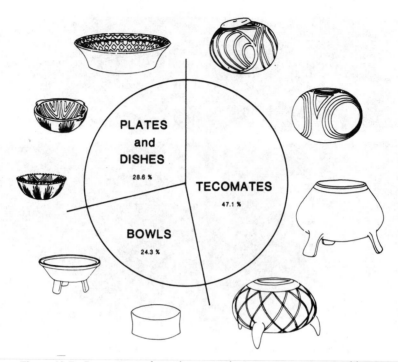

Figure 12.7   Percentages of vessel types in the Locona ceramic assemblage.

Table 12.1   Consumption of tecomates during the Early Formative, based upon the minimum number of individual (MNI) pots. MNI calculated by refitting and analyzing rim sherds

Tecomates	Barra phase[*]		Locona phase[**]	
	MNI	MNI/m^3	MNI	MNI/m^3
Fancy, slipped	74	9.7	118	10.0
Grooved	6	0.8	44	3.7
Plain	0	0.0	44	3.7
Total	80	10.5	206	17.4

[*] based upon 7.5 m^3 of deposit.
[**] based upon 11.8 m^3 of deposit.

appropriating materials from outside areas in their never-ending quest for self-promotion (see Hayden 1990). Domesticated corn and beans were both clearly present in Mazatan by Locona times, and we suspect that these highland cultigens were first brought into the area during the Late Archaic. But several lines of evidence sug-

gest that maize may not have been very important in the diet. We cannot evaluate the importance of beans at this time.

Corn cobs in Locona deposits are quite small (3–4 cm long) and not very productive. Our analysis of C13/C12 ratios from twenty-eight human bone collagen samples spanning the Late Archaic to Late Postclassic periods show that maize (or other C-4 plants) was not a significant part of the diet until the Middle Formative Conchas phase (ca. 850–650 BC). For all Early Formative samples, the stable carbon isotope ratios are as low as those for hunter-fisher-gatherers in many other regions of the world (Blake, Chisholm, et al. 1992).

We suggest that the adoption of maize may have been linked to the adoption of ceramic technology. Clearly, maize was imported into a system already self-sufficient in basic foodstuffs. Even the highland peoples who domesticated maize were still not fully sedentary agriculturalists at this time (MacNeish 1964; Flannery and Marcus 1983; Flannery 1986); Mesoamerican corn was not that productive 4,000 years ago. In line with our model, we suggest that maize may have been adopted as a status food and not as some sort of far-sighted, prehistoric agricultural improvement project. We should not assume that plants were imported to Mazatan 4,000 years ago for reasons having to do with their function today.

We have argued that Barra ceramics were designed for liquids, presumably liquids with ritual significance and prestige value for the giver. Maize may have been part of this complex, introduced to the coastal area prior to the adoption of ceramics primarily for making corn beer, or *chicha*. Alternatively, it may have been used with chocolate or as a drink in its own right such as *atole; atole* is still an important ritual drink in Chiapas. Hayden (1990) argues that the domestication of plants and animals resulted from their deployment as status foods. While this may not explain the development of agriculture, it may explain the spread of some cultigens. Use of corn as a ritual ingredient, or as an alcoholic beverage could explain (1) the initial importation and special cultivation of this unproductive highland cereal, (2) the rarity of seed-processing implements, and (3) the minor contribution of maize in the overall diet during the Early Formative period.

Summary and Conclusions

Our explanation of the emergence of permanent social inequality from egalitarian socio-political structures rests on six propositions:

1 Egalitarian social systems contain the seeds of permanent social inequality in their structure of age, kin, gender, and aptitude distinctions.
2 The development of permanent social inequality is an unanticipated consequence of individuals pursuing self-interests and personal aggrandizement.
3 Temporary positions of prestige become hereditary and legitimate positions of authority under limited social and natural environmental conditions.

4 These changes result from the purposive action of individuals pursuing individual strategies and agendas within the structural constraints of their cultural system.
5 The engine of change is competition for prestige – constituted as public recognition of status, rights, and responsibilities – among a network of aggrandizers.
6 Effective competition within one's community requires that aggrandizers traffic outside their respective communities and establish enduring ties with individuals elsewhere.

These propositions have archaeological implications that differ significantly from those generated by functionalist/ecological approaches. Ecological approaches see hierarchical, chiefly political organization as an adaptive, structural response to social/ecological needs. Therefore, to explain the change it is sufficient to document the conditions or needs stimulating the adaptive response. In contrast, we suggest that chiefdom emergence must be explained in terms of the political process.

Anterior social structure as well as perceived environmental constraints shape the emergent system. This means that a great deal of variability may be expected in the paths to permanent inequality taken by different societies. Aggrandizers in different cultural-environmental contexts may employ some but not all of the various options available. Although the broad outlines of structural change may be similar, specific conditions of inequality will vary considerably from case to case as each will have its own history.

But the focus on individual historical sequences need not degenerate into a particularistic view of social process that negates generalization and the search for patterns. Our model for the transition to institutionalized inequality has several implications which can be verified archaeologically for any test case. First, if the emergence of hereditary inequality is indeed an unanticipated consequence of competition among aggrandizers in transegalitarian systems, this transitional period from egalitarian societies to chiefdoms should appear, archaeologically, neither egalitarian nor ranked. Many of the standard trappings of chiefly societies will be absent during the transitional period because they are still unnecessary or, in some cases, not permitted. Once clear evidence of hereditary inequality appears, the transition is long past. On the other hand, if in emergent chiefdoms constraints to wealth accumulation and public display were undergoing modification, aggrandizers would be allowed to produce and distribute subsistence and craft items in excess of existing norms. Therefore, one might find archaeological evidence of elaboration and experimentation with status objects and social structures which might become embedded in subsequent chiefdoms.

Second, change would be rapid in transitional societies because innovation would be useful for competing aggrandizers. In contrast, material culture, symbols, and sociopolitical structure in both egalitarian societies and developed chiefdoms would be more stable with an emphasis on perpetuating the traditional bases of power. As sociopolitical structures develop so does the symbolism of chiefly power and interregional alliances. Their very existence leads to conservatism, thereby dampening their own rates of change. Elite competition within a chiefdom or among chiefdoms takes place within the newly established, legitimate symbol system based upon a limited range of recognized status markers. Radical and innovative changes in symbol systems accompany major social structural changes.

Third, aggrandizers, like big-men and chiefs, must control or maintain access to a large labor pool in order to sustain the high levels of production that both demonstrate and further their influence. Thus, an aggrandizer will value all innovations that (1) attract more followers and (2) increase production to sustain those followers. Novelties, whether arising from emulation or invention, will be valued, especially those items that can be controlled, managed, or manipulated by aggrandizers.

In evaluating this model of chiefdom emergence we reviewed three lines of archaeological evidence as they relate to population dynamics, development of ceramic technology, and adoption of agriculture. As noted, we expect population growth and nucleation to occur during the transition to non-egalitarian society. At the very least, population should not remain stable or decline within the region of the aggrandizer interaction network as long as resources can be intensified and the system does not collapse. Survey data for the Mazatan region show significant population increase and nucleation during the early part of the Early Formative period. The first evidence of population growth is coeval with the first indications for competition among aggrandizers, during the Barra phase. This suggests that population growth and nucleation – and the increasing labor pool they imply – could have been consequences of social and political strategies.

New technology is another expectation for a competitive political environment favoring innovation. In the Mokaya case, the first use of ceramics began during the Barra phase. These highly decorated and well-made ceramic containers were probably first used in beverage preparation and consumption as an adjunct to public feasting rather than in utilitarian functions such as cooking. Such activities would have been crucial for an aggrandizer trying to attract, impress, and retain followers.

Finally, the adoption of agriculture in coastal Chiapas suggests a sociopolitical dynamic quite different from those postulated for other parts of Mesoamerica. Maize and bean cultivation in the highland valleys go back several millennia before the Chiapas Early Formative period. By the Locona phase (ca. 1350–1250 BC) in Mazalan, maize and beans were used frequently enough to enter the archaeological record. However, it was not until the Middle Formative that maize became significant enough in the diet to influence the stable carbon isotope ratio in human bone collagen. One possibility is that aggrandizers adopted an agricultural complex as a means of growing new foods, one of which (maize) could be used in making alcoholic beverages useful in competitive feasting. They may also have cultivated a range of other plants of which we have no material evidence. However, the faunal evidence clearly indicates that the Early Formative Mokaya were fishers, hunters, and gatherers. Hunter-fisher-gatherers in other highly productive regions of the world developed simple chiefdoms. The Mokaya appear to have done so also. Maize cultivation may have initially been a dietary supplement of greater political than nutritional value.

Much more research remains to be done to understand the transition from egalitarian to permanently ranked social organizations. We are confident, however, that the avenues for inquiry suggested by a focus on transitional political processes differ substantially from traditional functionalist/ecological approaches – especially those that consider established, early chiefdoms. Once the transitional process began, the sociopolitical order became fundamentally different, both from what it had been and from what it was to become.

ACKNOWLEDGMENTS

Our research was generously funded by the New World Archaeological Foundation of Brigham Young University, then directed by Gareth W. Lowe. We are grateful for the opportunity to undertake the Mazatan Project. Barbara Stark, Barbara Voorhies, Jim Brown, Brian Hayden, Peter Peregrine, Elizabeth Brumfiel, and John Fox offered many constructive suggestions on previous drafts of this paper, for which we extend our appreciation. The second half of this paper is a modification of our paper presented at the Circum-Pacific conference.

NOTES

1 Our use of masculine pronouns is intentional. Female aggrandizers remain a theoretical possibility, but their minor representation in the ethnographic record requires explanation. An aggrandizer's competitive ability derives in large part from his immediate access to the productive labor of his wife (or wives) and children, a form of familial exploitation socially justified by gender ideology. Schrijvers (1986: 25–6) observes that "women cannot achieve political power [since] women cannot marry wives to work for them and increase their wealth."

2 Two objections to our interpretation of Barra tecomates as vessels used for brewing, storing, and/or serving liquids have been raised. First, tecomates are poorly designed to pour or dispense liquids – but pouring liquids is not implicated in our argument. Some of the smaller tecomates could have been passed among participants, or participants could drink from one large tecomate with straws (illustrated by Katz and Voigt 1986: 28; fig. 6a for the Tiriki of Kenya). Small gourd tecomates are still used by Maya groups in Chiapas for ritual drinking. The second objection, that large gourd tecomates are used today to store tortillas and so may have served this function in the past, stems from a naïve use of ethnographic analogy. The first clear evidence of tortillas in Chiapas dates only to the Early Postclassic period, ca. AD 1000. If tortillas or tamales were involved with the function of these early ceramic vessels, we would expect to find evidence of a greater contribution of corn to the diet and evidence of using vessels in cooking.

REFERENCES

Allen, M. 1984. Elders, chiefs and big men: authority legitimation and political evolution in Melanesia. *American Ethnologist* 11: 20–41.

Bailey, Frederick G. 1977. The definition of factionalism. In M. Silverman and R. F. Salisbury, eds, *A House Divided? Anthropological Studies of Factionalism*, pp. 21–32. Toronto: University of Toronto Press.

——1988. *Humbuggery and Manipulation: The Art of Leadership*. Ithaca: Cornell University Press.

Berger, Peter L. and Thomas Luckmann. 1966. *The Social Construction of Reality: A Treatise in the Sociology of Knowledge*. Garden City, NY: Doubleday.

Béteille, André. 1977. *Inequality Among Men*. Oxford: Basil Blackwell.

Binford, Lewis R. 1983. *In Pursuit of the Past: Decoding the Archaeological Record*, New York: Thames and Hudson.

Blake, M., B. S. Chisholm, J. E. Clark, B. Voorhies, and M. Love. 1992. Prehistoric subsistence in the Soconusco region. *Current Anthropology* 33: 83–94.

Blake, M., J. E. Clark, V. Feddema, M. Ryan, and R. Lesure. 1993. Early Formative architecture at Paso de la Amada, Chiapas, Mexico. *Latin American Antiquity* 4.

Blake, M., J. E. Clark, B. Voorhies, G. Michaels, M. Love, A. A. Demarest, M. Pye, and B. Arroyo. 1993. The Archaic and Early Formative chronology for the Soconusco region of Mexico and Guatemala. *Ancient Mesoamerica* 4.

Blau, Peter M. 1964. *Exchange and Power in Social Life*. New York: John Wiley and Sons.

Blumer, Herbert. 1969. *Symbolic Interactionism: Perspective and Method*. Berkeley: University of California Press.

Bourdieu, Pierre. 1977. *Outline of a Theory of Practice*. Cambridge: Cambridge University Press.

Callinicos, Alex. 1988. *Making History*. Ithaca: Cornell University Press.

Carneiro, Robert L. 1970. A theory of the origin of the state. *Science* 169: 733–8.

Cherniak, Christopher. 1986. *Minimal Rationality*. Cambridge MA: MIT Press.

Clark, John E. 1991. The beginnings of Mesoamerican: apologia for the Soconusco Early Formative. In W. R. Fowler, Jr., ed., *The Formation of Complex Society in Southeastern Mesoamerica*, pp. 13–16. Boca Raton: CRC Press.

Clark, John E. and William J. Parry. 1990. Craft specialization and cultural complexity. *Research in Economic Anthropology* 12: 289–346.

Clastres, Pierre. 1977. *Society Against the State: The Leader as Servant and the Humane Uses of Power among the Indians of America*. Trans. R. Hurley, New York: Urizen Books.

Coe, Michael D. 1960. Archaeological linkages with North and South America at La Victoria, Guatemala. *American Anthropologist* 62: 363–93.

Cohen, Abner. 1974. *Two-Dimensional Man: An Essay on the Anthropology of Power and Symbolism in Complex Society*. Berkeley: University of California Press.

Cohen, A. P. and J. L. Comaroff. 1976. The management of meaning: on the phenomenology of political transactions. In B. Kapferer, ed., *Transaction and Meaning: Directions in the Anthropology of Exchange and Symbolic Behavior*, pp. 87–107. Philadelphia: Institute for the Study of Human Issues.

Cohen, Mark N. 1985. Prehistoric hunter-gatherers: the meaning of social complexity. In T. D. Price and J. A. Brown, eds, *Prehistoric Hunter-Gatherers: The Emergence of Cultural Complexity*, pp. 99–119. New York: Academic Press.

Collier, Jane. 1988. *Marriage and Inequality in Classless Societies*. Stanford: Stanford University Press.

Coontz, Stephanie and Peta Henderson. 1986. Introduction: 'explanations' of male dominance. In S. Coontz, and P. Henderson, eds, *Women's Work, Men's Property: The Origins of Gender and Class*, pp. 1–42. London: Verso.

Coupland, Gary. 1985. Restricted access, resource control and the evolution of status inequality among hunter-gatherers. In M. Thompson, M. T. Garcia, and F. J. Kense, eds, *Status, Structure and Stratification: Current Archaeological Reconstructions*, pp. 217–26. Calgary: Archaeological Association, Department of Archaeology, University of Calgary.

Dahrendorf, Ralf. 1968. *Essays in the Theory of Society*. Stanford: Stanford University Press.

Doob, Leonard W. 1983. *Personality, Power and Authority: A View from the Behavioral Sciences*. Westport, CT: Greenwood Press.

Earle, Timothy K. 1987. Chiefdoms in archaeological and ethnohistorical perspective. *Annual Review of Anthropology* 16: 279–308.

Fischer, David Hackett. 1970. *Historian's Fallacies: Toward a Logic of Historical Thought*. New York: Harper and Row.

Flannery, Kent V., ed. 1986. *Guilá Naquitz: Archaic Foraging and Early Agriculture in Oaxaca, Mexico*. New York: Academic Press.

Flannery, Kent V. and J. Marcus, eds, 1983. *The Cloud People: Divergent Evolution of the Zapotec and Mixtec Civilizations*. New York: Academic Press.

Fried, Morton H. 1967. *The Evolution of Political Society: An Essay in Political Anthropology*. New York: Random House.

——1975. *The Notion of Tribe*. Menlo Park, CA: Cummings.

Friedman, Jonathan. 1975. Tribes, states, and transformations. In M. Bloch, ed., *Marxist Analyses and Social Anthropology*, pp. 161–202. New York: John Wiley and Sons.

Freidman, Jonathan and Michael J. Rowlands. 1978. Notes toward an epigenetic model of the evolution of "civilisation." In J. Friedman and M. J. Rowlands, eds, *The Evolution of Social Systems*, pp. 201–76. Pittsburgh: University of Pittsburgh Press.

Giddens, Anthony. 1979. *Central Problems in Social Theory: Action, Structures and Contradiction in Social Analysis*. Cambridge: Cambridge University Press.

Godelier, Maurice. 1986. *The Menial and the Material*. Trans. M. Thom, London: Verso.

Gosden, Chris. 1989. Debt, production, and prehistory. *Journal of Anthropological Archaeology* 8: 355–87.

Gulliver, P. H. 1977. Networks and factions: two Ndendeuli communities. In M. Silverman and R. F. Salisbury, eds, *A House Divided? Anthropological Studies of Factionalism*, pp. 37–65. Toronto: University of Toronto Press.

Hayden, Brian. 1986. Resources, rivalry, and reproduction: the influence of basic resource characteristics on reproductive behavior. In W. P. Handwerker, ed., *Culture and Reproduction: An Anthropological Critique of Demographic Transition Theory*, pp. 176–95. Boulder, CO: Westview Press.

——1990. Nimrods, piscators, pluckers, and planters: the emergence of food production. *Journal of Anthropological Archaeology* 9: 31–69.

——1992. Conclusions: ecology and complex hunter-gatherers. In B. Hayden, ed., *Complex Culture of the British Columbia Plateau*, pp. 525–63. Vancouver: University of British Columbia Press.

Hayden, Brian and Rob Gargett. 1990. Big man, big heart? A Mesoamerican view of the emergence of complex society. *Ancient Mesoamerica* 1: 3–20.

Helms, Mary W. 1988. *Ulysses' Sail: An Ethnographic Odyssey of Power, Knowledge and Geographical Distance*. Princeton: Princeton University Press.

Hoopes, John W. 1987. Early ceramics and the origins of village life in lower Central America. Ph.D. dissertation, Harvard University, Ann Arbor: University Microfilms.

Johnson, Gregory A. 1977. Aspects of regional analysis in archaeology. *Annual Review of Anthropology* 6: 479–508.

Josephides, Lisette. 1985. *The Production of Inequality: Gender and Exchange among the Kewa*. London: Tavistock.

Katz, Solomon H. and Mary M. Voigt. 1986. Bread and beer: the early use of cereals in the human diet. *Expedition* 28: 23–34.

Keeley, Lawrence H. 1988. Hunter-gatherer economic complexity and "population pressure": a cross-cultural analysis. *Journal of Anthropological Archaeology* 7(4): 373–411.

Kirch, Patrick V. 1984. *The Evolution of the Polynesian Chiefdoms*. Cambridge: Cambridge University Press.

Kirkby, Anne V. T. 1973. *The Use of Land and Water Resources in the Past and Present Valley of Oaxaca, Mexico*. Ann Arbor: The University of Michigan Museum of Anthropology, Memoir 5.

Lathrap, Donald W. 1977. Our father the cayman, our mother the gourd: Spinden revisited, or a unitary model for the emergence of agriculture in the New World. In C. A. Reed, ed., *Origins of Agriculture*, pp. 713–51. The Hague: Mouton.

Lederman, Rena. 1986. *What Gifts Engender: Social Relations and Politics in Mendi, Highland Papua New Guinea*. Cambridge: Cambridge University Press.

Lee, Richard B. 1990. Primitive communism and the origin of social inequality. In S. Upham, ed., *The Evolution of Political Systems: Sociopolitics in Small-Scale Sedentary Societies*, pp. 225–46. Cambridge: Cambridge University Press.

Lowe, Gareth W. 1975. *The Early Preclassic Barra Phase of Altamira, Chiapas: A Review with New Data*. Provo, UT: New World Archaeological Foundation, Papers 38.

McCracken, Grant. 1987. Clothing as language: an object lesson study of the expressive properties of material culture. In B. Reynolds and M. A. Scott, eds, *Material Anthropology: Contemporary Approaches to Material Culture*, pp. 103–28. Lanham, MD: University Press of America.

MacNeish, Richard S. 1964. Ancient Mesoamerican civilization. *Science* 143: 531–7.

Marcus, Joyce. 1983. The Espiridion complex and the origins of the Oaxacan Formative. In Flannery and Marcus 1983: 42–3.

Matson, R. G. 1985. The relationship between sedentism and status inequalities among hunters and gatherers. In M. Thompson, M. T. Garcia, and F. J. Kense, eds, *Status, Structure and Stratification: Current Archaeological Reconstructions*, pp. 245–51. Calgary: Archaeological Association, Department of Archaeology, University of Calgary.

Nelson, Fred W. and Barbara Voorhies. 1980. Trace element analysis of obsidian artifacts from three shell midden sites in the littoral zone. Chiapas, Mexico. *American Antiquity*, 45(3): 540–50.

Netting, Robert McC. 1990. Population, permanent agriculture, and polities: unpacking the evolutionary portmanteau. In S. Upham, ed., *The Evolution of Political Systems: Sociopolitics in Small-Scale Sedentary Societies*, pp. 21–61. Cambridge: Cambridge University Press.

Orenstein, Henry. 1980. Asymmetrical reciprocity: a contribution to the theory of political legitimacy. *Current Anthropology* 21: 69–91.

Otterbein, Keith F. 1985. *The Evolution of War: A Cross-Cultural Study.* New Haven: Human Relations Area File Press.

Paynter, Robert and John W. Cole. 1980. Ethnographic overproduction, tribal political economy, and the Kapauku of Irian Jaya. In E. B. Ross, ed., *Beyond The Myths of Culture: Essays in Cultural Materialism*, pp. 61–99. New York: Academic Press.

Price, Barbara J. 1977. Shifts in production and organization: a cluster-interaction model. *Current Anthropology* 18: 209–33.

—— 1984. Competition, productive intensification, and ranked society: speculations from evolutionary theory. In R. B. Ferguson, ed., *Warfare, Culture and Environment*, pp. 209–40. Orlando: Academic Press.

Price, T. Douglas and James A. Brown, eds. 1985. *Prehistoric Hunter-Gatherers: The Emergence of Cultural Complexity.* Orlando, NJ: Academic Press.

Renfrew, Colin and John F. Cherry, eds. 1986. *Peer Polity Interaction and Socio-Political Change.* Cambridge: Cambridge University Press.

Sack, Robert David. 1986. *Human Territoriality: Its Theory and History.* Cambridge: Cambridge University Press.

Sahlins, Marshall D. 1968. *Tribesmen.* Englewood Cliffs, NJ: Prentice-Hall.

Salisbury, Richard F. and Marilyn Silverman. 1977. An introduction: factions and the dialectic. In Silverman and Salisbury 1977, pp. 1–20.

Schmookler, Andrew Bard. 1984. *The Parable of the Tribes: The Problem of Power in Social Evolution.* Boston: Houghton Mifflin Company.

Schrijvers, Joke. 1986. Make your son a king: political power through matronage and motherhood. In M. A. van Bakel, R. R. Hagesteijn, and P. van de Velde, eds, *Private Politics: A Multi-Disciplinary Approach to "Big-Man" Systems*, pp. 13–32. Leiden: E. J. Brill.

Service, Elman R. 1975. *Origins of the State and Civilization.* New York: W. W. Norton.

Silverman, Marilyn. 1977. Village council and factionalism: definition and contextual issues. In Silverman and Salisbury 1977, pp. 66–98.

Silverman, Marilyn and Richard Salisbury (eds). 1977. *A House Divided? Anthropological Studies of Factionalism.* Institute of Social and Economic Research, Memorial University of Newfoundland, St John's.

Steinberg, Arthur. 1977. Technology and culture: technological styles in the bronzes of Shang Chin, Phrygia and Urnfield Central Europe. In H. Lechtman and R. Merrill, eds, *Material Culture: Styles, Organization, and Dynamics of Technology*, pp. 53–86. New York: West.

Strathern, Andrew J. 1966. Despots and directors in the New Guinea highlands. *Man* 1: 356–67.

Vincent, Joan. 1978. Political anthropology: manipulative strategies. *Annual Review of Anthropology* 7: 175–94.

Voorhies, Barbara. 1976. *The Chantuto People: An Archaic Period Society of the Chiapas Littoral, Mexico.* Provo, UT: New World Archaeological Foundation, Papers 41.

—— 1990. *Ancient Economies of the Soconusco: The Prehistory and History of the Economic Development in the Coastal Lowlands of Chiapas, Mexico.* Salt Lake City: University of Utah Press.

Wobst, H. Martin. 1974. Locational relationships in Paleolithic society. *Journal of Human Evolution* 5: 49–58.

Wolf, Eric R. 1966. Kinship, friendship and patron–client relationship in complex societies. In M. Banton, ed., *The Social Anthropology of Complex Societies*, pp. 1–22. London: Tavistock.

Woodburn, James. 1982. Egalitarian societies. *Man* 17: 431–51.

CHAPTER 13

Classic Maya Emblem Glyphs

Peter Mathews

One of the great breakthroughs in the decipherment of Maya hieroglyphic writing was the discovery by Heinrich Berlin in 1958 of a particular category of hieroglyph that he called "Emblem" Glyphs (Berlin 1958). Berlin had noticed that Emblem Glyphs had a fairly standard position and form in Maya texts: they occurred towards the end of passages, and they usually consisted of three signs – a prefix, a superfix, and a "main sign" (figure 13.1). The main sign of Emblem Glyphs, Berlin noted, was different from site to site but fairly consistent within each site's inscriptions. Copan's Emblem Glyph, for example, occurs very commonly in the inscriptions of Copan, but only rarely in texts outside that site.

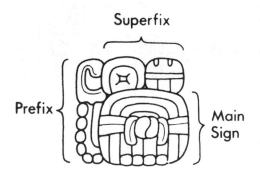

Figure 13.1 The standard form of the Emblem Glyph, using Yaxchilan as an example. The prefix is commonly known as the "water group." The main sign is usually a single sign, but in some Emblem Glyphs is a consistent combination of two or more signs.

Berlin was not the first to notice the homogeneity of these glyphs: J. Eric S. Thompson had already isolated several Emblem Glyphs through the common use of their prefix (Thompson 1950: figure 43). Berlin, however, was the first to notice the geographical implications of this set of glyphs. He called them Emblem Glyphs because they seemed to be emblematic, in some ways, of the site in which they predominantly occurred. Berlin left open, however, the question of their precise significance, i.e., whether Emblem Glyphs represent the name of the city itself, or of the patron deity or ruling dynasty of the city.

In his article Berlin illustrated the Emblem Glyphs of eight Classic Maya sites and discussed possible Emblem Glyphs at six others. In the years following the publication of his article, many additional Emblem Glyphs have been noted, so that there are now some three dozen sites with securely identified Emblem Glyphs. In addition, Classic Maya inscriptions contain several Emblem Glyphs which are still not identified as to site (figure 13.2).

There is still considerable debate over the precise role of Emblem Glyphs. Proskouriakoff (1960: 471) believed that they functioned as lineage or dynastic names; Barthel (1968a), who analyzed Emblem Glyphs in considerable detail, suggested that the prefix and superfix have a titular function, and that the main sign "seems to concern placenames as well as ethnic names" (Barthel 1968b: 120, translation mine). Kelley

Reprinted from Peter Mathews. 1991. Classic Maya Emblem Glyphs. In *Classic Maya Political History: Hieroglyphic and Archaeological Evidence*, edited by T. Patrick Bulbert (Cambridge University Press, New York), pp. 19–29.

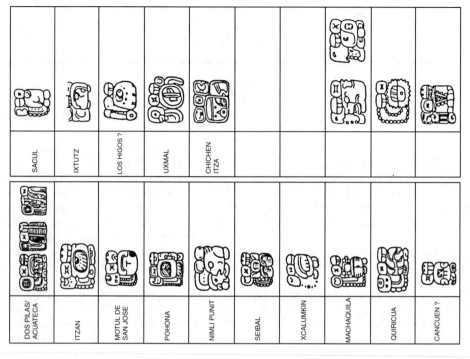

Figure 13.2 Known Emblem Glyphs (in approximate order of appearance).

(1976: 215), on the other hand, argued cogently that the main signs of Emblem Glyphs are place-names.

Most, if not all, of today's generation of epigraphers follow Kelley in regarding Emblem Glyph main signs as toponyms. However, there is still some disagreement on two key questions concerning Emblem Glyphs. First, what is the specific function of the prefix and superfix of Emblem Glyphs, and hence what is the overall reading and function of Emblem Glyphs? Second, what are the implications of Emblem Glyphs for the sociopolitical and geopolitical organization of the Classic Maya? As we shall see shortly, the second of these questions is the more hotly debated at the present time, despite continuing uncertainty over the solution to the first.

The Structure and Function of Emblem Glyphs

We have seen that Emblem Glyphs were isolated by Berlin largely because of their general consistency in form: usually they have a prefix, a superfix and a main sign. Ironically, it is the *inconsistencies* of their form – the rarer variants of Emblem Glyphs – that give us the best clues as to their specific functions and reading (figure 13.3). Many Emblem Glyphs can, on occasion, have a subfix below their main sign. By far the most common subfix is T130 (T number from Thompson's [1962] catalog of glyphs), a sign whose value *wa* or *−w* is accepted by most epigraphers. Although it is possible that this sign acts as a grammatical suffix, it is more likely that it functions as a phonetic complement, indicating the final *−w* of some word. Since it is subfixed to the Emblem Glyph main sign, it might be reasonable to deduce that the T130 *−w* suffix is a phonetic complement to the main signs of Emblem Glyphs. However, this would have the implication that all Emblem Glyph main signs – and there are some forty different ones known – are words that end in *−w*. This seems highly unlikely. Whenever the T130 subfix is present in an Emblem Glyph, T168 occurs as superfix, and so it is

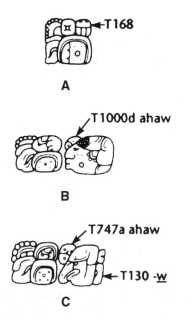

Figure 13.3 Variant forms of Emblem Glyphs: *(A)* "standard" form of Piedras Negras Emblem Glyph; *(B)* early variant of the Piedras Negras Emblem Glyph with T1000d ahau replacing the T168 superfix; *(C)* early variant of the Piedras Negras Emblem Glyph with T747a ahau replacing the T168 superfix. Note the T130 *−w* postfix to T747a.

possible to hypothesize the subfix as a phonetic complement to the *superfix*, the two signs perhaps qualifying the main sign that they embrace.

T168 is a sign whose derivation has been brilliantly worked out by Lounsbury (1973) as *ahpo* or *ahpop*, "ruler." Lounsbury argued that T168 later came to be read (especially in the Maya lowlands) *ahaw* (*ahau*), "lord." This reading makes good sense in the context of Emblem Glyphs, in view of the T130 *−w* phonetic complement associated with them. It also makes good sense in view of the context of Emblem Glyphs, for they invariably occur towards the end of name phrases of Maya rulers and nobles, and thus presumably have a general function as royal or noble titles. I have argued elsewhere (Mathews 1985: 32; Mathews and Justeson 1984: 216–19) that occasionally there are aberrant Emblem Glyph compounds in which no

T168 superfix occurs; in such cases, however, the glyph *following* the "Emblem Glyph" is a royal title. In most cases this title has the form T1000d or T747a, often with a T130 suffix (figure 13.3). These two signs are well recognized as head-variants of ahau (both occur, for example, as head variants of the day name Ahau). These variant Emblem Glyph forms show the substitution for T168 (as superfix to the main sign) of compounds that can be read ahau (and that follow the main sign). They therefore indicate that T168 is to be read ahau, and that the reading order of Emblem Glyphs was probably prefix + main sign + ahau.

The prefixes of Emblem Glyphs occur in several slightly variant forms, all belonging to what Thompson (1950: 274–81) referred to as the "water group" of prefixes, owing to the presence of a row of dots or droplets in most examples. In addition to interpretations of water, the droplets have been interpreted as kernels of maize, beads of incense, and pebbles used in divination. Barthel (1968a: 169–70) regarded Emblem Glyph prefixes as "patrilineal symbols." More recently, the droplets have been interpreted as drops of blood (Stuart 1984; Schele and Miller 1986: 175–208), perhaps to be read as "precious, holy, divine" or some such. Whether or not any of these interpretations is correct, the Emblem Glyph prefix does appear to be less important to the compound as a whole than the superfix and main sign, for it is frequently absent from Emblem Glyphs, apparently without radically changing their meaning.

So far we have looked at the affixes of Emblem Glyphs, and have seen that they functioned as titles, even though the prefix is still not well understood. The main sign and its interpretation have yet to be discussed. We have seen that there are several possible interpretations: place-name, patron deity, dynasty, or lineage name, and ethnic group. Each of these has been argued for to some extent, but most epigraphers nowadays accept place-name as the most likely candidate. There are several reasons for this. First, several Emblem Glyph main signs occur in a verbal compound signifying "war" (figure 13.4), a compound first interpreted by Riese (1984). In this compound they substitute with T526, *cab*, "earth" – a place-name *par excellence*. Second, in two examples from Seibal (see figure 13.4 G, H), the Emblem Glyph main sign is prefixed by T59, *ti/ta*. While there are several possible functions of *ti/ta*, the one that seems to fit here is that of spatial locative preposition "in, at (a place)." Finally, as Kelley (1976: 215) has pointed out, most of the major categories of Maya glyphs have now been deciphered or at least are understood. If Emblem Glyphs do not include references to the individual sites or polities, then there seems to be no such reference in the Maya inscriptions. In view of the historical and political nature of the texts, this absence would be most odd.

We are left, then, with an interpretation of Emblem Glyphs that sees them functioning as royal titles (they invariably occur in royal name phrases) and read perhaps as "divine Tikal lord," etc. The "divine" interpretation of the prefix is still far from proven but is viewed favorably by many epigraphers. The main sign is viewed by most epigraphers as a place-name, referring either to the city itself or to the territory that it controlled or to both. And the "lord" is precisely the title that we would expect to find in a royal name phrase.

Sociopolitical Implications of Emblem Glyphs

Even if we are correct in the above interpretation of Emblem Glyphs, we are still left with the question of the main sign and its implications. Does the main sign of Emblem Glyphs – which most epigraphers now see as a place-name – refer to the city itself (or to part of the city), or to the territory controlled by the city, the polity? Do Emblem Glyphs occur as equals in the political landscape of the Classic Maya, or do they occur in some sort of hierarchical arrangement? The second of these questions is the most contentious issue currently concerning Emblem Glyphs, as we shall see in the following paragraphs.

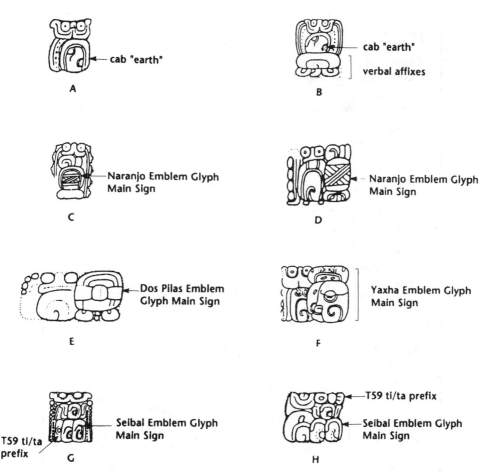

Figure 13.4 War compounds with *cab* "earth" or Emblem Glyph main signs.

Regarding the first question, there now seems to be considerable agreement that Emblem Glyphs refer to a wider geographical area than just the city. Marcus (1973: 913), for example, believes that Emblem Glyphs refer to "the site, as well as the territory subject to it." Whether or not this is the case (I believe that Marcus is correct), Emblem Glyphs can certainly be used in interpretations of Classic Maya political geography, for their very presence implies the functioning of local dynasties, and therefore of individual Maya sites. By looking at which Emblem Glyph sites were functioning at the same time, we can begin to attempt reconstructions of Classic Maya geography,

and by considering other details, such as individual dynasties and their external contacts, we can begin to determine the relationships between the sites and attempt reconstructions of the Classic Maya political landscape.

As early as 1968 Barthel argued that Emblem Glyphs could be arranged in a hierarchical structure, and also that on occasion groups of four Emblem Glyph sites could be seen as directional capitals of the Maya world (Barthel 1968a). Barthel's arguments were embraced and greatly developed by Marcus (1973, 1976), who has done more than any other scholar to develop our knowledge and understanding of Emblem

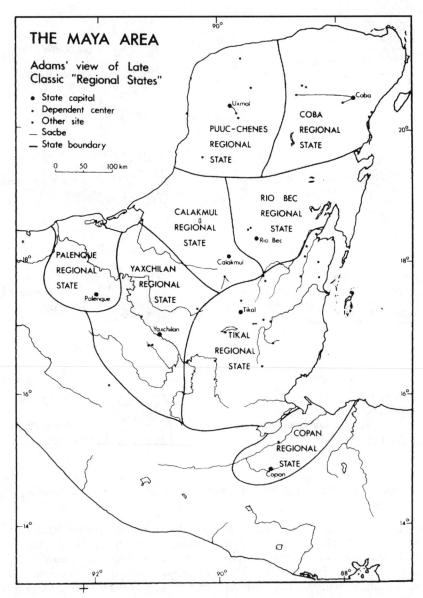

THE MAYA AREA

Adams' view of Late
Classic "Regional States"

- State capital
- Dependent center
- Other site
— Sacbe
— State boundary

0   50   100 km

Figure 13.5   Adams' (1986b) view of Late Classic political organization.

Glyphs. Marcus argued that sites with Emblem Glyphs were politically more important than those with none. Furthermore, she argued that a hierarchy existed among sites with Emblem Glyphs: "If Site A was dependent to Site B, I expected Site A to mention Site B more often than Site B mentioned Site A" (Marcus 1976: 10).

Marcus arrived at a five-tiered hierarchy of Maya sites, in which centers with Emblem Glyphs comprise the first two ranks, sites in levels 3 and 4 have monuments but no Emblem Glyphs, and shifting hamlets comprise the lowest level. Into this hierarchy, Marcus incorporated Barthel's groups of four Emblem Glyph sites, recorded on

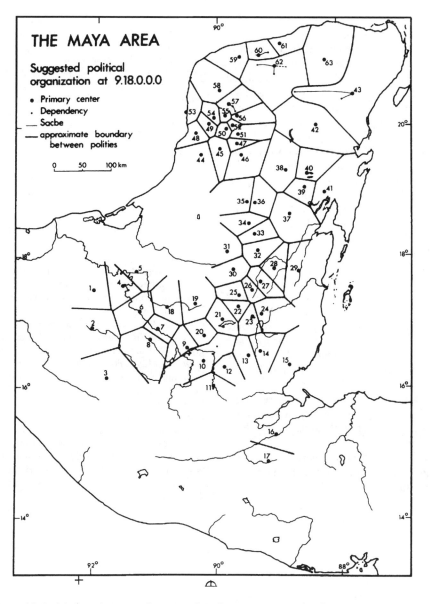

THE MAYA AREA

Suggested political
organization at 9.18.0.0.0

- Primary center
- Dependency
— Sacbe
— approximate boundary
 between polities

0   50   100 km

Figure 13.6 Mathews' suggested Maya political organization and polity centers at 9.18.0.0.0
(AD 790).

Copan Stela A (9.15.0.0.0; AD 731) and Seibal Stela 10 (10.1.0.0.0; AD 849). Marcus considered these monuments to refer to the four capitals of the Maya world at their respective dates. The four sites (and they differed slightly on the two monuments) held sway politically over other sites, even those with Emblem Glyphs, in their respective regions. In other words, the lords of the four capitals were overlords of the Maya world, and other dynasts were inferior. This view leads to the argument for very large polities during the Classic Maya period: R. E. W. Adams (1986: 437) –

largely following Marcus – has reconstructed eight "regional states" in the Late Classic Maya lowlands, with an average area of some 30,000 km^2 (figure 13.5).

My own view of Classic Maya political geography is somewhat different, for I do not see any hierarchical structure implied by Emblem Glyph patterns of occurrence. Rather, I see Emblem Glyphs, occurring in title phrases of Maya lords, as implying the *same* political rank – for the title involved is ahau, "lord." The Maya seem to have gone to some length when stating hierarchical political relationships (see Houston and Mathews 1985: figure 12); there is no implication of differential status in Emblem Glyph references.

If one considers all Emblem Glyphs to be references to sites and dynasties of equal political status, then there were at least as many polities functioning throughout the Classic Maya lowlands as there were Emblem Glyphs. I have argued for as many as two dozen independent polities in the southern Maya lowlands at 9.18.0.0.0 (AD 790; figure 13.6), and throughout the entire Maya lowlands at that date there might have been sixty or seventy autonomous "city-states," most with an area of about 2,500 km^2.

Which of these models is the more likely will no doubt be a matter of debate for some time to come.

REFERENCES

Adams, Richard E. W. 1986. Rio Azul. *National Geographic* 169: 420–51.

Barthel, Thomas S. 1968a. El Complejo Emblema. *Estudios de Cultura Maya* 7: 159–93.

——1968b. Historisches in den klassischen Mayainschriften. *Zeitschrift für Ethnologie* 93: 119–56.

Berlin, Heinrich. 1958. El Glifo "Emblema" en las Inscripciones Mayas. *Journal de la Société des Americanistes* (n.s.) 47: 111–19.

Houston, Stephen D. and Peter Mathews. 1985. *The Dynastic Sequence of Dos Pilas, Guatemala*. Pre-Columbian Art Research Institute Monograph 1. San Francisco.

Kelley, David H. 1976. *Deciphering Maya Script*. University of Texas Press, Austin.

Lounsbury, Floyd G. 1973. On the Derivation and Reading of the Ben-ich Prefix. In *Mesoamerican Writing Systems*, edited by Elizabeth P. Benson, pp. 9–143. Carnegie Institution, Washington, DC.

Marcus, Joyce. 1973. Territorial Organization of the Lowland Classic Maya. *Science* 180: 911–16.

——1976. *Emblem and State in the Classic Maya Lowlands*. Dumbarton Oaks, Washington, DC.

Mathews, Peter. 1985. Maya Early Classic Monuments and Inscriptions. In *A Consideration of the Early Classic Period in the Maya Lowlands*, edited by Gordon R. Willey and Peter Mathews, pp. 5–54. Institute of Mesoamerican Studies, State University of New York, Albany.

Mathews, Peter and John S. Justeson. 1984. Patterns of Sign Substitution in Maya Hieroglyphic Writing: The Affix Cluster. In *Phoneticism in Maya Hieroglyphic Writing*, edited by Johns S. Justeson and Lyle Campbell, pp. 185–231. Institute for Mesoamerican Studies Publication 9. State University of New York, Albany.

Proskouriakoff, Tatiana. 1960. Historical Implications of a Pattern of Dates at Piedras Negras, Guatemala. *American Antiquity* 25: 454–75.

Riese, Berthold. 1984. Kriegsberichte der Klassischen Maya. *Baessler-Archiv* (n.f.) 30: 255–321.

Schele, Linda and Mary Ellen Miller. 1986. *The Blood of Kings: Dynasty and Ritual in Maya Art*. George Braziller, New York.

Stuart, David. 1984. Royal Auto-sacrifice among the Maya: A Study in Image and Meaning. *Res: Anthropology and Aesthetics* 7/8: 6–20.

Thompson, J. Eric. 1950. *Maya Hieroglyphic Writing: An Introduction*. Carnegie Institute of Washington Publication 589. Carnegie Institution, Washington, DC.

——1962. *A Catalog of Maya Hieroglyphs*. University of Oklahoma Press, Norman.

CHAPTER 14

Ideology in Ancient Maya Cultural Evolution

The Dynamics of Galactic Polities

Arthur A. Demarest

White (1949: 364–5) defines ideology as systems of religion, values, beliefs, or symbols through which human experience finds its interpretation. Here, I would prefer to apply the term more narrowly as it refers to ritual, religion, and explicit cosmology. In most of this chapter, I stress what might be called *religious ideology*, including formal religion as well as the precise guidance of formalized religious institutions or dogmas. In this sense an *ideology* is a set of interrelated ideas that provides the members of a group with a rationale for their existence. A formal *religion* is a particular kind of religious ideology, one based on beliefs in supernatural beings or forces, with a more standardized presentation of these beliefs and, generally, an institutional structure. The political and economic impact of these ideologies is the issue of central concern here, but we should avoid definitions of ideology that are so broad as to be synonymous with political relations, world view, or even "culture." I would prefer to bind my definition more closely to formal, explicit ritual, religion, and cosmology, and only subsequently to examine their broader impact and implications.

The Maya civilization left us with among the richest sets of pre-Columbian evidence on these aspects of culture. Their art, iconography, artifacts, and written texts given detailed views of Maya religion, ritual, and cosmology. Mayanists now have a vast knowledge of Classic Maya world view, myths, and political ideology. It should not, then, be difficult to address the issue of the role of ideology in the history and evolution of the Classic Maya civilization of Central America. Yet, the uneven and incomplete nature of the evidence on Classic Maya economics and subsistence systems makes it difficult to speculate on the relationship between their ideology and their material base. The ongoing revolution in hieroglyphic decipherment and recent discoveries in chronology and subsistence have further complicated the situation by rendering obsolete most of the earlier reconstructions of the nature and dynamics of the Maya state.

It is necessary, then, to begin by assessing the problems of Maya archaeology and the most plausible current interpretations of the Classic Maya state, including its still uncertain functions, its volatile political dynamics, and the apparent sources of power and authority for Maya rulers. In assessing the new evidence on each of these issues, I speculate on the role of ideology and its relationship to other factors in Maya cultural history. Finally, I expand earlier discussions (Demarest 1984a, 1986, 1988) of a specific set of analogies drawn

Reprinted from Arthur A. Demarest. 1992. Ideology in Ancient Maya Cultural Evolution: The Dynamics of Galactic Polities. In *Ideology and Pre-Columbian Civilizations*, edited by Arthur A. Demarest and Geoffrey W. Conrad (School of American Research Press, Santa Fe), pp. 135–58. Copyright 1992 by the School of American Research, Santa Fe, New Mexico.

from Southeast Asian history that might provide insights into the role of ideology in the evolution and unstable political dynamics of Classic Maya society.

The Problematic Maya Civilization: The Enigmas and Materialist Solutions

The Maya civilization has always presented a challenge to archaeologists and anthropologists interested in cultural evolution. Unlike the arid river valley systems in which most early states flourished, the Classic Maya civilization flourished in a lowland jungle environment. Moreover, their settlement strategy was dispersed rather than nucleated. Most specific models of cultural evolution have emphasized the role of ecological parameters, such as geographical circumscription, irrigation in arid environments, resource deficiency, and environmental diversity. Yet the Mayas raised their cities and ceremonial centers in seeming contradiction to ecological rationality and achieved their florescence in a dense, subtropical rain forest with generally thin and poor soils, unstable fresh-water supplies, few navigable rivers, and less environmental diversity or environmental circumscription than their highland neighbors.

In light of this ecological situation, it is also interesting that Maya culture was unusually heavily invested in both collective ritual life and individual symbols of ideological power. This investment is manifest in their monuments – ideological statements expressed in millions of tons of stone. Interpreters of ancient Maya culture history have puzzled over a possible relationship between the Maya obsession with ritual and its unusual ecological circumstances as a rain-forest civilization. The easiest solution was simply to dismiss this exasperating tropical civilization by suggesting that the Mayas were a unique culture, that they were a short-lived anomaly, that they never really attained the level of a state, or that Maya states were secondary by-products of more ecologically "normal" highland civilizations (cf. Meggers 1954; Price 1978; Sanders

1962; Sanders and Price 1968; Thompson 1966). These suggestions have never been convincing to most scholars, and archaeologists have continued to puzzle over how and why the Classic Maya sustained elaborate public ritual and architecture in their rain-forest environment.

In the 1960s and 1970s, great strides were made in improving our understanding of lowland Maya ecology, settlement patterns, and written history. Building on these discoveries, some scholars sought to understand Maya civilization by reexamining its ecology and reworking earlier interpretive concepts. Changes in Maya chronology, ecology, and demography seemed to allow for a less paradoxical reconstruction of the early rise of Maya civilization and the managerial functions of the early Maya state. Drawing on this new evidence, the participants in the 1975 School of American Research advanced seminar on Maya origins agreed on a general ecological/demographic model to account for the rise of Maya civilization (e.g. Adams 1977; Ball 1977; Rathje 1977; Sanders 1977; Webster 1977; Willey 1977). This interpretation held that, by the end of the Late Preclassic period, ecological circumstances required a managerial elite and provided them with the means to achieve coercive power. New demographic estimates were believed to show population pressure by Late Preclassic times (Ball 1977). New subsistence evidence seemed to indicate that the Mayas responded to this pressure by intensification of agriculture and the creation of terraces, canals, and raised fields (Adams, Brown, and Culbert 1981; Netting 1977). In turn, these systems would have increased the need for management in their construction and maintenance. Finally, evidence of fortifications implied that in the Late Preclassic period population pressure might have culminated in conflict over resources, creating the need for military leadership (Ball 1977; Webster 1977).

Meanwhile, the ecology and environment of the Maya lowlands was redefined, bringing it into closer alignment with patterns observed for other civilizations. Carneiro

(1970) and Webster (1975, 1977) applied a flexible concept of "social circumscription" to redefine the sprawling limestone plain of the Maya lowlands as "socially circumscribed" – presumably because of the absence of unoccupied zones around it. Sanders (1977) argued that the Maya lowlands could be redefined as "environmentally diverse" since soil qualities, water accessibility, and areas of uplands varied between zones. Rathje (1977) argued that the lack of volcanic stone, salt, and other commodities would further necessitate interregional exchange and symbiosis, creating additional needs for a managerial elite. After these revisions of the evidence, all the factors that had been defined in central Mexico and other world regions as ecological prime movers seemed to apply to the Mayas as well. The Maya lowlanders were believed to have bred themselves into an ecological crisis leading to state formation. By the end of the Preclassic, the responses were agricultural intensification, regional and interregional exchange, and warfare – all responses that helped to generate state leadership.

In the past decade, however, new discoveries have undermined many of these reworkings of the Maya civilization. Recent findings (1) push back the entire chronology for the rise of Maya civilization by four to five centuries, (2) leave the archaeological evidence for warfare several centuries too late for it to be a major factor in the initial rise of Maya states, and (3) generally indicate that settlement patterns suggesting demographic pressure also postdate state formation by at least several centuries (e.g. Andrews V 1981; Andrews V et al. 1984; Demarest 1984a; Freidel 1979; Hansen 1989; Laporte 1986; Matheny 1980; Pendergast 1981; Robertson and Freidel 1986).

In retrospect, it is now clear that we had played some games with terms like "social circumscription," "environmental diversity," and "resource deficiency" in the popular theories of the 1970s. We failed to recognize that these terms are *relative*. Any region can be interpreted as being socially circumscribed or environmentally diverse. Yet, an objective assessment must judge the

Maya lowlands as geologically and ecologically *less* diverse and *less* circumscribed than any area of comparable size in Mesoamerica south of the northern Mesa Central of Mexico. Similarly, it is hard to argue for demographic pressure and circumscription before about 100 BC. Rathje's alleged "resource deficiency" of the Maya lowlands disappears with recent evidence that "needed" goods were available locally (e.g. salt, chert, limestone metates) and long-distance imports were primarily ideological in function (e.g. quetzal feathers, obsidian blades, jade). Thus, problems of both logic and evidence are evident in all of the proposed materialist solutions.

The Instability of Maya States: The Many "Rises" and "Falls" of Lowland Maya Civilization

In the end, efforts to understand Maya ecology and state formation were misled by a flawed chronology. Indeed, current evidence indicates that we may not find a single trajectory and set of causes for the rise of Maya civilization. Instead, we find a complex and heterogeneous civilization, one that may have experienced multiple rises and falls, florescences and declines. The recent research at El Mirador, Cerros, Nohmul, Nakbe, the Mundo Perdido zone of Tikal, and other sites not only provides an earlier general history for the Mayas, it also reveals a multiplicity of contradictory developmental sequences for ancient Maya states (Demarest 1984a; Freidel 1979; Hansen 1989; Laporte 1989; Matheny 1986). Although the rise and decline of El Mirador, Cerros, and Nakbe occurred within the Preclassic period, later and different evolutionary trajectories have been found for other sites.

There is also now evidence for at least three crises between AD 1 and 1000: the "decline" at the beginning of the Early Classic, the mid-Classic hiatus, and the southern lowland collapse in the Terminal Classic. Some explanations of these three declines have once again proposed uniform, pan-lowland ecological processes. For example,

Dahlin (1983, 1984) has invoked desiccation to explain the Protoclassic or initial Classic collapse of El Mirador, Cerros, and other sites. Sheets (1979, 1983), Sharer (1982), and Dahlin (1979) have suggested that the eruption of the volcano Ilopango in El Salvador was a major factor in the decline of the Late Preclassic centers in the highlands, setting the stage for a Classic-period recovery centered on Tikal and the northeastern Peten.

None of these new hypotheses account for the fact that most "declines" of the Maya polities are not chronologically aligned. For example, the Early Classic decline in ceremonial construction activity at El Mirador probably occurs earlier than the parallel declines in Belize. It is also probable that, at least at some lowland sites, the Early Classic population decline has been exaggerated by the persistence of Late Preclassic domestic wares into the Classic period, falsely dating Early Classic houses to the Late Preclassic period (e.g. Hester 1979; Valdez 1987, personal communication 1988; Willey and Mathews 1985). At other centers the Early Classic was a period of great prosperity. For example, Laporte's excavations in the Mundo Perdido zone of Tikal (Laporte 1989; Laporte and Fialko 1985; Laporte and Vega de Zea 1987) exposed a flourishing epicenter with wealth, control over labor, and political development that grew at an accelerated pace right through the Preclassic – Classic interface and into the Early Classic. So, the declines in fortune at some centers, such as El Mirador, were paralleled by florescence elsewhere, as at Tikal. Slightly later Early Classic boom periods were experienced at Altun Ha (Pendergast 1979), Rio Azul (Adams 1986; Adams et al. 1984), and other sites (Mathews 1985).

The so-called sixth-century hiatus has likewise proven to reflect *variability* in the power and construction activity of the major centers rather than a general epoch of decline. Indeed, epigraphic evidence now shows that the sixth- and seventh-century hiatus in northeast Peten was in fact a period of political expansion by centers like Caracol, Belize, and later Dos Pilas, which eclipsed the Tikal regional state (Chase and Chase 1987; Culbert 1988b; Demarest and Houston 1990). The result was a reduction of construction activity by Tikal and its allies. Tikal recovered in the Late Classic, drawing labor and power through its domination of Uaxactun and other sites (Culbert 1988b), but this recovery caused an apparent eighth-century "decline" in construction activity at other sites within Tikal's sphere of influence.

Similar inversely correlated power relations are documented in the hieroglyphic inscriptions, public architecture, and population estimates of other Classic-period centers (cf. Willey 1986). Breakthroughs in hieroglyphic decipherments have enabled Mathews and others (e.g. Beetz and Satterthwaite 1981; Culbert 1988b; Houston and Mathews 1985; Mathews 1985, 1988; Mathews and Willey 1990; Riese 1980; Schele and Mathews 1990; Schele and Miller 1986) to plot the boundaries of Maya regional states in the Classic period. These studies have shown that their area was generally small (less than 2,000 square kilometers). Stable, large-scale, unified political hierarchies may never have existed in the lowlands (Culbert 1988b; Mathews 1988; cf. Adams 1986; Marcus 1976), but areas controlled by even small centers could expand or contract by 100 percent in less than a century (Mathews 1988). Some centers, such as Tikal (Culbert 1988b), Caracol (Chase and Chase 1987), and Dos Pilas (Demarest and Houston 1989, 1990; Houston 1987; Houston and Mathews 1985) had episodes of rapid expansion that allowed them to generate large, loose hegemonies.

The picture that emerges from all of the evidence is one of a volatile political dynamic with the fortunes of centers rising and falling throughout the Classic period, and with the networks of subordinate centers correspondingly expanding and contracting. We can presume that their control over labor (voluntary or tributary) for monuments and public architecture varied with these fluctuations, as reflected in episodes of frenzied construction followed by periods of little activity. Similar bursts and declines in construction activity have even been demonstrated in the Preclassic period at Nakbe (Hansen 1989), El Mirador (Demarest 1984a; Matheny 1986), and Cerros (Robertson and Freidel 1986) and in the Classic period at Tikal, Copan, Caracol, and other sites (Ashmore and Sharer 1975; Chase and Chase 1987; Dahlin 1976; Fash 1983). Yet these myriad Maya states were linked together by elite interaction, trade, and ideology into a single, ethnically distinct cultural system – what Freidel, Sabloff, and others have referred to as a "peerpolity" network (Freidel 1986; Sabloff 1986).

It should be clear from this new historical and archaeological evidence that we can no longer hope to trace a single linear trajectory for lowland Maya civilization. Instead, each regional polity had its own individual developmental history, with large numbers of centers (but not all) aligning only during the ninth-century collapse. In this respect the Maya political landscape resembles that of early competitive states in Mesopotamia and Southeast Asia rather than the more centralized regional polities like Teotihuacan, Tiahuanaco, or Early Dynastic Egypt.

Why is the Maya civilization characterized by heterogeneous and regionalized culture histories? More important, why did they continue to maintain this pattern throughout the Classic period without ever achieving the unification of large regional polities? Local variation in ecology and climate may be a partial explanation, but civilizations that sprawled across far more variable terrains have had much more developmental uniformity and achieved more centralized polities than those characteristic of the Mayas. Any study of Maya history must now address the question of the causes and implications of the political instability as indicated by the archaeological and epigraphic evidence. In turn, the key to understanding the complexity and variability of lowland Maya development may lie in the sources of power in ancient Maya society and the political dynamics that these sources would generate.

Sources of Power and Authority in the Classic Maya States

As in most world regions, discussion of Maya state power has been dominated by functionalist or managerial theories. These theories have designated ecological parameters like arid riverine landscapes (Wittfogel 1955), environmental diversity (Sanders 1968), circumscription (Carneiro 1970), resource deficiency (Rathje 1971), or verticality (Isbell 1978) as responsible for the specific cultural activities (irrigation, markets, territorial warfare, long-distance trade, etc.) that require the development of political leadership for their management or direction. As discussed above, however, because of the new evidence on chronology and environment, the functionalist and environmental theories did not survive the scrutiny of the past decade. Still, we must discover the precise nature of Maya state involvement in local or long-distance exchange, warfare, agriculture, and other activities if we are to understand the unusually volatile dynamics of Maya states. The hard data suggest that Maya rulers were usually most involved in the aspects of each of these activities that relate to ideological authority and political legitimation.

Classic Maya exchange systems, elite interaction, and ideology

Some theories have stressed the role of elite management in Maya exchange systems. Coordination was seen as vital because of ecological pressures for intercenter trade owing to lowland shortages of basic resources (Rathje 1971) or environmental diversity (Sanders 1977) – both of which I criticized above on several grounds (also see Culbert 1977; Dillon 1975; Sharer 1977). From the presently thin evidence on subsistence it would appear that no state-directed complex systems were necessary. The variety of Maya subsistence methods and cultigens (e.g. Hellmuth 1977; Marcus 1982) would have enabled them to balance out any resource deficiencies locally, and each regional Maya polity was probably largely self-sufficient in subsistence goods. Analyses of energetics and transport indicate that throughout Mesoamerica exchange of foodstuffs was limited to the local or intraregional level (e.g. Culbert 1988a; Drennan 1984; Sanders and Santley 1983).

The most recent studies of nonsubsistence exchange systems in the Maya area have also stressed the predominantly localized and intraregional nature of Classic Maya economies. Production and exchange of utilitarian objects appear to have been controlled at the level of local communities (Ball and Taschek 1989; Fry 1979; Rands and Bishop 1980; Rice 1987). Long-distance exchange of commodities like obsidian and salt may not have required complex administration (Clark 1986; Drennan 1984; Marcus 1983; Sanders and Webster 1988; Sidrys 1978), but the state was probably involved in trade in exotic goods and high-quality lithics (Belizean chert, obsidian, etc.). Overall, although evidence remains admittedly insufficient, it now appears unlikely that control or management of exchange systems in foodstuffs or utilitarian goods was a principal source of Maya state authority. There is no evidence that these systems were highly evolved or that they were state-controlled.

In contrast, it is clear that rulers and elites were very concerned with exchange of a specific set of nonutilitarian, status-reinforcing goods. Elite trade or gift exchange in status-reinforcing exotic goods was important in *political* interaction. Archaeological research by Ball and Taschek (1989) and compositional studies by Ronald L. Bishop (personal communication, 1988 and 1989) have demonstrated direct elite control of production and exchange of certain fine polychrome ceramic types, eccentric lithics, carved jade, and exotic objects. Other important items of long-distance trade were quetzal feathers, jade, and obsidian. The first two are symbols of rulership, whereas the third had utilitarian uses. However, very fine cherts or highland obsidian obtained by long-distance trade were often used to produce eccentrics for scepters, tools for bloodletting, exotics for tombs and

caches, and exquisite spearheads for ritual warfare (e.g. Gibson 1986). Freidel (1992) and Schele (1984) believe that even simple obsidian blades were often tools for autosacrifice, a hypothesis supported by recent contextual associations with dried blood and bloodletting bowls in temple caches (William L. Fash, personal communication 1986).

Although limited in quantity, these exotic goods were critical in identification of the divine elite class, enhancement of their prestige, and definition of their relations. Sabloff (1986) and Freidel (1986) have emphasized that these elite exchange networks were critical to peer polity interaction, while limited redistribution of exotics reinforced the loyalty and patronage of nobles and retainers. Thus, the managerial involvement of rulers in trade systems seems to have been focused on items of an *ideological* nature, items that formed a very limited, but politically critical, portion of the lowland economy.

Classic Maya warfare, interaction, and ideology

Warfare was another area in which Maya rulers had a managerial role, yet again the role generally focused on the ideology of political legitimation. Warfare had an early impact on the development of Maya society, probably as a pressure enabling chiefs to extend their power beyond kinship-defined systems (cf. Demarest 1978; Webster 1975). Yet its direct economic impact, positive or negative, appears relatively small when compared to its impact on central Mexico, Peru, or Bolivia (as described by other contributors to this volume). Warfare became less restricted during the last part of the Classic period and in situations of conflict across ethnic boundaries (Cowgill 1979; Demarest 1978; Webster 1975, 1977), but epigraphy and archaeology show that defeat in warfare did *not* usually lead to political domination of the defeated center. For example, it has been demonstrated that Quirigua's famous defeat of Copan (celebrated in many monuments) did not lead to territorial control of Copan by Quirigua or to an economic decline at Copan itself. Indeed, after this defeat, Copan went on to its greatest period of monumental construction. The same occurred after Tikal's defeat in AD 678 by Dos Pilas (Demarest and Houston 1990). Tikal's next king, Ruler A, was *not* a vassal of Dos Pilas; rather, he led Tikal into its greatest period of florescence.

Throughout most of the Preclassic and Classic periods, warfare was ritualized and culturally constrained to varying degrees (Demarest 1978, 1984b; Freidel 1986; Schele 1986). In most cases the spoils of war were probably sacrificial victims, the status reinforcement of the victory itself, access to some captives as slaves, and some amount of tribute (primarily in nonsubsistence exotic goods). As Freidel (1986) has pointed out, warfare was usually closer in its effects to interdynastic marriage than to territorial absorption; in other words, it was another form of elite interaction, alliance, and information exchange. Moreover, like all of the other forms of elite interaction, Maya warfare was deeply embedded in ritual and religious institutions. Like coronations, period-endings, births, funerals, and other royal events, warfare provided an occasion for the elite visits and elaborate public rituals that helped to hold the Classic Maya world together. Recent syntheses of deciphered Maya texts have detailed the elaborate webs of ritual events and contacts between elites (e.g. Mathews 1988; Miller 1986; Schele and Mathews 1990; Schele and Miller 1986).

Still, the economic and political impact of Maya warfare in some cases could be quite significant, especially in the cases of the territorial expansion of conquest states like those of Tikal (e.g. Culbert 1988b), Dos Pilas (Demarest and Houston 1989, 1990), and Caracol (Chase and Chase 1987). Yet even these largest of Maya conquest states controlled extended territories for less than a century before they retracted to "standard" size for Maya polities. In most cases the political or economic gains from warfare came indirectly from ideological effects – the enhancement of the prestige of the victorious ruler and his lineage. For example, the sacrifice of Copan's high king enhanced Quirigua's prestige, legitimated the power of its dynasty, and increased the local power of its rulers over their own populace (Fash 1988; Fash and Stuart 1990; Sharer 1978). The higher status of Quirigua's dynasty was ensured by the public ritual of royal captive sacrifice repeatedly advertised in public monumental sculptures and inscriptions. Thus, the dynasty strengthened its power over the populace and increased its ability to draw on the labor and loyalty of the citizens – an ideological effect that led to very concrete material gains. The same occurred in the case of the defeat of Tikal by Dos Pilas in AD 678. Tikal was not dominated, nor did it lapse into deeper decline, but the prestige of Dos Pilas's Ruler 1 was greatly enhanced by the victory, which was celebrated in many stone monuments. The increased prestige helped to launch this young center on its own campaign of expansionism.

Intensive agriculture and the economic role of Maya leadership

The role of the state in constructing or managing agricultural intensification or hydraulics is as yet unclear. In Yucatan, polities may have been involved in the management of fairly substantial agricultural and water-management systems (Harrison and Turner 1978; Matheny 1976; Turner 1974). In the rain forest of the southern lowlands, these managerial activities might have been less crucial. The discovery of raised field and canal systems in some areas led Mayanists to envision intensive agricultural systems across wide stretches of the Peten (Adams 1983; Adams, Brown, and Culbert 1981; Culbert, Magers, and Spencer 1978; Matheny 1976), some of which were identified using SLAR and other satellite and aerial imagery. Some of the SLAR imagery interpretations were questionable, however, and subsequent ground checking has disproven the existence of most proposed systems (e.g. Dahlin, Foss, and Chambers 1980; Dunning and Demarest 1990; Pope and Dahlin 1989). In most areas, soil types and lacustrine hydrology are inappropriate for extensive raised field agriculture (Dunning and Demarest 1990; Pope and Dahlin 1989). These findings cast doubt on theories that raised field agriculture, state-directed or otherwise, was a major subsistence base for the lowlands.

The most recent studies of rain-forest eco-systems view them as incredibly complex and fragile with a wide diversity and dispersal of species. Human systems successfully adapt to rain forests by mimicking this dispersed nature and complexity. Thus, Maya agriculture was probably a complex mix of techniques, each in relatively small units, adapted to the limits and possibilities of specific types of econiches (Dunning and Demarest 1990; Nations and Nigh 1980; Ruthenberg 1981). Again, this finding casts doubt on the need for centralized management – or even its desirability (cf. Flannery 1968). Certainly, the specific types of agricultural regimes in the lowlands could have been managed by local corporate groups.

Even if large-scale intensive agricultural systems were present in some areas, it does not follow that state control existed. Mayanists sometimes overlook the implications of decades of research in Mesopotamia, which demonstrate that extensive irrigation systems in Ubaid and Early Uruk times were probably locally constructed and managed without major state intervention (Adams 1965, 1966, 1981; Adams and Nissen 1972). In the southern Maya lowlands the irregular distribution and alternation of swidden plots, raised fields extending outward from uplands, and irregular canal systems can be compared to the Ubaid pattern: growth by accretion of many small, local efforts. An even better example of the disjunction between political power and economic infrastructure can be seen in the rain-forest civilizations of Southeast Asia, the so-called galactic polities or theater states (Bentley 1986; Geertz 1980; Gesick 1983; Tambiah 1976). Some of these states have complex systems of intensive agriculture with an elaborate bureaucracy, yet most

analysts agree that the state itself probably had no control over local economic systems (Bentley 1986; Gesick, ed. 1983).

Direct archaeological evidence for state involvement in agricultural management is lacking in the southern lowlands. Hierarchies of administrative centers, unpopulated agrarian landscapes, and highly organized and aligned fields, canals, or raised field systems have not been found. The state-controlled agricultural landscape described by Kolata (1992) in the Titicaca basin contrasts sharply with the Maya patchwork of garden, slash-and-burn, terrace, and occasionally raised fields. Nor is there evidence or representations of rulers' involvement in agriculture in the extensive, propagandistic Maya monumental art, murals, ceramic art, and artifacts, unlike that found in Egypt, Mesopotamia, and elsewhere. The kinds of metaphorical claims of Maya control over nature described by Freidel (1992), Freidel and Schele (1988a, 1988b), and Taube (1985) were statements of only a broad spiritual power to invoke prosperity or fecundity. This negative evidence is hardly conclusive, but it does raise doubts about the common assumption of state management based on the mere presence of extensive field or terrace systems in the Maya area.

Thus there is an absence of any clear iconographic, settlement, or administrative evidence for state involvement, and the specific Maya agricultural regimes identified in any one zone were apparently autonomous, diverse, and not extensive. It is probable, then, that the agricultural managerial function was weakly developed in the Maya state. It is rather distressing that after more than a century of archaeological research in the Maya lowlands, we still do not really know the role of the state in Maya agriculture or even the precise nature of the agricultural system itself. Ongoing research is exploring southern lowland agricultural systems on a regional level and looking for evidence of any degree of management or involvement by the elites of regional centers. Given current evidence, however, it seems highly unlikely that control of agricultural systems was a major element of Maya state power.

The role of ideology in Maya polities

One inescapable deduction from the discussion presented above is that both local power and interpolity connections were based heavily on ideological support and sanction: in other words, the role of ritual, religion, public display, and monumental propaganda was central to Classic Maya society. We have seen that this ideological component was critical to elite involvement in both long-distance trade and warfare, and that other economic functions for state leadership may have been poorly developed. Here I would like to stress what should be obvious: religion itself was a principal source, perhaps *the* source, of the power of Maya rulers.

In a recent series of works, Schele, Freidel, Miller, Stuart, and others have detailed the ideology of kingship that held Maya polities together by legitimating the ruler's role, sacralizing the elite class, and specifying rulers' ritual and shamanistic functions (Freidel 1981, 1986; Freidel and Schele 1988a, 1988b; Schele 1985; Schele and Freidel 1990; Schele and Miller 1986; Stuart 1984). As Freidel (1992) demonstrates, the Mayas viewed their leaders as embodiments of the axis of the universe and conduits of communication between the secular and divine worlds. The latter included the world of the Maya earth-sky deities, the world of the revered ancestors, and the world of other divine rulers here on earth. The glyphic and iconographic evidence leaves no doubt that the Mayas themselves considered these roles of *axis mundi*, source of sacred blood, prognosticator, and royal shaman to be the principal functions of the ruler. The bulk of Maya labor was spent in construction of the elaborate stages of their ceremonial centers – plazas, temples, facades, monuments, costumes, exotics, and paraphernalia – all for these ritual events. Warfare and long-distance trade provided, respectively, the captives and goods needed to stage and costume these awe-inspiring displays.

The interaction between elites of different centers reinforced the power drawn from local rituals and religion by sharply defining the class that had access to this power. As Helms has shown (e.g. 1979), the interaction of rulers with their distant peers was similar in its legitimating effect to Maya rulers' claims of contact with the upper worlds of the sky gods or the lower worlds of ancestors and deities. Thus, elite interaction not only defined relations between centers but also enhanced the ruler in his local role as a spiritual leader. We have seen that long-distance trade and warfare were especially concerned with interpolity interaction and elite peer definition.

Other mechanisms of intrapolity interaction reinforced the ties between the major center and its local subordinate centers or rural populations. For example, Vogt (1983, 1985) emphasizes the importance of ritual circuits and movements from center to periphery in ancient and ethnographic Maya culture. The movement of idols from the center to the periphery of sites was critical in all periods as indicated by the ethnohistorical record (Coe 1965; Tozzer 1941) and by the archaeological presence of ceremonial causeways connecting temple complexes within and between sites. On a wider scale, Freidel has stressed the role of religious pilgrimages and periodic markets in Maya settlement patterns (1981). He points out that these mechanisms enabled the Maya to hold states together against the centrifugal force of the ecologically adaptive rain-forest settlement pattern of residential dispersion.

Thus, the ideological role of leaders cannot be dismissed as their own "emic" delusions; they were a very real, direct source of prestige, charisma, and, thus, access to labor and resources. A recent study by Monaghan (1990) of contemporary and ancient Mixtec sacrifice and tribute shows how elites acquired resources through direct payment for religious services. These "gifts" often took the form of status-reinforcing goods that symbolically defined membership in the ruler class. In exchange for privilege and power, elites provided religious services and their role as intermediaries with the spiritual world. Similarly, the impressive public displays carried out on the stage of Maya ceremonial centers were a direct source of support – not merely legitimating, but generating power. The epistemology of many archaeologists in recent years has dictated that ideological factors must be regarded as a reinforcement, legitimation, or simply a "phantasmic representation" of the "real" (generally economic) sources of power. But studies analyzing state power in Southeast Asia and elsewhere have proven that in some states the rituals themselves are a true source of power, and sometimes it is state control of the underlying economic base that is "phantasmic."

Southeast Asian and Maya Galactic Polities: The Dynamics of Ideologically Dependent States

The previous observation leads us inevitably to consider the remarkable similarities between political dynamics in the Maya area and those of Southeast Asia. Striking parallels to lowland Classic Maya states can be found in the historically known polities of Southeast Asia (Coe 1961; Demarest 1984a, 1986, 1988), variously called "galactic polities," *negara, mandala*, or "theater states." I have already reviewed salient characteristics of Maya states, including the competitive dynamics of the peer-polity landscape, the instability of individual polities, and the critical role of rulers in warfare, in trade for prestige goods, and in grand ritual display in the ceremonial centers. All of these features and many more similar traits are found in the polities of Southeast Asia.

Galactic polities and theater states

To improve our understanding of Maya political dynamics and the role of ideology, particular insights can be gained through application and modification of concepts developed by historians and archaeologists studying Southeast Asian polities (e.g. Bentley 1986; Fritz 1985, 1986; Fritz, Michell,

and Rao 1985; Geertz 1980; Gesick 1983; Higham 1989; Tambiah 1976, 1982, 1984; van Liere 1980). Through comparisons we can benefit from the more complete record of the historical kingdoms of Southeast Asia, a long scholarly tradition of analysis, and the past two decades of debate on the nature and sources of power in these polities. We can also hope that the striking similarities among these rain-forest civilizations might reveal some broader explanatory factors.

All conceptions of the segmentary states of Southeast Asia view them as forming a volatile, competitive, peer-polity landscape (*sensu* Renfrew and Cherry 1986). Like the Classic Maya kingdoms, Southeast Asian polities were highly unstable and had inversely correlated fortunes. Yet, as in the Maya case, these polities shared cultural values and traits that gave the regional civilization an enduring character. Together they formed "a vast political arena in southeast Asia, made up of a number of principalities, changing boundaries and affiliations and possessing an identity by virtue of commitment to a religious political ideology, on the one hand, and of sharing similar economic, demographic, and logistical features, on the other" (Tambiah 1982: 18). As with the Mayas, Southeast Asian civilization endured for millennia, but individual states had complex and volatile political histories. Each polity consisted of a loose hegemony with a principal center surrounded by a galaxy of smaller subordinate centers, which in turn dominated local centers and populations.

The major characteristics of what Tambiah termed the "galactic polities" of Southeast Asia are largely parallel to those of segmentary states elsewhere, but they are especially similar in structure to the Maya hegemonies described above, particularly in their political dynamics and state ritual. Tambiah (1976, 1977), Geertz (1980), and Fritz (1986) describe how the structure of these states and even the physical characteristics of their centers reflect a cosmological model (*mandala, negara*): an emic vision of the kingdom and the role of the ruler that reinforces both the ideological functions of the state and its structural instability. The most salient characteristic of these polities is the great importance of ritual performances in their ceremonial centers and the awe (and authority) that these displays generated (Geertz 1980; Tambiah 1976, 1977). Other important features include (1) the organization of hegemonies into capital centers loosely controlling a cluster or galaxy of subordinate centers; (2) a redundancy of structure and functions between the capital center and dependencies; (3) an emphasis on control over labor and allegiance rather than territory; (4) little direct control by the rulers over local economic infrastructure; (5) an extreme dependency on the personal performance of the ruler in warfare, marriage alliances, and above all, ritual; and (6) the tendency of these states to expand and contract in territory, reflecting the dynamics resulting from all of these features, as dependencies struggle against authority or shift allegiances or as expanding capitals impose short-lived attempts at centralization.

Like Maya political structure – and unlike idealized central-place models – the elements in these Southeast Asian hegemonies were hierarchically organized in power and status but did not represent a strong hierarchy of functions. According to Tambiah, the major center and its principal satellites were "a decentralized constellation of units that replicate one another in that they show minimal differentiation of function" (1976: 113) or, as Bentley puts it, "a nested hierarchy of functionally undifferentiated units" (1986: 292). Because of this redundancy, subordinate centers had less *need* for the affiliation with the capital center than the center had for affiliation with its subordinates, and there was a large potential pool of usurpers for each capital. The rulers of each subordinate center also had their own claims to divine authority, which created circumstances conductive to rebellion by satellites and to competition for those satellites between adjacent major hegemonies. The result was an unstable political landscape that very much resembles the shifting alliances of the Classic Maya world.

The source of power in galactic polities was control over networks of human relationships and labor, rather than physical control of territory. In Southeast Asia this emphasis on labor, rather than land, was related to low population densities and dispersed settlement patterns. As Bentley notes, "the limiting factor on political development throughout the region was not territory but mobilizing sufficient labor to exploit it" (1986: 298; see also Bilgalke 1983; Kirch 1984; Wheatley 1983; Wyatt 1984). "Such labor could be obtained by capturing it or by attracting it" (Bentley 1986: 290). Thus, as with the Mayas, the emphasis is on warfare between elites and on charismatic ritual performance to maintain and expand ideological control of the population. Political allegiance, power, and the degree of centralization of the state were dependent on these networks of personal, political, and religious control that radiated out from the ruler himself through subordinate centers and to their populations. In this sense the *mandala*, like Maya polities, were flexible "center-oriented" networks rather than sharply delineated, "bounded" territories (Tambiah 1977: 74).

Many of these features may relate to the general characteristic discussed earlier: weak involvement of these Southeast Asian states in management, control, or administration of economic infrastructure. "The actual control over men and resources (the political center, so to speak) sat very low in the system" (Geertz 1980: 134). The upper tiers of the political hierarchy extracted labor and support from below, but not efficiently and with little or no administrative control of local units and their agricultural activities. This characterization is remarkable given that these societies were originally considered examples of Wittfogel's coercive "Oriental despotisms." Nonetheless, the past two decades of research in Southeast Asia have produced a consensus on the unusually limited degree of state involvement in intensive agriculture and irrigation: "it appears that in these states both large and small, irrigation control was a localized cooperative affair" (Gesick 1983:

3–4) and "there were no state-owned or state-managed waterworks of any sort" (Geertz 1980: 69). Terrace systems were similarly controlled entirely at the local end (Geertz 1980: 68–86). A few late, unusually large states may have imposed state order on some aspects of agricultural systems, but even this possibility is in doubt. For example, some archaeologists and historians studying the "ultimate" water control system around Angkor Wat have concluded that at this

> locus classicus of "hydraulic despotism," recent archaeological evidence suggests that the foregoing observations are also applicable there, that is, that the irrigation systems of Khmer villages in Angkorian times appear to have been quite separate, localized affairs, unconnected with the spectacular waterworks of the temple complexes, which were designed wholly with ceremonial uses in mind.
> (Gesick 1983: 3–4; cf. van Liere 1980)

As discussed earlier, in the Maya case the data on local economies are too scant to justify a similar conclusion. However, the probable limited economic involvement of the Maya states could help to explain other parallels to the Southeast Asian mandala.

The central role of ideology in Asian and Maya theater states

A principal source of a king's power in the Southeast Asian polities was even more directly ideological than that of Maya rulers. His status was most enhanced by (1) the ruler's role in the center's rituals; (2) his supervision of politico-religious rites in subordinate centers; (3) his celebrated periods of study with revered holy men; (4) his acquisition and public worship of heirlooms and renowned idols; and (5) other mechanisms of public ritual and ideological interaction (Geertz 1980; Tambiah 1976, 1977, 1982, 1984; cf. Gesick, ed. 1983). In turn, this increased spiritual status attracted the loyalty of subordinate centers, often manifest in their desire for linkage through political alliance, especially royal marriages. Thus, the expansion of galactic realms was

based, above all, on ideological power and prestige generated by these activities and by the ruler's performance in elaborate public ritual. Tambiah notes that the central ruler controls his satellites "not so much by the real exercise of power as by devices and mechanisms of a ritual kind that have performative validity" (1976: 125). Similarly, Geertz's elegant presentation of the rituals of Bali's "theater states" shows how "the state drew its force, which was real enough, from its imaginative energies, its semiotic capacity to make inequality enchant" (1980: 123).

In fact, the specific, detailed descriptions of Southeast Asian rulers' competitive invocations and manipulations of the spiritual framework of the mandala or negara are again strikingly similar to the growing body of evidence on the Maya theater states. Descriptions of the Maya cosmogram and its political implications by Freidel and Schele (1988a, 1988b; Schele and Freidel 1990; Schele and Miller 1986; Freidel 1992) perfectly fit the theater-state model of the "whole polity being held together as an ordered unity by the king's enactment of cosmic rites and his role as the validator of his satellites' credentials" (Tambiah 1976: 123). Even the specific mechanisms used to hold the satellites to the center were similar, including movement of idols, installment rites of local rulers, positions similar to those in cargo hierarchies for local leaders in the kings' courts, and reification of the cosmogram (and its politically legitimating effect) in frequent rites defined by time cycles and involving directional movement and rotation. The historical descriptions (Geertz 1980; Tambiah 1976, 1982) indicate the importance of the central role of public ritual displays in maintaining the power of kings. Like the Maya ahau described by Freidel (1992), the ruler of a Thai polity was the central axis of state ritual and the personal embodiment of the cosmological principles of the state. The capitals themselves – in both Southeast Asia and the Maya area – incorporate a series of settings for public performances that reenact and reinforce the divine model of the state, structurally replicating the order of the cosmos with the ruler always at its center.

The spectacular and complex nature of the ideological reinforcement (art, ritual, architecture, etc.) involved in maintaining the galactic polities should not seduce archaeologists or historians into misreading them as indicative of great coercive power, centralization, or stability. This heavy investment in ideology was built on little or no control of the economic base and no direct provision of local economic benefits. Because of this ideological dependence, state hegemonies were highly vulnerable to short-term ecological crises, military defeats, interruptions of trade in exotics, or any other factor that might reduce the charisma of the ruler: "behind the doctrines of the exemplary center, of graded spirituality, and of the theater state ... behind these ritually inflated notions we see the dynamics of polities that were modulated by pulsating alliances, shifting territorial control, and frequent rebellions and succession disputes" (Tambiah 1976: 123).

Ideology and the "Pulsations" of Classic-period southern lowland Maya polities

In Southeast Asia, far-flung polities did sometimes arise that were comparable to the larger Maya hegemonies maintained by Tikal, Caracol, and Dos Pilas for one or two generations. The expansion of these hegemonies occurred when a charismatic leader came to rule a major center and expanded his alliance through warfare, marriages, and ritual display. Also important in episodes of expansionism were exchange and contact with the world beyond Southeast Asia, which were symbolized in exotic goods that reinforced the prestige of the ruler and subordinates by displaying "other worldly" knowledge structurally equivalent to spiritual knowledge (see especially Tambiah 1976, 1984; cf. Helms 1979). Yet, among the Southeast Asian *mandala*, the more widespread hegemonies would usually last at most a few generations, and ultimately,

"this process of centralization was abortive" (Tambiah 1976: 127). The ideological framework of these theater states held the cultural system together but could not sustain larger, individual states.

The similarities of this system to Maya political dynamics boldly highlight the role of ideology in the Maya world. The Classic southern lowland Maya centers may have had the same redundancy of functions and economic weakness as those in Southeast Asia, along with the corresponding emphasis on ritual, shared cosmology, and elite interaction to hold polities together. In the Maya case these weaknesses also led to the same instability in political control. The rapid but short-lived expansions of the political networks of centers like Tikal, Dos Pilas, and Caracol were also initiated by charismatic leaders who extended their alliances through public performance, marriage alliances, warfare, prestige-reinforcing connections to distant realms, and redistribution to subordinate leaders of exotic symbols of power from those realms.

Specific and now well-documented histories of the expansion and contraction of Maya hegemonies are remarkably parallel to the volatile histories of the segmentary theater states of Southeast Asia. The complex history of the kingdom of Tikal is one example. The impressive religious architecture, sculpture, and ritual settings of the Tikal center in the Middle and Late Classic periods reflect the central ideological component of their expanding hegemony in the fourth and fifth and in the seventh and eighth centuries (Culbert 1988b; Jones 1977, 1990; Laporte 1989; Laporte and Fialko 1985; Mathews 1985, 1988). However, the Tikal hegemony also relied heavily on status reinforcement through contacts with distant capitals like Teotihuacan, redistribution of exotic goods from those regions, and dynastic marriage alliances (Coggins 1975, 1976; Culbert 1988b; Demarest and Foias 1991; Jones 1977; Schele 1986; Schele and Mathews 1990; Taube 1992). Both Early and Late Classic episodes of Tikal's expansion of influence ended with a corresponding contraction of their power and political alliances. Status-shattering defeats reduced both tribute and the ideological pull of that great center (Chase and Chase 1987; Demarest 1990; Houston and Stuart 1990). This contraction is reflected in Tikal's archaeology in dramatic reductions in the monuments and architecture that functioned as the stages of its ritual displays, created and staffed through the state's control of loyal corporate labor.

Another episode of expansion of a galactic polity, that of the eighth-century Dos Pilas hegemony, is currently being documented by archaeology and epigraphy (Demarest 1990; Demarest and Houston 1989, 1990; Houston 1987; Houston and Stuart 1990). Dos Pilas probably relied more heavily than Tikal on warfare and the ideology of militarism. Note, however, that the direction of expansionism (up and down the Pasión River) suggests that control over highland trade routes in exotics was one probable motive for the warfare, again reflecting the demands of elite ideological competition for status-reinforcing goods. The victories of Dos Pilas and subsequent public sacrifice of high-status captives are celebrated in the many stela monuments and hieroglyphic stairways of the Petexbatun and Pasión regions (Houston 1987; Houston and Mathews 1985; Houston and Stuart 1990). Unlike much of the ritualized warfare of the Classic Maya, the wars in the Petexbatun region during the seventh and eighth centuries often resulted in actual conquest and territorial expansion. The ability of the Dos Pilas hegemony to expand, however, may have resulted as much from the success of its propagandistic advertising of the defeat and sacrifice of rivals as from military occupation; the combination of victories, their accompanying rituals, and the monumental propaganda enhanced the prestige of the Dos Pilas rulers and, thus, their ability to contract subordinates through marriage alliances or ritual ties (Demarest 1990: 611–12).

In comparisons of the Maya and Southeast Asian political histories, we see remarkable similarity in the specific sets of ideological mechanisms and institutions used to generate, legitimate, and expand royal power. Rituals of temporal cyclicality, center–periphery movements, and rotation of offices and idols were used by both civilizations in their futile attempts to make the center hold. Both civilizations shared an emphasis in art, ritual, and myth on a framing cosmogram, a sacred geography for political action (cf. Tambiah 1976; Freidel and Schele 1988a, 1988b), and both regions have left us a rich corpus of politico-religious art, elaborate rituals, and complex regional histories documenting rulers' charismatic performances or disappointing and brief runs on the stages of these "theater states."

Perhaps, then, the central role of ideology and its particular manifestations in ancient Maya "galactic polities" also can help to explain the contradictory trajectories of Maya regional culture histories – the enigma of the inversely correlated rises and falls of some of the greatest Maya centers. These events need not be seen as idiosyncratic and based on the appearance of "great men" or on imagined ecological crises. Rather, they have a basis in the structural characteristics of the system: the weakness of economic control by centers and the heavy dependence on ideology for state authority. This political framework sets a stage for expansion of spheres of influence through the force of an individual leader's charisma and ability, through propaganda victories in warfare among elites, or through the ideological manipulation of economically trivial foreign contacts. Unfortunately for centers like El Mirador, Cerros, Caracol, Tikal, and Dos Pilas, this political framework was as fragile as it was fluid, resulting in the repeated collapse of the hegemonies it generated.

Concluding Speculations

I have argued that Maya civilization existed in a state of dynamic instability because of its particular institutional and structural characteristics. In so doing, I seem to contradict ecological and materialist functionalism in positing that a major civilization had states in which economic functions were weak and in which power was heavily based on ideology. The existence of these state-level societies in Southeast Asia, Africa, and the Maya world underscores the problems of the distinction between the *legitimation* of power and the *generation* of power. When embedded in a cultural context with historical inertia, what were identified as the ideological "legitimating" activities of the state may actually be the primary source of power for that state.

Issues of causality must be resolved by demonstrations of chronological priority, but owing to the constant feedback between ideological power and the *reinforcement* of political or economic power, it may not be possible to make chronological and causal distinctions. Still, it is clear that an imposition of a materialist paradigm could *not* explain the inception or the continued existence for thousands of years of either the Southeast Asian kingdoms or southern lowland Maya systems of galactic polities. Only by accepting a major role for ideology as a direct source of power can one understand the institutions of these civilizations, their history, and the elaborate cultural concepts that sustained them.

Despite the apparent disagreement with materialist approaches over the importance of ideology, there is also an implicit admission in this discussion that in long-term cultural evolution, economic and ecologically based power may be more enduring than power based on ideology. The more secure material and coercive bases of power held by states like Teotihuacan or Tiahuanaco may have made them more stable polities. More important, subsequent states built on their economic and cultural institutions, which led to ever more extensive, populous, and energy-intensive political systems. In contrast, the ideologically dependent galactic polities of the Classic Maya lowlands and Southeast Asia seemed doomed to repeat perpetual cycles of internal expansion and decline. In the end, these fragile systems faced overall disintegration, absorption, or externally stimulated transformations to more economically oriented polities. These aspects of the system, especially its dependency on ideology and charismatic leadership, may have resulted in political involution, rather than evolution. Thus, common ground between culture-ecologists and "holists" interested in ideology may be found by focusing on cultural evolution in its longest terms and most grand scale.

REFERENCES

Adams, Richard E. W. 1977. *The Origins of Maya Civilization.* University of New Mexico Press, Albuquerque.

——1983. Ancient Land Use and Culture History in the Pasion River Region. In *Prehistoric Settlement Patterns: Essays in Honor of Gordon R. Willey,* edited by Evon Z. Vogt and Richard M. Leventhal, pp. 319–36. University of New Mexico Press, Albuquerque.

——1986. Rio Azul. *National Geographic* 169: 420–51.

Adams, Richard E. W., W. E. Brown, Jr., and T. Patrick Culbert. 1981. Radar Mapping, Archaeology, and Ancient Maya Land Use. *Science* 213: 1457–63.

Adams, Richard E. W., Grant D. Hall, Ian Graham, Fred Valdez, Stephen L. Black, Daniel Potter, D. J. Connell, and B. Connell. 1984. *Rio Azul Project Report 1: Final 1983 Report.* Center for Archaeological Research, University of Texas Press, San Antonio.

Adams, Robert McC. 1965. *Land Behind Baghdad: A History of Settlement on the Diyala Plains.* University of Chicago Press, Chicago.

——1966. *The Evolution of Urban Society: Early Mesopotamia and Prehistoric Mexico.* Aldine, Chicago.

——1968. The Study of Ancient Mesopotamian Settlement Patterns and the Problem of Urban Origins. *Sumer* 25: 111–24.

——1981. *Heartland of cities: Surveys of Ancient Settlement and Land Use on the Central Floodplain of the Euphrates.* University of Chicago Press, Chicago.

Adams, Robert McC. and Nissen, H. 1972. *The Uruk Countryside: The Natural Setting of Urban Societies.* University of Chicago Press, Chicago.

Andrews, E. Wyllys V. 1981. Dzibilchaltun. In *Supplement to the Handbook of Middle American Indians: Archaeology,* vol. 1; pp. 113–41, edited by Jeremy A. Sabloff. University of Texas Press, Austin.

Andrews, E. Wyllys V., William M. Ringle, Philip J. Barnes, Alfredo Barrera R., and Tomas Gallareta N. 1984. *Komchen: An Early Maya Community in Northeast Yucatan*. Proceedings of the XVII Mesa Redonda de la Sociedad Mexicana de Antropología. San Cristobal, Chiapas, Mexico.

Ashmore, Wendy A. and Robert J. Sharer. 1975. A Revitalization Movement at Late Classic Tikal. Paper presented at the Area Seminar in Ongoing Research. West Chester State College, New York.

Ball, Joseph. 1977. *Archaeological Ceramics of Becan, Campeche, Mexico*. Middle American Research Institute Publication 43. Tulane University, New Orleans.

Ball, Joseph and Jennifer Taschek. 1989. Small Center Archaeology and Classic Maya Political Organization: The Mopan–Macal Triangle Project. Paper presented at the Society for American Archaeology Meetings.

Beetz, Carl and Linton Satterthwaite. 1981. *The Monuments and Inscriptions of Caracol, Belize*. Monographs of the University Museum 45. University of Pennsylvania, Philadelphia.

Bentley, G. Carter. 1986. Indigenous States of Southeast Asia. *Annual Review of Anthropology* 15: 275–305.

Bigalke, T. 1983. Dynamics of the Torajan Slave Trade in South Sulawesi. In *Slavery, Bondage, and Dependency in Southeast Asia*, edited by A. Reid. St Martin's Press, New York.

Carneiro, Robert L. 1970. A Theory of the Origin of the State. *Science* 169: 733–8.

Chase, Arlen F. and Diane Z. Chase. 1987. *Investigations at the Classic Maya City of Caracol, Belize: 1985–1987*. Pre-Columbian Art Research Institute Monograph 3. San Francisco.

Clark, John E. 1986. From Mountains to Molehills: A Critical Review of Teotihuacan's Obsidian Industry. *Research in Economic Anthropology Supplement* 2: 23–74.

Coe, Michael D. 1961. Social Typologies and Tropical Forest Civilizations. *Comparative Studies in Society and History* 4: 65–86.

——1965. A Model of Ancient Community Structure in the Maya Lowlands. *Southwestern Journal of Anthropology* 21: 97–114.

Coggins, Clemency C. 1975. Painting and Drawing Styles at Tikal: An Historical and Iconographic Reconstruction. Ph.D. dissertation, Department of Anthropology, Harvard University.

——1976. Teotihuacan at Tikal in the Early Classic Period. *Acts of the 42nd International Congress of Americanists* 8: 251–69.

Cowgill, George L. 1979. Teotihuacan, Internal Militaristic Competition, and the Fall of the Classic Maya. In *Maya Archaeology and Ethnohistory*, edited by Norman Hammond and Gordon R. Willey, pp. 51–62. University of Texas Press, Austin.

Culbert, T. Patrick. 1977. Maya Development and Collapse: An Economic Perspective. In *Social Process in Maya Prehistory: Essays in Honor of Sir J. Eric S. Thompson*, edited by Norman Hammond, pp. 510–31. Academic Press, New York.

——1988a. The Collapse of Classic Maya Civilization. In *The Collapse of Ancient States and Civilizations*, edited by Norman Yoffee and George L. Cowgill, pp. 69–101. University of Arizona Press, Tucson.

——1988b. Political History and the Decipherment of Maya Glyphs. *Antiquity* 62: 135–152.

Culbert, T. Patrick, P. Magers, and M. Spencer. 1978. Regional Variability in Maya Lowland Agriculture. In *Prehispanic Maya Agriculture*, edited by Peter D. Harrison and Billie Lee Turner II. University of New Mexico Press, Albuquerque.

Dahlin, Bruce H. 1976. An Anthropologist Looks at the Pyramids: A Late Classic Revitalization Movement at Tikal, Guatemala. Ph.D. dissertation, Department of Anthropology, Temple University.

——1979. Cropping Cash in the Protoclassic: A Cultural Impact Statement. In *Maya Archaeology and Ethnohistory*, edited by Norman Hammond and Gordon R. Willey, pp. 21–37. University of Texas Press, Austin.

——1983. Climate and Prehistory on the Yucatan Peninsula. *Climate Change* 5: 245–63.

——1984. A Colossus in Guatemala: The Preclassic City of El Mirador. *Archaeology* 37(3): 18–25.

Dahlin, Bruce H., John E. Foss, and Mary Elizabeth Chambers. 1980. Project Acalches. In *El Mirador, Peten, Guatemala: An Interim Report*, edited by Ray T. Matheny. Papers of the New World Archaeological Foundation No. 45. Brigham Young University, Provo, Utah.

Demarest, Arthur A. 1978. Interregional Conflict and "Situational Ethics" in Classic Maya Warfare. In *Codex Wauchope: Festschrift in Honor of Robert Wauchope*, edited by Monroe Edmonson and Winifred Creamer, pp. 101–11. Tulane University, New Orleans.

——1984a. Conclusiones y Especulaciones. In *Proyecto El Mirador*, edited by Arthur A. Demarest. Mesoamérica 7, Centro de Investigaciones Regionales de Mesoamérica. South Woodstock, Vermont.

—— 1984b. Overview: Mesoamerican Human Sacrifice in Evolutionary Perspective. In *Ritual Human Sacrifice in Mesoamerica*, edited by Elizabeth H. Boone. Dumbarton Oaks, Washington, DC.

—— 1986. *The Archaeology of Santa Leticia and the Rise of Maya Civilization*. Middle American Research Institute Publication 52. Tulane University, New Orleans.

—— 1988. Political Evolution in the Maya Borderlands: The Salvadoran Frontier. In *The Southeast Classic Maya Zone*, edited by Elizabeth H. Boone and Gordon R. Willey, pp. 335–94. Dumbarton Oaks, Washington, DC.

—— 1990. Resumen de los Resultados de la Segunda Temporada. In Informe Preliminar No. 2: Segunda Temporada (1990) del Proyecto Arqueológico Regional Petexbatun, edited by Arthur A. Demarest and Stephen D. Houston. Report submitted to the Instituto de Antropología e Historia de Guatemala.

Demarest, Arthur A. and Antonia Foias. 1991. Mesoamerican Horizons and the Cultural Transformations of Maya Civilization. In *Latin American Horizons*, edited by Don S. Rice, pp. 147–92. Dumbarton Oaks, Washington, DC.

Demarest, Arthur A. and Stephen D. Houston. 1989. Informe Preliminar de la Primera Temporada (1989) del Proyecto Arqueológico Regional Petexbatun. Report submitted to the Instituto de Antropología e Historia de Guatemala.

—— —— 1990. Informe Preliminar No. 2 Segunda Temporada (1990) del Proyecto Arqueológico Regional Petexbatun. Report submitted to the Instituto de Antropología e Historia de Guatemala.

Dillon, Brian D. 1975. Notes on Trade in Ancient Mesoamerica. *Contributions of the University of California Archaeological Research Facility* No. 24: 80–135.

Drennan, Robert D. 1984. Long-Distance Movement of Goods in the Mesoamerican Formative and Classic. *American Antiquity* 49: 27–43.

Dunning, Nicholas P. and Arthur A. Demarest. 1990. Sustainable Agricultural Systems in the Petexbatun, Pasion, and Peten Regions of Guatemala: Perspectives from Contemporary Ecology and Ancient Settlement. Proposal submitted to the United States Agency for International Development.

Fash, William L., Jr. 1983. Maya State Formation: A Case Study and its Implications. Ph.D.

dissertation, Department of Anthropology, Harvard University.

—— 1988. A New Look at Maya Statecraft from Copan, Honduras. *Antiquity* 62: 157–69.

Fash, William L., Jr. and David Stuart. 1990. Interaction and Political Process in Copan. In *Classic Maya Political History: Archaeological and Hieroglyphic Evidence*, edited by T. Patrick Culbert, pp. 147–79. School of American Research Advanced Seminar Series. Cambridge University Press, Cambridge.

Flannery, Kent V. 1968. Archaeological Systems Theory and Early Mesoamerica. In *Anthropological Archaeology in the Americas*, edited by Betty J. Meggers, pp. 67–87. Anthropological Society of Washington, Washington, DC.

Freidel, David A. 1979. Culture Areas and Interaction Spheres: Contrasting Approaches to the Emergence of Civilization in the Maya Lowlands. *American Antiquity* 44: 36–54.

—— 1981. Civilization as a State of Mind: The Cultural Evolution of the Lowland Maya. In *The Transition to Statehood in the New World*, edited by Grant D. Jones and Robert R. Kautz, pp. 188–227. Cambridge University Press, Cambridge.

—— 1986. Maya Warfare: An Example of Peer Polity Interaction. In *Peer Polity Interaction and the Development of Sociopolitical Complexity*, edited by Colin Renfrew and John F. Cherry, pp. 93–108. Cambridge University Press, Cambridge.

—— 1992. The Trees of Life: *Ahau* as Idea and Artifact in Classic Lowland Maya Civilization. In *Ideology and Pre-Columbian Civilizations*, edited by Arthur A. Demarest and Geoffrey W. Conrad, pp. 115–34. School of American Research Press, Santa Fe.

Freidel, David A. and Linda Schele. 1988a. Kingship in the Late Preclassic Lowlands: The Instruments and Places of Ritual Power. *American Anthropologist* 90: 547–67.

—— —— 1988b. Symbol and Power: A History of the Lowland Maya Cosmogram. In *Maya Iconography*, edited by Elizabeth Benson and Gillette Griffin, pp. 44–93. Princeton University Press, Princeton.

Fritz, John M. 1985. Is Vijayanagara a Cosmic City? In *Vijayanagara: City and Empire*, edited by S. Dallapicola and S. Zingel-Ave Lallement. South Asia Institute, Heidelberg.

—— 1986. Vijayanagara: Authority and Meaning of a South Indian Imperial Capital. *American Anthropologist* 88: 44–55.

Fritz, John M., G. A. Mitchell, and M. S. Nagara Rao. 1985. *Where Kings and Gods Meet: The*

Royal Center of Vijayanagara, India. University of Arizona Press, Tucson.

Fry, Robert E. 1979. The Economics of Pottery at Tikal, Guatemala: Models of Exchange for Serving Vessels. *American Antiquity* 44: 494–512.

Geertz, Clifford. 1980. *Negara: The Theatre State in Nineteenth-Century Bali.* Princeton University Press, Princeton.

Gesick, Loraine. 1983. Introduction. In *Centers, Symbols, and Hierarchies: Essays on the Classical States of Southeast Asia*, edited by Loraine Gesick, pp. 1–8. Southeast Asia Studies Monograph Series No. 26. Yale University Press, New Haven.

Gibson, Eric C. 1986. Diachronic Patterns of Lithic Production, Use, and Exchange in the Southern Maya Lowlands. Ph.D. dissertation, Department of Anthropology, Harvard University.

Hansen, Richard D. 1989. Las Investigaciones del Sitio Nakbe, Peten, Guatemala. Paper presented at the Tercer Simposio de Arqueología Guatemalteca, Museo Nacional de Arqueología y Etnología, Guatemala City.

Harrison, Peter D. and Billie Lee Turner II. 1978. *Prehispanic Maya Agriculture.* University of New Mexico Press, Albuquerque.

Hellmuth, Nicholas M. 1977. Cholti-Lacandon (Chiapas) and Peten-Ytsa Agriculture, Settlement Pattern, and Population. In *Social Process in Maya Prehistory: Essays in Honor of J. Eric S. Thompson*, edited by Norman Hammond, pp. 421–48. Academic Press, New York.

Helms, Mary W. 1979. *Ancient Panama: Chiefs in Search of Power.* University of Texas Press, Austin.

Hester, Thomas R. 1979. The Colha Project: A Collection of Interim Papers. Center for Archaeological Research. University of Texas, San Antonio.

Higham, Charles. 1989. *The Archaeology of Mainland Southeast Asia.* Cambridge University Press, Cambridge.

Houston, Stephen D. 1987. The Inscriptions and Monumental Art of Dos Pilas, Guatemala: A Study of Classic Maya History and Politics. Ph.D. dissertation, Department of Anthropology, Yale University.

Houston, Stephen D. and Peter Mathews. 1985. *The Dynastic Sequence of Dos Pilas, Guatemala.* Pre-Columbian Art Research Institute Monograph 1. San Francisco.

Houston, Stephen D. and David Stuart. 1990. Resultados Generales de los Estudios Epigráficos del Proyecto Petexbatun. In Informe Preliminar No. 2 Segunda Temporada (1990) del Proyecto Arqueológico Regional Petexbatun, edited by Arthur A. Demarest and Stephen D. Houston. Report submitted to the Instituto de Antropología e Historia de Guatemala.

Isbell, William H. 1978. Environmental Perturbations and the Origin of the Andean State. In *Social Archaeology: Beyond Subsistence and Dating*, edited by Charles L. Redman, Mary Jane Berman, Edward V. Curtin, William T. Langhorne, Jr., Nina M. Versaggi, and Jeffery C. Wanser, pp. 303–14. Academic Press, New York.

Jones, Christopher. 1977. Inauguration Dates of Three Late Classic Rulers of Tikal, Guatemala. *American Antiquity* 42: 28–60.

—— 1990. Cycles of Growth at Tikal. In *Classic Maya Political History: Archaeological and Hieroglyphic Evidence*, edited by T. Patrick Culbert, pp. 102–27. School of American Research Advanced Seminar Series. Cambridge University Press, Cambridge.

Kirch, Patrick V. 1984. *The Evolution of Polynesian Chiefdoms.* Cambridge University Press, Cambridge.

Kolata, Alan L. 1992. Economy, Ideology, and Imperialism in the South-Central Andes, In *Ideology and Pre-Columbian Civilizations*, edited by Arthur A. Demarest and Geoffrey W. Conrad, pp. 65–86. School of American Research Press, Santa Fe.

Laporte, Juan P.

—— 1986. El "Talud-Tablero" en Tikal, Peten: Nuevos datos. Paper presented at the Symposium "Vida y Obra de Román Piña Chán," Mexico City.

—— 1989. Alternativas del Clásico Temprano en la Relación Tikal-Teotihuacán: Grupo 6C-XVI, Tikal, Peten, Guatemala. Ph.D. dissertation, Department of Anthropology, Universidad Nacional Autónoma de México.

Laporte, Juan P. and Vilma Fialko. 1985. *Reporte Arqueológico: Mundo Perdido y Zonas de Habitación, Tikal.* Instituto de Antropología e Historia, Guatemala.

Laporte, Juan P. and Lillian Vega de Zea. 1987. *Aspectos Dinásticos para el Clásico Temprano de Mundo Perdido, Tikal.* In Primer Simposio Mundial Sobre Epigrafía Maya. Guatemala Association Tikal.

Marcus, Joyce. 1976. *Emblem and State in the Classic Maya Lowlands.* Dumbarton Oaks, Washington, DC.

—— 1982. The Plant World of the Lowland Maya. In *Maya Subsistence: Studies in Memory of Dennis Puleston*, edited by Kent V. Flannery. Academic Press, New York.

—— 1983. Lowland Maya Archaeology at the Crossroads. *American Antiquity* 48: 454–88.

Matheny, Ray T. 1976. Maya Lowland Hydraulic Systems. *Science* 193: 639–46.

—— 1980. *El Mirador, Peten, Guatemala: An Interim Report*. Papers of the New World Archaeological Foundation No. 45. Brigham Young University, Provo.

—— 1986. Early States in the Maya Lowlands During the Late Preclassic Period: Edzna and El Mirador. In *The Maya State*, edited by Elizabeth P. Benson, pp. 1–44. Rocky Mountain Institute for Precolumbian Studies, Denver.

Mathews, Peter. 1985. Maya Early Classic Monuments and Inscriptions. In *A Consideration of the Early Classic Period in the Maya Lowlands*, edited by Gordon R. Willey and Peter Mathews, pp. 5–55. Institute of Mesoamerican Studies, State University of New York, Albany.

—— 1988. The Sculptures of Yaxchilan. Ph.D. dissertation, Department of Anthropology, Yale University.

Mathews, Peter and Gordon R. Willey. 1990. Prehistoric Polities of the Pasion Region: Hieroglyphic Texts and their Archaeological Settings. In *Classic Maya Political History: Archaeological and Hieroglyphic Evidence*, edited by T. Patrick Culbert, pp. 30–71. School of American Research Advanced Seminar Series. Cambridge University Press, Cambridge.

Meggers, Betty J. 1954. Environmental Limitations on the Development of Culture. *American Anthropologist* 56: 801–24.

Miller, Mary E. 1986. *The Murals of Bonampak*. Princeton University Press, Princeton.

Monaghan, John. 1990. Sacrifice and the Symbolics of Power in Ancient Mesoamerica. Manuscript in possession of the author. Department of Anthropology, Vanderbilt University.

Nations, James D. and R. B. Nigh. 1980. The Evolutionary Potential of Lacandon Maya Sustained-Yield Forest Agriculture. *Journal of Anthropological Research* 35: 1–26.

Netting, Robert McC. 1977. Maya Subsistence: Mythologies, Analogies, Possibilities. In *The Origins of Maya Civilization*, edited by Richard E. W. Adams. School of American Research Advanced Seminar, University of New Mexico, Albuquerque.

Pendergast, David M. 1979. *Excavations at Altun Ha, Belize, 1964–1970*, vol. 1. Royal Ontario Museum, Toronto.

—— 1981. Lamanai, Belize: Summary of Excavation Results 1974–1980. *Journal of Field Archaeology* 8: 29–53.

Pope, Kevin O. and Bruce S. Dahlin. 1989. Ancient Maya Wetland Agriculture: New Insights from Ecological and Remote Sensing Research. *Journal of Field Archaeology* 16: 87–106.

Price, Barbara J. 1978. Secondary State Formation: An Explanatory Model. In *Origins of the State: The Anthropology of Political Evolution*, edited by Ronald Cohen and Elman R. Service, pp. 161–86. Institute for the Study of Human Issues (ISH), Philadelphia.

Rands, Robert L. and Ronald L. Bishop. 1980. Resource Procurement Zones and Patterns of Ceramic Exchange in the Palenque Region, Mexico. In *Models and Methods in Regional Exchange*, edited by Robert E. Fry, pp. 19–46. Society for American Archaeology Papers No. 1, Washington, DC.

Rathje, William L. 1971. The Origins and Development of Lowland Classic Maya Civilization. *American Antiquity* 36: 275–85.

—— 1977. The Tikal Connection. In *The Origins of Maya Civilization*, edited by Richard E. W. Adams. University of New Mexico Press, Albuquerque.

Renfrew, Colin and John F. Cherry. 1986. *Peer Polity Interaction and Socio-Political Change*. Cambridge University Press, Cambridge.

Rice, Prudence M. 1987. Economic Change in the Lowland Maya Late Classic Period. In *Specialization, Exchange, and Complex Societies*, edited by Elizabeth Brumfiel and Timothy Earle, pp. 67–82. Cambridge University Press, Cambridge.

Riese, Berthold. 1980. Katun-altersagaben. *Baessler-Archiv, Beitrage zür Volkerkunde* 28: 155–80.

Robertson, Robin A. and David A. Freidel. 1986. *Archaeology at Cerros, Belize, Central America: vol. 1: An Interim Report*. Southern Methodist University Press, Dallas.

Ruthenberg, H. 1981. *Farming Systems in the Tropics*. Oxford University Press, Oxford.

Sabloff, Jeremy A. 1986. Interaction Among Classic Maya Polities: A Preliminary Examination. In *Peer Polity Interaction and Socio-Political Change*, edited by Colin Renfrew and John F. Cherry. Cambridge University Press, Cambridge.

Sanders, William T. 1962. Cultural Ecology of Nuclear Mesoamerica. *American Anthropologist* 64: 34–44.

—— 1968. Hydraulic Agriculture, Economic Symbiosis, and the Evolution of the States in

Central Mexico. In *Anthropological Archaeology in the Americas*, edited by Betty J. Meggers, pp. 88–107. Anthropological Society of Washington, Washington, DC.

—— 1977. Environmental Heterogeneity and the Evolution of the Lowland Maya Civilization. In *The Origins of Maya Civilization*, edited by Richard E. W. Adams. University of New Mexico Press, Albuquerque.

Sanders, William T. and Barbara J. Price. 1968. *Mesoamerica: The Evolution of a Civilization*. Random House, New York.

Sanders, William T. and Robert S. Santley. 1983. A Tale of Three Cities: Energetics and Urbanization in Pre-hispanic Central Mexico. In *Prehistoric Settlement Patterns: Essays in Honor of Gordon R. Willey*, edited by Evon Z. Vogt and Richard M. Leventhal, pp. 243–92. University of New Mexico Press, Albuquerque.

Sanders, William T. and David Webster. 1988. The Mesoamerican Urban Tradition. *American Anthropologist* 90: 521–46.

Schele, Linda. 1984. Human Sacrifice Among the Classic Maya. In *Ritual Human Sacrifice in Mesoamerica*, edited by Elizabeth Boone, pp. 7–49. Dumbarton Oaks, Washington, DC.

—— 1985. The Hauberg Stela: Bloodletting and the Mythos of Maya Rulership. *Fifth Palenque Round Table*, vol. 7, pp. 135–49. Pre-Columbian Art Research Institute, San Francisco.

—— 1986. Architectural Development and Political History at Palenque. In *City-states of the Maya: Art and Architecture*, edited by Elizabeth P. Benson, pp. 110–38. Rocky Mountain Institute for Pre-Columbian Studies.

Schele, Linda and David A. Freidel. 1990. *A Forest of Kings: The Untold Story of the Ancient Maya*. William Morrow Company, New York.

Schele, Linda and Peter Mathews. 1990. Royal Visits Along the Usumacinta. In *Classic Maya Political History: Archaeological and Hieroglyphic Evidence*, edited by T. Patrick Culbert, pp. 226–52. School of American Research Advanced Seminar Series, Cambridge University Press, Cambridge.

Schele, Linda and Mary Ellen Miller. 1986. *The Blood of Kings: Dynasty and Ritual in Maya Art*. George Braziller, New York.

Sharer, Robert J. 1977. The Maya Collapse Revisited: Internal and External Perspectives. In *Social Process in Maya Prehistory: Essays in Honour of Sir J. Eric S. Thompson*, edited by Norman Hammond, pp. 532–52. Academic Press, New York.

—— 1978. Archaeology and History at Quirigua, Guatemala. *Journal of Field Archaeology* 5: 51–70.

—— 1982. Did the Maya Collapse? A New World Perspective on the Demise of Harappan Civilization. In *Harappan Civilization: A Contemporary Perspective*, edited by Gregory A. Possehl. American Institute of Indian Studies, New Delhi.

Sheets, Payson D. 1979. Maya Recovery from Volcanic Disaster. *Archaeology* 32(3): 32–42.

—— 1983. Summary and Conclusions. In *Archaeology and Volcanism in Central America: The Zapotitan Valley of El Salvador*, edited by Payson D. Sheets, pp. 275–94. University of Texas Press, Austin.

Sidrys, Raymond D. 1978. Notes on Obsidian Prismatic Blades at Seibal and Altar de Sacrificios. In *Excavations at Seibal, Department of Peten, Guatemala: Artifacts*, edited by Gordon R. Willey, pp. 146–52. Peabody Museum Memoirs 14, No. 1. Harvard University, Cambridge.

Stuart, David. 1984. Royal Auto-sacrifice Among the Maya: A Study in Image and Meaning. *Res: Anthropology and Aesthetics* 7/8: 6–20.

Tambiah, Stanley J. 1976. *World Conqueror and World Renouncer*. Cambridge University Press, Cambridge.

—— 1977. The Galactic Polity: The Structure of Traditional Kingdoms in Southeast Asia. *Annals of the New York Academy of Sciences* 293: 69–97.

—— 1982. Famous Buddha Images and the Legitimization of Kings. *Res: Anthropology and Aesthetics* 4: 5–19.

—— 1984. *The Buddhist Saints of the Forest and the Cult of the Amulets: A Study in Charisma, Hagiography, Sectarianism, and Millenial Buddhism*. Cambridge University Press, Cambridge.

Taube, Karl. 1985. The Classic Maya Maize God: A Reappraisal. *Fifth Palenque Round Table*, vol. 7, pp. 171–81. The Pre-Columbian Art Research Institute, San Francisco.

—— 1992. The Temple of Quetzalcoatl and the Cult of Sacred War at Teotihuacan. *Res: Anthropology and Aesthetics*. 21: 53–87.

Thompson, J. Eric S. 1966. *The Rise and Fall of Maya Civilization*. Revised edn. University of Oklahoma Press, Norman.

Tozzer, Alfred M. 1941. *Landa's Relacion de las Cosas de Yucatan: A Translation*. Papers of the Peabody Museum of American Archaeology and Ethnology, vol. 18. Harvard University, Cambridge.

Turner, Billie Lee II. 1974. Prehistoric Intensive Agriculture in the Mayan Lowlands. *Science* 185: 118–24.

Van Liere, W. J. 1980. Traditional Water Management in the Lower Mekong Basin. *World Archaeology* 11: 265–80.

Valdez, Fred, Jr. 1987. The Prehistoric Ceramics of Colha, Northern Belize. Ph.D. dissertation, Department of Anthropology, Harvard University.

Vogt, Evon Z. 1983. Ancient and Contemporary Maya Settlement Patterns: A New Look from the Chiapas Highlands. In *Prehistoric Settlement Patterns: Essays in Honor of Gordon R. Willey*, edited by Evon Z. Vogt and Richard M. Leventhal, pp. 89–114. University of New Mexico Press, Albuquerque.

——1985. Cardinal Directions and Ceremonial Circuits in Mayan and Southwestern Cosmology. *National Geographic Research Reports* 21: 487–96.

Webster, David L. 1975. Warfare and the Evolution of the State: A Reconsideration. *American Antiquity* 40: 464–70.

——1977. Warfare and the Evolution of Maya Civilization. In *The Origins of Maya Civilization*, edited by Richard E. W. Adams. School of American Research Series, University of New Mexico Press, Albuquerque.

Wheatley, Paul. 1983. *Niagara and Commandery*. Department of Geography Research Papers Nos. 207–8. University of Chicago, Chicago.

White, Leslie. 1949. *The Science of Culture*. Grove Press, New York.

Willey, Gordon R. 1977. The Rise of Maya Civilization: A Summary View. In *The Origins of Maya Civilization*, edited by Richard E. W. Adams. School of American Research Advanced Seminar, University of New Mexico, Albuquerque.

——1986. The Classic Maya Sociopolitical Order: A Study in Coherence and Instability. In *Research and Reflections in Archaeology and History: Essays in Honor of Doris Stone*, edited by E. Wyllys Andrews V, pp. 189–98. Middle American Research Institute Publication 57. Tulane University, New Orleans.

Willey, Gordon R. and Peter D. Mathews. 1985. *A Consideration of the Early Classic Period of the Maya Lowlands*. Institute for Mesoamerican Studies, State University of New York, Albany.

Wittfogel, Karl. 1955. Developmental Aspects of Hydraulic Societies. In *Irrigation Civilizations: A Comparative Study*. Social Science Monograph 1. Pan American Union, Washington, DC.

Wyatt, D. K. 1984. *Thailand*. Yale University, New Haven.

CHAPTER 15

State and Society at Teotihuacan, Mexico

George L. Cowgill

Introduction

Teotihuacan is an immense prehistoric city in the semi-arid highlands of central Mexico. It rose in the first or second century BCE and lasted into the 600s or 700s (figure 15.1 outlines the ceramic chronology). Its early growth was rapid, and by the 100s it covered about 20 km^2 with a population estimated to be around 60,000–80,000 (Cowgill 1979: 55; Millon 1992: 351). Subsequently, there was little change in area, and population grew more slowly, apparently reaching a plateau of 100,000 or more by the 300s or earlier. No other Mesoamerican city had such a large and dense urban concentration before Aztec Tenochtitlan, in the late 1400s. By the 200s Teo (as I will henceforth call it) also had the largest integrated complex of monumental structures in Mesoamerica: the gigantic Sun Pyramid (with a base area close to that of the largest Egyptian pyramid), the Moon Pyramid, the 16-ha Ciudadela enclosure with its Feathered Serpent Pyramid, and the broad 5-km-long Avenue of the Dead, along whose northern 2 km these and many other pyramids, platforms, and elite residences are arranged (figure 15.2).

Millon et al. (1973) published map sheets of the whole city at a scale of 1:2000, based on an intensive surface survey. A 1:40,000 version appears in Millon (1973, 1974, 1976, 1981, 1988a). Articles by Millon (1981, 1988a, 1992) and Cowgill (1992a, 1992b) include reviews of research and literature on Teo. I concentrate here on publications since the mid-1960s that bear especially on state and society. I emphasize relatively accessible sources and do not always identify earliest publications of specific ideas. Edited volumes with papers on a wide range of Teo topics include Berlo (1992a), Berrin (1988), Berrin and Pasztory (1993), Cabrera Castro et al. (1982a, 1982b), 1991a), Cardós (1990), de la Fuente (1995), Diehl and Berlo (1989), McClung, de Tapia, and Rattray (1987), Rattray et al. (1981), Sanders (1994–6), Sociedad Mexicana de Antropología (1967, 1972), and special sections of *Ancient Mesoamerica* (1991: vol. 2 [1, 2]) and *Arqueología* (1991). The proceedings of a 1993 Instituto Nacional de Antropología e Historia (INAH) workshop on Teo chronology, edited by Cabrera and Brambila, are in press, and a book by Pasztory (1997) has just appeared. Sugiyama has created a web site: http://archaeology.la.asu.edu/vm/mesoam/teo.

Method and Theory

We still only glimpse the outlines of polity and society in the city and the state it dominated. Surviving inscriptions are few, brief, and hard to read. Teo society was destroyed by the 700s or earlier, and to the Aztecs, about whom we have a wealth of ethnohistoric data, Teo was a place of mysterious ruins; more mythical than historical. These problems mean that theoretical preconceptions and methodological assumptions play a large role in determining which interpretations seem intrinsically plausible or even

Reprinted from Geoge L. Cowgill. 1997. State and Society at Teotihuacan, Mexico. *Annual Review of Anthropology* 26: 129–61.

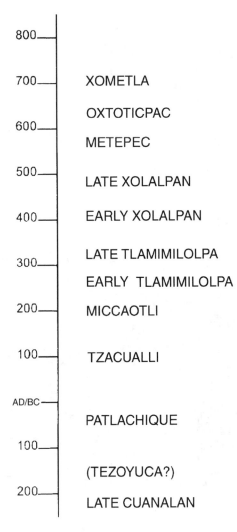

800—

700— XOMETLA

      OXTOTICPAC
600—
      METEPEC

500— LATE XOLALPAN

400— EARLY XOLALPAN

      LATE TLAMIMILOLPA
300—
      EARLY TLAMIMILOLPA

200— MICCAOTLI

100— TZACUALLI

AD/BC—

      PATLACHIQUE
100—

      (TEZOYUCA?)
200—
      LATE CUANALAN

Figure 15.1 Teotihuacan ceramic chronology.

empirically well founded. Sanders et al. (1979) and Santley (1983, 1984, 1989) are strongly cultural-materialist and favor interpretations and explanations in terms of environmental and economic factors, relatively neglecting warfare and nearly excluding religion and other ideational aspects and the agency of individual actors. Others give more weight to ideation and individual agency.

Teo is in a challenging twilight zone for direct historical approaches; close enough to the 1500s to make it wasteful to neglect evidence from later societies, yet distant enough to make it unsound to project ethnohistoric data uncritically. Linguistic evidence suggests that Nahua speakers were absent or at least not influential in the Basin of Mexico before the decline of Teo (Justeson et al. 1983). The Aztecs and other Nahua in-migrants adopted much from earlier central Mexican traditions, but the possibility of significant ethnic discontinuity adds to the uncertainties of direct historical projections. Kubler (1967) went to a skeptical extreme; Pasztory (1992) has returned to this extreme and favors a "semiotic" approach. López Austin et al. (1991) and Coe (1981) are at the opposite pole. A more nuanced approach is preferable to either extreme. Using knowledge from the 1500s to understand Teo is neither impossible nor easy, and it is best to proceed piecemeal, case by case. Many Teo images have no obvious later counterparts. Others do but must be used cautiously; meanings and clusters of meanings may have shifted.

Growth of the City

It is notoriously difficult to derive accurate population estimates from archaeological data. Millon (1973) estimated the Xolalpan Phase population by using sizes, layouts, and inferred uses of rooms in excavated apartment compounds to infer that a 60 x 60-m compound would have housed about 60 to 100 people. His surface survey indicated that over 2000 such compounds were occupied during Xolalpan times. Making allowances for those larger or smaller than 60 x 60 m, he arrived at an estimate of 100,000 to 200,000 for the whole city, with 125,000 a reasonable middle value (Millon 1992: 344). Architectural data for other phases are less clear, so Cowgill (1974, 1979) extrapolated the Xolalpan estimate by comparing quantities of phased sherds collected by the Mapping Project, with adjustments for estimated phase durations, assuming that per capita sherd production remained approximately constant. He did not find a Xolalpan peak. Instead, early rapid growth was followed by a long

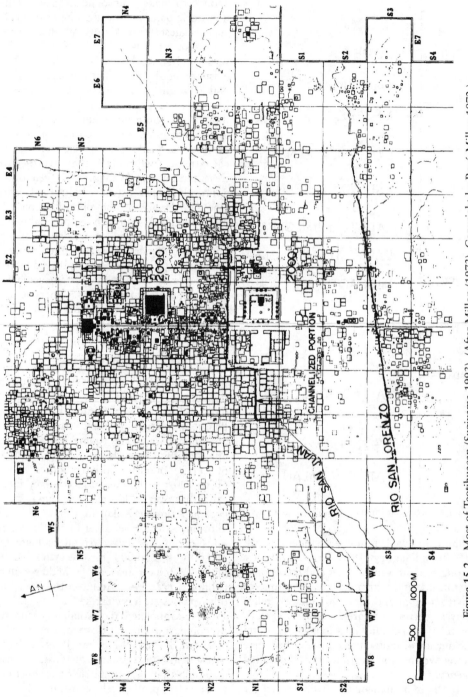

Figure 15.2 Most of Teotihuacan (Sugiyama 1993). (After Millon (1973). Copyright by René Millon 1972.)

plateau. By ca. 1 BCE the city covered about 8 km² and probably had a population of 20,000 to 40,000 (Cowgill 1979: 55). In the century before any known monumental structures were built, Teo was already a city of exceptional size. During the Tzacualli phase (ca. 1–150 CE) increase continued to around 60,000–80,000, aided by movement into the city of most people in the Basin of Mexico. After that, growth was much slower. Urban population may have reached its maximum by the Miccaotli phase, ca. 200 CE. Perhaps Teo had reached a ceiling imposed by difficulties in provisioning a larger city with the resources and means of transportation available. Most of the farming population was concentrated in and near the city, and Teo seems to have underutilized the southern Basin, including the lands most suited for *chinampa* cultivation.

It is also possible, if Storey's (1985, 1992) estimates for one low-status compound can be generalized, that very high infant and child mortality rates set a limit to the city's growth. In any case, Teo's population seems to have been fairly stable for several centuries. This suggests that whatever environmental degradation may have occurred must have been gradual.

Extent of Teotihuacan Rule

Teo was the capital of an important state, but we know little about it. Teo is in the northeastern part of the Basin of Mexico, about 45 km from modern Mexico City. The Basin is about 80 x 50 km, ca. 5000 km², ringed on most sides by volcanoes and high mountains, but more open to the north and northeast, so Teo was well situated for movement in and out. The Basin is high (ca. 2,250 m) but relatively flat and generally suitable for growing maize, beans, and other food crops, though tracts suitable for canal irrigation are limited and localized, a major one being a few thousand hectares just west of the city. Teo clearly dominated the Basin politically, as shown by its drastic interference with the settlement system.

Very likely Teo's administrative control extended somewhat beyond the Basin of Mexico, but perhaps not much beyond. It covered at least 25,000 km² (Millon 1988a), a radius of about 90 km, and may have reached considerably farther. Beyond that, Teo probably concentrated on controlling key settlements and routes between them, rather than solid blocks of territory; "hegemonic" in Hassig's (1992: 57–9) terms. Teo's immense prestige, however, surely exceeded its political sphere, and we still know little about specific outposts. Hassig's lucid account is a fascinating source of conjectures to be tested, but it presents much as fact that is highly uncertain or sometimes wrong. Studies such as Kurtz's (1987) and Algaze's (1993) also fit ambiguous or problematic data into preconceived patterns.

Relations between Teo and Cholula, 90 km away, in the next major upland plain to the southeast, are unclear (McCafferty 1996), though the weight of evidence suggests it may have been independent. Cantona, further northeast, on the way to the Gulf lowlands, may also have resisted Teo (García Cook 1994). Teo moved south to control the eastern Valley of Morelos where, unlike the Basin of Mexico, cotton could be grown, a key resource for a textile industry (Hirth 1978, 1980; Hirth and Angulo Villaseñor 1981).

Northwest, there is a Teo presence in the area around Tula, Hidalgo, notably at the site of Chingú (Díaz Oyarzábal 1980). It is uncertain how far Teo influence went west or north of Tula. Aveni et al. (1982) argued for Teo presence at Alta Vista, in Zacatecas. Some features at Alta Vista have astronomical significance, and its location on the Tropic of Cancer is probably intentional. We should not assume, however, that local people were unlikely to make the needed observations without tutelage from Teo "merchant-scientists-priests." Ceramic resemblances suggest only remote, indirect connections. A cross-in-circle petroglyph motif is shared with Teo, but it is widespread in Mesoamerica; its occurrence need not mean Teo presence. Teo may have received minerals from this area, but its impact on local societies is unclear.

In Oaxaca, the Zapotec state was independent and maintained diplomatic relations with Teo (Marcus and Flannery 1996). Some sort of Teo presence is known for Matacapan in southern Veracruz (Santley 1989), Mirador in Chiapas (Agrinier 1975), Kaminaljuyú, and other sites in highland and Pacific coastal Guatemala (Berlo 1983, 1984; Demarest and Foias 1993, Kidder et al. 1946; Sanders and Michels 1977). Santley's (1989; Santley et al. 1987) exaggerated claims about a Teo outpost at Matacapan have created much confusion. Most of the Matacapan ceramics are strikingly different (Arnold et al. 1993), and the Teo impact seems weaker than at Kaminaljuyú. Matacapan cylinder tripod vases, for example, show generic resemblances to Teo forms, but very few, if any, are specific Teo subtypes. Small, relatively crude twin-chambered incense burners (candeleros) are a stronger point of similarity. A relief from Soyoltepec in a style closely similar to Teo shows a figure with flaming torches and a rattlesnake headdress, suggesting military action in the lowlands (Sugiyama 1989b; von Winning 1987).

A Teo connection is manifest at Altun Ha in Belize by the early 200s (Pendergast 1990), but most Teo influences in the Maya lowlands do not seem earlier than the late 300s, which suggests that the spread of Teo prestige occurred considerably later than the rapid rise of the city. They are especially strong at Tikal (Kowalski 1997; Laporte and Fialko 1990) but are unlikely to represent control by Teo. Many reflect adoption of a limited number of Teo-related symbols by local elites for their own purposes (Stone 1989; Demarest and Foias 1993).

Writing and Literacy

Teo had nothing like the writing systems of the contemporary Lowland Maya or earlier neighbors in Veracruz, though some Teotihuacanos must have been aware of these systems. There is ample evidence, however, of standardized signs and a notational system comparable to those of the Aztecs, though few specific signs are shared (Berlo 1989). Langley (1986) provided an indispensable study and catalog of signs, whereas his later works deal with specific clusters and compounds (Langley 1991, 1992). Cowgill (1992c) identified a sign cluster ("red bone-flower") semantically equivalent to a term used by Aztecs. However, no examples of phoneticism have been identified, nor any grammatical elements, so, even when meanings can be inferred, the signs have not helped to identify the dominant language or languages of the city.

A remarkable find in recent work in the La Ventilla district directed by Rubén Cabrera, not far southwest of the Great Compound, consists of over 30 signs and sign clusters painted on the floor of a patio (de la Fuente 1995). They stand alone, unassociated with representational scenes. They were made quickly and show a control of line that bespeaks an experienced hand. Their meaning and purpose are obscure, but there can no longer be any doubt that Teotihuacanos had a notational system adequate for the information-handling needs of their society. What remains noteworthy is the sparing use of this system in sculpture, mural painting, and decorated ceramics; one aspect of the near lack of public celebration of named specific individuals.

Pasztory (1992) suggested that Teo was almost secretive and made a point of being different from other Mesoamerican societies. It is easy for us, in our frustration, to feel they were deliberately being difficult, but I suspect most meanings of their scenes and signs were intended to be clear to the average Teotihuacano, and we have trouble only because we still lack many keys. They seem, however, not to have been very interested in exotic ideas. Some fine foreign ceramics were imported, but most exotic goods were raw materials intended for working by Teo artisans. The contrast with the Aztec interest in finished products from afar, seen in the Templo Mayor offerings (Matos Moctezuma 1988), is striking. Persons in other societies adopted Teo symbols for their own ends, but there was little flow in the opposite direction; Teotihuacanos seem to have been satisfied with their local style and symbols (Pasztory 1990: p. 187). The great value placed on the exotic in many societies (Helms 1993) is not evident at Teo.

One exception is adoption of interlocking scroll motifs from the lowlands of central Veracruz (Stark 1995). The earliest cylinder tripod vases were probably imports from this region (Bennyhoff 1967: 26). Teotihuacanos, however, may have recognized an affinity with Gulf lowland neighbors, and the adoptions occurred during Miccaotli and/or Early Tlamimilolpa, when Teo may have been more receptive to new ideas than it was later.

Personality and Socialization

Approaches that take serious account of individual agency imply that we should also take account of individual personality. Archaeologists, however, have done little along this line, and there is almost no explicit discussion of this topic for Teo. Foucault's notion of governmentality looks useful but has not yet been applied. Pasztory (e.g. 1992) characterizes the art as remote and impersonal, and Cowgill (1993: 564–8) touches on the topic of personality. No scenes glorify specific individuals, and human beings are shown subordinate only to deities, not to other human beings. This has implications about the political system, or about how the system was represented, but it also suggests something about socialization of children and about preferred character traits.

Beginning as early as the repeated images on the Feathered Serpent Pyramid (FSP), identical figures are repeated in numerous copies. Some scenes (especially of fierce animals) convey tension and vibrant power, as in the "Mythological Animals" mural (de la Fuente 1995: 93–101), and elsewhere (e.g. Berrin 1988: 187), but much of the art is stiff, and human faces look expressionless to modern viewers. Sometimes small human figures are shown simply clad, in free and playful poses, as in a scene from Tepantitla that reminds us how small a fraction of Teotihuacano life was depicted in

Teo art. Most scenes show human beings so loaded with clothing and insignia that faces and other body parts are barely visible. Emphasis is on acts rather than actors; on offices rather than office-holders. This, together with the multiplicity of identical scenes, suggests an ethos in which individuals were interchangeable and replaceable. These properties are found not only in sculpture and paintings that must have been elite-sponsored, but also in ubiquitous objects such as composite censers and clay figurines. Whether or not impersonality and multiplicity were deliberately encouraged by state policy, they are themes that pervaded all classes and social sectors. No evidence of resistance or dissent has been recognized so far.

Nonelite Elements of the Society

Households and apartment compounds

We know little of Teo housing during the early centuries when the great temples were being built. In the 200s and 300s, more than 2,000 "apartment compounds" were built to house nearly the whole city, of all socioeconomic statuses. Millon uses "apartment" because each building contains several distinct suites of rooms, indicating occupation by multiple domestic units, and "compound" rather than "complex" because they are bounded by thick outer walls with few entrances and are separated from one another, often by narrow streets. Contrary to widespread belief, in many districts compound sizes are not highly standardized, and they vary widely around an average of roughly 60×60 m. Internal layouts are diverse, although the core of most apartments is a patio surrounded by rooms and platforms. Yet the facts that compounds are so substantially built (of rubble walls faced with thick concrete covered with lime plaster) and approximate the canonical Teo orientation of $15.5°$ east of true north, even in outlying areas where they are widely spaced, suggest some sort of state interest. Possibly   the   state   aided   in   their construction. Very likely occupants of a compound formed an important sociopolitical unit, composed of several households but smaller than a neighborhood (Millon 1976). Societies with most of the population organized in units of this size are not common.

Construction quality and size of rooms vary considerably, between compounds and within single compounds. Some have spacious rooms and abundant mural paintings (e.g. Zacuala "Palace" [Séjourné 1959]); others are far more modest (e.g. Tlajinga 33 [Storey 1985, 1991, 1992; Widmer 1991; Widmer and Storey 1993]). When less was known about the compounds it seemed reasonable to call some of them "palaces," but over-broad application of the term has been misleading. Millon (1976) suggests at least six socioeconomic levels, with uppermost elite residences in the Ciudadela and elsewhere near the Avenue of the Dead. He would put Zacuala "Palace" in about the third level from the top. Sempowski (1994) has tabulated information on offerings in Teo burials, mostly in apartment compounds, and her analyses suggest status differences and changes over time in these differences.[1] Spence's (1974, 1994) studies of nonmetric skeletal traits suggest a preference for patrilocal postmarital residence in most compounds.

It is unclear whether there was any distinct material gap between the elite and the merely prosperous, and proportions of residences of varying quality are also unclear. Further analyses of Mapping Project surface collections may clarify these questions (Robertson 1999). Even the proportion of compounds with mural paintings is debatable. Fine murals were not common, and many compounds had only white-plastered walls, with at most a few borders outlined in red. Most floors were plaster over concrete; some were of cobbles or earth.

We need excavations of many more compounds using the best methods and concepts of household archaeology. Good examples already exist, in a residential area in the Oztoyahualco district (Manzanilla 1993, 1996; Manzanilla and Barba 1990), in the Oaxaca enclave (Spence 1989, 1992), in the

"Merchants' Barrio" (Rattray 1989, 1990), and in the Tlajinga 33 ceramic and lapidary residential workshop. Manzanilla and her colleagues have used chemical analyses of residues on plaster floors to infer highly localized activities within rooms.

Barrios, enclaves, and districts

Occupants of the city must have recognized distinct neighborhoods. Millon (1976: 225) said that many spatial clusters of apartment compounds can be identified. Some, such as the block that includes the Tepantitla compound (figure 15.2, NE part of square N4E2), look clear. Craft workshops often form spatial clusters. Unambiguous distinct small neighborhoods, however, seem hard to define in much of the city. Most freestanding pyramids are not plausible barrio temples, and they are absent in large tracts of the city. The excavated plan of one compound, Yayahuala, suggests that it may have housed a barrio headman (Millon 1976) but other examples would be hard to recognize without excavation. J. Altschul (personal communication) suggests that the importance of apartment compounds as multihousehold social and political units may have meant that small neighborhoods were not very important administrative units.

There are at least two enclaves with foreign affiliations. Toward the western edge of the city, centered in square N1W6, is a cluster of about a dozen compounds with Oaxacan affinities (Rattray 1993; Spence 1989, 1992). Architecture and most ceramics are typically Teo. A small percentage of the ceramics, however, mostly locally made, are Late Monte Albán II (formerly called II/IIIA transition) in style, and a few vessels are imports. Stratigraphic evidence suggests that this early style continued to be used from Tlamimilolpa through Metepec times, which implies either remarkable conservatism (Spence 1992) or some unresolved problem in ceramic chronology. A further Oaxacan tie is collective tombs, quite different from the Teo pattern of individual inhumations beneath floors. Socioeconomic status of the enclave occupants looks no more than average. Their role in Teo society is unclear, but similar ceramics in a lime-producing district near Tula (Crespo and Mastache 1981) suggest they may have been masons.

Another enclave with foreign ties is the "Merchants' Barrio" on the eastern edge of the city. Most ceramics are Teo, but some are imports from the Gulf lowlands, and a smaller number are from the Maya lowlands. Some structures are Teo-like, but others are circular, a form associated with the lowlands (Rattray 1989, 1990). Probably the enclave specialized in lowlands imports, including perhaps cotton and other perishable materials.

It is not clear whether Teo was as ethnically diverse as is often suggested. The early influx from within the Basin would have brought in people with different local affinities, but they may not have differed much in language or culture. Later, foreigners seem to have been handled by spatial segregation, to judge from the enclaves described above. Even without ethnic frictions, factions would have posed sociopolitical management problems.

Aztec Tenochtitlan was divided into four quarters that were important sociopolitical units. Teo is divided into quarters by the Avenue of the Dead and "East" and "West" Avenues, whose axes pass through the Great Compound and the Ciudadela. Sugiyama (1993: 110) questions the existence of the east and west avenues, but Millon's survey found ample evidence of them. They differ sharply, however, from the northern part of the Avenue of the Dead in not being lined by pyramids, platforms, or other obviously special structures. Teo has no long and architecturally prominent east–west alignments comparable to the north–south Avenue of the Dead. Division of the city is more bipartite than quadripartite.

There is evidence for socially meaningful districts larger than barrios and enclaves, but smaller than whole quarters (Altschul 1987; Cowgill et al. 1984). Freestanding walls bound a number of precincts, especially near the Avenue of the Dead. They are 1–2 m thick at their bases, but nearly all have been eroded to ground level. A Mapping Project excavation (TE5) found that the top of one wall joined the northwest corner of the Moon Pyramid at a height of about 5 m. Other walls are much farther from the ceremonial center. Starting at the "Plaza One" three-pyramid complex in square N5W2 (figure 15.2), a wall can be traced eastward for more than 1 km and southward for nearly 1 km. Traces of other walls several 100 m long are at the east edge of N5W4 and near the south edge of N6W3. There is no suggestion that the city was enclosed by walls, and walls may or may not have been militarily significant. They, however, as well as watercourses, would have strongly affected movement within the city.

Some abrupt changes in density of apartment compounds coincide with walls outside the central ceremonial district, but changes in socioeconomic status indicators have not been obvious. A possible exception is the so-called "Old City," centered in square N6W3. Millon (1973) recognized during the 1960s survey that structures in this area were different from most apartment compounds, and excavations by Manzanilla (1993) bear this out. Millon suggested that the apartment compound innovation and concomitant social changes did not spread to this area, which preserved an earlier style of housing. I am not sure whether it was earlier or just different, but it is unlike most of the city. It is outside the outermost known walls, population density was high, and it has two of the largest three-pyramid complexes outside the city center. Some artifact categories, such as composite censers, occur in unusually high proportions, but no categories unique to this district have been recognized. A search for distinctions at the microtradition level might be rewarding.

The Tlajinga district, in S3W2, S3W1, S4W2, and S4W1, is near the southern extreme of the city, separated from the rest by the Río San Lorenzo. The Mapping Project survey found exceptional proportions of San Martín Orange, a utility ware, on a number of sites, and excavations at one of

these, Tlajinga 33, have confirmed its manufacture there (Sheehy 1992; Storey 1991;
Widmer and Storey 1993). This was probably a district of low-status artisans. Specialized ceramic production was plausibly
situated in this remote area to shield
higher-status Teotihuacanos from the
smoke of pottery firing.

Lineages?

Even modest apartment compounds or
room complexes, such as Tlajinga 33 and
Tlamimilolpa (Linné 1942) tend to have
one or a few relatively richly stocked graves,
which may have been those of founders (e.g.
Millon 1976; Headrick 1996). Millon
points out that the inflexible sizes of compounds with fixed outer walls are ill-suited
to the inevitable fluctuations of strictly uni-
lineal descent groups, and Spence (1974)
cites one case in which shared nonmetric
skeletal traits suggest a group of related
women who stayed home while their hus-
bands moved in from elsewhere. Nevertheless, consistent with most of Spence's
findings, each apartment compound probably was associated with a core of individuals claiming descent from a common
ancestor, plus others whose rights to residence were based on marriage, some more
tenuous kin tie, or a wide variety of special
circumstances, perhaps including servants
and apprentices.

Headrick (1996) proposed that descent
groups at the apartment compound level
may have been hierarchically organized
into much larger groups, whose heads
would have been of elite status. Different
apartment compound groups may have
been roughly ranked according to the degree
to which they could claim connection with
the apical ancestor through senior links.
Many such systems exist elsewhere in the
world. If such higher-level units existed,
many of their head families may have
resided on or near the Avenue of the Dead,
while member lineages may have been dispersed in various districts, rather than being
spatially concentrated. A few three-pyramid
complexes in the northwest part of the city,

not associated with the Avenue, could be
headquarters for more independent lineages,
although other interpretations are possible
(Cowgill et al. 1984).

Household religion and ritual

Pasztory (1992) argued that a good deal of
village-level religion persisted in urban Teo.
Assuredly, much was distinct from the
"state" religion, but it dealt with domestic
and familial concerns that would have persisted no matter how large and complex the
state became. Many such rituals may have
been of no interest to the state. Others, however, may reflect the "long arm" of the state
imposing itself at the household level. I
know of nothing that suggests conscious
resistance to the state.

Standardized stone bowls supported on
the back of a thin and bent old man, ubiquitous in apartment compounds of all socioeconomic statuses, probably belong to a cult
of the hearth. They are called "Huehue-
teotls," but use of this Aztec term is
problematic; an Aztec revival of the form
(López Luján 1989, Umberger 1987) rein-
terprets it and shows that Aztecs did not
recognize its Teo meaning. Except that the
state had an interest in promoting domestic
tranquillity, it is unlikely that these stone
carvings had much political significance.

Composite censers are also ubiquitous.
These are built from coarse flowerpot-like
bowls, often on a high pedestal base, with a
similar inverted bowl as a lid, from which
rises a tubular chimney. Panels, frames, and
a profusion of appliqué ornaments largely
conceal the chimney. Often the central element is a human face. From Late Tlamimilolpa onward, faces and other ornaments are
moldmade. Some censers are associated
with burials, but many are not. Nevertheless, they were probably used in rituals commemorating the dead. Headrick (1996) and
others have argued that Teo stone masks
were attached to mortuary bundles containing remains of deceased elites. Composite
censers were probably an equivalent for
commemorating honored but less illustrious
compound residents. As such, it might seem

that the state would have little interest in them. One of the clearest instances of a state-related workshop at Teo, however, is in the large enclosure attached to the north side of the Ciudadela, where great numbers of censer ornaments and molds for their manufacture were found (Múnera 1985). Múnera and Sugiyama have prepared an unpublished catalog of these finds. The nature of the state interest in composite censers will become clearer through further studies of the multitude of standard signs on their ornaments.

Another indication that beliefs and practices associated with composite censers may have been connected with the Teo state is that they disappear with the collapse of that state. Dominant post-Teo censer forms are ladles, much more portable and adapted for quite different activities. The shift, however, may simply reflect ethnic discontinuity. This may also be the case with twin-chambered "candeleros," small, simple, and often crude incense burners that occur in great numbers at Teo but that do not survive the city. They are ubiquitous but are less common in the city center. Probably they were for modest house hold or individual rituals. Twin-chambered Teo-like varieties occur rarely in Maya sites and elsewhere in Mesoamerica, but are not scarce at Matacapan.[2]

Pasztory (1992) also linked "Tlaloc" jars with popular religion. Some occur in sites of no obvious prominence, but they are more abundant in high-status contexts, such as the FSP. Most are well polished, elaborately hand-modeled, and represent (by Teo standards) a high level of skill and manufacturing effort. In murals, the Storm God often carries similar jars, and they are probably associated with state religion.

Infants' burials are often associated with patio altars. It is not clear whether any were sacrificial victims; high infant mortality probably accounts for the number observed. In recent Tlaxcala they are seen as especially effective intermediaries between human beings and the supernatural because they have spent so little time in this world (Headrick 1996; Nutini 1988). This analogy makes great sense of the Teo data.

Designs pecked on rocks or impressed in plaster floors are common at Teo. These include rectangles, Maltese crosses, and other forms, but many consist of a cross and two concentric circles. This motif is widespread, from north of Alta Vista (Zacatecas) to Uaxactun. Among the first found at Teo were a pair, several kilometers apart, that formed a perpendicular to the Avenue of the Dead, suggesting that they were important in astronomical alignments and city planning. So many more have since been found at Teo, often within buildings where long-distance sightings would have been unfeasible, that their use for astronomy and surveying has become uncertain. Some consist of approximately 260 dots, and the case is better for a connection with the 260-day sacred calendar, perhaps divination, and possibly gaming. Many outside the city are on prominences suitable for distant sightings, but within the city many are in seemingly unremarkable buildings. This, plus their abundance and simplicity, makes state involvement somewhat unlikely. Pecked cross-and-circles and other motifs are especially profuse in a recently uncovered floor near the Sun Plaza, but even here they could reflect a popular cult.

The term "temple" has been used at Teo to refer to freestanding pyramids and also to the platforms that are ubiquitous in apartment compounds. The former must represent public religion, whether at the state or at some intermediate level. The latter are standard Teo "talud-tablero" platforms, which usually support a room fronted by a portico. Typically there are three such platforms, on the north, east, and south sides of a patio to which they connect by short stairways and in whose center there is often an altar; the eastern platform is most prominent. Millon (1976) suggested that a patio-platform group in the Yayahuala compound, because of its size and accessibility, may have served as a barrio temple, and the compound may have housed a barrio headman. Many of these patio-platform groups, however, were more likely used only by compound occupants, and often there is more than one such group in a single

compound. They are architecturally substantial, and they were probably used for
some mundane activities as well as for ceremonial occasions.

Craft Production and Trade

We have learned much about Teo technology, but scale and organization of craft
production are still poorly understood.
Depopulation of the countryside implies
that farming was a major activity of many
households. Earlier estimates on the order of
400 obsidian workshops have been revised
downward. Clark (1986) thinks the scale of
production and exchange was much smaller.
He overstates his case and perhaps underestimates the immense quantities of obsidian
debitage at Teo. Assessments of the obsidian
industry by Spence (1981, 1984, 1987,
1996) are more reasonable. The Mapping
Project made test pits in or near obsidian
and lapidary workshops, but more extensive
excavations of obsidian and other workshops are needed.

Obsidian from the nearby Otumba source
is of moderate quality and was used mainly
for local consumption. Teo controlled the
Pachuca source of superior green obsidian.
Much was consumed in the city, and it is
found in small amounts widely in Mesoamerica. There is good evidence, however,
that Teo did not monopolize obsidian
production and exchange (Drennan et al.
1990). Sources unlikely to have been
controlled by Teo continued to export obsidian (Stark et al. 1992). Teo emissaries
could be backed by the city's prestige and
could carry fine stucco-decorated ceramics
and perhaps perishable manufactures, but
green obsidian was the only locally obtained
valuable raw material they could offer
abroad, which may account for its wide distribution. Commerce in obsidian and other
materials may have been fairly important,
although we have recognized no evidence
of a distinct merchant class (Manzanilla
[1992] doubts that one existed), but the
scale of trade postulated by Santley (1983,
1984; Santley et al. 1986) is not supported
by evidence. Emphasis on trade alone under-

plays military and ideational bases for Teo's
wide influence.

Sheehy (1992) and Hopkins (1995) have
studied Teo ceramic production techniques,
and the late Paula Krotser began a review of
Mapping Project evidence for production
sites, but we still lack a comprehensive
picture of the organization and spatial distribution of pottery making. San Martín
Orange utility ware was a specialization in
the Tlajinga district. Other utility wares,
such as burnished ollas and cazuelas, may
have been made on a smaller scale in less
specialized households. Significant state
involvement seems unlikely, except for the
mold-made censer parts noted above.

Turner (1987, 1992) reported on a barrio
of lapidary craftsmen on the eastern outskirts of the city, and other evidence suggests
some lapidary work in fine stone and marine
shell under state sponsorship. Lapidary
work at Tlajinga 33 (Widmer 1991) was
probably not state directed. An obsidian
concentration in a walled precinct just west
of the Moon Pyramid (Spence 1981, 1984,
1987) implies at least part-time work sponsored by temple or state. This, as well as the
censer ornament workshop in the enclosure
attached to the Ciudadela, indicates that
some craftsmen worked outside household
contexts at least part of the time. Some may
have been attached specialists, but most or
all may have been providing periodic labor
services. A great deal of production seems
household-based, however, possibly taxed
and regulated to some degree by the state
but not state-sponsored.

War and the Military

By the 1960s it was clear that Teo was not a
very peaceable society (C. Millon 1973; R.
Millon 1976). Recognized military symbolism, however, was mostly late, and it seemed
that emphasis on military elements
increased over time. New finds and reinter-
pretations of old data now show that military emphasis began early. About 200
persons were sacrificed as part of the FSP
construction activities, ca. 200 CE (Cabrera
Castro et al. 1991b; Sugiyama 1989a,

1989b, 1993, 1995; *Arqueología* 1991: vol. 6). Many, but not all, were in military garb and accompanied by weapons. Two large pits, underneath the pyramid and at the foot of its stairway, may have contained bodies of Teo rulers, but they were looted anciently, so it is not clear whether the victims accompanied a dead ruler. In any case, victims and grave goods were arranged in highly structured patterns, which Sugiyama (1995) argued were related to the calendar and creation symbolism. The victims may have been enemies or low-status Teotihuacanos dressed as soldiers and dignitaries, but I suspect they belonged to the royal household and that the soldiers were elite guardsmen. Anatomical, chemical, and cultural studies of bones, teeth, and grave goods, now under way, may resolve these issues.

Many now see the symbolism of the FSP facade as associated with war (Carlson 1991; López Austin et al. 1991; Sugiyama 1989b, 1995; Taube 1992). For most, the Feathered Serpent itself reflects sacred Venus-related war; Taube makes the connection by interpreting the figure that alternates with the Feathered Serpent as a solar fire/war serpent.

"Portrait" clay figurines are abundant at Teo. Their heads, stamped in molds, are anything but portraits of individuals. Their contorted body positions have been puzzling (figure 15.3). W. Barbour (in Berrin and Pasztory 1993: and 228) suggested convincingly that they are poised to hurl a spear (of perishable material) in the right hand and held a shield in the left hand. They probably wore perishable clothing. These figurines also point to the salience of war in Teo thought.

It is unlikely that Teo could have gained preeminence – however aided by its sacred significance, location on a strategic trade route, and proximity to canal-irrigated fields – unless it had been able to overcome armed resistance from rival centers. Defensible locations of sites of the poorly understood Tezoyuca phase (Sanders et al. 1979) suggest warring polities in the Basin of Mexico just before or early in Teo's rise. Pasztory

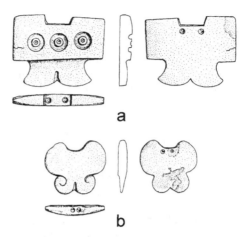

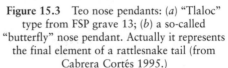

Figure 15.3   Teo nose pendants: (*a*) "Tlaloc" type from FSP grave 13; (*b*) a so-called "butterfly" nose pendant. Actually it represents the final element of a rattlesnake tail (from Cabrera Cortés 1995.)

(1990; 1993: 138) thinks Teo emphasis on war was mainly symbolic, but it was probably very real, at least initially. Hassig (1992) argued convincingly that Teo armies were highly effective not only because of their atlatl-propelled darts and other weapons but because they fought in disciplined masses, using many commoners as well as elites. This is consonant with everything else we know of Teo. It is less clear that organization was what Hassig (1992) calls "meritocratic," i.e. that commoners were motivated by the chance for upward mobility if they performed well; this view underestimates the power of ideology.

Berlo (1983, 1984) emphasizes military symbolism in Teo-derived composite censers in Pacific coastal Guatemala, and war is prominent in Teo symbolism adopted by the lowland Maya (Schele and Freidel 1990; Stone 1989). Conquest of the lowland Maya is unlikely, but the city's military prestige traveled well. Teo weapons and possibly some tactics seem to have been adopted by the Maya, at least for a while. But military successes would have been attributed at least as much to potency of the Teo War God as to weapons and tactics, and this would have been a powerful incentive for adopting elements of Teo religion. Teo's military prestige may have lasted long after its real military effectiveness waned.

Teo soldiers were associated with fierce animals, especially rattlesnakes, jaguars, coyotes, and raptorial birds. There were probably military orders something like the Aztec eagle and jaguar knights, as suggested by C. Millon (1973, 1988) and argued especially by Headrick (1996). These may have been sodalities that crosscut kin ties and provided politically important cohesive institutions. The earliest prominent fierce animal is the Feathered Serpent, depicted as a rattlesnake, though with avian feathers and a feline snout. Many nose pendants of the "butterfly" type (figure 15.3b) were in the burial at the center of the FSP. Oralia Cabrera Cortés (1995) recognized that they are not butterflies (prominent in other Teo war symbolism), but final segments of rattlesnake rattles. Wearers of this type of nose pendant were identified with the Feathered Rattlesnake. Whether there was such a sodality is unclear.

Canid jaws were worn by a few sacrificed soldiers at the FSP, and a few eagle and felid bones were found. Symbolic importance of these animals seems to have increased over time, since they are shown more centrally and more engaged in activities in later murals, where serpents occur mainly in bordering frames. Serpents seem to have a (literally) overarching importance, whereas human beings and symbolic animals carry out the actions. In the West Plaza Group of the Avenue of the Dead Complex, an earlier balustrade of the central pyramid stairway has projecting monumental heads that are serpent-like, replaced in a later stage by more feline heads (Morelos García 1993). Many war birds have been identified as owls, but most may be eagles. There may have been an early period, until the mid-200s, dominated by the Feathered Rattlesnake, followed by growing emphasis on coyote, jaguar, and owl/eagle orders. This may reflect the rise of military sodalities that limited the power of the ruler.

C. Millon (1973, 1988) has recognized a distinctive tasseled headdress as a symbol of high war-related office, probably approximately what we would call "general." It may represent a level above the postulated sodalities.

State/Public Religion

State interests were probably represented by a few major deities. One was the Feathered Serpent, discussed above. Like all Teo deities, it had multiple aspects, and besides its military associations it often occurs associated with vegetation and the fruitful earth. Another reptilian being was prominent and is represented by the head-like object that pairs with the Feathered Serpent in the FSP facades. This is often called "Tlaloc," but it shows few traits of that god. Sugiyama (1993: 116) and Taube (1992) argued that it is a headdress. Drucker (1974), Sugiyama (1989b), and López Austin et al. (1991) linked it to Aztec Cipactli, the Primordial Crocodile and the beginning of calendrical time, whereas Taube linked it with the Xiuhcoatl solar fire serpent.

The Storm/war god

This deity is identifiable by his fangs, distinctive upper lip, receding or absent lower jaw, and goggles around the eyes. Other attributes, such as aquatic vegetation in the mouth, a distinctive headdress, and a lightning bolt in the hand, are more variable and emphasize different aspects. Pasztory's (1974) distinction between "Tlaloc A" and "Tlaloc B" no longer seems clearcut, but she rightly pointed out a range of contexts and meanings for this god. He is associated with beneficent rain and fertility, but also with lightning, thunderstorms, and the crop-devastating hail that often accompanies them. Sometimes weapons associate him with warfare. The state would have had a profound interest in maintaining good relations with this god in all his aspects. He may differ in details but is broadly similar to Aztec Tlaloc and to other Mesoamerican deities such as Zapotec Cociyo and Maya Chac.

Death and underworld gods

Several large skull carvings come from within or near the Sun Plaza (Berrin and Pasztory 1993: 168; Millon 1973). Possibly these and jaguar sculptures from the Sun Plaza pertain to death, the underworld, and the night sun, and they may be related to the cave under the Sun Pyramid. The pyramid may have been associated with a sun god, in day and night aspects.

The "great goddess" and rulership

Pasztory (1977) identified certain images, characterized by a nose pendant and a bird in the headdress, as a goddess. Others tend to agree (C. Millon 1988; Berlo 1983, 1992b; Taube 1983; von Winning 1987). Pasztory (1992: 281) says there is a near consensus that there was a single Great Goddess with several aspects, including a military persona, whose image became progressively more important from about 200 CE, who is shown superior to the Storm God, and who was apparently the major deity of Teo.

Among the multiplicity of Teo images of deities it has not been possible to decide how many distinct individuals there are, and how many iconographic complexes represent aspects of a single deity. Teotihuacanos may not have felt a need to settle this question. Gender identification is also a problem. Most Teo figures are too heavily clad for biological sex to be inferred from physical features, so usually we must rely on costume to infer socially constructed gender. One deity with female dress is the "Diosa de Agua" found near the Moon Pyramid (Pasztory 1992), which is 3.9 m high and weighs 22 tons. Some much smaller stone figures wearing female dress may also be deities (Berlo 1992b: 138 figure 11, 144 figure 18; Pasztory 1992: 309 figure 23). None of these figures in female dress has nose pendants or other supposed Great Goddess diagnostics. The unfinished and somewhat damaged Colossus of Coatlinchan (moved in the 1960s to the front of the Museo

Nacional), which weighs 180 tons and is over 7 m tall (Berlo 1992b: 138 figure 10) is said to wear female clothing, but I find its dress ambiguous.

A female goddess with multiple aspects was certainly important in the state religion, but I am not convinced that she was as important or pervasive as Pasztory and others argue. The difficulty is that attributes that may be only diacritical are treated as diagnostic. For example, a goddess is shown in a mural at Tepantitla, wearing a distinctive nose pendant consisting of a bar in which there are three circles, and from which fangs depend (Berlo 1992b: 130 figure 1; Langley 1986: 277 no. 153, type E nose pendant). Rather than treating the pendant as a diacritical element that emphasizes some aspect of the goddess, it is treated as a diagnostic that marks any other figure that bears it as a manifestation of the Great Goddess. This, as well as a headdress with birds, is what led Pasztory (1992) to identify a frieze from the West Plaza Group in the Avenue of the Dead Complex as probably a depiction of the Goddess (figure 15.4). If one does not take the nose pendant or the birds in the headdress as diagnostic of the Goddess, however, nothing else in the figure proves it to be female. Further doubts are raised by the discovery of very similar nose pendants of green stone in Burial 13 of the FSP (figure 15.3a), one of them associated with an unusually robust male.

The figure in this frieze holds a torch in each hand, from which flames and smoke emerge, together with budding plant stalks. The torches are wrapped rods with "year-sign" variants on their fronts. Torches were symbols of rulership in Preclassic Mesoamerica (Grove 1987). The frieze probably symbolizes rulership rather than the Great Goddess (Cowgill 1992a, 1992b). Linda Schele (personal communication) has independently reached a similar conclusion.

One could read the frieze as an example of the Great Goddess's identification with rulership. Pasztory (1992) (in one of the few explicit considerations of gender ideology at Teo) suggested that a female was chosen as the supreme deity because a

Figure 15.4 Frieze from the West Plaza Group of the Avenue of the Dead Complex. It has been identified as the Great Goddess by some scholars, but it probably represents rulership (from Berlo 1992a: 282.)

female could be seen as benevolent, maternal, and impartially transcending factions associated with male heroes. This makes assumptions about Teo social construction of gender that are plausible but need further testing. I think any connection between this frieze and the Great Goddess is questionable.

This is not to say that the frieze represents a specific individual. Morelos García (1993: figure F.2) illustrated additional fragments of two more figures from the same context, apparently identical to the relatively complete one. It seems that the idea or office of rulership, rather than any specific rulers, is represented. It is interesting that this frieze comes from the West Plaza Group of the Avenue of the Dead Complex, which I think may have been a setting for top-level government activities (Cowgill 1983).

The colossal figure in female dress that was found near the Moon Pyramid might be connected with the moon. This would be consonant with the idea, developed most fully by Sugiyama (1993), that the Sun and Moon Pyramids and the Venus-related Ciudadela represent a triad of astral deities, a concept widespread in Mesoamerica.

The Nature of Teotihuacan Rulership

Palaces

The Ciudadela apartment compounds flanking the FSP have been interpreted as residences of the heads of the Teo state (Armillas 1964; Coe 1981; Cowgill 1983; Millon 1973, Taube 1992). Sugiyama (1993, pp. 110, 123) appears to be skeptical, perhaps because he believes the Ciudadela was associated with the underworld, while administrative centers for the "present" world would more likely have been near the Sun and Moon and/or along the Avenue of the Dead. The Ciudadela and the Great Compound, however, are very different from any other Teo complexes, which suggests that they served unique purposes. Nevertheless, the Ciudadela is unlike many better-known royal palaces, such as those in Tenochtitlan when the Spaniards arrived. The Templo Mayor shows the practice of rebuilding a temple on the same spot, each new structure enlarging on and covering its predecessors. In sharp contrast, Aztec rulers tended to build new palaces; in 1519 Axayacatl's was still standing, not far from that of Motecuhzoma II. Aztec palaces were luxurious, with numerous facilities for large staffs and a wide range of civic and private activities.

The Aztec pattern is similar to many palaces in European and other traditions. Frequent major changes are most likely when rulers have relatively unrestricted control over a large fraction of state resources and can command the construction of residences as much for their personal glorification as for the state. When heads of state directly control fewer resources, and especially if their residence cannot be viewed as family property, as, for example, the US White House, major changes are less likely. The Ciudadela fits this second pattern better (Cowgill 1983). It is about three-fourths the volume of the Sun Pyramid, but most of the mass is in the great outer platforms and the FSP. The total area of apartments would only accommodate a few hundred occupants. To begin with, there seems to have been little differentiation among apartments. Probably it was designed to serve a ruler who could command great resources but was accustomed to operating with a small staff. The South Palace remained nearly unchanged, but some doorways in the North Palace were blocked to make it less public, it was enlarged by another room complex that projected into the great plaza of the Ciudadela, and it had relatively good access to the large walled compound immediately to the north, where specialists in moldmade censer adornos and perhaps other artisans worked. These look like features intended to facilitate administrative purposes at relatively low cost and without too drastically changing outward appearances.

Another macrocomplex that may have been used for high-level government and may possibly have housed rulers is the "Avenue of the Dead Complex" (Cowgill 1983). It straddles the Avenue of the Dead, is partially enclosed by large walls, extends about 350×350 m, and has many groups of rooms, apartment compounds, pyramids, platforms, and plazas. Their number and variety would have provided for more administrative activities than could easily be accommodated by the Ciudadela. It includes the luxurious Viking Group compound, the Superposed Buildings group, and, in its west center, the "West Plaza Group" (Morelos García 1993). Much remains unexcavated. Earliest major structures are probably a little later than the Ciudadela, although we need greater chronological precision. Major rebuildings followed. Perhaps the rulers' residence shifted to the Avenue of the Dead Complex during the political changes that may have occurred somewhere between 250 and 350 CE.

An oligarchic republic?

Supreme Teo political authority may not always have been strongly concentrated in a single person or lineage. R. Millon (1976) suggested that Teo might have been an oligarchic republic. The case now seems stronger, though not yet overwhelming. Rulership in early states was not always monarchic. It is no longer widely thought that states arose as responses to social and/or environmental problems and benefited commoners as well as elites. The main explanations, however, of how elites could exploit the rest are that they could threaten force and that they promoted ideologies in which the gods and the very nature of the universe made inequality right, or at least unavoidable. Undoubtedly force and religious ideology were used by the Teo state. However, a more mundane civic consciousness, a sense of the virtue of "good citizenship," may also have been a factor. Given the prominence of this theme in modern societies, it is surprising that ancient Mesoamericans are not often credited with such perceptions and sentiments.

Pasztory's (1992) concept of a "utopian" society touches on similar issues, but I do not think Teo was utopian in any reasonable sense. Nevertheless, civic pride and a sense of citizenship, and not just submission to overawing deities and overpowering rulers, may explain much about Teo's stability and why there was no abundance of self-glorifying rulers. Blanton et al. (1996) are probably correct in considering the Teo state "corporate,"[3] at least in its later stages.

An oligarchic republic is not necessarily democratic or egalitarian. There are many Old World examples. Romila Thapar (1966) described republics in early India. Other cases are the city states of Classical Greece, Rome before the Empire, and some of the small states of medieval and Renaissance northern Italy. Venice is a notable example.

Venice

Venice differed greatly from Teo (Muir 1981), yet it is interesting to compare. By the 800s this island city was ruled by a duke subject to the Byzantine emperor in Constantinople. Over time, Venice gained its independence and the duke (called "doge;" "ducal" is the adjective) was chosen by popular acclamation. By around 1300 this was formalized in a system that lasted until the Napoleonic conquest of 1797, wherein the adult males of specified elite families comprised a "Great Council," whose members were the only ones eligible to elect the doge and to hold that and a number of other high offices. The doge was elected for life by an intricate system of balloting and lottery intended as much to counteract factionalism (a recognized problem in other Italian states) as to ensure representation of elite majority will. The office circulated widely among leading families. Venetians thought themselves remarkably free of factions, and many outsiders saw them that way. Factions were probably more important than Venetians liked to admit, but they seem to have been less divisive than in other Italian states.

Many restrictions were imposed on doges' use of public funds or their private resources; for example, gift-giving was sharply restricted. In Eisenstadt's (1969) terms, doges commanded limited "free-floating resources." Some doges tried to subvert the system and gain more personal power, but with little success. The elite were also relatively successful in keeping popular resistance under control; some disturbances occurred but the masses never overthrew regimes, as they sometimes did in other Italian states.

Individual doges were more celebrated than Teo rulers appear to us, but their pedigrees seem to have been unimportant, as long as they belonged to elite Great Council families. There are numerous portraits of doges, and many had fine tombs (at least one was criticized for living and dying too simply), but these seem by way of keeping up a certain dignity for the prestige of the state, and I do not believe any ducal tombs or images became important in state ritual and myth (as did the relics of various saints, especially St Mark). If we had as little data on Venice as we do on Teo, visibility of the doges would probably be low.

The doge's palace immediately adjoins the basilica of St Mark, the principal religious structure of the state. An earlier ducal palace on this site was destroyed by fire, but the present one has persisted for many centuries. Occasional efforts to move the ducal residence to another site were successfully resisted. Each new doge would move his immediate family and household furnishings into the palace, but upon his death the survivors had only a few days to remove themselves and their goods. Although various doges renovated or modified the palace, its location and basic structure remained unchanged for a long time. It sounds something like the Ciudadela palaces.

Early autocracy?

How much did the Teo political system change over time? Teo probably never emphasized inheritance and validation of rulership through pedigree as much as the Classic Maya, yet early rulers may have been powerful and self-glorifying. All the awe-inspiring monuments are early, and they represent an audacious plan imposed on several square kilometers of landscape. Millon (1992) thinks the layout developed over time in several stages, beginning shortly after the concentration of most of the population of the Basin of Mexico in the city around 1 CE. Sugiyama (1993) argued that all major elements of the layout were probably envisioned as an integrated plan from the beginning, although it may have taken some time to complete the construction project. He relies most strongly on key linear dimensions of structures and distances between them, which he feels translated key calendrical numbers into a unified spatial pattern, and he downplays ceramic evidence for the length of time that elapsed between the earliest Sun Pyramid and the Ciudadela.

Whoever is more nearly correct about how much of the present pattern was fully conceived from its inception, the layout of the monumental part of Teo was created in two centuries or less. Teo began its urban growth in the last centuries BCE and already covered about 8 km^2, with a population of 20,000–40,000, before anything very monumental was constructed. The great surge of building does not seem to represent the thought of weak rulers or of persons strongly beholden to advisory councils. Moreover, it is just at the beginning of this interval that virtually the entire population disappeared elsewhere in the Basin of Mexico (Sanders et al. 1979). People were evidently resettled in Teo. The official ideology may or may not have been collective, but in any case it looks as if there were a few very powerful, very able, and very imaginative rulers, who were probably not self-effacing persons. The immense structures were probably seen as lasting monuments to these rulers, who needed no inscriptions and no statues to reinforce the messages of the buildings. Sugiyama (1993) and Millon (1992) suspect that a royal tomb is associated with the Sun Pyramid; Millon suspects one also at the Moon Pyramid.

Absence of different plans for different city districts contrasts significantly with many other Mesoamerican centers, where there is coordinated planning within large segments but no single plan that encompasses all segments. Imposition of one plan for almost the whole city is another sign of early strength of the central authority at Teo and suggests relative weakness of intermediate social units, such as large lineages.

A shift to more collective governance?

In the ensuing centuries, from about the middle of the 200s to the 600s or 700s, the city's population remained high and the total volume of monumental construction was quite large. It consisted, however, of enlargements and modifications of existing complexes. It was also at this time that architecturally substantial apartment compounds were built. These soon housed nearly all residents, of low as well as intermediate and high status. Emphasis on building apartment compounds rather than new pyramids may have been part of a conscious shift to greater concern for general well-being than for individual glory.

There is evidence that this change began violently. Our 1988–1989 excavations revealed that the FSP and the temple atop it were burned in a hot fire, and large fragments of modeled clay walls and other debris from the temple were used as part of the fill for the stepped platform ("Plataforma Adosada") that covered (and preserved) most of the front of the FSP. Instead of being buried by some grander pyramid, most of the ruined FSP was left exposed, perhaps a reminder to any future ruler tempted to overstep, and it suffered further damage.[4] It was probably at this time that looters tunneled into the FSP and removed most contents of the largest pits. If these events happened soon after the FSP was built, and if FSP victims were in fact loyal high-status Teotihuacanos, it may be that elites saw the sacrifices as excessive and reacted strongly (Millon 1988b, Pasztory 1988). Identities of the victims, however, are not yet established, and incomplete ceramic analyses suggest that a century or more may have elapsed before the Plataforma

Adosada was built. Perhaps several auto-
cratic rulers succeeded the one responsible
for the FSP and the sacrifices, and perhaps it
was some time before a less able ruler made
revolt possible.

Whether reaction was swift or delayed, it
seems to have initiated a period of more
collective rule. There may have been a con-
sciously new theory of governance. Possibly,
however, Teo political theory always
favored collective rule, and the time of
powerful rulers may have been seen as a
tyrannical aberration. If so, the reaction
would have been perceived as the restoration of traditional government.

Teotihuacanos living from infancy in sight
of the great pyramids may no longer have
been overawed by them, but they must have
taken immense pride in them; one likely
reason for their disinterest in things foreign.

The scarcity of obvious boasting by Teo
rulers has prompted comparisons with the
Harappan civilization of the Indus Valley.
Teo differs markedly, however. Harappan
sites do not have the monumental civic–religious structures of Teo nor the wealth of
pictorial art, and settlement patterns are
very different.

Decline and Collapse

Metepec-period decline?

During Teo's last century the city's population may have declined significantly. The
extent of decline, however, will not be clear
until there is more agreement on Metepec
period ceramic diagnostics. Some households remained quite prosperous, but dispa-
rities among households may have been
increasing (Sempowski 1994). Centers such
as Xochicalco and Cacaxtla possibly developed only after the fall of Teo but may have
begun earlier, as a declining Teo lost its ability to punish upstarts. Better control of the
chronology of Teo's decline and the rise of
other central Mexican sites is crucial. It is
easy to imagine ways in which Teo government and society might have been in
trouble, through some combination of
bureaucratic proliferation; failure to adapt

to "Epiclassic" styles of government, commerce, and religion that were developing
elsewhere; and possibly environmental problems. Without new income from new conquests and without crises posed by outside
threats, rulers may have found it hard to
break free of increasingly stultifying constraints and unable to adjust to changes
even if they had the will and wisdom (Cowgill 1992a; Millon 1988b).

Fiery (but selective) destruction

The Teo state was physically destroyed by
the burning of temples and elite residences
and the smashing of idols, especially in the
central part of the city. R. Millon emphasizes how selective the destruction was. It
was intended to destroy the artifacts and
physical facilities of the Teo state. Millon
(1988a) believes it could only have been
done by insiders, but I think surrounding
societies may have gained power and numbers to the point where they, or some combination, perhaps including dissident
insiders, could have defeated a weakened
and no longer well-led city. A sizable population, perhaps 40,000, survived or resettled
the city, which has remained a town of some
importance ever since. But Teo was never
again the capital of a regional state.

ACKNOWLEDGMENTS

Preparation of this article was aided by work on a
manuscript in press, during a 1992–3 Fellowship
at the Center for Advanced Study in the Behavioral Sciences, Stanford, California. I am grateful for financial support provided by NSF grant
SES-9022192. Oralia Cabrera Cortés, John E.
Clark, René Millon, Ian Robertson, Barbara L.
Stark, and Saburo Sugiyama made useful suggestions on an earlier draft, but I am solely responsible for this version.

NOTES

1 Rattray (1992) also provided data on burials
  and offerings. See Millon's corrections in Sempowski and Spence (1994).
2 Bove (personal communication) finds them in
  Pacific coast Guatemalan sites that also have
  composite censers.

3 Millon (1992) noted that "corporate state" commonly refers to systems and ideologies that glorify personal rule and the cult of the leader – the opposite of how Mesoamericanists have used the term. "Collective" would be preferable, but "corporate," in the sense of collective, may be too entrenched to be changed easily.

4 Conceivably this was when work on the idol of Coatlinchan halted; it may have been a ruler's try at personal glorification.

REFERENCES

Agrinier, P. 1975. *Mounds 9 and 10 at Mirador, Chiapas, Mexico*. New World Archaeological Foundation, Paper 39, Provo, UT.

Algaze, G. 1993. Expansionary dynamics of some early pristine states. *American Anthropologist* 95: 304–33.

Altschul, J. H. 1987. Social districts of Teotihuacan. In McClung de Tapia and Rattray 1987, pp. 191–217.

Armillas, P. 1964. Northern Mesoamerica. In *Prehistoric Man in the New World*, ed. J. D. Jennings and E. Norbeck, pp. 291–321. Chicago: University Chicago Press.

Arnold, P. J., Pool, C. A., Kneebone, R. R., and Santley R. S. 1993. Intensive ceramic production and Classic-period political economy in the sierra de los Tuxtlas, Veracruz, Mexico. *Ancient Mesoamerica* 4(2): 175–91.

Aveni, A. F., Hartung, H., and Kelley, J. C. 1982. Alta Vista (Chalchihuites), astronomical implications of a mesoamerican ceremonial outpost at the tropic of Cancer. *American Antiquity* 47(2): 316–35.

Bambrila, R. and Cabrera R. (eds). 1998. *Los ritmos del cambio en Teotihuacán, reflexiones y discusiones de su cronología*. Colección Científica, vol. 366. Instituto Nacional de Antropología e Historia, Mexico City.

Bennyhoff, J. A. 1967. Chronology and change in the Teotihuacan ceramic tradition. See Sociedad Mexicana de Antropología 1967, pp. 19–29.

Berlo, J. C. 1983. The warrior and the butterfly: central Mexican ideologies of sacred warfare and Teotihuacan iconography. In *Text and Image in Pre-Columbian Art*, ed. J. C. Berlo, pp. 79–117. British Archaeological Reports International Series 180, Oxford.

——1984. *Teotihuacan Art Abroad*. British Archaeological Reports International Series 199, Oxford.

——1989. Early writing in central Mexico: *in tlilli, in tlapalli* before AD 1000. In Diehl and Berlo 1989, pp. 19–47.

——(ed.). 1992a. *Art, Ideology, and the City of Teotihuacan*. Washington, DC: Dumbarton Oaks.

——1992b. Icons and ideology at Teotihuacan: the Great Goddess reconsidered. In Berlo 1992a, pp. 129–68.

Berrin, K. (ed.). 1988. *Feathered Serpents and Flowering Trees: Reconstructing the Murals of Teotihuacan*. San Francisco: The Fine Arts Museums of San Francisco.

Berrin, K. and Pasztory, E. (eds). 1993. *Teotihuacan: Art from the City of the Gods*. New York: Thames & Hudson.

Blanton, R. E., Feinman, G. M., Kowalewski, S. A., and Peregine, P. N. 1996. A dual-processual theory for the evolution of Mesoamerican civilization. *Current Anthropology* 37(1): 1–14.

Cabrera Castro, R., Rodríguez, I., and Morelos, N. (eds). 1982a. *Teotihuacan 80–82: Primeros Resultados*. Mexico City: Instituto Nacional de Antropología e Historia.

——, ——, ——(eds). 1982b. *Memoria del Proyecto Arqueológico Teotihuacan 80–82*. Mexico City: Instituto Nacional de Antropología e Historia.

——, ——, ——(eds). 1991a. *Teotihuacan 1980–1982: Nuevas Interpretaciones*. Mexico City: Instituto Nacional de Antropología e Historia.

Cabrera Castro, R., Sugiyama S., and Cowgill, G. L. 1991b. The Templo de Quetzalcoatl project at Teotihuacan. *Ancient Mesoamerica* 2(1): 77–92.

Cabrera Cortés, M. O. 1995. *La lapidaria del Proyecto Templo de Quetzalcoatl 1988–1989*. Licentiate thesis. Escuela Nacional de Antropología e Historia, Mexico City.

Cardós, A. (ed.). 1990. *La Epoca Clásica*. Mexico City: Instituto Nacional de Antropología e Historia.

Carlson, J. B. 1991. *Venus-Regulated Warfare and Ritual Sacrifice in Mesoamerica: Teotihuacan and the Cacaxtla "Star Wars" Connection*. College Park, MD: Center for Archaeoastronomy, Technical Publication 7.

Clark, J. E. 1986. From mountains to molehills: a critical review of Teotihuacan's obsidian industry. In Isaac 1986, pp. 23–74.

Coe, M. D. 1981. Religion and the rise of mesoamerican states. In *The Transition to Statehood in the New World*, ed. G. D. Jones and R. R. Kautz, pp. 157–71. Cambridge: Cambridge University Press.

Cowgill, G. L. 1974. Quantitative studies of urbanization at Teotihuacan. In Hammond 1974, pp. 363–96.

—— 1979. Teotihuacan, internal militaristic competition, and the fall of the Classic Maya. In *Maya Archaeology and Ethnohistory*, ed. N. Hammond and G. R. Willey, pp. 51–62. Austin: University of Texas Press.

—— 1983. Rulership and the Ciudadela: political inferences from Teotihuacan architecture. In *Civilization in the Ancient Americas*, ed. R. M. Leventhal and A. L. Kolata, pp. 313–43. Cambridge, MA: University of New Mexico Press and the Peabody Museum, Harvard University.

—— 1992a. Toward a political history of Teotihuacan. In *Ideology and Pre-Columbian Civilizations*, ed. A. A. Demarest and G. W. Conrad, pp. 87–114. Santa Fe, New Mexico: School of American Research Press.

—— 1992b. Social differentiation at Teotihuacan. In *Mesoamerican Elites: An Archaeological Assessment*, ed. D. Z. Chase and A. F. Chase, pp. 206–20. Norman: University of Oklahama Press.

—— 1992c. Teotihuacan glyphs and imagery in the light of some early colonial texts. In Berlo 1992a, pp. 231–46.

—— 1993. Distinguished lecture in archeology: beyond criticizing New Archeology. *American Anthropologist* 95(3): 551–73.

Cowgill, G. L., Altschul, J. H., and Sload, R. S. 1984. Spatial analysis of Teotihuacan: a mesoamerican metropolis. In *Intrasite Spatial Analysis in Archaeology*, ed. H. J. Hietala, pp. 154–95. Cambridge: Cambridge University Press.

Crespo, A. M. and Mastache, A. G. 1981. La presencia en el área de Tula, Hidalgo, de grupos relacionados con el barrio de Oaxaca en Teotihuacan. In Rattray et al. 1981, pp. 99–106.

de la Fuente, B. (ed.). 1995. *La Pintura Mural Prehispánica en México I: Teotihuacan. Vol. 1: Catálogo*. Mexico City: Instituto de Investigaciones Estéticas, Universidad Nacional Autónoma de México.

Demarest, A. A. and Foias, A. E. 1993. Mesoamerican horizons and the cultural transformation of Maya civilization. In *Latin American Horizons*, ed. D. S. Rice, pp. 147–91. Washington, DC: Dumbarton Oaks.

Díaz Oyarzábal, C. L. 1980. *Chingú: un sitio clásico del área de Tula, Hgo*. Mexico City: Instituto Nacional de Antropología e Historia.

Diehl, R. A. and Berlo, J. C. (eds). 1989. *Mesoamerica After the Decline of Teotihuacan*. Washington, DC: Dumbarton Oaks.

Drennan, R. D., Fitzgibbons, P. T., and Dehn, H. 1990. Imports and exports in Classic Mesoamerican political economy: the Tehuacan Valley and the Teotihuacan obsidian industry. *Research in Economic Anthropology* 12: 177–99.

Drucker, R. D. 1974. Renovating a Reconstruction: The Ciudadela at Teotihuacan, Mexico. Ph.D. thesis. University of Rochester.

Eisenstadt, S. N. 1969. *The Political Systems of Empires*. New York: Free Press.

García Cook, A. 1994. *Cantona*. Mexico City: Salvat.

Grove, D. C. 1987. Torches, "knuckle dusters" and the legitimization of Formative Period rulership. *Mexicon* 9(3): 60–5.

Hammond, N. (ed.). 1974. *Mesoamerican Archaeology: New Approaches*. London: Duckworth.

Hassig, R. 1992. *War and Society in Ancient Mesoamerica*. Berkeley: University of California Press.

Headrick, A. 1996. The Teotihuacan Trinity: unMASKing the Political Structure. Ph.D. thesis. University of Texas, Austin.

Helms, M. 1993. *Craft and the Kingly Ideal*. Austin: University of Texas Press.

Hirth, K. G. 1978. Teotihuacan regional population administration in eastern Morelos. *World Archaeology* 9(3): 320–33.

—— 1980. *Eastern Morelos and Teotihuacan*. Nashville, TN: Vanderbilt University Publications in Anthropology 25.

—— (ed.). 1984. *Trade and Exchange in Early Mesoamerica*. Albuquerque: University of New Mexico Press.

Hirth, K. G. and Angulo Villaseñor, J. 1981. Early state expansion in central Mexico: Teotihuacan in Morelos. *Journal of Field Archaeology* 8(2): 135–50.

Hopkins, M. R. 1995. Teotihuacan Cooking Pots: Scale of Production and Product Variability. Ph.D. thesis. Brandeis University Waltham, MA.

Isaac, B. L. (ed.). 1986. *Economic Aspects of Prehispanic Highland Mexico*. Greenwich, CT: JAI Press.

Justeson, J. S., Norman, W. M., Campbell L., and Kaufman T. 1983. The foreign impact on lowland Mayan language and script: a summary. In Miller 1983, pp. 147–58.

Kidder, A. V., Jennings, J. D., and Shook, E. M. 1946. *Excavations at Kaminaljuyu, Guatemala*. Washington, DC: Carnegie Institute Washington, DC.

Kowalski, J. K. 1997. Natural order, social order, political legitimacy and the sacred city: the architecture of Teotihuacan. In *Mesoamerican Architecture as a Sacred Symbol*, ed. J. K. Kowalski. New York/Oxford: Oxford University Press.

Kubler, G. 1967. *The Iconography of the Art of Teotihuacan*. Washington, DC: Dumbarton Oaks.

Kurtz, D. V. 1987. The economics of urbanization and state formation at Teotihuacan. *Current Anthropology* 28(3): 329–53.

Langley, J. C. 1986. *Symbolic Notation of Teotihuacan*. British Archaeological Reports International Series 313, Oxford.

—— 1991. The forms and usage of notation at Teotihuacan. *Ancient Mesoamerica* 2(2): 285–98.

—— 1992. Teotihuacan sign clusters: emblem or articulation? In Berlo 1992a, pp. 247–80.

Laporte, J. P. and Fialko, V. 1990. New perspectives on old problems: dynastic references for the Early Classic at Tikal. In *Vision and Revision in Maya Studies*, ed. F. S. Clancy and P. D. Harrison, pp. 33–66. Albuquerque: University of New Mexico Press.

Linné, S. 1942. *Mexican Highland Cultures*. Stockholm: Ethnographic Museum, Sweden.

López Austin, A., López Luján, L., and Sugiyama, S. 1991. The Temple of Quetzalcoatl at Teotihuacan: its possible ideological significance. *Ancient Mesoamerica* 2(1): 93–105.

López Luján, L. 1989. *La Recuperación Mexica del Pasado Teotihuacano*. Mexico City: Instituto Nacional de Antropología e Historia.

Manzanilla, L. 1992. The economic organization of the Teotihuacan priesthood: hypotheses and considerations. In Berlo 1992a, pp. 321–38.

—— (ed.). 1993. *Anatomía de un Conjunto Residencial Teotihuacano en Oztoyahualco*, 2 vols. Mexico City: Instituto de Investigaciones Antropológicas, Universidad Nacional Autónoma de México.

—— 1996. Corporate groups and domestic activities at Teotihuacan. *Latin American Antiquities* 7(3): 228–46.

Manzanilla, L. and Barba, L. 1990. The study of activities in classic households. *Ancient Mesoamerica* 1: 41–9.

Marcus, J. and Flannery, K. V. 1996. *Zapotec Civilization*. London: Thames & Hudson.

Matos Moctezuma, E. 1988. *The Great Temple of the Aztecs*. London: Thames & Hudson.

McCafferty, G. G. 1996. Reinterpreting the great pyramid of Cholula, Mexico. *Ancient Mesoamerica* 7(1): 1–17.

McClung de Tapia, E. and Rattray, E. C. (eds.) 1987. *Teotihuacan: Nuevos Datos, Nuevas Síntesis, Nuevos Problemas*. Mexico City: Instituto de Investigaciones Antropológicas, Universidad Nacional Autónoma de México.

Miller, A. G. (ed.). 1983. *Highland–Lowland Interaction in Mesoamerica*. Washington, DC: Dumbarton Oaks.

Millon, C. 1973. Painting, writing, and polity in Teotihuacan, Mexico. *American Antiquities* 38(3): 294–314.

—— 1988. A reexamination of the Teotihuacan tassel headdress. In Berrin 1988, pp. 114–34.

Millon, R. 1973. *Urbanization at Teotihuacan, Mexico*, vol. 1: *The Teotihuacan Map, part 1: Text*. Austin: University of Texas Press.

—— 1974. The study of urbanism at Teotihuacán, Mexico. See Hammond 1974, pp. 335–62.

—— 1976. Social relations in ancient Teotihuacan. In *The Valley of Mexico*, ed. E. R. Wolf, pp. 205–48. Albuquerque: University of New Mexico Press.

—— 1981. Teotihuacan: city, state, and civilization. In *Supplement to the Handbook of Middle American Indians*, vol. 1: *Archaeology*, ed. J. A. Sabloff, pp. 198–243. Austin: University of Texas Press.

—— 1988a. The last years of Teotihuacan dominance. In *The Collapse of Ancient States and Civilizations*, ed. N. Yoffee and G. L. Cowgill, pp. 102–64. Tucson: University of Arizona Press.

—— 1988b. Where *do* they all come from? The provenance of the Wagner murals from Teotihuacan. In Berrin 1988, pp. 78–113.

—— 1992. Teotihuacan studies: from 1950 to 1990 and beyond. In Berlo 1992a, pp. 339–429.

Millon, R. Drewitt, R. B., and Cowgill, G. L. 1973. *Urbanization at Teotihuacan, Mexico*, vol. 1: *The Teotihuacan Map. Part 2: Maps*. Austin: University of Texas Press.

Morelos García, N. 1993. *Proceso de Producción de Espacios y Estructuras en Teotihuacán*. Mexico City: Instituto Nacional de Antropología e Historia.

Muir, E. 1981. *Civic Ritual in Renaissance Venice*. Princeton, NJ: Princeton University Press.

Múnera, L. C. 1985. *Un Taller de Cerámica Ritual en la Ciudadela, Teotihuacan*. Licentiate thesis. Escuela Nacional de Antropología e Historia, Mexico City.

Nutini, H. G. 1988. *Todos Santos in Rural Tlaxcala*. Princeton, NJ: Princeton University Press.

Pasztory, E. 1974. *The Iconography of the Teotihuacan Tlaloc*. Washington, DC: Dumbarton Oaks.

—— 1977. (1973). The gods of Teotihuacan. In *Proceedings of the 40th International Congress of Americanists Rome–Genoa, 1972*. 1: 147–59. Reprinted in *Pre-Columbian Art History*, ed.

A. Cordy-Collins and J. Stern, pp. 81–95. Palo Alto, CA: Peek.

—— 1988. A reinterpretation of Teotihuacan and its mural painting tradition. In Berrin 1988, pp. 45–77.

—— 1990. El poder militar como realidad y metáfora en Teotihuacan. In Cardós 1990, pp. 181–204.

—— 1992. Abstraction and the rise of a utopian state at Teotihuacan. In Berlo 1992a, pp. 281–320.

—— 1993. An image is worth a thousand words: Teotihuacan and the meanings of style in Classic Mesoamerica. In *Latin American Horizons*, ed. D. S. Rice, pp. 113–45. Washington, DC: Dumbarton Oaks.

—— 1997. *Teotihuacan: An Experiment in Living*. Norman: University of Oklahoma Press.

Pendergast, D. M. 1990. *Excavations at Altun Ha, Belize, 1964–1970*, vol. 3. Toronto: Royal Museum of Ontario.

Rattray, E. C. 1989. El barrio de los comerciantes y el conjunto Tlamimilolpa. *Arqueología* 5: 105–29.

—— 1990. The identification of ethnic affiliation at the Merchants' barrio, Teotihuacan. In *Etnoarqueología: Primer Coloquio Bosch-Gimpera*, ed. Y. Sugiura and M. C. Serra, pp. 113–38. Instituto de Investigaciones Antropológicas, Universidad Nacional Autónoma de México.

—— 1992. *The Teotihuacan Burials and Offerings*. Nashville: Vanderbilt University Publications, *Anthropology* 42.

—— 1993. *The Oaxaca Barrio at Teotihuacan*. Puebla: University of the Americas, Monographs in Mesoamerica 1.

Rattray, E. C., Litvak, J. and Díaz, C. (eds). 1981. *Interacción Cultural en Mexico Central*. Mexico City: Instituto de Investigaciones Antropológicas, Universidad Nacional Autónoma de México.

Robertson, I. 1999. Spacial and Multivariate Analysis, Random Sampling Error, and Analytical Noise: Empirical Bayesian Methods at Teotihuacan, Mexico. *American Antiquity* 64: 137–52.

Sanders, W. T. (ed). 1994–6. *The Teotihuacan Valley Project Final Report*, vol. 3: *The Teotihuacan Period Occupation of the Valley*. 4 parts. University Park: Matson Museum of Anthropology, Pennsylvania State University Press.

Sanders, W. T. and Michels J. W. (eds). 1977. *Teotihuacan and Kaminaljuyu*. University Park, Pa.: Pennsylvania State University Press.

Sanders, W. T., Parsons, J. R., and Santley R. S. 1979. *The Basin of Mexico*. New York: Academic.

Santley, R. S. 1983. Obsidian trade and Teotihuacan influence in Mesoamerica. In Miller 1983, pp. 69–124.

—— 1984. Obsidian exchange, economic stratification, and the evolution of complex society in the Basin of Mexico. In Hirth 1984, pp. 43–86.

—— 1989. Obsidian working, long-distance exchange, and the Teotihuacan presence on the south Gulf Coast. In Diehl and Berlo 1989, pp. 131–51.

Santley, R. S., Kerley, J. M., and Kneebone, R. R. 1986. Obsidian working, long-distance exchange, and the politico-economic organization of early states in central Mexico. In Isaac 1986, pp. 101–32.

Santley, R. S., Yarborough, C., and Hall, B. 1987. Enclaves, ethnicity, and the archaeological record at Matacapan. In *Ethnicity and Culture*, ed. R. Auger, M. Glass, S. MacEachern, and P. McCartney, pp. 85–100. Calgary: University of Calgary.

Schele, L. and Freidel, D. 1990. *A Forest of Kings*. New York: Morrow.

Séjourné, L. 1959. *Un Palacio en la Ciudad de los Dioses*. Mexico City: Instituto Nacional de Antropología e Historia.

Sempowski, M. 1994. Mortuary practices at Teotihuacan. In Sempowski and Spence 1994, pp. 1–314.

Sempowski, M. L. and Spence, M. W. (eds). 1994. *Mortuary Practices and Skeletal Remains at Teotihuacan*. Salt Lake City: University of Utah Press.

Sheehy, J. J. 1992. Ceramic Production in ancient Teotihuacan, Mexico: A Case Study of Tlajinga 33. Ph.D. thesis. Pennsylvania State University.

Sociedad Mexicana de Antropología. 1967. *Teotihuacan, Onceava Mesa Redonda*. Mexico City.

—— 1972. *Teotihuacan, XI Mesa Redonda*. Mexico City.

Spence, M. W. 1974. Residential practices and the distribution of skeletal traits in Teotihuacan, Mexico. *Man* 9(2): 262–73.

—— 1981. Obsidian production and the state in Teotihuacan. *American Antiquity* 46(4): 769–88.

—— 1984. Craft production and polity in early Teotihuacan. In Hirth 1984, pp. 87–114.

—— 1987. The scale and structure of obsidian production in Teotihuacan. In McClung de Tapia and Rattray 1987, pp. 429–50.

—— 1989. Excavaciones recientes en Tlailotlacan, el barrio oaxaqueño de Teotihuacan. *Arqueología* 5: 82–104.

—— 1992. Tlailotlacan, a Zapotec enclave in Teotihuacan. In Berlo 1992a, pp. 59–88.

—— 1994. Human skeletal material from Teotihuacan. In Sempowski and Spence 1994, pp. 315–445.

—— 1996. Commodity or gift: Teotihuacan obsidian in the Maya region. *Latin American Antiquity* 7(3): 21–39.

Stark, B. L. 1995. Estilos de volutas en el período clásico. In *Rutas de Intercambio en Mesoamérica*, ed. E. C. Rattray. Mexico City: Universidad Nacional Autónoma de México.

Stark, B. L., Heller, L., Glascock, M. D., Elam, J. M., and Neff, H. 1992. Obsidian-artifact source analysis for the Mixtequilla region, south-central Veracruz, Mexico. *Latin American Antiquity* 3(3): 221–39.

Stone, A. 1989. Disconnection, foreign insignia, and political expansion: Teotihuacan and the warrior stelae of Piedras Negras. In Diehl and Berlo 1989, pp. 153–73.

Storey, R. 1985. An estimate of mortality in a pre-Columbian urban population. *American Anthropology* 87: 519–35.

—— 1991. Residential compound organization and the evolution of the Teotihuacan state. *Ancient Mesoamerica* 2(1): 107–18.

—— 1992. *Life and Death in the Ancient City of Teotihuacan*. Tuscaloosa: University of Alabama Press.

Sugiyama, S. 1989a. Burials dedicated to the Old Temple of Quetzalcoatl at Teotihuacan, Mexico. *American Antiquity* 54(1): 85–106.

—— 1989b. Iconographic interpretation of the Temple of Quetzalcoatl at Teotihuacan. *Mexicon* 11(4): 68–74.

—— 1993. Worldview materialized in Teotihuacan, Mexico. *Latin American Antiquity* 4(2): 103–29.

—— 1995. Mass Human Sacrifice and Symbolism of the Feathered Serpent Pyramid in Teotihuacan, Mexico. Ph.D. thesis. Arizona State University, Tempe.

Taube, K. A. 1983. The Teotihuacan Spider Woman, *Journal of Latin American Lore* 9(2): 107–89.

—— 1992. The Temple of Quetzalcoatl and the cult of sacred war at Teotihuacan. *Res* 21: 53–87.

Thapar, R. 1966. *A History of India*, vol. 1: New York: Penguin.

Turner, M. H. 1987. The Lapidary Industry of Teotihuacan, Mexico. Ph.D. thesis. University of Rochester.

—— 1992. Style in lapidary technology. In Berlo 1992a, pp. 89–112.

Umberger, E. 1987. Antiques, revivals, and references to the past in Aztec art. *Res* 13: 61–105.

von Winning, H. 1987. *La Iconografia de Teotihuacan*. Mexico City: Universidad Nacional Autónoma de México.

Widmer, R. J. 1991. Lapidary craft specialization at Teotihuacan: implications for community structure at 33:S3W1 and economic organization in the city. *Ancient Mesoamerica* 2(1): 131–41.

Widmer, R. J. and Storey, R. 1993. Social organization and household structure of a Teotihuacan apartment compound: S3W1:33 of the Tlajinga barrio. In *Prehispanic Domestic Units in Western Mesoamerica*, ed. R. S. Santley and K. G. Hirth, pp. 87–104. Boca Raton: CRC Press.

CHAPTER 16

Militarism and Social Organization at Xochicalco, Morelos

Kenneth G. Hirth

Introduction

The Epiclassic period (AD 650–900) is one of the most important and least understood periods in Central Mexican prehistory. It was important because it marked a series of broad social and political changes within areas formerly under Teotihuacan control. New cultural traditions emerged, and independent state-level societies appeared and flourished in many areas of the central highlands. The appearance of new state systems heightened the competition for scarce resources, resulting in an increase in state-sponsored militarism both within Central Mexico and beyond.

One of the concerns of this paper is to examine the evidence for, and importance of, state-sponsored militarism in structuring Epiclassic society. Studies examining the topic have used diverse data ranging from settlement patterns and artistic evidence to ethnohistoric references (Blanton 1975; Nicholson 1960; Jiménez Moreno 1966; Webb 1978). Although Epiclassic militarism is frequently alluded to, it is rarely discussed in terms of individual societies at specific points in time. This study takes a different perspective: it focuses specifically on the role and importance of militarism in the organization of Epiclassic society at Xochicalco.

Xochicalco is located in western Morelos (figure 16.1) and was one of the first independent urban centers to appear during the

Epiclassic period. Although its militaristic characteristics have been discussed by numerous researchers and travelers visiting the site (Togno 1993; Armillas 1951; Litvak King 1971), recent studies have tended to emphasize its mercantile (Litvak King 1970) and religious (Piña Chan 1977) functions over its political ones. I begin, therefore, by examining and summarizing the available evidence for militarism in Xochicalco. This task is fundamental to identifying the presence of military activity and reconstructing the size, composition, and organization of its corresponding social and political units. Once this is accomplished it will be possible to examine the organizational structure of the Xochicalco polity.

Although warfare is a condition of political relations, evidence for conflict by itself does not specify how warfare was organized or used in structuring social relationships within competing societies. For example, despite a number of excellent studies documenting militaristic themes in the Middle Horizon art and iconography of Teotihuacan (Millon 1973; Pasztory 1974; Berlo 1983) and Monte Alban (Marcus 1983), we still lack a comprehensive understanding of the role of militarism in the structure, growth, and maintenance of the early states. The key issue in Central Mexico is how the early state was organized in Teotihuacan. Unresolved is whether the militaristic

Reprinted from Kenneth G. Hirth. 1989. Militarism and Social Organization at Xochicalco, Morelos. In *Mesoamerica After the Decline of Teotihuacan, AD 700–900*, edited by Richard Diehl and Janet Berlo (Dumbarton Oaks Publications, Washington DC), pp. 69–81.

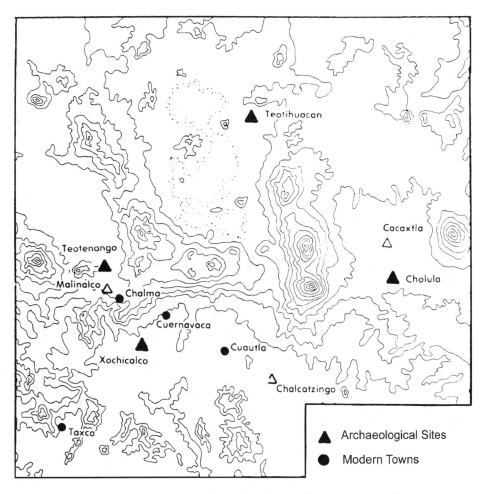

Figure 16.1 Location of important archaeological sites mentioned in the text.

themes found at Teotihuacan reflect its organization as conquest state, the operation of armed merchant groups (Berlo 1983), or the appearance of warrior societies/sodalities alongside local militias organized through kinship and community lines. This study examines the role of militarism during the Epiclassic for which the documentary evidence is both more abundant and more specific in meaning.

The question to be addressed is whether the growth of Xochicalco as a political center was linked to the appearance of state-dependent military sodalities. It is becoming increasingly clear that Epiclassic

societies were organized in a way analogous to the Late Horizon conquest states. Intergroup warfare was a condition of the times and was important in structuring the social, economic, and political aspects of society. The data suggest that political systems grew through military conquest and that tribute was extracted from conquered provinces to support an administrative elite. Warrior societies were present and appear to have been characterized by both the internal stratification and upward social mobility found among the *quauhpipiltzin* of the Late Horizon Mexica. Religious themes suggest the presence of the human sacrifice/god nourishment complex which legitimized the role and social position of warrior sodalities (*quauhpipiltzin*) within the society. The significance of the warrior societies is that they cut across social classes and allowed the acquisition of status and rewards for service to the state.

This paper concludes with a few brief comments on the size of the Xochicalco state. More important, I attempt to show that Central Mexico was divided sharply into several competing political and economic systems during the Epiclassic. Political competition is reflected in the limited economic interaction between these systems which are differentiated from one another by their regionally distinct archaeological assemblages. Western Morelos was clearly outside of the Valley of Mexico economic sphere; this suggests that Xochicalco was an independent and active competitor of Teotihuacan and other centers throughout the valley's southern lakes region.

Evidence for Militarism in Architecture and Settlement Patterns

Xochicalco is located on a hilltop 15 km southwest of the modern town of Cuernavaca. Its hilltop location has prompted comments about the militaristic character of the site by many of its early visitors. Alzate y Ramirez (1791) described the site's defensive architecture and characterized it as a military fortress as early as 1777. Togno (1903) believed that Xochicalco's internal organizational design was an early version of the polygonal fortress plan used during the nineteenth century throughout Europe. In 1978 the Xochicalco Mapping Project was initiated to study the development of urban-state political systems in western Morelos. Since that time the project has assembled quite a variety of data reflecting militarism, including defensive fortifications, the internal organization of the Xochicalco site, the configuration of regional settlement patterns, iconographic themes portrayed on stone sculpture, and the occurrence of artifact classes specifically associated with the practice of human sacrifice.

Intensive reconnaissance of Cerro Xochicalco has supported earlier suggestions that the site was constructed as a fortified urban precinct. Barrier walls, ramparts, dry moats, and trenches were mapped. On the basis of their size and location, these appear to be defensive features. Barrier walls and ramparts vary from 2–4 m in height and are usually found together with a dry moat or trench. Moats and trenches are equally formidable and are cut directly into the bedrock up to 3 m in depth.

The distribution of these architectural features (figure 16.2) reveals several interesting characteristics about defensive strategy during the Epiclassic. First, Xochicalco's primary defenses were provided by its hilltop location and the long terraces and platforms that have downslope facades from 3–5 m in height. Walls and moats were constructed as supplementary defenses which, together with interconnecting terraces and platforms, provide a formidable barrier around the base of the hill. Second, these supplementary constructions did not create a continuous defensive perimeter around the entire site. Although the lower portions of Cerro Xochicalco were fortified with ditches and ramparts on its southern and eastern flanks, these constructions end where the slope steepens and the terrain provides some natural defense for the site occupants. Even though a discontinuous defensive perimeter would be ineffective against a western military strategy, this is precisely what some early conquistadors describe as a tactical feature of Pre-Hispanic warfare in some areas of Mesoamerica (Dávila in Chamberlain 1948: 114).

An important characteristic of Xochicalco's organizational design is that it provided site occupants with a multiple series of internal defensive perimeters. These perimeters were created by constructing long terraces with steep downslope facades in a series of concentric bands extending up the slope of the hill. The occurrence of fortifications with several of these internal perimeters provides proof that the concentric terrace arrangement was designed specifically for defense. Freestanding defensive walls were

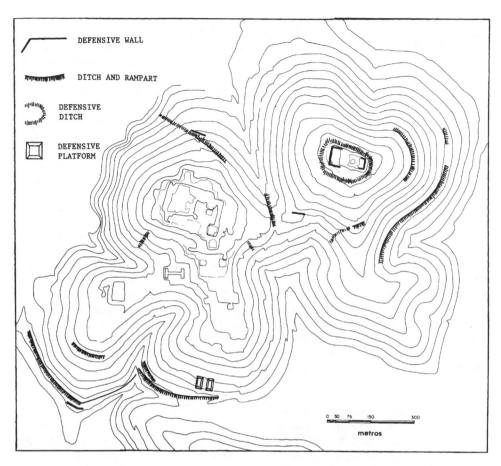

Figure 16.2 Distribution of defensive architecture at Xochicalco, Morelos.

incorporated into the internal defenses to bolster the downslope edge of terraces (T14 and T8) and to enclose separate precincts (Plaza Ceremonial). Trenches were also used on the North Hill to divide the site into horizontal rather than vertical segments. It is possible that some of the internal defensive perimeters were established along the boundaries between barrios or other social divisions within the site.

Division of the site into multiple concentric compartments was a practical defensive strategy. Access between them was restricted by a series of paved ramps or accessways which ascended the hillside in specific locales. Accessways were the weakest part of the concentric design and were

defended by large flanking platforms where they crossed internal site segments. While the main purpose of these accessways was to restrict vertical movement throughout the site, many were enclosed on both sides by masonry walls which increased the horizontal dissection of the site into pie-shaped segments.

Another interesting characteristic of the region's Epiclassic defensive architecture is that a great deal of effort was invested in fortifying small precincts within one kilometer of the major defensive perimeter of Cerro Xochicalco. Six small civic-ceremonial precincts identified by the Mapping Project (La Bodega, La Silla, Temascal, La Fosa, La Maqueta, Tlacuatzingo) are fortified with a combination of moats, ramparts, walls, and platforms. This is surprising not only because of their proximity to the Cerro Xochicalco defenses but also because four of the six precincts appear to have been special-purpose zones with little or no associated residential habitation. I believe that these precincts were the fortified retreats of groups residing in the outlying hinterland surrounding Xochicalco. A similar, although not identical, situation is recorded for Utatlan, Guatemala, where major lineage heads maintained a palace complex in the urban center while their vassals and clansmen resided in the surrounding rural areas (Carmack 1981). In a similar vein, the village of Tlacuatzingo and the more distant community at Cerro Jumil constructed their own defenses rather than relying on those of Cerro Xochicalco. The presence of multiple defensive precincts perhaps reflects a segmented social system where individual communities maintained a high degree of internal autonomy but were linked in a mutually beneficial political league under the hegemony of the Xochicalco elite.

Regional settlement survey of 250 km^2 in the Coatlan region has provided useful information on changing demographic relationships in an area 12 km southwest of Xochicalco. During the Classic period preceding Xochicalco's rise to power, the Coatlan region was characterized by a poorly developed settlement hierarchy. The majority of the population was dispersed throughout small hamlets located alongside good agricultural land. Small villages provided the primary social and administrative functions for dispersed groups throughout the region (Hirth and Angulo 1981: fig. 4). These villages averaged 100–200 persons in size and rarely contain civic-ceremonial structures greater than 2 m in height. The area has moderately weak cultural linkages with the Valley of Mexico; Teotihuacan culture is not strongly reflected in either ceramic or architectural assemblages except at the site of Miahuatlan (RCT-133) located along the Amacusac River. Miahuatlan was the only large Classic period site located in the Coatlan region and may have been an important regional administrative center and outpost for trade leading south into Guerrero and beyond to the Pacific coast.

During the Epiclassic several significant changes occurred in the settlement patterns throughout the Coatlan region which may be related to increased militarism and the integration of rural populations under Xochicalco's political control. First, there was a clear trend of nucleating population into fewer but larger sites in good agricultural zones. Second, the location of village communities with ceremonial architecture shifted from the valley floor to defendable locales on hills and ridgetops overlooking the alluvial bottoms. The construction of terraces was the principal means of fortifying the large hilltop sites of Coatlan del Rio (RCT-1) and Miahuatlan Pueblo (RCT-119). No auxiliary defensive features, such as moats, ramparts, or defensive walls, were identified throughout the region. It is likely that Xochicalco and its associated fortified precincts provided the strategic defenses for groups in western Morelos.

Xochicalco Militarism: Art and Artifacts

Some of the best information on militarism is that portrayed on the carved stone monuments located in the Plaza Ceremonial on the summit of Cerro Xochicalco. The best known of these monuments is the Pyramid of the Plumed Serpent (figure 16.3) whose carved surfaces contain a variety of liturgical, calendric, historic, and conquest information. The multiple messages depicted on the Pyramid of the Plumed Serpent have been discussed by others; it is only the militaristic themes that I am concerned with here.

Militarism in its simplest form is portrayed on the Pyramid of the Plumed Serpent as warriors arrayed in battle costume and carrying a shield and darts (figure 16.4a). Most of these figures are located on the masonry temple on the top of the pyramid which was already badly destroyed at the time of Leopoldo Batres' (1912) partial restoration in the late nineteenth century. Twelve armed warriors are depicted on the

Figure 16.3   The Pyramid of the Plumed Serpent, as seen from the southwest.

exterior walls of this building. It once contained many additional figures, judging from the loose carvings scattered around the base of the monument which could not be repositioned in the upper facade. Warrior figures also occupy prominent locations on the sides of the stairway leading to the summit of the pyramid. Past interpretations of this monument have overlooked the frequency and location of warrior figures in favor of the better preserved and boldly depicted carvings on the base of the pyramid. There is no question that the Pyramid of the Plumed Serpent was one of the most spectacular and important temple structures at Xochicalco. The prevalence of warrior figures as the dominant theme in the upper temple decoration indicates that they had both a prominent social and ceremonial role in the society and suggests that they were either intricately related to the maintenance of cult deities or involved in the ritual associated with this important temple.

I believe that militaristic themes are also portrayed by the carvings on the *tablero* of the temple platform (figures 16.4b, 16.5). The recurrent theme across the *tablero* is a seated figure holding a bag or jar who faces an open mouth devouring a four-part circle with associated symbols (figure 16.4b). The *tablero* images frequently have been interpreted as conveying messages of religious significance (Peñafiel 1890; Noguera 1946;

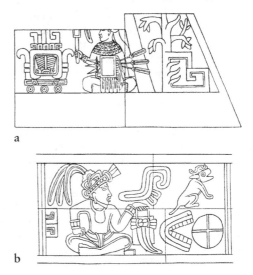

Figure 16.4   Sculptural elements on the Pyramid of the Plumed Serpent: (a) warrior on the upper masonry temple; (b) *tablero* cluster of seated figure, devouring motif, and toponym. After Peñafiel 1890.

Piña Chan 1977). The seated figures have been interpreted as Tlaloc priests because of the circular goggles placed over their eyes and the presence of the year signs in their headdresses. Correspondingly, the jaws and circle associated with these priests have been interpreted either as eclipse information (Noguera 1946; Angulo 1978: 24) in harmony with calendric notations on the structure's western *talud* or as a generalized depiction for the passage of time (Peñafiel 1890; Abadino 1910).

The alternative interpretation that I propose here is that the *tablero* element cluster depicts the three-part association of warrior, conquest, and tribute. I believe that the seated figures portrayed on the *tablero* depict warriors or members of a warrior cult rather than priests.[1] Individuals with similar costume elements are depicted clearly as warriors in the Battle Murals at Cacaxtla (Foncerrada de Molina 1982). Cacaxtla warriors wear the year sign motif in their headdresses and display Tlaloc imagery both in their belts and in the mask elements suspended in front of their faces. The year sign and facial Tlaloc imagery occur at Cacaxtla only within scenes of war and militarism and only then with the ornately embellished, most prominent, and presumably highest ranking members of the victorious group. This imagery is similar to that found at Teotihuacan where Pasztory (1974: 15) has observed that human figures associated with war and sacrifice are frequently portrayed with rings over their eyes. The seated *tablero* figures at Xochicalco are portrayed as speaking, so it is probable that the associated symbols are meant to be interpreted as the subject of their message. Similarly, Linda Schele and Mary Miller (1986: 177) have determined that the year sign headdress and Tlaloc imagery (Millon 1973) were closely associated with warfare and human sacrifice on public monuments in the Maya region.

Immediately adjacent to the seated *tablero* figure is an open jaw devouring a four-part circle. I believe that this depiction is meant to be interpreted literally; that is, the jaws portray the action to eat, consume, or put inside. The four-part circle or *kan* sign in Mesoamerican epigraphy was often used to represent the idea of something precious (Thompson 1971: 275). I believe that the jaw and circle association is a hieroglyphic text portrayed in ideo-pictographic form. Since the seated figures are always depicted as speaking, the content of the

message is "I eat or consume something precious" or, alternatively, "I put something precious inside." It is interesting that the Nahuatl verb meaning "to put something precious or valuable inside" is *calaquia* (Molina 1977). If the message was spoken in Nahuatl, the seated figure would have said *nitla, calaquia*. The word for tribute in Nahuatl is *tlacalaquilli*, and the verb to pay tribute is *nitlacalaquia* (Molina 1977).

Located above the open jaw and four-part circle are a series of nonrepeating iconographic elements which have been interpreted as a form of calendric designation (Peñafiel 1980; Abadino 1910; Roque 1928). In an early article Leopoldo Batres (1886) suggested that some of these elements might properly be interpreted as the toponymic depictions of specific places. I favor this interpretation since the organization of the iconography is consistent with the principles of Nahuatl place-name construction when using the picto-ideographic approach (Dibble 1971: 324; Peñafiel 1885). In the discussion that follows I use Nahuatl to decipher and propose place-name equivalents for these toponyms. In doing this I would like to make two points clear. First, I do not mean to imply that the inhabitants of Xochicalco were necessarily Nahuatl speakers. Since place names referred to real things or actions, the meaning and symbolism of indigenous names were maintained despite the translation of the name into various languages. Second, what I want to demonstrate is that these *tablero* elements can be interpreted plausibly and logically as toponyms. I am *not* concerned with identifying or correlating these toponyms with *specific* places known from contact period sources. References to specific places or geographic regions are intended merely to illustrate a possible reading of the toponym.

Only seven of the original twenty-eight toponyms in the *tablero* register are complete enough to be read. Six of these are located on the north *tablero* where the late nineteenth-century photographs taken prior to Batres' reconstruction show the facade to be complete and well preserved (Saville

NORTH TABLERO

SOUTH TABLERO

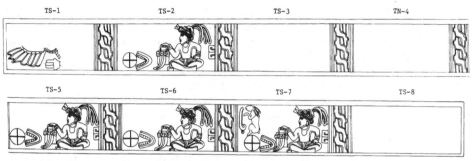

Figure 16.5 Preserved sculptural elements on the north and south *tableros* of the Pyramid of the Plumed Serpent. Courtesy of Virginia Grady Smith.

1928; Peñafiel 1890). The single remaining toponym is located on the pyramid's south *tablero*. Figure 16.5 illustrates these toponyms.[2]

Toponym TN-I is located on the north *tablero* and is a carving of a flower (*xochitl*) accompanied by a curved bar or staff (*topilli*). If we presume an implied locational ending such as *can* (place of) or *tlan* (near, together), a possible translation for this toponym would be Xochitopilan (place of the flowered staff). The next toponym on the north *tablero* (TN-2) is a human arm holding or throwing a spear. Alternative translations for this could be Tlacochcalco (place of the house of spears) or Miacatlan (abundant place of spears). This glyph may refer to the large Epiclassic site located on the hill overlooking the modern town of Miacatlan approximately 8 km southwest of Cerro Xochicalco. The third toponym

on the north *tablero* (TN-3) portrays an iguana or lizard (*cuetzpallin*) which could be translated as Cuetzpalan (place of the iguana) or by dropping the "p" as Cuetzalan (green place, place of the quetzal birds).

Translation of toponym TN-4 is more secure because of its similarity with the depiction of some Aztec place names. The figure is that of a dog or coyote (*coyotl*) with a flourish or crest on its forehead. A literal translation for this toponym would be Coyoacan (place of the coyote). In the codices the toponym for Coyoacan was drawn simply as a coyote portrayed with a black spot (a double entendre with *coyoctic* meaning hole) painted on its side. Another way of translating Coyoacan is "place of the crest of the head of the coyote," as it was among the Otomi. Ecker (1940: 200) suggests that this was the ancient way of indicating Coyoacan, and it is what I believe is depicted here.[3] It is possible that this toponym is meant to refer to the old town of Yacapixtlan in northeastern Morelos which was called Coyoacan (Chimalpahin 1965: 154) prior to its resettlement by the Tlacochcalco during the late fourteenth or early fifteenth century.

Toponym TN-5 portrays two legs placed over the symbol for water. One of the legs is inclined inward to indicate action. I believe that this toponym is meant to be interpreted as a whole action, namely, to walk on or pass over water. The verb to cross a river is *pano*, while the noun for a river ford or water crossing is *panoayan*. The toponym can be translated directly as Panoayan (crossing over water), which may refer either to the archaeological site of Pantitlan near Huastepec in central Morelos or perhaps an unidentified Epiclassic town in the Amecameca area leading north into the Valley of Mexico which was known ethnohistorically as Panohuayan Amaquemecan (Chimalpahin 1965: 25).

The last undamaged toponym on the north *tablero* is TN-8 which displays human legs wearing a pair of elaborate sandals adorned with the heads of birds. These represent eagle sandals (*quauhcatli*) which were worn during the Postclassic period by royal or important personages. The flourish between the legs is interesting because the postfix *tlan* was used to signify "between" (Peñafiel 1885: 28). A logical translation for this toponym would be Quauhcatlan or Quauhcatitlan, a possible reference to a town somewhere in eastern Morelos along the Rio Cuautla.

Only one toponym is complete enough to be read on the south *tablero*. Figure TS-7 portrays a rabbit (*tochtli*) depicted as singing or speaking. Several alternative interpretations can be given for this toponym. It can be interpreted as Tuchtlan (place of the rabbits) or Tuxpan (among the rabbits) by focusing on the rabbit representation. An alternative possibility is that the speech scroll (*cuicatl*) carries the major meaning in which case the toponym could be read as Cuicatlan. If the latter interpretation is taken, it may refer to a Cuicatenco town

somewhere in the state of Oaxaca (Macazaga Ordoño 1978).

I would like to suggest that the main purpose of the *tablero* sculpture on the Pyramid of the Plumed Serpent was to portray a list of the towns paying tribute to Xochicalco. Furthermore, the depiction of the seated figure in warrior regalia was intended to convey the idea that the towns were conquered and/or the tribute can be credited to the actions of a warrior group. The same symbolism was used to convey the idea of tribute in the Battle Mural at Cacaxtla, although in a somewhat different context. In Late Horizon religious cosmology warriors killed in battle were considered to be divine offerings to the gods. The blood of fallen warriors and sacrificial victims was perceived as a blood tribute needed to nourish the gods and maintain stability in the universe.

At Cacaxtla the symbolism for tribute occurs in the context of "blood tribute" associated with the killing and sacrifice of warriors on the field of battle. The idea of blood tribute is portrayed as a composite association of three separate elements including the four-part circle meaning precious, a row of teeth representing the jaw equivalent or action of eating, and the heart or blood symbol (figure 16.6a). This glyph occurs six times in the Cacaxtla mural either in front of or attached to a warrior

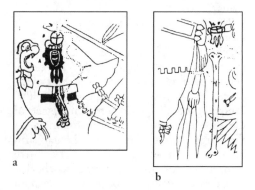

a

b

Figure 16.6 Portions of the Cacaxtla Battle Mural displaying aspects of militarism: (a) blood tribute symbol; (b) human femur, part of costume of Individual 7. (After Foncerrada de Molina 1982, figs. 20 and 30.)

in the process of killing a fallen enemy. The blood tribute glyph may also be attached to the weapon doing the killing and in one instance is actually attached to the wrist of a warrior (Individual 10 in the mural) who is graphically thrusting a spear into a wounded opponent (Foncerrada de Molina 1982: fig. 20). The rationalization of warfare as service to the gods is a significant theme in the development of the Central Mexican conquest state. From the available evidence, this appears to have been present during the Epiclassic period.

At Xochicalco we find the relationship between religion and warfare represented by evidence for human sacrifice during the Epiclassic period. Visitors in the eighteenth and nineteenth centuries report many loose stone carvings in the Plaza Ceremonial, some of which were illustrated by Peñafiel (1890). One of the most interesting of these monuments is a full-round sculpture in the form of a human torso which I believe depicts the practice of human sacrifice (figure 16.7). The torso is portrayed as decapitated and severed from its lower legs. The ribs are exposed by a deep incision into the central chest cavity which was presumably made to remove the victim's heart. This monument was probably used as a sacrificial altar which can be associated with

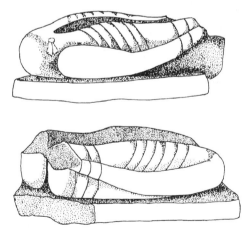

Figure 16.7 Xochicalco sculpture portraying human sacrifice. (Courtesy of Virginia Grady Smith.)

warfare and militarism on the basis of three circumstantial bits of data. First, Peñafiel (1890: 32) locates this monument at the base of the Pyramid of the Plumed Serpent. I believe that this provenience is not accidental and that the monument was originally associated with the temple on the summit of the pyramid where other warfare elements are portrayed. A knotted cord or rope is clearly depicted on the right shoulder of the torso; this was often used as the symbol for captive or capture in Lowland Maya stonework (Marcus 1974; Baudez and Mathews 1978). The dismembered victim was probably a captive taken in battle and subsequently sacrificed. Finally, the portrayal of a human torso with both its head and legs removed may have been meant to symbolize the taking of war trophies from sacrificial victims. Among the Late Horizon Aztecs, the state claimed the head of the sacrificial victim which was mounted on a *tzompantli*, or skull rack, while the arms and legs were distributed to the warriors participating in the capture. It is significant that the sculpture is depicted without its head and thighs, which may have symbolized the mutual participation and cooperation of the state and the individual in the taking and offering of sacrifical victims to the gods.

The suggestion of trophy taking in the context of human sacrifice is significant because it would be a means of verifying the presence of warrior associations and the acquisition of status through participation in warfare. Among the Aztecs trophy taking validated that a warrior had taken part in the capture of a sacrificial victim, and trophies were believed to be endowed with special mystical properties of benefit to the individual who possessed them (Duran 1964: 164). Two carved human crania, recovered in excavations at Cerro Xochicalco in 1977, have been interpreted as probable sacrificial trophies because of their similarity to human trophy masks used by the Aztecs. Artifact 1 (figure 16.8a) is a cut segment of the frontal and nasal bones of the human face. The artifact was covered with red cinnabar but does not

Figure 16.8 Human skeletal trophies from Xochicalco: (a) frontal portion of a cut human cranium covered with hematite; (b) mask carved from the occipital of a human cranium.

bear traces of the mosaic or inlay found on later Aztec pieces (Noguera 1971). Artifact 2 (figure 16.8b) was cut from the occipital at the back of the skull. A human face was carved on the surface of the bone and then polished to a high luster. Holes drilled around the perimeter of the piece were used to attach adornments or to tie it to another object. The image on the mask is portrayed wearing tubular earspools and has a glyph on its forehead; the mouth of the image is formed by the opening of the foramen magnum.

Excavations at Cholula (Lopez, Lagunas, and Serrano 1970) have uncovered decapit-

ated and dismembered human corpses which may also have been related to the curation of human skeletal heirlooms from vanquished opponents. The relationship between skeletal trophies and Epiclassic warfare is clearly depicted in the Battle Mural at Cacaxtla. Individual 7, one of the victorious jaguar warriors, is shown in battle wearing a decorated human femur as part of his costume (Nagao 1989). Display of a human trophy in this context was probably meant to indicate the individual's rank, ferocity, and, I presume, prior participation in the taking of sacrificial captives in warfare (figure 16. 6b).

The Meaning of Militarism at Xochicalco

The data from Xochicalco and the surrounding region support the position that there was a significant amount of conflict and militarism during the Epiclassic period. The shift of regional settlement to nucleated and defendable locales, the construction of formal fortifications and defensive enclosures, and the presence of militaristic themes in the iconography at Xochicalco all support this conclusion. Epiclassic militarism was not characterized by endemic regional competition between communities but rather appears to have been the power and prerogative of Xochicalco's state elite. This is evident in its simplest form by the distribution of fortifications in and around Xochicalco. Instead of being distributed throughout the region, as would be expected under conditions of intraregional conflict, defensive fortifications were concentrated at Xochicalco to protect the central state and its highest-ranking elite.

Imagery on the lower *tablero* of the Pyramid of the Plumed Serpent indicates that militarism at Xochicalco was oriented specifically toward the formation of a tribute-paying conquest state. Toponymic information on the Pyramid of the Plumed Serpent provides valuable, although imprecise, clues about the size and configuration of the Xochicalco state. When taken in conjunction with the distribution of regional ceramic types it appears that Xochicalco's conquest domain extended from Morelos north into the Ajusco Mountains bordering the Valley of Mexico and south and west into the Mixteca baja and the Balsas depression. Perhaps the most important characteristic of Xochicalco and other Epiclassic conquest states is that they had the ability to conquer, integrate, and administer a political domain that stretched beyond the confines of their respective physiographic regions. It is precisely this capability that resulted in the interregional conflict depicted at Cacaxtla where local highland warriors are victorious over a distinct ethnic group with Maya affiliation presumably from some where in the Gulf Coast region (see also Nagao 1989).

During the Epiclassic we see the consolidation of the Central Mexican lifeway described in ethnohistoric accounts of social and political organization at the time of the Spanish Conquest. Evidence from Xochicalco and elsewhere suggests that the Epiclassic conquest state was based on the support of warrior sodalities, or *quauhpipiltzin*, which were characterized by internal ranking, achieved status, and materialist rewards. Clavijero (1787: 365) points out that Mexican groups were very attentive in distinguishing military rank which was carefully depicted on the battlefield by a warrior's costume. Evidence for this kind of social stratification can be found in the Cacaxtla Battle Mural where distinctive battle costumes portray differences in rank between the warriors. Several of the more elaborately dressed individuals among the victors (Individuals 3 and 29) wear the insignia of Tlaloc with the cross trapeze emblem in their headdress (Nagao 1989), while other warriors wear the skins and tunics of the spotted ocelot. It is significant that Individuals 10 and 34 in the Cacaxtla mural are depicted wearing the whole skin of the ocelot which was emblematic of the *Ocelotl* warrior sodality at the time of the Spanish Conquest (Canseco Vincourt 1966: III). That the Tlaloc and Ocelot warriors are both depicted twice in the murals may be an attempt to convey the notion of paired combatants, which according to some ethnohistoric sources is how *quauhpipiltzin* engaged in combat (Sahagún 1979: book 8; 88).

It is possible that at least one of the warriors in the Cacaxtla mural is meant to depict a pre-initiate to one of the *quauhpipiltzin* warrior sodalities. Individual 25 at the far eastern end of the mural is depicted naked and wearing body paint rather than being dressed in a fashion similar to any of the victorious or vanquished warriors in the battle (Nagao 1989). Among the Aztecs, undistinguished commoners and those going into battle for the first time were not allowed to wear any badge of distinction and usually wore only a simple breechcloth. As a result, undistinguished members of the militia frequently counterfeited the prestigious attire of the rank they wanted to emulate by painting their bodies with the colors and designs of the corresponding costumes (Clavijero 1787: 364–7). Portrayal of this individual in the fray of battle suggests that stratification of society on the basis of deeds in battle already may have existed during the Epiclassic.

Evidence for warrior sodalities at Xochicalco is less direct and resides primarily in the symbolism for human sacrifice and its relationship to the warfare-god nourishment complex which was an integral part of political expansion among the Late Horizon Aztecs. The religious beliefs underlying the warfare-god nourishment complex and its function in the expansion of the Aztec state have been extensively discussed by other investigators (Nicholson 1971; Townsend 1979). Central Mexican groups believed that the world was unstable and could be perpetuated only by nourishing their gods with human blood supplied through death in combat or the periodic sacrifice of human supplicants. Although the origin of this belief is still not known, we find evidence for blood ritual and the importance of bloodletting at least as early as the Classic period at Teotihuacan (Pasztory 1974). The emphasis on bloodletting and the taking of live captives in the Cacaxtla Battle Mural is significant because it places blood ritual specifically within the context of state-sponsored militarism during the Epiclassic.

Repeated use of the glyphic representation for blood tribute and its association with warriors as instruments in the sacrificial act suggests that warfare, as the mechanism for providing nourishment for the gods, had become established as an important principle in Central Mexican religious philosophy. At Xochicalco, human sacrifice is similar in form to that found among the Aztecs and involved the removal of the heart, decapitation, and dismemberment of war captives. The curation of skeletal trophies at Xochicalco is perhaps best understood using a Late Horizon analogy: the trophies functioned as symbols of power and were the evidence of heroic deeds that legitimized the right of membership in a warrior sodality.

Xochicalco in Regional Perspective

The Epiclassic period is poorly understood because it cannot be studied within the narrow regional research boundaries in which archaeologists work. There is significant diversity throughout Central Mexico both in the structure, composition, and interaction of Epiclassic groups as they adapted to changing social and political conditions within their respective areas. For example, research in the Valley of Mexico provides a distinct and uncharacteristic picture of Epiclassic social and political conditions when compared to other areas of Central Mexico at the same time. Recent research indicates that Teotihuacan did not collapse at the end of the Classic period but remained the largest single community in the Valley of Mexico during the Epiclassic, decreasing gradually in both size and prestige as the period progressed (Sanders, Parsons, and Santley 1979). Local sociopolitical relationships probably were structured similarly to what they had been during the Classic period. Teotihuacan appears to have been the region's dominant administrative center and may have kept control over much of its former political domain within the valley proper.

Outside the Valley of Mexico, sociopolitical conditions were substantially different.

Contact with Teotihuacan was quite variable, and the city appears to have lost direct control over most of Central Mexico by the start of the Epiclassic period. Independent state centers such as Xochicalco, Cacaxtla, and perhaps Teotenango appeared which were concerned with the governance and exploitation of their own respective regions. One question that remains to be answered is how much direct contact these new centers had with Teotihuacan or other centers in the Valley of Mexico. Were they economic and political competitors, or did they share a common culture through political coexistence and overlapping and interacting economic relationships?

Data collected by the Xochicalco Mapping Project indicate that Epiclassic groups in western Morelos developed and maintained a distinct cultural tradition from that found in the Valley of Mexico. Western Morelos was not strongly dominated by Teotihuacan during the several centuries prior to Xochicalco's rise to power. Although Teotihuacan-style ceramics occur throughout the area during the Classic period (AD 250–650), they are less abundant and include a greater number of poorly made local imitations than are found elsewhere in Central Mexico at the same time (Hirth and Angulo 1981).

Growth in the size and prestige of Xochicalco was matched by a corollary decrease in the number of ceramic similarities with the Valley of Mexico. During the first half of the Epiclassic period ceramic comparability between the two areas was restricted to general similarities in the form and decoration of storage jars and simple tripod bowls. Western Morelos lacked all of the common Metepec phase trade wares found at Teotihuacan, including Thin Orange, and appears to have established independent trade relationships resulting in the importation of metamorphic and micaceous paste wares from Guerrero and the Mixteca. By the Late Epiclassic we find two distinct, noninteracting ceramic spheres appearing in the Highlands. In the Valley of Mexico we find the distinctive Coyotlatelco ceramic tradition with its characteristic red-on-brown decorative painting (Rattray 1966), while Xochicalco maintains a simple orange-and-brown monochrome tradition with limited use of bichrome design (Cyphers Guillén 1980). What is important here is that virtually *none* of the Coyotlatelco painted ceramic types have been recovered from Xochicalco or other sites in western Morelos. This is unusual because Coyotlatelco decorated ware is abundant throughout the Valley of Mexico and the Valley of Toluca (Vargas Pacheco 1980; Sugiura Yamamoto, personal communication) and even occurs in the Amatzinac region in eastern Morelos (Hirth 1977). The absence of ceramic ties to the Valley of Mexico is significant in light of the long-distance contacts Xochicalco established during this time with such areas as the Valley of Oaxaca, Veracruz, and the Maya region (Sáenz 1963, 1964; Litvak King 1972).

Recent source analysis of obsidian from archaeological sites in western Morelos indicates a similar change in obsidian procurement networks between the Classic and Epiclassic periods (Sorensen, Hirth, and Ferguson n.d.). During the Classic period, lithic workshops at Teotihuacan produced large quantities of obsidian artifacts for export throughout Central Mexico and beyond (Spence 1981; Santley 1984). Most of the artifacts produced in these workshops were manufactured from obsidian coming from the Otumba and Pachuca sources which were under the direct control of the Teotihuacan state. Analysis of seventeen obsidian artifacts from Late Classic deposits at Miahuatlan (RCT-119) indicates that the

majority of the obsidian reaching sites in western Morelos originated from Teotihuacan controlled obsidian sources (table 16.1).

The situation changed substantially during the Epiclassic period (table 16.2). Source analysis of 116 obsidian artifacts from Xochicalco indicates a decline in the procurement and utilization of obsidian from the traditional Teotihuacan sources. The quantity of Pachuca obsidian declined significantly in western Morelos, and Otumba obsidian all but disappeared despite the continued operation of large production workshops at Teotihuacan. Instead, Xochicalco appears to have relied heavily on the importation of obsidian from the more distant Ucareo source near Zinepecuaro, Michoacan. This is significant because the Ucareo source is much farther from Xochicalco than either the Otumba or Pachuca obsidian mines; the distance from Xochicalco to the Ucareo source is 197 km, while Otumba and Pachuca are only 98 and 125 km from the site. Obsidian from Ucareo probably reached western Morelos by circuitous trade routes which bypassed the western edge of the Valley of Mexico.

The differences in the material culture remains between western Morelos and the Valley of Mexico appear to be the result of their polarization under separate and competing political centers. During previous periods similarities in ceramic assemblages indicated communication flow and/or economic interaction between these regions. Interruption of these linkages and the coexistence of two distinct ceramic spheres are significant, reflecting a breakdown of

Table 16.1 Source analysis of Late Classic obsidian from the site of Miahuatlan Pueblo (RCT-119) in western Morelos

| | Identified obsidian sources | | | |
	Pachuca	Otumba	Zinapecuaro	Total
Excavation B	7	1	2	10
Excavation E	5	1	1	7
TOTAL	12	2	3	17
Percentage of Total	(70.6)	(11.8)	(17.6)	(100.0)

Table 16.2   Source analysis of obsidian from Epiclassic contexts at Xochicalco and Tlacuatzingo, Morelos

	Identified obsidian sources						
	Zinapecuaro	Otumba	Paredon	Metzquititlan	Pachuca	Unknown	Total
Xochicalco surface collections							
Workshop 1	22	2	0	2	1	0	27
Workshop 3	20	0	0	0	0	0	20
Xochicalco excavations							
La Maqueta	7	1	0	1	1	1	11
Terrace 2	14	1	0	1	1	1	18
Campo Santo	18	0	0	2	0	0	20
Tlacuatzingo							
Exc. D	18	1	1	0	0	0	20
TOTAL	99	5	1	6	3	2	116
Percentage of Total	(85.3)	(4.3)	(.9)	(5.2)	(2.6)	(1.7)	(100.0)

former interdependencies established over a long period of time. The preference for obsidian from the more distant Ucareo source over closer ones is more likely a reflection of political and/or social boundaries rather than of expected economic behavior without corollary constraints.

I believe that this situation reflects the emergence of Xochicalco as a powerful and independent political competitor within the old Teotihuacan domain. Whether Xochicalco was in direct competition with Teotihuacan or some of the other large sites in the southern lakes region is not particularly clear. What is certain, however, is that important symbiotic relationships had developed between the Valley of Morelos and the Valley of Mexico during the Classic period (Hirth 1980; Hirth and Angulo 1981). I believe that elites in the Valley of Mexico had become dependent upon Morelos and other areas of the Tierra Templada as sources for the production of cotton, paper, and other tropical products which could not be produced in the Valley of Mexico. The breakup of the old Teotihuacan domain and the growth of independent polities throughout Central Mexico reduced the number of alternative source areas for these goods. This only intensified the need for Valley of Mexico elites to maintain access to or control over portions of More-

los which was their closest and most accessible source for tropical products. Despite the continued demand for Tierra Templada products, I believe western Morelos was largely free of Valley of Mexico control during the Epiclassic. Socioeconomic independence was possible only through the emergence of a regional polity capable of establishing and maintaining its local autonomy. Xochicalco's rise to power represents the coalition of political authority in western Morelos. Its regionally distinct cultural assemblage indicates an absence of economic interdependencies with the Valley of Mexico.

Conclusion

In this paper I have attempted to summarize the available data and interpret the significance of militarism for explaining the development of Xochicalco. The Epiclassic was a period of conflict and regional militarism brought on, at least in part, by the destabilization of Teotihuacan administrative control throughout Central Mexico. Xochicalco is one of several independent states emerging during this era through regional conquest and the collection of tribute.

What is surprising about the available data on the Epiclassic is not that there is evidence for militarism, but rather that it so closely parallels the pattern of militarism found in Central Mexico at the time of the conquest. The Epiclassic conquest state may have been based upon the appearance of warrior sodalities, where participation in warfare provided a vehicle for upward social mobility through the acquisition of rank, privilege, and material reward. Evidence was also found for a range of related activities including human sacrifice and the curation of trophies from vanquished enemies. It would appear that militarism during this period was reinforced by a belief system that advocated warfare and blood sacrifice as a necessary aspect of the religious complex.

The point on which I would like to conclude is that societies during the Epiclassic period display all the characteristics manifested by the Late Horizon conquest states. Militarism during this period was the central theme in the organization of conquest states supported by internally stratified warrior sodalities. Investigators interested in the origin of the Central Mexican conquest state must now turn their attention to the Middle Horizon when warrior themes became prevalent at Teotihuacan (Millon 1973; Berlo 1983).

NOTES

1 Although I have suggested that the figures represent warriors or members of a warrior cult, a compatible alternative would be that they represent a ruler arrayed in a warrior's regalia. I am not so much concerned with either the status or specific identity of the seated figures as I am with the fact that they contain elements indicative of militarism.

2 Illustrations of the *tablero* sculpture (figure 16.5) and the sculpted human monument (figure 16.7) were graciously provided by Virginia Grady Smith whose 1988 doctoral at the University of Kentucky provides a more detailed discussion of Xochicalco iconography. Renderings of the *tablero* sculpture were made by Ms Smith using Peñafiel's original drawings, pre-restoration photographs, and careful on-site study and photography of bas-relief carvings.

3 According to Ecker (1940), the translation of Coyoacan in Otomi is Demin'yo composed of *Min'yo* (coyote) and *de* (forehead or crest).

REFERENCES

Abadino, Francisco. 1910. Xochicalco-Chico-moztoc-Culhuacan. In *Dos monografías arqueológicas:* 13–25. Mexico City.

Alzate y Ramirez, Joseph Antonio. 1791. *Descripción de las antiquedades de Xochicalco dedicada a los señores de la actual expedición maritima al rededor del orbe.* Suplemento a la Gazeta de Literatura, Mexico City.

Angulo Villaseñor, Jorge. 1978. *El museo de Cuahtetelco: Guía Oficial.* Instituto Nacional de Antropología e Historia, Mexico City.

Armillas, Pedro. 1951. Mesoamerican Fortifications. *Antiquity* 25 (8): 77–86.

Batres, Leopoldo. 1886. Les ruines de Xochicalco au Mexique. *La nature* 14: 308–10.

——1912. Las ruinas de Xochicalco. *Proceedings of the 17th International Congress of Americanists:* 406–10.

Baudez, Claude and Peter Mathews. 1978. Capture and Sacrifice at Palenque. In *Tercera Mesa Redonda de Palenque:* 31–40. Pre-Columbian Art Research Center, Palenque.

Berlo, Janet C. 1983. The Warrior and the Butterfly: Central Mexican Ideologies of Sacred Warfare and Teotihuacan Iconography. In *Text and Image in Pre-Columbian Art*, ed. Janet C. Berlo, pp. 79–117. BAR International Series 180, Oxford.

Blanton, Richard. 1975. Texcoco Region Archaeology. *American Antiquity* 40: 227–230.

Canseco Vincourt, Jorge. 1966. *La guerra sagrada.* Instituto Nacional de Antropología e Historia, Mexico City.

Carmack, Robert M. 1981. *The Quiche Maya of Utatlan.* University of Oklahoma Press, Norman.

Chamberlain, Robert. 1948. *The Conquest and Colonization of Yucatan 1517–1550.* Carnegie Institution of Washington, Publication 582, Washington, DC.

Chimalpahin, Francisco de San Antón Muñón. 1965. *Relaciones originales de Chalco Amaquemecan*, trans. Silvia Rendon. Fondo de Cultura Económica, Mexico City.

Clavijero, D. Francesco Saverio. 1787. *The History of Mexico*, trans. Charles Cullen. 2 vols. G. J. and J. Robinson, London.

Cyphers Guillén, Ann. 1980. Una secuencia preliminar para el valle de Xochicalco. *Anales de Antropología* 17: 33–52.

Dibble, Charles E. 1971. Writing in Central Mexico. In *Archaeology of Northern Mesoamerica*, part 1, ed. Gordon Ekholm and Ignacio Bernal, pp. 322–32. *Handbook of Middle American Indians*, Vol. 10. University of Texas Press, Austin.

Durán, Diego. 1964. *The History of the Indies of New Spain*, trans. Doris Heyden and Fernando Horcasitas. Orion Press, New York.

Ecker, Lawrence. 1940. Testimonio otomi sobre la etimología de "Mexico" y "Coyoacan." *El México Antiguo* 5(6): 198–201.

Foncerrada de Molina, Marta. 1982. Signos glíficos relacionados con Tlaloc en los murales de la batalla en Cacaxtla. *Anales del Instituto de Investigaciones Estéticas* 50(1): 23–34.

Hirth, Kenneth G. 1977. Toltec-Mazapan Influence in Eastern Morelos, Mexico. *Journal of New World Archaeology* 2: 40–6.

—— 1980. *The Teotihuacan Classic: A Regional Perspective from Eastern Morelos*. Vanderbilt University, Publications in Anthropology 25, Nashville.

Hirth, Kenneth G. and Jorge Angulo Villaseñor. 1981. Early State Expansion in Central Mexico: Teotihuacan in Morelos. *Journal of Field Archaeology* 8: 135–50.

Jiménez Moreno, Wigberto. 1966. Mesoamerica before the Toltecs. In *Ancient Oaxaca*, ed. John Paddock, pp. 1–82. Stanford University Press, Stanford.

Litvak King, Jaime. 1970. Xochicalco en la caída del clásico: Una hipótesis. *Anales de Antropología* 7: 131–44.

—— 1971. Investigaciones en el Valle de Xochicalco, 1569–1970. *Anales de Antropología* 8: 102–24.

—— 1972. Las relaciones externas de Xochicalco: Una evaluación en su posible significado. *Anales de Antropología* 9: 53–76.

Lopez, Sergio, Zaid Lagunas, and Carlos Serrano. 1970. Sección de antropología física. In *Proyecto Cholula*, ed. Ignacio Marquina, pp. 143–52. Instituto Nacional de Antropología e Historia, Investigaciones 15, Mexico City.

Macazaga Ordoño, César. 1978. *Nombres geográficos de México*. Editorial Innovación, Mexico City.

Marcus, Joyce. 1974. The Iconography of Power among the Classic Maya. *World Archaeology* 6: 83–94.

—— 1983. The Conquest Slabs of Building J, Monte Alban. In *The Cloud People: Divergent Evolution of the Zapotec and Mixtec Civilizations*, ed. Kent Flannery and Joyce Marcus, pp. 106–8. Academic Press, New York.

Millon, Clara. 1973. Painting, Writing and Polity at Teotihuacan, Mexico. *American Antiquity* 38: 294–314.

Molina, Alfonso De. 1977. *Vocabulario en lengua castellana y mexicana y mexicana y castellana*. Editorial Porrúa, Mexico City.

Nagao, Debra. 1989. Public Proclamation in the Art of Cacaxtla and Xochicalco. In *Mesoamerica After the Fall of Teotihuacan, AD 700–900*, edited by Richard Diehl and Janet Berlos, pp. 83–104. Dumbarton Oaks, Washington, DC.

Nicholson, Henry B. 1960. The Mixteca-Puebla Concept in Mesoamerican Archaeology: A Re-examination. In *Man and Cultures: Selected Papers of the Fifth International Congress of Anthropological and Ethnological Sciences*, ed. Anthony Wallace, pp. 612–17. University of Pennsylvania Press, Philadelphia.

—— 1971. Religion in Pre-Hispanic Central Mexico. In *Archaeology of Northern Mesoamerica*, part 1, ed. Gordon F. Ekholm and Ignacio Bernal, pp. 395–446. Handbook of Middle American Indians, vol. 10. University of Texas Press, Austin.

Noguera, Eduardo. 1946. Cultura de Xochicalco. In *Mexico prehispánico: Antología de Esta Semana, This Week, 1935–1946* (Jorge Vivo, ed.), 185–93. Editorial Emma Hurtado, Mexico.

—— 1971. Minor Arts in the Central Valleys. In *Archaeology of Northern Mesoamerica*, part 1, ed. Gordon F. Ekholm and Ignacio Bernal, pp. 258–69. Handbook of Middle American Indians, vol. 10. University of Texas Press, Austin.

Pasztory, Esther. 1974. *The Iconography of the Teotihuacan Tlaloc*. Studies in Pre-Columbian Art and Archaeology 15, Dumbarton Oaks, Washington, DC.

Peñafiel, Antonio. 1885. *Catálogo alfabético de los nombres de lugar pertenecientes al idioma "nahuatl." Estudio jeroglífico de la Matrícula de los Tributos del Codice Mendocino*. Secretaría de Fomento, Mexico City.

—— 1890. *Monumentos del arte mexicano antiguo*. A. Asher, Berlin.

Piña Chan, Román. 1977. *Quetzalcoatl serpiente emplumada*. Fondo de Cultura Económica, Mexico City.

Rattray, Evelyn. 1966. An Archaeological and Stylistic Study of Coyotlatelco Pottery. *Mesoamerican Notes* 7–8: 87–211.

Roque, J. Ceballos Novelo. 1928. Teopoztlan, Teopanzolco y Xochicalco. In *Estado actual de los principales edificios arqueológicos de México*: 100–16. Secretaría de Educación Pública, Mexico City.

Sáenz, César. 1963. Exploraciones en la piramide de las serpientes emplumadas, Xochicalco, Morelos. *Revista Mexicana de Estudios Antropológicos* 19: 7–26.

——1964. *Ultimos descubrimientos en Xochicalco*. Instituto Nacional de Antropología e Historia, Departamento de Monumentos Prehispánicos, Informes 12, Mexico City.

Sahagún, Bernardino de. 1979. *Florentine Codex: General History of the Things of New Spain. Book 8, Kings and Lords*, ed. and trans. Arthur Anderson and Charles Dibble. School of American Research and the University of Utah Press, Santa Fe and Provo.

Sanders, William, Jefrey Parsons, and Robert Santley. 1979. *The Basin of Mexico: Ecological Processes in the Evolution of a Civilization*. Academic Press, New York.

Santley, Robert. 1984. Obsidian Exchange, Economic Stratification and the Evolution of Complex Society in the Basin of Mexico. In *Trade and Exchange in Early Mesoamerica* (Kenneth Hirth, ed.), pp. 43–86. University of New Mexico Press, Albuquerque.

Saville, Marshall H. 1928. *Bibliographic Notes on Xochicalco, Mexico*. Museum of the American Indian, Heye Foundation, Indian Notes and Monographs 6(6), New York.

Schele, Linda and Mary Miller. 1986. *The Blood of Kings: Dynasty and Ritual in Maya Art*. Kimbell Art Museum and George Braziller, Fort Worth and New York.

Smith, Virginia, Grady. n.d. The Iconography of Power at Xochicalco, Morelos. Ph.D. dissertation, Department of Anthropology, University of Kentucky, Lexington, 1988.

Sorensen, Jerrel, Kenneth Hirth, and Steve Ferguson. n.d. The Contents of Seven Obsidian Workshops around Xochicalco, Morelos. Paper presented at the Simposio La Obsidiana en Mesoamerica, Pachuca, Hidalgo, 1981.

Spence, Michael. 1981. Obsidian Production and the State in Teotihuacan. *American Antiquity* 46: 769–88.

Thompson, J. Eric S. 1971. *Maya Hieroglyphic Writing*. University of Oklahoma Press, Norman.

Togno, Juan B. 1903. Xochicalco, 1892. In *Colección de documentos para la historia mexicana*, ed. Antonio Peñafiel, 6. Secretaría de Fomento, Mexico City.

Townsend, Richard Fraser. 1979. *State and Cosmos in the Art of Tenochtitlan*. Studies in Pre-Columbian Art and Archaeology 20, Dumbarton Oaks, Washington, DC.

Vargas Pacheco, Ernesto. 1980. Consideraciones sobre Teotenango y Ojo de Agua, Estado de Mexico. *Anales de Antropología* 17(1): 53–67.

Webb, Malcolm. 1978. The Significance of the "Epiclassic" Period in Mesoamerican Prehistory. In *Cultural Continuity in Mesoamerica*, ed. David Browman, pp. 155–78. Mouton, The Hague.

CHAPTER 17

The Four Priests

Political Stability

John M. D. Pohl

Most administrative systems in traditional societies employ persons who not only smooth the transition of high authority following the death of the paramount but provide checks and balances to the ambitions of those hoping to succeed. The positions these personages hold are integrated into the hierarchy of government. This study considers the nature of a hierarchical system maintained by the Postclassic Mixtec as reflected in the codices. The object of this chapter is to (1) define the roles that priests played in the system, as officials ("regidores" or "gobernadores" to the Spaniards) who provided checks and balances to high authority, and (2) to illuminate the general structure and function of ancient Mixtec government in general.

Unfortunately, the documentary evidence on the management of authority within these factionalized realms is scanty. The Mixtec were not subject to the initial shock created by the Conquistadors, and during the Colonial period the Spanish found it more convenient to incorporate native regional control rather than reorganize it. There was no significant relocation plan, and the control of many cacicazgos (a Spanish term for native territorial units) was maintained within a native royal line. Spores (1984) proposes that the integration of Mixtec culture into Spanish Colonial society was greatly facilitated not by overt subjugation by an intrusive Spanish elite, but by the efforts of the Dominicans, who sought to insert themselves into existing social patterns. These early Dominican friars did not, however, produce the detailed studies of native culture provided by Sahagún, Durán, and others for the Aztec. Fray Francisco de Burgoa's works were written in the late seventeenth century, nearly 150 years after the Conquest.

On the other hand, political interactions are portrayed in considerable detail throughout the pictorial manuscripts of the Mixtec, and careful analysis of the painted narratives can reveal much about administrative management. In this chapter, I will first discuss some basic characteristics of social stratification rooted in elite kinship and the roles nonparamount personnel played during the transition of authority in such systems. Next I will discuss the roles of priests in the more detailed codical narratives, and finally, with ethnohistorical data, I will suggest how the positions these persons occupied related to the paramount as parts of an administrative system. Specifically, I will concentrate on a group of judicial personnel who functioned as counselors to the king.

Social Stratification and Elite Kinship

The development of social organization in the Mixteca during the Postclassic was

Reprinted from John M. D. Pohl. 1994. The Four Priests: Political Stability. In *The Politics of Symbolism in the Mixtec Codices*, Vanderbilt University Publications in Anthropology, no. 46 (Department of Anthropology, Vanderbilt University, Nashville), pp. 19–41.

closely tied to shifts in settlement, population increase, and the intensification of terraced agricultural practices (Spores 1967, 1972, 1983, 1984; Byland 1980; Byland and Pohl 1994). As the Mixtec adapted to these environmental and cultural changes, so evolved the need for administrative authority to promote organization. At the time of the Conquest, elite administration was rooted in an extended kinship system composed of multiple royal descent groups or lineages called *tnuhu* in Mixtec (see Pastor 1987). Burgoa (1934: vol. 1, 276, 369) stated that the highest ranked of these lineages was the royal house of Tilantongo. Rank in Mixtec social organization consequently became contingent on descent. This is nowhere more evident than in the codical records themselves. Codex Bodley reverse, for example, presents over 500 years of descent reckoning for the kings of Tilantongo. Regarding descent, Irving Goldman proposed that:

Descent can be understood as rules of affiliation or as rules of subdivision of kin groups. Since membership in a kin group conveys a variety of rights and corresponding responsibilities, descent may be considered more specifically as the valid, the truly authentic way of participating in such rights and responsibilities. Whether seen as the means of forming kin groups, as a method of affiliation to kin groups, or as the vehicle for transmitting rights and exacting responsibilities, descent appears in general social theory as technical rule, as a device for establishing effective order among kin.

(Goldman 1970: 419)

Seniority in rank is reckoned through descent by primogeniture, a fundamental aspect of many elite kinship systems. It was a "preferred" system for the transference of authority among the Mixtec. At the family level the consequences of being a junior member are not so serious as at the administrative level. This is because an individual's proximity to the ancestor of the royal line not only directs inheritance of family property but also justifies control over the government of society. The possibility of gaining the high position was of serious concern among royal siblings. Therefore, primogeniture not only served as a convenient means of granting authority, but it also firmly established a traditional means of electing a successor. Furthermore, primogeniture served to limit the size of the elite class. Sahlins stated:

As a consequence of seniority, the descendants of an older brother rank higher than the descendants of a younger brother. In any given group which is descendant from a common ancestor, we can distinguish a senior line from a number of junior lines. Every individual within this group of descendants from a common ancestor holds a different status, one precisely in proportion to his distance from the senior line of descent in the group.

(Sahlins 1958: 141)

Thus, rank within the royal line effectively produced a paramountcy and a system of downward mobility through time as junior members of a ruling family produced lines which became successively more distant from the ancestor, consequently filling the lower ranks. For the Mixtec, these ranks formed a class of princes called *tay toho* (Spores 1984: 64). Among the Zapotec, the priesthood was selected from this same junior nobility (Burgoa 1934: vol. 2, 168). The system of primogeniture therefore ideally ensured that the firstborn would continue the most direct line to the founding ancestor.

Goldman sees a general evolutionary trend in many societies from what he has labeled "Traditional," to "Oper," to "Stratified" forms of organization based on an analysis of cultural evolution in Polynesia. Warfare becomes characteristic of "Open" societies as kinship groups begin to dominate one another by force and militarily stronger groups focus their authority at the top of the social hierarchy. Indeed the Oaxacan Formative period (Monte Alban I and II) was characterized by intensive raiding patterns which allowed Monte Alban eventually to overcome its neighbors by military domination (Flannery and Marcus 1983: 79–83; Marcus 1983: 106–8).

In "Stratified" societies, the high authority and members of his line often become deified as the title passes to descendants by rule of primogeniture (or some other predetermined positions of heredity). The Mixtec term for the "authority of the lord," for instance, means "to be held by god" (Pastor 1987: 26). The deification process has the effect of further ensuring the ritual sanctity of the royal line but more importantly of preserving the order of the hierarchy now so basic to governmental administration. Since important rituals involving the deified paramount are essentially "religious," persons who administer the religion as priests necessarily play important roles both in the sacred and secular realms of authority. They control the ritual basis for popular belief in royal sanctity through a deified ancestor and thereby handle the sacred objects involved in both the cult and the rights to hereditary authority by the royal line. In religious and political systems characterized by elaborate rituals like those of the Mixtec, an examination of the ceremonies of succession can therefore reveal much about social hierarchy and the roles of authorities.

Succession is a critical event to a study of rank because it is a time, when the high authority changes, that the elite class reestablishes its relationships both within itself and to the paramount position by reevaluating the rules of descent. During ceremonies of succession, priests, noblemen, and members of the high authority's family must meet to decide who will succeed and to formalize – often with great ritual – the installation of a new head administrator. Succession to high office is seldom a smooth operation. This is especially clear in the highly competitive universe of Mixtec factionalism portrayed in the codices, a universe where problems in the transition of authority are resolved by war.

Where the royal family is concerned, the transference of property also entails the position of head of state. The power factor involved stimulates the ambitions of not only junior members of the royal family, but also higher-ranking officials of the whole elite class (generals, priests, lesser noblemen who try to begin new dynasties). Few will bypass the opportunity to elevate their positions. However, the pressure from persons of lower rank to elevate themselves in the administrative hierarchy runs against the current of downward mobility idealized in the primogeniture system of the sacred royal line. Thus, ambition for status can lead individuals to try to alter the system by intrigue or by force. Such persons put themselves before the preservation of the governmental administration, and they become dangerous to the framework of society. An evolving social system with defined ranking only has to experience once the turmoil brought about by the failure of a high authority to produce a viable heir before it learns that controls over succession practices must be maintained.

Jack Goody (1966: 10–12) has defined two types of authority that can act to smooth the transition of power during an interregnum: stand-ins and stake-holders. Summarizing material from African kingdoms, he described the nature of these positions in five societies. The stand-in serves as a temporary high authority and usually the position is filled by a person who, by order of birth or distance from the royal line, is excluded from making permanent claim to the high position. Stake-holders, on the other hand, are persons who take charge of the emblems of authority, the royal regalia, during the interregnum. These emblems are the material means by which the high authority publicly demonstrates his position. The emblems themselves become charged with the authoritative power of tradition as they are passed from one generation to the next.

Like the stand-ins, stake-holders are also excluded from permanent control through their distance from the royal line. For instance, among the Bemba (Goody 1966: 11), a group of priest-counselor takes over, while among the Ashanti it is a more generalized group of lower administrative officials. R. S. Rattray (1929: 83–8) outlines the process of succession among the Ashanti chiefs.

The real hereditary power of chiefs is attributed to stools. Upon the death of a chief, the ancestral stools (literally the seats of authority of former chiefs) are taken by the *wirempefo*, the body of lower officials, together with the white stool belonging to the dead chief, which is blackened, to become an ancestral stool. The blackened stools, normally kept in the royal household, are both the focus of the ruling family's ancestor cult and the principal objects used in the accession ceremony. The *wirempefo*, however, maintain the stools until the proper time after the dead chief has been interred and the heir has been ceremoniously recognized...

The enstoolment ceremony proper, which in many cases only a select few ever witness, consists in the new chief being led forward to where the most important of the blackened stools of his dead ancestors is placed. This stool...is the shrine in which a departed spirit rests. Upon it the new chief is placed for a second, and lifted up; and the process is repeated three times. Then and not until then has he been "enstooled." From now onwards he is invested with all the sanctity and the power of the dead until such time as he dies or is destooled, i.e., made to sever by force the spiritual connection.

(Rattray 1929: 84)

Ashanti religious ideology attributes a sacred ancestral power to the stool. Therefore, one who possesses the stool also possesses the power of the ancestors: the prerogative of rulership. However, only within the possession of a person of royal blood can the power of the stool be activated, and blood is defined through kinship. Consequently, one means by which the Ashanti ensure that the power of the high authority is transferred smoothly is by the symbolic and temporary seizure of the emblems of power by non-royal persons.

Sacred Bundles and the *Ñuhu* Cult

"Power" objects imbued with the sanctity of royal authority through ancestral descent, much like the Ashanti stools, were manifested in Mixtec society through sacred bundles (Byland and Pohl 1994; Furst 1986: 62). Bundle cults have been found at the core of American Indian religious practices and social organization from Alaska to the Amazon. Nowhere has their traditional form and use been described in more detail than in the religious practices of many Great Plains United States–Canadian tribes, particularly the Blackfeet and Pawnee (see Wissler 1912, 1920).

The Blackfeet of Southern Alberta and Montana are distinguished by their veneration of sacred bundles in connection with virtually all religious practices (McClintock 1935; Reeves 1993). The opening of bundles and the handling of the objects within them are the most holy of acts accompanied by elaborate rituals, prayers, singing, dancing, and recitations of tribal history. Bundles are associated with powerful dreams that were experienced by culture heroes during which mortals actually spoke with the most potent spirit powers (Bullchild 1985). The spirit powers then gave the bundles to man along with the proper songs for invoking their magic (figures 17.1 and 17.2).

The possession of sacred bundles is tied to political organization through membership in "societies," resulting in the creation of one of the most complex social systems to have evolved on the western plains (Reeves 1993). It is notable that members of warrior societies (see McClintock 1938) are traditionally prohibited from possessing the most powerful bundles. The Beaver bundle, for example, is synonymous with concepts of tribal unity, and restrictions in possession point to checks in the authority of the militant components of tribal organization. The possessor of the Beaver bundle, on the other hand, could be a tribal judge (McClintock 1935: 6).

B. O. K. Reeves (1993) has proposed that the songs and prayers performed with bundle-opening rituals invoke cycles of legends that are associated with place-naming in the Piegan landscape. These locations are archaeologically significant (the "Head's Smashed In" Bison Jump is a prime example) and had been critical to seasonal migration and environmental exploitation patterns in hunting and gathering (Reeves 1978). To the Blackfeet, sacred bundles are not simply holy objects in and of themselves,

Figure 17.1 A Piegan culture hero descends from heaven on a rope with the Ancient Pipe Bundle (redrawn after a hide painting by Percy Bullchild, 1985: 286). Blackfeet sacred bundles are not only a primary focus of religious veneration, they serve as symbolic objects to be manipulated in the course of critical information exchanges in the society. Tribal members gain prestige through possession of bundles and each bundle entails different kinds of social obligations. The possessor may also be entrusted with memorizing hundreds of songs and stories containing cognitive maps prerequisite to environmental exploitation.

Figure 17.2 (a) The Blackfeet Sacred Beaver Bundle (McClintock 1935: 14); (b) the Pawnee Evening Star Bundle with fire-making implements (Chamberlain 1982); (c) the Pawnee Skull Bundle surmounted by skull of first Pawnee man (Chamberlain 1982).

but serve as ritual symbols for critical forms of information exchange and the definition of tribal cohesion.

Werner Stenzel (1972: 351) has likewise outlined fundamental elements of bundle worship in ancient Mesoamerica. The bundles were and still are holy objects wrapped in layers of cloth. They are viewed as containing supernatural "power" or "energy," often likened to wind (Mendelson 1958: 123). The opening and closing of bundles constitute important social rituals which provide access to "power." At such times

invocations are made to the bundles, usually as prayers for social welfare, weather control, and war.

Bundles are commonly associated with the creation of the world and the migrations of the group. There is often a connection between the bundles and some form of kinship group hierarchy which includes a supreme sacred bundle which is viewed as the chief focus of social unity. Finally, chieftaincy or kingship is based on and/or traced back to the possession, preservation, or taking care of sacred bundles.

Sacred bundles are found with uncommonly high frequency in the accounts of

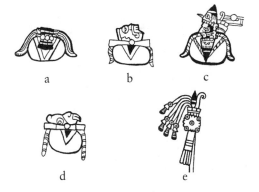

Figure 17.3 Sacred bundles in the Mixtec codices: (a) bundle wrapped in layers of white cloth and tied with a red and white triple-knot bow (Zouche-Nuttall 69); (b) bundle surmounted by an effigy head of *dzahui*, the rain deity as in figure 17.5 (Selden 3); (c) bundle surmounted by flint effigy of the culture hero, 9 Wind (Zouche-Nuttall 15); (d) bundle surmounted by effigy head of the *ñuhu* or earth spirit-force (Selden 3); the "venus" staff that often accompanies the sacred bundle.

divine origin in Codex Zouche-Nuttall obverse and in the 8 Deer story, in both Zouche-Nuttall reverse and Colombino-Becker (figure 17.3). In the Zouche-Nuttall reverse it appears five times. It is present at the beginning of the account on page 42, and displays the head of the culture hero 9 Wind as a qualifier. On page 52 it appears before Lord 4 Jaguar from whom 8 Deer receives a nose ornament making him a lineage head. On page 68 it is shown being borne by one of three priests for 8 Deer and his half-brother, Lord 12 Movement, on a peregrination. This act culminates in a sacrifice performed before a fourth appearance of the bundle by another priest, 8 Deer's brother, Priest 9 Flower. Finally, on page 83, it is present at the sacrifice of 8 Deer's two half-nephews, Lords 10 Dog and 6 House.

In the Colombino-Becker, the sacred bundle appears more frequently, including cognates to the scenes in Codex Zouche-Nuttall just discussed. It is carried on 8 Deer's behalf to Tututepec (6II, 5II, and 5I), where the conqueror and his brother,

Lord 12 Movement, appear. Smith (1973a: 67–8) proposes that 8 Deer became ruler of that kingdom. Later on (Colombino 14III), the bundle is carried by a personage during 8 Deer's peregrination to see 4 Jaguar and to receive the nose ornament. The group travels through several successive places, each of which has its own sacred bundle (Colombino 14III-II).

A significant detail of the bundles portrayed in Colombino-Becker is that they are surmounted by the head of a deity unique to Mixtec codices, very rarely, if ever, appearing in the art of other Mesoamerican traditions (figure 17.3d). Although badly damaged, the first and third place signs on Colombino 14III and 14II show that the head is colored red with a large round eye, two sets of knobby "horns," and the remnants of fanged teeth. This figure makes its most frequent appearances in the Codex Vindobonensis Obverse. Here it is found over twenty-five times in highly ritualistic contexts. On page 27 it appears as a limbless dwarf with an ear of corn growing from its head. Just to the lower left is the same figure directing the falling rain (figure 17.4).

The creature seems to be some sort of supernatural, not only because of its unusual form, but because of its highly symbolic usage. It may serve as a personal name, a place sign qualifier, and a bundle qualifier. Smith (1973b: 65–71) has identified Spanish glosses in the Codices Muro and Egerton associated with personages bearing name glyphs that include the dwarf-like figure.

Figure 17.4 The *ñuhu* figure in Vindobonensis 22 and 27.

From her work we know that the figure is called a *ñuhu (ñoho)* a term possessing some very significant linguistic associations that are borne out iconographically. According to the Arana and Swadesh (1965: 110–11) dictionary, *ñuhu* means:

- God
- Spirit
- Land, Earth
- Sun

It would appear, therefore, that the *ñuhu* figure represents a primary spirit force in Mixtec religious ideology. In place sign qualifiers and personal names, the *ñuhu* is sometimes shown emerging from the earth or a jewel, displaying the same pose and gesture peculiar only to the first ancestors who emerge from the earth or trees. The god steps out of a crevice, usually with its arms upraised, with its hands outstretched or pointing (for instance, compare Selden 13IV, 14II, 14IV, and Becker I: 9II with Zouche-Nuttall: 9A or Selden 2I). The *ñuhu* head qualifies the contents of the sacred bundles in many Codex Selden accession scenes. Page 14III–IV is typical in showing a lord burning incense to such a bundle before becoming a ruler of Jaltepec and marrying. The word for temple in the Alvarado dictionary is *huahi ñuhu* or "*ñuhu* temple," and the ruins of the Postclassic temple at Jaltepec are still called *vehe ñuhu*, or "*ñuhu* house" (Byland and Pohl: 1994).

Depiction of the head of the *ñuhu* spirit or an ancestral deity surmounting the sacred bundle may refer to the bundle's contents. Codex Selden 3I–II shows the preparation of twenty bundles for the first lord of Jaltepec by two aged priests. The first bundle is surmounted by the head of the lord's mother who appeared in a previous scene. The 1544–6 Inquisitions of Yanhuitlan likewise describe twenty sacred bundles which contained idols. One was called *zaguii (dzahui)*, after the name for the Mixtec rain god. Among the greenstone images (called penates) found so commonly in the Mixteca, several portray the rain deity *dzahui* and were doubtless included in sacred bundles

Figure 17.5   Greenstone effigy mask of *dzahui* in the collection of the Metropolitan Museum of Art.

(figure 17.5). John Monaghan (1987) found that *dzahui* is perceived as the chief of the *ñuhu* in the Mixtec community of Nuuyoo. The Mixtec refer to themselves as the *ñuu dzahui* or "People of *dzahui*."

The principal idol of Yanhuitlan was called the "idolo del pueblo" (Jiménez-Moreno and Mateos Higuera 1940: 40). Burgoa (1934: vol. 1, 332) describes an idol at Achiutla that was similarly referred to as the "corazon del pueblo." It was about the size of a pepper and made of green stone. A fascinating wooden image of a *ñuhu* is also found in the Vienna Museum of Natural History. Because of its diminutive size and form, it was probably contained in a sacred bundle as well (Nowotny 1949; Pohl n.d.). It is distinguished by the large round eyes, fanged teeth, and horns. What is so curious is that the Vienna *ñuhu* is giving birth to a tiny king who emerges between its legs, even though the figure also possesses male genitalia (figure 17.6).

From both the pictorial and linguistic evidence, we begin to form a picture of Mixtec religion that focuses not only on ancestor worship but on a more generalized spirit force as well. The two may even be synonymous. Caso found that the term for a dead king, *ñu*, is a conjunction for *ñuhu*, the spirit force (Caso 1962: 126). Indeed, the modern

Figure 17.7   Stone *ñuhu* heads from Yucunama,
Mixteca Alta.

Figure 17.6   Wooden *ñuhu* effigy in the collection
of the Museum für Völkerkunde, Vienna.

Mixtec still maintain a strong link with the
ñuhu. According to Robert Ravicz and Kimball Romney (1969: 373, 394), the earth is
seen as a living dynamic force that has
become an integral part of the Mixtec personality. Springs, streams, and swamps, for
instance, are especially invested with the
power of a spirit who dwells there or is
simply imbued with some kind of supernatural energy.

More recent research has found that many
of these spirits are in fact seen as *ñuhus*
(Monaghan 1987). They appear to be a
Mixtec variation of the *dueño*, or "earth
lord" concept that is so widespread in

Mesoamerica today (see Jansen 1982: 295–
311). The modern people of Apoala address
as *ñuhus* huge stone fragments that have
fallen from the valley walls (Jansen 1976,
1980, 1982), and the people of Tilantongo
refer to *dueños* or spirits in the valley that
are called *ñutilus* (*ñuhu tilu*). Figure 17.7
shows four stone heads from San Pedro
Yucunama near Texupan. They are typical
of carvings found throughout the Mixteca
today, and although the Yucunama people
could not identify them for this author,
Kathryn Josserand (personal communication) has seen them in Peñoles where they
are addressed as *ñuhus*. Even in stone relief
they bear the large round eyes and fanged
teeth of this being.

The *ñuhu* deity concept was and still is at
the center of a traditional form of Mixtec
spiritualism. It is noteworthy that the power
embodied in the god is represented in the
bundle that was the most important object
of veneration for Mixtec lords. It will
become clearer below, however, that there
were different kinds of bundles, some of
which represented specific founder lords
such as the culture hero, 9 Wind.

Perhaps the reason for venerating the
ñuhu can be seen in a myth recorded by
Antonio de los Reyes (1976: I–II). The

lords who were born from trees in Apoala and who divided the land and established the first kingdoms were not the original inhabitants. These kings had to subdue an indigenous group of Mixtec who were called the *tay ñuhu* because they were said to have come from the center of the earth (*tay* – people, *ñuhu* – earth) (see Smith 1973b).

The Bundle Priests

Codex Vindobonensis 14–15 depicts a scene in which four individuals present objects before Lady 9 Grass. We know that Lady 9 Grass was a highly venerated authority in Mixtec political affairs. She is commonly involved with lords and ladies exhibiting ambition or displacement during turmoil in the codices. She was also one of the first ancestors and presided over a religious cult important to the royalty of Tilantongo and Jaltepec (Byland and Pohl: 1994).

The roles of the four other individuals are not so clear, and we may only describe them by their most distinctive costume attributes (figure 17.8). They are all wearing black face and body paint, their hair is twisted, and two of them wear skeletal jaws. These personages also appear on page 36 of Vindobonensis where all four wear the death mask. Herrera (1945: 168–9) said that the black body paint was distinctive of Mixtec priests, being the result of rubbing henbane into the skin and the continuous burning of pine pitch in their "monasteries." He goes on to say that their clothing was often white and daubed with black color from rubber

"gum," doubtless a reference to the black-and-white *xicollis* of priests in the codices.

Zouche-Nuttall 4 B–C shows a scene very similar to that just described. Again we see four priests with twisted hair, black body paint, and skeletal features; two are wearing black and white shirt-like "xicollis" (Anawalt 1981: 135). They present sacred objects to a lord wearing secular garments, here expressing personal and military prestige. The similarity between these scenes suggests a kind of institutionalized ritual, and in fact there are a number of similar events depicted throughout the pictorials, in which a body of priests, often four, interacts with the most powerful rulers. In many instances, the priests appear as caretakers of the sacred *ñuhu* bundles and emblems of authority for the lord. One title for a Mixtec religious leader was "*dzutu sandidzo ñuhu*" or "priest who carries the *ñuhu*" (Alvarado 1962: 185b).

A behavioral analysis of the pictorial representations of priests in the codices reveals specific activity patterns both in relation to the veneration of sacred bundles and to periods of succession to paramount authority. Codex Zouche-Nuttall obverse features events in the lives of two priests, 5 Flower and 12 Wind, who establish the first religious institutions by bringing the sacred bundles and regalia to several different kingdoms located in the Tilantongo Valley. Lord 5 Crocodile, the father of 8 Deer, lived shortly after 12 Wind, becoming head of a council of four priests at Tilantongo (Byland and Pohl 1994). His story is described

Figure 17.8 Four priests venerate the oracle 9 Grass (Vindobonensis 14–15).

within the context of the collapse of Tilantongo's first dynasty, after the death of a
royal heir and the eventual usurpation of
the realm by 8 Deer.

Case Studies

5 Flower

Page 15A of the Codex Zouche-Nuttall
shows three priests bearing a sacred bundle,
an heraldic "venus" staff, and other
emblems associated with royal authority.
They accompany Lady 3 Flint, wife of the
chief priest, 5 Flower. Two of the priests are
recognizable by the wearing of black-and-
white xicollis and black facial/body paint.
Apparently Priest 5 Flower and Lady 3
Flint had miraculously emerged from a
cave at a Cliff of Heaven on page 14. From
there they arrived at the large temple with a
conical roof encircled by a plumed serpent
on page 15B. A sacred bundle sits inside the
temple. Upon the bundle is placed the head
of the culture hero 9 Wind. The red-and-
white frieze which qualifies the temple platform is part of the name for Hill or Place of
Flints (Zouche-Nuttall 21A; Bodley 14III),
a site located in the southern Tilantongo Valley (Pohl and Byland 1990; Byland and Pohl
1994).

Priest 5 Flower appears a second time on
Zouche-Nuttall 15. He is now dressed in a
black-and-white xicolli and black body
paint in the same way as those who had
accompanied him earlier. He sheds blood
from his ear with a bone awl, as a sacrificial
offering before the sacred bundle of 9 Wind
(figure 17.9). 5 Flower appears three more
times in the codex on pages 16 and 17; twice
he is dressed with the attributes of a priest.
In the last instance he sits inside a palace in
the act of marrying Lady 3 Flint.

The interpretation of these scenes has
been a source of considerable debate in Mixtec codical studies (Nuttall 1902; Dennis
1990). The problem surrounds confusion
over the identity of not one, but two Lady
3 Flints (mother and daughter?) who are the
principal subjects of the narrative. Regardless of the confusion, it is clear that page 14

Figure 17.9 Priest 5 Flower sheds blood from
his ears (Zouche-Nuttall 15).

depicts a Cliff of Heaven within the context
of other significant geographical locations.
Two elders and two priests accompany 5
Flower and Lady 3 Flint to establish the
cult of 9 Wind Ehecatl-Quetzalcoatl at a
location in the Tilantongo Valley. 5 Flower's
first act as a priest is to make an offering of
blood from his ear at the institution of the
temple and its cult.

The *Relación de Tilantongo* says that the
offering of blood from the ears was a characteristic ritual for the veneration of idols by
the priesthood (Acuña 1984: 233). Herrera
(1945: 169) said that after a certain period
of years in religious service, a priest was
admitted to the king's council and permitted
to marry. Unlike most of the accounts of
marriage in the codices, no children are
given as the offsprings of the Priest 5 Flower
and Lady 3 Flint indicating that the marriage was deemed more important to the
institution of the cult than to dynastic reckoning.

12 Wind

Following the account of Priest 5 Flower,
Zouche-Nuttall 19 shows the descent of
four new priests from "Heaven" by means
of a rope ladder (figure 17.10). The leader,

12 Wind—

Figure 17.10   Priest 12 Wind descends from Place of Heaven on a rope ladder carrying a temple on his back. Three cohorts bear other sacred objects, including the sacred bundle (Zouche-Nuttall 19).

carrying a temple on his back, is named 12 Wind "Smoke Eye." Before him sits a sacred bundle. What is curious about this scene is its similarity to three other pages in the codex (19, 21, 22), in which Priest 12 Wind and his assistants are engaged in similar events. In each case, the sacred bundle, the "venus" staff, the temple, and other royal regalia are born by Priests 12 Wind, 3 Flint or an aide, but after the descent from Place of Heaven they arrive at four different kingdoms.

On page 18, 12 Wind appears a second time, burning copal in a sahumador before a temple at Red and White Bundle. The place sign has been correlated with a site lying a few kilometers to the east of Tilantongo (Pohl and Byland 1990; Byland and Pohl 1994). Again, the temple is encircled by a plumed serpent and contains a sacred bundle like that venerated by Priest 5 Flower.

On page 19 of Zouche-Nuttall, 12 Wind is seated before two gods, who present him with the temple and fire-making instruments which so often accompany the sacred bundle. After the presentation, 12 Wind again descends on the rope ladder from Place of Heaven. He is dressed in a black-and-white xicolli and black face/body paint as are his three assistants. They arrive at a large, composite place sign. In the upper right-hand corner is a temple in which sit a "venus" staff and a sacred bundle surmounted by a flint and the fire-making instruments given to 12 Wind in the previous scene. The temple is located at the site of *Yucu Yoco* or Hill of the Wasp, a prominent late Classic site located on a mountain above Tilantongo (Pohl and Byland 1990; Byland and Pohl 1994).

In the lower left-hand corner is another place sign for Hill of Flints. Here sits the bundle of the culture hero 9 Wind that was brought to that place by Priest 5 Flower. The significance of page 19 is not only the magnificent portrayal of the descent from heaven but the pageantry of 12 Wind's marriage to Lady 3 Flint, a daughter(?) of Lady 3 Flint who married priest 5 Flower. On page 20 the marriage scene is repeated, but no children are listed. On page 21, 12 Wind and his chief assistant, 3 Flint, descend from heaven to Hill of the Sun (the Classic occupation site of Achiutla), where they are met by Lady 1 Death and Lord 4 Crocodile, the first progenitors of the royal house of Tilantongo in Bodley 1–2V. Finally, on page 22 Priests 12 Wind, 3 Flint, and 5 Dog appear at a compound place sign representing Tilantongo itself. They are led by the culture hero 9 Wind himself in this instance, who stands with the sacred bundle in the Temple of Heaven, a prominent shrine in Tilantongo (Pohl and Byland 1990).

To summarize briefly, 12 Wind, like 5 Flower, emerges from Place of Heaven. The action emulates the scene in Codex Vindobonensis in which 9 Wind himself is given the sacred bundle and emblems of royal authority, after which he descends on a rope ladder. The results of 12 Wind's activities, much like those of 5 Flower, are the institutionalization of the cult of the culture hero 9 Wind at various communities in the southern end of the Nochixtlan Valley, including Tilantongo itself.

5 Crocodile

Codex Zouche-Nuttall 25 B–C shows three men in priestly costume meeting with a fourth, 5 Crocodile, the father of 8 Deer (figure 17.11). 5 Crocodile's ancestry is listed on the same page, beginning with his grandparents. According to Bodley 6I, his father was a lord of Mouth of the River or Place of the River, a place sign for Ayuta/Atoyaquillo in the Achiutla Valley. Caso (1960: 32) proposed that his mother, Lady 1 Vulture, was a niece of Lord 12 Lizard, king of Tilantongo. Caso originally believed that 5 Crocodile started a new Tilantongo dynasty after the mysterious death of his cousin, 2 Rain Ocoñaña, a legitimate heir to the throne (Caso 1960: 32). Nevertheless, the meeting between the four priests is unusual because it seems to show an event involving strictly religious authorities rather than "rulers." Because of Emily Rabin's revised chronology, we now know that this event took place at Tilantongo at a time when either Lord 12 Lizard Arrow Legs was king, or his son Lord 5 Movement. Other than the significance of there being four priests involved, we do not know why they are meeting and making offerings.

The *Relación de Tilantongo* on the other hand, gives us a clue in the description of four priests who acted as the administrative council for the king of Tilantongo:

A los quinze capítulos dixeron que señor natural tenía quatro regidores los quales le governan todo el Reyno y ante ellos pasaban todos sus pleytos, y despúes para determinallos yban a su señor a darle cuenta dellos. Y el más sabio de éstos here presidente y los demás heran sus quavjutores. Y éstos determinaban las cosas de sus sacrificios y de quándo alguno se abía de bender. Y los demás negocios que entre ellos pasaban. Y el sacerdote y patriarca dellos here al que determinabe las cosas de las guerras, y cosas que se abían de hazer, y estos quarto regidores andaban besttidos con unas capas largas de mantas de algodon pintadas a manera de capas de licenciados. Y el sacerdote se bestía el día del sacrificio de muncha plumería y mantas muy galanas y pintadas, y en la cabeça se ponía una mitra, a manera de Obisbo; y quando faltabe presidente elegían al sacerdote que en aquel tienpo here, y el sacerdote no abía de dormir de noche ni beber bino ni illegar muger. Y para hazelle que se desytiese del sacerdocio y no pudiese husar dél, le hazian beber bino y casar.
(Paso y Troncoso 1905: 74; Acuña 1984: 233)

They say that the natural lord [i.e., king] had four officials that governed the whole kingdom, and before them passed all disputes. Later to determine their outcome the officials went before the king to give an account of the disputes. The wisest [of the four officials] was the president and the others were his associates. And these officials determined the details of sacrifices, and the times when one had to sell, and the rest of the business that passed before them. And the priest and patriarch among them was the one who determined the details of wars, and of things that had to be done. And these four officials went about dressed in long cotton capes painted in the

Figure 17.11   Priest 5 Crocodile meets with other members of the sacred council of four at Tilantongo (Zouche-Nuttall 25).

manner of scholars' robes. And on the day of the sacrifice the priest dressed with many feathers and elegant painted robes, and he put on a headdress like a bishop's mitre. When the president was absent they selected another priest, and this priest was not allowed to sleep at night nor drink wine nor have a woman. And when the priest was finished and there was no more use for him, they made him drink wine and marry.

It seems therefore that the three priests meeting with 5 Crocodile are involved with his institution as head of the holy council of four, and not as king of Tilantongo. This hypothesis is confirmed by Jansen's (1982: 378–9) observation that the event follows a series of "awards" in the form of various xicollis given to 5 Crocodile every four years. Herrera (1945: 169), in fact, said that priests were promoted for their service to more prestigious "cargos" every four years by the king.

Following the meeting with the three priests, 5 Crocodile next appears before the Temple of Heaven at Tilantongo, shedding blood from his ear onto a sacred bundle. This is the same act associated with the Priest 5 Flower on Zouche-Nuttall 15 discussed above. A cognate scene appears in Codex Bodley, this time, however, 5 Crocodile burns incense in a sahumador before the bundle, as his counterpart 12 Wind had done in Zouche-Nuttall 18.

Clearly, the bloodletting by 5 Crocodile onto a sacred bundle does not refer to an accession event but rather to a symbolic act associated with the head of the council of four priests at Tilantongo. The reverse of the Codex Vindobonensis 5–6 shows the same presentation scene as Zouche-Nuttall 25. It is notable that here 5 Crocodile is given an additional name or title. It is composed of a small red man with a skeletal head bearing a ñuhu spirit with the blood-letter stuck into it. As we have seen, a common appearance of the ñuhu is on sacred bundles, and it relates the bundle to the first ancestors and the primary Mixtec spirit force. The symbolic configuration matches the term for priest, as "the bearer of the ñuhu" listed in the Alvarado dictionary.

At the time that 5 Crocodile is head of the sacred council at Tilantongo, a series of events unfolds that ultimately leads to the collapse of the ruling dynasty when Tilantongo's king, 2 Rain Ocoñaña, mysteriously dies on Bodley 51. 2 Rain was the son of 5 Movement, a lord of both Red-and-White Bundle and Tilantongo according to Codex Bodley 6II and the Mapa de Teozacoalco. Apparently, 5 Movement's marriage to a Jaltepec woman, and his relationship with Red-and-White Bundle stood in direct conflict to another arrangement that developed between the Jaltepec Lady 6 Monkey and the Red-and-White Bundle Lord 11 Wind. A war broke out in which 5 Movement's son, 2 Rain Ocoñaña, is represented by a champion defeated in a war at Jaltepec. A few years after this setback, 2 Rain himself dies. Given that the place sign with which 2 Rain is associated in Zouche-Nuttall 24 is not Tilantongo, it may be that he was residing with his parents elsewhere, and that 5 Crocodile is operating as both high priest and regent or stake-holder at Tilantongo.

Figure 17.12 illustrates specific forms of behavior enacted not only by Priests 5 Flower, 12 Wind, and 5 Crocodile, but by the culture hero 9 Wind Ehecatl-Quetzalcoatl and other priests who appear throughout the codices. Priests in the codices appear in black-and-white or gray-and-white garments. Often, their shirt-like xicollis are decorated with greca motifs or white flowers. Priests also wear black facial and body paint. Many wear a skeletal jaw or mask. These forms of symbolic imagery doubtless supported their roles as holy men specifically involved with the worship of the dead and the maintenance of the ancestor cult.

Just as their costume is characteristic of their rank and position, so is their behavior. Priests appear in foundation myths in which they transport the sacred bundles and regalia of rulership from a Place of Heaven to several different kingdoms. They are the personages most closely associated with the ñuhu bundles, before which they are seen either burning incense or making auto-sacrifices. There is virtually no case in the codices in which the "king" himself physically

The council works in groups of four

They perform auto-sacrifice before sacred bundles

They burn incense before sacred bundles

dzutu sandidzo ñuhu: "priests who carry the ñuhu"

Figure 17.12 Behavioral characteristics of the council of priests.

handles a sacred bundle. The Codex Selden scenes in which many of the rulers of Jaltepec appear before the Temple of the *ñuhu* at Jaltepec and burn incense before a sacred bundle conform with Herrera's (1945) state-ment that before acceding to the throne, some Mixtec kings were required to spend a year serving as a priest.

It is clear that more than one bureaucratic organization, the paramountcy of kingship, is being portrayed in the codices. The four priests discussed here specifically conform to descriptions in the *Relación de Tilantongo* and elsewhere of a body of judges who administered the realm for the king. The head of this council was also the war leader.

Further evidence for the political roles of priests as pictorialized in the codices is found in the accounts of the 1544–6 Inquisition of Yanhuitlan. When the Dominicans brought the "gobernadores" (governors) Don Domingo, Don Francisco, and Don Juan to trial, numerous witnesses testified as to the kinds of behavior in which the defendants were involved. While Don Domingo was acting as regent/cacique, Don Francisco supervised four priests who took care of twenty sacred bundles containing idols for Don Domingo. The four priests, clearly equivalents to the "regidores" described for Tilantongo, were accused of making blood offerings to idols and burning copal just as did the holy men in the codices. According to one of these native priests, also named Domingo, the idols were later seized by the encomendero Francisco de las Casas when Don Francisco was arrested. This event suggests that the accusations of idolatry were in some way connected to a power play on the part of de las Casas (Spores 1967: 230–31; Greenleaf 1969).

The role of Don Domingo bears resemblance to the behavior of his distant ancestor Priest 5 Crocodile as well. As brother to Doña Maria de Coquahu, Don Domingo was not in line to become cacique of Yanhuitlan (Spores 1967: 135). Consequently, he had been educated as a native priest, like Don Francisco and Don Juan. When the rightful heir to Yanhuitlan (Doña Maria's son, Gabriel) was deemed too young to inherit on his mother's death, Don Domingo served as a stake-holder in Yanhuitlan, perhaps in much the same way as 5 Crocodile had at Tilantongo.

To summarize, this discussion of the role of kinship as a means of defining a social hierarchy focused on the traditional selection of an heir by rules of birthright in order to preserve the sanctity of the royal line. I emphasized primogeniture because it

was the "preferred" system by the Mixtec. However, even a political system founded on phenomena so basic as marriage and the production of offspring can become upset if a viable heir is not produced. A perfect example is the tragic fate of Lord 2 Rain Ocoñaña of Tilantongo. For this reason, good administrations maintain alternative systems of ensuring that the economic and social fabric are preserved, despite problems in the transference of royal authority. The question is where to place that administrative safeguard within the hierarchy.

In his discussion of the mechanisms of succession, Jack Goody emphasized the need for stake-holders during an interregnum. From comparisons of several traditional societies, he proposed that such officials are most effectively recruited from among the priesthood, for they are the caretakers of the emblems of sacred authority so important to both popular religion and kingship. They are ideally suited because they may be members of the royal line with a vested interest in the maintenance of social order yet, because of their membership in junior descent groups, lack strong claims to the paramount position themselves.

Mixtec priests, both in powers described in Colonial sources and in their activities portrayed in codices, precisely fit the roles of stake-holders in a system of governmental checks and balances. They were members of the upper class often shown with little or no genealogical background in the codices, in striking contrast to the extensive inheritance lists given for kings. We may perceive analogues for such authority in the management of bundles by medicine men in Blackfeet social organization for example. Pronounced similarities in theology are sufficient to suggest a common origin for Blackfoot and Mixtec bundle cults. This could either be traced back to the Archaic roots of native religion or to an emulation (though probably not direct) of certain forms of ritualism by either the Blackfeet or the Mixtec at a later time.

Admittedly, both cultures have experienced significant changes in social organization concomitant with various environmental adaptations. Nevertheless, by functional comparison alone, we may glimpse something of the processes that may have led to the development of Mixtec religion and aristocratic history. For example, obvious differences in the contents of the bundles are indicative of the concerns of the people who used them. The Blackfeet beaver bundle, a symbol of tribal unity, contained the pelts of animals that represented not only the principal spirit powers but game animals exploited by tribal hunters. Mixtec bundles on the other hand were imbued with the spirit powers of rain, corn, and the earth, reflecting uniquely agrarian concerns.

Both cults are reflective of two differing exploitation strategies associated with the tribal organization of hunters and gatherers on one hand, and the chiefly organization of settled villages on the other. Marked differences appear in control over the bundles. Among the Blackfeet, the beaver bundle is given to a member of the tribe based upon the individual's predilection to the spiritualism with which a bundle is associated, regardless of clan affiliation. Possession of a Blackfeet beaver bundle is a means of physically displaying one's status as the possessor of critical elements of tribal history and legends, including songs that recount geographical locations critical to a seasonal hunting strategy (Reeves 1993).

By comparison, the Mixtec usage of the bundle not only as a symbol of community identity, but also as the focus of a royal ancestor cult, implies that, at some point, control over critical information had passed into the hands of a single kinship group. This could have happened by direct seizure during a formative period, when one clan came to dominate the society (militarily), or perhaps through some later form of religious specialization, when the ability to learn songs and perform acts associated with the bundle became the task of a single descent group (charismatically). The fact that the chief Mixtec bundle priest was a relative of the king, head of the war council, and a specialized religious practitioner by the Postclassic period points to a combination of all three factors.

At the tribal level, sacred bundles may symbolize social unity or define special roles through membership in "societies." The most sacred bundles, however, are not imbued with the power of an individual or even specific ancestors, but rather with more generalized culture heroes or spirits invoked from an overall tribal history or environmental animism. At some point, Mixtec social order symbolized in such beliefs became fused with the establishment of a paramount position no longer dependent upon election by tribal consent. Early Mixtec chiefs no doubt discovered that the most effective means of symbolically consolidating their authority was to infuse their personal ancestral history into that of the group (i.e. *ñuhu* as both deceased king and the spirit force of the environment).

This contributed to what Goldman described as a "Stratified" level of social organization in which the paramount and his ancestors are thereby deemed divine. The act is a form of seizure on the part of ambitious individuals who seek to fix the most authoritative positions within their family and to preserve this power through descent.

In order to stress the sanctity of a royal line the paramount would by necessity depend upon relatives who were the caretakers of sacred bundles in order to focus popular attention on the cult of the individual. This process is nowhere more evident than in the codices. It is not the kings themselves who descend from "Heaven" on rope ladders bringing the holy regalia of rulership, but rather the four priests led by such culture heroes as 5 Flower and 12 Wind. Likewise, Lord 8 Deer seeks the support of his brother 9 Flower as his chief priest and keeper of the sacred bundle in his bid to usurp the throne of Tilantongo.

REFERENCES

Acuña, René. 1984. Relación de Tilantongo. In *Relaciones Geográficas del Siglo XVI: Antequera*, edited by René Acuña, vol. 2, pp. 223–48. Universidad Nacional Autónoma de México, Mexico City.

Alvarado, Francisco de. 1962. *Vocabulario en Lengua Mixteco por Fray Francisco de Alvarado*. Reproducción facsimilar con un estudio de Wigberto Jiménez Moreno. Instituto Nacional Indigenista e Instituto Nacional de Antropología e Historia, Mexico City.

Anawalt, Patricia R. 1981. *Indian Clothing Before Cortes: Mesoamerican Costumes from the Codices*. University of Oklahoma Press, Norman.

Arana, Evangelina and Mauricio Swadish. 1965. *Los Elementos del Mixteco Antiguo*. Instituto Nacional Indigenista and Instituto Nacional de Antropología e Historia, Mexico City.

Bullchild, Percy. 1985. *The Sun Came Down: The History of the World as my Blackfeet Elders Told It*. Harper and Row, San Francisco.

Burgoa, Francisco de. 1934. *Geográfica descripción*, vols 25–6. Publicaciones del Archivo General de la Nación, Mexico City.

Byland, Bruce E. 1980. Political and Economic Evolution in the Tamazulapan Valley, Mixteca Alta, Oaxaca, Mexico: A Regional Approach. Ph.D. dissertation, Pennsylvania State University.

Byland, Bruce E. and John M. D. Pohl. 1994. *In the Realm of 8 Deer: The Archaeology of the Mixtec Codices*. University of Oklahoma Press, Norman.

Caso, Alfonso. 1960. *Interpretation of the Codex Bodley 2858*. Sociedad Mexicana de Antropología, Mexico City.

—— 1962. Vocabulario Sacado del Arte en Lengua Mixteca de Fray Antonio de los Reyes. In *Vocabulario en Lengua Mixteco por Fray Francisco de Alvarado*. Reproducción facsimilar con un estudio de Wigberto Jiménez Moreno. Instituto Nacional Indigenista e Instituto Nacional de Antropología e Historia, Mexico City.

Chamberlain, Von del. 1982. *When Stars Came Down to Earth. Cosmology of the Skidi Pawnee Indians of North America*. Ballena Press Anthropological Papers No. 26, Los Altos.

Dennis, Bryan J. 1990. Establishing the Mixtec Dynasties of the Tilantongo Valley: An Interpretation of Codex Zouche-Nuttall Pages 14–22. Unpublished master's thesis, University of California, Los Angeles.

Flannery, Kent and Joyce Marcus. 1983. The Origins of the State in Oaxaca. In *The Cloud People: Divergent Evolution of the Zapotec and Mixtec Civilizations*, edited by K. Flannery and J. Marcus, pp. 79–83. Academic Press, New York.

Furst, Jill Leslie. 1986. The Lords of "Place of the Ascending Serpent:" Dynastic Succession on the Nuttall Obverse. In *Symbol and Meaning Beyond the Closed Community: Essays in Mesoamerican Idea*, edited by Gary H. Gossen, pp. 57–68. Studies on Culture and Society, vol. 1, Institute for Mesoamerican Studies, State University of New York.

Goldman, Irving. 1970. *Ancient Polynesian Society*. University of Chicago Press, Chicago.

Goody, Jack. 1966. *Succession to High Office*. Cambridge Papers in Social Anthropology No. 4. Cambridge University Press, Cambridge.

Greenleaf, Richard E. 1969. *The Mexican Inquisition of the Sixteenth Century*. The University of New Mexico Press, Albuquerque.

Herrera, Antonio de. 1945. *Historia general de los hechos de los Castellanos, en las islas, y tierra-firma de el mar oceano*, vol. 4. Editorial Guariana, Buenos Aires.

Jansen, Maarten E. R. G. N. 1976. El lugar donde estaba el cielo. Master's thesis, University of Leiden, Holland.

—— 1980. *Tnuhu Niquidza iya: Temas principales de la historiografía Mixteca*. Ediciones del Gobierno Constitutional del Estado de Oaxaca. Dirección General de Social de Oaxaca, Oaxaca.

—— 1982. *Huisi Tacu, estudio interpretivo de un libro mixteco antiguo: Codex Vindobonensis Mexicanus I*. CEDLA, Incidentale Publicaties 24, vols 1 and 2, Amsterdam.

Jiménez Moreno, Wigberto and Salvador Mateos Higuera. 1940. *Códice de Yanhuitlán*. Museo Nacional del INAH, Mexico City.

Marcus, Joyce. 1983. The Conquest Slabs of Building J, Monte Alban. In *The Cloud People: Divergent Evolution of the Zapotec and Mixtec Civilizations*, edited by K. Flannery and J. Marcus, pp. 106–8. Academic Press, New York.

McClintock, Walter. 1935. *The Blackfoot Beaver Bundle*. Southwest Museum Leaflets Nos 2 and 3. Southwest Museum, Los Angeles.

—— 1938. *Blackfoot Warrior Societies*. Southwest Museum Leaflets No. 8. Southwest Museum, Los Angeles.

Mendelson, E. Michael. 1958. A Guatemalan Sacred Bundle. *Man* 58 (170): 121–6.

Monaghan, John. 1987. We Are People Who Eat Tortillas: Household and Community in the Mixteca. Ph.D. dissertation, Department of Anthropology, University of Pennsylvania, Philadelphia.

Nowotny, Karl Anton. 1949. A Unique Wooden Figure from Ancient Mexico. *American Antiquity* 15(1): 57–61.

Nuttall, Zelia. 1902. *Codex Nuttall: Facsimile of an Ancient Mexican Codex Belonging to Lord Zouche of Harryngworth*. Harvard University, Peabody Museum of American Archaeology and Ethnology, Cambridge.

Paso y Troncoso, Francisco del. 1905. *Papeles de Nueva España. Secundo Serie*. Volume II: *Relaciones geográficas de la diócesis de Oaxaca*. Est. Tipográfico, Madrid.

Pastor, Rodolfo. 1987. *Campesinos y reformas: La Mixteca 1700–1856*. Secretaría de Educación Pública, Mexico City.

Pohl, John M. D. n.d. Xipe Totec and Zapotec Lordship. Manuscript in author's possession.

Pohl, John M. D. and Bruce E. Byland. 1990. Mixtec Landscape Perception and Archaeological Settlement Patterns. *Ancient Mesoamerica* 1(1): 113–31.

Rattray, R. S. 1929. *Ashanti Law and Constitution*. Clarendon Press, Oxford.

Ravicz, Robert, and Kimball Romney. 1969. The Mixtec. In *Handbook of Middle American Indians* 7: 367–99.

Reeves, Brian O. K. 1978. Head-Smashed-In: 5500 Years of Bison Jumping in the Alberta Plains. *Plains Anthropologist Memoir* 14(23–82, part 2): 151–74.

——1993. Iniskim: A Sacred Nitsitapii Religious Tradition. In *Kunaitupii: Coming Together on Native Sacred Sites, their Sacredness, Conservation, and Interpretation*, edited by Brian O. K. Reeves and Margaret A. Kennedy, pp. 194–259. Archeological Society of Alberta, Calgary.

Reyes, Antonio de los. 1976. *Arte en Lengua Mixteca*. Vanderbilt University Publications in Anthropology No. 14, Nashville.

Sahlins, Marshall. 1958. *Social Stratification in Polynesia*. University of Washington Press, Seattle.

Smith, Mary E. 1973a. *Picture Writing from Ancient Southern Mexico: Mixtec Place Signs and Maps*. University of Oklahoma Press, Norman.

——1973b The Relationship Between Mixtec Manuscript Painting and the Mixtec Language: A Study of Some Personal Names in Codices Muro and Sanchez Solis. In *Dumbarton Oaks Conference on Mesoamerican Writing Systems*, edited by E. Benson, pp. 47–98. Dumbarton Oaks, Washington, DC.

Spores, Ronald. 1967. *The Mixtec Kings and their People*. University of Oklahoma Press, Norman.

——1972. *An Archaeological Settlement Survey of the Nochixtlan Valley, Oaxaca*. Vanderbilt University Publications in Anthropology No. 1, Nashville.

——1983 The Origin and Evolution of the Mixtec Systems of Social Stratification. In *The Cloud People: Divergent Evolution of the Zapotec and Mixtec Civilizations*, edited by K. Flannery and J. Marcus, pp. 227–38. Academic Press, New York.

——1984 *The Mixtecs in Ancient and Colonial Times*. University of Oklahoma Press, Norman.

Stenzel, Werner. 1972. The Sacred Bundles in Mesoamerican Religion. *Actas del XXXVIII Congreso Internacional de Americanistas* 2: 347–52. Stuttgart.

Wissler, Clark. 1912. Ceremonial Bundles of the Blackfeet Indians. *American Museum of Natural History Anthropological Papers* 7(2): 65–289.

——1920. The Sacred Bundles of the Pawnee. *Natural History* 20: 569–71.

PART IV

Religion and Ideology

Editors' Introduction

The Mesoamerican archaeological record contains abundant features and artifacts that represent ritual activity. The material remains of rituals are recovered from all kinds of archaeological contexts, from the smallest house structure to the grandest temple. Through studying the diverse expressions of religious belief in public and private settings, we can see how religious practice reflected social and political realities. It is also possible to reconstruct systems of beliefs and cosmology from an indigenous point of view by comparing ritual deposits to historic and modern accounts of ritual practice. The study of Mesoamerican religion is aided by the preservation of numerous Prehispanic indigenous texts such as Maya hieroglyphs which specifically refer to the use and meaning of religious architecture and paraphernalia.

The study of Mesoamerican ideology, like the study of economic, social, and political institutions, also provides a vast amount of information about regional and interregional patterns of cultural development and interaction. Local and long-distance elite interaction was often highly ritualized in Mesoamerica, and political meetings were accompanied by ceremonies and the use of interregionally understood ritual symbols and language. The possession of this knowledge and the accouterments of ceremony represented an important means by which high-status individuals were able to distinguish themselves from commoners in Mesoamerican societies, as Clark and Blake (chapter 12) discuss. Although evidence suggests that similar religious beliefs were held by commoners and elites, ritual was practiced on a larger and more elabor-ate scale in elite contexts, and in some Mesoamerican cultures elites possessed greater amounts of ritual materials such as ceramic censers, shell, mercury, and jade than did commoners. Mesoamerican religious practice was thus closely linked to the realms of political strategy and status differentiation. Certain religious institutions, such as ancestor veneration, were also tied to economic foundations of society as McAnany argues (chapter 23). She presents evidence which suggests that through symbolizing a "genealogy of place," the sacred interments of previous generations legitimized social groups' links to the land and orchards that were the basis for their wealth and sustenance.

Approaches to the Study of Mesoamerican Religion

The articles in this section illustrate various scales of religious practice in Mesoamerica from households to temples. Household perspectives include Masson's study of a small Postclassic Maya island community (chapter 21) and Brumfiel's consideration of Aztec state ideology at the domestic level (chapter 22). Early elite religious practices are described for the chiefly centers of a Middle Formative interregional interaction sphere (Reilly, chapter 18) and the center of San José Mogote (Marcus and Flannery, chapter 19). The religious and cosmological foundations of the emergence of Maya kingship at the Late Formative center of Cerros are analyzed by Freidel and Schele (chapter 20). Students should compare the strategies of elite legitimization reflected in each of the three articles which address royal rituals (chapters 18, 19, and 20). McAnany's (chapter 23) discussion of links between the doctrines of divine Classic kingship and the rituals of Formative agrarian households bridges the gap between social extremes and suggests that the former developed out of the latter.

These contributions crosscut various approaches to the study of religion in archaeology, anthropology, and other disciplines, including Marxian, functional, and cognitive frameworks for the analysis of ideological systems. Traditional Marxian perspectives approach religion as a force that serves elite class interests by shaping the consciousness of working-class supporting populations (Marx and Engels 1970). Marxian analyses of religion in archaeology are quite diverse and typically focus on the role of ideology in masking, legitimizing, and resisting institutionalized social inequalities (Miller et al. 1989; McGuire 1992: 140–2; see Brumfiel, chapter 22). Functionalists stress the integrative role of religious beliefs and behaviors which serve to maintain fundamental social institutions which comprise social systems (Durkheim 1965). Cognitive approaches explore aspects of religion which provide mental templates for interpreting life experiences within a particular society (Geertz 1966: 45–6; Sahlins 1981).

Research on Mesoamerican religious institutions has embraced all three of these approaches. The purpose of elite ideologies as strategies of domination has been analyzed for Aztec society (Brumfiel, chapter 22). Much public art and writing at monumental centers represents billboards of propaganda for political regimes (Pasztory 1988, 1997; Schele and Freidel 1990; Marcus 1992; Umberger 1996). Ethnographic studies in modern Mesoamerica reveal the integrative effects of religious practice which link poor and wealthy members (and those in between) of modern communities and regions (Vogt 1969; Freidel et al. 1993; Gossen and Leventhal 1993; Lewis 1951). These data support functionalist interpretations of the role of religion in modern Mesoamerican villages, and evidence suggests that

rituals were powerful integrative events for ancient communities as well. Links in ritual expression observed among settlements of different sizes located across contemporary Maya landscapes have recently been described as manifestations of "cults of the center and periphery" (Gossen and Leventhal 1993: 207).

Evon Vogt (1969: 572) was one of the first anthropologists to observe the fact that religious ceremony occurred at various scales throughout highland Maya communities surrounding the primary village of Zinacantan. More centrally located, politically significant communities generally put on a bigger show, but religious holidays were celebrated at settlements throughout the region in varying degrees of elaboration. Ethnography and archaeology in regions outside of Mesoamerica have documented the existence of many layers of ideological practice, and rituals that outwardly appear to be similar can have a range of meanings over space and time, or multiple levels of meaning may be perceived simultaneously by different participants (McGuire 1992: 141–2). Archaeological investigations suggest that fundamental elements of Mesoamerican religions endured for many centuries. Certain beliefs that have their origins in antiquity have remained useful to agriculturalist societies such as the Maya (Schele and Freidel 1990: 401; Freidel et al. 1993: 39–44). Indeed, McAnany (chapter 23) notes that the state religions of the Classic-period Maya drew on their pre-state, agrarian origins. This argument suggests that Maya kings couched themselves in agrarian metaphors precisely because these symbols represented an established association of ties to the land through the sanction of inheritance that was accepted by society and practiced across many social scales.

The observation that continuities in religious belief and ritual practice can last for many centuries in a given society does not imply that regional religions or other cultural institutions were static and unchanging through time (Sahlins 1981). One important aspect of Mesoamerican belief systems was a reverence for the past (Dahlin

1976: 256–63; Schele and Freidel 1990: 84, 203–4; McAnany, chapter 23). Meso-american religions were heavily concerned with conventions, objects, and personages of earlier times, which were frequently referred to in later revitalistic political ideologies. This reinvention of regional history is one strategy which encouraged the long-term survival of ancient traditions, however newly interpreted by later generations. Crucial here is the cyclical view of time held by the Maya as expressed in the Maya chronicles (Barrera Vasquez and Morley 1949; Bricker 1981; Jones 1989). The manipulation of history in revitalization and revival movements was not unique to Mesoamerica (Wallace 1956), but is found in all societies precisely because the past represented a powerful motivational and integrative force.

Another approach to the study of religion has been evolutionary. Religious institutions of various degrees of complexity were originally equated with political complexity in early anthropological syntheses (Frazer 1922). The institution of shamanism in particular was originally thought to represent a form of religious practice associated primarily with hunter-gatherer peoples, and religion was thought to evolve out of preceding traditions of magic, antedating the development of science in ancient societies (Frazer 1922). Studies in Mesoamerica (Furst 1976; Freidel et al. 1993) and North Asia (Eliade 1964; Chang 1989) suggest that this early view of shamanism is inadequate because shamanistic practice can be manifested on different scales of cultural complexity. Similarly, Marcus and Flannery (chapter 19) point out that institutions such as animism (the belief that inanimate objects can be imbued with a life force or soul), often thought to be associated with simple societies, can also be integral to chiefdom and state religions. In his original examination of animism, Tylor (1958: 443) also defined several scales of complexity at which this property is observed among living societies.

Archaeologists employ a number of methods to study belief systems in ancient Mesoamerica. The use of analogy is central

to many approaches. Information about regional religions gleaned from the descendants of ancient cultures in both historical and modern times has formed a primary basis for interpretation of archaeological data. Ethnographically documented rituals which involve the use of facilities and objects similar to those found in the archaeological record are often used to infer meaning. Generally speaking, the closer in space and time the historical or ethnographic source is to the archaeological data set, the more reliable the analogy. In Mesoamerica, living indigenous peoples provide a rich ethnographic record from which analogies can be drawn (e.g. Deal 1988; Flannery 1976). This region is also fortunate to have a large number of surviving Colonial texts (such as Landa 1941; Sahagún 1950–89) and pre-conquest indigenous hieroglyphic monuments and codices which offer rich sources of information about religion. Marcus and Flannery (chapter 19) and Brumfiel (chapter 22) make the greatest use of ethnohistorical information among the articles compiled in this section, but this method is also found in other works throughout this volume as well.

The study of Mesoamerican religion requires approaches that cross academic disciplines. Archaeologists must work with ethnohistoric and ethnographic data as described above, as well as linguistic data or epigraphic (hieroglyphic) information. Some art historical approaches in Mesoamerica embrace an interdisciplinary approach and make extensive use of cross-cultural analogy. This kind of approach is demonstrated in Reilly's chapter on Olmec cosmology (chapter 18), and the article by Freidel and Schele (chapter 20) provides an example of a collaborative effort of an archaeologist and art historian/epigrapher. The excerpt from McAnany's book (chapter 23), weaves together evidence from ethnohistorical, ethnographic, and archaeological data to such a skillful extent that it is difficult to distinguish where one line of evidence ends and another begins in the flow of the argument. A useful exercise for students would be to attempt to pinpoint the approaches used among the different articles in this reader.

Although collaboration and interdisciplinary research can be highly productive, scholars from different disciplines can be interested in very different issues. Reilly (chapter 18) and Freidel and Schele (chapter 20) are interested in strategies of early lowland rulership and cosmology as expressed in public art. The article by Marcus and Flannery (chapter 19) endeavors to infer meaning of early Zapotec ritual features and the control of ritual by elite members of Zapotec society by using analogies to historic times. Masson (chapter 22) also examines the control of ritual by upper-status members of a small community, and seeks to identify scales of ritual practice at a specialized ritual shrine, an elite household, and nonelite households at a single site. Brumfiel (chapter 22) uses figurines recovered from Aztec-period households to examine the roles of women in Aztec society and the influence of state ideology on women's perception of themselves. The final chapter of this volume (McAnany, chapter 23) examines the meaning of a single religious institution, ancestor worship, across many agrarian and royal contexts of Maya society and the importance of this institution to social groups and their territorial prerogatives.

Common Elements of Mesoamerican Religions

Mesoamerican religions from different regions share several common institutions of belief and cosmology. In fact, many living and archaeological societies in the New World share similar underlying basic attributes which are exhibited in specific regional traditions. Similarities in shamanistic aspects of religion observed in China, Siberia, and the Americas led Furst (1972: 261–78, 1976: 149–57) and Chang (1989: 162–3) to propose that these belief systems evolved regionally from a shared template that originated in Paleoindian times, when Siberian ancestors of Native Americans crossed over from the Bering Strait and settled the New World. The shared shamanistic beliefs identified by these authors include the following: (1) a cosmology which includes the belief in tiered worlds; (2) a belief in the capacity for humans and supernaturals to travel back and forth between these tiered worlds; (3) a belief in the capacity for magical flight, where the soul can travel separate from the body during sleep or trance; (4), a belief in an animal or other supernatural alterego or companion spirit and the capacity of some people to transform themselves into this companion spirit; and (5) a well-developed tradition of ancestor veneration, including the practices of ancestor communication, conjuring to sanction events in this world, and ancestor intervention on behalf of the living in the other world. The manifestations of these elements of belief are not identical or of equal importance in the diverse cultures of the New World. Many Mesoamerican religions exhibit several of these traits, however. Studying the variation in the development of these institutions within regions of cultural areas like Mesoamerica provides an important basis for understanding different paths of cultural evolution and ways in which cultural and natural environments have shaped these regional societies.

Three articles in this reader (chapters 18, 19, 20) present examples of regionally distinct religious beliefs and their affiliated political strategies. A Middle Formative Ceremonial Complex found in both the Olmec heartland and more distant areas includes the following attributes: depictions of rulers as the central axis of the world (*axis mundi*) or world tree, rulers as performers of auto-sacrifice and conjurers of ancestors, rulers as sacrificers, rulers participating in cave rituals in the otherworld, ruler transformation into feline animal companion form, and other themes (Reilly, chapter 18).

Lowland Maya temples, including Structure 5C-2nd from the site of Cerros analyzed by Freidel and Schele (chapter 20), were created as cosmograms in which Maya rulers portrayed themselves at the center of the universe. The creation of sacred space as a stage for divine kings involved not only architectural design and orientation, but also important arrangements of offerings. Ritual adornments of kingly costumes also examined in this work symbolize the role of these leaders as intermediaries with the supernatural realm. This article illustrates the close relationship between claims of supernatural power and political power in the Maya institution of "ahawship." Rituals documented at the site of San José Mogote (Marcus and Flannery, chapter 19) include bloodletting, sacrifice, incense burning, and the ritual use of narcotics, which may have been performed by ancient priests in a manner analogous to priestly rituals recorded during Spanish Colonial times as the authors observe. They suggest that such rituals occurred in temples similar to those recorded by the Spanish. Figurine scenes provide additional clues regarding rituals directed at ancestors and supernatural entities.

Two other articles in this section (chapters 21, 22) examine the manifestation of ideology not from this top-down perspective, but from the bottom up, in the realm of ritual practice in domestic settings. The final chapter of this volume by McAnany (chapter 23) examines the underlying commonalities of a religious institution that is utilized across a range of social tiers in space and time, as the "living make use of the dead." The works in this section on religious institutions provide only a sample of the broad array of approaches to studying the ideological foundations of Mesoamerican civilizations. Additional aspects of Mesoamerican religion are also addressed in the articles included in the section on political organization (part III). Students should think about the relationships between religion and politics in ancient Mesoamerica: are these topics that can be separated, or are they different expressions of the same underlying forces?

REFERENCES

Barrera Vasquez, A. and Sylvanus G. Morley. 1949. *The Maya Chronicles*. Carnegie Institute of Washington Publication 585, contribution 48. Washington, DC.

Bricker, Victoria Reifler. 1981. *The Indian Christ, The Indian King: The Historical Substrate of Maya Myth and Ritual*. University of Texas Press, Austin.

Chang, Kwang-Chih. 1989. Ancient China and its Anthropological Significance. In *Archaeological Thought in America*, edited by C. C. Lamberg-Karlovsky, pp. 155–66. Cambridge University Press, Cambridge.

Dahlin, Bruce Harrison. 1976. An Anthropologist Looks at the Pyramids: A Late Classic Revitalization Movement at Tikal, Guatemala. Ph.D. dissertation, Temple University. University Microfilms, Ann Arbor.

Deal, Michael. 1988. Recognition of Ritual Pottery in Residential Units: An Ethnoarchaeological Model of the Maya Family Altar Tradition. In *Ethnoarchaeology Among the Highland Maya of Chiapas, Mexico*, edited by Thomas A. Lee and Brian Hayden, Vol. 56, pp. 61–90. New World Archaeological Foundation, Provo, UT.

Durkheim, Emile. 1965. *The Elementary Forms of Religious Life*. Translated by Joseph Ward Swain (from the original edn, 1915). The Free Press, New York.

Eliade, Mircea. 1964. *Shamanism: Archaic Techniques of Ecstasy*. Translated from the French by Willard R. Trask. Bollingen Series LXXVI, Princeton University Press, Princeton, NJ.

Flannery, Kent V. 1976. Contextual Analysis of Ritual Paraphernalia from Formative Oaxaca. In *The Early Mesoamerican Village*, edited by Kent V. Flannery, pp. 333–45. Academic Press, New York.

Frazer, James G. 1922. Magic and Religion. In *The Golden Bough: A Study in Magic and Religion*, vol. 1, by Sir James George Frazer. Originally published by Macmillan Publishing Company, New York and London. Excerpt reprinted in *Ritual and Belief: Readings in the Anthropology of Religion*, edited by David Hicks, pp. 78–82. McGraw-Hill, Boston.

Freidel, David A., Linda Schele, and Joy Parker. 1993. *Maya Cosmos: Three Thousand Years on the Shaman's Path*. William Morrow and Company, New York.

Furst, Peter T. 1972. Hallucinogens and the Shamanic Origins of Religions. In *Flesh of the Gods: The Ritual Use of Hallucinogens*, edited by Peter D. Furst. Praeger, New York.

—— 1976. Shamanistic Survivals in Mesoamerican Religion. *Actas del XLI Congreso Internacional de Americanistas III*, pp. 149–57. Mexico City.

Geertz, Clifford. 1966. Religion as a Cultural System. In *Anthropological Approaches to the Study of Religion*, edited by Michael Blanton, pp. 1–45. Tavistock Publications, London.

Gossen, Gary H. and Richard M. Leventhal. 1993. The Topography of Ancient Maya Religious Pluralism. In *Lowland Maya Civilization in the Eighth Century AD*, edited by Jeremy Sabloff and John Henderson, pp. 185–218. Dumbarton Oaks, Washington, DC.

Jones, Grant D. 1989. *Maya Resistance to Spanish Rule: Time and History on a Colonial Frontier*. University of New Mexico Press, Albuquerque.

Landa, Friar Diego de. 1941. *Landa's Relaciones de las Cosas de Yucatan*. Translated by Alfred Tozzer. Papers of the Peabody Museum of Archaeology and Ethnology 18. Harvard University Press, Cambridge.

Lewis, Oscar. 1951. *Life in a Mexican Village: Tepoztlan Restudied*. University of Illinois Press, Urbana.

Marcus, Joyce. 1992. *Mesoamerican Writing Systems: Propaganda, Myth, and History in Four Ancient Civilizations*. Princeton University Press, Princeton.

Marx, Karl and Frederick Engels. 1970. *The German Ideology*. International Publishers, New York.

McGuire, Randall H. 1992. *A Marxist Archaeology*. Academic Press, New York.

Miller, Daniel, Michael Rowlands, and Christopher Tilley (ed.) 1989. *Domination and Resistance*. Unwin and Hyman, London.

Pasztory, Esther. 1988. A Reinterpretation of Teotihuacan and its Mural Painting Tradition. In *Feathered Serpents and Flowering Trees: Reconstructing the Murals of Teotihuacan*, edited by K. Berrin, pp. 45–77. The Fine Arts Museum of San Francisco, San Francisco.

—— 1997. *Teotihuacan: An Experiment in Living*. University of Oklahoma Press, Norman.

Sahagún, Fray Bernardino de. 1950–89. *Florentine Codex, General History of the Things of New Spain*. 12 books. Translated and edited by Arthur J. O. Anderson and Charles E. Dibble. School of American Research and the University of Utah Press, Santa Fe and Salt Lake City.

Sahlins, Marshall. 1981. *Historical Metaphors and Mythical Realities: Structure in the Early History of the Sandwich Islands Kingdom*. University of Michigan Press, Ann Arbor.

Schele, Linda and David A. Freidel. 1990. *A Forest of Kings: The Untold Story of the Ancient Maya*. William Morrow, New York.

Tylor, Edward Bunnette. 1958. *Religion in Primitive Culture*. 2nd edn. Harper and Row, New York.

Umberger, Emily. 1996. Art and Imperial Strategy in Tenochtitlan. In *Aztec Imperial Strategies*, edited by Frances F. Berdan et al., pp. 85–106. Dumbarton Oaks, Washington, DC.

Wallace, Anthony F. C. 1956. Revitalization Movements: Some Theoretical Considerations for their Comparative Study. *American Anthropologist* 58: 264–81.

Vogt, Evon Z. 1969. *Zinacantan: A Maya Community in the Highlands of Chiapas*. The Belknap Press of Harvard University Press, Cambridge, Massachusetts.

CHAPTER 18

Art, Ritual, and Rulership in the Olmec World

F. Kent Reilly III

When Mesoamerican scholars discuss the origin of civilized life in Mexico, they always begin with references to Olmec culture. In the ongoing debates that accompany such discussions, however, different researchers use the term *Olmec* in different ways. Moreover, the definition of Olmec has changed as new artifacts of uncertain provenance have been added as data to the debate. Confusion has resulted from scholars' various emphases, biases, and points of view. Thus, Olmec has come to mean many different things. In the most commonly applied definition,

Figure 18.1   La Venta Altar 4.

Reprinted from F. Kent Reilly III. 1995. Art, Ritual, and Rulership in the Olmec World. In *The Olmec World: Ritual and Rulership* (The Art Museum, Princeton University, Princeton, NJ), pp. 27–45.

Olmec refers both to an archaeological culture centered in the Mexican Gulf Coast and an early, geographically dispersed pre-Columbian art style that shares features with the material remains of the archaeological Olmec culture, especially in Guerrero.

Despite the lack of consensus on what the term Olmec embraces, scholars agree that Olmec was the dominant cultural expression of the Early and Middle Formative periods in Mesoamerica (1500–300 BC). Because some current definitions of Olmec have been based partially on material evidence supplied by Olmec-style objects of unknown provenance, however, many researchers have been reluctant to enter the definition debate. Nevertheless, these objects, while unaligned in any archaeological context – and many of unparalleled beauty – have been pivotal in determining the current stylistic and iconographic identification of Olmec art. Therefore, hard evidence in the form of archaeological data, when available, both in and outside of the Olmec heartland, has become an even more critical resource.

The Olmec Gulf Coast archaeological culture is now firmly dated at 1200–600 BC. The seven-hundred-year life span of the Gulf Coast Olmec is generally divided into two archaeological temporal periods, or horizons: the San Lorenzo Horizon 1200–900 BC and the La Venta Horizon 900–600 BC. Within the Gulf Coast heartland, Olmec subsistence patterns were a mixture of swidden, river levee, and horticultural systems.[1] Material evidence also suggests that the heartland Olmec were connected to other Mesoamerican cultures through long-distance trade. Recent ethnographic and linguistic research strongly suggests that the Gulf Coast archaeological Olmec spoke a language belonging to the Mixe-Zoque linguistic family.[2] On Olmec sociopolitical organization, archaeological evidence is much more tenuous.[3] Hypotheses define the Olmec as an empire, theocracy, chiefdom, early state, or fully developed state. Current research favors a protostate or at least a paramount chiefdom

level of political organization within the Olmec heartland.[4]

In contrast to the geographic limits of the heartland-centered *Olmec archaeological culture*, objects created in the *Olmec art style* are found throughout Mesoamerica. The many symbolic elements and motifs that have been important factors in defining the Olmec style can be seen on small-scale objects created in wood, clay, and stone as well as on monumental sculpture found both in the heartland and far beyond. While the majority of Olmec-style art objects are small and easily carried, the hallmarks of the archaeological Olmec heartland culture are the enormous earthen platforms; colossal basalt heads; table-top altars; and representations in sculpture of individuals, executed with such realism they approach modern concepts of portraiture.

Few scholars question the hypothesis that the Mesoamerican monolithic sculpture tradition originated in the Olmec heartland. This tradition also began to spread beyond the heartland in the La Venta Horizon. Investigations at Abaj Takalik, in Guatemala, and at Chalcatzingo, Morelos; Teopantecuanitlan, Guerrero; and other areas of highland Mexico show those sites erecting free-standing examples of monolithic sculpture after 900 BC.[5]

Proof of an Olmec presence outside the Gulf Coast heartland, however, has never been determined solely by the presence of monolithic sculpture, but rather by the presence of objects executed in the Olmec style. This usually means objects incised or painted with elements of the Olmec symbol system or, if a human or zoomorphic supernatural depiction, carrying the stylistic, classically Olmec attributes of the drooping were-jaguar mouth and the cleft forehead.

The Olmec of the Gulf Coast were not, however, the only Formative period culture producing specialized categories of artifacts. Graves dating to the Early Formative period have yielded a treasure trove of distinctive ceramic artifacts, several of which were unknown in the Olmec heartland. In the Valley of Mexico, at Tlatilco and

Tlapacoya, artisans working in clay produced stirrup-necked bottles, large hollow figurines, solid female figurines, and exquisite zoomorphic vessels shaped in the form of fish, ducks, and other aquatic animals native to the lake that covered a large part of the valley floor. The inhabitants of ancient Tlatilco placed these distinctive ceramics in the tombs of their honored dead, but they also included ceramic vessels marked with Olmec-style symbols. The existence of Olmec-style material in the graves of a non-Olmec people is currently interpreted by most observers as evidence of Olmec influence in the Valley of Mexico. However, as we shall see, a few scholars believe that the appearance of Olmec symbols in Tlatilco graves proves that it was not the Olmec alone who were responsible for many of the symbols and artifacts now attributed to them.

In a large riverine valley on the border of the modern Mexican states of Morelos and Puebla, the graves of a number of Early Formative villages, collectively known as Las Bocas, have yielded ceramic objects rivaling and, in some instances, surpassing those of Tlatilco and Tlapacoya. As at Tlatilco, the graves at Las Bocas yielded two types of objects – those distinctive to the site and village culture and those carrying Olmec symbols and motifs (figure 18.2; cat. nos 246a, 109). The Olmec zoomorphic ceramics share with the vessels of Tlatilco the theme of the fauna of the natural world, and the large Olmec kaolin hollow figures are finer than any others. However, Las Bocas also produced a large number of stylized ivory-slipped ceramic figurines that seemingly depict the activities of the elite inhabitants of this early central Mexican village. These expressive, mostly solid figures show the Las Bocas villagers in various shapes and sizes. Some of them have Olmec symbols incorporated into their coiffures (figure 18.3; cat. no. 236). The figurines are often in indolent or lecherous postures (figure 18.4; cat. no. 240). A few small figurines are hollow and have Olmec-style symbols cut into their bodies (figure 18.5; cat. no. 237). The fact that these figures

Figure 18.2a Plate, 1200–900 BC, Las Bocas, Puebla. Blackware with traces of cinnabar, h. 3.2 cm; diam. 14.5 cm. (Anonymous loan to The Art Museum, Princeton University.)

Figure 18.2b Carved Bottle, 1200–900 BC, Las Bocas, Puebla. Blackware with traces of red pigment, h. 21 cm; diam. 14 cm. (Private collection.)

carry symbols of Olmec ideology identifies them as more than just representations of village life. The recovery of many of them from graves strongly suggests they are portrayals of the dead in the supernatural otherworld.

Over the years, arguments have persisted about the origins of the Olmec symbols and style and the realistic human forms

Figure 18.5   Reclining Hollow Figure, 1200–900 BC, Las Bocas, Puebla. Clay with traces of red pigment, h. 6 cm; w. 12 cm; d. 3 cm. (Private collection.)

Figure 18.3   Seated Figure, 1200–900 BC, Las Bocas, Puebla. Clay with traces of red pigment, h. 6.2 cm; w. 5.1 cm; d. 4.2 cm. (Private collection.)

Figure 18.4   Man and Woman Embracing, 1200–900 BC, Las Bocas, Puebla. Clay with ivory slip and traces of red pigment, h. 9 cm; w. 5 cm; d. 6 cm. (Private collection.)

commonly thought to be an Olmec trait. The continuing doubts concerning what makes an object "Olmec" have caused some researchers to challenge the generally accepted heartland origin of the Olmec style and symbol system.[6] David Grove, the most recent excavator of the highland site of Chalcatzingo, has questioned whether artifacts known to originate from highland and Pacific Coast Formative period sites and bearing "Olmec-style" symbols and motifs

are Olmec at all.[7] But if all the objects created in the Olmec style and carrying Olmec symbols did not originate in the Olmec heartland, from where did they come? Explanations of the extensive presence of Olmec-style objects throughout Formative period Mesoamerica currently range from conquest, to colonization, to missionary activity. The precise mechanisms by which these objects and symbols spread throughout Mesoamerica are still a topic of debate.

A plausible theory, supported by archaeological evidence, favors the long-distance trade and interaction sphere hypothesis, in which lowland coastal products – including marine shells, tropical birds' feathers, and, possibly, cotton and cacao beans – were exchanged for highland serpentine, obsidian, and other stones.[8] Yet, economics alone fails to explain the wide distribution of the Olmec art style and the many stylistic and thematic variations within that style. Economics together with ideology provide a more satisfactory account.

The proven antiquity of the Olmec style in the Gulf Coast heartland, and the recognizable stylistic and motif variations within the large corpus of Olmec-style objects recovered outside that heartland, have led to extended discussions and, sometimes, controversy about the social and economic mechanisms accounting for the Olmec phenomena.[9] Given the ongoing nature of this controversy, I believe a reexamination of

Olmec definitions and, if necessary, the development of a new and dynamic template explaining the stylistic and thematic variations in the Olmec art style, without denigrating the formidable achievements of the Gulf Coast heartland Olmec, are required. In pursuit of this template, I have proposed that many of the Olmec-style artifacts created between 900 and 500 BC would be better classified as ritual objects that functioned in a geographically dispersed *Middle Formative Period Ceremonial Complex*.[10] This hypothesis explains the stylistic and material evidence far better than conquest, missionaries, or even long-distance trade. Based on what is known now, there can be little argument that within the broad geographical limits of this ceremonial complex throughout both the Early and Middle Formative periods, the Olmec heartland held the most concentrated remains of these ritual objects. However, many of the other ethnic groups participating in the ceremonial complex must have contributed a large portion of the symbols, motifs, and artifacts that are hallmarks of Middle Formative ceremonial life.

The Middle Formative Ceremonial Complex Model

Simply stated, the Middle Formative Ceremonial Complex consists of the physical evidence – artifacts, symbols, motifs, and architectural groupings – for the rituals practiced by, and the ideology and political structures of, the numerous ethnic groups forming the demographic and cultural landscape of Middle Formative period Mesoamerica. The methodology used to recover the underlying ideology visualized by Olmec objects is the structural analysis of Olmec-style iconography.[11] When this is combined with an ethnohistorical approach, the political ideology can be recovered as well. The inhabitants of the Olmec heartland were the primary source for this ceremonial complex, but other contemporary Mesoamerican ethnic groups contributed, too.[12]

Ceremonial complexes are no more rare in the Americas than in the Old World.[13] The Formative period was not the only time in which ceremonial complexes flourished in Mesoamerica. The presence of Teotihuacan war imagery among the Classic period Maya (AD 200–900) represents a Mesoamerica-wide Classic Period Ceremonial Complex. The combination of Classic period Teotihuacan and Maya iconography at such Epiclassic sites as Xochicalco, Morelos and Cacaxtla, Tlaxcala indicates an Epiclassic Ceremonial Complex in these highland areas. The forced adoption of Aztec ideology and rituals by non-Aztec elite groups in Late Postclassic Mesoamerica can also be discussed in terms of an Aztec Ceremonial Complex.

The Mesoamerican Middle Formative period was an era of increasing political complexity and enormous artistic output. Monumental sculpture, until then restricted to the Olmec Gulf Coast heartland, began to be created at centers both in the Mexican highlands and along the Pacific coast state of Guerrero. Many symbols and motifs that in the Early Formative period may have been restricted mostly to the easily accessible medium of clay, in the Middle Formative are found over a wide area on small-scale ritual objects carved in the Olmec style from jade and other forms of greenstone.[14] These easily transportable, greenstone objects can be classified in four categories: celts or hand axes; seated and standing human figures; zoomorphic supernaturals; and ritual objects such as masks, bloodletting instruments, and divinatory apparatus.[15] The function of these objects was twofold: to act as props in shamanic rituals and to provide, through the symbolic information they bore, visual validation for the political authority of the rulers who manipulated them in these rituals. In order to understand the interrelatedness of these two essentially ideological functions, it is important to know the role art played in shamanic rituals and the meaning, as well as ritual function, of Olmec-style motifs and symbols.

Shamanism

An ancient, but living worldwide religious tradition, shamanism is based on the belief that the spirits of ancestors and the controlling forces of the natural world, or gods, can be contacted by religious specialists in altered states of consciousness.[16] Fundamental to shamanism is the conviction that the cosmos and everything in it are imbued with a life force or soul and are interconnected. Shamanism centers on techniques of ecstasy used by a religious practitioner called a shaman in rituals of supernatural communication. Individuals may become shamans by being chosen directly by the spirits of the supernatural or inheriting shamanic power from an ancestor or apprenticing to a practicing shaman.

In shamanic rituals the shaman achieves the trance state. In this trance, the shaman is understood to travel to the supernatural otherworld and upon his return to communicate his revelations to the community. The trance state itself is often described as the act of flying between different planes of reality. It can be brought on by a variety of ecstatic techniques, such as meditation, drumming, dance, pain, sensory deprivation, and the taking of hallucinogens. In the shamanic view, these techniques, since they open the portals between the natural and the supernatural realms, are held sacred. Thus, "the pre-eminently shamanic technique is the passage from one cosmic region to another – from earth to sky or from earth to the underworld. The shaman knows the mystery of the break-through in plane."[17]

Shamanic Organization

The internal organization of shamanism and the shaman's sociopolitical function vary greatly from culture to culture. In many shamanic societies the shaman's role may overlap with the priest's, medicinal curer's, and sorcerer's. Shamanic religious organization may be individualistic, collective, or institutional. Individualistic shamanism is traditional shamanism: a single individual

(the shaman) has access to the supernatural in trance and relates the experience to the community. Collective shamanism allows a number of individuals to participate in the shamanic trance journey. Institutional shamanism exists in "state"-level cultures where political leaders validate their power through the ritual medium of the trance journey.

Shamanistic trance is rarely the basis for political authority in societies that are more complex than a tribe or, perhaps, a chiefdom. Recent hieroglyphic discoveries demonstrate conclusively, however, that Classic period Maya kings validated their right to royal power by publicly proclaiming their ability to perform the shamanic trance journey and transform into power animals.[18] Linda Schele's and David Freidel's iconographic and epigraphic discoveries successfully show how shamanism's ideology was the foundation of Classic period Maya political validation.[19]

Formative period Mesoamerica was not alone in validating political authority through shamanic authority. In the Old World, Shang Dynasty China (1726–1122 BC),[20] early Yamato period Japan (ca. AD 50–300),[21] and Silla Dynasty Korea (AD 668–935)[22] are prime examples of state-level political authority based on shamanism. Presently, controversy surrounds the origins of institutionalized shamanism. However, as we shall see, investigation of Olmec-style artifacts should help to define the origins of political structures based on institutional shamanism in Mesoamerica and, perhaps, other areas of the world.

Shamanic Human–Animal Transformation

Trance and the trance-induced journey are the focus of shamanic worship. Shamans worldwide are often aided in their trance journey or shamanic flight by *nagualo*, animal spirit companions. These spirit companions can either carry the shaman into the supernatural otherworld or guard against malevolent spirits who might harm or even kill him. They take the form of both deceased shamans and power animals, such as the jaguar, eagle, or bear. In the trance state some shamans achieve animal–human transformation. "On these occasions the shaman projects his consciousness into an animal form on an imaginal level and it is in this 'body' that he or she goes forth on the spirit journey."[23] In the otherworld, shamans, in the forms of their power animals, are known to have spirit battles with other shamans. Such battles can result in the death of one or both of the opponents, in which case the shaman's human body also dies.

The Shamanic Ritual Costume

Few shamanic ritual objects play a greater role in the visualization of the shamanic trance journey and the shaman's spirit companions than the shamanic costume. It is central, researchers have shown, to the public acceptance and thus legitimization of the shaman. Though much of the shamanic experience is interior and personal, the shaman's success depends on his tribe's or group's acceptance and sanction. However, "the mode of expression whereby the shaman relates to the social system is not standardized or ritually fixed."[24] Ritual and "the shaman's accessories provide a dramatic means by which the tribal audience can affirm and participate in the shaman's visionary experience."[25] "The shaman's costume itself constitutes a religious hierophany and cosmography; it discloses not only sacred presence but also cosmic symbols and metaphysic itineraries. Properly studied, it reveals the system of shamanism as clearly as do the shamanic myths and techniques."[26] In effect, the shamanic costume is a symbolic map of the cosmological structure in which the shaman travels to the supernatural otherworld.

Many details of the shamanic costume are closely related to the concept of the ecstatic journey or shaman's flight, taking the form of avian symbols attached as single feathers dangling from the shirt, small wings affixed to the shoulders of the costume, or collars of feathers worn around the neck. The species

from which the feathers come vary, but the most prominent are owls and eagles. Many groups believe the eagle is the ancestral, first shaman. Furthermore, the eagle plays a central role not only in many shamanic initiations, but also in a symbolic complex focusing on the cosmological function of the world tree as the *axis mundi* and the mechanism of ascent in the shaman's ecstatic journey.[27]

Shamanic Cosmology

The cosmos described by the shaman's costume and other ritual accouterments is a multitiered configuration centered on the *axis mundi*. The number of tiers, or planes, in the shamanic cosmos varies from culture to culture, but generally there are three, consisting of sky, earth, and underworld. The underworld and sky realms are also perceived as supernatural otherworld locations. For some Mesoamerican peoples the underworld was understood to rotate up at sunset from under the earthly realm to become the night sky. The stars and other celestial bodies were thus perceived as inhabitants of the supernatural otherworld.[28] Like all other shamanic cosmological models, the center point in the Maya earthly grid was the *axis mundi*. In Mesoamerican and other cultures, the *axis mundi* was conceived as a great tree or mountain linking all three levels of the cosmos. This world tree or mountain connected the human world to the realm of the supernatural.[29] Shamanic vision quests are sometimes described as ascensions to the other world via the *axis mundi*.

Analyzing Shamanic Art

Discussions of shamanic costumes and the art objects integral to these costumes often focus on whether they are the origins of art itself.[30] Esther Pasztory, however, pointed out that "visual art is not essential to shamanism" and that "shamanism is primarily linked with aural traditions and only secondarily with the visual." Nevertheless, she concludes that "when art objects are used by shamans, they acquire characteristics that fit in with shamanic values... [that] much of the emphasis in shamanic art is directed toward the visualization of the shamanic trance journey... [and that when] art objects in shamanism are made to help communicate certain ideas, more emphasis is placed on the subjects they represent than on their formal appearance."[31]

Pasztory divided shamanic art into four thematic categories: "human figures, animals, animal–human contact, and cosmic charts." She suggests that human or anthropomorphic figures may represent the "shaman, or a mythical first shaman, as a human individual with magical powers." This shamanic control of magical powers is artfully conveyed by anthropomorphic figures in frontal poses with orant gestures. Anthropomorphic figures also function as the shaman's helping spirits or as specific deities. Magical powers manipulated by the shaman in trance and in trance rituals are often transmitted through objects carved to portray parts of the human and animal body (hearts, skeletons, horns, etc.) and, most strikingly, transformation masks. The power of shamanic masks to transport the wearer from the natural to the supernatural plane and to reveal supernaturals encountered in trance states is common in shamanic rituals. Pasztory cautioned, however, "without ethnographic information, it is often impossible to tell shamans, spirits, and deities apart: all partake of similar power attributes and have interchangeable iconographic traits."[32]

Pasztory is convinced that, like the anthropomorphic, the animals category is ambiguous: "The animals represented include the hunted animals... as well as power animals. The power animals may be animal versions of the supernatural deity who controls the animals, the helping spirit of the shaman, or the shaman in animal disguise."[33] Power animals and animal spirit companions are often depicted as fabulous, composite, zoomorphic supernaturals, whose combined body parts create visual metaphors for creatures that cross different levels of reality.

Pasztory's final thematic category is cosmology: "A three-dimensional representation of the cosmos is often an integral part of the shamanic performance."[34] This three-dimensional cosmic model is frequently the ceremonial space in which the shamanic ritual is conducted, although two-dimensional cosmic models are not unknown.

Analyzing Olmec-Style Art

Generally, the term *style*, when applied to objects identified as works of art, refers to the "formal qualities" linking the specific object to other works of art. With works of art produced by a prehistoric people, the definition of style can encompass a larger meaning. For archaeologists and prehistorians, style can be central to any attempt to understand the belief system of a prehistoric people. The anthropologist Robert Layton broadened the definition of style to include the efforts of prehistoric people to communicate *ideas* through art.[35] In this context, Layton defined style as: "one of the necessary components of visual communication but... it acquires special qualities when it becomes part of art – qualities which express the artist's sensitivity to form and significance. Because of this, it is possible to study how a culture fills the world around it with meaning."[36]

In any discussion of Formative period art, Layton's definition of style provides a methodology for the recovery of meaning. In an anthropological approach to the Olmec style, style itself becomes a term implying the ability of an object to communicate messages from the past. Objects are billboards and framing devices that provide structure for the iconographic information incised on their surfaces. Using this approach to style, Olmec objects are both prehistoric data and communication devices. In the context of a specific theoretical approach, Olmec-style objects can be understood as a symbolic system for the visualization of ideology.

Much of the difficulty in formulating a successful definition of the Olmec style is compounded by the seven-hundred-year period during which it was produced. We must contend not only with the style's regional differences, but with its long-term evolution and change.[37] The archaeological record makes clear, however, that Olmec art can be traced largely to the Gulf Coast Olmec heartland.

Miguel Covarrubias was the first scholar and artist to use a systematic approach in defining the formal qualities of the Olmec style.[38] Objects created in the Olmec style first came to his notice on excursions in Guerrero. Searching for local folk art, he dropped in at *pulquerias* and traded drinks with the local *campesinos* in exchange for "small idols of fat personages of extraordinary mongoloid traits and with thick unpleasant-looking mouths."[39] Stunned by the power and integrity of these objects, Covarrubias was impressed with the consummate skill of the carvings and the dark greenstone and blue jade from which they were made.

Using an ethnographic and physiographic approach, Covarrubias compared Olmec-style human depictions with contemporary Mexican ethnic groups. He found the humans depicted on the ancient objects "made up of solid ample masses, powerful and squat, quite in accord with the physical build of some Indians of Southern Mexico."[40] His most useful tool in the interpretation of Olmec-style art was his own artistic insights. Covarrubias interpreted Olmec art as a style centered on human beings depicted as "short and fat, with wide jaws, a prominent chin, short and flat noses with the septum perforated, mongoloid eyes with swollen eyelids, and with artificially deformed heads in the shape of a pear."[41] He thought the most important characteristic of these grotesque human depictions was the drooping, downturned, often toothless mouth. This trapezoidal-shaped mouth with its thickened upper lip, Covarrubias believed, gave the figures a "fierce and evil-looking appearance, with a bold protruding upper lip like that of a prowling jaguar" (figure 18.6; cat. no. 36).[42]

In Covarrubias's eyes, the Olmec style stood apart from the rest of ancient Mexican art because its artists chose to represent "almost exclusively man, that is to say,

Figure 18.6 Supernatural Effigy Plaque, 900–400 BC, Cuautla, Morelos. Greenstone, h. 14.9 cm; w. 6.7 cm; d. 2 cm. (William P. Palmer III Collection, Hudson Museum, University of Maine.)

themselves, or at least their esthetic ideal."[43] Other ancient Mexican art was "generally subordinated to religious ideas and frequently limited by its traditional stylizations."[44]

He linked the extraordinary Olmec stone carvings, many from Guerrero, with the equally accomplished ceramic arts of the Formative period. In his view, the "'Olmecs' modeled clay with the same masterly sensitivity with which they carved jade."[45]

The skill of these ancient stone carvers captivated him: "'Olmec' artists dominated the material to impose the form required, carving it with the same realistic looseness with which they modeled clay. So advanced a lapidary technique employed all imaginable methods: cutting the stone, abrading, crumbling by percussion, and an unknown manner of obtaining the splendid polish of the pieces. The 'Olmec' lapidaries were able to make the most amazing perforations in jade objects – holes in thin plaques and tubular beads several inches long, some so minute that it is difficult to string them."[46]

Michael D. Coe has pointed out that identifying meaning in an art style based on a different concept of reality than our own is difficult. But an important iconographic clue to interpreting Olmec art is provided by the metaphoric functions of zoomorphic supernaturals in Formative period cosmology.[47] The primary zoomorphic supernatural, the Olmec Dragon, has been isolated by Peter David Joralemon.[48] He demonstrated that the Olmec Dragon dominates much of the thematic content of Olmec art and that Olmec artists used four general methods to convey the symbolic elements defining this ubiquitous supernatural in either a full-figured *pars pro toto*, frontally faced, or profile variant.[49]

Joralemon's Olmec Dragon is a composite beast whose several body parts derive from natural animals (figure 18.7). In identifying an Olmec zoomorph as a supernatural hybrid the locomotive body parts are decisive. Thus, a single motif – i.e., the hand-paw-wing, a composite of a human's hand, animal's paw, and bird's wing – on the body of an avian- or saurian-derived zoomorph alerts the viewer to the fact that it is able to move among several cosmic realms.

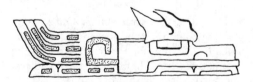

Figure 18.7 A *pars pro toto* Olmec Dragon.

Another recent insight into the formal qualities of the Olmec style is the principle of multiple perspective, or multiple horizons. Many incised compositions are best understood when their distinct elements are placed in relative spatial position.[50] This principle creates visual fields in which a four-by-four orientation, as in a courtyard, is shown top view, while objects within the field are in profile. The use of multiple points of view, which in Olmec art resembles the sections of a paper castle before it is cut out, folded, and assembled, is not restricted in Mesoamerica to Middle Formative artists.

This cut-out and fold-up concept was also used by Maya artists in drawings accompanying hieroglyphic texts in the four surviving Postclassic codices. A cosmic diagram in the Madrid Codex is a four-by-four orientation of the cosmic directions conflated into a single, one-dimensional plane (figure 18.8a). The deities and the world tree within that plane are rendered in profile. When European spatial convention is applied to this illustration, the central world tree and its flanking deities stand in the middle of a flat plane (figure 18.8b). The corners of this cosmic model are marked by the cardinal and intercardinal directions. The continued use of the principle of multiple perspective, or multiple points of view by later cultures is further proof that the templates of Mesoamerican art, political structure, and religion were first created in a permanent medium by the Olmec and other Formative period cultures.

Identifying the Shamanic Content of Middle Formative Olmec Art

Linking archaeological artifacts with shamanic ideology is a difficult task. Connecting certain Olmec-style motifs, symbolic elements, and stylistic variations with political validation is even more difficult. Any such attempts should be made within the prescribed boundaries of what is known about the function of shamanic art in general and Mesoamerican art in particular. But if my model is correct – i.e., that a ranked or

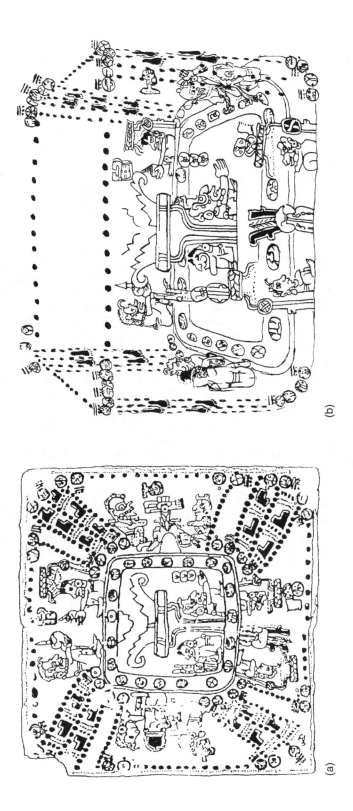

(b)

(a)

Figure 18.8a The Creation page from the Postclassic Maya Madrid Codex.

b. The Creation page from the Postclassic Maya Madrid Codex, reinterpreted within European spatial convention.

stratified social order is the product of economic and political power gained through institutionalized shamanic ritual performance – supporting evidence must be provided by the artifacts manipulated by elites. The ritual functions of these artifacts must then be identified by placing them in Pasztory's categories of shamanic art. In search of such evidence, I shall now examine Middle Formative costume details and ritual artifacts and show how they are examples of the shamanic trance journey, cosmological diagram, or human–animal transformation.

Olmec and Middle Formative Cosmology

Olmec and Middle Formative cosmology is fueled by shamanic magic. The Olmec and other Middle Formative peoples perceived their universe as multileveled, containing natural and supernatural oppositions. An axis described iconographically as maize or a cosmic mountain connected the levels. These ancient Mesoamericans did not view the cosmic levels as separate and distinct constructions, but as a living and interconnected universe.

Close study of Olmec iconography reveals that Middle Formative cosmology was almost certainly a blend of myth and natural phenomena. The growth cycle of maize, habits of particular species of animals, meteorological events, and motion of astral bodies generated symbolic metaphors for describing the cosmic order. The metaphors took the form of zoomorphic supernaturals or dragons who possessed the ability to cross cosmic boundaries.[51] Individual elements on the dragons' chimerical bodies identified their cosmological realms.[52]

Bloodletting played a significant role in the cosmology of Olmec and Middle Formative ceremonies, as it continued to do in later Mesoamerican cultures.[53] Blood was a magical substance opening the portal between the natural and supernatural cosmic divisions. Though scenes of bloodletting are not as numerous in Olmec art as they seem to be in the art of the Classic Maya, strong evidence for bloodletting and human sacrifice exists in Middle Formative period art. Chalcatzingo Monument 2 appears to depict a ritual human sacrifice in which two masked performers dispatch a bound and seated captive with paddle-shaped clubs, while a third elevates a bundle of vegetation (figure 18.9).

Among the Olmec-style artifacts is a category of objects shaped like ice picks

Figure 18.9   Bas-relief from Chalcatzingo Monument 2, which appears to depict a ritual human sacrifice.

Figure 18.10 Perforator, 900–600 BC, Río Pesquero. Gray-green jadeite, h. 8.9 cm; w. 3.1 cm; d. 5 cm. (Private collection.)

identified as bloodletters. Peter T. Furst pointed out that this category may be too all encompassing and that many of these objects may, in fact, be weaving picks.[54] Two, however, are unquestionably ritual bloodletters. The first has a blade carved to represent a stingray spine (figure 18.10; cat. no. 77), a preferred bloodletting instrument since it came from the underwater otherworld. The second, beautifully carved from blue-green jade, lost its pointed end sometime in antiquity (figure 18.11; cat. no. 78). An incised line for a beak and the ubiquitous "flame eyebrows" identify the handle as an avian zoomorph. The handle carries secondary, incised information about the ideological function of blood in Olmec religion. The underside is incised with a four-dots-and-bar motif, an abstract symbol of the terrestrial Olmec Dragon – the earth (figure 18.12; cat. no. 78).[55] The now broken point of this bloodletter drew forth the magical fluid – blood – that opened a path of communication between the two cosmic realms.

The Earthly Realm

Iconographic investigations reveal that the Olmec Dragon, like later Mesoamerican primordial monsters, floated on the surface of the waters of creation.[56] In some titanic struggle in the mythic past, the body of this great leviathan was broken apart to form the earth and sky realms.[57] The terrestrial aspect of this saurian supernatural – represented as a full-figure in monumental sculpture, and in abstract form on Early

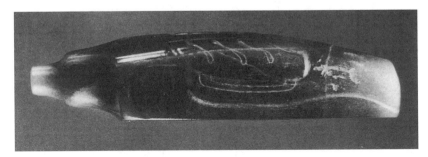

Figure 18.11 Perforator Handle, 900–600 BC, Guerrero. Blue-green jade, h. 1.2 cm; w. 7.2 cm; d. 2.5 cm. (Anonymous loan to The Art Museum, Princeton University.)

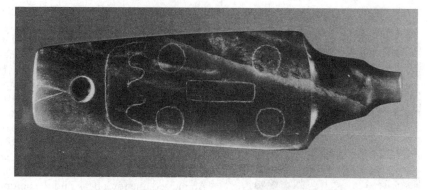

Figure 18.12   Incisions on the underside of figure 18.11.

Formative ceramics – is a dominant theme in Middle Formative sculpture and ceramics.[58]

The largest full-figured sculptural depiction of the Olmec Dragon is La Venta Monument 6, a sandstone sarcophagus (length 2.8 meters, width 0.96 meters, height approximately 0.86 meters) carved sometime around 400 BC in the form of the Olmec terrestrial dragon (figure 18.13).[59] Shown floating on the primordial waters of creation, split-stemmed vegetation emerges from its back. The La Venta ruler buried in this sarcophagus was literally interred within the body of the Olmec Dragon itself.

While not all Olmec dragons are equipped with distinct physical attributes, many have ones occurring with enough frequency they can be considered definitive. Among these are backward L-shaped eyes on dragons viewed in profile, trough-shaped eyes on dragons viewed frontally, and eyes topped with flame eyebrows. The dragons' locomotion is supplied by the hand-paw-wing motif (figure 18.14). Olmec dragons have few teeth and gumlines with downturning brackets.

Inturning gum brackets, except when descending fangs are explicitly depicted, are standard equipment on zoomorphic earth monsters. Gum brackets are also prominent in the *pars pro toto* representations of the Olmec Dragon. A line of gum brackets came to represent the surface of the earth itself in Middle Formative Olmec-style sculptural compositions, for example, the rock carving from the site of San Isidro Piedra Parada, El Salvador (figure 18.15). Ultimately, a single inturning gum bracket symbolized the surface of the earth, as on both an incised tablet and incised vessel (figure 18.16; cat. nos 131, 198).

The great, gaping maw, a feature of most frontal Olmec dragons, could function as the portal between the natural and

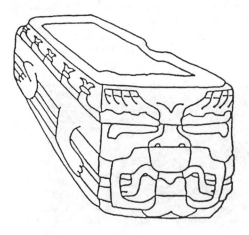

Figure 18.13   La Venta Monument 6 in the form of the Olmec terrestrial dragon.

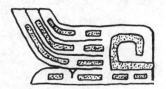

Figure 18.14   Hand-paw-wing motif from a ceramic vessel from Tlatilco.

Figure 18.15 Carved relief at San Isidro Piedra Parada, El Salvador.

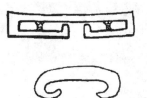

Figure 18.16 Details of an Incised Tablet (bottom) and Vessel (top).

Figure 18.17 Chalcatzingo Monument 9, 700–500 BC?, Chalcatzingo, Morelos. Granodorite, h. 183 cm; w. 142 cm; d. 15.2 cm. (Munson-Williams-Proctor Institute Museum of Art, Utica, New York.)

supernatural divisions of the Olmec cosmos.[60] Supernatural gateways thus served as paths of access to and communication with supernatural power. In the highland areas of Middle Formative Mesoamerica, the gaping maw was frequently quatrefoil-shaped. Monument 9 from Chalcatzingo is a superb illustration of the frontal view of this gaping maw (figure 18.17; cat. no. 37).

The Sky Realm

For Mesoamericans, the celestial realm was closely related to the underworld/otherworld, which they also conceived of as an underwater domain. The exquisite renderings of fish, ducks, turtles, and other aquatic creatures, hallmarks of Early Formative ceramics, are almost certainly metaphors of this underwater/otherworld (cat. nos 52–6, 60). The presence of these zoomorphic vessels in tombs at the sites of Tlatilco and Las

Bocas in the Mexico-Puebla highlands indicates that the tombs and their contents were regarded as gateways to the underwater/otherworld.[61] I believe future research will show that the dwarfs, fetuslike creatures, and hunchbacks who inhabited this otherworld had their counterparts in the celestial realm as well.[62]

The celestial/otherworld domain was also symbolized by a zoomorphic supernatural, the celestial dragon which, like its terrestrial counterpart, was artistically rendered in either a full-figured, abstract, or *pars pro toto* representation. Occasionally both of these zoomorphic supernaturals are shown together: a ceramic vessel from the Valley of Mexico Formative period site of Tlapacoya has carvings of the Olmec Dragon in both its sky and its earth manifestations (figure 18.18). The frontal and profile views of the Olmec dragons on the Tlapacoya vessel are similar in several respects. Most details in the frontal view can be matched with those in the profile view. They share crested eye ridges, gum bracket markings in their mouths, and nostril configuration. The

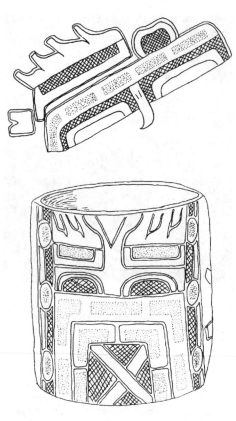

Figure 18.18   Ceramic vessel from Tlapacoya with frontal and profile view of the Olmec Dragon.

frontal image has trough-shaped eyes and the profile, backward L-shaped eyes. One interesting problem was how to render the prominent cleft between the eyes on the frontal view in the profile view. This was solved by disengaging the cleft from the profile image and rotating it behind the head as a separate element.

The crossed-bands motif, present only in the mouth of the frontal image on the Tlapacoya vessel, is noticeable on many Olmec dragons with strong sky realm associations. In the Classic Maya iconographic system, the crossed-bands, if not the hieroglyph for the sky itself, symbolizes a celestial location. In a remark made to Coe, Charles Smiley suggested that the crossed-bands is a symbolic replication of the crossing point of the ecliptic and the Milky Way.[63] If true, the

crossed-bands would symbolize the center of the sky.

The crossed-bands appears most frequently in Olmec-style art on pectorals and on the front pieces of belts worn by both humans and anthropomorphic supernaturals (figure 18.19; cat. no. 143). It also often occurs as a body marking associated with Olmec celestial dragons. On the Tlapacoya ceramic vessel, the crossed-bands on the frontal but not the profile Olmec Dragon indicates more than a stylistic variation. Furthermore, some Early Formative abstract dragons have the crossed-bands and others do not. Because of its strong celestial associations, the crossed-bands in

Figure 18.19   Standing Figure Holding Crossed-Bands, 900–600 BC, Guerrero. Light green serpentine, h. 7.8 cm; w. 4 cm; d. 3.5 cm. (Private collection.)

the mouth of the frontal dragon on the Tlapacoya vessel most likely suggest that this creature is a sky beast.[64] Chalcatzingo Monument 5 is certainly a full-figured Olmec sky dragon: it is not only marked with the crossed-bands, but floats above a motif (the Lazy-S) recently shown to be the symbol of a celestial location (figure 18.20).[65]

The placement of the celestial monster in paired opposition with the profile image on the Tlapacoya vessel probably can be read as a cosmic diagram of the earth and sky. Since the crossed-bands is a specific sky location or celestial marker, the Olmec Dragon is either two separate creatures or a single monster with both terrestrial and celestial aspects.[66]

Another celestial motif on the Olmec Dragon is the diamond-shaped symbol named and identified by Coe in its Formative period context as a star glyph, the ancestor of the Maya Venus/Lamat hieroglyph (figure 18.21a).[67] A potsherd from Tlapacoya dramatically illustrates this association of the celestial symbol with the Olmec Dragon (figure 18.21b). The incised frontal supernatural image, with its almond-shaped eyes surrounded by trough eyes and flame eyebrows, has, in the middle of its face, a symbol identical to the Maya Lamat glyph instead of a mouth and nose. More recently, Coe's astral interpretation of this diamond-shaped star symbol has been dramatically

confirmed by a ceramic bottle from the Middle Formative region of Puebla (Las Bocas) on which six diamond-shaped elements marking the sinuous body of a bicephalic supernatural prove to be ancestral to the double-headed serpent ecliptic monsters of Classic Maya cosmology (cat. no. 107).

In its *pars pro toto* representation, the Olmec celestial realm can appear as a sky band, with repeated inward-angled horizontal bands derived from the frontal Olmec Dragon's V-shaped cleft (figure 18.22a). Just as for the earth the symbol can be a single row of gum brackets, so for the sky it can be a series of V-shaped clefts.

On La Venta Stela 1 (figure 18.22b) the Olmec Dragon's abstracted open mouth has become a portal in which a single figure

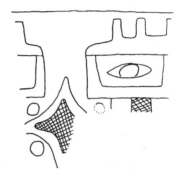

Figure 18.21b Incised frontal image of Olmec celestial dragon from a potsherd from Tlapacoya.

Figure 18.20 Chalcatzingo Monument 5, the Olmec sky dragon.

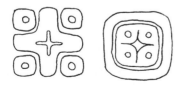

Figure 18.21a Maya Venus/Lamat hieroglyph.

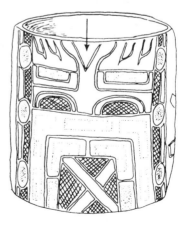

Figure 18.22a Incised vase from Tlapacoya showing Olmec Dragon with V-shaped cleft.

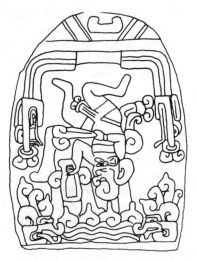

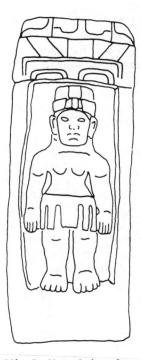

Figure 18.23a Izapa Stela 23, figure falling from a sky band.

Figure 18.22b La Venta Stela 1, figure standing in the open mouth of the Olmec Dragon.

stands. The cleft in the top register of this composition is a single pair of inward-angled horizontal bands. A striking example of the fusion of the full-figured Olmec celestial dragon and the horizontal bands sky symbol is seen incised on an enormous jade bead (cat. no. 211). Here, the Olmec celestial dragon carries the bands sky symbol on its back in much the same way the later Classic Maya sky dragon carries celestial symbols.

By the Late Formative period (300 BC–AD 1) the bands sky motif is used to identify the location of celestial events, for example, on the monuments of Izapa. On Izapa Stela 23 from Izapa Stela Group 1, a figure falls from a sky band (figure 18.23a). From this sky band a bicephalic ecliptic monster is hung. On Stela 2 from Izapa Stela Group 5, a celestial bird falls from an identical sky band (figure 18.23b). However, on Stela 60 from the same group, the sky band has migrated to the bottom of the composition and the celestial bird kneels on top of it

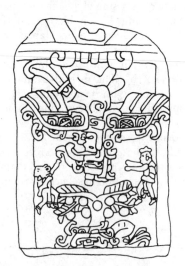

Figure 18.23b Izapa Stela 2, celestial bird falling from an identical sky band.

(figure 18.23c).[68] Undoubtedly, the action should be understood as taking place in the sky realm.

The *Axis Mundi* as the World Tree

All shamanic cosmologies have an *axis mundi* linking the celestial, terrestrial, and underworld realms. In the New World, the

Figure 18.23c Izapa Stela 60, celestial bird kneeling on top of sky band.

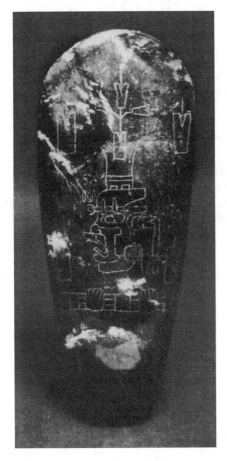

Figure 18.24 Incised celt, 900–600 BC, Río Pesquero. Jade, h. 24.8 cm; w. 10.2 cm. (Private collection.)

concept of the world tree as *axis mundi* is not limited to the pre-Columbian populations of Mesoamerica. Many Native American groups, including modern Maya populations and Zoque communities in Chiapas, still possess a cosmology in which the world tree functions prominently.[69] The *axis mundi* is no less fundamental to Olmec and Middle Formative cosmology and political validation. The world tree is rendered either as an upended saurian supernatural whose tail or upper body sprouts vegetation or, more naturalistically, as a sprouting maize plant. In *pars pro toto* representations, the world tree is reduced to a trefoil worn in the headdresses of Middle Formative supernaturals and rulers (figure 18.24). The wearers are thus identified as occupants of the cosmic center and the interface of the natural and supernatural oppositions in nature. The saurian world tree must have emerged from constant recombinations of the symbols of the Olmec Dragon. An upended saurian appears as the world tree on a Middle Formative serpentine statue referred to as the "Young Lord" (figure 18.25; cat. no. 193).

Fusing the Images of the Ruler and the World Tree

Middle Formative political validation was obtained by ritually defining the political leader as the world tree. In Olmec cosmograms where the world tree/ruler is central, the other four points are identified as sprouting maize seeds.[70] An example of this five-point cosmogram/political validation is incised on a Middle Formative jade celt from the heartland site of Río Pesquero (figure 18.26). The central point of this cosmogram is a human figure wearing a buccal mask and a headdress topped by a bifurcated fringe, perhaps feathers, from which trefoil vegetation emerges.[71] Virginia M. Fields researched the origins of this trefoil in the center of the Classic Maya royal headband, determining that its real-life source is maize. She also suggested that the two pairs of sprouts flanking the central trefoil of the Maya headband are maize seeds.[72]

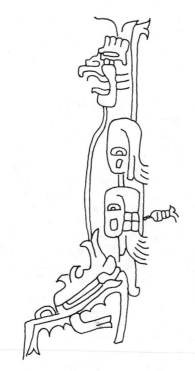

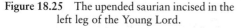

Figure 18.25 The upended saurian incised in the left leg of the Young Lord.

Figure 18.26 Incised jade celt from Río Pesquero.

More recently, Schele has hypothesized that two types of vegetation are the sources for the symbols in the royal headdress.[73] Working from a suggestion by Matthew Looper, Schele believes that the trefoil is derived from a dicot, specifically, beans or squash, and that the four flanking elements, as Fields suggested, are a sprouting monocot – in this case, maize.[74] Building on a proposal of Freidel, Schele concluded that the vegetative elements "not only encompass the major components of the food production system – that is, corn as monocot, beans and squash as dicots, and cuttings of fruit and nut bearing trees – but they also are associated with the major methods by which plants are hybridized in the process of domestication. These are cross-fertilization and grafting."[75] Another of Freidel's observations adds an important shamanic aspect to this pattern of rulership and vegetative symbolism, Schele further stated: "In the archaic hunter-gatherer societies that

preceded the Olmec, the individuals that were responsible eventually for the domestication of plants were shamans and *curanderos*. They were the ones who kept track of plant lore and who regularly planted and harvested those plants important to their craft." Freidel set forth that the shamans' and *curanderos*' domestication of plants resulted in the special role of sprouts and plant husbandry in the symbolism of Olmec rulership and later royal symbolism.[76]

As we have seen, the world tree has reptilian as well as maize associations. The connection between the standing figure on the Río Pesquero celt and the upended saurian world tree is made clear on examining the lower part of the standing figure's body closely. This reveals that his legs are inset with the flame eyebrows, backward L-shaped eyes, protruding nostril, and gum brackets identified with the upended Olmec dragon in his role as the upended crocodilian world tree. Thus, the body of this ruler is incorporated into the upended crocodilian world tree itself.

To demonstrate that this ruler occupies the center of the five-point cosmogram, it is necessary to reinterpret the incised image by European conventions of spatial illusion. Shadows give the incised images real dimensions, making the central position of the ruler obvious; the corners marked by the cleft and sprouting maize seeds become the other four directions (figure 18.27). The legs of the standing figure also form the mouth of the upended crocodilian world tree, offering further proof that the standing figure is the interface between the natural and supernatural.

Among depictions of the world tree in the iconography of Middle Formative cosmology and rulership, the saurian, while important, is not the dominant form. The world tree is most often rendered as cruciform-shaped vegetation, sprouting from the heads of anthropomorphic figures on the surface of celts or appearing in cruciform-shaped arrangements of celts. At La Venta, celts in this cruciform shape were buried as caches beneath ritual space. These deposits

marked the cosmic stage on which the Olmec ruler performed the rituals of both the *axis mundi* and the shamanic trance journey into the otherworld.

The Shamanic Trance-Journey (or Flight) Costume

The elaborate clothing worn by an enthroned individual in Mural 1 on a cliff face above the north grotto at Oxtotitlan Cave identifies the painting's subject: a specific moment in a shamanic flight or cosmic travel ceremony (figure 18.28). Large (width 3.8 meters by height 2.5 meters) and remarkably well preserved (considering it has been exposed to the elements for some twenty-seven hundred years), the Oxtotitlan mural is located with other paintings in a series of shallow grottos near the city of Chilpancingo, Guerrero.[77] The Oxtotitlan murals join those of Juxtlahuaca Cave, also in Guerrero, as the only known examples of large-scale Formative period polychrome paintings.[78]

Enough of Oxtotitlan Mural 1 has survived to allow an excellent reconstruction by the Mexican artist Felipe Dávalos. The enthroned figure's most striking article of costume is his complex bird helmet or mask,

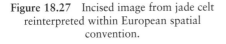

Figure 18.27 Incised image from jade celt reinterpreted within European spatial convention.

Figure 18.28 Drawing of the polychrome mural above the grotto at Oxtotitlan Cave, Guerrero.

which was once physically connected to a feather cape and backrack. The resemblance of the bird helmet's features to an owl's is too striking to go unmentioned. The iris of the hollowed-out, large round eye, Grove suggested, "once held an object such as a piece of jade or a polished magnetite mirror." This owl mask is cut away in shamanic X-ray style to provide a view of the human face under the mask, leaving no doubt in the mind of the beholder that this is a human in ritual costume, not a zoomorphic supernatural.[79]

The rest of the costume reiterates the avian theme. A feathered cape suspended from the arms replicates the wings of a bird. Both the down-pointing right hand and arm and the uplifted left arm are hung with what are almost certainly jade bracelets, with bands to which the feathered cape is attached. When the arms are outstretched, these allow the cape to spread like the wings of a bird. Behind the seated individual is a backrack with an intricate feathered-tail assemblage. Around his waist is an apron or loincloth hanging over a brown, possibly hide, skirt, which is painted with two hand-paw-wing motifs, each containing an inturning spiral. The association between the hand-paw-wing motif and the inturning spiral and avian themes serves to identify this figure as a cosmic flier, which is further

supported by the crossed-bands pectoral on the chest.

The throne on which this cosmic flier sits is made up of three zoomorphic faces. The eyes of the upper, frontal face, which is the best preserved, are marked with the crossed-bands, a strong indication this zoomorph is a variant of the Olmec sky dragon, and are framed by eyebrows identical to those on the throne, Monument 22, in the sunken patio at Chalcatzingo (figure 18.29).[80] From the upper jaw, two downturned fangs descend. Between the two fangs runs a striped, horizontal band, undoubtedly a sky band. At Oxtotitlan and on La Venta Altar 4, the horizontal band motif identifies the seats as sky thrones. Though the incised motifs on the upper register, or ledge, of Chalcatzingo Monument 22 are badly damaged, some form of banding, though not horizontal, also appears to have existed on this monument. However, in the case of the Chalcatzingo throne zoomorph, the eyes are not marked with the crossed-bands, which suggests that it is the Olmec earth dragon. The features of the other two zoomorph faces, which form the "legs" of the Oxtotitlan throne, have been obscured by the ravages of time, but in each case at least an eye and a blunt fang are visible. Overall, the Oxtotitlan throne is strikingly similar to a supernatural image incised on a

Figure 18.29   Monument 22, throne in sunken patio of Chalcatzingo, Morelos.

stone bowl from Xochipala (figure 18.30). The Oxtotitlan throne may well originally have had a fourth face like the image on the Xochipala bowl, but the mural is too badly damaged in its lower section to allow such a reconstruction.

The mouth of the tricephalic throne monster in Oxtotitlan Mural 1 is actually formed by the grotto beneath. Grove reports that "in times past the cave contained lagoons of water during the rainy season; on occasion this water would overflow the mouth of the cave and cascade into the fields below."[81] The enthroned figure's legs dangle over the edge of the throne in what Anne-Louise Schaffer identified, in reference to the Maya, as the "posture of royal ease."[82] The figure at Oxtotitlan is depicted at the precise moment before he will lift off and fly through the thin membrane of the cosmic portal into another reality.

La Venta Altar 4 and the Olmec Heartland Shamanic Flight Costume

Sky thrones, like the one in Oxtotitlan Mural 1, played a critical role in Middle Formative iconography and the ritual accouterments of shamanic flight. No single throne exemplifies this concept more than La Venta Altar 4, a truly monumental example of heartland sculpture (height 160 centimeters, width 319 centimeters, depth 190 centimeters), first identified as a royal seat or throne by Grove (figure 18.31).[83] Now that Olmec altars are recognized as the seats or thrones of Olmec rulers, it makes sense that they would also be used to convey the iconography of rulership, which would support a heartland origin for much of the Olmec-style symbol system.

The central image on the front of La Venta Altar 4 is a life-size human figure seated cross-legged in a niche surrounded by a ropelike element, attached to which are four symbols that have been interpreted as plants. This interpretation may be correct – the four symbols are positioned similarly to the four elements of sprouting vegetation at the corners of Chalcatzingo Monument 9 – but the symbols could also be plates with smoking jars or incense burners placed in them. A pattern has been established

Figure 18.31 Front of La Venta Altar 4.

Figure 18.30 Incised bowl, 900–600 BC, Xochipala, Guerrero. Stone, h. 6.4 cm; diam. 15.5 cm. (Private collection.)

associating such plates with elite burials at both La Venta and Chalcatzingo.[84]

The La Venta Altar 4 figure, like his Oxtotitlan counterpart, wears an intricate, raptorial avian helmet or headdress. Whereas the Oxtotitlan helmet covers the wearer's face completely and uses the X-ray style to reveal the human face beneath the mask, La Venta Altar 4's avian helmet is tied to the wearer's head with a strap but it does not have a mask. The human features are thus visible beneath what would have been the avian beak. Grove is convinced, and I concur, that the elaborate crest on the back of the bird helmet pinpoints the species as the harpy eagle (*Harpia harpyja*).[85]

In Postclassic Mesoamerican iconography, the harpy eagle is affiliated with the sun and human sacrifice.[86] Owls, on the other hand, are nocturnal birds, messengers between the supernatural realm and human beings.[87] Considering the day and night associations of these two avians incorporated into the shamanic flying costumes at two Middle Formative sites – the owl at Oxtotitlan and the harpy eagle at La Venta – an opposition between day and night at these sites may have been incorporated into the shamanic flight costumes of the rulers.

La Venta Altar 4's niche figure holds the end of a rope in his right hand; the end of another rope passes under his left knee. The rope held in his right hand goes around the side of the altar where it ends tied around the wrist of a seated human figure, whose facial features have been recarved in modern times (figure 18.32). The left side of the altar is too extensively damaged to determine whether there was a counterpart to the figure on the right side. Grove argues that the rope symbolizes kinship and ancestral or lineage relationships.[88] However, the fact that the rope is tied around the seated figure's wrist and not held in his hand and that his other hand is held across his chest in a posture of submission leads me to conclude that he is a captive whose blood will open

Figure 18.32   Right side of La Venta Altar 4.

the supernatural ritual in which the central figure participates.

The altar's ledge, which overhangs the seated central figure, is incised with five identifiable symbols: a double merlon motif at each corner; a sky band; an earth band; and, overlapping both the sky and earth bands, the head of a feline, perhaps a jaguar, who holds the crossed-bands in his open mouth. The ledge as a whole is a one-dimensional cosmic model. Within this, the function of the sky and earth bands is self-evident, but what of the double merlon, jaguar, and crossed-bands motifs?

The double merlon motif can mark the entrance or portal to the supernatural otherworld as well as the Olmec sacred mountain and the otherworld contained within.[89] The double merlons on the corners of this ledge in effect mark those corners and perhaps Altar 4 itself as the location of portals. The jaguar with the crossed-bands in his mouth is best understood if we keep in mind that Altar 4, like its Oxtotitlan and Chalcatzingo counterparts, is a throne. In Oxtotitlan Mural 1, the zoomorphic throne is shown with its occupant. In order to view La Venta Altar 4 in the same light, we can imagine the life-size central figure from the niche seated atop Altar 4, directly above the frontal jaguar (figure 18.33).

Figure 18.33   Top of La Venta Altar 4.

La Venta Altar 4 is thus both a throne and a cosmological model. The throne visualizes the Olmec ruler as the interface between the natural and supernatural realms. The feline/jaguar, the ruler's animal spirit companion, is his means of locomotion in his trance journey into the other world. Peter T. Furst, in his article first identifying the shamanic content of Olmec art and ideology, discussed several South American myths in which jaguars are the instrument of human travel to the otherworld.[90] He observed that the seat or stool on which a Yecuana shaman sits while performing nocturnal curing rituals is carved in the shape of a jaguar. The felines on Altar 4 and La Venta Monument 59, which I discuss below, can also be interpreted as jaguar-shaped shaman's stools. On Altar 4, the fact that the feline image overlaps both the sky and earth bands and holds the crossed-bands motif in his mouth underscores his role in supernatural travel.

Without a more explicit example of a jaguar throne, my conjecture would remain simply that. Happily for my argument, such a throne exists: La Venta Monument 59 (height 95 centimeters, width 65 centimeters, length 113 centimeters), a three-dimensional, snarling supernatural jaguar with a ledge on its back (figure 18.34). Undoubtedly, Monument 59 is a three-dimensional depiction of the jaguar carved on the ledge of Altar 4.

My interpretation of Altar 4's symbolic function is further confirmed by a small carved jade showing a supernatural being transported on the back of a sinuous feline (figure 18.35; cat. no. 63).[91] In this case, the supernatural rides his feline transporter, holding onto its tail for dear life. The round shape of this feline's ears is identical to that of the feline's on the ledge of Altar 4.

Another carved jade, the handle of a jade blood-letter, has a thematically similar scene (figure 18.36). Here, the transporter is marked with what appear to be dragon more than feline characteristics. The human figure stretched out on his stomach along the supernatural's back clings to its

Figure 18.34   La Venta Monument 59.

head to keep from being thrown off. On each of these two carved jades, a supernatural aids in the action of cosmic flight.

Returning to the throne in Oxtotilan Mural 1, I am convinced the three zoomorphs with their crossed-bands eyes are supernatural transporters and portals. Since La Venta Altar 4 is the same as the kind of throne depicted at Oxtotitlan, it was probably also a supernatural aid to cosmic flight. The flying costumes worn by Olmec rulers and other Middle Formative ritual practitioners underscore the importance of shamanic ideology to Middle Formative political validation.

The trance journey remains at the heart of shamanic ideology. The existence of diverse images such as the depictions of rulers wear-ing the shamanic flier and world tree costume suggests the possibility of regional and perhaps ethnic variations within the larger body of Middle Formative Olmec-style objects. The wide geographical range and the overarching theme of access to supernatural power and political validation conveyed by these objects reinforces my hypothesis that behind this tradition lay the Middle Formative Ceremonial Complex. Olmec-style objects first appeared in the Gulf Coast heartland of the archaeological Olmec, indicating that the complex originated with that people. With our knowledge of the iconographic content of Olmec-style art, we may soon be able to test a given geographical and linguistic area to see whether ideology and political structure were indeed based on this complex.

Figure 18.35 Supernatural Riding a Jaguar, 900–600 BC, Río Pesquero, Veracruz. Gray-green jadeite with a milky patina and a vein of softer mineral, h. 8.9 cm; w. 3.1 cm; d. 3 cm. (Private collection.)

Figure 18.36 Bloodletter handle, 900–600 BC, Mexico. Greenstone. (Private collection.)

NOTES

1 Richard A. Diehl, "Olmec Archaeology: What We Know and What We Wish We Knew," in *Regional Perspectives on the Olmec*, ed. Robert J. Sharer and David C. Grove (Cambridge, 1989), 23–6.

2 For a discussion of the Olmec/Mixe-Zoque connection, see Lyle R. Campbell and Terrence S. Kaufman, "A Linguistic Look at the Olmec," *American Antiquity* 41 (1976): 80–9.

3 Ibid., 26–31.

4 For a discussion of Olmec political organization, see Philip Drucker, "On the Nature of the Olmec Polity," in *The Olmec and Their Neighbors: Essays in Memory of Matthew W. Stirling*, ed. Elizabeth P. Benson (Washington, DC, 1981), 29–48.

5 For a discussion of the spread of monumental sculpture throughout large areas of Middle Formative Mesoamerica, see David C. Grove, "'Olmec' Horizons in Formative Period Mesoamerica: Diffusion or Social Evolution?," in *Latin American Horizons*, ed. Donald S. Rice (Washington, DC, 1993), 83–112.

6 Miguel Covarrubias argued early on for a Guerrero or Mixteca Alta genesis for the Olmec in *Indian Art of Mexico and Central America* (New York, 1957). Covarrubias's conclusions have been supported by Gillett G. Griffin of The Art Museum, Princeton University, and the Olmec scholar Carlo T. E. Gay.

7 David C. Grove, "Olmec: What's in a Name?" in *Regional Perspectives on the Olmec*, ed. Sharer and Grove (as in note 1), 8–14.

8 For the original proposal for the interaction sphere model, see Kent V. Flannery, "The Olmec and the Valley of Oaxaca: A Model For Inter-regional Interaction in Formative Times," in *Dumbarton Oaks Conference on the Olmec*, ed. Elizabeth P. Benson (Washington, DC, 1968), 79–110.

9 In an attempt to resolve this controversy, David Grove and Robert Sharer organized a symposium entitled "Regional Perspectives on the Olmec," at the School of American Research, Santa Fe, 1984, which ultimately led to the volume of essays by the same name (as in note 1), xix–xxiv.

10 For the original proposal for a Middle Formative Ceremonial Complex, see F. Kent Reilly III, "Cosmos and Rulership: The Function of

Olmec-Style Symbols in Formative Period Mesoamerica," *Visible Language* 24 (1990): 12–37. The term Middle Formative Period Ceremonial Complex arose from investigations to discover an archaeological model that would best describe what I believe happened in Formative period Mesoamerica. This model proved to be the Southeastern Ceremonial Complex, a label used to define the art style and ritual activity associated with it produced by the cultures of the eastern United States during the Mississippian period (AD 900–1600).

11 A technique developed primarily within the discipline of linguistics, structural analysis is fundamentally the identification of substitution sets. Because writing is absent from the cultures of the Middle Formative period, I propose a principle of iconographic substitution equivalent to the structural analysis used in linguistics. This principle argues that if two or more symbolic elements substitute for each other in a similar iconographic context, they probably carry similar – if not exactly the same – meanings.

12 For a discussion of the role of other ethnic groups within my proposed ceremonial complex model, see Joyce Marcus, "Zapotec Chiefdoms and the Nature of Formative Religions," in *Regional Perspectives on the Olmec*, ed. Sharer and Grove (as in note 1), 148–97.

13 Other unified, yet ethnically diverse, cultural or ideological expressions are those of the Hellenistic Levant, Christian Medieval Europe, and the spread of Islam and Buddhism across wide areas of Asia.

14 For the archaeological evidence for this change, see Grove (as in note 5).

15 See Tate, "Art in Olmec Culture," in *The Olmec World: Ritual and Rulership* (The Art Museum, Princeton University, Princeton, NJ), 47–68.

16 See Furst, "Shamanism, Transformation, and Olmec Art," ibid., 69–82.

17 Mircea Eliade, *Shamanism: Archaic Techniques of Ecstasy*, trans. Willard R. Trask, Bollingen Series 76 (Princeton, NJ, 1970), 259.

18 Stephen Houston and David Stuart, "The *Way* Glyph: Evidence for 'Co-Essences' among the Classic Maya," in *Research Reports on Ancient Maya Writing*, no. 30 (Washington, DC, 1989).

19 Linda Schele and David Freidel, *A Forest of Kings: The Untold Story of the Ancient Maya* (New York, 1990); Linda Schele, David Frei-

del, and Joy Parker, *Maya Cosmos: Three Thousand Years on the Shaman's Path* (New York, 1993).

20 K. C. Chang, *Art, Myth, and Ritual: The Path to Political Authority in Ancient China* (Cambridge, Mass., 1983), 44–55. A leading scholar on ancient China, Chang gives conclusive evidence in his chapter on "Shamanism and Politics" that Shang Dynasty Chinese rulers acted as chief shamans. According to Chang, the imperial ancestors spoke through the medium of the oracle bones, but the Shang emperor was the one who interpreted the symbols.

21 Joseph W. Kitagawa, *Religion in Japanese History* (New York, 1966), 3–45.

22 K. C. Chang, "An Introduction to Korean Shamanism," in *Shamanism: The Spirit World of Korea*, ed. Chai-shin Yu and Richard W. I. Guisso (Berkeley, 1988), 30–51.

23 Nevill Drury, *The Elements of Shamanism* (Longmead, England, 1989), 28–9.

24 John A. Grim, *The Shaman: Patterns of Religious Healing among the Ojibway Indians* (Norman, Okla., 1983), 41.

25 Ibid.

26 Eliade (as in note 17), 145.

27 Ibid., 156–8.

28 Schele, Freidel, and Parker (as in note 19), 75–107.

29 J. Eric S. Thompson, *Maya History and Religion* (Norman, Okla., 1970), 195.

30 For a more in-depth examination of the origins of shamanic art, see Andreas Lommel, *Shamanism, the Beginnings of Art* (New York, 1967); and Ann T. Brodzky, Rose Daneswich, and Nick Johnson, "Stones, Bones and Skin: Ritual and Shamanic Art," *Artscanada* (Toronto, 1977).

31 Esther Pasztory, "Shamanism and North American Indian Art," in *Native North American Art History: Selected Readings*, ed. Zena P. Mathews and Aldona Jonaitis (Palo Alto, Cal., 1982), 9.

32 Ibid.

33 Ibid.

34 Ibid., 17.

35 Robert Layton, *The Anthropology of Art* (New York, 1981).

36 Ibid., 170–1.

37 For a discussion of the chronology of Olmec sculpture, see Susan Milbrath, "A Study of Olmec Sculptural Chronology," *Studies in Pre-Columbian Art and Archaeology*, no. 23 (Washington, DC, 1979).

38 Miguel Covarrubias, "El arte 'Olmeca' o de La Venta," *Cuadernos Americanos* 28, no. 4 (1946): 153–79; and idem (as in note 6), 13–83.

39 Miguel Covarrubias, "Olmec Art or the Art of La Venta," trans. Robert Thomas Pirazzini, in *Pre-Columbian Art History: Selected Readings*, ed. Alana Cordy-Collins and Jean Stern (Palo Alto, Cal.), 1.

40 Covarrubias, *Indian Art* (as in note 6), 54.

41 Covarrubias, "Olmec Art or the Art of La Venta" (as in note 39), 4.

42 Ibid., 5.

43 Ibid., 4.

44 Ibid.

45 Covarrubias, *Indian Art* (as in note 6), 55.

46 Ibid.

47 Reilly (as in note 10), 12–37.

48 Peter David Joralemon, "The Olmec Dragon: A Study in Pre-Columbian Iconography," in *Origins of Religious Art and Iconography in Preclassic Mesoamerica*, ed. Henry B. Nicholson (Los Angeles, 1976), 27–71.

49 Ibid., 37–40.

50 Reilly (as in note 10), 30–4. This conflation of the cosmological divisions is not unknown in Mesoamerican art. It was a technique also used by the Classic period Maya (AD 200–900), the most striking example of which is the composition carved along the front edge of a bench discovered by David Webster at the site of Copan. Within this horizontal space, the Maya artist executed a cosmic model consisting of motifs and symbols representing the divisions of the cosmos into realms of sky, earth, and underworld. What the viewer has to understand is that the edge of the bench is carved to represent a vertically stacked model of sky over earth and earth over underworld. What the viewer actually sees are the symbols and motifs of the three cosmic realms laid out in a horizontal composition.

51 Joralemon (as in note 48), 37–40; F. Kent Reilly III, "Visions to Another World: Art, Shamanism, and Political Power in Middle Formative Mesoamerica," Ph.D. diss., University of Texas at Austin, 1994.

52 For a full definition of the Olmec Dragon, see Joralemon (as in note 48).

53 For a discussion of bloodletting among the ancient Maya, see Linda Schele and Mary E. Miller, *The Blood of Kings: Dynasty and Ritual in Maya Art* (Fort Worth, Tex., 1986); David Stuart, "Blood Symbolism in Maya Iconography," in *Maya Iconography*,

ed. Gillett G. Griffin and Elizabeth P. Benson (Princeton, NJ, 1988), 175–221.

54 Peter T. Furst, personal communication, April 1994.

55 For the linkage of the four-dots-and-bar motif with the Olmec Dragon, see Joralemon (as in note 48), 47.

56 Reilly (as in note 10), 12–37.

57 In Aztec mythology the primordial dragon was identified as Cipactli. While floating on the surface of the primordial sea, Cipactli is torn apart by Quetzalcoatl and Tezcatlipoca. These two deities create the earth from the lower part of Cipactli's body, the sky from the upper part. For a brief account of this myth, see B. C. Bundage, *The Fifth Sun: Aztec Gods, Aztec World* (Austin, Tex., 1979), 31–2.

58 Peter David Joralemon, "A Study of Olmec Iconography," *Studies in Pre-Columbian Art and Archaeology*, no. 7 (Washington, DC, 1971), 35.

59 For a full account of the excavation of La Venta Monument 6, see Matthew W. Stirling and Marion Stirling, "Finding Jewels of Jade in a Mexican Swamp," *National Geographic Magazine* 82 (1942): 635–61.

60 David C. Grove, "The Olmec Paintings of Oxtotitlan Cave. Guerrero, Mexico," *Studies in Pre-Columbian Art and Archaeology*, no. 6 (Washington, DC, 1970), 11, 32: Joralemon (as in note 48), 37–40.

61 In a personal communication (1992), Muriel Porter Weaver, who excavated at Tlatilco, informed me of the presence of several unfired examples of these aquatic, zoomorphic ceramic vessels in the tombs. She stated that their condition supports my interpretation that this category of ceramics was intended for tomb, not daily, use.

62 See Tate, as in note 15.

63 Charles Smiley in Michael D. Coe, "Olmec and Maya: A Study in Relationships," in *The Origins of Maya Civilization*, ed. Richard E. W. Adams (Albuquerque, NM, 1977), 189.

64 In Classic Maya art the sky was often depicted as a great, crocodilian-derived, zoomorphic supernatural. The Classic Maya cosmic monster is often marked with the crossed-bands motif as well as other celestial symbols. For a description of the Maya cosmic monster, see Schele and Freidel (as in note 19), 66.

65 Iconographic analysis of the recently discovered Monument 31 from the highland site of Chalcatzingo demonstrates for the first time that at least by the Middle Formative period,

the Lazy-S motif, like its Classic Maya counterpart, was associated with clouds, bloodletting, and a celestial location. Although the Lazy-S motif figures prominently in the iconographic corpus at Chalcatzingo, until the analysis of Monument 31 no context existed for its meanings. For a more complete analysis of the Lazy-S, see F. Kent Reilly III, "The Lazy-S: Evidence for a Formative Period Iconographic Loan to Maya Hieroglyphic Writing," in *Seventh Palenque Round Table, 1989*, ed. Merle Green Robertson (in press).

66 Joralemon summarizes the ideological implications of the dual nature of the Olmec dragon in "The Olmec Dragon" (as in note 48), 37–47.

67 Coe (as in note 63), 189.

68 The Izapan origin of the celestial bird iconographic complex is fully developed by Constance Cortez, "The Principal Bird Deity in Preclassic and Early Classic Maya Art," Master's thesis, University of Texas at Austin, 1986. Current investigations of the ideological function of the celestial bird (see Schele, Freidel, and Parker [as in note 19]) have determined that this supernatural is the avatar of Itzam-Na, the Classic Maya, primordial shaman deity. The image of the celestial bird – Itzam-Ye – on any man-made or supernatural object symbolizes that the object is animated and magical.

69 Susana Villasana Benitez, "La Organización social de los Zoques de Tapalap, Chiapas," in *Estudios Recientes en el Area Zoque* (Chiapas, 1988).

70 Throughout much of Mesoamerican cosmological thought was a perception of not one, but five world trees corresponding to the five world directions of east, west, north, south, and center. These five directional world trees served as conduits for the movement of supernatural power from one cosmic realm to another.

71 My current research leads me to believe that if the incised image on this celt is a human figure, then he wears the costume of the Middle Formative maize lord in his Milky Way manifestation.

72 In 1984 Virginia M. Fields was the first to link the Formative period three-pronged motif, or trefoil, to the Maya jester god headdress. The story of her discovery is told in two pivotal works in which she developed her hypothesis: "The Origins of Kingship among the Lowland Classic Maya," Ph.D. diss., University of Texas at Austin, 1989, and "The Iconographic Heritage of the Maya Jester God," in *Sixth Palenque Round Table, 1986*, ed. Virginia M. Fields (Norman, Okla., 1991), 167–74.

73 Linda Schele, "Sprouts and the Early Symbolism of Rulers in Mesoamerica," paper delivered at the Conference on Early Symbolism in the Writing of the Maya, Hildesheim, Germany, 1993.

74 Ibid.

75 Ibid.

76 Ibid.

77 David C. Grove was the first researcher to bring the Oxtotitlan murals to public attention in "The Olmec Paintings of Oxtotitlan Cave" (as in note 60).

78 The Juxtlahuaca Cave paintings and their identification as Olmec-style works of art was first proposed by Carlo T. E. Gay, "Oldest Paintings in the New World," *Natural History* 76 (1967): 28–35.

79 For a full discussion of the function of the "X-ray style" in shamanic art forms, see Lommel (as in note 30), 129–33.

80 William Fash, "The Altar and Associated Features," in *Ancient Chalcatzingo*, ed. David C. Grove (Austin, Tex., 1987), 82–94.

81 Grove (as in note 60), 31.

82 Anne-Louise Schaffer. "The Maya 'Posture of Royal Ease,'" in *Sixth Palenque Round Table*, ed. Fields (as in note 72), 203–10.

83 David C. Grove, "Olmec Altars and Myths," *Archaeology* 26 (1973): 128–35.

84 For a more complete discussion of the relationship between Middle Formative grave goods at Chalcatzingo and the burial practices at La Venta, see David C. Grove, *Chalcatzingo: Excavations on the Olmec Frontier* (New York, 1984), 75; Marcia Merry de Morales, "Chalcatzingo Burials as Indicators of Social Ranking," in *Ancient Chalcatzingo* (as in note 80), 95–114.

85 Grove (as in note 83): 130.

86 Joralemon (as in note 48), 52–8.

87 Mary Ellen Miller and Karl A. Taube, *The Gods and Symbols of Ancient Mexico and the Maya: An Illustrated Dictionary of Mesoamerican Religion* (New York, 1993), 128.

88 Grove (as in note 83): 130–4.

89 For a more complete discussion of the origin and function of the "double merlon" motif, see Elizabeth P. Benson, "An Olmec Figure at Dumbarton Oaks," *Studies in Pre-Columbian Art and Archaeology*, no. 8 (Washington, DC,

1971), 10 n. 2; F. Kent Reilly III, "Olmec Iconographic Influences on the Symbols of Maya Rulership: An Examination of Possible Sources," in *Sixth Palenque Round Table*, ed. Fields (as in note 72), 151–66.

90 Peter T. Furst, "The Olmec Were-Jaguar Motif in the Light of Ethnographic Reality," in *Dumbarton Oaks Conference on the Olmec*, ed. Elizabeth P. Benson (Washington, DC 1968), 151.

CHAPTER 19

Ancient Zapotec Ritual and Religion

An Application of the Direct Historical Approach

Joyce Marcus and Kent V. Flannery

This chapter is dedicated to José Luis Lorenzo, whose thoughtful advice in 1979 led to the discovery of the temple sequence below Structure 13 at San José Mogote

We see today a growing interest in cognitive approaches to archaeology, a genuine desire to reach back for the mental templates that underlie human behaviour. While this interest is surely commendable, we should guard against two possible negative outcomes. One such outcome would be the conversion of cognitive archaeology into a fad or a narrow speciality that ignores all other aspects of prehistory. The other would be the delusion that our search for the ancient mind is a recent advance for which our generation is solely responsible.

To avoid the first pitfall, we prefer to speak not of 'cognitive archaeology' but rather of 'holistic archaeology', a discipline in which cognitive variables would be given equal weight with ecological, economic and sociopolitical variables. As far back as 1976 we called for 'a framework for analysis which is neither a mindless ecology nor a glorification of mind divorced from the land' (Flannery and Marcus 1976a: 383).

To avoid the second pitfall, we remind ourselves that many previous generations of archaeologists were just as interested in topics such as ideology, cosmology, iconography and religion (e.g. Caso 1945, 1958; Thompson 1950, 1966, 1970, 1973). Consider, for example, the brilliant writings of Frankfort et al. (1946) on the mind of ancient Egypt and Mesopotamia nearly half a century ago. Even the so-called 'processual archaeologists' of the 1960s and 1970s, with their love of subsistence, optimal foraging, human ecology and locational analysis, did not always ignore the roles of ideology and cosmology in shaping human societies. To be sure, some archaeologists concentrated so hard on the way prehistoric societies provisioned themselves with food and *matériel* that they allowed the realm of the mind to be claimed by humanists.

When processual archaeologists – most of whom are anthropologists – waive their right to include cosmology and ideology in their reconstructions, one gets the kind of dichotomy which we have seen in Mesoamerica: anthropologists writing about

Reprinted from Joyce Marcus and Kent V. Flannery. 1994. Ancient Zapotec Ritual and Religion: An Application of the Direct Historical Approach. In *The Ancient Mind: Elements of Cognitive Archaeology*, edited by Colin Renfrew and Ezra B. W. Zubrow (Cambridge University Press, New York), pp. 55–74.

settlement and subsistence, while humanists write about religion and cosmology. And the humanists, for the most part, do not have the ecological and evolutionary perspective of the anthropological archaeologists. Thus we have Aztec gods like Tezcatlipoca and Tlaloc projected back onto Formative societies such as the Olmec (e.g. Covarrubias 1942; M. D. Coe 1973), and polytheistic state religions used as models for the early village religions which preceded them by 2,000 years (e.g. Joralemon 1971). In this paper, we will try to show that ideological and cosmological principles evolved (and were readapted over time) as Mesoamerican cultures went from egalitarian village societies to ranked societies or chiefdoms, and finally to urban civilizations.

No archaeologist who works for any length of time with the Indians of North, Middle, or South America can fail to see the important roles that religion, cosmology and ideology have played in shaping their societies (Marcus 1978). The problem comes when we try to decide by which *scientific method* we will study those subjects. It is simply not enough to rely on one's intuition and assert what we believe to be true, as some of our humanistic colleagues have done of late. Cognitive archaeology needs a methodology, just as 'settlement and subsistence archaeology' does.

Potentially, there are a number of methodological approaches that could be used. In this chapter, we will combine three which we feel suit the problem of ancient Zapotec ritual and religion. These approaches are (1) the Direct Historical Approach; (2) the analysis of public space and religious architecture; and (3) the contextual analysis of religious paraphernalia.

The Direct Historical Approach

Throughout the late nineteenth and early twentieth centuries, New World archaeologists used ethnographic data from elderly living informants, as well as ethnohistoric records, to interpret the archaeological sites they were excavating. For a long time this approach constituted a traditional method, although it had not been given a formal name.

Classic examples of the method can be found in Arthur C. Parker's *Archaeological History of New York* (1922); William Duncan Strong's *An Introduction to Nebraska Archaeology* (1935); and William A. Ritchie's two works, 'The Algonkin sequence in New York' (1932) and 'A perspective of northeastern archaeology' (1938). Finally, in an article entitled 'The Direct-Historical Approach in Pawnee archaeology', Waldo R. Wedel (1938) gave the approach its name.

The Direct Historical Approach (DHA) was seen as a way of working back in time from the known to the unknown, using ethnographic and ethnohistoric data to interpret prehistoric remains. For example, both Wedel and Strong used Pawnee ethnographic and ethnohistoric data to enhance their reconstructions of the protohistoric and Upper Republican cultures of Nebraska, which preceded the historic Pawnee. Archaeologists using the approach made it clear that they felt most comfortable with their reconstructions when they could show *continuity from the archaeological record to the ethnographic present* – in other words, when they could plausibly show that the same ethnic and linguistic group had continuously occupied the area from prehistoric to historic times.

It would be a mistake, however, to assume that the DHA only emphasizes continuity while ignoring change, even in such supposedly 'conservative' areas as ideologies, religious beliefs, and ritual institutions. The fact is that most American archaeologists, especially since the 1930s, have been concerned with both continuity and change. For example, Strong's (1933) paper on 'The Plains culture area in the light of archaeology' documents the way the introduction of the horse from Europe transformed Plains horticulturalists into mounted nomads. Indeed, one reason the approach was so widely used at that time is because so many archaeologists of Strong's generation were well-rounded anthropologists who knew ethnology and ethnohistory as well as they knew archaeology.

In southern Mexico, both Alfonso Caso (1932, 1966) and Ignacio Bernal (1949, 1958, 1965, 1966) used ethnohistoric data on the Zapotec and Mixtec of Oaxaca to enhance their reconstructions of prehistoric cultures in that region. The Valley of Oaxaca is one of those 'fortunate' areas (from the perspective of archaeology) where there was great continuity from prehistoric to Spanish Colonial times. In 1983, a group of our colleagues joined us in taking advantage of that continuity to trace the Zapotec and Mixtec civilizations out of their common ancestral culture (Flannery and Marcus 1983). In that symposium, we used a kind of DHA to the Oaxaca region, looking for both continuity and change through time.

One reason ritual and religion could be seen as appropriate themes for a DHA in Mesoamerica is that the ethnohistoric and ethnographic data from that region emphasize how conservative and slow to change those aspects of culture were. Within the realm of the sacred, a high premium was placed on maintaining tradition and preserving anachronisms. Despite long-term continuity, however, one can see adjustments being made over time as the sociopolitical infrastructure of society evolved.

Architecture and the Public Use of Space

A second approach to recovering cognitive information from prehistory lies in the study of changing patterns of public architecture or the use of public space, where many religious and ideological principles are expressed in physical remains (e.g. Flannery and Marcus 1976a, 1976b). For example, the careful excavation of a sequence of super-imposed temples at sites such as Kaminaljuyú (Kidder, Jennings, and Shook 1946), Uaxactún (Ricketson and Ricketson 1937; Smith 1950) and Tikal (W. R. Coe 1990) has given us data on the evolution of Maya temples and the range of activities that took place on their floors. Later in this chapter we will present a comparable sequence of temples from a secondary administrative centre within the Zapotec state centred at Monte Albán, Oaxaca.

Contextual Analysis of Ritual Paraphernalia

A third approach to the study of ancient ritual and religion is the 'contextual analysis' defined and described by Flannery (1976) for Formative Oaxaca villages. This type of analysis is based on Rappaport's (1979: 176) observation that ritual *must be performed*, and that to be valid it must be performed over and over again in certain prescribed ways. This means that those artefacts used in ritual should exhibit a pattern of use and discard which is non-random and yields insights into the nature of the ritual itself. In other words, although religious beliefs are mental constructs which cannot themselves be directly recovered archaeologically, those beliefs may direct ritual practices which are performed with artefacts that *can* be directly recovered. In this paper we will show that certain artefacts left behind in Zapotec temples reflect rituals of human and animal sacrifice which follow from the religious beliefs recorded in ethnohistoric documents.

Relationships Among Approaches

Let us now briefly review the three approaches used in this paper and the way in which they are related. First, our DHA begins with descriptions of the ideology, religion and ritual practices of the Zapotec of Oaxaca, Mexico, as they were described by the sixteenth-century Spaniards. This historic information gives us some insight into the cognitive world of the Zapotec, as well as certain expectations about the kinds of public buildings and ritual artefacts we might find in the archaeological record. We can then examine the archaeological record to see if, and when, such buildings and ritual paraphernalia appear, and whether their form and pattern fit our expectations.

It seems to us almost certain that some of our expectations will be met and others will not; it also seems likely that the archaeological record will contain unexpected types of information, for which the Spanish accounts do not prepare us. Resolving the contradictions between our ethnohistoric expectations and our archaeological observations will be one challenge of the method; another will be to decide whether those cases in which our observations and expectations fit are genuine continuities, or only superficial similarities.

Zapotec Ethnohistory

Sixteenth- and seventeenth-century documents written by the Spaniards (or by Indian nobles at the Spaniards' request) constitute a very rich body of material for the study of prehispanic philosophy, religion and ideology. Among these documents are (1) Spanish friars' accounts of 'pagan' religious practices such as human and animal sacrifices, incense burning and bloodletting; (2) dictionaries of indigenous languages, containing many religious and philosophical terms; (3) answers to standardized questionnaires (relaciones) elicited from indigenous nobles between 1579 and 1581 at the request of the Spanish throne; (4) prehispanic and early Colonial native maps on deer hide or cloth; and (5) prehispanic and early Colonial manuscripts (codices) that contain calendric, ritual, genealogical and pilgrimage data.

While these documents are rich in detail, their use requires a careful attempt to 'factor out' Colonial Spanish prejudices. After all, many of the Spaniards were missionaries whose goal it was to eliminate 'heathen' practices which they regarded as barbaric and repugnant. The Spaniards also had Classical Greco-Roman religion as their subconscious paradigm for 'pagan' beliefs, and tended to speak of things such as 'pantheons of gods' when they were more likely seeing lists of deified royal ancestors (Marcus 1978, 1983a, 1983b).

The principal ethnohistoric sources for Zapotec religion date from the sixteenth and seventeenth centuries, and were written by Spanish friars and administrators. First

and foremost as a source was Fray Juan de Córdova, who in 1578 published both a dictionary (Vocabulario en Lengua Zapoteca) and a grammar (Arte en Lengua Zapoteca) which contained important data on religion (Córdova 1578a, 1578b). His work built on that of his superior, Fray Bernardo de Alburquerque, who had arrived in Mexico around 1535. By 1540, Fray Alburquerque was the vicar of Tehuantepec and the city of Oaxaca. Fray Juan de Córdova joined Alburquerque in 1547 in the convent of Antequera (modern Oaxaca City). Both friars learned Zapotec well, since their conversion of the Indians required them to master the language in all its subtlety. Alburquerque wrote an important manuscript (Doctrina Cristiana en Lengua Zapoteca) which was never published, but was used by other friars in their sermons. Ultimately, Córdova was assigned to the convent at Teticpac (modern San Juan Teitipac), and later was named vicar at Tlacochahuaya in the Valley of Oaxaca (see figure 19.1).

A second source on Zapotec religion is the work of Fray Gonzalo de Balsalobre (1656; Berlin 1957; Marcus 1983b) who from 1634 to 1665 was a priest in what is today Sola de Vega, Oaxaca. Balsalobre recorded 'survivals of pagan beliefs', eliciting some of his data from a Zapotec cacique or native lord who had been baptized 'Diego Luis'.

A third source are the works of Fray Francisco de Burgoa (1670, 1674), whose two seventeenth-century books supply important data on Zapotec religion. Still a fourth major source are the well-known Relaciones Geográficas (Paso y Troncoso 1905: vol. 4), written between 1579 and 1581 by Spanish scribes who were completing questionnaires at the behest of Charles V of Spain.

Zapotec Religion

From the ethnohistoric sources given above, it appears that sixteenth-century Zapotec religion had at least four principal features. First, it was an animatistic religion, which attributed life to many things we consider inanimate. Second, it emphasized the

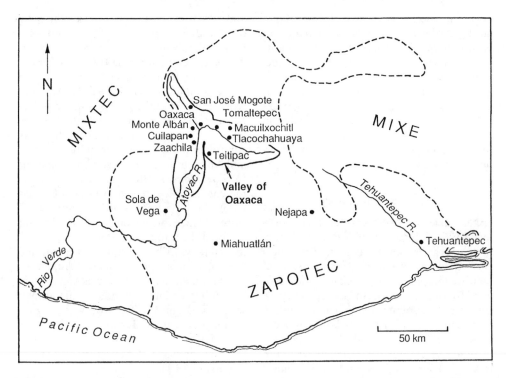

Figure 19.1 The heartland of Zapotec civilization was the valley of Oaxaca, Mexico, which lies some 380 km southeast of Mexico City at an elevation of 1,500 m. By the time of the Spanish Conquest, however, Zapotec speakers had spread northeast into rugged mountains, and south and east to the Pacific Coast. On this map, which gives localities mentioned in the text, the irregular dashed line separates the Zapotec from speakers of Mixtec or Mixe languages.

worship of natural forces, such as lightning and earthquake. Third, one of its fundamental components was reverence for human ancestors, especially royal ancestors. And fourth, man's relationship with great natural forces and supernatural phenomena was governed by reciprocity: each supernatural blessing required an appropriate sacrifice by the recipient.

Ironically, anthropologists have often associated most of these features with 'primitive' societies. Complex societies, such as chiefdoms and states, have often been assumed to have one of two kinds of religions – either monotheism or an elaborate pantheon of gods and goddesses, often in human form. These preconceptions are the result of our Greco-Roman bias and do not fit the religions of most prehispanic civilizations.

Natural and Supernatural Forces

The Zapotec had a concept of vital force that distinguished 'living' from 'nonliving' matter. They used the word *pèe* or *pi*, a word which can be translated as 'breath', 'spirit' or 'wind', to designate this vital force. Anything lacking *pèe* was considered inanimate and could be manipulated by technology, such as the irrigation systems used for rainwater after it had reached the ground. However, the clouds from which rain came were conceived of as animate, and therefore had to be approached through religious ritual.

Anything with *pèe* – a river in flood, the moon, the foam on top of a cup of hot chocolate, or a bolt of lightning – could move, and thus was considered alive and sacred. All items with *pèe* were deserving of respect and could not simply be manipulated; they had to be addressed respectfully during ritual, and a reciprocal relationship established with them.

The Zapotec addressed items with *pèe* by invoking the life force within them. For example, they used the expression '*Pitào Cociyo*'[1] or 'Great Spirit [within] Lightning' to petition Lightning to pierce the clouds, to send rain down to earth where it could be directly manipulated by humans; as long as the rain stayed up in the clouds, man could not utilize it for his own purposes. They used '*Pitào Xòo*' or 'Great Spirit [within] the Earthquake' when asking Earthquake to stop shaking the earth. In return for the granting of these requests, the Zapotec made appropriate offerings of their own blood, of incense, of food, of sacrificed animals and humans, and of non-perishable exotics such as jade, shell, obsidian and so forth.

Most deserving of respect were great universal forces, such as the lightning and earthquake mentioned above, and also fire, wind, hail and clouds (figure 19.2). In fact, clouds were regarded as the beings into which Zapotec ancestors – *penigòlazaa*,

Figure 19.2 Zapotec effigy vessel showing an anthropomorphic Cociyo, or Lightning, with 4 containers on his back (h. 15 cm). Ethnohistoric data suggest that these containers were for rain, wind, hail, and clouds, the major elements associated with Lightning. (Drawn from a photo in Caso and Bernal 1952: fig. 54.)

'old people of the clouds' – had metamorphosed after death. Royal ancestors, in particular, were thought to have the power to intercede with powerful supernaturals on behalf of their descendants on earth, but only if those earthly descendants made the appropriate offerings and petitions. Something was offered in anticipation of a request being met, and also in return for a concession. The kinds of offerings ranged from food and drink to one's own blood, a sacrificed quail, a turkey, a child or an adult human, depending on the request, the severity of one's need or the magnitude of one's gratitude. The smoke from burning incense was thought to rise upward until it eventually reached the clouds; so, too, did the smoke from a human heart burned in a charcoal brazier.

Just as the smoke from burning incense was a way of communicating with royal ancestors and supernatural beings, various narcotics were used by the Zapotec to communicate with the spirit world. One of these was *Datura* or *pinijchi-pitào* ('ghost of the great spirit'), with which the Spaniards said the Zapotec 'saw visions' (Marcus and Flannery 1978: 73–4). Others included tobacco (*Nicotiana* sp.) and hallucinogenic mushrooms (*Psilocybe* sp.), the latter generally taken only by very experienced religious specialists because an overdose could be toxic.

As the transformation of deceased royalty into clouds demonstrates, the concept of metamorphosis from one life form to another was an important concept in Zapotec philosophy and religion. Partially metamorphosed figures are frequently seen in Oaxaca art (figure 19.3), and an example from our own excavations will be given below.

Finally, some rituals among the Zapotec were calendrically scheduled. Like other Mesoamerican peoples, the Zapotec had two calendars, one secular (365 days) and one ritual (260 days). The 260-day ritual calendar was called the *piye*, a term whose initial phoneme suggests that it had *pèe* or vital force. Thus ritual time was alive, it moved, and its calculations were in the

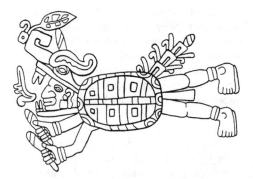

Figure 19.3 Flying 'cloud person' modelled in stucco on the wall of a late prehistoric tomb from Zaachila, Oaxaca. Sixteenth-century Oaxaca peoples conceived of the clouds from which ancestors had descended as flying turtles (Marcus 1983d: 195), which explains the turtle carapace of the flying figure.

hands of religious specialists. The 260-day calendar was divided into four equal parts called *cociyos* or 'lightnings', each 65 days long. Another name used for these 65-day periods was *pitào*, or 'great spirit'.

On a cosmological level, the Zapotec world was divided into four great quarters, each associated with a colour. The main axis of this division was the east–west path of the sun, the result being that many ancient maps have east at the top, and many temples face east or west.

Archaeologically Recoverable Features of Zapotec Religion

Before beginning our search for ritual or religious data in Oaxaca prehistory, let us consider those features of Zapotec religion that might be archaeologically recoverable. One of the most obvious would be the standardized two-room temple known as *yoho pèe*, 'sacred house' or 'house of the vital force'. At the time of the Spanish Conquest, such temples were manned by full-time priests. To the less sacred outer room came persons who wished to make an offering; the actual sacrifice would be performed by full-time specialists in the more sacred inner room. No layman was allowed to enter the inner room, while the priests rarely

left it (virtually 'living in it', according to ethnohistoric source).

The Zapotec priesthood had a hierarchy of high priests (*uija-tào*), ordinary priests (*copa pitào*), lesser religious personnel, and young men educated to enter the priesthood (*bigaña*). One seventeenth-century source (Burgoa 1674) says that the high priest or *uija-tào* had as his chief function the consultation with the supernatural on important matters, and then the transmitting of this information to his assistants and to others down the hierarchy. This high priest had the power to place himself into an ecstatic state (possibly with the aid of drugs), and he believed what he saw in his visions. The Zapotec ruler treated the high priest with great respect, principally because the latter had close contact with the supernatural and could see into the future. The ruler often turned to his high priest for advice and followed it diligently (Seler 1904: 248). Some of the high priests were, in fact, brothers or other relatives of the ruler.

Hierarchically below were other priests, also recruited from the nobility. At the lowest level were diviners (*colanij*), who probably were not always drawn from the nobility. These diviners usually interacted directly with the common people, helping them with individual decisions – whom to marry, when to marry, the naming of one's children, when to plant, etc. Such diviners took the decision-making out of the hands of the individual and left the decision up to 'fate' or 'fortune', whose will was determined by casting lots (often with maize kernels or beans) in groups of 2s, 3s, 4s, and so forth.

The ancient Zapotec distinguished between two kinds of blood: flowing blood (*tini*) and dried blood (*rini*). Flowing blood was preferred for a whole range of rituals, and it was collected on papers, feathers and other perishable items for inclusion in caches. While special priests sacrificed humans and animals, almost all Zapotec practised autosacrifice of small amounts of their own blood, using distinctive paraphernalia such as stingray spines, shark's teeth, obsidian lancets and leaf spines of maguey (*Agave* sp.) to perforate veins or skin. Some priests even let their fingernails grow long in order to use them as bloodletting instruments. When the act of bloodletting – removing blood from the fleshy parts of the body, especially the ears and tongue (Burgoa 1674) – was completed, the person would leave his bloodletting paraphernalia in a cache or in the temple itself. Since the blood itself was often caught on grass, feathers, papers placed in a basket, and other perishable materials, such offerings would be difficult to recover archaeologically. However, slips of bark paper similar to those used to catch drops of flowing blood have been found in the deposits of dry ritual caves (Moser 1983).

Many animals, including quail, turkeys, deer and dogs, were offered in sacrifice. Quail were considered especially appropriate for sacrifice because the Zapotec regarded them as 'clean' or 'pure' animals. That is because the Zapotec observed quail drinking from dew drops; even today, Zapotec who observe them doing so comment that quail 'will not drink dirty water'. In Oaxaca, the two quail most frequently encountered are the Montezuma quail (*Cyrtonyx montezumae*), which inhabits pine-oak forests, and the common Bobwhite (*Colinus virginianus*), which inhabits the weedy borders of maize fields (figure 19.4).

Figure 19.4   The two species of quail most often sacrificed in Zapotec temples. Left, the Montezuma quail (*Cyrtonyx montezumae*). Right, the common Bobwhite (*Colinus virginianus*). Both birds are 20–25 cm in total length.

Evidence for human sacrifice is also clear in the ethnohistoric record. For example, sixteenth-century information indicates that infants, children and adults were sacrificed to Lightning, the most powerful supernatural depicted in Zapotec art. Slaves and captives taken in war were the most common adult sacrifices, with specially-trained priests cutting out their hearts with leaf-shaped flint or obsidian daggers while the victim was still alive. This was done so that the heart would still be beating, i.e. it would still possess *pèe* when offered to Lightning.

The Zapotec accompanied their rituals with the burning of incense (*yàla*), believing that the aromatic smoke rose to join with the clouds in the sky above – an effective way to address one's ancestors so that they could intercede on one's behalf. The resin of the copal tree (*Bursera* sp.), which is native to the Valley of Oaxaca and much of southern Mexico, was a preferred incense.

Given this brief discussion, it should be clear what some of the archaeologically preserved evidence for ancient Zapotec religious ritual might be. First, we might expect to find two-room temples, often oriented to the east–west axis of the sun. Second, we should look for the braziers in which offerings of incense (and sometimes human hearts) were burned. Third, we should look for flint or obsidian daggers of the type used in human sacrifice, and for the kinds of smaller tools used in ritual bloodletting – stingray spines, shark teeth, obsidian lancets and so on. Fourth, we should look for the skeletal remains of those animals regarded as appropriate for sacrifice, such as quail, dogs, turkeys, deer and others. Fifth, we should look for the use of ritual drugs such as *Datura*, *Psilocybe*, or even *Nicotiana*, which might appear among the archaeological plant remains. Sixth, we should look for evidence of the 260-day *piye* or ritual calendar. Seventh, we should look for depictions of Lightning, Earthquake, and other supernatural beings in the art of the ancient Zapotec. Finally, we should look for evidence of ancestor worship and the metamorphosis of ancestors into *penigòlazaa* or 'cloud people'. If any or all of these features are present, it may be possible to reconstruct parts of ancient Zapotec religion by use of the Direct Historical Approach.

Obviously, some of the elements on this list are likely to be harder to find than others. There are also major unanswered questions about their relationships. When the Spaniards arrived, all these features were part of an impressive complex of religious practices engaged in by hundreds of thousands of Indians sharing a common language and political system. Did all the features of this complex appear at once, or did they appear one by one during the long archaeological record in Oaxaca? If the latter were the case, in what order did the features appear, and does that order tell us something about the course of Zapotec cultural evolution? Finally, does the archaeological record give us any additional information, not mentioned by the Spanish chroniclers of the sixteenth century? In the remainder of this paper, we look back over three millennia of Oaxaca prehistory in an attempt to answer those questions.

Early Evidence of Zapotec Ritual

As we look back over Oaxaca's archaeological record, we can see that the various elements of Zapotec religion did *not* all appear simultaneously. Some were in evidence almost as soon as permanent village life began, while others did not appear until after the state had formed. Moreover, even those elements which appeared early did not remain static over time; they were reworked and reinterpreted as ideologies changed with each stage of cultural evolution.

One of the first practices for which we have indirect evidence is the ritual use of narcotics. At least one of Oaxaca's early villages has a stratigraphic sequence of small public buildings which may be analogous to the 'men's houses' used by egalitarian village societies elsewhere (Flannery and Marcus 1990: 23–9). A significant feature of such buildings was a small, centrally placed circular pit filled with finely powdered lime (Flannery and Marcus 1990: fig.

2.3). This lime might have been stored for ritual purposes, such as mixing with narcotics like tobacco. The use of tobacco was widespread among the Zapotec, and is mentioned in sixteenth-century *relaciones* from Macuilxochitl, Miahuatlán, Nejapa and other places in Oaxaca (Paso y Troncoso 1905). Unfortunately, actual macrofossils of *Nicotiana* have not yet been found in archaeological contexts.

Prismatic obsidian blades of the type used for ritual bloodletting appear in the archaeological record by 1150 BC, but owing to the many purposes to which these tools could be put, they cannot be used as proof of bloodletting. A better case can be made for the stingray spines which appear between 1000 and 850 BC (figure 19.5a). In a previous contextual analysis of ritual paraphernalia, Flannery (1976) showed that during this period, autosacrifice had begun to reflect emerging hereditary inequality: relatively high-status individuals used genuine stingray spines, lower-status individuals used imitation stingray spines whittled from deer bone, and very high-status elites of the Mexican Gulf Coast used imitation stingray spines carved from jade (Flannery 1976: fig. 11.7). Now we can add the fact that between 700 and 500 BC, high-status individuals in both Oaxaca and the Valley of Morelos used imitation stingray spines chipped from large obsidian blades (see figure 19.5b and Parry 1987: 125–31).

It is also during the period 1150–850 BC that lightning first appeared in Oaxaca art. Marcus (1989) has suggested that certain designs on the pottery of this period reflect a dichotomy between sky and earth, with sky represented by lightning (the 'fire serpent' or 'sky dragon') and earth represented by the 'were jaguar' or 'earth monster'. As shown in figure 19.6, lightning could be represented as a realistic serpent with flames rising from his eyebrows, or by a stylized design where U-elements represent the serpent's gums and sine curves represent his eyebrow flames. While certain artistic representations of this supernatural force were specific to Oaxaca, they were apparently only local versions of what seems to

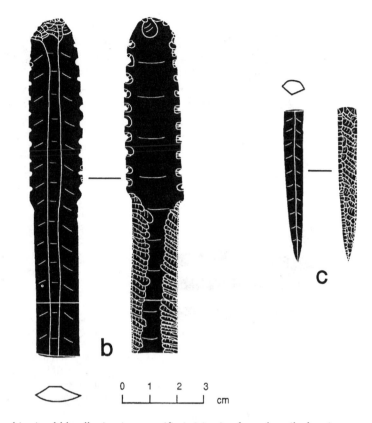

a

b

c

0 1 2 3 cm

Figure 19.5 Artefacts used in ritual bloodletting (autosacrifice): (a) spine from the tail of a stingray (family *Dasyatidae*), House 17, San José Mogote (900–850 BC). An attempt has been made to drill a hole in the base, presumably so that it could be worn round the owner's neck; (b) basal half of a large, broken, imitation stingray spine made from an obsidian blade, Structure 28 patio, San José Mogote (600–500 BC); (c) tip of an obsidian bloodletting lancet (600–500 BC). (b, c redrawn from Parry 1987: fig. 52.)

have been a pan-Mesoamerican motif (Marcus 1989). It would therefore not be accurate to refer to these early motifs as representing a specifically 'Zapotec' deity.

Another ritual behaviour of this period was the use of small, handmade pottery figurines to create ritual scenes. Because some of these figurines were posed in the most common burial position of the period, we have argued elsewhere that they may depict deceased ancestors (Flannery and Marcus 1976a). Even today, when such figurines are found by the Zapotec of Tehuantepec, they are referred to as *penigòlazaa*, 'old people of the clouds' (Marcus and Flannery 1978: 55; Marcus 1983b: 347). Assuming

that we have interpreted those figurines correctly, they would constitute our first evidence for the important role played by the ancestors in Zapotec religion.

Several new elements appeared between 700 and 500 BC, when the archaeological site of San José Mogote had become the largest settlement in the Valley of Oaxaca. By that time, San José Mogote was the ceremonial centre for a network of some 18–20 villages in the northern part of the valley, serving an estimated 1,300–1,400 persons. A carved stone monument located between two public buildings on the site's most prominent pyramidal mound gives us our oldest depiction of a human sacrificial victim,

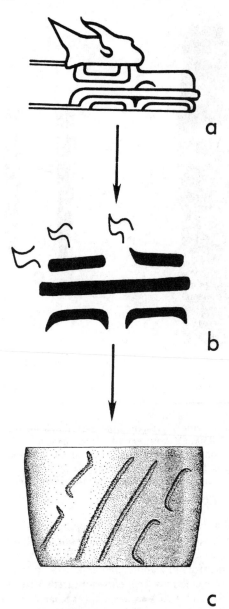

Figure 19.7 Top view and eastern edge of Monument 3 at San José Mogote, a carved stone which depicts a sacrificed individual with the date (or personal name) '1 Earthquake' between his feet. A ribbon of blood runs east from the complex scroll design on his chest and ends in two stylized drops which run down the edge of the stone.

Figure 19.6 Representations of the 'fire-serpent' or 'sky-dragon' in the art of 1150–850 BC: (a) shows a naturalistic representation found on pottery at sites near Mexico City; (b) shows an abstract version carved on pottery vessels in Oaxaca, where the serpent's gums become inverted Us and his eyebrow flames become simple curving lines; (c) shows a burial vessel from Oaxaca with an even more abstract version of (b).

possibly a captive taken in raiding (figure 19.7). The victim is shown naked but with a complex scroll covering his chest, possibly depicting blood issuing from an open wound like that made for removal of the heart during sacrifice. Between his feet are two hieroglyphs which give the day '1 Earthquake' in the Zapotec *piye* or 260-day ritual calendar (Marcus 1976). While this may be the personal name of the victim (taken from the date of his birth), its significance here is that it shows that by this period the ritual calendar was already in existence.

The Rise of the Zapotec State

A major turning point in Zapotec prehistory was the founding of Monte Albán, the fortified mountain-top city which, for roughly a millennium, was the capital of the Zapotec state (Blanton 1978). While Monte Albán was founded some time around 500 BC, it is not until its second archaeological period, Monte Albán II (200 BC–AD 100) that we see overwhelming evidence for the diagnostic characteristics of an archaic state.

During Monte Albán II, Monte Albán was a city of 416 hectares, with an estimated population of 10,650–19,000 persons. Below it was a hierarchy of settlements with at least four tiers: secondary administrative centres of up to 70 hectares, tertiary centres of 2–8 hectares, and more than 400 small farming villages with no apparent administrative functions.

At the top two tiers of this hierarchy were rulers who lived not merely in elite residences, but in actual palaces whose construction required corvée labour. At the top three tiers of the hierarchy there were standardized, two-room temples which fit the description of the Zapotec *yoho pèe*, or 'house of the vital force', seen at the time of the Spanish Conquest. Each consisted of a more sacred inner room, to which we presume only the priests had access, and a less sacred outer room, to which we presume other worshippers could come. Although both rooms had doorways flanked by columns (figure 19.8), the inner room had a narrower doorway and was reached only after a step up of 20–30 centimetres above the level of the outer room. At its peak, Monte Albán's Main Plaza may have had twenty such temples; San José Mogote, a secondary centre during Period II, had ten; and Tomaltepec, perhaps a tertiary centre, had a single temple.

Other archaeological manifestations of the Zapotec state were ball courts (more than one at the capital, usually only one at secondary centres); royal tombs with ceramic effigies of apotheosized royal ancestors at both the capital and secondary centres; and monuments at the capital commemorating military conquests. These monuments included a list of more than forty places evidently conquered by Monte Albán between 200 BC and AD 100 (Marcus 1980, 1983c: 106–8; 1988). Monte Albán – only one of several communities located on defensible hilltops during this period – had 3 kilometres of defensive walls built

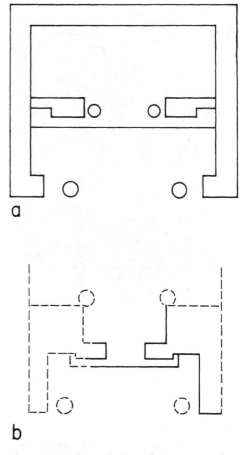

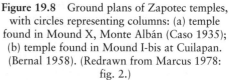

Figure 19.8 Ground plans of Zapotec temples, with circles representing columns: (a) temple found in Mound X, Monte Albán (Caso 1935); (b) temple found in Mound I-bis at Cuilapan. (Bernal 1958). (Redrawn from Marcus 1978: fig. 2.)

along the gentler and more easily climbed slopes of the mountain. In other words, by ca. 200 BC we are dealing with an urban, expansionist, militaristic state with royal families living in palaces, priests directing a state religion in standardized temples, and royal ancestor worship. By now the depictions of Lightning in Zapotec art were no longer generalized 'fire-serpents' or 'sky-dragons', but recognizable depictions of the powerful supernatural *Cociyo* (figure 19.9).

More temples have been excavated at Monte Albán than at any other Oaxaca

5 cm

Figure 19.9 By Period I of Monte Albán, according to Caso and Bernal (1952: 24), there were representations of Lightning which are recognizable as the supernatural Cociyo of Zapotec ethnohistory. This battered fragment of a larger vessel from the Valley of Oaxaca shows an anthropomorphic figure with a typical buccal mask, serpent tongue, flat nose, and gaping mouth of Cociyo; note also the heavy, serrated eyebrows, which probably evolved from the flame eyebrows of the earlier 'fire serpent'. At this early date (perhaps 300 BC) depictions of Cociyo did not yet have the protruding fangs of later versions like those shown in figure 19.16. (Drawn by John Klausmeyer, from an illustration by Abel Mendoza (Caso and Bernal 1952: fig. 26).)

site, but much of this excavation was carried out in the 1930s and 1940s and has never been published in detail. There is evidence that some temples had important offerings under their floors or in their foundations, perhaps left during 'rituals of sanctification' (Rappaport 1971, 1979) which converted secular ground into sacred ground. For example, in Mound 'g' – the pyramidal plat-

form for a temple of such limited accessibility that it may have been used only by the Zapotec royal family – archaeologists found two skeletons, probably both female, associated with a mother-of-pearl mosaic, two necklaces of greenstone and shell, and six pottery vessels. At a depth of 9.5 metres inside Building I – the platform for a more accessible temple in the Main Plaza – was a Monte Albán II offering inside a stone masonry 'offering box' typical of Zapotec temples. This offering included a necklace of marine shell, flower-shaped jade ear ornaments, two mosaic masks (one of jade and turquoise, the other of iron pyrite and shell), and a bone carved in the shape of a chess pawn (Flannery 1983: 103–4). Below and around the offering box were the remains of sacrificed birds, unfortunately never identified. It would be interesting to know if they included quail, doves, macaws or turkeys.

Even the temples at secondary centres, such as Cuilapan (Bernal 1958) and San José Mogote (see below) had important subfloor offerings. For example, a temple in Mound I-bis at Cuilapan (figure 19.8b), excavated by Saville in 1902, had a dedicatory offering which included an apparent sacrificed child covered with hematite pigment and accompanied by 17 jade figurines, 400 jade beads, 35 marine shells, 2 pottery ear ornaments, and disintegrated mosaics of shell, obsidian and hematite (Bernal 1958: 25). Interestingly enough, such offerings are not described by the sixteenth-century Spaniards, who saw the final temple at each community but were not present when the foundations were laid and the dedicatory offerings deposited.

Temples at San José Mogote

Some of the details of Zapotec ritual can be inferred from a sequence of Monte Albán II temples on Mound 1 at San José Mogote. This series of three stratigraphically superimposed buildings – Structures 36, 35, and 13 – was excavated by Marcus during two field seasons, 1974 and 1980.

The sequence of temples appears in figure 19.10. Structure 36, the oldest, dates to the

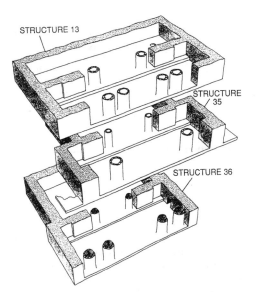

STRUCTURE 13

STRUCTURE 35

STRUCTURE 36

Figure 19.10 Reconstruction drawings of superimposed Monte Albán II temples on Mound I, San José Mogote. All temples face west. The artist has preserved the actual position of each building above or below the others, while exaggerating the vertical separation slightly so that the layout of the lower temples can be seen clearly. (Drawing by D. West Reynolds.)

very beginnings of Monte Albán II (200 BC–150 BC?). It measured roughly 11 m × 11 m and was slightly T-shaped, the inner room being smaller than the outer. Interestingly enough, both columns flanking the inner doorway and all four columns flanking the outer doorway were tree trunks of bald-cypress (*Taxodium* sp.), covered first with a layer of small stones and then white stucco. So hardy is this wood that much of it was still preserved in identifiable form in the column bases below the floor. (Unfortunately *Taxodium* is not much help for radiocarbon dating, since individual trees can live 1,000 years.)

Other details of Structure 36 included a niche in the south wall of the outer room, in which the priests may have stored an incense burner – or one of those Zapotec effigy vessels the Spaniards (drawing on their European background) called 'idols' or 'demons'. The floor of the temple was burned or stained grey with smoke wherever incense burners had been allowed to sit for any length of time, and the circular stains from this activity allowed us to see which areas had been favoured locations for burning copal. Especially common were sooty circles in the centres of the inner and outer rooms, signs of burning along the back wall of the inner room, and stains atop the step between the outer and inner rooms. The white-plastered interior walls of the temple bore geometric designs in polychrome paint like those seen on certain stuccoed ceramics of Monte Albán II (see Caso, Bernal and Acosta 1967: Lám. III–IV).

Structure 35, built over the deliberately razed and levelled remains of Structure 36, dated to the middle of Monte Albán II (ca. 50 BC?). It was larger than Structure 36 (measuring roughly 12 m × 13.5 m) and also slightly T-shaped like its predecessor. In the rubble layer between the two buildings we recovered occasional bird bones, including the remains of a Montezuma quail which might have been sacrificed in the earlier temple. Structure 35 was the best preserved of the temples on this spot and will be described in detail below. Its columns – one on either side of the inner and outer doorways – were made from large stones stacked one above the other and surrounded by small, stony rubble covered over with white stucco. Evidently these rubble columns, also characteristic of later Zapotec temples, had now replaced tree trunks.

Finally, above the deliberately razed and levelled remains of Structure 35, sat Structure 13. This temple dated to the end of Monte Albán II (AD 100–200?). Though poorly preserved, it seems to have measured about 15 m × 8 m and to have been rectangular rather than T-shaped. Its columns – two flanking the inner doorway and four flanking the outer doorway – were of rubble with a core of larger stones, like those of Structure 35. One of the building's most distinctive features was a basin 75 cm in diameter and 22 cm deep, built into the floor near the southeast corner of the inner room. There were no signs of burning in this basin; on the basis of ethnohistoric analogy, it may have served either (1) to hold water for washing the artefacts of sacrifice, or (2) to receive blood from some type of sacrifice.

Structure 35

Like Structure 36 below it, Structure 35 had circular stains on its floor in certain places where incense burners had been fuelled with charcoal. Figure 19.11 shows an artist's conception of the temple, with incense burners set in the most frequently burned or stained areas. (The artist's placement of those *incensarios* is only designed to indicate the most favoured locations, since we doubt that so many burners would all be in use at one time. Indeed, it is possible that certain locations were appropriate for some rituals and not for others.)

While most Zapotec temples that we have excavated appear to have been swept peri-odically (with the debris dumped in extra-ordinarily large cylindrical or bottle-shaped trash pits in the talus slope behind them), in the case of Structure 35 we were lucky enough to find some artefacts still on the floor. All those artefacts, as shown in figure 19.12, were in the extreme southern part of the smoky, windowless inner room, and especially its southwest corner – perhaps an area where the shadows were deepest, and the final sweeping was less thorough. The artefacts – all of obsidian – included two broken, leaf-shaped bifacial daggers of the type usually called 'sacrificial knives', the tip of a bifacial lancet, forty-two prismatic blades and five flakes (figure 19.13). While the lancet and prismatic blades are artefacts usually associated with autosacrifice (ritual bloodletting) by priests, the bifacial daggers are of the type shown in scenes of human sacrifice. This collection of tools, evidently overlooked when the floor was swept for the

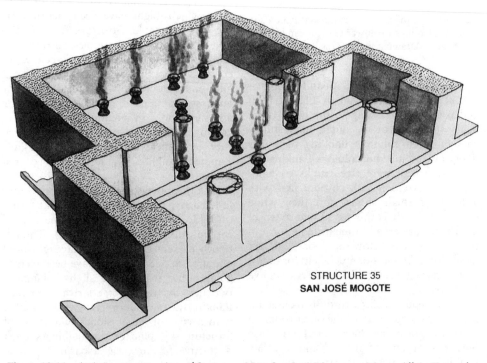

STRUCTURE 35
SAN JOSÉ MOGOTE

Figure 19.11 Artist's reconstruction of Structure 35 at San José Mogote, a Monte Albán II temple. Incense burners are shown on those parts of the floor which displayed the highest frequency of repeated burning and soot-staining. (Drawing by D. West Reynolds.)

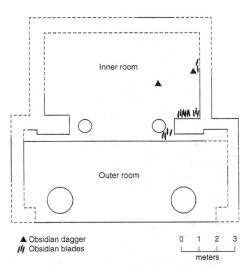

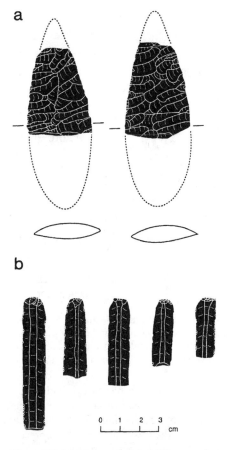

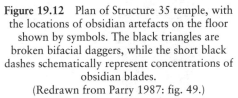

▲ Obsidian dagger
/// Obsidian blades

0   1   2   3
meters

Figure 19.12 Plan of Structure 35 temple, with the locations of obsidian artefacts on the floor shown by symbols. The black triangles are broken bifacial daggers, while the short black dashes schematically represent concentrations of obsidian blades.
(Redrawn from Parry 1987: fig. 49.)

0   1   2   3   cm

Figure 19.13 A sample of obsidian artefacts found on the floor of Structure 35 (see figure 19.12): (a) fragments of broken bifacial daggers; (b) examples of prismatic obsidian blades. The dagger blades in (a) would originally have been hafted.
(Redrawn from Parry 1987: figs 50, 51.)

last time, probably represents only a tiny fraction of what was used during the lifetime of the temple.

The most spectacular artefacts of Structure 35, however, were not found on the floor or in nearby trash pits. They lay in the offering boxes beneath the floor, where they had been left following 'rituals of sanctification' at the dedication of the temple.

There were five offering boxes below Structure 35. Two of these – Features 92 and 93 – lay below the northern and southern halves of the outer room. No artefacts were discovered in either, but this may only mean that their contents were perishable. Feature 93 contained two bones of quail, including *Cyrtonyx montezumae*.

Under the northern half of the inner room were two stone masonry offering boxes, Features 94 and 95, arranged in the form of a T (figure 19.14). Feature 95, the larger, contained no artefacts. Feature 94, the smaller, contained two jade statues, two jade beads and several small fragments which could have been by-products of

jade-working.[2] All objects lay in a dense vermilion powder which appeared to be hematite or ochre. The larger of the two statues was 49 cm tall, while the smaller measured around 15 cm (figure 19.15).

The larger statue stands stiffly erect, arms held rigidly at his sides, his feet ending in flat soles with no delineation of toes. He has the typical slab-shaped ears common in Monte Albán II and the lobes are pierced, perhaps for perishable ornaments which have since disintegrated. The top of his head has a drilled hollow which could have held the

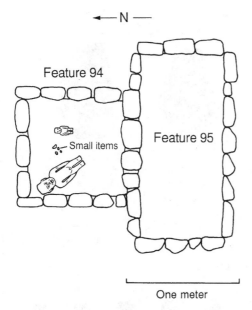

Figure 19.14 Features 94 and 95, two stone masonry offering boxes found below the floor of the Structure 35 temple. Feature 94 contained the two jade statues shown in figure 19.15.

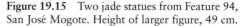

Figure 19.15 Two jade statues from Feature 94, San José Mogote. Height of larger figure, 49 cm.

base of a perishable headdress. This allowance for ear and head ornaments, combined with the fact that the figure is clearly a nude male, raises the possibility that he represents a sacrificed noble carved in jade.

The smaller figure also stands erect and has its earlobes drilled to receive ornaments; its neck is drilled through from side to side, possibly so that the figure could be worn as a pendant. Its hairdo, which features two isolated locks on each side of the head, resembles that of the sexually mutilated prisoner called 'Danzante 12', a carved stone monument from Monte Albán (Caso 1965: fig. 3). Although no sex organs are depicted on the smaller statue, the figure appears to be a male. We cannot claim to understand the full meaning of the Feature 94 offering, but it certainly involved many hours of invested craftsmanship. Perhaps these two figures were intended to 'stand in' for a pair of sacrificed elite males. If so, their semiprecious raw material gave them one advantage over human victims: they would never decay in the ground.

Under the south half of the inner room of Structure 35 was Feature 96, an offering box made of adobes rather than stone. This more complex offering consisted of seven ceramic piece arranged in the form of a scene, with each piece held in place by the earthen fill of the box. An artist's reconstruction of the scene is shown in figure 19.16.

At the centre of the scene was a miniature tomb whose walls were made of adobes set on edge, and whose roof was a slab of volcanic tuff. Inside this miniature tomb was an open bowl, and inside the bowl was an effigy vessel of the type known colloquially to Oaxaca specialists as an *accompañante* because of its frequent occurrence in tombs.[3] Resting against the north side of the open bowl was the complete skeleton of a sacrificed Bobwhite quail (*Colinus virginianus*). Immediately to the south of the volcanic tuff slab was a pair of deer antlers,

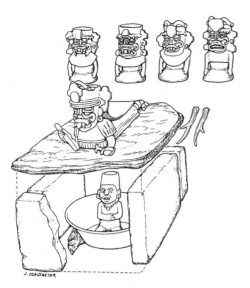

Figure 19.16 Artist's reconstruction of the ritual scene from Feature 96, an offering box below the floor of the Structure 35 temple. The scene consisted of a miniature adobe tomb with a stone roof, containing a pottery bowl, a ceramic effigy, and a sacrificed quail; a flying figure on the tomb roof, with a pair of deer antlers nearby; and four grotesque effigy figures in the background (see text). (Drawing by John Klausmeyer.)

like those used by the Zapotec to play the indigenous turtle shell drum.

The *accompañante* is a human figure, identified as a member of the hereditary nobility by his large, spool-shaped ear ornaments and a necklace which probably represents jade beads. He kneels with his arms folded across his chest – an arm position seen in Oaxaca burials for thousands of years – and has dry red pigment on his face and arms. Both the red pigment and the arm position suggest that he may represent a buried noble of some kind, with the bowl serving as the floor of his tomb and the stone slab as its roof.

Lying full length on the roof slab of the miniature tomb is a flying human figure with a long cape flowing behind him. He wears a facial mask depicting *Cociyo* or Lightning, his feet are in sandals, and his anklets bear 'dog-collar' spikes of the type

frequently seen on Zapotec incense burners. In his right hand he holds a wooden stick, and in his left he holds a bifid serpent tongue whose base is so long that it wraps around his wrist. There are several reasons why these objects may symbolize the relationship between lightning, rain and agriculture. First of all, the Zapotec words for 'young maize' and 'serpent' are homonyms (*zee* or *ziy*), with one frequently standing in for the other. What we may see here is a figure masked as Lightning, carrying an agricultural dibble stick in one hand and the tongue of a serpent (metaphoric of newly sprouted maize) in the other.

The symbolism of Cociyo is reinforced by the four ceramic effigies who sit in a row behind the flying figure, witnessing the scene. Each figure is shown as a kneeling woman with a grotesque Cociyo mask and a set of ear ornaments which vary from figure to figure. Almost certainly these women – each of whose heads is a hollow receptacle – represent clouds, rain, hail and wind, the four elements which we already saw accompanying Cociyo in figure 19.2.

What this scene may depict is the metamorphosis of a deceased Zapotec lord into a 'cloud person' or flying figure who is now in contact with Lightning. The flying figure could be a royal ancestor of the kneeling man in the miniature tomb or, just as likely, he may represent the partial metamorphosis of that very same buried noble, caught by the sculptor at a stage where his body is still that of a human, but his face is Cociyo's and he now can fly. It is frustrating indeed to look at this scene and realize that there must be much more information contained in it, even more than the ethnohistoric documents can help us decipher.

Before leaving Feature 96, we should point out that scenes of this type were evidently not rare at other Zapotec archaeological sites. We have seen numerous pieces, which also appear to have been part of arranged scenes, in museums and private collections of Zapotec art. Unfortunately, because they were found by looters rather than professional archaeologists, the pieces have been divided among different collections and their relationship destroyed, so that one can only guess what the original scene looked like.

Summary and Conclusions

Many of the ethnographically known elements of Zapotec ritual and religion can be found in the archaeological record, some as far back as the origins of village life. At this early stage, however, many of those elements appear as generalized features or ritual artefacts shared with several other Mesoamerican ethnic groups. Not until Monte Albán II (200 BC–AD 100), when the state had formed, do we finally see all those elements come together as a 'package' that resembles sixteenth-century Spanish descriptions of Zapotec religion. Clearly, therefore, what the Spaniards were describing was *Zapotec state religion*; we know much less about the household ritual conducted by commoners.

As early as 1350 BC, public buildings had storage pits for powdered lime that may have been used with narcotics or hallucinogens. By 1000 BC we see possible depictions in art of lightning and earthquake, and ritual scenes composed of small solid figurines that may represent ancestors. Stingray spines for ritual bloodletting were also present by that time, and between 700 and 500 BC, elite individuals were using obsidian artefacts chipped to resemble such spines. By 500 BC, we also have evidence for human sacrifice and the 260-day ritual calendar, two additional elements of Zapotec ritual.

A new plateau was reached by 200 BC, when standardized two-room temples became widespread at major sites. Those buildings match our sixteenth-century descriptions of temples in whose inner rooms the *bigaña*, or Zapotec priests, actually resided. The *bigaña* are described as letting their own blood with prismatic obsidian blades, and using flint or obsidian daggers to sacrifice slaves and war captives. They are also said to have sacrificed quail and turkeys, and to have burned great quantities of incense. Evidence for all these activities has been archaeologically recovered at temples like Structure 35 at San José Mogote. It is accompanied by the disappearance of many of the elements of pre-state religion, such as small solid figurines and depictions of the 'fire-serpent' and 'were-jaguar'.

What the Spaniards did not tell us – presumably because it took place before their arrival – is that the Zapotec had turned secular ground into sacred ground by placing valuable, labour-intensive offerings in the foundations of their temples. It remained for archaeologists to discover this. The DHA therefore, lies at the interface between archaeology and history. First, ethnohistory tells us what a temple should look like and accurately predicts that we should discover obsidian blades, sacrificial knives, incense burners and quail. Archaeology then reveals unpredicted offerings beneath the temples, but ethnohistory gives us some clues for interpreting them. In the case of Feature 96 at San José Mogote, it suggests that we are seeing metamorphosis, a major career transition of deceased royalty. Ethnohistory makes us less surprised that metamorphosed 'cloud people' wear the grotesque mask of Cociyo – the most powerful supernatural seen in Zapotec art, the version of Lightning preferred by the Classic Zapotec state.

The longer we work with the Zapotec, the more indebted we feel to the earlier generation of anthropological archaeologists who pioneered the DHA. Of course, our debt also extends to the sixteenth- and seventeenth-century Spaniards, without whose accounts it would be impossible to interpret meaning, symbolism, ideology and context in Zapotec archaeological remains. 'Cognitive archaeology' is not easy under any circumstances, but it is made easier when there is so much continuity between prehistoric and historic cultures.

ACKNOWLEDGEMENTS

We would like to thank Jeremy Sabloff for his very useful comments on this paper.

NOTES

1 Córdova (1578a) spelled Lightning *Cocijo*, which has for years been the standard spelling. However, he also made it clear that he was using the Latin *j* in his dictionary, reflecting the pronunciation *co-ci-yo*.

2 'Jade' is used colloquially here for jadeite, nephrite, and related metamorphics, since there is no true jade in Mexico.

3 In some Zapotec tombs, *acompañante* figures are so numerous as to seem almost analogous to the *ushabtis*, or servant figures, seen in Egyptian tombs. However, their earspools and necklaces make it clear that they are not depictions of commoners and therefore do not represent servants.

REFERENCES

Balsalobre, G. de. 1656. Relación auténtica de las idolatrías, supersticiones, vanas observaciones de los indios del Obispado de Oaxaca. Reprinted 1892 in *Anales del Museo Nacional de México*, Primera Epoca 6: 225–60.

Berlin, H. 1957. Las antiguas creencias en San Miguel Sola, Oaxaca, México. In *Beiträge zur mittelamerikanischen Völkerkunde*, herausgegeben von Hamburgischen Museum für Völkerkunde und Vorgeschichte, No. 4.

Bernal, I. 1949. Exploraciones en Coixtlahuaca, Oaxaca. *Revista Mexicana de Estudios Antropológicos* 10: 5–76.

——— 1958. Exploraciones en Cuilapan de Guerrero, 1902–1954. *Informes 7*, Dirección de Monumentos Prehispánicos. Mexico City: Instituto Nacional de Antropología e Historia.

——— 1965. Archaeological synthesis of Oaxaca. In *Handbook of Middle American Indians. Vol. III: Archaeology of Southern Mesoamerica*, part 2, ed. R. Wauchope and G. R. Willey, pp. 788–813. Austin: University of Texas Press.

——— 1966. The Mixtecs in the archaeology of the valley of Oaxaca. In *Ancient Oaxaca: Discoveries in Mexican Archaeology and History*, ed. J. Paddock, pp. 345–66. Stanford: Stanford University Press.

Blanton, R. E. 1978. *Monte Albán: Settlement Patterns at the Ancient Zapotec Capital*. New York: Academic Press.

Burgoa, F. de. 1670. Palestra historial de virtudes y exemplares apostólicos... Reprinted 1934 in *Publicaciones del Archivo General de la Nación*, vol. 24. Mexico City: Talleres Gráficos de la Nación.

——— 1674. Geográfica descripción. Reprinted 1934 in *Publicaciones del Archivo General de la Nación*, vols 25–6. Mexico City: Talleres Gráficos de la Nación.

Caso, A. 1932. La tumba 7 de Monte Albán es mixteca. *Universidad de México* 4 (20): 117–50.

——— 1935. *Las Exploraciones en Monte Albán, temporada 1934–5*. Instituto Panamericano de Geografía e Historia, Publicaciones No. 18. Mexico City.

——— 1945. *La religión de los aztecas*. Mexico City: Secretaría de Educación Pública.

——— 1958. *The Aztecs: People of the Sun*. Translated by Lowell Dunham. Norman: University of Oklahoma Press.

——— 1965. Sculpture and mural painting of Oaxaca. In *Handbook of Middle American Indians. Vol. III: Archaeology of Southern Mesoamerica*, part 2, ed. R. Wauchope and G. R. Willey, pp. 849–70. Austin: University of Texas Press.

——— 1966. The lords of Yanhuitlán. In *Ancient Oaxaca: Discoveries in Mexican Archaeology and History*, ed. J. Paddock, pp. 313–35. Stanford: Stanford University Press.

Caso, A. and I. Bernal. 1952. Urnas de Oaxaca. *Memorias del Instituto Nacional de Antropología e Historia*, No. 2. Mexico City.

Caso, A., I. Bernal, and J. R. Acosta. 1967. La cerámica de Monte Albán. *Memorias del Instituto Nacional de Antropología e Historia*, No. 13. Mexico City.

Coe, M. D. 1973. The iconology of Olmec art. In *The Iconography of Middle American Sculpture*, pp. 1–12. New York: The Metropolitan Museum of Art.

Coe, W. R. 1990. *Tikal Report 14. Excavations in the Great Plaza, North Terrace and North Acropolis of Tikal*. University Museum Monograph No. 61. Philadelphia: University of Pennsylvania.

Córdova, Fray J. de. 1578a. *Vocabulario en Lengua Zapoteca*. Mexico City: Pedro Charte y Antonio Ricardo. Reprinted 1942.

——— 1578b. *Arte en Lengua Zapoteca*. Mexico, Pedro Balli. Reprinted 1886.

Covarrubias, M. 1942. Origen y desarrollo del estilo artístico 'Olmeca'. In *Mayas y Olmecas*, pp. 46–9. Mexico City: Sociedad Mexicana de Antropología.

Flannery, K. V. 1976. Contextual analysis of ritual paraphernalia from formative Oaxaca. In *The Early Mesoamerican Village*, ed. K. V. Flannery, pp. 333–45. New York: Academic Press.

——— 1983. The development of Monte Albán's main plaza in period II. In *The Cloud People: Divergent Evolution of the Zapotec and Mixtec*

Civilizations, ed. K. V. Flannery and J. Marcus, pp. 102–4. New York: Academic Press.

Flannery, K. V. and J. Marcus. 1976a. Formative Oaxaca and the Zapotec cosmos. *American Scientist* 64(4): 374–83.

—— and ——1976b. Evolution of the public building informative Oaxaca. In *Cultural Change and Continuity: Essays in Honor of James Bennett Griffin*, ed. C. E. Cleland, pp. 205–21. New York: Academic Press.

—— and ——1990. Borrón, y Cuenta Nueva: setting Oaxaca's archaeological record straight. In *Debating Oaxaca Archaeology*, ed. J. Marcus, pp. 17–69. Museum of Anthropology, University of Michigan, Anthropological Papers, No. 84, Ann Arbor.

Flannery, K. V. and J. Marcus (eds). 1983. *The Cloud People: Divergent Evolution of the Zapotec and Mixtec Civilizations*. New York: Academic Press.

Frankfort, H., H. A. Frankfort, J. A. Wilson, and T. Jacobsen. 1946. *The Intellectual Adventure of Ancient Man*. Chicago: University of Chicago Press. Reprinted 1949 as *Before Philosophy*. Baltimore: Penguin Books.

Joralemon, P. D. 1971. A study of Olmec iconography. *Studies in Pre-Columbian Art and Archaeology*, No. 7. Washington, DC: Dumbarton Oaks.

Kidder, A. V., J. D. Jennings, and E. M. Shook. 1946. *Excavations at Kaminaljuyu, Guatemala*. Carnegie Institution of Washington, Publication 561. Washington, DC.

Marcus, J. 1976. The origins of Mesoamerican writing. *Annual Review of Anthropology* 5: 35–67.

——1978. Archaeology and religion: a comparison of the Zapotec and Maya. *World Archaeology* 10(2): 172–91.

——1980. Zapotec writing. *Scientific American* 242: 50–64.

——1983a. Rethinking the Zapotec urn. In *The Cloud People: Divergent Evolution of the Zapotec and Mixtec Civilizations*, ed. K. V. Flannery and J. Marcus, pp. 144–8. New York: Academic Press.

——1983b. Zapotec Religion. In *The Cloud People: Divergent Evolution of the Zapotec and Mixtec Civilizations*, ed. K. V. Flannery and J. Marcus, pp. 345–51. New York: Academic Press.

——1983c. The conquest slabs of Building J, Monte Albán. In *The Cloud People: Divergent Evolution of the Zapotec and Mixtec Civilizations*, ed. K. V. Flannery and J. Marcus, pp. 106–8. New York: Academic Press.

——1983d. Changing patterns of stone monuments after the fall of Monte Albán, AD 600–900. In *The Cloud People: Divergent Evolution of the Zapotec and Mixtec Civilizations*, ed. K. V. Flannery and J. Marcus, pp. 191–7. New York: Academic Press.

——1988. Comments on 'Ecological theory and cultural evolution in the Valley of Oaxaca' by William T. Sanders and Deborah L. Nichols. *Current Anthropology* 29(1): 60–1.

——1989. Zapotec chiefdoms and the nature of formative religions. In *Regional Perspectives on the Olmec*, ed. R. J. Sharer and D. C. Grove, pp. 148–97. Cambridge: Cambridge University Press.

Marcus, J. and K. V. Flannery. 1978. Ethnoscience of the sixteenth-century valley Zapotec. In *The Nature and Status of Ethnobotany*, ed. R. I. Ford, pp. 51–79. Museum of Anthropology, University of Michigan, Anthropological Papers, No. 67. Ann Arbor.

Moser, C. L. 1983. A Postclassic burial cave in the Southern Cañada. In *The Cloud People: Divergent Evolution of the Zapotec and Mixtec Civilizations*, ed. K. V. Flannery and J. Marcus, pp. 270–2. New York: Academic Press.

Parker, A. C. 1922. Archaeological history of New York. *New York State Museum Bulletin*, 235–8. Albany, New York.

Parry, W. J. 1987. Chipped stone tools in Formative Oaxaca, Mexico: their procurement, production and use. In *Prehistory and Human Ecology of the Valley of Oaxaca*, vol. 8, ed. K. V. Flannery. Memoirs of the University of Michigan Museum of Anthropology, No. 20. Ann Arbor.

Paso y Troncoso, F. del. 1905–6. *Papeles de Nueva España: segunda serie, geografía y estadística*, 7 volumes. Madrid, Est. Tipográfico 'Sucesores de Rivadeneyra'.

Rappaport, R. A. 1971. Ritual, sanctity and cybernetics. *American Anthropologist* 73: 59–76.

Rappaport, R. A. (ed.). 1979. *Ecology, Meaning, and Religion*. Richmond, California: North Atlantic Books.

Ricketson, O. G. and E. B. Ricketson. 1937. *Uaxactún, Guatemala, Group E. 1926–1931*. Carnegie Institution of Washington, Publication 477. Washington, DC.

Ritchie, W. A. 1932. The Algonkin sequence in New York. *American Anthropologist* 34: 406–14.

——1938. A perspective of northeastern archaeology. *American Antiquity* 4(2): 94–112.

Seler, E. 1904. The wall paintings of Mitla, a Mexican picture writing in fresco. In Mexican and Central American antiquities, calendar systems, and history (24 papers by Seler, Förstemann, Schellhas, Sapper, Dieseldorff, translated from the German by Charles P. Bowditch). *Bureau of American Ethnology Bulletin* 28: 247–324. Washington, DC: US Government Printing Office.

Smith, A. L. 1950. *Uaxactún, Guatemala: Excavations of 1931–1937*. Carnegie Institution of Washington, Publication 588. Washington, DC.

Strong, W. D. 1933. The Plains culture area in the light of archaeology. *American Anthropologist* 35(2): 271–87.

—— 1935. *An Introduction to Nebraska Archaeology*. Smithsonian Miscellaneous Collections, vol. 93, No. 10. Washington, DC: Smithsonian Institution.

Thompson, J. E. S. 1950. *Maya Hieroglyphic Writing: An Introduction*. Carnegie Institution of Washington, Publication 589. Washington, DC.

—— 1966. *The Rise and Fall of Maya Civilization*. Norman: University of Oklahoma Press.

—— 1970. *Maya History and Religion*. Norman, University of Oklahoma Press.

—— 1973. Maya rulers of the Classic Period and the Divine Right of Kings. In *The Iconography of Middle American Sculpture*, pp. 52–71. New York: The Metropolitan Museum of Art.

Wedel, W. R. 1938. The Direct-Historical Approach in Pawnee archaeology. *Smithsonian Miscellaneous Collections*, vol. 97, No. 7. Washington, DC: Smithsonian Institution.

CHAPTER 20

Kingship in the Late Preclassic Maya Lowlands

The Instruments and Places of Ritual Power

David A. Freidel and Linda Schele

The ancient Lowland Maya civilization is now recognized as an example of a truly literate society in the pre-Columbian New World. Fundamental breakthroughs in the decipherment and translation of Maya hieroglyphic texts from the Classic period (AD 200–900) over the last two decades (Proskouriakoff 1960, 1961, 1963–4; Berlin 1958, 1959; Kelley 1962; Lounsbury 1974, 1985; Mathews and Schele 1974; Schele 1978–87, 1982; Schele and J. Miller 1983) have demonstrated that these texts deal primarily with the history and ritual activities of kings and nobles as legitimated by theological and mythological precepts shared by the many Maya polities. Furthermore, the decipherment of Maya glyphs has allowed the systematic and testable identification of the meanings attached to central icons and artistic compositions carved on stone, painted on pottery, and found decorating public buildings, among many other media (cf. Schele 1976, 1979; Schele and M. Miller 1986). One of the issues emerging in light of these breakthroughs is the legitimation of royal status and the manner in which kingship both defined and responded to the changing social conditions of the Maya world.

The Evolution of Maya Kingship

Archeological research during the last decade in the Maya lowlands has demonstrated that Late Preclassic (350 BC–AD 100) society was complex, hierarchical, and centralized in capitals of substantial scale (figure 20.1; Freidel 1979, 1981; Matheny 1987; Pendergast 1981; Andrews 1981; Hammond 1985a, 1985b). But while scholars acknowledge the existence of an elite in this period (Willey 1977), the institutional form of Late Preclassic government has remained undefined and unidentified. As the nature of Classic Maya kingship has come into better focus through text translation, we can now discern diagnostics of the central Classic period institution of *ahaw*, ruler, in Late Preclassic period facilities and implements. We regard the identification of the institution of *ahaw* in the material symbol systems of the Late Preclassic period as a central issue. The coeval appearance of the symbols of rulership and the sudden elaboration of public centers in the first century BC (Freidel 1979, 1981; Freidel and Schele 1988) suggests that this initial florescence of Maya civilization hinged upon the invention of this institution.

Reprinted from David A. Freidel and Linda Schele. 1988. Kingship in the Late Preclassic Lowlands: The Instruments and Places of Ritual Power. *American Anthropologist* 90: 3 (Sept. 1988) 547–67. Reproduced by permission of the American Anthropological Association. Not for further reproduction.

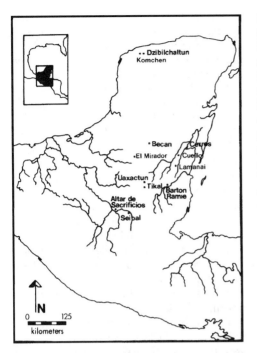

Figure 20.1 Map of the Maya area showing key sites discussed in the text.

The Lowland Maya concept of kingship has been recently summarized by Schele and M. Miller (1986), but some salient characteristics of the institution of *ahaw* are as follows. First, beings of this category are endowed with divine or supernatural power. Second, it is a category that includes dead ancestors and gods as well as human beings. Third, individuals who are in this category appear to be essentially equivalent to each other in that a human *ahaw* can be the incarnation of the Maya Ancestral Heroes. Fourth, humans of this category are capable of ritual conflation and substitution – particularly in sacrifice (Freidel 1986). Finally, Maya rulers are the pivotal actors in the celebration of rituals that have at their base a common theology of divine ancestors who ordered the world and established the contractual obligations of human and divine beings.

We propose (Freidel and Schele 1988; Schele 1985; Freidel 1986a) that the institution of *ahaw* originated in the first century

BC; that it was invented to accommodate severe contradictions in Maya society between an ethos of egalitarianism and an actual condition of flourishing elitism brought on by successful trade and interaction between the Lowland Maya and their hierarchically organized neighbors over the course of the Preclassic era. We further suggest that the invention of this institution constituted the successful transformation of a mythology focusing on Heroic Ancestor Twins from an ideological affirmation of ethnic brotherhood across a vast segmentary society into a celebration of hierarchical division of that society into living representatives of those ancestors and their worshipers. The consequence of this transformation of Maya ideology was a sudden surge of construction in centers throughout the southern lowlands (Freidel 1979) accompanied by a rapid elaboration of the material implements of power used by rulers and other elite.

An empirical difficulty with investigating the origins of the Late Preclassic institution of *ahaw* is the paucity of antecedent evidence pertaining to ideology because of the simplicity and ambiguity of the material symbol systems prior to the Late Preclassic transformation. The next major transformation we can identify in the Maya record spans the shift from the Late Preclassic period to the Early Classic period (AD 200–600). While this episode remains sparsely documented in the archeological record (Willey and Mathews 1985), we do at least have command of material symbol systems on both sides of the posited transformation.

The Late Preclassic–Early Classic transition is marked by some significant changes: El Mirador (Matheny 1987), an enormous center in northwestern Peten, Guatemala, collapsed at the end of the Preclassic era. Other smaller but still impressive centers like Cerros and the industrial community of Colha (Potter 1985; Shafer and Hester 1983) in northern Belize were likewise abandoned. Tikal in Guatemala experienced a period of stasis in construction (W. Coe 1965) and so, evidently, did the major center of Lamanai in Belize (Pendergast 1981).

It is also during this period, roughly the first two centuries of the present era (cf. Willey 1977), that interaction intensified between the Maya lowlands and the neighboring highland and Pacific slope societies to the south – societies evincing substantial complexity and scale (Sharer 1974). Several key features of Classic Maya kingship and elite technology occurred in more developed form among the Late Preclassic period societies of this southern highland and Pacific slopes region, principally the depiction of royal personages upon carved stone stelae accompanied by hieroglyphic texts and calendrical statements (Schele 1985). Indeed, these features of Lowland Maya kingship are so central that many scholars of the Maya regard the innovation of this institution as contingent upon interaction between the Maya highlands and lowlands, if not upon outright migration of highlanders into the lowlands during this transitional period (Willey 1977, 1985).

Our position in this article is that while Lowland Maya kingship certainly changed between the Late Preclassic and Early Classic periods, the institution of *ahaw* was established in the lowlands in the context of the first great centers of the last 100 years BC and not in the intervening centuries between the collapse of the major Late Preclassic centers and the establishment of the Early Classic centers. What occurred between the Late Preclassic period and the Early Classic period, then, was not the invention of Lowland Maya kingship, but rather a transformation of this institution.

From our present evidence, we believe that the southern Highland and Pacific Slope Maya of the Late Preclassic first harnessed the principle of the temporal cycles of history to the policy of kingship as expressed in hieroglyphic texts accompanying the portraits of kings on stelae. This principle of history specified and legitimated the personage of the king as to name and place, and hence as to dynasty. It also specified the actions that confirmed his status as *ahaw* (Schele 1985). These major features of kingship, however, succeeded in the Classic period lowlands because they were grafted onto a Late Preclassic institution of kingship that appealed more to the principle of personal charismatic power endowed in the role of the shaman than to the principles of lineage and genealogy.

The advantages of a political ideology emphasizing personal charismatic power and the ritual roles of a village-level specialist in the supernatural make sense in light of a constituency that had maintained an egalitarian ethos for centuries in the face of emerging elitism. The transformation to the Early Classic is characterized by the adoption of firm genealogical principles of succession and firm ritual formulae, as carved on stone stelae, for achieving the status of *ahaw*. These products of the transformation suggest that the major problem with Late Preclassic kingship was the absence of a mechanism to ensure the stable transmission of central leadership over generations.

The problems of succession remained a major theme of Classic Maya texts and imagery, but evidently these were manageable in the context of hieroglyphic commentary and a material symbol system displaying the personage of the ruler and his cohorts. In practical terms, Classic period art displays kings graphically engaged in their ritual action, while the agent is missing from the scene in the Preclassic and his actions must be deduced from the correspondence between his instruments of power and the cosmic frames within which his actions were performed.

Interpreting Maya Symbol Systems

The methodology employed in this essay follows Linda Schele and Jeffrey Miller's (1983) analysis of Classic Maya royal accession texts and rituals in that it marshals evidence of the correspondence between form and meaning from several independent sources: glyphic texts, iconic compositions, ethnohistoric dictionaries and descriptions, Colonial period Maya texts, and archeological contexts. Specifically, the crux of the argument both in Schele and Miller (1983: 1) and in the present analysis is a correlation between a visual – here artifactual – model for a particular grapheme and the meaning that can be postulated for that grapheme through grammatical or syntactical context, phonetic decipherment, linguistic definition, social function, and finally archeological patterning. Here the central model is the stone of prophecy used by Maya shamans and, we argue, by Maya kings.

One specific bridge between the epigraphic, iconographic, and contextual that we attempt to build below is the application of the principle of syntax derived from epigraphy to the design of an exemplary Maya building and its accompanying iconographic composition (figures 20.2–20.5). The premise is that the ancient Maya read their art and witnessed their rituals using the same kind of positional codes as found in their hieroglyphic texts. In texts, that syntax is predominantly verb-object-subject. As described below, we postulate a comparable three-part visual syntax for Maya artistic compositions. In contrast to the primarily linear arrangement of textual syntax, however, the visual syntax is capable of concentric design (in addition to linear sequencing). As described below, the ability of visual syntax to arrange meaningful positions concentrically is of central importance to the Maya.

Iconographic Syntax

In essence, there are three primary positions in Maya iconographic composition: the central agent, the objects with which the agent (usually the king) communes with the supernatural, and the framing supernatural powers and beings. In the Late Preclassic period, this visual syntax is well established and expressed in panels of modeled and painted stucco (Freidel 1985).

For example, on Structure 5C-2nd at Cerros (figure 20.2), the main task on the lower west panel depicts the Jaguar Sun – second born of the Ancestral Heroes[1] – identified by the *k'in*, Sun, day or light, glyph on his cheeks (Freidel and Schele 1988; Freidel 1986a). Flanking the Sun are his objects. Since the image of the agent is reduced to the head alone, the object positions are

helmet, chin-strap, and earflares. Finally, these categories are framed by the double-headed serpent motif, expressing the homophony linking the words for snake and sky (*chan-chan*) and depicting the path along which the Sun and his brother Venus travel. As the being sustaining their movement, the sky-serpent is a prime example of supernatural force.

Within the entire composition, the eastern sets of earflares are marked with a category of "word" or written information by glyph signs attached to their knots (figure 20.3). This "word" tag is *yax*, meaning "first," which in this context identifies the eastern heads, Sun and Venus morning star, as the "first" or rising. The western heads, unmarked and vomited downwards by a distinctive split representation of the sky entity in the top register, are the setting Sun and Venus evening star. The earflares are all further qualified by flanking profile polymorphic heads denoting their power, *wah*, which in this Maya case is specifically composed of the blood of sacrifice and its primary classification set: fire, smoke, and water (Freidel 1985).

The human agent is invisible and ephemeral in this composition, but the syntactical principle allows for "reading" his presence upon the stairway flanked by such panels. First, the principle of framing and flanking the supernatural agents (the deity heads) by the objects and serpent-sky frame on the individual panels is physically analogous to the framing of the stairway by the four masks on Structure 5C-2nd (figure 20.4; Schele 1985). Second, we may conclude from architectural and engineering decisions that the stairs were built between the panels in order to place a human standing on the landing or at the summit in the pivotal position central to these four cycling manifestations of ancestral and cosmic power.

The Objects of Kingship

Certain symbols carved on objects of the Late Preclassic period can be confidently identified as insignia of royal status because of their consistent and enduring associations

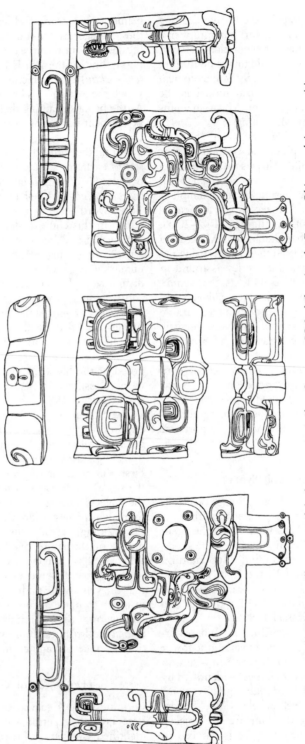

Figure 20.2   Blow-out illustration of the lower west panel on Structure 5C-2nd showing the Frame, Object, and Agent positions.

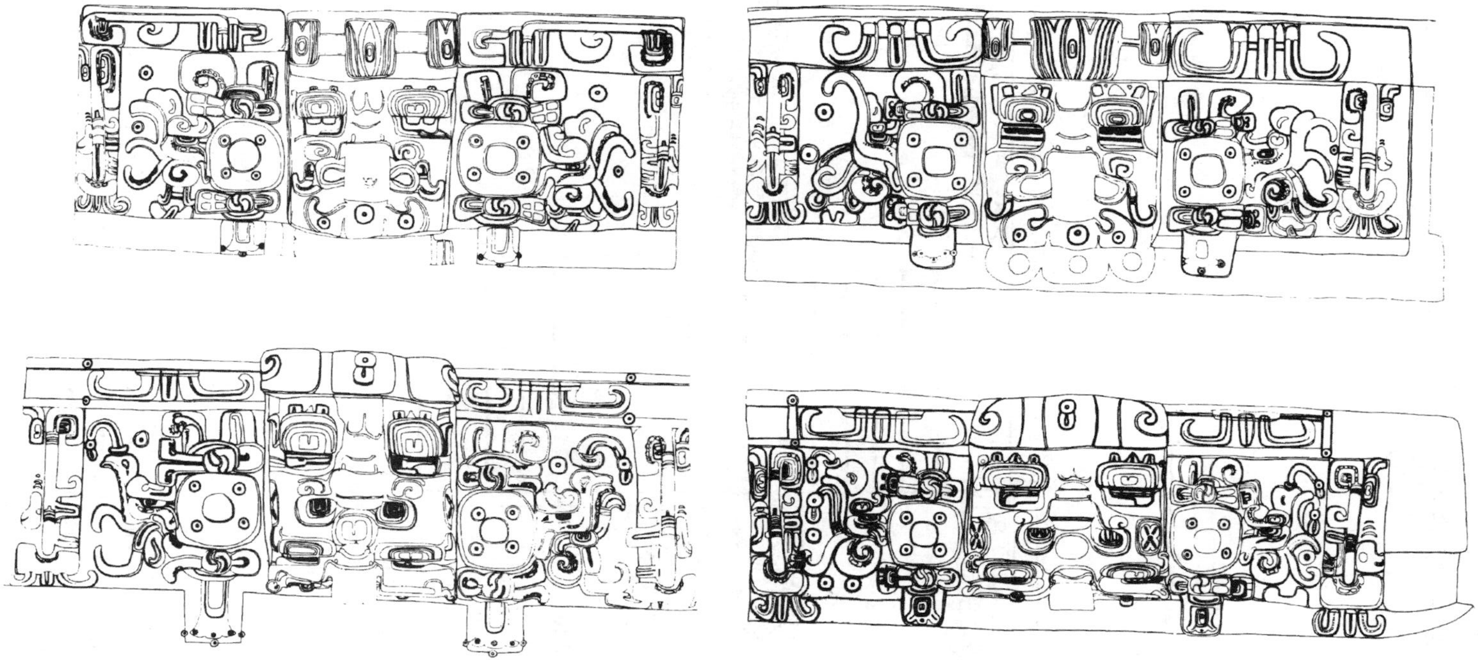

Figure 20.3   Restoration drawing of the facade of Structure 5C-2nd at Cerros.

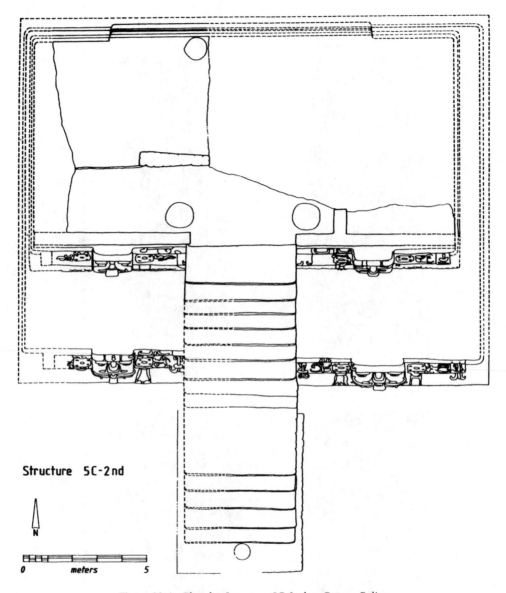

Figure 20.4   Plan for Structure 5C-2nd at Cerros, Belize.

through the Classic period. Among such Late Preclassic objects is the incised back of the Dumbarton Oaks pectoral (figure 20.5; M. Coe 1966), an unprovenienced object, stylistically and iconographically identified as a Late Preclassic portrayal of a king on a power object (Schele and M. Miller 1986: 119–20). The original front of this pectoral displays an Olmec-style face marking it as an heirloom, but the incised ruler on the back wears one of the major Maya power objects: the Jester God diadem. The accompanying text, furthermore, clearly states the event portrayed as the "seating" of the person as king, and this sentence employs the tri-pointed symbol of the Jester God.

The Jester God, a clearly identified signal of kingship in the Classic period, occurs as

Figure 20.5 Late Preclassic ruler incised on the back of the Dumbarton Oaks Plaque, and associated inscription.

an object worn or handled, as a glyph denoting kingship, and as a semantic determinative for the status of king, *ahaw*. The Jester God diadem appears as the crown of a fuschite head (Clancy et al. 1985: pl. 16), found in Late Preclassic period Burial 85 (W. Coe 1965: 43) at Tikal, affirming a Preclassic context for this emblem of Maya kingship. Although this object was placed upon a bundle containing a headless body, it is pierced for suspension and for hanging cylinders and beads along its lower edge. These features show that it was a chest pectoral or girdle ornament like those so often

shown in the costuming of Classic period rulers. The presence of the Jester God symbol on the headband marks the portrayed wearer as *ahaw*. At the same time, because the Jester God is a semantic determinative of *ahaw*, this mask is part of the category of *ahaw* masks found throughout the Classic period (Schele and J. Miller 1983: fig. 4).

While this Tikal object conveniently confirms two *ahaw* object positions – pectoral and diadem – it raises the question: Where are the actual Jester God diadems as worn by Late Preclassic kings? The diagnostic feature of the Jester God is the three-part pointed cap, and this is found on a green stone pendant pierced for suspension which was part of a Late Preclassic cache deposited in Structure 6B at Cerros (figures 20.6 and 20.7; Freidel 1979; Garber 1983, 1986).

The Jester God is distinguished by the tripointed division of its headdress, and this form can be seen in figure 20.7c. While other pendants of the "bibbed head" style have tripartite divisions of helmets, the diagnostic feature of this early form of the Jester is the deliberately pointed shape of the headdress. The pendant, furthermore, is the appropriate size and weight to serve as a diadem, and is pierced for suspension or to be sewn onto a headband. Another diagnostic feature of early depictions of the Jester God diadem is that it is flanked by other icons, particularly a pair of bifurcated shapes (figure 20.5). In a number of examples these flanking shapes can also be shown as additional Jester Gods or other personified symbols. The three additional pendants (figure 20.7 b, d, and e), each of which is drilled for suspension, appear to have functioned as these flanking heads. One (figure 20.7b) displays the tripartite rectilinear helmet shared by the Jaguar Sun and early *ahaw* masks (figure 20.2).

The presence of four such pendants in the Cerros cache suggests that the Late Preclassic diadems could be a four-part set as well as the three-part headband shown on the Tikal pectoral. Moreover, the bifurcated shapes flanking the early variants of the Jester God headdress, such as on the Dumbarton Oaks plaque and the Loltun Bas Relief

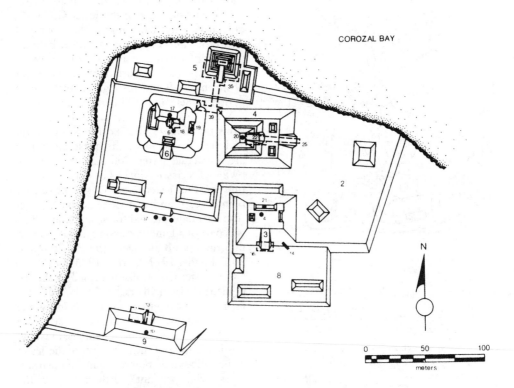

Figure 20.6 Map of the site of Cerros, Belize.

in Yucatan (Andrews 1981), appear to be related to the Early Classic "u" glyph that marks an array of objects iconographically identifiable as stone jewelry: beads, flares, and so forth (e.g. Stela 31, Jones and Satterthwaite 1982: fig. 91). The flanking shapes on Late Preclassic royal headbands may thus signal the presence of stone jewels.

The larger head in the Cerros cache (figure 20.7a) is of the size and style appropriate for use as a generalized "young lord" *ahaw* pectoral, and it is drilled for suspension. Furthermore, its human features, excised cheek, and the three-part division of the headdress match closely such a pectoral found in a burial near Kendal, Belize (Price 1899; Schele and M. Miller 1986: pl. 19). Although slightly later in style, the Kendal pectoral was found with drill holes along its lower edge and with cylinders and alligator beads (Price 1899) that leave no doubt of

its function as a pectoral. The excised circles on the cheeks of the Kendal pectoral match the position and size of the face circles characteristic of the human *ahaw* glyph and generalized pectoral of the Classic period. The close similarity of detail and image between the Kendal and Cerros pectorals allows us to deduce that the Cerros pectoral is a Late Preclassic prototype for the *ahaw* pectorals of Classic period portraiture.

The arrangement of the head pendants in the Cerros cache was deliberate: the four smaller heads were placed down at the edges of the base of the ceramic bucket, forming a quadrangle around the central pectoral, which was face upwards. This pattern closely replicates the *quincunx* design (fourfold pattern of dots surrounding a central depression) characteristic of earflares as represented on Structure 5C-2nd (figures 20.2 and 20.3) and throughout the Classic

a

b

c

d

e

Figure 20.7 The carved stone head pendants from Cache 1, Structure 6B, Cerros.

period. Since other objects in the cache vessel, such as spondylus shell and volcanic hematite mirror fragments, were found in the layers above the pectoral and pendants, we infer that all of the cache objects were set in some kind of matrix prior to interment to hold their relative positions. Commensurate with this interpretation, one might regard the large human head pectoral in the center of the Cerros cache as the king surrounded by his objects. The comparable pectoral in Burial 85 at Tikal represents the head of a king otherwise present in postcranial fragments.

The correspondences between the materials and design of the cached offering on Structure 6B and the object categories on monumental panels – particularly the earflare assemblage – are sufficient to indicate intentional connections by the users of these objects and facilities. In addition to the *quincunx* pattern on the earflare proper, analysis of the earflare assemblages on the Structure 5C-2nd panels (figure 20.2) shows the presence of mirrors, bundle-knots, suspended trilobate shapes reminiscent of the Jester God insignia, and rising bifurcate scrolls. Each of these symbols came to be used in the T712/757 accession phrase for Classic Maya kings (Mathews and Schele 1974). In sum, the four smaller head pendants in the Cerros cache appear to be elements in a royal crown. The most unequivocal feature of this hypothesis is the presence of a Jester God image among them.

A further correspondence can be seen in the three-part rectilinear helmet associated with GIII, the Jaguar Sun, found on both the central *ahaw* pectoral and one of the smaller pendants. That the three-part rectilinear design is intended to register the GIII association even without the curls found on the panels of Structure 5C-2nd (figure 20.2) is suggested by another stone pectoral reported from Early Classic context at Santa Rita (Chase and Chase 1986: 13). This pectoral is clearly the human *ahaw* face, with the three-part helmet, but in this case the diagnostic curls of GIII are present. The Kendal *ahaw* pectoral (Schele and

M. Miller 1986: pl. 19) displays the segmented helmet decorated with the central droplet element seen on the Jaguar Sun at Cerros (figure 20.2). The royal association with the Ancestral Twins is established in the Late Preclassic period, both in implements and in facilities.

The Fourfold Path of Power

The arrangement of the Cerros pendants and pectoral inside the bucket in a *quincunx* pattern prompts the hypothesis that quadripartition and concentric dualism were important structures in the ritual function of these objects. Preliminary confirmation of this hypothesis is found in the Pomona Flare, another important Late Preclassic artifact from Belize (Justeson, Norman, and Hammond 1988; Hammond 1987; Schele and M. Miller 1986). The sentences on the Pomona flare pair an actor marked by *k'in*, Sun, day, or light, to one marked by *akbal*, darkness. Later in the Classic period, the same opposition appears in the form of the Paddler Gods, who are named glyphically either with their portrait heads or with *k'in* and *akbal* glyphs inserted in special notched cartouches (Stuart 1984: 13–15). These are entities born in the blood of royal sacrifice in the scattering rite (Stuart 1984: 14–15; Schele and M. Miller 1986: 52) and are associated with the vision rite and the dedication of a "blood house" on an Early Classic cache vessel from the Central Acropolis at Tikal (MT 140; W. Coe 1967: 70). This paired opposition and its companion – the sun god and the maize god (or the numbers four and eight) – are embedded in the *quincunx* pattern.

A recently reported Early Classic painted tomb at the site of Rio Azul (Adams 1986) supplies a vital architectural and epigraphic set of clues to the ritual function and meaning of the four-part arrangement of icons. The walls of the tomb (Graham 1986: 456) are oriented to the cardinal directions and display the directional glyphs for east, north, west and south on the appropriate walls. In this case, of course, the *quincunx* pattern was completed by the interred individual,

whose skeleton was destroyed by looters. Four other glyphs were placed in the corners of the tombs at the intercardinal points. Each directional glyph was paired with another sign placed immediately above it. In each, the main sign is constant, but each has a superfix consisting of a variable sign and the sign *ah*. The variables change with the direction: *k'in* with east, *akbal* with west, the moon with north, and *lamat* (Venus) with south. The constant main sign is a relatively rare glyph; it appears with an *ah k'in* superfix in a phrase related to the Palenque Triad on Caracol Stela 14 and is the day sign *men* (T613, Thompson 1962). Its most important occurrence, however, is in the name of God D, which epigraphers accept as a phonetic rendering of the name *Itzamna*, in both the Classic inscriptions and the codices. Since this glyph appears as the second in a three-sign collocation which must read either *itz-am-na* or *I-tzam-na*, we can propose a value of either *tzam* or *am* for the sign. We hypothesize that the correct reading for this glyph is *am*, for this word is most germane to quadripartition, prognostication, and power.

The Stones of Prophecy

Landa gives this description of festival in the month of Zip:

> On the following day the physicians and the sorcerers assembled in one of their houses ... they opened the bundles of their medicine, in which they kept many little trifles, and each having his own, little idols of the goddess of medicine, whom they call Ix Chel ... as well as some small stones, called *am*, of the kind which they used for casting lots.
> *(Landa, quoted in Tozzer 1941: 154)*

Landa also notes, "And if he was a sorcerer, they buried him with some of his stones for witchcraft and instruments of his profession" (Tozzer 1941: 130). Further, in *Ritual of the Bacabs*, Roys gives the following incantation of the spider:

> First spider, second spider, third spider, fourth spider! Green spider of wood (*am-te*), green

spider of stone (*am-tun*)! Three days were you apart in the trough of the earth (cab)...This, then, is the virgin stone needle (or bodkin) of the virgin Ix Chel, Sacal Ix Chel, Chacal Ix Chel. This is the symbol of your sting...

(Roys 1965: 53)

Tozzer goes on to associate these stones with spiders, also called *am*, in one of his detailed footnotes: "the Motul definition of the word *am*, 'Certain small black spiders with red spots on the back,' etc. In a *Relacion* (RY 1: 301) we read, 'It stings with its tail.'" (Tozzer 1941: 154).

One sort of "black stone" that "stings" to elicit "red spots" is obsidian, and Kidder (1947: fig. 72) illustrates a cache of three carefully incised obsidian flakes from under a stela at Tikal. These three stones repeat the *am* glyphs of the Rio Azul tomb, giving us the same directional associations for a stela cache of Early Classic dating. At Tikal, the glyph compounds are arranged in a slightly different order giving the readings, *Ak'bal Am ahaw*, *Uh Am ahaw*, and *K'in Am ahaw* and the directional association of west-*ak'bal*, north-moon, and east-*k'in*. We can reconstruct the fourth obsidian from the established pattern as north-Venus *am*. The obsidian flakes were used in a stela that used the same quadripartite division as the Cerros cache and the Rio Azul tomb. The correspondence between this set of objects and the architectonic expression in the Rio Azul Tomb is clear and substantial. Moreover, Kidder (1947: figs 69–71) illustrates other cached obsidian flakes incised variously with God K, the Jester God, God C, the Maize Lord, the Moon Goddess, and the Sun. These artifacts were the standard stela offerings used at Tikal and Uaxactun. It is reasonable to propose that such materials were germane to the ritual activities carried out by the people portrayed on the monuments. Such ritual is discussed below in light of the Hauberg Stela.

The *am* described in the Colonial sources above is a green stone, and W. Coe, in his analysis of cached offerings from Classic contexts at Piedras Negras (1959: figs 45–6), illustrates some 46 incised green stone objects, small, flat, and generally of irregular outline. The predominant icon is the Jester God in profile, but there are also a probable God K (W. Coe 1959: figs 55v and 46s) and mat motifs which also occur on the obsidians from Tikal.

We believe, then, that the stones of prophecy of the Classic period, like those of the Conquest period, were made of green stone pebbles and flakes, as well as of obsidian flakes. It is not unreasonable to suppose that the Jester God diadem and accompanying icons depicted on green stone pebbles carry such meaning when they occur in offerings of the Late Preclassic period, and that both the Late Preclassic and Classic used paired oppositions as the principle of organization and meaning in rituals employing these implements.

If the head pendants found in Late Preclassic caches are indeed stones of prophecy, *am*, used for casting lots by sorcerers and curers, then it follows that a key feature of the charismatic office of ruler was the ability of the king to confront personally the supernatural as a sorcerer, curer, and prophet on behalf of his people. Indeed, in addition to the head pendants, the Cerros cache also contained little jadeite spangles of the kind associated with casting lots in ethnohistorical and ethnographic contexts (Garber 1983). This connection of the political office of ruler with the power to cure, sustain, protect, and prognosticate is common in the anthropological literature and hence not surprising in the Maya case.

The Place of Four Posts

The *quincunx* pattern of the earflares and cache deposits also appears as a sign in the glyphic system. Appearing in Landa's alphabet as the letter *b* and in well-defined phonetic contexts in the Classic inscriptions, this sign is accepted as *be* (or in Cholan languages, *bi*). In both language families, *be/bi* means road or path and can be extended to include not only human and animal types of paths, but canals as the "path of water" (*u be ha*) or veins as the "path of blood" (*u be k'ik'*). In Yucatec, it has also come to mean work, occupation, office, vocation, and cargo. The meaning of path is consistent with the rituals we have associated with the *quincunx* arrangement, and since the Late Preclassic examples are profoundly associated with the architectural and ritual manifestations of the newly emerged social system as well as with the symbols of ruling office, the meanings of work, social cargo, office in government, life vocation again seem more than fortuitous. We further suggest that the use of the *quincunx* glyph as the sound *be* may well have its roots in these Late Preclassic rituals and in the structure of the Late Preclassic community as it relates to these rituals.

Foremost among the physical facilities associated with *quincunx* ritual patterns are the *acantun* or *acante*, which are described by Roys as follows:

> The acantun ("stone set up on a foundation") was a monument, also considered to be a god, erected to honor the birth of each New Year at one of the four ritual entrances to a town and anointed with the blood of worshipers. *Acantuns* were also set up at the four cardinal points around the fenced hut where the idol makers smeared them with their own blood....I surmise that the "arbors" elsewhere mentioned in this manuscript were considered to be ceremonial huts, like those used by the idol makers.
>
> *(Roys 1965: 5)*

We have identified *te-tun* "three-stone" as the Classic glyph for stela (Schele and Stuart 1986) and confirmed that this metaphor is still used by Mayan and Spanish speakers in western Honduras and eastern Guatemala as the term for "a very large stone." The *acan te* is an *ac-a'an* "set up" *te'* "tree", and an *aca'an-tun* is a "set-up stone," but since we know that the Classic peoples called stelae *te'-tun*, both classes of objects can easily refer to stelae, whether they were made of stone or wood and whether they did or did not display writing.

The concept of tree and stela are additionally related in ways that figure prominently in incantations, as well as to a structure with four posts of stone or wood (figure 20.4):

A certain tree is ascribed to every person, its species apparently depending on the name of the day on which he was born. Such trees are also assigned to the personified diseases treated in these incantations.....Closely associated with the personified tree in this manuscript is the arbor (*dzubal*, also called *dzulub*), which is named for some species of tree or shrub. In the Chumayel manuscript, where the *dzubal* is also called a *pasel* ("small hut") in the same context, the arbor is ascribed to the "first men" of certain lineages in the ritual of a lineage-cult.... Frequently, though by no means always, the arbor is associated with an *acantun* ("stone shaft") and, less often, an *acante* ("wooden shaft").

> *(Roys 1965: xiii–xvii)*

The specific description of idol carving in the context of such a hut is given as follows:

> The Chacs whom they had chosen for this purpose, as well as the priest and the workman, began their fastings. While they were fasting the man to whom the idols belonged went in person to the forests for the wood for them, and this was always cedar. When the wood had arrived, they built a hut of straw, fenced in, where they put the wood and a great urn in which to place the idols and keep them under cover, while they were making them. They put incense to burn to four gods called *Acantuns*, which they located and placed at the four cardinal points.
>
> *(Landa, quoted in Tozzer 1941: 160)*

Tozzer makes the further comment: "The manufacture of idols has been recognized both by Thomas (1882) and by Förstemann (1902) as pictured in Tro-Cortesanius 97–101.... In practically every case the idol is represented by the face of God C" (1941: 161). Recall that the blood of sacrifice is also represented by God C in Classic period iconography and that the mannikin scepter God K, the most pervasive "idol" of the Classic period, is yet another expression of blood (Stuart 1984).

The creation of "wooden dolls" may involve not only the *acantuns* of the curers, but also their divining. For in the First Creation of the *Popol Vuh* of the Quiche Maya, the creation of people from wood – an antecedent to their successful creation from maize – involves the casting of lots (maize kernels and red seeds) by their creators (Edmonson 1971: 22). These ethnohistorical materials suggest that there were important links between the four-posted "hut" of the ritual creation of gods, the four-posted space that was the community in the year renewal ceremonies, the four-posted space that was the place of supernatural confrontation for diviners and curers – particularly in confrontation with disease – and the "hut" of lineage rituals carried out by their leaders.

The quadripartite principle, along with the tripartite principle (Freidel 1979), is a key feature of Late Preclassic Maya architecture. As noted earlier, the structure into which the offering described in this article was placed, Structure 6B, supplanted an earlier structure to the north and east of it, Structure 5C. Structure 5C-2nd is extraordinarily well preserved (figures 20.3 and 20.4) and shows the material spaces in which ceremonies organized in four-part or *quincunx* arrangements, as described in ethnohistorical literature, would have occurred.

On the outside of the building (figure 20.3; Freidel and Schele 1988), there is the four-part design of the panels depicting the cycle of the Ancestral Heroes, the Sun and Venus. When the agent stood upon the landing (figure 20.4), four steps up from the base or nine steps down from the threshold, visually he would have been in the center of the facade and would have completed the *quincunx* design.

Here then, are four icons, faces, like the faces on the head pendants in the offering, but rendered at monumental and public scale. Within the structure above, there are four enormous post-holes (Freidel 1986b). These are much too deep and large to have functioned as roof supports. Rather, they must have held great poles such as are found illustrated as animate tree frames on Izapan monuments (Garth Norman, personal communication, 1986; Norman 1976). This four-part architectural design is also seen in Structure E-VII-Sub at Uaxactun (Ricketson and Ricketson 1937), where there are not only the four decorated terraces, but also the four great post-holes on the summit platform. These are the potential Preclassic analogues of the *acantes*, the set-up trees. Within such four-part enclosures, the kings of the Late Preclassic might well have encountered the supernatural, as did their historical counterparts. There can be no doubt that the set-up tree existed in the Protoclassic period, for a carved bone haft (Schele and M. Miller 1986: 269–85) of this time shows such a tree growing from the base of a pyramid. It now seems clear that Classic Maya cosmology included the concept that "world trees" emerged from all temples in an analog of the tropical forest (Schele and M. Miller 1986: 269).

Enter the King: Ritual Displayed

The advent of carved stone stelae in Lowland Maya centers marks the beginning of the Classic period for archeologists dealing with the material symbol systems of the civilization. Socially, carved stelae herald the emergence of the king as the principal focus of religious and political power. Just as important as this change in the material display of central power, however, are the clear continuities in the activities and implements that link Late Preclassic kings to their Classic counterparts. Consideration of the Hauberg Stela (figure 20.8) shows these continuities in light of the above discussion of Late Preclassic royal ritual. The Hauberg Stela displays the sort of encounter proposed between the ruler and the supernatural. The protagonist, *Bac-T'ul*, is shown in an action defined glyphically as bloodletting (Schele 1985). His right hand is shown in the "scattering" gesture. In his other arm, he holds a Vision Serpent rearing through his arm to emit its visionary personage above the head of the king. On his back, the ruler wears the tree which arches from behind his shoulder toward the ground. The mutilated sacrificial victims fall down their tree on their way to the Underworld, for this tree is the path on which the Vision and the sacrificial victim travels (Schele and M. Miller 1986: 269–70, 304, 310–12). This, then, is a Maya king of AD 200 displaying himself as the *acante*. The

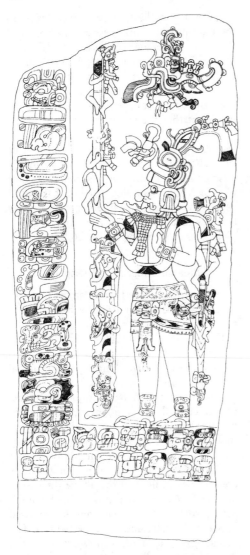

Figure 20.8 Rendering of the Hauberg Stela, showing key iconographic features of the ritual.

identification with trees is seen earlier in a surmounting element on the headdress of the king shown on the Dumbarton Oaks Plaque (figure 20.5), and perhaps most important, the ubiquitous serpent-fretted loincloth of Classic royal costume is also the *acante* in the form of the World Tree (Schele and M. Miller 1986: 77).

Four miniature beings climb the Vision Serpent. One of these is an early version of

Chac-Xib-Chac, closely tied to GI of the Triad Gods; another carries a Venus glyph in his headdress; and a third has features associated with early images of GIII, the Sun, at Tikal. Whatever the exact identities of these climbers, they are iconographically linked to the ancestral Hero Twins and the head pendants found in Late Preclassic and Early Classic offerings. Like the actual green stone objects, the heads of these climbers are bibbed (cf. Schele 1985: fig. 5). As the physical stones encircled and crowned the ruler, so these climbers frame *Bac-T'ul*: two on his left, two on his right; two above his shoulders, two below.

The three sacrificial victims falling down the tree have been cut in half and bifurcate blood scrolls flow from the wound. The bifurcate scroll is the icon of the generic substance of power, and blood and its cognates, transformed by the king ultimately into life-giving water (Freidel 1985). Unlike the four figures on the Vision Serpent, these are not bibbed, and their triadic pattern connects them to another concept, the Triad God. Maya kings of the Classic period literally give birth to the gods through blood sacrifice (Stuart 1984), as the priests of the Postclassic gave birth to the gods when they carved them of "god wood" within the four-part sacred enclosures and smeared them with sacrificial blood.

The king's right hand is the pivot of the whole composition; it overlays the point at which the tree path and the Vision Serpent intersect. Through this act of personal artifacts, he gives birth to the climbers and to the god emerging from the mouth of the Vision Serpent; through his sacrifice of the falling victims he sends them down the path to speak with the residents of the Underworld. His body as the tree is the path of both motions. The *ams*, the stones of prophecy, are cast out into the frame to become the fourfold deities who are the companions of the king in his journeys beyond this world.

Stuart (1984) has persuasively argued that the material cast by Maya kings in stela portrayals of ritual is in fact their own blood. In Classic iconography, these bloodstreams can be shown in various ways, but the one most distinctive form, both iconographically and glyphically, is a bifurcate scroll (trifurcate in front view), often marked with a beaded contour. In the glyphic version (Thompson's "water group") and in many iconic forms, the blood stream is marked by *yax, chac, k'an,* and "zero" signs, as well as by small pieces of jade, obsidian, shell, bone, and jade beads. These, we believe, are the *am* stones of the Colonial sources and the bibbed heads, shell, mirrors, and other offerings of the Late Preclassic and Early Classic caches.

What is portrayed, then, is not simply an act of communion, but also an act of creation: the creation of the paired oppositions and the gods the Maya depicted as twins; and the laying out of the *acante* (the garden plot), the farmer's field with its four sides and fourfold patrons, the four corners of the community, the four quadrants of time and the cycle of four yearbearers of the New Year rituals, all welded to the sacred obligations of kingship, incarnation, and carnation with the ancestors as first leader of all lineages. It is the creation of the future itself, in the act of divination, in the casting of lots, and in the visions of the other side of reality in the land of fright brought forth by blood.

Conclusions

The Classic period institution of *ahaw* resulted in a powerful focus upon the dynastic lineage and upon the concordance of royal actions and great cycles of history. The success of these innovations (and their material technology is carved stelae and written texts) built upon existing and enduring ritual practices and theological precepts that defined the ruler as a conduit of supernatural power and direct divine inspiration. What is extraordinary in the Maya case is not the existence of such power, or even the nature of Maya religion and ritual in the larger context of the ethnographic record of shamanism, but the fact that archeologists of a pre-Columbian society can address such specific issues to an empirical material record.

ACKNOWLEDGMENTS

We wish to thank several colleagues who have supported our efforts at interpreting Maya royal ritual through epigraphy. David Stuart, Peter Mathews, and Floyd Lounsbury have been especially influential. We are grateful to Nancy Troike for her pivotal role in the Hieroglyphic Workshop at Austin, where the discovery of the meaning of *am,* like so many discoveries, took place. An earlier version of this article was presented at a symposium at the Society for American Archaeology by the invitation of Susan Gillespie, David Grove, and Rosemary Joyce; we thank these friends and colleagues for that opportunity. The research at Cerros was supported by private benefactors and by National Science Foundation grants BNS-77-07959, BNS-78-24708, BNS-78-15905, and BNS-2-17620. Finally, we thank the editors of *American Anthropologist* and the outside reviewers for useful recommendations in the revision of the manuscript for publication. Any errors of fact or interpretation are our responsibility.

NOTES

1 The lower masks can be directly associated with the images of the cruller-eyed jaguar god of Classic period depictions. The birth of this god and his genealogical descent from the mother of the gods is explicitly recorded in the text of the Temple of the Sun at Palenque; he is the second born of the Palenque Triad of Gods first identified by Berlin (1963). Kelley (1965) identified the birth passages of these gods in the Group of the Cross, and Lounsbury (1985) associated GI and GIII as the prototypes of the *Popol Vuh* Hero Twins. The political purpose of the texts in the Group of the Cross is to document the descent of the Palenque from this set of divine borders. It is reasonable to presume that the Palenque rulers did not invent the mythology.

REFERENCES

Adams, R. E. W. 1986. Archaeologists Explore Guatemala's Lost City of the Maya: Rio Azul. *National Geographic* 169(4): 420–50.

Andrews, Anthony P. 1981. El "Guerrero" de Loltun: Commentario Analitico. *Boletin de la Escuela de Ciencas Antropologicas de la Universidad de Yucatan* 8–9 (48–9): 36–50.

Berlin, Heinrich. 1958. El Glifo "Emblema" en las Inscripciones Mayas. *Journal de la Société des Americanistes* 47 (n.s.): 111–19.

—— 1959. Glifos Nominales en el Sarcófago de Palenque. *Humanidades* 2(10): 1–8.

—— 1963. The Palenque Triad. *Journal de la Société des Americanistes* (n.s.) 52: 91–9.

Chase, Diane Z. and Arlen F. Chase. 1986. *Offerings to the Gods: Maya Archaeology at Santa Rita, Corozal*. Orlando: University of Central Florida.

Clancy, Flora S., Clemency C. Coggins, T. Patrick Culbert, Charles Gallenkamp, Peter D. Harrison, and Jeremy A. Sabloff. 1985. In *Maya, Treasures of an Ancient Civilization*, ed. Charles Gallenkamp and Regina E. Johnson. New York: Harry N. Abrams in association with the Albuquerque Museum.

Coe, Michael D. 1966. *An Early Stone Pectoral from Southwestern Mexico*. Studies in Pre-Columbian Art and Archaeology 1. Washington, DC: Dumbarton Oaks.

Coe, William R. 1959. *Piedras Negras Archaeology: Artifacts, Caches, and Burials*. University Museum Monograph 18, University of Pennsylvania.

—— 1965. Tikal, Guatemala, and Emergent Maya Civilization. *Science* 147: 1401–19.

—— 1967. *Tikal, A Handbook of the Ancient Maya Ruins*. Philadelphia: The University Museum, University of Pennsylvania.

Edmonson, Munro S. 1971. *The Book of Counsel: The Popol Vuh of the Quiche Maya of Guatemala*. Middle American Research Institute Publication 35, Tulane University, New Orleans.

Förstemann, Ernst. 1902. *Commentar zur Madrider Mayahandschrift (Codex Tro-Cortesianus)*. Danzig.

Freidel, David A. 1979. Culture Areas and Interaction Spheres: Contrasting Approaches to the Emergence of Civilization in the Maya Lowlands. *American Antiquity* 44(1): 36–54.

—— 1981. Civilization as a State of Mind: The Cultural Evolution of the Lowland Maya. In *The Transition to Statehood in the New World*, ed., G. D. Jones and R. R. Kautz, pp. 188–227. Cambridge: Cambridge University Press.

—— 1985. Polychrome Facades of the Lowland Maya Preclassic. In *Painted Architecture and Polychrome Monumental Sculpture in Mesoamerica*, ed. E. Boone, pp. 5–30. Washington, DC: Dumbarton Oaks.

—— 1986a. Maya Warfare: An Example of Peer Polity Interaction. In *Peer Polity Interaction and the Development of Sociopolitical Complexity*, ed. Colin Renfrew and John F.

Cherry, pp. 93–108. Cambridge: Cambridge University Press.

—— 1986b. The Monumental Architecture. In *Archaeology at Cerros, Belize, Central America* vol. 1: *An Interim Report*, ed. Robin A. Robertson and David A. Freidel, pp. 1–22. Dallas: Southern Methodist University Press.

Freidel, David A. and Linda Schele. 1988. Symbol and Power: A History of the Lowland Maya Cosmogram. In *Maya Iconography*, ed. E. Benson and G. Griffin, Princeton, NJ: Princeton University Press.

Garber, James F. 1983. Patterns of Jade Consumption and Disposal at Cerros, Northern Belize. *American Antiquity* 48(4): 800–7.

—— 1986. The Artifacts. In *Archaeology at Cerros, Belize, Central America*, vol. 1: *An Interim Report*, ed. Robin A. Robertson and David A. Freidel, pp. 117–26. Dallas: Southern Methodist University Press.

Graham, Ian. 1986. Looters Rob Graves and History. *National Geographic* 169(4): 453–61.

Hammond, Norman. 1985a. The Emergence of Maya Civilization. *Scientific American* 255(2): 106–15.

—— 1985b. New Light on the Most Ancient Maya. *Man* 21(3): 399–413.

—— 1987. *The Sun Also Rises: Iconographic Syntax of the Pomona Flare*. Research Reports on Ancient Maya Writing, Nos 6 and 7. Washington: Center for Maya Research.

Jones, Christopher and Linton Satterthwaite. 1982. *The Monuments and Inscriptions of Tikal: The Carved Monuments*. Tikal Report No. 33, part A. University Museum Monograph 44. Philadelphia: University Museum, University of Pennsylvania.

Justeson, John, William Norman, and Norman Hammond. 1988. The Pomona Jade Flare: A Preclassic Mayan Hieroglyphic Text. In *Maya Iconography*, ed. E. Benson and G. Griffin, Princeton: Princeton University Press.

Kelley, David. 1962. Glyphic Evidence for a Dynastic Sequence at Quirigua, Guatemala. *American Antiquity* 27: 323–35.

—— 1965. The Birth of the Gods at Palenque. In *Estudios de Cultura Maya* 5, pp. 93–134. Universidad Nacional Autónoma de México, Mexico City.

Kidder, A. V. 1947. *The Artifacts of Uaxactun, Guatemala*. Carnegie Institution of Washington Publication 576. Washington, DC: Carnegie Institution.

Lounsbury, Floyd G. 1974. The Inscription of the Sarcophagus Lid at Palenque. In *Primera Mesa Redonda de Palenque*, part II, ed. Merle Greene

Robertson, pp. 5–20. Pebble Beach: Robert Louis Stevenson School.

—— 1985. The Identities of the Mythological Figures in the "Cross Group" of Inscriptions at Palenque. In *Fourth Round Table of Palenque, 1980*, vol. 6, ed. Elizabeth Benson, pp. 45–58. San Francisco: Pre-Columbian Art Research Institute.

Matheny, Ray T. 1987. Early States in the Maya Lowlands During the Late Preclassic Period: Edzna and El Mirador. In *The Maya State*, ed. Elizabeth B. Benson, Denver: Rocky Mountain Institute for Precolumbian Studies.

Mathews, Peter and Linda Schele. 1974. Lords of Palenque – The Glyphic Evidence. In *Primera Mesa Redonda de Palenque*, part I, ed. Merle Greene Robertson, pp. 63–76. Pebble Beach: Robert Louis Stevenson School.

Norman, V. Garth. 1976. *Izapa Sculpture*. Part 2: *Text*. Provo, UT: Brigham Young University, Papers of the New World Archaeological Foundation 30.

Pendergast, David M. 1981. Lamanai, Belize: Summary of Excavation Results, 1974–1980. *Journal of Field Archaeology* 8: 29–53.

Potter, Daniel R. 1985. Settlement. In *A Consideration of the Early Classic Period in the Maya Lowlands*, ed. Gordon R. Willey and Peter Mathews, pp. 135–44. Publication No. 10. Institute for Mesoamerican Studies, State University of New York at Albany.

Price, H. W. 1899. *Proceedings of the Society of Antiquaries* 17: 339–44.

Proskouriakoff, Tatiana. 1960. Historical Implications of a Pattern of Dates at Piedras Negras, Guatemala. *American Antiquity* 25: 454–75.

—— 1961. Lords of the Maya Realm. *Expedition* 4(1): 14–21.

—— 1963–4. Historical Data in the Inscriptions of Yaxchilan, Parts I and II. *Estudios de Cultura Maya* 3: 149–67, and 4: 177–201.

Ricketson, Oliver G. and Edith B. Ricketson. 1937. *Uaxactun, Guatemala: Group E, 1926–1931*. Carnegie Institution of Washington, Publication 477. Washington, DC: Carnegie Institution.

Roys, Ralph L. 1965. *Ritual of the Bacabs*. Norman: University of Oklahoma Press.

Schele, Linda. 1976. Accession Iconography of Chan-Bahlum in the Group of the Cross at Palenque. In *The Art, Iconography and Dynastic History of Palenque*, part III, ed. Merle Greene Robertson, pp. 9–34. Pebble Beach: Robert Louis Stevenson School.

—— 1978–87. Notebooks of the Maya Hieroglyphic Workshop at Austin. Institute for Latin American Studies, University of Texas at Austin, Texas.

—— 1979. Genealogical Documentation on the Tri-Figure Panels at Palenque. In *Tercera Mesa Redonda de Palenque, 1978*, part I, ed. Merle Greene Robertson and Donnan Call Jeffers, pp. 41–70. Monterey, CA: Pre-Columbian Art Research.

—— 1982. *Maya Glyphs: The Verbs*. Austin: University of Texas Press.

—— 1985. The Hauberg Stela: Bloodletting and the Mythos of Maya Rulership. In *Fifth Palenque Round Table, 1983*, vol. 7, ed. Virginia M. Fields, pp. 135–49. San Francisco: Pre-Columbian Art Research Institute.

Schele, Linda and Jeffrey H. Miller. 1983. *The Mirror, The Rabbit, and The Bundle: "Accession" Expressions from the Classic Maya Inscriptions*. Studies in Pre-Columbian Art and Archaeology, No. 25. Washington, DC: Dumbarton Oaks Research Library and Collection.

Schele, Linda and Mary Ellen Miller. 1986. *The Blood of Kings: Dynasty and Ritual in Maya Art*. Fort Worth: Kimbell Art Museum.

Schele, Linda and David Stuart. 1986. *Te-tun as the Glyph for Stela*. Copán Note 1. Copán Mosaics Project and the Instituto Hondureño de Antropología e Historia. Copán, Honduras.

Shafer, Harry J. and Tom R. Hester. 1983. Ancient Maya Chert Workshops in Northern Belize, Central America. *American Antiquity* 48: 519–43.

Sharer, Robert J. 1974. The Prehistory of the Southeastern Maya Periphery. *Current Anthropology* 15(2): 165–87.

Stuart, David. 1984. Royal Auto-Sacrifice Among the Maya: A Study of Image and Meaning. In *Maya Iconography*, ed. E. P. Benson and G. Griffin, Princeton: Princeton University Press.

Thomas, Cyrus. 1882. *A Study of the Manuscript Troano*. Contributions to North American Ethnology, vol. 5, pt. 3, Washington, DC.

Thompson, J. Eric S. 1962. *A Catalog of Maya Hieroglyphics*. Norman: University of Oklahoma Press.

—— 1972. *A Commentary on the Dresden Codex*. Philadelphia: American Philosophical Society.

Tozzer, Alfred M. 1941. *Landa's Relación de las Cosas de Yucatan: A Translation*. Cambridge, MA: Papers of the Peabody Museum of American Archaeology and Ethnology, vol. 18.

Wauchope, Robert. 1938. *Modern Maya Houses: A Study of their Archaeological Significance*. Carnegie Institution of Washington, Publication No. 502. Washington, DC: Carnegie Institution.

Willey, Gordon R. 1977. The Rise of Maya Civilization: A Summary View. In *The Origins of Maya Civilization*, ed. R. E. W. Adams, pp. 383–425. Albuquerque: University of New Mexico Press.

——1985. The Early Classic in the Maya Lowlands: An Overview. In *A Consideration of the Early Classic Period in the Maya Lowlands*, ed.

Gordon R. Willey and Peter Mathews, pp. 5–54. Albany: Institute for Mesoamerican Studies, State University of New York at Albany.

Willey, Gordon R. and Peter Mathews (eds.) 1985. *A Consideration of the Early Classic Period in the Maya Lowlands*. Albany: Institute for Mesoamerican Studies, State University of New York at Albany.

CHAPTER 21

Postclassic Maya Ritual at Laguna de On Island, Belize

Marilyn A. Masson

Recent investigations at the Postclassic site of Laguna de On, Belize, provide evidence of an increase in ritual activity at the site during the Late Postclassic within a single, centrally located domestic zone. This paper examines the features and assemblages that signify Late Facet Late Postclassic (AD 1250–1450) ritual activity at this island settlement. Two contexts for ritual are identified at this site: a residential building (Structure I) and a rubble platform (Structure II) of specialized ritual function. Both structures form part of the same residential group, amid a zone of other domestic features in the north-central area of the site. In this paper, the examination of ritual contexts at Laguna de On employs a detailed analysis of features, artifacts, and depositional processes. A domestic-to-ritual continuum in assemblage composition is identified at these structures, and comparative frequencies demonstrate assemblage signatures that express the degree of ritual practice in each context examined. Late Postclassic Maya ritual at the community of Laguna de On illustrates a clear link between ritual activities and social status, and was a primary manner in which social power was manifested at this site. This examination of ritual contexts and assemblages at a small, rural community addresses the important issue of the degree of religious "secularization" in Postclassic Maya society.

The Site and its Setting

The Postclassic community of Laguna de On was located on an island and the shores of Honey Camp Lagoon in northern Belize (figure 21.1). Investigations at this site under the auspices of the Belize Postclassic Project (Masson and Rosenswig 1997, 1998a) and the Honey Camp–El Cacao Project (Masson 1993, 1997; Valdez et al. 1992) have examined diachronic patterns of community organization after the collapse of southern-lowland, Classic-period polities in northern Belize. This Postclassic community was located in a rural setting at a considerable distance (see figure 21.1) from political centers of this period, such as Lamanai (Pendergast 1981, 1986), Santa Rita (Chase 1982, 1986; Chase and Chase 1988), and Caye Coco (Masson and Rosenswig 1998b). Laguna de On was likely in the political domain of the newly discovered Postclassic center of Caye Coco on Progresso Lagoon (Masson and Rosenswig 1998b), located 20 km north down the Freshwater Creek drainage (see figure 21.1).

Laguna de On is thought to have occupied a third-tier position in the Late Postclassic political hierarchy of northern Belize, based on a three-tier model of centralized province organization originally proposed by Roys (1957) and recently reexamined by Marcus (1993). Laguna de On's classification is based on the spatial extent of the settlement

Reprinted from Marilyn A. Masson. 1999. Postclassic Maya Ritual at Laguna de On Island, Belize. *Ancient Mesoamerica* 10, pp. 51–68.

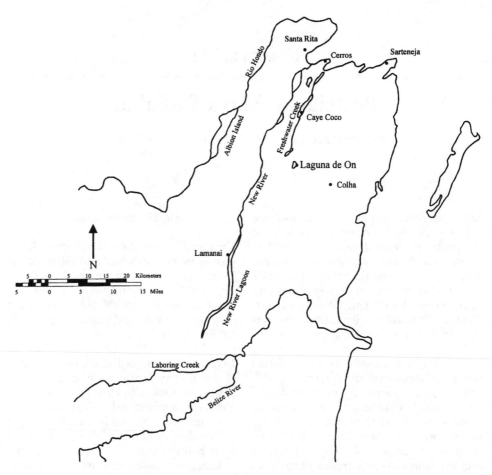

Figure 21.1 Location of Laguna de On and other selected Late Postclassic Maya sites.

around the shore (Waid and Masson 1998) and on the island, and the lack of elevated platform architecture of Postclassic date at this site. Laguna de On is tentatively classified as a third-tier site that would not have served as the seat of a primary (*halac uinic*) or secondary (*batab*) administrator in this region.

Settlement data suggest that Laguna de On was positioned within a nested hierarchy of communities (Masson 1998: fig. 2.1). At least four Late Postclassic centers have been identified within the Chetumal-province parameters (as defined by Jones [1989: map 21]) to which Laguna de On was probably linked. These Chetumal-province centers include Caye Coco (Masson and Rosenswig 1998b), Santa Rita (Chase and Chase 1988), Ichpaatun, and Sarteneja (Sidrys 1983). Laguna de On may have been part of a geopolitical unit formed by the Freshwater Creek drainage to the north, which linked it to the center of Caye Coco at Progresso Lagoon, the Last Resort site at Laguna Seca, and perhaps other communities along this waterway that are yet to be identified (see figure 21.1; Masson 1998: fig. 2.1). Four such linear aquatic political systems may have existed in northern Belize, organized along such prominent features as the Río Hondo, the New River, the Freshwater Creek drainage, and the Belize coast and cayes (Masson 1998).

Laguna de On Stratigraphy and Chronology

The island site of Laguna de On comprises three basic stratigraphic units (Masson and Stafford 1998). The lowest and earliest of these (Level 4) includes fine white clays intermingled with marl *sascab* limestone bedrock (Rosenswig and Stafford 1998). The clays are located in patches across the east side of the island and are absent in other locations tested, in which only bedrock was encountered. Overlying bedrock and white clays, Level 3 is defined as an interface zone (a mixture of two deposits) that combines overlying brown-gray loam deposits (Level 2) and bedrock. Level 2 is a layer of brown-gray loam that extends across the island in a 30-cm-thick layer from 15 to 45 cm below the surface. Level 1 is a layer of humic topsoil, riddled with roots, which overlies the brown-gray loam across the island. This topsoil layer extends from the surface to an average depth of 15 cm (Masson and Stafford 1998).

Two facets of Late Postclassic occupation are defined in these deposits at Laguna de On (Masson and Stafford 1998: fig. 1), the Early Facet (AD 1050–1250) and the Late Facet (AD 1250–1450). Thought to represent a linked, continuous occupation, these facets are defined on the basis of stratigraphic position and radiocarbon dating (Masson and Stafford 1998). Features and artifacts from the island's Early Facet Postclassic deposits are found within the brown-gray loam (Levels 2 and 3) that overlies bedrock across the island. A subsequent assemblage of Late Facet features and artifacts is found within the humic topsoil (Level 1) across the site.

Clear breaks in ceramic traditions are not observed among these two facets of occupation, which include primarily Payil Red, Rita Red, Zakpah Orange Red, Santa Unslipped, and unslipped censer forms (Mock 1997, 1998). The sherds at this site are highly fragmented and eroded, which makes the identification of types difficult, especially when vessel form is the most diagnostic attribute

(Mock 1998). The assemblage is dominated by Payil Red ceramics that link deposits of the Early and Late Facets in a continuum of ceramic production, despite an increase through time in the amounts of Rita Red and effigy censer forms observed at the site (Masson and Stafford 1998: fig. 3).

In spite of ceramic similarities, differences are observed between the types of features occurring in the Early Facet deposits (Levels 2 and 3) and those associated with Late Facet deposits (Level 1). Radiocarbon dating of lower and upper feature clusters suggests that these stratigraphic patterns are temporal, rather than horizontal, phenomena (Masson 1998; Stafford 1998; Masson and Stafford 1998). The assignment of stratigraphic deposits to the Early and Late Facet components is, thus, based on radiocarbon dating of vertically distinct features.

Changes in Early and Late Facet Features and Assemblages at Laguna de On Island

Early Facet features and artifacts found within Levels 2–3 across the island suggest that Laguna de On was a stable, prosperous community focused on the economic production of ceramics, textiles, and agricultural products; chalcedony quarrying; and extracting forest resources. Few Early Facet features or artifact distributions from the island appear to be related to a concern with public works or ritual. Household architecture is difficult to detect, limited to eroded dirt and marl floor surfaces and occasional postholes (Aguilera 1998; Sheldon 1998). Five large pits found at these lower levels were filled with ashy soil and other debris (e.g. broken metates, stone slab linings, and large sherds) that suggest they were used for firing ceramics (Aguilera 1998; Masson et al. 1997; Rosenswig and Becker 1997; Wharton 1998a).

It is clear from the presence of utilized stone tools and cores (Masson 1997; Oland 1998), large amounts of debitage (Masson 1993, 1997), a range of utilitarian ceramic forms (Mock 1998), spindle whorls (Murray 1998), manos and metates (Masson n.d.), faunal remains (Masson 1993; Wharton 1997, 1998b), and post molds, hearths, and fire pits (Aguilera 1998; Sheldon 1998) that the island was the site of domestic occupation and that a variety of household maintenance and production activities were performed there. Domestic debris is associated with architectural remains and is also found in sheet midden deposits that extend across the entire island. The settlement at the island was part of an occupation also found on the shores of the lagoon (Masson 1993, 1997; Waid and Masson 1998). Differences are not observed in the utilitarian debris found in Early Facet and Late Facet deposits, and all of the categories of debris listed above are included in each component. Like the ceramic assemblages, other utilitarian artifacts do not significantly change from the Early to the Late Facet. It is, thus, within a context of domestic continuity that the acceleration of ritual activities is observed between the Early and Late Facets.

Features of the Late Facet suggest an additional suite of community activities at this site that are not observed among Early Facet features. Five additional behavioural patterns reflected in Late Facet features include: (1) the construction of a defensive fortification (Barnhart and Howard 1997), (2) increased investment in household architecture (Aguilera 1998; West 1998; Wharton 1998a), (3) increased status differentiation in household assemblages (Masson n.d.), (4) increased ritual activity practiced in higher-status domestic zones, (Masson n.d.), and (5) the construction of formal ritual facilities (Masson n.d.). The first three patterns are described elsewhere (as referenced above), and the latter two patterns are the focus of the descriptions and analyses below.

A continuum of ritual-to-domestic zones is identified in Late Facet features at Laguna de On through variability observed in artifact assemblages (Masson 1998). The phrase "domestic zone" refers to an area that was either the site of a domestic structure or a sheet midden that is presumed to have derived from nearby structures. Ritual activity is identified in this study by the following indicators: the presence of concentrated,

broken incense-burner ceramics; caching of exotic or whole, unused, formal lithic tools; concentrations of cranial elements of large game animals; and concentrations of burned rock that do not appear to represent domestic activities. Although some features were constructed and reserved primarily for ritual practice (e.g. Structure II; figure 21.2), ritual activities are also found in upper-status domestic zones (primarily Structure I, but also Suboperation [Subop] 5; see figure 21.2). Some domestic zones exhibit no ritual indicators at all (e.g. Subops 17, 2/3, 7, 9–11, 15, 16, and 18; see figure 21.2), even though two of these zones (Subops 2/3, 17) were located in proximity to ritual activities performed at Structures I and II and are thought to form part of the same upper-status domestic group as these structures at the site (Aguilera 1998; Masson 1993). Household architecture across the site includes stone wall alignments, cobble floor foundations, and plaster floors; this architecture does not appear to vary according to social status at the site (Aguilera 1998; West 1998; Wharton 1998a). In fact, ritual activity is one of the primary indicators of status differentiation among

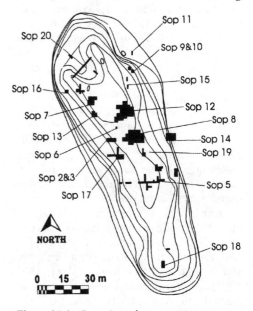

Figure 21.2   Location of excavation units on Laguna de On Island.

domestic groups. This pattern suggests that ritual at Laguna was not completely "secularized"; access to ritual knowledge and paraphernalia was not equal for all occupants of this settlement as has been previously suggested for Postclassic society (Smith 1962: 267; Thompson 1957: 634).

Ritual Activity in the Late Facet Occupation of Laguna de On

The remainder of this paper will present the analysis of ritual indicators at Laguna de On Island, as observed at the Structure I upper-status residence where ritual activity was concentrated and at the Structure II rubble platform. This examination will also address key issues of how ritual activity can be identified through assemblage analysis, and how domestic and ritual activities were combined in the Late Facet of the Postclassic occupation of Laguna de On Island.

Structure I: architecture and features of a ritual and domestic nature

The stone alignment that marks Structure I overlies two fire-pit features, 30 cm of brown loam sheet midden, and three burials

(Masson et al. 1997). A portion of this underlying midden dates to the Late Facet, as a fire feature yielded a calibrated radiocarbon date of AD 1280–1420 (Stafford 1998). Structure I overlies this feature and is, therefore, at least this old.

Structure I is defined by a three-sided wall foundation comprised of a single-course line of stones located on the north, west, and south sides (figures 21.3 and 21.4). An area of 67 square meters was excavated to expose features located within and outside of this foundation. The structure is open to the east, where no foundation stones were located (see figure 21.4). The upper portion of the building would have had perishable pole walls and a thatch roof. Three-sided "C-shaped" configurations have been reported among Classic and Postclassic architectural forms from northern Yucatan (Bey et al. 1997; Pollock 1965. fig. 10) to the Peten (Rice 1986; Tourtellot 1988: 247–60), and from earlier in the Classic period at Uaxactun (Pollock 1965: fig. 22). At the southwest corner of the building, a west-running alignment may have framed part of an additional room.

Near the southwest corner of the structure, a God K effigy eccentric chert artifact

Figure 21.3 Structure I, facing east. Stone alignment overlies 30 cm of brown loam deposits. Stones at bedrock level in foreground mark fire features that underlie Structure I and intrude into bedrock.

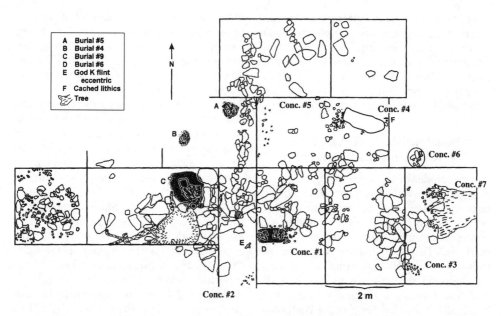

Figure 21.4 Composite map of features, Structure I.

(figure 21.5) was found at a depth of 15 cm below the surface. The artifact was probably cached in this location, but depositional evidence for near-surface caching is difficult to document in root-riddled humic topsoil and its transition to underlying brown loam, which does not preserve evidence of intrusive sediment features. However, the artifact was found below the humic root mat at the base of Level 1 topsoil deposits that contain Late Facet deposits and artifact concentrations at this location. In addition, the artifact was 40 cm southwest of a child burial (Burial 6), which was located at a slightly lower depth (20 cm below the surface; Masson et al. 1997: 17). Over this child burial was one of the most extensive concentrations of smashed censers and animal skulls found at the site (described later). The God K eccentric may be associated with these additional ritual features, further suggesting that it was buried beneath the surface at this location as an offering.

The God K effigy form of this artifact is identified by the smoking torch feature on each of the two heads depicted (see figure 21.5; Masson 1997). Such elaborate eccentrics are unknown from other

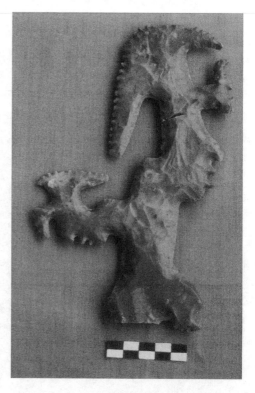

Figure 21.5 God K effigy eccentric flint from Structure I.

Postclassic contexts, and deity eccentrics from the Classic period are rare. Finely made eccentrics are recovered primarily from Classic-period funerary or cache contexts at such political centers as Altun Ha (Pendergast 1982: 121–4), Copan (Fash 1991: figs 53–7), El Palmar (Morley et al. 1983: 448), El Pozito (Hester et al. 1991), and Quirigua (Morley et al. 1983: 448). Eccentrics in northern Belize were made at the site of Colha (Eaton et al. 1994; Shafer and Hester 1983), and the Laguna de On eccentric is made of Colha chert. It is probably in secondary context, looted during the Postclassic period from a Classic-period monumental structure nearby. The base of the artifact is broken. Caching of eccentrics or other lithics in Postclassic contexts has been observed at Santa Rita (Gann 1918: 68), though it is unclear whether these artifacts were manufactured in the Postclassic. God K effigy flints were used as scepters of political authority in the Classic period (Coggins 1988; Schele 1976). This deity

had close symbolic associations with royal ancestors and passage into death (Grube 1992: 209–10; Schele and Miller 1986: 73, 286, pl. 114). The God K deity was also an important figure in the Postclassic codices, and retained its association with offices of political authority (Love 1994: 18). Thus, this object may have symbolized important links to the past, as well as current political authority for the agents of ritual at Structure I (Masson 1997).

Concentrations of artifacts at Structure I

Seven concentrations of ceramics and other artifacts were mapped around Structure I (figure 21.6). Each concentration included various amounts of censer sherds, red slipped and unslipped or eroded ceramics, animal bones, freshwater snail shells, flakes, and (rarely) obsidian (Masson et al. 1997). One of these, in the base of a tree root in Subop 8L (see figure 21.4), was highly

Figure 21.6 Ceramic and bone concentration Lot 27/36 (Concentration 1), south side of Structure I.

Table 21.1 Contents of artifact concentrations at Structure I

Concentration #, Location at Structure I Lot #	Lithic tools	Lithic flakes	Faunal remains	Slipped ceramics	Unslipped ceramics	Eroded ceramics	Censer fragments	Total
Concentration #1, south exterior (Lot 27/36)	3 (2.8%)	61 (5.4%)	174 (15.4%)	60 (61.4%)	38 (3.4%)	103 (9.1%)	27 (2.4%)	1,127
Concentration #2, southwest exterior (Lot 21/44)	3 (14.3%)	56 (25.1%)	36 (16.1%)	39 (17.5%)	12 (5.4%)	40 (17.9%)	8 (3.6%)	223
Concentration #3, southeast exterior (Lot 135/142)	3 (15.4%)	25 (12.0%)	10 (4.8%)	38 (18.3%)	5 (2.4%)	98 (47.1%)	?	208
Concentration #4, east interior (Lot 91/100/104)	1 (.5%)	104 (48.4%)	85 (39.5%)	8 (3.7%)	2 (.9%)	15 (7.0%)	?	215
Concentration #5, interior (Lot 92/101)	0	11 (5.9%)	99 (52.7%)	20 (10.6%)	43 (22.9%)	13 (6.9%)	2 (3.6%)	188
Concentration #6, east exterior (Lot 167)	0	8 (80%)	0	0	0	2 (20%)	?	10

Note: Percent shown is that within each concentration.

disturbed. The contents of the other six are listed in table 21.1, which lists the number of lithic tools, lithic flakes, faunal bone, and types of ceramics recovered from these concentrations and defines the material signature of a high-status domestic context for ritual.

The depositional context of these concentrations is unclear. No concentrations contained the remains of a single reconstructable vessel. Pieces of several vessels are represented in most concentrations, a pattern best demonstrated in Concentration 1 (figure 21.6), which had portions of at least eight bowls (direct rim, basal break, tripod, collared, and incised forms), one plate, one jar, one chalice, one *comal*, and two censer vessels represented by the sherds recovered. Censer forms included Cehachunacti Composite, Thul Appliqué, Onha Perforated (colander), and Kol Modeled, according to Mock (1997, 1998 [partially following Walker 1990]). Unslipped wares primarily included Santa Unslipped (Mock 1998), and slipped wares included Payil Red, Rita Red, and Zakpah Orange Red (Mock 1997, 1998 [following Chase 1982; Mock 1994]). Forms were not as diagnostic in concentrations other than Concentration 1 because of the lower number of sherds found in them (see table 21.1).

Lithic tools in the concentrations included six utilized flakes (in Concentrations 1, 2, 3), two cores (in Concentrations 2 and 3), and two formal-tool fragments (in Concentrations 1 and 4). A proximal lenticular biface fragment was found in Concentration 4, and a medial oval biface fragment was found in Concentration 1, typed according to lithic classifications established at Colha (Hester and Shafer 1991; Michaels 1987; Shafer and Hester 1983; Hester and Shafer 1991). Lithic tools were recovered primarily from south side concentrations (Concentrations 1–3), except for the lenticular biface found to the east (in Concentration 4). It is unclear whether they were used for ritual purposes or whether they represent domestic debris mixed into these concentrations.

Concentration 1 is the most extensive of all those recorded at the site. It was located on the south exterior side of the building, 10–20 cm above the child burial mentioned above. Other concentrations were noted along the east side of the building (see figure 21.4) and inside the building. Concentrations were not found on the north side of the building, but isolated Kol Modeled effigy-censer elements were found on all four exterior sides of it. In fact, four different sherds recovered from four sides of Structure I were refitted to form part of an hourglass censer vessel (figure 21.7). The location of these sherds suggests that they and other ceramic vessel fragments recovered with them were intentionally broken and scattered prior to deposition. Concentrations listed in table 21.1, other than Concentration 1, exhibited low quantities of expedient lithic tools, occasional formal-tool fragments, and various quantities of flakes and faunal remains. The faunal assemblage from Structure I features is distinguished from the rest of the site by the inclusion of cranial elements of large game animals, including brocket and white-tailed deer, peccary, tapir, and alligator (Masson 1993; Wharton 1997, 1998b), which are not found elsewhere at the site. The cranial elements of these species resemble the ceramics in their broken, disarticulated state. Reconstructable skulls were not represented in any single concentration, but whole jaws of deer and peccary were occasionally found. The materials found in concentrations around Structure I (see table 21.1) resemble the materials found in the entire assemblage of Late Facet sediments around the building (discussed later). Censers, cranial elements of large game, and lithics are generally found in the sediments surrounding this structure, although they are concentrated in certain areas. This pattern is attributed to diachronic activities occurring at this location that collectively contributed to concentrated features and a general spread of debris that provides this assemblage with its mixed residential and ritual signature.

Variability is observed in the percentages of materials comprising different concentrations, which may indicate functional

Figure 21.7   Censer fragments from Structure I.

variability in the kinds of activities that occurred around this building. Minimally, this variability indicates the range of activities that occurred through time at Structure I. The percentages shown in table 21.1 indicate that material classes are not uniformly found in each concentration. Lithic tools are low in most concentrations, and only form significant percentages of two concentrations that are located at the southwest (Concentration 2) and southeast (Concentration 3) vicinities of the building (see table 21.1). Lithic flakes were most common along the east side of the building, in percentages indicated for Concentration 4 (48.4%) and Lot 167 of Concentration 6 (80%). These high numbers of flakes may attest to a high index of domestic activities at the east side of the building. As the building opened to the east,

this may have been a frontal patio zone where general household production activities were performed. Concentration 4 also has one of the highest percentages of faunal remains (39.5%), although even more faunal remains were found within a concentration inside of the structure's walls (Concentration 5; 52.7%). Slipped ceramics are most commonly found in concentrations on the south side of the building, notably in Concentration 1 (61.4%), and also in Concentration 2 (17.5%) and Concentration 3 (18.3%). Unslipped ceramics are shown in low percentages, but many of these sherds may be masked in the "eroded" category, as they were difficult to identify to type in initial preliminary lab identifications. Censers, as identified by appliqué or effigy elements, are present in three concentrations (i.e. Concentrations 1, 2, and 5), and are most numerous in those located along the south exterior of the building (see table 21.1).

These comparisons indicate that the south concentrations contained greater percentages of slipped ceramics and censers. Other concentrations on the east side and in the interior of the structure had greater percentages of faunal remains and lithic flakes. This variation in contents suggests that much of the ritual activity at Structure I may have been concentrated along the south side of the building. It is possible that this activity was related to the location of Burial 6 in this vicinity. However, the recovery of refitting pieces to a single effigy censer from around all sides of the building (see figure 21.7) and the presence of censer sherds and large-animal cranial elements in general lots (outside of concentrations) suggests that the practice of ritual at this domestic location was not an isolated event, but part of ongoing activities that resulted in the mixture of features and ritual and domestic assemblages at this location.

Structure II: artifacts and features from a nondomestic rubble platform

Structure II was constructed in the Late Facet, based on a calibrated radiocarbon date of AD 1228–1390 from a carbonized wooden disk recovered from within its rubble matrix (Stafford 1998). One Colonial-period ceramic cup was recovered from its surface (Gann 1928; Masson 1997: fig. 9), suggesting its continued use in some capacity into the historical period. No ritual indicators were found beneath Structure II. A 40-cm-thick zone of brown-loam sheet midden or midden fill was encountered below the structure, above bedrock (Rosenswig and Becker 1997).

Structure II is located at the high point of the island, 10 m north of Structure I (see figure 21.2). An area of 77 m² was excavated around this building. The top portion of much of the rubble from this building was visible on the surface prior to excavation. Also visible from the surface was a row of vertical stones embedded into the rubble along the west half of the north edge of the building. Structure II's appearance and dimensions prior to excavation match a description of a "pavement of stone" reported by Thomas Gann (1928: 54), who visited the island in 1927.

Excavations at Structure II revealed a 3×4m rubble platform (figures 21.8 and 21.9) raised 25–40 cm above the surrounding terrain. Along the south, presumably frontal, edge of the rubble platform, a rubble patio (2 × 9 m) extends to the southeast (see figure 21.9). The platform and patio are oriented 10° west of magnetic north and face Structure I. This architecture was probably originally covered in limestone plaster that has since eroded because of its proximity to the surface. The platform consisted of two distinct spatial features on its east and west halves (Rosenswig and Becker 1997: 31–2) (see figure 21.9). The west side is framed by a vertical wall alignment on the north and contains less surface rubble, which appears to indicate the location of an enclosed room. The east side consisted of densely packed rubble. Both sides of the platform, including the west room and the east rubble surface, were functionally linked by dense concentrations of burned rock and other features and artifacts.

Ten burned-rock concentrations were identified in the rubble of Structure II (see figure 21.9), from 20 to 50 cm in diameter. They consisted of clusters of 5–30 highly charred, cube-shaped, golf-ball-sized limestone rocks. These clusters did not form depressions, and very few artifacts were recovered among them that might indicate their function. No burned matrix is associated with them, but their proximity to the surface could have resulted in the erosion of such sediments. The locations of these burned-rock features is plotted on figure 21.9. They generally encircle the rubble platform located on the east, south, west, and north sides of it. Three burned-rock concentrations are located farther away from the platform than the others, aligned along the east edge of the rubble patio (see figure 21.9). Two burned-rock

Figure 21.8   Structure II, facing northwest from far southeast corner of patio. Rubble platform in background, rubble patio in foreground.

concentrations are adjacent to the platform on the east and north sides, and one concentration is located on the south edge. Four additional concentrations are lined up in a row along the west side of the platform. They lie directly south of a vertical stone wall alignment that defines the rear (north) boundary of the room located on the west of Structure II; they appear to be located within this room and to define its east boundary.

Unique artifacts at the site were also recovered from the surface of this rubble platform (figure 21.10). One carbonized-disk wooden artifact was found embedded in the rubble of Structure II near the south (front) edge. One engraved ceramic object was found on the surface of the platform (figure 21.10a). An unused, complete, triangular biface (figure 21.10b) was found on top of the stones in the east side of the building. This tool may represent a cached lithic item, although the same difficulties in identifying topsoil caching for the God K

eccentric (discussed earlier) also apply to this artifact. Its complete, unused state suggests that it may have been placed in this location as an offering. Other stone tools were found embedded in the rubble patio in front of Structure II (Rosenwig and Becker 1997: 33), although these artifacts were heavily used and utilitarian in nature. It is unknown whether they are related to activities performed at this location or if they were part of the rubble fill in which they were found. One sherd from Structure II was refitted with a sherd from Structure I (figure 21.10c), suggesting that the structures were used contemporaneously.

Concentrations of artifacts at Structure II

Nine concentrations of artifacts were documented around this structure (see figure 21.9). The contents of eight fully excavated concentrations are shown in table 21.2 (omitting Concentration 9, which was not

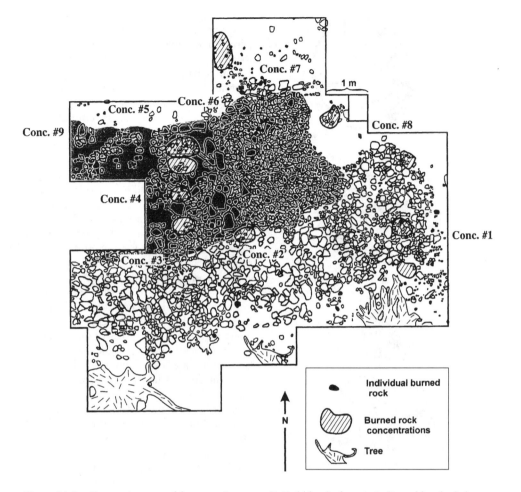

Figure 21.9 Composite map of features, Structure II. Rubble platform is indicated by shaded area, rubble patio is unshaded.

fully excavated). The artifact concentrations follow the same pattern of spatial distribution around the structure as the burned-rock features. In general, they are found on all four sides of the structure, or adjacent to its edges, with one outlier located at the far southeast corner of the rubble patio (Concentration 1; see figure 21.9). Concentration 2 is located (adjacent to a burned-rock feature) near the south edge of the platform, and four features (Features 3–5 and one incompletely excavated feature, Feature 9) are located on the west side of Structure II. Two additional concentrations (Concentrations 6 and 7) are located north of the rear

wall or edge of this structure, and one (Concentration 8) is located off of its east edge. Most concentrations appear paired with one or more burned-rock features, but functional links between these deposits are unclear.

The highest percentages of flakes are found on the west side (Concentrations 3 and 5; 24% and 36%, respectively). Faunal remains are also common in features to the west (Concentration 3, 72%), far southeast (Concentration 1, 42%), and north (Concentration 7, 34%). High frequencies of flakes and faunal remains are not found in the same features, but the highest

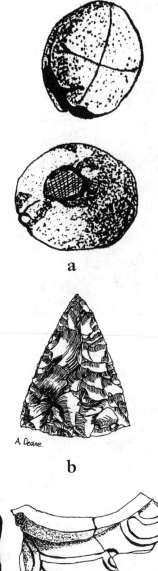

a

b

A. Deane.

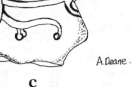

c

Figure 21.10 Artifacts found on surface of
Structure II: (a) engraved ceramic object;
(b) triangular biface; (c) engraved ceramic
(refitted with piece from Structure I); (b) and (c)
reduced to 50% of actual size. (Illustrations by
Anne Deane.)

percentages of each were found within the
west portion of the structure. Although high
percentages of flakes are reflected in features
located to the west, higher quantities of
faunal remains occur in features dispersed
around the structure. Faunal remains from
Structure II do not include the specialized
assemblage of large-game cranial parts
observed at Structure I. Fish, turtle, and
bird bones, as well as various mammal-
bone fragments, are common in this vicinity.
Slipped ceramics occur in higher percentages
in concentrations on the west side (Concentrations 4, 76.2%; 6, 39.3%) and off the
east edge (Concentration 8, 62%). These
figures functionally link the east and west
sides of the platform, both on and off of the
rubble surface. Slipped ceramics were less
common in other concentrations (see table
21.2). Ceramic-vessel forms were determined for several concentrations (identifications made by Shirley Mock), as follows:
Concentration 1 had pieces of an outflaring
bowl; Concentration 2 had a mixture of
bowl and plate forms and an unslipped jar;
Concentration 4 had portions of a shallow
bowl, a basal break bowl, and an effigy-
support bowl; Concentration 6 had portions
of a basal break bowl and a direct rim bowl,
and Concentration 7 had pieces of a small
jar or bowl, an incised jar, and a parenthesis-
rim jar. These vessel forms indicate that serving dishes were used extensively at Structure II. Mixed pieces of different vessels in
these concentrations follow the pattern
observed for Structure I.

Unslipped ceramics and censers in concentrations on the platform were most
common off the northeast edge (in Concentration 8). Unslipped sherds were also common to the west of the structure (in
Concentration 5). Although highest on the
northeast (in Concentration 8), censers were
also found on the west side (in Concentration 4), off the south edge (in Concentration
2); a ladle-censer fragment was found off the
north side (in Concentration 7). The distribution of censers (in low identified numbers), thus, follows that of high percentages
of slipped ceramics in east and west Concentrations 4 and 8. The co-occurrence of high

Table 21.2 Contents of artifact concentrations at Structure II

Concentration #, Location, Lot	Lithic tools	Lithic flakes	Faunal remains	Slipped ceramics	Unslipped ceramics	Eroded ceramics	Censer fragments	Total
Concentration #1, southeast corner, patio (Lot 41)	0	13 (15.3%)	36 (42.4%)	19 (22.4%)	1 (1.2%)	16 (18.8%)	0	85
Concentration #2, south/center, off platform (Lots 33/10)	2 (1.2%)	27 (16.3%)	38 (22.9%)	21 (12.7%)	12 (7.2%)	64 (38.6%)	2 (1.2%)	166
Concentration #3, west side, interior (Lot 102)	0	12 (24%)	36 (72%)	0	2 (4%)	0	0	50
Concentration #4, west side, interior (Lot 29)	0	2 (9.5%)	1 (4.8%)	16 (76.2%)	0	1 (4.8%)	1 (4.8%)	21
Concentration #5, west side, interior (Lot 52/42)	0	26 (36.6%)	17 (23.9%)	11 (15.5%)	16 (22.5%)	1 (1.4%)	0	71
Concentration #6, north exterior, rear wall (Lot 23/194)	0	3 (10.7%)	3 (10.7%)	11 (39.3%)	0	11 (39.3%)	0	28
Concentration #7, north side, off platform (Lot 71)	0	7 (10.9%)	22 (34.4%)	10 (15.6%)	3 (4.7%)	22 (34.4%)	0	64
Concentration #8, east side, off platform (Lot 198)	0	0	8 (11.3%)	44 (62%)	9 (12.7%)	4 (5.6%)	6 (8.5%)	71

Note: Percent shown is that within each concentration.

frequencies of slipped-ware censer sherds was previously observed within concentrations at Structure I.

Subop 17: A domestic zone near Structure I

Subop 17 represents a domestic zone that is located 5 m southwest of Structure I (see figure 21.2; Aguilera 1998). Its identification as a domestic zone is based on the recovery of a marl-covered cobble platform, hearth feature, ground stone, and large quantities of utilitarian debris (Aguilera 1998). Although concentrations of *Pomacea* shell and scattered ceramics were found in the top soil zones above and surrounding the cobble platform, few censers were recovered from this location. Subop 17, a domestic zone lacking evidence for ritual activity, is used in the assemblage analysis below as an index of comparison for Structures I and II. Subop 17 is one of the largest domestic-zone excavations on the island (see figure 21.2), and, therefore, possesses the greatest sample size of materials for comparison to Structures I and II. Comparing Structure I and Subop 17 provides a productive contrast, as they are located in the same central area of the site and share common utilitarian assemblages.

Assemblage comparisons

What does the variation in feature content at Structures I and II signify? The interpretation that Structure II was used for special ritual purposes must account for the fact that lithic tools, flakes, and nonspecialized faunal remains are found within concentrations of materials at this location. Structure II's ritual function may be more realistically identified based on relatively low numbers of domestic materials, rather than an absence of them altogether. Although this rubble platform may have been used for special purposes, it was located within a busy domestic zone represented by Structure I, and surrounding domestic sheet-midden deposits and house platforms detected in Subops 17, 2/3, 6, 7, 9/10, 13, and 15 (see figure 21.2). It is, thus, likely that domestic materials resulting from nearby activities would infiltrate the deposits of Structure II, and it is even possible that domestic activities were conducted at this location at various times in the structure's use. The identification of a "ritual" feature is, therefore, dependent on the degree of domestic materials relative to specialized features, and also the quantity of the materials recovered. Tables 21.3–21.6 illustrate the characteristics of Structure II's materials relative to Structure I and Subop 17, where a greater degree of domestic activity is represented.

Differences observed in the content and range of features around Structures I and II are described relative to the set of features at each structure in the paragraphs above. Some important patterns emerge when the concentrations as a group are compared between structures. Concentrations around Structure I contained more crania of large game, whereas Structure II features had a more mixed faunal signature of mammalian, aquatic, and avian species. Structure I also lacked the burned-rock concentrations that were common at Structure II. Ceramic concentrations at Structure II did not have many censer fragments in them as compared to Structure I. Concentrations at Structure II had less materials than did those of Structure I, with only one feature exceeding 100 pieces, whereas all but one of Structure I's features had more than 100 pieces. Most features in Structure II had 50–85 artifacts or bone fragments (with one outlier, n = 166), while features in Structure I most commonly ranged from 188 to 215 pieces (with two outliers: n = 10, n = 1,127). This pattern reveals an important differentiation between Structure I and Structure II; the latter has far less debris and contains far more ceramics relative to other categories of material than has Structure I (figure 21.11).

When the entire material assemblages are compared, Structures I and II exhibit very different compositions (see tables 21.3–21.6). The data described below document these patterns through comparison of the content of the entire assemblage of each

Table 21.3   Raw counts of materials recovered at three Laguna de On Late Facet structures, by material class

Structure, Function	Lithic tools	Lithic debris	Faunal remains	Obsidian	Slipped ceramics	Unslipped ceramics	Censer (appliqué) fragments	Total	Volume
Structure II, ritual	25	138	799	73	616	716	3	2,370	11.55
Structure I, residence/ritual	73	3,596	3,249	219	1,012	1,649	80	9,878	9.9
Subop 17, residence	36	3,220	575	81	541	671	0	5,124	2.025
Whole site	216	12,220	7,149	809	2,349	4,390	83	27,216	—[a]

[a] Not available.

Table 21.4   Percentages of artifacts at three Laguna de On Late Facet structures, by material class

Structure, Function	Lithic tools	Lithic debris	Faunal remains	Obsidian	Slipped ceramics	Unslipped ceramics	Total materials/structure	Materials/volume
Structure II, ritual	1.1%	5.8%	33.8%	3.1%	26.0%	30.2%	2,367	204.9
Structure I, residence/ritual	.7%	36.4%	32.9%	2.2%	10.2%	16.7%	9,878	997.8
Subop 17, residence	.7%	70.9%	12.7%	1.8%	6.2%	7.7%	5,124	2,530
Whole Site	0.8%	44.9%	26.3%	3.0%	8.6%	16.1%	27,216	—[a]

[a] Not available.

Table 21.5 Materials per cubic meter [N/volume] at three Laguna de On Late Facet structures, by material class

Structure, function	Lithic Tools	Lithic Debris	Faunal Remains	Obsidian	Slipped Ceramics	Unslipped Ceramics	Volume
Structure II, ritual	2.2	11.9	69.2	6.3	53.3	62.0	11.55
Structure I, residence/ritual	7.4	363.2	328.2	22.1	102.2	166.6	9.9
Subop 17, residence	17.8	1,590.1	284.0	40.0	267.1	331.3	2.025

Table 21.6 Ratio of lithic tools, lithic debris, faunal remains, and obsidian to total ceramics at three Laguna de On Late Facet structures

Structure, Function	Lithic Tools	Lithic Debris	Faunal Remains	Obsidian	Ceramics (Total #)	Ratio Ceramics/All Lithics and Faunal Remains
Structure II, ritual	18.8	103.6	599.8	54.8	1,332	1.29
Structure I, residence/ritual	27.4	1,351.4	1,221.0	82.3	2,661	.37
Subop 17 (residence)	29.7	2,656.8	474.4	66.8	1,212	.31
Whole site	32.1	1,813.3	1,060.8	120.0	6,739	.25

Note: Quotients multiplied by 1,000.

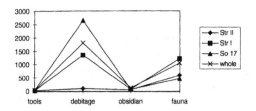

Figure 21.11 Ratio of nonceramic artifacts (and ecofacts) to ceramics by area at Laguna de On. Subop 17 and the entire site show higher amounts of debitage than the elite dwelling area of Structure I or the ritual zone of Structure II.

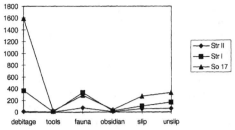

Figure 21.12 Material count per cubic meter by area at Laguna de On. Subop 17 shows much more debitage than the other elite or ritual zones. Fauna distinguishes residential zones Subop 17 and Structure I from Structure II. Slipped and unslipped ceramics are found in far greater numbers at Subop 17 than in the other two areas.

structure (features and general soil lots), which illustrates important differences in the function of activities performed at these two places. In tables 21.3–21.6, these structures are compared to a domestic zone, Subop 17, and to the entire site (Late Facet deposits). The data from the entire site include deposits from domestic zones in addition to Subop 17, as well as areas of ritual activity.

Tables 21.3–21.6 reveal an important contrast between Structure II and Structure I and Subop 17. These data help to distinguish primarily ritual deposits from primarily domestic deposits at this site, as well as deposits that represent a mixture of both activities. Despite having the greatest excavation area and volume of any excavation at the site (see table 21.4), Structure II has a low overall artifact density (204.9 items per m³) when compared to that of Structure I (997.8 items per m³). This relatively low density suggests that fewer domestic production and maintenance activities were performed in this location. Low artifact density may be linked to concepts of cleanliness or purity that universally define ritual places (McGee 1990: 55; Renfrew and Bahn 1991: 359). Structure I has almost five times more materials than does Structure II, and Subop 17 has more than twice as many materials as does Structure I. These figures place Structure I midway between Structure II and Subop 17 in terms of density of materials, in keeping with the interpretation that this structure represents an upper-status residence where ritual was performed.

Mixed activities at this location appear to result in a mixed material assemblage.

An examination of the quantity of each class of material by volume (see table 21.5) indicates that Structure II has fewer of each artifact category than do the areas with residential components (figure 21.12). Specifically, when material per cubic meter is compared, Structure I has about three times more lithic tools, more than 30 times more lithic debris, more than four times as many faunal remains and obsidian, more than two times the slipped ceramics, and more than three times as many unslipped ceramics. When various lithic and faunal remains to ceramic ratios are compared between these structures (see table 21.6), some proportions are the same, and some differences are reduced. However, the overall pattern of Structure I far exceeding Structure II in the quantity of utilitarian debris is maintained. The lithic tool to ceramic ratio continues to indicate that Structure I has three times more lithic tools than does Structure II. According to these ratios, lithic debris is 10 times greater in Structure I, the amount of faunal remains is doubled, and the amount of obsidian is tripled. The ratios of lithics or faunal remains to ceramics is dependent on the amount of ceramics within each assemblage. Structure II has proportionately far greater quantities of ceramics than do the other areas. The ceramics to all lithics and faunal remains ratio for Structure

II is 1.29, four times greater than for Structure I (.37). This value for Structure I is close to that of Subop 17 (.31) and of the entire site (.25).

Structure I continues to lie midway between Structure II and Subop 17 in most comparisons (see tables 21.5 and 21.6). Subop 17 exceeds the density of materials (see table 21.5) from Structure I in lithic artifacts, including lithic tools and obsidian (more than twice as much); lithic debris (five times as much); and slipped and unslipped ceramics (twice as much). Subop 17 has slightly fewer faunal remains than does Structure I. These relationships are also reflected in the ratios of various materials to ceramics (see table 21.6). Lithic tools are almost identically proportioned, but Subop 17 has twice the lithic debris, one-third the faunal debris, and less obsidian than Structure I. Ratios calculated for the entire site resemble Structure I for lithic tools, lithic debris, and faunal remains. The obsidian to ceramic ratio of the site is higher than for Structure I or Subop 17. In most categories, then, Structure I broadly resembles the entire site, and Structure II appears anomalous. Subop 17 has comparable amounts of lithic tools, but higher percentages of lithic flakes, relative to Structure I, probably attesting to its domestic function.

Table 21.4 allows the relative percentages of materials that comprise the assemblages of each area to be compared (figure 21.13). The aforementioned relatively high proportion of ceramics in Structure II when

compared to the other areas is expressed in these percentages, which show that 56.2% of Structure II's materials are ceramics. The structure has over 2.5 times the amount of slipped ceramics, and almost double the amount of unslipped ceramics, as Structure I. Structure I has more of each category of ceramics than does Subop 17. The percentages of slipped ceramics are closer between these two assemblages than are those of unslipped ceramics, probably because of the high number of unslipped censer fragments (body sherds not specifically identified as censers) in Structure I. Censer fragments tabulated in table 21.3 represent only appliqué, effigy, or rim elements that can be conclusively identified as being from censers. Structure I has proportions of unslipped sherds comparable to the entire site (16%; see table 21.4), although more of these may be censers as few censer elements are identified outside of Structure I (N = 6 for the entire site).

Discussion

Comparison of materials recovered from Structures I and II suggests that these buildings were the focus of ritual activity. Variability within concentrations located at each structure illustrates a continuum of domestic and ritual materials and activities at each location. At each structure, more specialized ritual concentrations are identified by higher percentages of slipped sherds and appliqué or effigy censer sherds, with the additional large-game cranial elements found at Structure I. At Structure I, the south side of the building was the location of concentrated materials with these ritual indicators. The east and interior areas of this building contained higher numbers of lithic flakes and nonspecialized faunal remains, perhaps indicating that more domestic activities were performed at this location. At Structure II, concentrations with greater numbers of slipped ceramics and censers were found at east and west areas of the rubble platform, but high quantities of slipped ceramics were found to the north, and censers were found on all sides. This pattern suggests a more

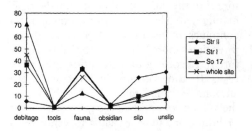

Figure 21.13   When relative percentages of materials within each zone are compared, Structure II, the ritual area, is distinguished from other zones by higher proportions of ceramics and lesser amounts of debitage.

generalized dispersal of ceramic types at Structure II as compared to Structure I. Flakes and faunal remains formed the greatest proportion of concentrations on the west side of Structure II; perhaps this was related to activities performed within this interior room.

Some degree of mixture with "background noise" of general midden debris probably occurred in concentrations at both structures and is to be expected. Chase (1986: 177) has noted the difficulty of differentiating between domestic and ritual deposits using comparisons of ceramic frequencies, advocating the use of whole vessels for such determinations. However, as no whole vessels were recovered from Laguna de On, the comparison of sherd frequencies appears to be an effective method at this site. At Mayapan, Smith (1971: tables 12–19) demonstrated clear utilitarian and ceremonial ceramic-assemblage dichotomies according to structure type. He used diagnostic forms (i.e. censers, cups, effigies, and vases), rather than comparing slipped and unslipped ceramics and censers to other artifact categories as in this investigation of Laguna de On. There are, thus, several methods that have been developed in studies of the Maya Postclassic to determine the degree of ritual activity and type of ritual context. Despite inevitable mixture with domestic debris, relatively low quantities of materials, high proportions of slipped ceramics, and the presence of censers appear to be the best indicators of degrees of ritual function at Laguna de On. An examination of variation among individual feature content at Structures I and II indicates that some features have greater quantities of slipped sherds and censers than do others. Partial testing of either building may have resulted in the recovery of concentrations with greater quantities of faunal remains or flakes, which would not fully represent ritual activities conducted at each of these places. The variation observed in concentration content at each structure also indicates that uniform patterns of directional symbolism are not reflected, with the south-side features exhibiting the greatest frequencies

of slipped sherds and censers at Structure I and the east and west sides exhibiting these trends at Structure II. Comparative information from other sites is needed to fully determine whether vessel breakage varies consistently according to direction among structures at Postclassic Maya sites.

While the assemblages of Structures I and II may indicate degrees of mixing of ritual and domestic debris, they may also represent overlap in dual contexts for the use of utilitarian objects. McGee (1990: 55) notes that Lacandon god houses are places "where everyday items become sacred offerings;" plainware cooking jars are primary components of altar assemblages recorded ethnographically (Deal 1988: 74). Food and alcohol are important components of ethnographic ritual, as are the serving vessels that contained them (Deal 1988: 86). At Laguna de On, however, relative percentages of ceramic types indicate that the overlap in domestic and ritual assemblages does not render them indistinguishable from one another.

The analysis of the entire assemblage of features and artifacts at Structures I and II reveals that ritual activities occurred in an upper-status domestic zone (Structure I) and a specialized structure (Structure II) at this site. The comparison of these structures to Subop 17 (and elsewhere) indicates that ritual activities did not take place at all domestic localities on the island. This pattern addresses important questions pertaining to the organization of ritual in Postclassic society. Postclassic religion is often described as "secularized" when compared to the Classic period (Pollock 1962: 16–17; Proskouriakoff 1962: 136; Smith 1962: 267; Thompson 1957: 634). In the secularization model, common households are inferred to have had unrestrained access to religious paraphernalia in the Postclassic period – in contrast to the Classic period, when religious practice was monopolized by royal sectors of society (Smith 1962: 263). This model is primarily based on the distribution of religious artifacts at Mayapan, where a typology of household altars and shrines was defined by the Carnegie

Institution (Smith 1962). It must, however, be remembered that Mayapan was a Postclassic political capital. If religious practice was a prerogative of those in political power during the Late Postclassic period, Mayapan would definitely be a location where this privilege would be exercised. In fact, comparative research at other sites indicates that religious paraphernalia was not generally available to all sectors of society during the Late Postclassic (Freidel and Sabloff 1984: 184). Mayapan appears anomalous when compared to such sites as Cozumel, where ritual facilities were distinct from domestic facilities and were dispersed in a carefully organized pattern (Freidel and Sabloff 1984: 184). Even within Mayapan itself, variability is noted in the spatial distribution of public buildings – with most of this architecture concentrated in a plaza complex in Quadrant Q of the site (Pollock et al. 1962) or not far from it (Chase 1992: 128–30, fig. 8.4). The distribution of caches (Chase 1992: 128–30, fig. 8.6) and sculptures also suggests that ritual paraphernalia was hierarchically distributed within Mayapan. Distribution of ritual features outside the center may more reflect a pattern of barrio elite settlement (Chase 1986: 362–7, 1992: 123–31) than generalized household practice in commoner contexts.

Despite the fact that ritual artifacts and features may conform to a hierarchical distribution at Mayapan and other Postclassic-period sites, it is probable that household religion was practiced to some degree regardless of social status. However, household practice is not strictly a Postclassic pattern, nor is it necessarily evidence of increased religious "secularization." The prevalence of household religion, at least in terms of the construction of household shrines or temples, has roots in the Maya formative (McAnany 1995: 55–60). Classic-period household groups have long been noted to include lineage temples or shrines in their midst (Becker 1971; Gossen and Leventhal 1993: 211; Leventhal 1983: 75–6, McAnany 1995: 53). Such structures replicated on a household scale the larger, more public versions of royal temples found

in political centers. This phenomenon was observed ethnographically by Vogt (1969: 572), who noted that ceremonial practice was manifested through ascending scales of social order between the political center of Zinacantan and its surrounding communities. This phenomenon has more recently been referred to by Gossen and Leventhal (1993: 207) as integrated cults of "periphery" and "center." As scales of social status are reflected in Postclassic domestic settlement at sites such as Cozumel (Sabloff et al. 1974: 406–8) and Santa Rita (Chase 1986: 356, 1992), scales of religious practice may also be reflected among them. Indeed, this pattern has been observed in the distribution of household shrines among various barrios at Santa Rita (Chase 1986: 365–6) and among communities of living highland Maya (Deal 1988: 72).

Identifying ritual in the Postclassic period can thus occur in the context of a domestic dwelling, in the context of a specialized household-group ritual structure, or in a public monumental context. Ethnographically, household altars throughout the Maya area are placed either in the "main" structure of a household cluster or in a separate oratory (Deal 1988: 64). At Laguna de On, two out of three of these scales of ritual practice are observed. Structure I illustrates a household context, and Structure II represents a probable household shrine or oratory. Public-scale monumental structures are not located at Laguna de On, but have been documented at the nearby Postclassic center of Caye Coco (Masson and Rosenswig 1998b) and other Postclassic capitals such as Santa Rita (Gann 1900: 662–77) and Lamanai (Pendergast 1981), where they are represented in the use, modification, or construction of conspicuous, public, monumental architecture.

The Laguna de On structures examined here not only illustrate two contexts of Postclassic household ritual, but also the form of ritual that is found at a third-tier site in a regional hierarchy. Structure I differs from almost all other domestic zones in its smashed censer and animal-crania pieces, although a few censer fragments at this site were recovered in soils above burials in Subop 5. This site illustrates a continuum of domestic-to-ritual deposits, and demonstrates that ritual artifacts are primarily concentrated at one upper-status residence and its associated rubble-platform shrine. On a small scale, these patterns suggest that religious practice at Laguna de On was not "secularized," and equal access to ritual paraphernalia was not available to all members of this small community. One household group monopolized most of this activity.

A survey of the shore of the north end of the lagoon in 1997 (Waid and Masson 1998) revealed the existence of an extensive sheet midden, reflecting a dispersed Postclassic community along bluffs located to the west, north, and east of the lagoon. Only one ritual feature was located in that entire area, suggesting that specialized ritual facilities were constructed on the shore, as well, and that certain social groups sponsored ritual activity, whereas others did not. Censer fragments were not found in any of the 15 areas tested except for the single locality where a line-of-stone shrine was recovered. Chase (1982: 132) has similarly noted that censers do not occur in low-status households at Santa Rita, and the limited distribution of censers on the island and shores of Laguna de On indicates the same pattern.

Conclusion

This investigation of ritual and domestic features and assemblages at Laguna de On Island illustrates variation in the context of Postclassic ritual practice at a small community. Even in a rural settlement located at a considerable distance from political centers, the practice of religious activities occurred in the context of spatially distinct ritual zones. Although religious ritual was probably incorporated as part of the activities of a single household on the island (occupying Structure I and its vicinity), it was clearly not practiced by all households in this community. Not only does one household group exhibit a near monopoly on

domestic ritual, it also probably sponsored the operation of a specialized ritual building, Structure II. However subtly defined, the organization of ritual practice at this community suggests that an internal social hierarchy was present, and that one of its primary manifestations was the appropriation of ritual activity. The analysis of ritual deposits provides important clues regarding the organization of Postclassic Maya society, as well as the links of this society to its past and present legacies of ritual practice.

ACKNOWLEDGMENTS

Archaeological research at Laguna de On has been made possible by the sponsorship of the Department of Anthropology at the University at Albany – State University of New York, the Center for Field Research: Earthwatch, the Foundation for the Advancement of Mesoamerican Studies, and the Wenner-Gren Foundation. This research is conducted with the gracious permission of Archaeological Commissioner John Morris and the Department of Archaeology, Belmopan, Belize. I wish to thank an anonymous reviewer, Bruce Dickson, Boyd Dixon, Thomas Hester, and Robert Rosenswig for providing me with an extremely insightful and thought-provoking series of comments on the archaeology of Laguna de On Island and the contents of this paper. Timothy Hare and Pamela Headrick drafted the maps of Structures I and II, and Anne Deane illustrated the artifacts. All errors and assertions in this are solely the responsibility of the author.

REFERENCES

Aguilera, Miguel. 1998. Domestic Feature Investigations at Subop 17, Laguna de On Island. In *The Belize Postclassic Project 1997: Laguna de On, Progresso Lagoon, and Laguna Seca*, edited by Marilyn A. Masson and Robert Rosenswig, pp. 11–20. Occasional Publication No. 2. Institute of Mesoamerican Studies, University at Albany, State University of New York, Albany.

Barnhart, Ed and Sarah Howard. 1997. Testing Explorations at Laguna de On Island: Landscape Modification, a Burial Area, and Courtyard Walls. In *The Belize Postclassic Project: Laguna de On Island Excavations 1996*, edited by Marilyn A. Masson and Robert M. Rosenswig, pp. 43–60. Occasional Publication No. 1.

Institute of Mesoamerican Studies, University at Albany, State University of New York, Albany.

Becker, Marshall Thomas. 1971. The Identification of a Second Plaza Plan at Tikal, Guatemala, and its Implications for Ancient Maya Social Complexity. Unpublished Ph.D. dissertation, Department of Anthropology, University of Pennsylvania, Philadelphia.

Bey, George J. III, Craig A. Hanson, and William M. Ringle. 1997. Classic to Postclassic at Ek Balam, Yucatan: Architectural and Ceramic Evidence for Defining the Transition. *Latin American Antiquity* 8: 237–54.

Chase, Diane Z. 1982. Spatial and Temporal Variability in Postclassic Northern Belize. Ph.D. dissertation, Department of Anthropology, University of Pennsylvania, Philadelphia. University Microfilms International, Ann Arbor.

—— 1986. Social and Political Organization in the Land of Milk and Honey: Correlating the Archaeology and Ethnohistory of the Postclassic Lowland Maya, In *Late Lowland Maya Civilization: Classic to Postclassic*, edited by J. A. Sabloff and E. W. Andrews V, pp. 347–78. University of New Mexico Press, Albuquerque.

—— 1992. Postclassic Maya Elites: Ethnohistory and Archaeology. In *Mesoamerican Elites: An Archaeological Assessment*, edited by Diane Z. Chase and Arlen F. Chase, pp. 118–34. University of Oklahoma Press, Norman.

Chase, Diane Z. and Arlen F. Chase. 1988. *A Postclassic Perspective: Excavations at the Maya Site of Santa Rita Corozal, Belize*. Monograph No. 4. Precolumbian Art Research Institute, San Francisco.

Coggins, Clemency C. 1988. The Manikin Scepter: Emblem of Lineage. *Estudios de Cultura Maya* 17: 123–58.

Deal, Michael. 1988. Recognition of Ritual Pottery in Residential Units: An Ethnoarchaeological Model of the Maya Family Altar Tradition. In *Ethnoarchaeology among the Highland Maya of Chiapas*, edited by Thomas A. Lee, Jr. and Brian Hayden, pp. 61–89. Papers No. 56. New World Archaeological Foundation, Provo, UT.

Eaton, Jack D., Thomas R. Hester, and Fred Valdez, Jr. 1994. Notes on Eccentric Lithics from Colha and Northern Belize. In *Continuing Archaeology at Colha, Belize*, edited by Thomas R. Hester, Harry J. Shafer, and Jack Eaton, pp. 257–66. Studies in Archaeology No. 16. Texas Archeological Research Laboratory, University of Texas, Austin.

Fash, William L. 1991. *Scribes, Warriors, and Kings: The City of Copan and the Ancient Maya*. Thames and Hudson, London.

Freidel, David A. and Jeremy A. Sabloff. 1984. *Cozumel: Late Maya Settlement Patterns*. Academic Press, New York.

Gann, Thomas W. 1900. Mounds in Northern Honduras. In *Nineteenth Annual Report of the Bureau of American Ethnology 1897–1898*, Pt. 2, pp. 655–92. Smithsonian Institution, Washington, DC.

—— 1918. *The Maya Indians of Southern Yucatan and Northern British Honduras*. Bureau of American Ethnology No. 64. Smithsonian Institution, Washington, DC.

—— 1928. *Maya Cities*. Thomas W. Gann, London and New York.

Gossen, Gary H. and Richard M. Leventhal. 1993. The Topography of Ancient Maya Religious Pluralism. In *Lowland Maya Civilization in the Eighth Century AD*, edited by Jeremy Sabloff and John Henderson, pp. 185–218. Dumbarton Oaks Research Library and Collection, Washington, DC.

Grube, Nikolai. 1992. Classic Maya Dance: Evidence from Hieroglyphs and Iconography. *Ancient Mesoamerica* 3: 201–18.

Hester, Thomas R. and Harry J. Shafer. 1991. Lithics of the Early Postclassic at Colha, Belize. In *Maya Stone Tools*, edited by Thomas Hester and Harry Shafer, pp. 155–62. Monographs in World Prehistory No. 1. Prehistory Press, Madison, WI.

Hester, Thomas R., Harry J. Shafer, and Thena Berry. 1991. Technological and Comparative Analyses of the Chipped Stone Artifacts from El Pozito, Belize. In *Maya Stone Tools*, edited by Thomas Hester and Harry Shafer, pp. 67–84. Monographs in World Prehistory No. 1. Prehistory Press, Madison, WI.

Jones, Grant D. 1989. *Maya Resistance to Spanish Rule: Time and History on a Colonial Frontier*. University of New Mexico Press, Albuquerque.

Landa, Friar Diego de. 1941. *Landa's Relaciones de las cosas de Yucatan*. Translated by Alfred Tozzer. Papers of the Peabody Museum of Archaeology and Ethnology No. 18. Harvard University, Cambridge, MA.

Leventhal, Richard M. 1983. Household Groups and Classic Maya Religion. In *Prehistoric Settlement Patterns: Essays in Honor of Gordon R. Willey*, edited by Evon Z. Vogt and Richard M. Leventhal, pp. 55–76. University of New Mexico Press, Albuquerque, and Peabody Museum of Archaeology and Ethnology, Harvard University, Cambridge, MA.

Love, Bruce. 1994. *The Paris Codex: Handbook for a Maya Priest*. University of Texas Press, Austin.

McAnany, Patricia A. 1995. *Living with the Ancestors: Kinship and Kingship in Ancient Maya Society*. University of Texas Press, Austin.

McGee, R. Jon. 1990. *Life, Ritual, and Religion among the Lacandon Maya*. Wadsworth, Belmont, CA.

Marcus, Joyce. 1993. Ancient Maya Political Organization. In *Lowland Maya Civilization in the Eighth Century* AD, edited by Jeremy A. Sabloff and John Henderson, pp. 111–84. Dumbarton Oaks Research Library and Collections, Washington, DC.

Masson, Marilyn A. 1993. Changes in Maya Community Organization from the Classic to Postclassic Periods: A View from Laguna de On, Belize. Unpublished Ph.D. dissertation, Department of Anthropology, University of Texas, Austin.

——— 1997. Cultural Transformations at the Maya Postclassic Community of Laguna de On, Belize. *Latin American Antiquity* 8: 293–316.

——— 1998. Postclassic Maya Settlement along the Freshwater Creek Drainage, Belize. Manuscript accepted and in revision for the *Journal of Field Archaeology*.

——— n.d. In the Realm of Nachan Kan: Postclassic Maya Archaeology at Laguna de On, Belize. Book manuscript in review by the University of Colorado Press.

Masson, Marilyn A. and Robert M. Rosenswig (eds). 1997. *The Belize Postclassic Project 1996: Laguna de On Excavations 1996*. Occasional Publication No. 1. Institute of Mesoamerican Studies, University at Albany, State University of New York, Albany.

——— 1998a. *The Belize Postclassic Project 1997: Laguna de On, Progresso Lagoon, and Laguna Seca*, edited by M. A. Masson and R. M. Rosenswig. Occasional Publication No. 2. Institute of Mesoamerican Studies, University at Albany, State University of New York, Albany.

——— 1998b. Postclassic Monumental Center Discovered at Caye Coco, Belize. *Mexicon* 20(1): 4–5.

Masson, Marilyn A. and Thomas W. Stafford, Jr. 1998. The Role of Laguna de On in the Postclassic Political Hierarchy of Northern Belize. Paper presented at the 63rd Annual Meeting of the Society for American Archaeology, Seattle.

Masson, Marilyn A., Melissa Joy Shumake, and Evon Moan. 1997. Structure I, a C-shaped Building at Laguna de On Island. In *The Belize Postclassic Project: Laguna de On Island Excavations 1996*, edited by Marilyn A. Masson and Robert Rosenswig, pp. 11–24. Submitted to the Department of Archaeology, Belmopan, Belize.

Michaels, George H. 1987. A Description and Analysis of Early Postclassic Lithic Technology at Colha, Belize. Master's thesis, Texas A & M University, College Station.

Mock, Shirley Boteler. 1994. Yucatecan Presence in Northern Belize Postclassic Ceramics at Colha. In *Continuing Archaeology at Colha, Belize*, edited by Thomas R. Hester, Harry J. Shafer, and Jack D. Eaton, pp. 9–16. Studies in Archaeology No. 16. Texas Archaeological Research Laboratory, University of Texas, Austin.

——— 1997. Preliminary Ceramic Analysis: Laguna de On 1996 Season. In *The Belize Postclassic Project: Laguna de On Island Excavations 1996*, edited by Marilyn A. Masson and Robert Rosenswig, pp. 61–8. Submitted to the Department of Archaeology, Belmopan, Belize.

——— 1998. Ceramics from Laguna de On, 1996 and 1997. In *The Belize Postclassic Project 1997: Laguna de On, Progresso Lagoon, and Laguna Seca*, edited by M. A. Masson and R. M. Rosenswig, pp. 192–202. Occasional Publication No. 2. Institute of Mesoamerican Studies, University at Albany, State University of New York, Albany.

Morley, Sylvanus G., George Brainerd, and Robert J. Sharer. 1983. *The Ancient Maya*. 4th edn. Stanford University Press, Stanford, CA.

Murray, Elizabeth. 1998. Spindle Whorls from Laguna de On. In *The Belize Postclassic Project 1997: Laguna de On, Progresso Lagoon, and Laguna Seca*, edited by Marilyn A. Masson and Robert Rosenswig, pp. 157–62. Occasional Publication No. 2. Institute of Mesoamerican Studies, University at Albany, State University of New York, Albany.

Oland, Maxine. 1998. Lithic Raw Material Sources at the Southern End of the Freshwater Creek Drainage. In *The Belize Postclassic Project 1997: Laguna de On, Progresso Lagoon, and Laguna Seca*, edited by M. A. Masson and R. M. Rosenswig, pp. 163–76. Occasional Publication No. 2. Institute of Mesoamerican Studies, University at Albany, State University of New York, Albany.

Pendergast, David M. 1981. Lamanai, Belize: Summary of Excavation Results, 1974–1980. *Journal of Field Archaeology* 8: 29–53.

——— 1982. *Excavations at Altun Ha, Belize 1964–1970*. Archaeological Monographs of the Royal Ontario Museum. Alger Press, Toronto.

——— 1986. Stability through Change: Lamanai, Belize from the Ninth to the Seventeenth Century. In *Late Lowland Maya Civilization: Classic to Postclassic*, edited by J. A. Sabloff and

E. W. Andrews V, pp. 223–50. University of New Mexico Press, Albuquerque.

Pollock, Harry E. D. 1962. Introduction. In *Mayapan, Yucatan, Mexico*, edited by H. E. D. Pollock, Ralph Roys, Tatiana Proskouriakoff, and A. Ledyard Smith, pp. 1–22. Publication No. 619. Carnegie Institute of Washington, Washington, DC.

—— 1965. Architecture of the Maya Lowlands. In *Archaeology of Southern Mesoamerica*, Pt. 1, edited by Gordon R. Willey, pp. 378–440. *Handbook of American Indians*, vol. 2, Robert Wauchope, general editor. University of Texas Press, Austin.

Pollock, Harry E. D., Ralph L. Roys, Tatiana Proskouriakoff, and A. L. Smith. 1962. *Mayapan, Yucatan, Mexico*. Publication No. 619. Carnegie Institute of Washington, Washington, DC.

Proskouriakoff, Tatiana. 1962. Civic and Religious Structures of Mayapan. In *Mayapan Yucatan Mexico*, edited by Harry E. D. Pollock, Ralph Roys, Tatiana Proskouriakoff, and A. Ledyard Smith, pp. 87–164. Publication No. 619. Carnegie Institute of Washington, Washington, DC.

Renfrew, Colin and Paul Bahn. 1991. *Archaeology: Theories, Methods, and Practice*. Thames and Hudson, London.

Rice, Don S. 1986. The Peten Postclassic: A Settlement Perspective. In *Late Lowland Maya Civilization: Classic to Postclassic*, edited by J. A. Sabloff and E. W. Andrews V, pp. 301–46. University of New Mexico Press, Albuquerque.

Rosenswig, Robert and Joy Becker. 1997. Structure II, a Rubble Platform Shrine at Laguna de On Island. In *The Belize Postclassic Project: Laguna de On Island Excavations 1996*, edited by Marilyn A. Masson and Robert Rosenswig, pp. 27–38. Submitted to the Department of Archaeology, Belmopan, Belize.

Rosenswig, Robert M. and Thomas W. Stafford, Jr. 1998. Archaic Component beneath a Postclassic Terrace at Subop 19, Laguna de On Island. In *The Belize Postclassic Project 1997: Laguna de On, Progresso Lagoon, and Laguna Seca*, edited by Marilyn Masson and Robert Rosenswig, pp. 81–9. Occasional Publication No. 2. Institute of Mesoamerican Studies, University at Albany, State University of New York, Albany.

Roys, Ralph L. 1957. *The Political Geography of the Yucatan Maya*. Publication No. 613. Carnegie Institute of Washington, Washington, DC.

Sabloff, Jeremy A., William L. Rathje, David A. Freidel, Judith G. Connor, and Paula W. Sabloff. 1974. Trade and Power in Postclassic Yucatan: Initial Observations. In *Mesoamerican Archaeology, New Approaches*, edited by Norman Hammond, pp. 397–416. University of Texas Press, Austin.

Schele, Linda. 1976. Accession Iconography of Chan-Bahlum in the Group of the Cross at Palenque. In *The Art, Iconography, and Dynastic History of Palenque*, Pt. 3, edited by Merle Greene Robertson, p. 9–34. Robert Louis Stevenson School, Pebble Beach, CA.

Schele, Linda and Mary Ellen Miller. 1986. *The Blood of Kings: Dynasty and Ritual in Maya Art*. Kimbell Art Museum, Fort Worth, TX.

Shafer, Harry J. and Thomas R. Hester. 1983. Ancient Maya Chert Workshops in Northern Belize, Central America. *American Antiquity* 48: 519–43.

Sheldon, Stephanie M. 1998. Excavations at Subop 5: Testing for Cemetery Boundaries and Landscape Modification at Laguna de On Island. In *The Belize Postclassic Project 1997: Laguna de On, Progresso Lagoon, and Laguna Seca*, edited by Marilyn A. Masson and Robert Rosenswig, pp. 25–38. Occasional Publication No. 2. Institute of Mesoamerican Studies, University at Albany, State University of New York, Albany.

Sidrys, Raymond V. 1983. *Archaeological Excavations in Northern Belize, Central America*. Monograph No. XVII. Institute of Archaeology, University of California, Los Angeles.

Smith, A. Ledyard. 1962. Residential and Associated Structures at Mayapan. In *Mayapan Yucatan Mexico*, edited by Harry E. D. Pollock, Ralph Roys, Tatiana Proskouriakoff, and A. Ledyard Smith, pp. 165–320. Publication No. 619. Carnegie Institute of Washington, Washington, DC.

Smith, Robert E. 1971. *The Pottery of Mayapan*. Papers of the Peabody Museum of Archaeology and Ethnology No. 66. Harvard University, Cambridge, MA.

Stafford, Thomas W., Jr. 1998. Appendix A. Radiocarbon Dates from the 1996 Season. In *The Belize Postclassic Project 1997: Laguna de On, Progresso Lagoon, and Laguna Seca*, edited by Marilyn Masson and Robert Rosenswig, p. 183. Occasional Publication No. 2. Institute of Mesoamerican Studies, University at Albany, State University of New York, Albany.

Thompson, J. Eric S. 1957. *Deities Portrayed on Censers at Mayapan*. Current Reports No. 40.

Department of Archaeology, Carnegie Institute of Washington, Washington, DC.

—— 1970. *Maya History and Religion.* University of Oklahoma Press, Norman, OK.

Tourtellot, Gair III. 1988. *Excavations at Seibal, Department of Peten, Guatemala: Peripheral Survey and Excavation Settlement and Community Patterns.* Memoirs of the Peabody Museum of Archaeology and Ethnology, vol. 16. Harvard University Press, Cambridge, MA.

Valdez, Fred, Jr., Marilyn A. Masson, and Lenore Santone. 1992. Report from the 1991 Field Season at Laguna de On. Manuscript on file, Department of Archaeology, Belmopan, Belize.

Vogt, Evon Z. 1969. *Zinacantan: A Maya Community in the Highlands of Chiapas.* Belknap, Harvard University Press, Cambridge, MA.

Waid, Alice and Marilyn A. Masson. 1998. Laguna de On Shore Reconnaissance and Testing. In *The Belize Postclassic Project 1997: Laguna de On, Progresso Lagoon, and Laguna Seca,* edited by Marilyn Masson and Robert Rosenswig, pp. 93–106. Occasional Publication No. 2. Institute of Mesoamerican Studies, University at Albany, State University of New York, Albany.

Walker, Debra. 1990. Cerros Revisited: Ceramic Indicators of Terminal Classic and Postclassic Settlement and Pilgrimage in Northern Belize. Unpublished Ph.D. dissertation, Department of Anthropology, Southern Methodist University, Dallas, TX.

West, Georgia. 1998. Domestic Feature Investigations at Subops 15 & 16, Laguna de On Island. In *The Belize Postclassic Project 1997: Laguna de On, Progresso Lagoon, and Laguna Seca,* edited by Marilyn Masson and Robert Rosenswig, pp. 43–54. Occasional Publication No. 2. Institute of Mesoamerican Studies, University at Albany, State University of New York, Albany.

Wharton, Jennifer. 1997. A Preliminary Analysis of Faunal Remains at the Postclassic Site of Laguna de On Island, Belize. In *The Belize Postclassic Project: Laguna de On Island Excavations 1996,* edited by Marilyn A. Masson and Robert Rosenswig, pp. 69–76. Occasional Publication No. 1. Institute of Mesoamerican Studies, University at Albany, State University of New York, Albany.

—— 1998a. Domestic Feature Investigations at Subop 7, Laguna de On Island. In *The Belize Postclassic Project 1997: Laguna de On, Progresso Lagoon, and Laguna Seca,* edited by Marilyn Masson and Robert Rosenswig, pp. 67–70. Occasional Publication No. 2. Institute of Mesoamerican Studies, University at Albany, State University of New York, Albany.

—— 1998b. Postclassic Maya Ritual and Staple Faunas of Laguna de On. Paper presented at the 63rd Annual Meeting of the Society for American Archaeology, Seattle.

CHAPTER 22

Figurines and the Aztec State

Testing the Effectiveness of Ideological Domination

Elizabeth M. Brumfiel

According to Margaret Conkey and Joan Gero (1991), studying gender in prehistoric societies involves much more than determining which activities were carried out by women and which by men. A gendered prehistory presents gender roles, gender relations, and gender ideology, and it explores the ways in which gender intersects with and is influenced by other aspects of social life. Such a vision of a gendered past is both inspiring and daunting. It is inspiring because striving to realize it will teach us so much about women's and men's lives and the dynamics of social change. It is daunting because it seems to require a knowledge of mental categories and patterns of social interaction that are not easily gleaned from the archaeological record.

This problem can be attacked from two sides. On the one hand, we can refine techniques of symbolic interpretation and contextual study so that we can reconstruct the subjective meanings of gender categories. On the other hand, we can sidestep the issue of content momentarily and explore the structure of gender ideologies and their intersection with other aspects of social life without specifying the meanings attached to gender in a particular culture. I follow the latter strategy.

This chapter explores the changes in gender that occurred in Late Postclassic central Mexico under the influence of the Aztec state. A rich historical record exists for Aztec culture, but the current analysis relies primarily upon the analysis of archaeological materials. It is hoped that the strategies of inquiry employed in this chapter will be applicable to other cultures, particularly cultures in "deep" prehistory, which may lack a historical record but which, like the Aztecs, produced visual images of gendered subjects that are available for analysis.

Do definitions of gender change in communities that are incorporated into highly stratified regional states? If so, what is the direction of change? Do community definitions of gender come to resemble those disseminated by the state or do local communities retain a distinctive view? Answers to these questions are obtained by studying variation in the representation of women in Aztec material culture. Two types of variation are analyzed.

First, I examine temporal change in the abundance and style of representation in a single genre, ceramic figurines. As Sharisse McCafferty and Geoffrey McCafferty (1991) suggest, studying symbols diachronically enables us to monitor the construction of gender ideologies and transformations

Reprinted from Elizabeth M. Brumfiel. 1996. Figurines and the Aztec State: Testing the Effectiveness of Ideological Domination. In *Gender and Archaeology*, edited by Rita P. Wright (University of Pennsylvania Press, Pennsylvania), pp. 143–66.

in negotiation of gender. Second, I compare the representation of women in several media at a single point in time. As Susan Pollock (1991) observes, women in different representational media may be portrayed in inconsistent and contradictory ways, and these very inconsistencies can inform us of the synchronic variation in gender ideology within a single society, and how this variation was negotiated.

This study of change in Aztec gender systems suggests some general conclusions about the effectiveness of ideological domination in states. The flow of discussion from "gender" to "nongender" issues demonstrates how gender is entwined with other aspects of social life. It suggests the broad relevance of gender as a focus of archaeological investigation.

The Problem

In recent years, some sharp disagreement has developed concerning the status of women in Aztec society. The debate centers upon whether Aztec gender relations were hierarchical or complementary and whether Aztec women accepted an ideology of male dominance or vigorously contested it. In her classic article "The Aztecs and the Ideology of Male Dominance," June Nash (1978) argues that Aztec imperial expansion resulted in the subordination of Aztec women. Warfare and conquest were men's work, and while men gained wealth, power, and prestige from imperial conquests, the status of women declined. Older deities expressing the balanced opposition of masculine and feminine were replaced by male warrior deities. Blood sacrifice and ritualized battles became common forms of religious devotion that excluded women from participation. As the empire expanded, the cult of warfare and male dominance was elaborated.

However, Nash believes that the influence of the male dominant ideology was circumscribed. It was resisted by Aztec women.[1] And it was not accepted by commoners or by hinterland peoples among whom older patterns of balanced opposition between male and female continued. Militarism and ideologies of male dominance were strongest among the ruling elite in the Aztec capital.

Nash's depiction of heightened gender inequality among the Aztecs is confirmed and extended by María Rodríguez (1988) in her book La Mujer Azteca. Rodríguez differs from Nash in arguing that the oppression of women was by no means a fortuitous outcome of militarism; rather, the oppression of women was pursued by men of the Aztec ruling class because it was very much in their interests. Control of women's labor increased their wealth, and control of women's sexuality increased their ability to make advantageous alliances and to reward male participation in the economy of conquest and tribute extraction.

Aztec religion constituted a primary avenue of male domination. In Aztec hands, female deities became secondary figures: the spouses, concubines, and subordinates of powerful male gods. They also assumed warlike elements of costume and character, indicating that no separate sphere of supernatural power was reserved to women, outside the male sphere of warfare and conquest.

Rodríguez paints a bleak picture of extreme male dominance. She suggests that Aztec women were systematically exploited, demeaned, and controlled by both brutal coercion and psychological terror. Unlike Nash, Rodríguez argues that Aztec women accepted their subordination and even participated in its perpetuation: mothers encouraged their daughters to suppress all their autonomous impulses. In another departure from Nash, Rodríguez maintains that the statuses of noble and commoner women were not very different; both were subject to powerful mechanisms of ideological control and both were thoroughly dominated. Furthermore, this domination characterized not only the Aztec capital but most of central Mexico; Rodríguez's (1989) analysis of the status of women in Tlaxcala suggests conditions that were not significantly different from those in Tenochtitlan.

Rodríguez's views are clearly different from those of McCafferty and McCafferty (1988, 1989, 1991), who argue that, even at the height of the empire, Aztec gender roles were characterized by "structural complementarity" and "parallelism" rather than dominance and submission. They also argue that women controlled important spheres of activity in Aztec culture including household production and sexual reproduction. Control of these spheres was associated with an ideology of female power that women exercised vigorously to resist male dominance. Spinning and weaving, archetypical female activities, linked Aztec women to Tlazolteotl, Xochiquetzal, Mayahuel, and Toci, four aspects of the Aztec mother goddess who controlled human reproduction.

These differing views raise two interesting general questions. The first concerns the general relationship between state formation and the oppression of women. Rayna Rapp (1978), Christine Gailey (1985), and Irene Silverblatt (1987) have argued that the rulers of states will always make an effort to subordinate women because the control of women is both a metaphor and a mechanism for the state's control over kinship-based households. The figurine data provide one gauge of the subordination of women in the process of state expansion.

The second question concerns the effectiveness of ideology as a mechanism of state dominance. Rodríguez (1988: 102) argues that ideological state apparatuses (see Althusser 1971) played an important role in the subordination of Aztec women and that ideological domination serves as an effective means of implementing state goals. McCafferty and McCafferty (1988: 46), citing Silverblatt, argue that there is always reciprocal interplay between ideologies of domination and resistance, implying that ideological domination is a less important mechanism of control.

An examination of the frequencies of different types of ceramic figurines at three Aztec-period sites in the Basin of Mexico enables us to address these arguments.

Aztec Figurines

Figurines occur in low frequencies at almost every Aztec-period site in the Basin of Mexico. They are small, molded ceramic figures, between ten and twenty centimeters in height, and apparently made of the same orange paste that was used in Aztec orange ware pottery (Cook 1950: 94). Mary Parsons (1972) defined three varieties of Postclassic figurines in collections from the Teotihuacan Valley. Solid, standing, flat-backed figurines were the most common (accounting for 84 percent of the Teotihuacan collection). Jointed figurines, which have holes at the four corners of the trunk of the body for the attachment of limbs (which also have holes drilled through their ends), are quite rare (accounting for only 2 percent of the collection).

These figurines were apparently made by craft specialists. Possible figurine workshops have been reported from Tlatelolco (Cook 1950) and Otumba (Otis Charlton 1994). The figurines were used in household contexts, for they are usually found in association with household debris and, occasionally, in association with burials (Pasztory 1983: 282; Evans 1990). They very rarely occur as offerings; Esther Pasztory (1983: 282) reports that there were no ceramic figurines among the more than seven thousand objects excavated from the Aztec Templo Mayor in Mexico City.[2] Clearly, then, figurines were utilized in activities carried out at the household level.

Most figurines are anthropomorphic (77 percent of the figurines in Parsons's Teotihuacan collection), and many of these clearly bear the insignia of Aztec deities (Seler 1902–23: vol. 1, 305–13; Preuss 1901: 87–91; Barlow and Lehmann 1956: 157–76; Kaplan 1958; Parsons 1972; Millian 1981). This implies a ritual function for the figurines, but it has been difficult to define their use in any detail.

Various sixteenth-century chroniclers comment upon the Aztecs' use of effigies or idols. Toribio Motolinía (1969: 26), for example, states that the Aztecs had idols of stone, wood, fired clay, and dough. Diego Durán (1971: 235, 452) and Bernardino de Sahagún (1950–69: book 2, ch. 9, p. 16; ch. 12, p. 21; ch. 19, p. 36) mention that idols were kept on household altars; such images became the focus of ritual offerings during certain calendrical ceremonies and when household members were away at war. Durán (1971: 419) states that "small effigies, cloth images" were hung from ropes strung from tree to tree in the cornfields, perhaps to promote agricultural fertility.[3] Motolinía (1969: 201) and Durán (1971: 419) record that children were given idols as protection against evil and illness; they were given idols at birth and at the ages of one and four years. However, the chroniclers never specify whether the idols used in these various contexts were ceramic figurines.

The archaeological evidence pertaining to figurine function is also sparse. Susan Evans (1990) observes that most Aztec figurines have been found in archaeological contexts such as the plow zone and midden that reflect patterns of discard rather than patterns of use. However, at Cihuatecpan, Evans found that most (90 percent) of the figurines with good behavioral contexts occurred in habitation rooms or in courtyards containing steam baths; the latter suggests an association between figurines and female reproduction and curing rituals, which frequently employed steam baths as a ritual procedure.

Suggestions that the figurines were concerned with health and curing have also been based upon the appearance of the figurines themselves. One common figurine type (figure 22.1) depicts a bare-breasted woman with a looped headdress ending in two projections. Often, she holds one or two children in her arms. It has been suggested that this figurine represents either the Aztec goddess Xochiquetzal or Coatlicue, and that it expresses a concern with healthy sex, fertility, and birth (Cook 1950; Parsons 1972; Millian 1981; Evans 1990; cf. Pasztory 1983: 284). Alva Millian (1981) suggests that the male deities represented among the figurines were the patrons of various

Figure 22.1 Aztec-period ceramic figurine of a woman holding two children (h. 19 cm). Musée de l'Homme, Paris. (Courtesy of Elizabeth Brumfiel.)

diseases.[4] Another link between figurines and health and curing is suggested by several figurines that depict individuals with physical abnormalities: hunchbacks, dwarfs, people with protruding chests such as might be associated with rickets, and possibly individuals afflicted with dementia (Cook 1950; Morss 1952; Parsons 1972; Millian 1981; Evans 1990).

However, not all figurines are anthropomorphic, and not all can be related to health and curing. There are zoomorphic figurines of various types (monkeys, rabbits, birds, coyotes, toads, and mountain lions, Parsons 1972: 112–13). And there are replicas of temple pyramids that may reflect the integration of peasant households into the state religion (Parsons 1972: 105–8; Kaplan 1958, cited in Pasztory 1983: 291). In addition, figurine heads from the Formative and Classic eras sometimes occur in what are otherwise undisturbed Postclassic strata. This implies that Postclassic peoples collected and curated figurines from earlier periods, perhaps incorporating them into their own household rituals. While these figurines are anthropomorphic, they most commonly occur as figurine heads lacking bodies, and although some wear fairly elaborate headgear, most lack attributes that would specifically define them as male or female. Therefore, for Postclassic peoples, these Formative and Classic figurines may have been ungendered, representing the general domain of ancestral authority.

In summary, then, Aztec figurines appear to represent ritual activity at the household level. Whether this ritual was carried out by folk practitioners, heads of households, or any household member, the figurines should reflect popular estimations of the importance of various supernatural powers and popular concern over the spheres of life where wellbeing was threatened. Thus, the frequencies of different types of figurines in hinterland communities before and during the period of Aztec dominance should provide a valid gauge of the extent to which popular consciousness was affected by state ideology (also see Kann 1989).

If there are no differences in the composition of the figurine assemblage or in the presentation of the female figure, then popular gender ideologies would appear unaffected by Aztec dominance. Such evidence would indicate that while male-dominant ideologies may be elaborated by political elites, they are not necessarily accepted by the rural, nonelite segments of state systems. On the other hand, the existence of differences in the composition of the figurine assemblage or in the presentation of the male or female figure would indicate that existing gender ideologies among commoners were challenged by the male dominant ideology of the Aztec elites. Whether the response to the elite ideology was one of acceptance or resistance is indicated by the degree of similarity between popular images of men and women as seen

in the figurines from hinterland communities and elite images of men and women as presented in the official arts of the Aztec state, such as manuscript painting and monumental sculpture.

Figurine Frequencies at Huexotla, Xico, and Xaltocan

Representative samples of figurines are available from three Postclassic sites in the Basin of Mexico (see figure 22.2). Huexotla and Xico have been sampled using intensive systematic surface collection (Brumfiel 1976, 1980, 1985, 1991a, 1991b). Sample sizes range from 1 percent in the urban core at Huexotla to 11 percent in Huexotla's piedmont sector and at Xico. At Xaltocan, figurine samples are available from seventeen excavation units, each a two-by-two-meter square. All three sites were occupied during the Middle Postclassic

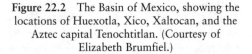

Figure 22.2 The Basin of Mexico, showing the locations of Huexotla, Xico, Xaltocan, and the Aztec capital Tenochtitlan. (Courtesy of Elizabeth Brumfiel.)

(AD 1150–1350) period, prior to Aztec rule; they were also occupied during the Late Postclassic (AD 1350–1521), the period of Aztec dominance. Figurines in collections with predominantly Middle Postclassic ceramics can be compared with figurines in collections with predominantly Late Postclassic ceramics. Observed differences in figurine frequencies or images provide a good indication of stability or change in gender ideologies. (Frequency is the number of figurines per 1,000 rim sherds in the collections. This ratio controls for differences in the extent and density of occupation debris dating to the Middle and Late Postclassic periods.)

Figurine data from the three sites are quite different, so it is best to discuss each site individually.

Huexotla was an important city-state in the eastern Basin of Mexico. Prior to Aztec dominance, Huexotla was an autonomous petty kingdom whose rulers were allied by marriage to the rulers of other major centers in the Basin of Mexico (Alva Ixtilxóchitl 1975–7: vol. 2, 22–5; Guzmán 1938: 92). With expansion of the Aztec empire, however, Huexotla became firmly affixed as one of the fourteen client states of nearby Texcoco. Huexotla's rulers served as counselors and judges in the Texcocan ruler's court, and Huexotla's commoners paid a tribute in goods and labor to their Texcocan overlord (Gibson 1956; Offner 1983: 97–114). The proximity of Huexotla to the imperial capital of Texcoco, less than five kilometers away, suggests an early and very intense level of interaction with an emerging imperial capital and its elite ideology.

Archaeologically, Huexotla consists of a three-hundred-hectare area of dense occupational debris in what was once Huexotla's urban core. This core contained both elite and commoner residences as well as several large, still preserved temple mounds. The urban core was occupied during both the Middle and Late Postclassic. Small scatters of prehistoric artifacts extend up the piedmont slopes east of Huexotla for a distance of ten kilometers; these small clusters probably mark the residences of rural agriculturalists, subjects of the urban-based nobility. The piedmont zone was occupied only during the Late Postclassic, the period of Aztec dominance.

Table 22.1 shows the distribution of figurines at Huexotla. It compares figurine frequencies for Middle Postclassic (pre-Aztec) collections from the urban core with figurine frequencies of Late Postclassic (Aztec) collections from both the urban core and the rural piedmont. These distributions have several interesting features. First of all, the overall frequency of figurines is about the same for Middle and Late Postclassic occupations. Figurines are somewhat more common in the rural piedmont than in the urban core, and this is consistent with the idea that figurines are a part of nonelite ritual activity.

Anthropomorphic figurines are very common at Huexotla. Counting only those figurines that could be identified using

Table 22.1   Ceramic figurines at Huexotla, Mexico

	Middle Postclassic urban sector	Late Postclassic urban sector	Late Postclassic piedmont
Female figurines	11 (46%)	44 (58%)	37 (63%)
Male figurines	8 (33%)	15 (20%)	8 (14%)
Human figurines (sex indeterminate)	—	2 (3%)	5 (7%)
Zoomorphic figurines	4 (17%)	9 (12%)	5 (7%)
Archaic figurines	1 (4%)	5 (7%)	1 (2%)
Temple replicas	—	1 (1%)	3 (5%)
Total	24	76	59
Rim sherds collected	3,225	11,874	7,659
Total per 1,000 rim sherds	7.4	6.4	7.7

Parsons's (1972) typology, anthropomorphic figurines account for 82 percent of all figurines from the site. Zoomorphic figurines are the next most common figurine category, accounting for 11 percent of the figurines. Archaic (that is, anthropomorphic, but clearly of a Formative, Classic, or Early Postclassic date) figurines account for 4 percent of the figurines, and temple replicas account for 3 percent.

Some interesting temporal differences are apparent. The proportion of female figurines increases from Middle to Late Postclassic times. Female figurines are particularly abundant in the piedmont collections where they outnumber male figurines by better than three to one.[5] At the same time, temple replicas are found only in Late Postclassic collections, and although the numbers are quite low, temple replicas are most common in the piedmont collections. Both these trends indicate a degree of penetration by the urban-based elite religion during the period of Aztec dominance. The temple replicas suggest growing popular concern with official religion, and the increasing ratio of female to male figurines suggests a changing gender role ideology under conditions of Aztec rule.

Xico is a nucleated Middle and Late Postclassic site of twenty-five hectares, located in the Chalco lakebed in the southern Basin of Mexico. It was a regional capital during the first half of the Early Postclassic, but its importance diminished by Middle Postclassic times. It was subject to Cuitlahuac during the Middle and Late Postclassic (*Anales de Cuauhtitlan* 1945: 17, 31), and Cuitlahuac became a client state of Tenochtitlan during the Late Postclassic. Thus, Xico was at least two steps removed from imperial rule during the Late Postclassic, suggesting a low level of interaction with imperial capitals. Nevertheless, Xico did serve as a tribute collection center for the Aztec Triple Alliance (*Codex Mendoza* 1992: folio 20$^\text{v}$), and the three substantial temple mounds on the site indicate elite-sponsored religion in the community.

Xico's figurine collection is quite different from Huexotla's (see table 22.2). Figurines are less abundant than at Huexotla, and only 38 percent of the figurines are anthropomorphic, while 46 percent of the figurines are in archaic styles (anthropomorphic figurines from the Formative, Classic, and Early Postclassic periods). Animal figurines account for 11 percent of the figurines, and the single temple replica constitutes 3 percent of the sample. There is no temporal trend for a change in the frequencies of female or male figurines. There is perhaps a lower frequency of archaic figurines during the Late Postclassic, and a higher frequency of zoomorphic figurines, but the counts are low, and these differences may be fortuitous. While Huexotla's figurines suggest changes in commoner ideology under Aztec rule, Xico's figurines provide little evidence of change. The low proportion of anthropomorphic figurines indicate that, at Xico, gender was not contested.

Table 22.2   Ceramic figurines at Xico, Mexico

	Middle Postclassic	Late Postclassic
Female figurines	5 (20%)	—
Male figurines	5 (20%)	3 (25%)
Human figurines (sex indeterminate)	1 (4%)	—
Zoomorphic figurines	—	4 (33%)
Archaic figurines	14 (56%)	3 (25%)
Temple replicas	—	1 (8%)
Other	—	1 (8%)
Total	25	12
Rim sherds collected	5,062	3,248
Total per 1,000 rim sherds	4.9	3.7

Xaltocan, in the northern Basin of Mexico, was first occupied during the Early Postclassic, around AD 950. By the Middle Postclassic, it had attained a position of great regional importance as the capital of all Otomí-speaking peoples in the southern Hidalgo–northern Basin of Mexico region (Alva Ixtlilxóchitl 1975–7: vol. 1, 321; Nazareo de Xaltocan 1940: 125–6; Carrasco 1950: 260–1). Xaltocan's rulers were allied by marriage to the rulers of other major centers in the Valley of Mexico (Alva Ixtlilxó-chitl 1975–7: vol. 2, 17, 18, 51; *Anales de Tlatelolco* 1947: 28; Nazareo 1940: 124). In 1395, Xaltocan was incorporated into the Tepanec empire, and after 1430 it was subject to the Aztec Triple Alliance.

After its defeat by the Tepanec, Xaltocan lay abandoned for thirty-five or forty years (*Anales de Cuauhtitlan* 1945: 50). On the basis of archival research, Hicks (1994) suggests that the repopulation of Xaltocan occurred under the direct control of Aztec nobles based in Tenochtitlan and Tlateloco. The Aztecs installed a military ruler to govern Xaltocan (Nazareo 1940: 125), and Xaltocan paid tribute to both the ruler of Texcoco and the ruler of Tenochtitlan (Alva Ixtlilxóchitl 1975–7: vol. 1, 380; Nazareo 1940: 120). Xaltocan represents a community whose level of interaction with imperial capitals was high, once it was brought under imperial control.

Archaeologically, Postclassic Xaltocan consists of sixty-eight hectares of archaeological debris within and surrounding the modern town of Xaltocan. Only sixteen figurines were recovered from the surface collections at Xaltocan, a much lower frequency than at Huexotla or Xico (table 22.3). The types of figurines in the collections are rather similar, to Xico: 38 percent are anthropomorphic, 50 percent are archaic, and 6 percent are zoomorphic. Again, there is no trend toward a higher frequency of female figurines in Late Postclassic collections. Few temporal differences of any kind can be discerned.

The very low frequency of figurines in surface collections from Xaltocan is probably a consequence of amateur collecting by modern residents of the town. This is suggested by recent excavations at the site, which produced figurine frequencies ten times greater than those obtained in the surface collections (table 22.4). With higher counts and less mixing, two important temporal shifts become apparent. First, the frequency of archaic figurines falls off steeply in the transition from Early to Middle Postclassic (around AD 1150). This decrease might indicate a decline in the importance of ancestral history in determining household rights and obligations as the strength of the rulers of autonomous city-states reached its height during Middle Postclassic times. Second, as at Huexotla, the proportion of female figurines increased from Middle to Late Postclassic times. Again, this increasing ratio of female to male figurines suggests a changing gender role ideology under conditions of Aztec rule.

Table 22.3 Surface collections of ceramic figurines at Xaltocan, Mexico

	Early and Middle Postclassic	Late Postclassic
Female figurines	4 (40%)	1 (17%)
Male figurines	1 (10%)	—
Human figurines (sex indeterminate)	—	—
Zoomorphic figurines	—	1 (17%)
Archaic figurines	4 (40%)	4 (67%)
Temple replicas	—	—
Other	1 (10%)	—
Total	10	6
Rim sherds collected	6,562	6,587
Total per 1,000 rim sherds	1.5	0.9

Table 22.4 Excavated ceramic figurines at Xaltocan, Mexico

	Early Postclassic	Middle Postclassic	Late Postclassic
Female figurines	5 (21%)	11 (39%)	12 (63%)
Male figurines	4 (17%)	14 (50%)	5 (26%)
Human figurines (sex indeterminate)	—	—	—
Zoomorphic figurines	4 (17%)	3 (11%)	1 (5%)
Archaic figurines	11 (46%)	—	1 (5%)
Temple replicas	—	—	—
Total	24	28	19
Rim sherds collected	2,816	3,348	2,091
Total per 1,000 rim sherds	8.5	8.4	9.1

The Female Subject: Official and Popular Images

The figurine collections from Huexotla and Xaltocan suggest that gender was a topic of increasing concern to some Basin of Mexico communities during the period of Aztec dominance. The question remains, was the attitude of nonelite segments of the hinterland population one of accepting or resisting the male-dominant ideology of the Aztec state? The striking differences between official and popular images of the female subject suggest that hinterland populations did not accept the elite ideology. In fact, the popular images provide evidence of an ideology of resistance that sharply contested the official gender ideology of the state.

The male-dominant ideology of the state is most obviously expressed in Aztec monumental sculpture. Two of the best known and most powerful pieces of Aztec sculpture present highly dramatic images of mutilated women. The colossal statue of Coatlicue (figure 22.3) presents a decapitated woman whose head is replaced by two snakes representing two streams of blood surging from her neck (Pasztory 1983: 158). The relief of Coyolxauhqui from the Templo Mayor presents a woman whose limbs and head have been severed from her naked body (figure 22.4). In both of these sculptures, images of mutilated women represent the Aztec state's subjugation of its enemies (Klein 1988); these images express the fundamental misogyny that Rodríguez (1988: 126) finds characteristic of Aztec culture. The sculptures also seem to condone the use of

Figure 22.3 The headless Coatlicue (h. 3.2 m). Museo Nacional de Antropología, Mexico City.

physical violence against women to achieve male goals (Rodríguez 1988: 140).

The ideology of male dominance is also expressed in Aztec manuscript painting. Goddesses are sometimes presented holding shields and phallic staffs (*Codex Magliabecchiano* 1983: vol. 1, 33; Pasztory 1983: colorplate 10; Sahagún 1950–69: book 1, illustrations 6–12). McCafferty and

Figure 22.4 The dismembered Coyolxauhqui (diam. 3.3 m). Templo Mayor, Mexico City. (Courtesy of Elizabeth Brumfiel.)

Figure 22.5 The goddess Coatlicue holding a shield and swordlike weaving batten, from the *Codex Magliabecchiano*. (Courtesy of Elizabeth Brumfiel.)

McCafferty (1988) argue that such images are an example of gender parallelism: female deities were powerful in the same terms as were male deities. But Yólotl González (1979: 17) and María Rodríguez (1988: 182) point out that such images are androgynous negations of a power grounded in femaleness. Rather than affirming an equivalence of male and female power, these images suggest that power can be obtained only through maleness. Androgynous goddesses are an artistic solution to the conceptual problem of representing powerful females under the prevailing ideology of male dominance (figure 22.5).[6]

Less dramatic, more common expressions of male dominance are provided by smaller stone sculptures from Tenochtitlan in which women are posed in a kneeling position (figure 22.6). This pose is so common in both sculpture and manuscript painting that it has been designated the "Aztec women's pose" (Caso 1960: 14; Robertson 1964: 430; Baird 1993: 127). According to Pasztory (1983: 210), the kneeling position "expressed the Aztec ideal of women, who were supposed to be modest and industrious. Quintessentially feminine activities,

such as weaving and grinding corn, were performed in a kneeling position." Such images are the visual counterparts of verbal statements that emphasize the role of women as producers of food and cloth in Aztec texts (Sahagún 1950–69: book 10, chs. 3, 6, and 18). Men are more often depicted in a crouched position that appears to be unrelated to their role in warfare. A standing position is sometimes used for both women and men, but it is more common for men.

Two images from official Aztec art, mutilated women and androgynous women, are not met with in popular representations of women in figurines.[7] Kneeling poses sometimes occur, but they are rare.[8] Most female figurines are posed standing, which, according to Pasztory (1983: 210), signifies higher status. In addition, female figurines often hold one or two children in their arms; such images are unknown in official Aztec art. In fact, official Aztec art contains only two cases of a woman being associated with children or reproduction. One is the *Codex Borbonicus* illustration of the goddess

Figure 22.6 Kneeling goddess with tasseled headdress (h. 30 cm). Museum für Völkerkunde, Basel. (Courtesy of Elizabeth Brumfiel.)

Tlazolteotl giving birth (Pasztory 1983: colorplate 32); the other is a realistic depiction in stone of a woman giving birth (Kubler 1984: fig. 57). This lack of reproductive imagery is consistent with the underemphasis of women's reproductive roles in Aztec verbal texts.[9]

Thus, official images and popular images of women have few areas of overlap. The official images depicted women as mutilated or androgynous or emphasized their roles in production; popular images more frequently associated women with reproduction. The official images of women lend credence to claims by Nash and Rodríguez that the Aztec state subscribed to a male-dominant ideology that diminished the status of women in Aztec society. However, the differences between official images and popular images of women sustain claims by Nash and McCafferty and McCafferty that

gender inequality had not suffused Aztec culture at all levels. In Huexotla and Xaltocan, Aztec dominance caused increased concern with gender ideology, but the result was not the acceptance of the state's point of view. Instead, the penetration of state ideology prompted a degree of ideological reformulation. Rejecting elements of official imagery, the reformulation stood in ideological opposition to official views; in other words, it constituted a kind of popular ideology of resistance.

Conclusions

Figurine data from Huexotla, Xico, and Xaltocan suggest two conclusions about the importance of dominant ideologies in premodern states. One is that dominant ideologies are dependent upon high levels of interaction with political capitals. If Black-on-Orange pottery is taken as a gauge of the level of interaction of hinterland communities with political (and market) centers in the Basin of Mexico, then Late Postclassic Huexotla and Xaltocan, with 13.3 and 14.2 percent Black-on-Orange pottery, respectively, show much higher levels of interaction than Xico, with only 7.2 percent Black-on-Orange pottery. Thus, the interaction that accompanied the highly integrated Basin of Mexico market economy (Smith 1979; Hassig 1985) was an important condition for the diffusion of the state ideology. In less commercialized economies with lower rates of capital–hinterland interaction, for example, premodern Europe, the apparatus of education and cultural transmission is much less effective (Abercrombie, Hill, and Turner 1980: 69–70).

Second, where the influence of the dominant ideology is felt, it does not always result in ideological dominance. Official images may be opposed by popular images that offer an effective critique. While states have the ability to place certain issues on the popular agenda, they do not have an unfailing capacity to dictate popular consciousness. Definition of the sources of popular ideologies of resistance constitutes a major problem for future research, but daily experience with the sharp contradiction between elite ideology and the material interests of subordinate classes must play an important role in enabling subordinate classes to formulate their own world views (Scott 1985).

ACKNOWLEDGEMENTS

An earlier version of this essay was presented at the session "The Engendered Subject: Practice and Representation in Mesoamerica," organized by Veronica M. Kann and Geoffrey G. McCafferty for the eighty-ninth annual meeting of the American Anthropological Association, New Orleans, 1990. This version has benefited greatly from comments offered by John Clark, Susan Evans, Veronica Kann, Helen Pollard, Michael Smith, Lynn Stephens, James Taggart, and Alison Wylie. However, they have not seen the current version of this chapter and cannot be held responsible for its contents.

I am grateful to Susan Evans for making available to me the results of her archaeological and ethnohistoric research on Aztec figurines. Fieldwork at Huexotla, Xico, and Xaltocan was supported by grants from the National Science Foundation (GS-38470 and BNS-89-19095), the Mellon Foundation, and the H. John Heinz III Charitable Trust. This essay was completed while I was a Fellow at the Center for Advanced Study in the Behavioral Sciences. I am grateful for financial support provided by the Andrew W. Mellon Foundation and the National Endowment for the Humanities. Maggie LaNoue produced the drawings that illustrate the chapter.

NOTES

1 As an instance of women's resistance to the male dominant ideology, Nash (1978) cites mourning that women assumed when warriors departed from Tenochtitlan; this she interprets as an expression of women's abhorrence of the destructiveness of war. Nash also suggests that when the women of Tlatelolco "flaunted their backsides" to insult visiting Tenochca warriors, they were protesting a military alliance negotiated between the two communities.

2 Recently, however, figurines were found in association with an offering at a public building in the ceremonial center of Tlatelolco (see Otis Charlton 1995).

3 Cook (1950: 94) notes that some of the figurines she inspected were perforated in ways that would permit their suspension.

4 For a summary of the illnesses associated with the various Aztec deities, see Aguilar (1946).

5 In contrast, Kaplan (1958: 217–18) reports that male figurines outnumbered female figurines at Nonoalco, a Late Postclassic site on the outskirts of Tenochtitlan-Tlatelolco.

6 However, Klein (1993) argues that the shield was a fundamentally feminine symbol, a visual metaphor for the female body itself.

7 Figurine heads attached to figurine bodies are very rarely encountered. Evans (1990) suggests that the heads may have been deliberately snapped from the body in an act of ritual sacrifice (in Aztec culture, women were conventionally sacrificed by decapitation; men were sacrificed by opening their chests to remove their still-beating hearts). However, as Evans notes, heads are rarely attached to figurine bodies even in workshop contexts so the breakage pattern may be due to technical factors. Heavy, solid figurine heads attached to solid or hollow bodies by slender necks may be responsible for the breakage patterns (Cook 1950).

8 Interestingly, there are four kneeling figurines among the five female figurines in a photograph of artifacts recovered in archaeological salvage during the construction of Mexico City's Metro (Arana and Cepeda 1967: 5). This suggests that the penetration of the state's male-dominant ideology was much greater in the imperial capital than in hinterland settlements such as Huexotla, Xico, and Xaltocan.

9 The popularity of reproductive imagery in female figurines may stem from a desire to define reproduction as a specifically female concern. This principle is also reflected in the symbolic association of women's implements such as spindles and cooking pots with human sexuality and childbirth (Sullivan 1982; McCafferty and McCafferty 1989, 1991; Brumfiel 1991c). This is consistent with McCafferty and McCafferty's (1991) observation that the goal of resistance was to delimit an arena within which female power could be negotiated. The popularity of reproductive imagery in female figurines may also reflect a growing concern with effective reproduction, perhaps because the state's demand for tribute, levied on a household basis, increased the need for household labor, and/or because the intensification of physical labor associated with

imperial domination made pregnancy and childbirth more difficult, and/or because the increasing levels of violence associated with imperial expansion and control made less certain the survival of children to support parents in their old age. James Taggart (1990, personal communication) points out that the domain of reproductive success might include the reproductive capacity of the earth as manifested in agricultural production. If so, then the popularity of reproductive imagery in female figurines might also be explained by the need to increase agricultural production to meet increased demands for tribute or market exchange while continuing to meet household subsistence needs.

REFERENCES

Abercrombie, Nicholas, Stephen Hill, and Bryan S. Turner. 1980. *The Dominant Ideology Thesis.* London: George Allen and Unwin.

Aguilar, Gilberto F. 1946. La medecina. In *México prehispánico*, edited by Jorge A. Vivó, 725–36. Mexico City: Emma Hurtado.

Althusser, Louis. 1971. Ideology and Ideological State Apparatuses. In *Lenin and Philosophy and Other Essays.* New York: Monthly Review Press.

Alva Ixtlilxóchitl, Fernando de. 1975–7. *Obras históricas*, edited by Edmundo O'Gorman. 2 vols. Mexico City: Universidad Nacional Autónoma de México, Instituto de Investigaciones Históricas.

Anales de Cuauhtitlan. 1945. *Anales de Cuauhtitlan.* In *Códice Chimalpopoca*, translated by P. F. Velázquez, 1–118. Mexico City: Universidad Nacional Autónoma de México, Instituto de Investigaciones Históricas.

Anales de Tlatelolco. 1947. *Anales de Tlatelolco*, translated by H. Berlin and R. Barlow. Mexico City: Antigua Librería Robredo.

Arana, Raúl and Gerardo Cepeda. 1967. Rescate arqueológico en la Ciudad de México. *INAH Boletín* 30: 3–9.

Baird, Ellen T. 1993. *The Drawings of Sahagún's Primeros Memoriales.* Norman: University of Oklahoma Press.

Barlow, Robert H. and H. Lehmann. 1956. Statuettes – Grelots Aztèques de la Vallée de México. *Tribus* 4–5: 157–76.

Brumfiel, Elizabeth M. 1976. *Specialization and Exchange at the Late Postclassic (Aztec) Community of Huexotla, Mexico.* Ann Arbor, Mich.: University Microfilms.

—— 1980. Specialization, Market Exchange, and the Aztec State: A View from Huexotla. *Current Anthropology* 21: 459–78.

—— 1985. The Division of Labor at Xico: The Chipped Stone Industry. In *Economic Aspects of Prehispanic Highland Mexico*, edited by B. L. Isaac, 245–79. Greenwich, Conn.: JAI Press.

—— 1987. Informe al Instituto Nacional de Antropología e Historia Sobre el Proyecto Xaltocan Azteca. Paper on file, Department of Anthropology and Sociology, Albion College, and the Instituto Nacional de Antropología e Historia, Mexico City.

—— 1991a. Agricultural Development and Class Stratification in the Southern Valley of Mexico. In *Land and Politics in the Valley of Mexico*, edited by H. R. Harvey, 43–62. Albuquerque: University of New Mexico Press.

—— 1991b. Tribute and Commerce in Imperial Cities: The Case of Xaltocan, Mexico. In *Early State Economics*, edited by H. J. M. Claessen and P. van de Velde, 177–98. New Brunswick: Transaction.

—— 1991c. Weaving and Cooking: Women's Production in Aztec Mexico. In *Engendering Archaeology: Women and Prehistory*, edited by Joan M. Gero and Margaret W. Conkey, 224–51. Oxford: Basil Blackwell.

Carrasco, Davíd. 1990. Give Me Some Skin: The Metamorphosis, Charisma, and Redistribution of the Aztec Warrior. Paper presented at the 55th annual meeting of the Society for American Archaeology, Las Vegas.

Carrasco, Pedro. 1950. *Los Otomíes: Cultura e historia prehispánica de los pueblos Mesoamericanos de habla Otomiana.* Mexico City: Biblioteca Enciclopédica del Estado de México.

Caso, Alfonso. 1960. *Interpretation of the Codex Bodley 2858.* Mexico City: Sociedad Mexicana de Antropología.

Codex Magliabecchiano. 1983. *The Codex Magliabecchiano.* Notes and commentary by E. J. Boone, 2 vols. Berkeley: University of California Press.

Codex Mendoza. 1992. *Codex Mendoza.* Edited by F. F. Berdan and P. R. Anawalt. Berkeley: University of California Press.

Conkey, Margaret W. and Joan M. Gero. 1991. Tensions, Pluralities, and Engendering Archaeology: An Introduction to Women and Prehistory. In *Engendering Archaeology: Women and Prehistory*, edited by Joan M. Gero and Margaret W. Conkey, 3–30. Oxford: Basil Blackwell.

Cook, Carmen. 1950. Figurillas de barro de Santiago Tlatelolco. *Memorias de la Academia*

Mexicana de la Historia (Tlatelolco a Través de los Tiempos) 9(1): 93–100.

Durán, Diego. 1964. *Historia de las Indias de Nueva España*. 2 vols. Mexico City: Porrua.

—— 1971. *Book of the Gods and Rites and the Ancient Calendar*. Translated by F. Horcasitas and D. Heyden. Norman: University of Oklahoma Press.

Evans, Susan. 1990. Household Ritual in Aztec Life. Paper presented at the 55th annual meeting of the Society for American Archaeology, Las Vegas.

Gailey, Christine Ward. 1985. The State of the State in Anthropology. *Dialectical Anthropology* 9: 65–89.

—— 1987. Culture Wars: Resistance to State Formation. In *Power Relations and State Formation*, edited by T. C. Patterson and C. W. Gailey, 35–56. Washington, DC: American Anthropological Association.

Gibson, Charles. 1956. Llamamiento General, Repartimiento, and the Empire of Acolhuacan. *Hispanic American Historical Review* 36: 1–27.

González Torres, Yólotl. 1979. El panteón mexica. *Antropología e Historia* 25: 9–19.

Guzmán, Eulalia. 1938. Un manuscrito de la colección Boturini que trata de los antiguos señores de Teotihuacán. *Ethnos* 3: 89–103.

Hassig, Ross. 1985. *Trade, Tribute and Transportation: The Sixteenth-Century Political Economy of the Valley of Mexico*. Norman: University of Oklahoma Press.

Hicks, Frederic. 1994. Xaltocan under Mexica Domination, 1435–1520. In *Caciques and their People*, edited by Joyce Marcus and J. F. Zeitlin, 67–85. Ann Arbor: Anthropological Papers 89. The University of Michigan Museum of Anthropology.

Kann, Veronica M. 1989. Late Classic Politics, Cloth Production, and Women's Labor: An Interpretation of Female Figurines from Matacapan, Veracruz. Paper presented at the 54th annual meeting of the Society for American Archaeology, Atlanta, Ga.

Kaplan, Flora. 1958. The Post-Classic Figurines of Central Mexico. Master's essay, Department of Anthropology, Columbia University, New York.

Klein, Cecelia F. 1988. Rethinking Cihuacoatl: Aztec Political Imagery of the Conquered Woman. In *Smoke and Mist: Mesoamerican Studies in Memory of Thelma D. Sullivan*, edited by J. K. Josserand and K. Dakin, 237–77. Oxford: British Archaeological Reports, International Series (402).

—— 1993. The Shield Women: Resolution of an Aztec Gender Paradox. In *Current Topics in Aztec Studies: Essays in Honor of Dr. H. B. Nicholson*, edited by A. Cordy-Collins and D. Sharon, 39–64. San Diego: San Diego Museum Papers (30).

Kubler, George. 1984. *The Art and Architecture of Ancient America*. 3rd edn. New York: Penguin Books.

McCafferty, Geoffrey G. and Sharisse D. McCafferty. 1989. Weapons of Resistance: Material Metaphors of Gender Identity in Postclassic Mexico. Paper presented at the 90th annual meeting of the American Anthropological Association, Washington, DC.

McCafferty, Sharisse D. and Geoffrey G. McCafferty. 1988. Powerful Women and the Myth of Male Dominance in Aztec Society. *Archaeological Review from Cambridge* 7: 45–59.

—— 1991. Spinning and Weaving as Female Gender Identity in Post-Classic Central Mexico. In *Textile Traditions of Mesoamerica and the Andes: An Anthology*, edited by M. Schevill, J. C. Berlo, and E. Dwyer, 19–46. New York: Garland.

Millian, Alva C. 1981. The Iconography of Aztec Ceramic Figurines. Master's essay, Department of Art History and Archaeology, Columbia University, New York.

Morss, Noel. 1952. Cradled Infant Figurines from Tennessee and Mexico. *American Antiquity* 18: 164–6.

Motolinía, Toribio. 1969. *Historia de los Indios de la Nueva España*. Mexico City: Porrúa.

Nash, June. 1978. The Aztecs and the Ideology of Male Dominance. *Signs* 4: 349–62.

Nazareo de Xaltocan, Don Pablo. 1940. Carta al Rey Don Felipe II. In *Epistolario de Nueva España*, edited by F. del Paso y Troncoso, 10: 109–29. Mexico City: Antigua Librería Robredo.

Offner, Jerome A. 1983. *Law and Politics in Aztec Texcoco*. Cambridge: Cambridge University Press.

Otis Charlton, Cynthia L. 1994. Plebeians and Patricians: Contrasting Patterns of Production and Distribution in the Aztec Figurine and Lapidary Industries. In *Economies and Polities in the Aztec Realm*, edited by M. G. Hodge and M. E. Smith, 195–219. Albany: State University of New York at Albany, Institute for Mesoamerican Studies.

—— 1995. Las figurillas prehispánicas y coloniales de Tlatelelco. Unpublished report submitted to the Subdirección Arqueológica, Instituto Nacional de Antropología e Historia, Mexico City.

Parsons, Mary H. 1972. Aztec Figurines from the Teotihuacan Valley, Mexico. In *Miscellaneous Studies in Mexican Prehistory*, by M. W. Spence, J. R. Parsons, and M. H. Parsons, 81–164. Ann Arbor: University of Michigan Museum of Anthropology, Anthropological Papers, 45.

Pasztory, Esther. 1983. *Aztec Art*. New York: Abrams.

Pollock, Susan. 1991. Women in a Men's World: Images of Sumerian Women. In *Engendering Archaeology: Women and Prehistory*, edited by Joan M. Gero and Margaret W. Conkey, 366–87. Oxford: Basil Blackwell.

Preuss, K. Th. 1901. Mexikanische Thonfiguren. *Globus* 79, no. 6: 85–91. Brunswick.

Rapp, Rayna. 1978. The Search for Origins: Unraveling the Threads of Gender Hierarchy. *Critique of Anthropology* 3: 5–24.

Robertson, Donald. 1964. Los manuscritos religiosos mixtecos. In *Thirty-fifth International Congress of Americanists, Mexico, 1962. Actas*, 1: 425–35.

Rodríguez, María J. 1988. *La Mujer Azteca*. Toluca: Universidad Autónoma del Estado de México.

—— 1989. La condición femenina en Tlaxcala según las fuentes. *Mesoamérica* 17: 1–23.

Sahagún, Bernardino de. 1950–69. *Florentine Codex: General History of the Things of New Spain*. Translated by A. Anderson and C. Dibble. 11 vols. Santa Fe, NM, and Salt Lake City: School of American Research and the University of Utah Press.

Scott, James C. 1985. *The Weapons of the Weak: Everyday Forms of Peasant Resistance*. New Haven, Conn.: Yale University Press.

Seler, Eduard. 1902–23. *Gesammelte Abhandlungen zur Amerikanischen Sprach- und Altertumskunde*. 4 vols. Berlin. Reprinted, 1960–1. Graz, Austria.

Silverblatt, Irene. 1987. *Moon, Sun, and Witches: Gender Ideologies and Class in Inca and Colonial Peru*. Princeton, NJ: Princeton University Press.

Smith, Michael E. 1979. The Aztec Marketing System and Settlement Pattern in the Valley of Mexico: A Central-Place Analysis. *American Antiquity* 44: 110–25.

Sullivan, Thelma D. 1982. Tlazolteotl-Ixcuina: The Great Spinner and Weaver. In *The Art and Iconography of Late Post-Classic Central Mexico*, edited by E. H. Boone, 7–35. Washington, DC: Dumbarton Oaks.

CHAPTER 23

Living with the Ancestors

Kinship and Kingship in Ancient Maya Society

Patricia A. McAnany

Ancestors as Place-Markers

Twenty-five years ago, Saxe (1970) suggested that burial practices were indicative of a developing linkage between people and places. Subsequent research (Brown 1981; Chapman, Kinnes, and Randsborg 1981; Goldstein 1981; Renfrew 1983) pursued this line of thought. Morris (1991) has contributed a reflexive revision to this theoretical premise, stressing the political uses to which ancestors are put. Oddly enough, this research has had virtually no impact on Maya mortuary studies, in which attention to ancestors is often viewed as the prerogative of the elite (as expressed in funerary pyramids), with deceased relatives of nonelites being simply buried under the floors of their houses or, worse yet, in domestic middens. Frequently, these interments are perceived as simply burials of the "hoi polloi" with less jade and fewer pots, to be analyzed for age, sex, and nutritional status so as to be disadvantageously compared to richly adorned elite burials. One could scarcely use the term "ancestor" in reference to these relatively modest interments!

On the contrary, I suggest that ancestors are exactly who these individuals were. Not ancestors in the generic sense of all deceased relatives, but ancestors as a select subgroup of a population who were venerated by name because particular resource rights and obligations were inherited through them by their descendants. This is precisely why ancestors "slept" within the construction mass of residential compounds – to insure the chain of continuity in resources as transmitted between the generations. These contexts are, in effect, domestic mausolea. Subfloor and shrine burials represent vital links in the chain of inheritance; thus, the placement of individuals in these residential contexts involved elaborate ritual, much of which is not preserved archaeologically. It is no wonder that Becker (1992) questioned the conceptual discreteness of Tikal contextual terms such as "burial" and "cache." At K'axob, careful excavation has revealed that Formative "burials" are so temporally and contextually connected with construction of a new structure that often they reside stratigraphically in a place betwixt an old and a new building. Burial of ancestors often marks the termination of the use of an older structure and the commencement of the construction of a new one. Over time, these places of the ancestors often become sacralized locales at which ritual structures such as temples or shrines completely replace domestic structures. I have cited one such sequence from K'axob, but the pattern is ubiquitous throughout the lowlands of Mesoamerica.

Reprinted from Patricia A. McAnany. 1995. Ancestors and the Archaeology of Place (extract), in chapter 6, *Living with the Ancestors: Kinship and Kingship in Ancient Maya Society* (University of Texas Press, Austin), pp. 160–5.

In the past, Quiché Maya of Chichicastenango expressed the sentiment that their
land and home belonged to their ancestors
and that they themselves were but
temporary lodgers in a protracted chain of
inheritance (Bunzel 1952). In the Andean
area, Salomon (1991: 20) has noted the
active role played by ancestors in establishing a sacred geography linking "territorial
places to ancestral time." To my mind,
these sentiments capture the manner in
which attention to ancestors is linked most
often to concerns with land and inheritance:
ancestors as markers of places. It follows,
therefore, that the emergence of the practice
of creating ancestors can be symptomatic of
the entrenchment of a pattern of land tenure
in which inheritance of fixed plots and orchards plays a primary role. In this regard, it is
most interesting that ancestor veneration
appears to be solidly rooted in the Formative period and, in some places, may be present at the onset of Middle Formative
settlement, although at K'axob it appears
during the Late Formative.

As markers of places and rights, sequential ancestral interments in ancient Maya
residences create a kind of text-free genealogy that is more subtle and difficult to interpret than genealogies written in hieroglyphic
texts. The "decipherment" of these "genealogies" is a critical area of study if we are to
recreate a social history of Maya society
giving full voice to the agrarian strategies
and practices of ancestor veneration of all
sectors of Maya society, elite and nonelite
alike.

The practice of ancestor veneration ultimately is not about the dead, but about how
the living make use of the dead. The title of
this study – *Living with the Ancestors* –
stresses the vibrant and proactive nature of
this social practice. Maya ancestor veneration is not a "cultic" practice engaged in by a
group sharing an obsessive or esoteric interest in the dead, and neither is it a mindless
worship of "idols;" rather, it is a type of
active discourse with the past and the future,
embodying what Carlsen and Prechtel
(1991: 35) have described as the centrality
of Maya understanding of death and rebirth

– called *jaloj-k'exoj* in the cosmology of the
Tzutujil Maya.

Inequality in Lineage and Residence

Traditional ethnographies of contemporary
Maya have hinted at the basic egalitarianism
of these societies. Less frequently mentioned
is the fact that many modern Mayan speakers, particularly those in Guatemala, live
under the subordination of what is essentially a conquest state. Employing an ill-
advised ethnographic analogy, Mayanists
of earlier times imputed a structural similarity between contemporary Maya and nonelite Maya of deep history. I have tried to
show how Maya society outside the web of
kingship was anything but egalitarian. On
the contrary, from a very early point in time
inequality in social, political, and economic
relations permeated the kinship structure.
Ancestor veneration in particular is not a
practice that promotes social equality;
rather, it promotes and perpetuates inequality and alienation from resources within the
household as well as the polity. The principle of first occupancy gave preferential
access to land to certain lineages and within
lineages to certain families. Lineage organization itself can be viewed as either a
mechanism for cementing land claims or
for alienating certain segments of society
from such claims. Inequality in political
power between lineages, within lineages,
and particularly within the multifamily
residential compounds that emerged in
the Maya lowlands during the Late Formative must have been particularly acute,
the conflict between household heads and
their heirs being the stuff of legends, laws,
and vivid ethnographic description. Con-
ceptualization of multifamily compounds
as socially heterogeneous...leads to the
realization of the ubiquity of multifarious
asymmetrical production relations between
residents and the household head. Even
in the absence of a divine king, inequality permeated Maya society, although
I have taken great pains to clarify the
critical differences between kinship and
kingship.

Forces of Divine Kingship

In this volume, I present a view of ancient Maya society in which kinship is cast in dynamic tension with the forces of divine kingship. Since I am suggesting an investiture of lineage organization into our model of Maya society and also inferring that these units of kinship were active players in the geopolitics of the Classic period, I realize that I run the risk of overly creative re-creation. Nevertheless, both settlement and epigraphic research are beginning to show that conflict between kinship and kingship was a significant political dynamic of Classic times, and this dynamic has already been documented for the Postclassic. The tension is between factions rather than classes – between two organizational forms in which the centripetal forces of divine kingship vie against the centrifugal forces of kinship. As divine kings gained control of labor, land, and exchange processes, so the power of traditional lineage leaders waned, particularly in the Petén heartland of kings. On the other hand, there were areas where lineages remained vital organizational forces throughout the Classic period, either coexisting with kings or living outside of the web of kingship. This is the case particularly in Belize, where mapping and excavation programs have shown time and again significant local variability in architectural elaboration and burial furnishings – indicators, I suggest, of the vitality of kinship structures and the role of lineage headship rather than of a "middle class" (cf. Chase 1992).

The waxing and waning of the power of kings and lineage leaders (*ah kuch kabob*) is captured in episodic "snapshot" fashion in sixteenth-century chronicles of northern Yucatán. Perhaps these accounts do not reflect an anomalous period of political balkanization. Rather, these chronicles, for all their inherent biases in original observation and later translation, give a reasonably accurate picture of the full range of variation in leadership positions and political dependencies – a range of institutional arrangements that certainly existed during the Classic period as well, even though the scholarship of this earlier period has given preferential attention to polities organized along the more centralized end of the political array.

Few would dispute that divine kingship in the Maya lowlands emerged from the agrarian matrix of Formative society. If the construction of tombs for the interment of deceased rulers can be used as a rough indicator of the emergence of this institution, then it is the first century BC before the first kings ruled Tikal (Haviland and Moholy-Nagy 1992: 58). Few have acknowledged, on the other hand, that one of the most salient features of divine kingship, that of ancestor veneration, also emerged from the identical matrix. As Fortes (1976: 3) has noted, ancestor veneration is located primarily in the familial domain of social life. It is about the perpetuation of links between descendants and the land and rights of their forebears. Thus, in the Maya region, as in China and Egypt, emergent elites appropriated the practice of ancestor veneration and converted it to an institution that cemented the transmission of political power rather than agrarian rights. It is this right to rule according to precedent set by ancestors that led Hocart to declare that "the first kings must have been dead kings" (Needham 1970).

In the Maya region, the politicization of ancestor veneration included the wholesale incorporation of the agrarian imagery of a lowland tropical environment – thus giving Maya kingship cosmology its distinctive "organic flavor." This imagery was born of fields, orchards, and swamps, and plants such as maize, avocados, and water lilies provided strong visual metaphors for kingly larger-than-life themes of life, death, inheritance, and continuity. The "ancestral orchard" of Pakal is one such example of the "borrowing" of agrarian imagery of inherited orchard crops for kingly purposes. Use of this imagery has been broadly misconstrued as an attempt by elites to use imagery that could be understood by the "illiterate masses;" I suggest instead that elites appropriated organic motifs precisely because of their powerful association with agrarian themes of regeneration and inheritance.

The presence of other motifs in mortuary contexts in Formative villages illustrates a similar point – that of appropriation of such images by elites to serve new ends. The quadripartite motif in particular is grounded in agrarian/calendrical expressions of the Formative period. As such, it packs a particular punch when used in the context of divine kingship. In general, then, iconography is a conservative type of expression, and iconographic motifs may be present across significant thresholds of political transformation. That is, the motifs are constant but the contextual meaning of the motifs changes as they are manipulated for political and economic ends.

Much of what has been written here challenges untested yet commonplace assumptions about Maya society, questions established wisdom, and I hope, therefore, will swing readers' perspectives away from the prevalent unitary view of Maya society. Excitement over the ongoing decipherment of Maya hieroglyphs has focused attention on the elite sector of Classic Maya society, and current popular publications often present a skewed view of ancient Maya society – one that dwells upon the material expressions of elites. Disregarded is the fact that elites did not invent the solar calendar or ancestor veneration; rather, they appropriated them from an ancient agrarian core of rituals, beliefs, and practices and selectively modified them for the political arena of elite rulership, succession, and competitive interaction. In this book, I have sought to place major ideological tenets of Maya society – such as the link between ancestors and resource rights – in proper historical context. In doing so, I have identified the study of ritual and practice in the residence as requiring further investigation. Through such research, Maya studies will begin to encompass the spirit of social historical research and leave behind the stigma of a terribly skewed, ahistorical perspective.

REFERENCES

Becker, Marshall J. 1992. Burials as Caches; Caches as Burials: A New Interpretation of the Meaning of Ritual Deposits among the Classic Period Lowland Maya. In *New Theories on the Ancient Maya*, edited by Ellen C. Danien and Robert J. Sharer, pp. 185–96. The University Museum, University of Pennsylvania, Philadelphia.

Brown, James A. 1981. The Search for Rank in Prehistoric Burials. In *The Archaeology of Death*, edited by D. Miller, Mark Rowlands, and Christopher Tilley, pp. 127–39. Unwin Hyman, London.

Bunzel, Ruth. 1952. Chichicastenango: A Guatemalan Village. *American Ethnological Society* 22. University of Washington Press, Seattle.

Carlsen, Robert S. and Martin Prechtel. 1991. The Flowering of the Dead: An Interpretation of Highland Maya Culture. *Man* 26: 23–42.

Chapman, Robert, Ian Kinnes, and Klavs Randsborg (eds). 1981. *The Archaeology of Death*. Cambridge University Press, Cambridge.

Chase, Arlen F. 1992. Elites and the Changing Organization of Classic Maya Society. In *Mesoamerican Elites: An Archaeological Assessment*, edited by Diane Z. Chase and Arlen F. Chase, pp. 31–49. University of Oklahoma Press, Norman.

Fortes, Meyer. 1976. An Introductory Commentary. In *Ancestors*, edited by W. H. Newell, pp. 1–16. Mouton, Paris.

Goldstein, Lynne. 1981. One-Dimensional Archaeology and Multi-Dimensional People: Spatial Organization and Mortuary Analysis. In *The Archaeology of Death*, edited by R. Chapman, I. Kinnes, and K. Randsborg, pp. 53–69. Cambridge University Press, Cambridge.

Haviland, William A. and Hattula Moholy-Nagy. 1992. Distinguishing the High and Mighty from the Hoi Polloi at Tikal, Guatemala. In *Mesoamerican Elites: An Archaeological Assessment*, edited by Diane Z. Chase and Arlen F. Chase, pp. 50–60. University of Oklahoma Press, Norman.

Morris, Ian. 1991. The Archaeology of Ancestors: The Saxe/Goldstein Hypothesis Revisited. *Cambridge Archaeological Journal* 1: 147–69.

Needham, Rodney. 1970. Editor's Introduction. In *Kings and Councillors: An Essay in Comparative Anatomy of Human Society*, by A. M. Hocart, pp. xiii–xcix. University of Chicago Press, Chicago.

Renfrew, Colin. 1983. The Social Archaeology of Megalithic Monuments. *Scientific American* 249: 152–63.

Salomon, Frank. 1991. Introductory Essay: The Huarochiri Manuscript. In *The Huarochiri Manuscript: A Testament of Ancient and Colo-nial Andean Religion*, edited by Frank Salomon and G. L. Urioste, pp. 1–38. University of Texas Press, Austin.

Saxe, Arthur A. 1970. Social Dimensions of Mortuary Practices. Ph.D. dissertation, Department of Anthropology, University of Michigan.

INDEX